27TH ANNUAL EDITION

2014

POET'S
MARKET

Robert Lee Brewer, Editor

WD
WRITER'S DIGEST
BOOKS
WritersDigest.com
Cincinnati, Ohio

Publisher: Phil Sexton

Writer's Market website: www.writersmarket.com
Writer's Digest website: www.writersdigest.com
Writer's Digest Bookstore: www.writersdigestshop.com

Distributed in Canada by Fraser Direct
100 Armstrong Avenue
Georgetown, Ontario, Canada L7G 5S4
Tel: (905) 877-4411

Distributed in the U.K and Europe by F&W Media International
Brunel House, Newton Abbot, Devon, TQ12 4PU, England
Tel: (+44) 1626-323200, Fax: (+44) 1626-323319
E-mail: postmaster@davidandcharles.co.uk

Distributed in Australia by Capricorn Link
P.O. Box 704, Windsor, NSW 2756 Australia
Tel: (02) 4577-3555

ISSN: 0883-5470
ISBN-13: 978-1-59963-730-3
ISBN-10: 1-59963-730-8

Attention Booksellers: This is an annual directory of F+W Media, Inc. Return deadline for this edition is December 31, 2014.

Edited by: Robert Lee Brewer
Cover designed by: Claudean Wheeler
Interior designed by: Claudean Wheeler
Page layout by: Geoff Raker
Production coordinated by: Greg Nock

CONTENTS

FROM THE EDITOR.. 1

BUSINESS OF POETRY

HOW TO USE POET'S MARKET.. 2

FREQUENTLY ASKED QUESTIONS... 7

HOW TO INCREASE YOUR ODDS OF PUBLICATION
    by Sage Cohen 19

READY YOUR WORK FOR PUBLICATION
    by Lauren Camp 25

THE ORGANIZED POET
    by Patricia Kennelly 30

1O CHAPBOOK DESIGN TIPS EVERY POET SHOULD KNOW
    by Amy Miller 36

MISTAKES POETS MAKE.. 41

DEALING WITH PROBLEM EDITORS.. 44

HOW TO WRITE A SUCCESSFUL GRANT TO FUND YOUR WRITING
    by Kris Bigalk 47

IS IT A 'CON'?.. 52

REVOLUTION ROAD
    by Nate Pritts.. 56

PROMOTION OF POETRY

WHY POETS NEED PLATFORMS
    by Sage Cohen 61

BLOGGING BASICS
    by Robert Lee Brewer.. 67

A YEAR IN THE LIFE OF A CITY POET LAUREATE
    by Jeannine Hall Gailey 74

POETRY READINGS
    by Scott Owens.. 79

HOW TO GIVE A GREAT POETRY READING
    by Jeannine Hall Gailey 84

SOCIAL MEDIA PRIMER FOR POETS
by Robert Lee Brewer..88

POET INTERVIEWS

TRACI BRIMHALL
by Robert Lee Brewer..92

CARMEN CALATAYUD
by Robert Lee Brewer..96

BARTON SMOCK
by Robert Lee Brewer..102

ERICA WRIGHT
by Robert Lee Brewer..105

HEATHER BELL
by Robert Lee Brewer..109

S. THOMAS SUMMERS
by Robert Lee Brewer..114

KAREN RIGBY
by Robert Lee Brewer..117

DEBORAH HAUSER
by Robert Lee Brewer..121

CRAFT OF POETRY

POETIC FORMS
by Robert Lee Brewer..125

HOW TO FOCUS ON REVISION
by Nate Pritts..140

FRESHEN YOUR POETRY BY REVISING STALE LANGUAGE
by Nancy Susanna Breen..145

POEMS

THE IMPORTANCE OF READING POETRY
by Nancy Susanna Breen..151

INVENTION OF EVERYTHING ELSE
by Susan Rich..156

BREAKING MORNING
    by Scott Owens..158

IF TESLA HAD AIMED HIS DEATH RAY AT VORTEX, KENTUCKY
    by Shaindel Beers..159

FIVE WAYS OF LOOKING AT A MUSHROOM CLOUD
    by Chris Haven..160

INTRODUCTION TO DISASTER PREPAREDNESS
    by Jeannine Hall Gailey..162

TROUBLE IN MIND
    by Nancy Posey..163

THE OFFERING OF HIS EYE
    by J.P. Dancing Bear..164

ALONE IN FADING LIGHT
    by Helen Losse..165

THE ARTISTS' HONEYMOON
    by Daniel Ari..167

ORIFICE
    by Terry Wolverton..168

TRESPASS WITH HORSEFLY
    by Kevin McLellan..169

RECIPE
    by Martha Silano..170

ELEGY
    by Amorak Huey..172

NINE GULLS
    by Maril Crabtree..173

POET BIOS..174

MARKETS

MAGAZINES/JOURNALS...177

BOOK/CHAPBOOK PUBLISHERS..377

CONTESTS & AWARDS...411

GRANTS..445

RESOURCES

CONFERENCES, WORKSHOPS & FESTIVALS 451

ORGANIZATIONS 464

POETS IN EDUCATION 474

GLOSSARY OF LISTING TERMS 477

GLOSSARY OF POETRY TERMS 481

INDEXES

SUBJECT INDEX 488

GENERAL INDEX 496

FROM THE EDITOR

In the most recent edition of *Poet's Market*, I shared how I started writing poetry. In this edition, I'm excited to share that my first full-length collection of poetry, *Solving the World's Problems*, will be published by Press 53 (released awfully close to when this title hits bookshelves, in fact).

It has been an exciting and enlightening process. For one, the editor who loved my manuscript "as is" challenged me to push beyond what was accepted for publication. So we cut poems that were published in nice publications. We completely revised (heck, re-wrote) other poems. We added in new poems. Plus, we took other poetic leaps.

Notice that I say "we," instead of "I," because publication is often a collaborative activity. Sure, my editor made amazing suggestions and asked incredible questions, but he let me decide how to attack them. When I came back with something, he asked more questions, made more suggestions.

Every year, I receive feedback from poets who find success in their own poetic careers and who want to credit me or *Poet's Market* for helping them get there. That's great! But it's a collaborative process. I only provide information; you make it work.

With that in mind, I hope the *2014 Poet's Market* will help you achieve more than you ever thought possible. Keep working on your craft and submitting to the markets. I know that you can do this.

Until next time, keep poeming!

Robert Lee Brewer
Senior Content Editor, *Poet's Market*
http://www.writersdigest.com/editor-blogs/poetic-asides
http://twitter.com/robertleebrewer

HOW TO USE
POET'S MARKET

Delving into the pages of *Poet's Market* indicates a commitment—you've decided to take that big step and begin submitting your poems for publication. How do you *really* begin, though? Here are eight quick tips to help make sense of the marketing/submission process:

1. BE AN AVID READER. The best way to hone your writing skills (besides writing) is to immerse yourself in poetry of all kinds. It's essential to study the masters; however, from a marketing standpoint, it's equally vital to read what your contemporaries are writing and publishing. Read journals and magazines, chapbooks and collections, anthologies for a variety of voices; scope out the many poetry sites on the Internet. Develop an eye for quality, and then use that eye to assess your own work. Don't rush to publish until you know you're writing the best poetry you're capable of producing.

2. KNOW WHAT YOU LIKE TO WRITE—AND WHAT YOU WRITE BEST. Ideally, you should be experimenting with all kinds of poetic forms, from free verse to villanelles. However, there's sure to be a certain style with which you feel most comfortable, that conveys your true "voice." Whether you favor more formal, traditional verse or avant-garde poetry that breaks all the rules, you should identify which markets publish work similar to yours. Those are the magazines and presses you should target to give your submissions the best chance of being read favorably—and accepted. (See the Subject Index to observe how some magazines and presses specify their needs.)

3. LEARN THE "BUSINESS" OF POETRY PUBLISHING. Poetry may not be a high-paying writing market, but there's still a right way to go about the "business" of submitting and publishing poems. Learn all you can by reading writing-related books and magazines. Read the articles and interviews in this book for plenty of helpful advice. Surf the Internet for a wealth of sites filled with writing advice, market news and informative links.

4. RESEARCH THE MARKETS. Study the listings in *Poet's Market* thoroughly; these present submission guidelines, editorial preferences and editors' comments as well as contact information (names, postal and e-mail addresses, website URLs). In addition, the indexes in the back of this book provide insights into what an editor or publisher may be looking for.

However, studying market listings alone won't cut it. The best way to gauge the kinds of poetry a market publishes is to read several issues of a magazine/journal or several of a press's books to get a feel for the style and content of each. If the market has a website, log on and take a look. Websites may include poetry samples, reviews, archives of past issues, exclusive content, and especially submission guidelines. (If the market is an online publication, the current issue will be available in its entirety.) If the market has no online presence, send for guidelines and sample copies (include a SASE—self-addressed stamped envelope—for guidelines; include appropriate cost for sample copy).

Submission guidelines are pure gold for the specific information they provide. However you acquire them—by SASE or e-mail, online, or in a magazine itself—make them an integral part of your market research.

⊕ market new to this edition

⊘ market does not accept unsolicited submissions

🍁 Canadian market

🌏 market located outside of the U.S. and Canada

↻ online opportunity

💲 market pays

⊶ tips to break into a specific market

○ market welcomes submissions from beginning poets

◑ market prefers submissions from skilled, experienced poets; will consider work from beginning poets

● market prefers submissions from poets with a high degree of skill and experience

◎ market has a specialized focus

5. START SLOWLY. It may be tempting to send your work directly to *The New Yorker* or *Poetry*, but try to adopt a more modest approach if you're just starting out. Most listings in this book display symbols that reflect the level of writing a magazine or publisher prefers to receive. The ○ symbol indicates a market that welcomes submissions from beginning or unpublished poets. As you gain confidence and experience (and increased skill in your writing), you can move on to markets coded with the ● symbol. Although it may tax your patience, slow and steady progress is a proven route to success.

6. BE PROFESSIONAL. Professionalism is not something you should "work up to." Make it show in your first submission, from the way you prepare your manuscript to the attitude you project in your communications with editors.

Follow those guidelines. Submit a polished manuscript. (See "Frequently Asked Questions" for details on manuscript formatting and preparation.) Choose poems carefully with the editor's needs in mind. *Always* include a SASE with any submission or inquiry. Such practices show respect for the editor, the publication and the process; and they reflect *your* self-respect and the fact that you take your work seriously. Editors love that; and even if your work is rejected, you've made a good first impression that could help your chances with your next submission.

7. KEEP TRACK OF YOUR SUBMISSIONS. First, do *not* send out the only copies of your work. There are no guarantees your submission won't get lost in the mail, misplaced in a busy editorial office, or vanish into a black hole if the publication or press closes down. Create a special file folder for poems you're submitting. Even if you use a word processing program and store your manuscripts on disk, keep a hard copy file as well (and be sure to back up your electronic files).

Second, establish a tracking system so you always know which poems are where. This can be extremely simple: index cards, a chart created with word processing or database software, or even a simple notebook used as a log. (You can enlarge and photocopy the Submission Tracker or use it as a model to design your own version.) Note the titles of the poems submitted (or the title of the collection if you're submitting a book/chapbook manuscript); the name of the publication, press, or contest; date sent; estimated response time; and date returned *or* date accepted. Additional information you may want to log: the name of the editor/contact, date the accepted piece is published and/or issue number of the magazine, type/amount of pay received, rights acquired by the publication or press, and any pertinent comments.

Without a tracking system, you risk forgetting where and when manuscripts were submitted. This is even more problematic if you simultaneously send the same manuscripts to different magazines, presses or contests. And if you learn of an acceptance by one magazine or publisher, you *must* notify the others that the poem or collection you sent them is no longer available. You run a bigger chance of overlooking someone without an organized approach. This causes hard feelings among editors you may have inconvenienced, hurting your chances with these markets in the future.

8. DON'T FEAR REJECTION. LEARN FROM IT. No one enjoys rejection, but every writer faces it. The best way to turn a negative into a positive is to learn as much as you can from your rejections. Don't let them get you down. A rejection slip isn't a permission slip to doubt yourself, condemn your poetry or give up.

Look over the rejection. Did the editor provide any comments about your work or reasons why your poems were rejected? Probably he or she didn't. Editors are extremely busy and don't necessarily have time to comment on rejections. If that's the case, move on to the next magazine or publisher you've targeted and send your work out again.

SUBMISSION TRACKER

Poem Title	Publication Contest	Editor/Contact	Date Sent	Date Returned	Date Accepted	Date Published	Pay Recieved	Comments

If, however, the editor *has* commented on your work, pay attention. It counts for something that the editor took the time and trouble to say anything, however brief, good or bad. And consider any remark or suggestion with an open mind. You don't have to agree, but you shouldn't automatically disregard the feedback, either. Tell your ego to sit down and be quiet, then use the editor's comments to review your work from a new perspective. You might be surprised by how much you'll learn from a single scribbled word in the margin; or how encouraged you'll feel from a simple "Try again!" written on the rejection slip.

GUIDE TO LISTING FEATURES

Below is an example of a Magazines/Journal listing (Book/Chapbook Publishers listings follow a similar format). Note the callouts that identify various format features of the listing. A key to the symbols displayed at the beginning of each listing is located on the inside cover of this book.

EASY-TO-USE
REFERENCE ICONS

E-MAIL ADDRESSES
AND WEBSITES

SPECIFIC
CONTACT NAMES

TYPES OF POETRY
CONSIDERED

DETAILED
SUBMISSION
GUIDELINES

EDITOR'S
COMMENTS

◑ ⑤ ALASKA QUARTERLY REVIEW

ESB 208, University of Alaska-Anchorage, 3211 Providence Dr., Anchorage AK 99508. (907)786-6916. E-mail: aqr@uaa.alaska.edu. Website: www.uaa.alaska.edu/aqr. **Contact:** Ronald Spatz. "*AQR* publishes fiction, poetry, literary nonfiction and short plays in traditional and experimental styles."

• *Alaska Quarterly* reports they are always looking for freelance material and new writers.

MAGAZINES NEEDS *Alaska Quarterly Review*, published in 2 double issues/year, is "devoted to contemporary literary art. We publish both traditional and experimental fiction, poetry, literary nonfiction, and short plays." Wants all styles and forms of poetry, "with the most emphasis perhaps on voice and content that displays 'risk,' or intriguing ideas or situations." Has published poetry by Maxine Kumin, Jane Hirshfield, David Lehman, Pattiann Rogers, Albert Goldbarth, David Wagoner, Robert Pinsky, Linda Pastan, Ted Kooser, Kay Ryan, W. S. Merwin, Sharon Olds and Billy Collins. *Alaska Quarterly Review* is 224-300 pages, digest-sized, professionally printed, perfect-bound, with card cover with color or b&w photo. Receives up to 6,000 submissions/year, accepts 40-90. Subscription: $18. Sample: $6. Pays $10-50 subject to availability of funds; pays in contributor's copies and subscriptions when funding is limited.

HOW TO CONTACT No fax or e-mail submissions. Reads submissions mid-August to mid-May; manuscripts are *not* read May 15-August 15. Responds in up to 5 months, "sometimes longer during peak periods in late winter."

ADDITIONAL INFORMATION Guest poetry editors have included Stuart Dybek, Jane Hirshfield, Stuart Dischell, Maxine Kumin, Pattiann Rogers, Dorianne Laux, Peggy Shumaker, Olena Kalytiak Davis, Nancy Eimers, Michael Ryan, and Billy Collins.

TIPS "All sections are open to freelancers. We rely almost exclusively on unsolicited manuscripts. *AQR* is a nonprofit literary magazine and does not always have funds to pay authors."

FREQUENTLY ASKED QUESTIONS

The following FAQ (Frequently Asked Questions) section provides the expert knowledge you need to submit your poetry in a professional manner. Answers to most basic questions, such as "How many poems should I send?," "How long should I wait for a reply?" and "Are simultaneous submissions okay?" can be found by simply reading the listings in the Magazines/Journals and Book/Chapbook Publishers sections. See the introduction to each section for an explanation of the information contained in the listings. Also, see the Glossary of Listing terms.

Is it okay to submit handwritten poems?

Usually, no. Now and then a publisher or editor makes an exception and accepts handwritten manuscripts. However, check the preferences stated in each listing. If no mention is made of handwritten submissions, assume your poetry should be typed or computer-generated.

How should I format my poems for submission to magazines and journals?

If you're submitting poems by regular mail (also referred to as *land mail*, *postal mail* or *snail mail*), follow this format:

Poems should be typed or computer-printed on white 8½×11 paper of at least 20 lb. weight. Left, right and bottom margins should be at least one inch. Starting ½ inch from the top of the page, type your name, address, telephone number, e-mail address (if you have one) and number of lines in the poem in the *upper right* corner, in individual lines, single-spaced. Space down about six lines and type the poem title, either centered or flush left. The title may appear in all caps or in upper and lower case. Space down another two lines (at least) and begin to type your poem. Poems are usually single-spaced,

MAILED SUBMISSION FORMAT

S.T. Coleridge
1796 Ancient Way
Mariner Heights OH 45007 **2**
(852) 555-5555
albatross@strophe.vv.cy
54 lines

KUBLA KHAN **4**

5 In Xanadu did Kubla Khan
a stately pleasure dome decree:
where Alph, the sacred river, ran
through caverns measureless to man
down to a sunless sea.
So twice five miles of furtile ground
with walls and towers were girdled round:
and there were gardens bright with sinuous rills,
where blossomed many an incense-bearing tree;
and here were forests ancient as the hills,
enfolding sunny spots of greenery.

6 But oh! that deep romantic chasm which slanted
down the green hill athwart a cedarn cover!
A savage place! as holy and enchanted
as e'er beneath a waning moon was haunted
by woman wailing for her demon lover!
And from this chasm, with ceaseless turmoil seething,
as if this earth in fast thick pants were breathing, **7**
a mighty fountain momentarily was forced:
amid whose swift half-intermitted burst
huge fragments vaulted like rebounding hail,
or chaffy grain beneath the thresher's flail;
And 'mid these dancing rocks at once and ever
it flung up momently the sacred river.

1 DO leave ½" margin on top, at least 1" on sides and bottom. **2** DO list contact information and number of lines in upper right corner. **3** DO space down about 6 lines. **4** DO type title in all caps or upper/lower case. Type flush with left margin. **5** DON'T type a by-line but DO space down at least 2 lines. **6** DO double-space between spaces. **7** DO type poems single-space unless guidelines specify double spacing. **8** For multi-page poems, DO show your name, keyword(s) from title, page number, and "continue stanza" or "new stanza." **9** DO space down at least 3 lines before resuming poem.

S.T. Coleridge
KUBLA KAHN, Page 2, continued stanza. ⑧

Five miles meandering with a mazy motion
through wood and dale the sacred river ran,
then reached the caverns measureless to man,
and sank in tumult to a lifeless ocean:
and 'mid this tumult Kubla heard from afar
ancestral voices prophesying war!

The shadow of the dome of pleasure
floated midway on the waves;
where was heard the mingled measure
from the fountain and the caves.
It was a miracle of rare device,
a sunny pleasure dome with caves of ice!

A damsel with a dulcimer
in a vision once I saw:
It was an Abyssinian maid,

although some magazines may request double-spaced submissions. (Be alert to each market's preferences.) Double-space between stanzas. Type one poem to a page. For poems longer than one page, type your name in the *upper left* corner; on the next line type a key word from the title of your poem, the page number, and indicate whether the stanza begins or is continued on the new page (i.e., MOTHMAN, Page 2, continue stanza *or* begin new stanza).

If you're submitting poems by e-mail:

First, make sure the publication accepts e-mail submissions. This information, when available, is included in all *Poet's Market* listings. In most cases, editors will request that poems be pasted within the body of your e-mail, *not* sent as attachments. Many editors prefer this format because of the danger of viruses, the possibility of software incompatibility, and other concerns associated with e-mail attachments. Editors who consider e-mail attachments taboo may even delete the message without opening the attachment.

Of course, other editors do accept, and even prefer e-mail submissions as attachments. This information should be clearly stated in the market listing. If it's not, you're probably safer submitting your poems in the body of the e-mail. (All the more reason to pay close attention to details given in the listings.)

Note, too, the number of poems the editor recommends including in the e-mail submission. If no quantity is given specifically for e-mails, go with the number of poems an editor recommends submitting in general. Identify your submission with a notation in the subject line. While some editors simply want the words "Poetry Submission," others want poem titles. Check the market listing for preferences. **Note:** Because of spam, filters and other concerns, some editors are strict about what must be printed in the subject line and how. If you're uncertain about any aspect of e-mail submission formats, double-check the website (if available) for information or contact the publication for directions.

What is a chapbook? How is it different from a regular poetry book?

A chapbook is a booklet, averaging 24-50 pages in length (some are shorter), usually digest-sized (5½×8½, although chapbooks can come in all sizes, even published within the pages of a magazine). Typically, a chapbook is saddle-stapled with a soft cover (card or special paper); chapbooks can also be produced with a plain paper cover the same weight as the pages, especially if the booklet is photocopied.

A chapbook is a much smaller collection of poetry than a full-length book (which runs anywhere from 50 pages to well over 100 pages, longer for "best of" collections and retrospectives). There are probably more poetry chapbooks being published than full-length books, and that's an important point to consider. Don't think of the chapbook as a poor relation to the full-length collection. While it's true a chapbook won't attract big

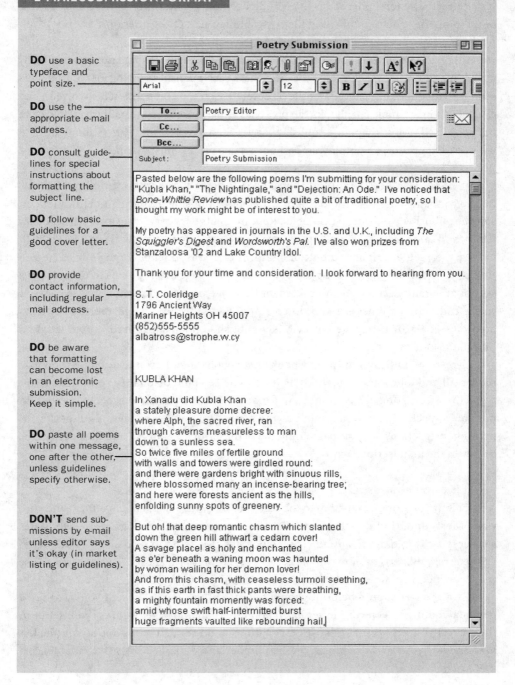

E-MAIL SUBMISSION FORMAT

DO use a basic typeface and point size.

DO use the appropriate e-mail address.

DO consult guidelines for special instructions about formatting the subject line.

DO follow basic guidelines for a good cover letter.

DO provide contact information, including regular mail address.

DO be aware that formatting can become lost in an electronic submission. Keep it simple.

DO paste all poems within one message, one after the other, unless guidelines specify otherwise.

DON'T send submissions by e-mail unless editor says it's okay (in market listing or guidelines).

Poetry Submission

Arial 12 **B** *I* U

To... Poetry Editor
Cc...
Bcc...
Subject: Poetry Submission

Pasted below are the following poems I'm submitting for your consideration: "Kubla Khan," "The Nightingale," and "Dejection: An Ode." I've noticed that *Bone-Whittle Review* has published quite a bit of traditional poetry, so I thought my work might be of interest to you.

My poetry has appeared in journals in the U.S. and U.K., including *The Squiggler's Digest* and *Wordsworth's Pal*. I've also won prizes from Stanzaloosa '02 and Lake Country Idol.

Thank you for your time and consideration. I look forward to hearing from you.

S. T. Coleridge
1796 Ancient Way
Mariner Heights OH 45007
(852)555-5555
albatross@strophe.w.cy

KUBLA KHAN

In Xanadu did Kubla Khan
a stately pleasure dome decree:
where Alph, the sacred river, ran
through caverns measureless to man
down to a sunless sea.
So twice five miles of fertile ground
with walls and towers were girdled round:
and there were gardens bright with sinuous rills,
where blossomed many an incense-bearing tree;
and here were forests ancient as the hills,
enfolding sunny spots of greenery.

But oh! that deep romantic chasm which slanted
down the green hill athwart a cedarn cover!
A savage place! as holy and enchanted
as e'er beneath a waning moon was haunted
by woman wailing for her demon lover!
And from this chasm, with ceaseless turmoil seething,
as if this earth in fast thick pants were breathing,
a mighty fountain momently was forced:
amid whose swift half-intermitted burst
huge fragments vaulted like rebounding hail,

reviews, qualify for major prizes or find national distribution through chain bookstores, it's a terrific way for a poet to build an audience (and reputation) in increments, while developing the kind of publishing history that may attract the attention of a book publisher one day.

Although some presses consider chapbooks through a regular submission process, many choose manuscripts through competitions. Check each publisher's listing for requirements, send for guidelines or visit the website (absolutely vital if a competition is involved), and check out some sample chapbooks the press has already produced (usually available from the press itself). Most chapbook publishers are as choosy as book publishers about the quality of work they accept. Submit your best poems in a professional manner.

How do I format a collection of poems to submit to a book/chapbook publisher?

Before you send a manuscript to a book/chapbook publisher, request guidelines (or consult the publisher's website, if available). Requirements vary regarding formatting, query letters and samples, length, and other considerations. Usually you will use 8½×11, 20 lb. white paper; set left, right and bottom margins of at least one inch; put your name and title of your collection in the top left corner of every page; limit poems to one per page (although poems certainly may run longer than one page); and number pages consecutively. Individual publisher requirements might include a title page, table of contents, credits page (indicating where previously published poems originally appeared) and biographical note.

If you're submitting your poetry book or chapbook manuscript to a competition, you *must* read and follow the guidelines. Failure to do so could disqualify your manuscript. Guidelines for a competition might call for an official entry form to accompany the submission, a special title page, a minimum and maximum number of pages, and specific formatting instructions (such as paginating the manuscript and not putting the poet's name on any of the manuscript pages).

What is a cover letter? Do I have to send one? What should it say?

A cover letter is your introduction to the editor, telling him a little about yourself and your work. Most editors indicate their cover letter preferences in their listings. If an editor states a cover letter is "required," absolutely send one! It's also better to send one if a cover letter is "preferred." Experts disagree on the necessity and appropriateness of cover letters, so use your own judgment when preferences aren't clear in the listing.

A cover letter should be professional but also allow you to present your work in a personal manner. Keep your letter brief, no more than one page. Address your letter to the correct contact person. (Use "Poetry Editor" if no contact name appears in the listing.) Include your name, address, phone number and e-mail address (if available). If a

PREPARING YOUR COVER LETTER

Perry Lineskanner ❶
1954 Eastern Blvd.
Pentameter OH 45007
(852) 555-5555
soneteer@trochee.vv.cy

April 24, 2009

Spack Saddlestaple, Editor
The Squiggler's Digest ❷
Double-Toe Press
P.O. Box 54X
Submission Junction AZ 85009

Dear Mr. Saddlestaple:

❸ Enclosed are three poems for your consideration for The Squiggler's Digest: "The Diamond Queen," "The Boy Who Was Gromit," and "The Maker of Everything."

❹ Although this is my first submission to your journal, I'm a long-time reader of The Squiggler's Digest and enjoy the scope of narrative poetry you feature. I especially enjoyed Sydney Dogwood's poetry cycle in Issue 4.

My own poetry has appeared recently in The Bone-Whittle Review, Bumper-Car Reverie, and Stock Still.

Thank you for considering my manuscript. I look forward to hearing from you.

Sincerely,

Perry Lineskanner

❶ DO type on one side of 8½ × 11 20lb. paper. ❷ DO use a standard 12-point typeface (like Times New Roman). ❸ DO list the poems you're submitting for consideration. ❹ DO mention something about the magazine and about yourself.

biographical note is requested, include 2-3 lines about your background, interests, why you write poetry, etc. Avoid praising yourself or your poems in your letter (your submission should speak for itself). Include titles (or first lines) of the poems you're submitting. You may list a few of your most recent publishing credits, but no more than five; and keep in mind that some editors find publishing credits tiresome—they're more interested in the quality of the work you're submitting to *them*.

Use a business-style format for a professional appearance and proofread carefully; typos, misspellings and other errors make a poor first impression.

Show your familiarity with the magazine to which you're submitting: comment on a poem the magazine published, tell the editor why you chose to submit to her magazine, mention poets the magazine has published. Use a business-style format for a professional appearance and proofread carefully; typos, misspellings and other errors make a poor first impression. Remember that editors are people, too. Respect, professionalism and kindness go a long way in poet/editor relationships.

What is a SASE? An IRC (with SAE)?

A SASE is a self-addressed, stamped envelope—and you should never send a submission by regular mail without one. Also include a SASE if you send an inquiry to an editor. If your submission is too large for an envelope (for instance, a bulky book-length collection of poems), use a box and include a self-addressed mailing label with adequate return postage paper-clipped to it.

An IRC is an International Reply Coupon, enclosed with a self-addressed envelope for manuscripts submitted to foreign markets. Each coupon is equivalent in value to the minimum postage rate for an unregistered airmail letter. IRCs may be exchanged for postage stamps at post offices in all foreign countries that are members of the Universal Postal Union (UPU). When you provide the adequate number of IRCs and a self-addressed envelope (SAE), you give a foreign editor financial means to return your submission (U.S. postage stamps cannot be used to send mail *to* the United States from outside the country). Purchase price is $2 per coupon. Call your local post office to check for availability (sometimes only larger post offices sell them).

IMPORTANT NOTE ABOUT IRCS: Foreign editors sometimes find the IRCs have been stamped incorrectly by the U.S. post office when purchased. This voids the IRCs and makes it impossible for the foreign editor to exchange the coupons for return postage for your manuscript. When buying IRCs, make sure yours have been stamped correctly before you leave the counter. (The Postal Service clerk must place a postmark in the block with the heading *control stamp of the country of origin*.) More information about International Reply Coupons is available on the USPS website (www.usps.com).

To save time and money, poets sometimes send disposable manuscripts to foreign markets and inform the editor to discard the manuscript after it's been read. Some enclose an IRC and SAE for reply only; others establish a deadline after which they will withdraw the manuscript from consideration and market it elsewhere.

How much postage does my submission need?

As much as it takes—you do *not* want your manuscript to arrive postage due. Purchase a postage scale or take your manuscript to the post office for weighing. Remember, you'll need postage on two envelopes: the one containing your submission and SASE, and the return envelope itself. Submissions without SASEs usually will not be returned (and possibly may not even be read).

Note: New postage rates went into effect in January, 2013. There is now a new fee structure for First-Class Postage. For letters and cards (including business-size envelopes), the First-Class rate is 46 cents for the first ounce, and 20 cents per additional ounce up to and including 3.5 ounces. **Letter-sized mail that weighs more than 3.5 ounces is charged the "flats" rate** ("flats" include any envelope large enough to mail an 8½×11 manuscript page unfolded) of 92 cents for the first ounce, and 20 cents for each additional ounce up to and including 13 ounces. This means if you send a large envelope that weighs only one ounce, it costs 92 cents at the First-Class flats rate instead of the 46 cents charged for First-Class letters and cards. (See the charts on the next page for First-Class rates for letters and flats, or go to www.usps.com for complete information on all rates questions.)

The USPS also offers its Click-N-Ship® program, which allows a customer to print domestic and international shipping labels with postage, buy insurance and pay for postage by credit card. See the USPS website for a one-time software download, to check system requirements and to register for an account.

The website is also your source for ordering supplies (such as a postage scale and labels), reviewing postal regulations, calculating postage and more. Canada Post information and services are available at www.canadapost.com.

POSTAGE INFORMATION

First Class Mail Rates: Letters & Cards

1 ounce	$0.46	3 ounces	$0.86
2 ounces	$0.66	3.5 ounces	$1.06
Postcard	$0.33		

First Class Mail Rates: Flats

Weight not over (ounces)	Rate	Weight not over (ounces)	Rate
1	$0.92	8	$2.32
2	$1.12	9	$2.52
3	$1.32	10	$2.72
4	$1.52	11	$2.92
5	$1.72	12	$3.12
6	$1.92	13	$3.32
7	$2.12		

Source: Website of the United States Postal Service (www.usps.com)

U.S. Postal Codes

AL	Alabama	KY	Kentucky	OK	Oklahoma
AK	Alaska	LA	Louisiana	OR	Oregon
AZ	Arizona	ME	Maine	PA	Pennsylvania
AR	Arkansas	MD	Maryland	PR	Puerto Rico
CA	California	MA	Massachusetts	RI	Rhode Island
CO	Colorado	MI	Michigan	SC	South Carolina
CT	Connecticut	MN	Minnesota	SD	South Dakota
DE	Delaware	MS	Mississippi	TN	Tennessee
DC	District of Columbia	MO	Missouri	TX	Texas
FL	Florida	NE	Montana	UT	Utah
GA	Georgia	NV	Nevada	VT	Vermont
GU	Guam	NH	New Hampshire	VI	Virgin Islands
HI	Hawaii	NJ	New Jersey	VA	Virginia
ID	Idaho	NM	New Mexico	WA	Washington
IL	Illinois	NY	New York	WV	West Virginia
IN	Indiana	NC	North Carolina	WI	Wisconsin
IA	Iowa	ND	North Dakota	WY	Wyoming
KS	Kansas	OH	Ohio		

Canadian Postal Codes

AB	Alberta	NS	Nova Scotia	QC	Quebec
BC	British Columbia	NT	Northwest Territories	SK	Saskatchewan
MB	Manitoba	NU	Nunavut	YT	Yukon
NB	New Brunswick	ON	Ontario		
NL	Newfoundland & Labrador	PE	Prince Edward Island		

What does it mean when an editor says "no previously published" poems? Does this include poems that have appeared in anthologies? What if one of my poems appeared online through a group or forum?

If your poem appears *anywhere* in print for a public audience, it's considered "previously" published. That includes magazines, anthologies, websites and online journals, and even printed programs (say for a church service, wedding, etc.). See the explanation for rights below, especially *second serial (reprint) rights* and *all rights* for additional concerns about previously published material.

One exception to the above guidelines is if your poem appears online in a *private* poetry forum, critique group, etc. As long as the site is private (i.e., a password is required to view and participate), your poem isn't considered "published." However, if your poem is printed on an online forum or bulletin board that's available for public viewing, even if you must use a password to post the poem or to comment, then your poem is considered "published" as far as rights are concerned.

What rights should I offer for my poems?
What do these different rights mean?

Editors usually indicate in their listings what rights they acquire. Most journals and magazines license *first rights* (a.k.a. *first serial rights*), which means the poet offers the right to publish the poem for the first time in any periodical. All other rights to the material remain with the poet. (Note that some editors state that rights to poems "revert to poets upon publication" when first rights are acquired.) When poems are excerpted from a book prior to publication and printed in a magazine/journal, this is also called *first serial rights*. The addition of *North American* indicates the editor is the first to publish a poem in a U.S. or Canadian periodical. The poem may still be submitted to editors outside of North America or to those who acquire reprint rights.

When a magazine/journal licenses *one-time rights* to a poem (also known as *simultaneous rights*), the editor has *nonexclusive* rights to publish the poem once. The poet may submit that same poem to other publications at the same time (usually markets that don't have overlapping audiences).

Editors/publishers open to submission of work already published elsewhere seek *second serial (reprint) rights*. The poet is obliged to inform them where and when the poem previously appeared so they can give proper credit to the original publication. In essence, chapbook or book collections license reprint rights, listing the magazines in which poems previously appeared somewhere in the book (usually on the copyright page or separate credits page).

If a publisher or editor requires you to relinquish *all rights*, be aware that you're giving up ownership of that poem or group of poems. You cannot resubmit the work elsewhere, nor can you include it in a poetry collection without permission or by negotiating for reprint rights to be returned to you. Before you agree to this type of arrangement, ask the editor first if he or she is willing to acquire first rights instead of all rights. If you receive a refusal and you don't want to relinquish all rights, simply write a letter withdrawing your work from consideration. Some editors will reassign rights to a writer after a given amount of time, such as one year.

With the growth in Internet publishing opportunities, *electronic rights* have become very important. These cover a broad range of electronic media, including online magazines, CD recordings of poetry readings and CD-ROM editions of magazines. When submitting to an electronic market of any kind, find out what rights the market acquires upfront (many online magazines also stipulate the right to archive poetry they've published so it's continually available on their websites).

What is a copyright? Should I have my poems copyrighted before I submit them for publication?

Copyright is a proprietary right that gives you the power to control your work's reproduction, distribution and public display or performance, as well as its adaptation to other forms. In other words, you have the legal right to the exclusive publication, sale or distribution of your poetry. What's more, your "original works of authorship" are protected as soon as they are "fixed in a tangible form of expression," i.e., written down or recorded. Since March 1989, copyright notices are no longer required to secure protection, so it's not necessary to include them on your poetry manuscript. Also, in many editors' minds, copyright notices signal the work of amateurs who are distrustful and paranoid about having work stolen.

If you still want to indicate copyright, use the © symbol or the word *copyright*, your name and the year. If you wish, you can register your copyright with the Copyright Office for a $45 fee, using Form TX (directions and form available for download from www.copyright.gov). Since paying $45 per poem is costly and impractical, you may prefer to copyright a group of unpublished poems for that single fee. Further information is available from the U.S. Copyright Office, Library of Congress, 101 Independence Ave. S.E., Washington DC 20559-6000; by download from www.copyright.gov; or by calling (202)707-3000 between 8:30 a.m. and 5:00 p.m. (EST) weekdays.

SPECIAL NOTE REGARDING COPYRIGHT OFFICE MAIL DELIVERY: The "effective date of registration" for copyright applications is usually the day the Copyright Office actually receives all elements of an application (application form, fee and copies of work being registered). Because of security concerns, all USPS and private-carrier mail is screened off-site prior to arrival at the Copyright Office. This can add 3-5 days to delivery time and could, therefore, impact the effective date of registration. See the website for details about proper packaging, special handling and other related information.

HOW TO INCREASE YOUR ODDS OF PUBLICATION

....

by Sage Cohen

Writing poetry is an art, and so is the process of submitting your poems for publication. If you'd like to increase your odds of getting noticed and getting published, this article can help you align your best work with the right opportunities—so you can give your poems the chance they deserve.

IDENTIFY THE RIGHT PUBLICATIONS FOR YOUR POETRY

You'll have the greatest odds of publication when you submit your poems to journals or contests that are most suited to your work—and therefore most likely to appreciate it. If you're not sure how to identify such possibilities, consider the following:

Read the work of poets you love

A good way to get a feel for publishing possibilities is by reviewing the acknowledgments pages of the poetry collections you admire. If you connect to a particular poet's work, chances are good that your poetry could also be well suited to the journals where s/he has been published.

Do your due diligence

Let's say you've collected a list of possible journals and contests based on the tip above. And let's say you've never sent out work for publication before. You can research here in *Poet's Market* to learn more about how your poetry and these opportunities might line up. For example, you'll want to submit only to journals that say they publish work by emerging as well as established poets. You'll want to confirm that contest submission fees and guidelines are in alignment with what you're willing to send and spend. And you may want to make sure your themes, poetic forms, and approach to language are compatible with the publication's description of what it is seeking. I also suggest learning what you can about the editors or contest judge(s)—and reading their poetry, if possible, so you get a feeling for their personal aesthetic.

Always experience a journal before submitting

Before submitting your work to a publication, purchase its latest issue or view content online to get a sense of the poets and poems it features. Also consider how the publication's front cover, inside art, website design, production, paper quality and font choice create a particular kind of experience. If you can imagine seeing your poetry in these pages, that's a good indication that the journal or site may be the right fit for you.

Track what you learn to grow your knowledge base

I suggest creating a simple system—a document, binder or folder—where you track what you've learned about each publication and record your thinking about how your poems align or do not align. This way, you'll have a growing knowledge base about the poetry market—and how various opportunities may be suited to your objectives—as you investigate, submit and publish over time.

CHOOSE THE RIGHT POEM/S

When you've chosen a publication or contest to which you'd like to submit, it's time to gather the poems for this opportunity. Consider running the poems you are considering through these filters of inquiry:

Does something significant or resonant happen?

Poems get editors' attention when they introduce a new possibility, provide a palpable experience or revelation, and say something in a way it has never been spoken (or written) before. Ask yourself:

- What happens in this poem? (Or, if the poem is non-narrative, do the language, sound and/or imagery create the kind of experience or journey I intended?)
- If this poem is about or addressed to someone I know, does it also reveal something meaningful or relevant to people outside of the dynamic?
- What is discovered or transformed or revealed?

Because it can be tricky to experience your own, highly subjective material objectively, you may want to share your poems with a reader or two you trust and ask these questions of them. If you're not sure you are creating an experience that has impact or resonance, your poem may not yet be ready for publication.

Have I found something fresh to say about a familiar theme?

If you're writing about a historical person or event or one that's been covered in the news in recent years, chances are good that most readers will have a good handle on the facts. To ensure that your poem makes an impact, ask yourself:

- What happens in this poem that is fresh, surprising, and different than the information already available on this topic?
- How is this poem departing from the work of "reporting" and moving into the territory of "illuminating"?
- How is this event or person serving as a leaping-off point for my own inquiry or discovery about myself, history, the natural world, or the human condition?

IS MY WORK AS POLISHED AS POSSIBLE?

These 10 revision tips may help you identify opportunities to nip, tuck, and shine. Ask yourself:

1. Could I trim exposition at the beginning or summary information at the end that is not serving the poem?
2. Could I use a different voice to influence the experience of this poem? (For example, consider changing a third-person voice into the first person and see if this shift in intimacy is of benefit.)
3. Could my similes and metaphors be more distilled or powerful? If I've used an extended metaphor, does it hold up throughout the poem?
4. Where can I bring more energy to the language I've used? Can I use more active language to communicate similar ideas? Can modifiers be cut?
5. What if I changed the past-tense verbs to the present tense (or vice versa)?
6. How might I shape the poem (line length, stanza breaks, white space) to more fully enact the emotion and rhythm of its content?
7. Are punctuation and capitalization and verb tense consistent? Would different choices (such as removing punctuation or capitalization) improve the experience?
8. Is there a music of repeating sounds throughout the poem? What words could I replace to create a more cohesive sound experience?

9. Are there opportunities to break lines in ways that give attention to important words or pace the momentum of the narrative more powerfully?

10. How might the title better encapsulate and add dimension to the experience of the poem? Could some of the exposition cut in step one be used to set the context of the poem in its title?

ARRANGE YOUR POEMS INTENTIONALLY

The order of the poems you've submitted can make a difference in an editor's experience and opinion of your work—even if you're just submitting three to five poems. Think about the arrangement as a single composition that provides a coherent reading journey. Where do you want the reader to start—and finish? How do you want them to enter the realm of your poetry, and how are you intending to send them off?

MAKE SUBMISSION GUIDELINES YOUR BIBLE

Every literary publication and contest will offer detailed guidelines about how and when they want to receive poems. Your job is to follow every single detail of those guidelines fanatically to ensure you don't rule yourself out with a simple oversight. Because it's easy to miss a detail when scanning instructions online, I recommend printing out the submission guidelines for any opportunity and then checking off each requirement as you meet it. Specifically:

- Follow simultaneous submission instructions. Some publications accept simultaneous submissions (meaning that you've sent the same poems to more than one publication for consideration at the same time) and others don't. Be careful to understand and honor each journal's parameters.
- Get your timing right. Publications have contest deadlines and specific reading windows. Make sure you are sending your work in advance of the specified deadline.
- Choose poems that fit. Ensure that you have chosen poems that match any specific requirements, such as: theme, form, length (number of lines or pages), number of poems allowed or required.
- Be deliberate about where you include your name. Some publications read and choose poems "blind," others don't. Be sure to understand whether the publication wants identifying information on the poems or not—and follow these guidelines carefully.
- Double-check the mailing address and editor names. No editor wants to see his or her name misspelled or receive mail addressed to his or her predecessor. It's also a

good idea to confirm the gender of the person you are addressing if you have any doubt.

- Follow binding requirements. Publications are often very specific about whether they want paper clips, staples or loose pages.
- Provide an SASE (self-addressed, stamped envelope) if this is required or requested by the publication. If they've made it clear that they intend to notify you some other way, follow whatever process is requested.
- Include a check if you are submitting to a contest that has a required reading fee. Make sure you make it out to the organization as requested in the amount required and specify the name of the contest to which you are submitting.

FORMAT, PROOF, AND POLISH

First impressions are often the last impression. Think of your submission package as a gift that an editor or selection committee will enjoy opening and experiencing—whether you're submitting online or by mail:

- Use a standard font that is easy to read—such as Times New Roman or Garamond or Calibri—using 12-point font, unless instructed otherwise. Your priority should be: legibility and ease for the person(s) who will be considering your poem.
- Unless you are doing so for a very specific reason, such as for dialogue or to distinguish a speaker's thoughts, think twice about bolding or italicizing fonts. Let your images, word choice and line breaks do the work of creating emphasis and momentum.
- Print your poems on white, unrumpled and unscented paper.
- Ensure that your toner is working or that your photocopies are clear and crisp.

WRITE A COVER LETTER THAT CONNECTS

Your cover letter should first and foremost provide whatever information is requested in the submission guidelines, if any. In the absence of specific instruction, write a concise note that covers the following:

- Explain that you are submitting poems for [name of contest, issue, or general consideration].
- Describe in a sentence or two what you admire about the publication and why you chose to submit your work—if you have something authentic to say. Or, if you've had a previous communication with an editor (such as, they sent an encouraging rejection with a note inviting you to submit again in the future) you can mention that here.

- Lists the names of the poems being submitted. If this is a simultaneous submission, it is good form to mention this and confirm that you intend to follow whatever process this publication has requested in its submission guidelines.
- Provide a brief biographical paragraph that describes key publishing or education highlights to reflect your literary experience and expertise. If you haven't published yet or don't have anything else relevant to report, no need to say anything here.
- Be polite and gracious.

Remember, this is a business communication. Some mistakes to avoid:

- Do not provide explanations about why you chose these poems for submission, why you wrote them, what they mean to you or your family, or how you have revised them.
- Do not advise editors about when you expect to hear back from them.
- Do not send a follow-up letter with a batch of poems that are edited versions of a previous submission.
- Do send a follow-up letter to withdraw any poems you have submitted as soon as they have been accepted elsewhere.

Over time, you'll get more efficient and adept with this process. Preparing your poems for submission will get faster, easier and more automatic as you know what steps to take and mistakes to avoid. Your commitment to consistently putting your best work forward—and willingness to learn from the feedback you get along the way—will give you the very best odds of publication.

SAGE COHEN is the author of *Writing the Life Poetic* and *The Productive Writer,* both from Writer's Digest Books, and the poetry collection Like the Heart, the World. She holds an MFA in creative writing from New York University and a BA from Brown University. Sage has won first place in the Ghost Road Press poetry contest, been nominated for a Pushcart Prize and published a number of articles in *Writer's Digest* magazine. In 2011, she judged the Writer's Digest contest for non-rhyming poetry. To learn more about Sage, visit pathofpossibility.com.

READY YOUR WORK FOR PUBLICATION

9 Techniques for Perfecting Poems

....

by Lauren Camp

Poetry is a sublime art form, but making it takes time. Breathtaking poems generally emerge from a slow, considered approach and a long gestation period.

Writing technical and magazine articles taught me structure, concision, and reporting strategies. Poetry teaches me to analyze the colors of each thought, and to look for ways to sculpt the statement. If every poem came out perfect right away, the experience would feel too clipped. I want the project to take a while, to "marinate" and evolve into language both exquisite and weirdly unexpected.

To ensure your poems get picked out from the editors' slush pile, take some time to prime your work for publication. Here are nine hands-on, critical techniques to help you assess your poems from different perspectives, and improve your writing.

TIP #1 — LISTEN TO MILES DAVIS.

On his 1959 album *Kind of Blue,* trumpeter and composer Miles Davis named a composition "So What." Ask that question of your poem. *So what* if you have a distinctive voice? *So what* if there's melody? Why should others care about your poem?

To create a poem with staying power, you have to be able to answer one tough question: is this worth saying? If you are writing the poem just to share an experience, the poem isn't done yet. Consider what the experience taught you. Would an audience be interested in that? Most experiences are universal in some way. Give readers an insight that they can connect to their lives.

TIP #2 — EATING THE BANANA.

Think hard about "the."

"The" means "the one and only." The ultimate. The whole enchilada. The all and everything of a subject.

Look at every single place you've used it. Is this what you're trying to infer? Did you really sit on "the" park bench? (I can think of a lot of benches – and a lot of parks). Did you really eat "the" banana? The one and only?

You see what I mean. It's easy to say it and write it, but when you start picking apart what you mean…well, maybe you shouldn't use "the." Try substituting "a" – a park bench, a banana, a trip to Peru – or see if the poem works without any articles at all.

TIP #3 — STOP GOING AND DOING.

Another easy fix is to shorten and tighten verbs. Why are you "going" when you could just "go" – or better yet, "fly," "meander," or "trudge"?

Gerunds ("ing" words) are so kind. They whisper over readers with a tinge of apology. They are almost always less effective than a lean verb — one without fat. Be insistent in your writing for a change. Make those verbs muscular. Ask them to really do something, to lift the line. Be more authoritative than you think you can; stop "ing-ing" around.

After you've made these changes, re-read your lines out loud in a big, vigorous, and certain voice. How does the poem sound now?

Clearly, you can't cut all "ing" words all the time. Look for a balance of tensile strength with breathing space.

TIP #4 — PULL YOURSELF OUT.

We all write about ourselves in some way, but sometimes poems are just loaded with… well, us.

How many times do you have to say "I" for your readers to know the poem is happening to you? I bet you could safely eliminate some references to self, and readers would still be clued in. Try it. Take one "I" out, and see if it matters. Take out another. Don't forget to read out loud to make sure you haven't lost the flow - or the human quality of the poem.

Remove yourself just enough that you aren't ever-present, but be careful. If you take yourself completely out, the poem will seem choppy and abstract.

TIP #5 — LOOK FOR SOFT SPOTS.

My students step into soft spots all the time. So do I, and you will, too, because you must write first for you, and then, revise for someone else.

Where readers sink is the quicksand of the poem. The weight of messy language pulls them down. Sometimes our writing is thick and circular – especially if we are trying to say too much. Because we often write to figure something out for ourselves, rather than writing what we already know, we may be uncertain how to draw the map of what we're exploring. What a writer thinks is solid might not always be so to a reader.

How can you avoid these spots? Let the poem sit for a while. The irony of this technique is that the quick answer to finding your soft spots is time. Let the poem exist on your hard drive, unopened, until it becomes a little unfamiliar to you – one month, three months even, if you can manage that.

Then, when a sufficient amount of time has passed, read it. Anything that is confusing or too abstract will now be evident. You will see where you have taken readers on a side journey, and forgotten to bring them back. Because the poem is again new to you, you will know if you have complicated its map, and if there is a more direct route.

You want readers to get somewhere specific: your revelation. Take out references that send them to the wrong places.

TIP #6 — WEAR THE STRONG SUIT OF SPECIFICITY.

Be particular in your writing. Give details without drowning your readers in adjectives. Tell us which street, which store, the hour it happened, the season, the type of insect you heard in the air, the color of buttons on his shirt.

Israeli poet Yehuda Amichai once wrote that you must "put real things in your poems." Ask the poem every possible question you can. Is everything defined precisely? One of my students wrote about how, as a young child, she was instructed to put her small, cold hand inside the pocket of her mother's wool coat as a way for her mother to keep her close on dangerous urban streets. Holding fast to the pocket, the girl felt the nubbly texture. Because she described it, I could also feel the pocket lining, and the sense of security that came with it.

TIP #7 — SMASH IT.

Auguste Rodin advised young sculptors to stop gently picking at the clay and plaster of their sculpture when something wasn't going well. Instead, he encouraged them to "drop it on the floor and see what it looks like then."

It's easy to draw an analogy between this and poetry revising. Both creative acts sometimes require drastic changes to find the form your piece needs. Revision is all about seeing new options, but you might not be able to do this when you're trying to stay true to your initial intent.

If you are convinced that a poem isn't working and will never work, you are free to do anything at all to it. Construction workers often relish demolition work. Why not use their approach? Destruction frees the poem of the ghost of its earlier structure. Rather than remedying little parts, rebuild the whole.

Pick a line or phrase that seems strong. Let that chosen line become a new jumping off place, and jump in an unexpected direction.

Of course, if you're an archivist, and the idea of tossing big parts of the poem gives you hives, by all means, save the gems. (I collect the lines that I still like in a separate document.) But eviscerate them if they don't serve the poem you're revising.

TIP #8 — INTERLACE.

Have you ever tried splicing two poems together? In a way, it's like braiding hair. You pull a line from here and a line from there, again and again, until you have created a more complex structure, woven with new thoughts.

Take those good lines, and plait them into another poem. If they are on the same subject, aha! an easy fit. If not, well… your job as poet becomes more challenging. How to match them together…?

In the mid-1960s, John Lennon wrote lyrics inspired by a news headline about a car accident and other events that were current at the time. His musical partner Paul McCartney had written a simple ditty about a man heading out late on a bus, and moving into a hazy dream. These were totally separate stories, neither quite complete in itself. Twined together, the lyrics became "A Day in the Life," an intriguing song on the *Sgt. Pepper's Lonely Hearts Club Band* album.

Lennon said, "I had the bulk of the song and the words, but [Paul] contributed this little lick floating around in his head that he couldn't use for anything."

Isn't that how it is sometimes with a poem – a perfect phrase that needs a new home? Move it to another poem. Encourage it to become a strand in something larger, something with a separate music – maybe even one you didn't realize could exist. Take it from two lyrical masters; poetry interspersed with poetry can double the emotional impact.

TIP #9 — CHANGE THE PACING.

Revision is about taking innumerable steps to write the best possible poem. One technique worth trying is to change the speed of the poem – how fast or slow it travels on the page.

If you're writing about something urgent or disturbing, and you want readers to keep moving through the poem – if, in fact, you believe readers should be nearly breathless when reading, try enjambment. In other words, don't let your lines end comfortably with commas or periods. Don't let anyone stop reading. Keep the thought in motion.

Think like a movie director for a thriller. When one of the characters is in danger, you want to design the scene to keep viewers on the edge of their seats, blood racing. How will you do this? Lighting, sound…whatever it takes to keep the suspense constant.

That's what you're after as a poet, too. Make your readers keep hurrying ahead to the next line, and the next. This doesn't mean you can't use punctuation. Instead, place those punctuation marks in the middle of lines, where periods are significantly less weighty and powerful.

For a different way to speed up, you might try incorporating a full line of monosyllables. You'll get a ticker-tape effect from the rapid short words, which will hurtle readers through the line.

What if you want to move more slowly, and let readers revel in your images? Lines that are end-stopped (with periods) allow them to pause deeply. Stanza breaks take this even further – a maximum full stop. A complete resting place.

So, try switching the stride of your poem. As the writer, you know whether it should meander along or hurtle forth; now you just need to make your line decisions fit the mood of the piece, so readers know how to "hear" the poem.

It can take a lot of work to get a poem right, but what seems like discipline can also be a joy. My students call this work "revisioning." Whatever techniques you employ, don't be too controlling. Remember to allow spontaneity to also guide the work.

Lauren Camp is the author of the poetry collection *This Business of Wisdom* (West End Press), an interdisciplinary artist, and an educator. Her poems have appeared in *J Journal, Linebreak, Beloit Poetry Journal*, and *you are here*, among other journals. Her work gets accepted almost as frequently as it gets turned down, which she considers good odds. She has also guest edited special sections for *World Literature Today* (on international jazz poetry) and for *Malpaís Review* (on the poetry of Iraq). Lauren blogs about poetry at *Which Silk Shirt*. On Sundays, she hosts "Audio Saucepan," a weekly global music and poetry program on Santa Fe Public Radio. www.laurencamp.com

THE ORGANIZED POET

by Patricia Kennelly

If you're like many poets I've talked with, it's not uncommon to have your poems everywhere. My desktop held overflowing notebooks, file folders and piles of random pieces of paper, scribbled with favorite words, lines, and poem starts. My computer's desktop wasn't any better. Although I knew most of my work was saved, my lack of organization made finding a particular poem time-consuming.

This wasn't too much of a problem until I started submitting my body of work. I struggled with getting my work to the right market. I missed good opportunities and important deadlines and created unnecessary stress by entering my poems at the last minute. Finding contests, markets and journals was the easy part; tracking down a poem or trying to read my illegible note about a "must enter" contest became challenging.

Most organizational experts agree that organizing any part of your life will save you time, money and help to eliminate stress. So why do so many poets have resistance to organizing their work? Some poets think that organization is the opposite of creativity and that being too businesslike will stifle their voices. I found the opposite to be true. Working on organization fueled my desire to write poetry and get my poems published.

The result? More published pieces and a clearer picture of where I wanted to go with my poetry.

When I decided to take ownership of my body of work and organize, I naturally approached the submission process in a professional manner. Doing the hard work ahead of time meant I had more time to find and research markets. The result? More published pieces and a clearer picture of where I wanted to go with my poetry.

Whatever system you choose (pen and paper, computer based, online or a combination of all) make sure it's one that will work for you. And if it doesn't work, consider trying another. The best organizational systems only function if you're ready to get organized and if they fit your personality. If any of these tips seem too daunting, consider asking a fellow poet to work with you in exchange for doing the same for them.

10 WAYS TO GET ORGANIZED

If you don't already have an uncluttered writing space, create one. It's difficult to work on organization if your space causes additional stress or distraction. These tips might help you become a more organized poet:

1. Find all of your publishable poems as well as your incomplete poems. This may take some time. Don't rush this process; finding, reading and organizing your forgotten words may inspire new work. Consider typing up your poem starts into one document so you know where to begin when you're stuck for inspiration.

2. Print hard copies of all work and separate publishable poems and poems that need revision into separate accordion files or three-ring binders. You can choose to file by title, subject/theme or type/form. Other poets include length of poem and tone.

3. Generate a virtual folder on your desktop. I titled mine "All Poetry" and created subfolders entitled "Publishable Poems," "Needs Work," and "Published Poems." Choose subfolder titles that make sense to you, you can use poem title, subject matter, form, or theme. Your goal is to be able to find your poems easily.

4. Create or find a submission tracker. If your goal is publication, having a system that tracks your submissions and that is easy to use and update will help create a sense of order.

5. Write or type up a list of goal markets for the year. I do this by going through *Poet's Market* and my favorite poetry newsletters and websites to find markets that seem to be a good fit. This document will grow every month as you discover more markets, contests and literary journals. Some poets find including the hyperlinks to be helpful.

6. Make an appointment with yourself. At least once every week I set aside some time to follow up with upcoming deadlines and to write a to-do list. More productive writers than myself do a to-do list every day, but with a full-time job I find that this weekly check-in is enough to keep me on task.

7. Subscribe to poetry newsletters and set Google alerts for specific contests you'd like to enter. Here is the challenging part–as soon as you receive the newsletter or alert, fill in your paper or virtual poetry calendar. And then delete the newsletter.

8. Keep office supplies including: envelopes, paper, file folders, printer ink and stamps stocked. While many magazines and journals are set up for e-mail submissions, there are still some journals that require a hard copy submission.

9. Organize your books by genre. I keep chapbooks, craft books, journals, and poetry magazines on one shelf for reference and inspiration. While the Internet makes it easy to access information, having all of your reference materials within easy reach could prevent you from getting distracted online.

10. Do set a date for completion of your new organizational system by choosing a realistic goal date and sticking to it. As Barbara Sher writes in *Wishcraft: How to Get What You Really Want*, "…your true goal, or target, has to be a concrete action or event, not only so you'll know for sure when you get there, but so that you can make that date with success in advance!"

SETTING UP A POETRY CALENDAR

At the beginning of every year or starting today, consider purchasing a large spaced desk calendar specifically for poetry. Because I'm sitting at the desk every day it's easy to jot down poetry contests and submission deadlines I don't want to miss, especially the "no-entry fee" contests. If it's on my goal market list, I use different colored highlighters to show when the journal is open to submissions.

Writer Phyllis Kaelin also uses a similar paper-based calendar system but uses colorful sticky notes to chart her progress on a particular project. Her paper calendar system works hand in hand with her computer files. She says, "Within the project folder, I keep a running "notes document" where I put comments, plans, progress, word count etc. When I decide to submit I make a note there too."

If you don't already use an online calendar specifically for poetry set one up. If you're serious about poetry this can be used to track submissions, deadlines and markets but also helps keep you on track with readings, writing groups and poetry events. Popular online calendars include: Google Calendar (www.google.com/calendar), Convenient Calendar (www.convenientcalendar.com), and 30 Boxes (www.30boxes.com). I like using an online calendar that integrates with my smartphone so that I can send reminders to my phone, email and/or virtual desktop.

WHY USE A SUBMISSION TRACKER?

Even if you have a good memory, once you get in the habit of sending out your poems it's very easy to lose track of when and where your poems were sent. And there's nothing more frustrating than finding a good market for a particular poem and not remembering where or if it was sent out.

Poet's Market includes a basic submission tracker that you can enlarge and copy. Or if you're feeling creative, you can design your own paper submission tracker using headlines that make sense to you. Another option many poets use is index cards or a simple journal log. Alternatively you can convert *Poet's Market*'s submission tracker to a computer spreadsheet program such as Excel. If you're not comfortable setting up your own tracking spreadsheet on your computer, there are several free submission trackers available online.

The most popular free submission trackers include: Duotrope (www.duotrope.com), Luminary Writer's Database (www.writersdb.com), Writers Market (www.writersmarket. com). *Note*: your purchase of *Poet's Market* includes a 1-year online poetry subscription.

The benefits of using a submission tracker far outweigh the time it will take to set one up.

Rooze, an award-winning poet who is currently pursuing her MFA, says about Duotrope, "I like that they have a theme calendar and a deadline calendar. For each journal, they also list the average response time, percentage of submissions accepted, and the last time a response was received. This gives me a better context to know what to expect. Duotrope also specifies additional criteria, such as requirements around simultaneous submissions and previously printed poems."

The benefits of using a submission tracker far outweigh the time it will take to set one up. If you choose to include comments you can easily recognize when a poem needs a second look. If you use an online submission tracker your timely follow-up can also help other poets who use the database. Knowing that we're all in this submission process together, helping fellow poets just feels right.

If spreadsheets and submission trackers seem too left-brain, you might consider poet Jessy Randall's process. She says, "I write, with my hand and a pen, a poem. I mess around with, cross things out, rewrite lines, for a day or two. Then I set it aside for, if possible, at least a month, or even better, three months. Then I take a look at it again. If I think it's any good, I type it into a giant Word document that contains typed versions of all my poems, with the newest ones at the top. I fiddle around with it some more as I type it. I set it aside again for a while, maybe another month. If I still like it after all that, I submit it to a journal, bundling it together with other poems that somehow go with it. I keep track of where I've sent it, and when, in a Word document (to tell the truth, it's the same giant document). I also try to keep track of the general response time so I know when I should send a query. So I'll have something like:

"Name of Journal: Poem Title 1, Poem Title 2, Poem Title 3, sent January 2012, should respond in 6 months."

For the submission process Randall adds that the "submission information is in the top of my Word document, along with a list of the poems that aren't sent out anywhere at the moment. Then come all the typed poems. At the bottom of this giant document is where I keep track of rejections, in alphabetical order by journal name. If I need to, I can do a word search in the document to see if a particular journal has already seen a particular poem."

YOU'RE PUBLISHED!

Unfortunately just being organized doesn't guarantee publication. But if you're committed to poetry and part of that commitment includes being organized and businesslike, with time and persistence, there's a very good chance that your work will be accepted.

> If the poem was a simultaneous submission, be professional and notify the other publications that you are withdrawing your work.

When you do receive the letter or e-mail that your work is being accepted make sure to follow through. Update your submission tracker as well as your computer and/or paper files. It's very rewarding to move the poem (physically or virtually) from the publishable folder to the published folder and/or to write where and when your poem will be published. If the poem was a simultaneous submission be professional and notify the other publications that you are withdrawing your work.

Blogger and poet Sonya Fehér of Mama True (www.mamatrue.com) includes a Published Worksheet as part of her organizational system.

"The Published Worksheet includes the following fields:

- **Market** – Name of market in which the poem was published
- **Details** – Volume # and other details from publication
- **Link** – If the poem was published online, this gives me the location."

For poet Jessy Randall, being organized makes poetry more gratifying: "This may sound weird, but I particularly enjoy the housekeeping side of poetry, the keeping-track-of-submissions part. When I open up the file that shows me what's where, what's been rejected, what's forthcoming, I feel a real sense of accomplishment even if I didn't write anything that day. Because look at all the stuff that's percolating along without me doing anything!"

That's the favorite part for me too; once I set my organizational system in place I had more fun with the submission process. I missed fewer deadlines and felt more in control of my poetic career. Whether your body of work consists of five or 50 poems there's no time like today to start organizing. Taking the time to organize your work goes beyond the practical; it's a way to honor your time, work, and commitment to craft. It could very well be the inspiration you need to get published.

PATRICIA KENNELLY is a published poet, business owner and editor in Colorado Springs, CO. Her poems have most recently appeared in *Haibun Today*, *Messages from the Hidden Lake* and *The Denver Post*. She gently nags about writing daily and creativity at http://www.writingnag.com.

10 CHAPBOOK DESIGN TIPS EVERY POET SHOULD KNOW

by Amy Miller

There's never been a better time to publish a chapbook. These days, desktop-publishing software is so easy to use that practically any poet who can turn on a computer can put together a chapbook—a small booklet of poems to sell at readings and book fairs. That's the good news. But the bad news is that it's easy to go mad with all that power and crank out a quick chapbook that doesn't do your poems justice. From cramped typography to scary author photos, there are lots of ways—some obvious, some subtle—to go wrong with a chapbook. But with a handful of tips and techniques, you can design a book that lures readers into its pages and presents your work in the best light.

And you don't have to be printing your own chapbook to take advantage of these tips. If you're just sending your work out to literary journals, some basic typography tweaks can help your poems look more polished on the page. And if you've been lucky enough to have your manuscript—chapbook-size or full-length—accepted by a publishing house, knowing a few tricks of the trade will help you communicate your wishes to your publisher in a language you both understand, perhaps making the difference between a book that just gets the job done and one that really pops.

FIGURE OUT THE BEST TYPE SIZE AND LEADING

This bit of typography-speak is one of the most important factors—some would say the most important—in making your poems look good on the page. Put simply, this is the relationship between the size of the letters (type size) and the vertical distance between the lines (leading). A common mistake is to make the leading too tight, resulting in lines that are too close together. It's a subtle business—this cramping won't make the type illegible, but even leading that's just a bit too tight will make it hard for the reader to discern one line from the next, making for an uncomfortable reading experience.

A good rule of thumb for poetry is to make your type size three points smaller than the leading: for instance, 11-point type on 14-point leading, or 12 on 15. But not all fonts are created equal; one font may look best at 11.5 on 15, while another may shine at 12 on 14.75. If you're trying to fit more lines onto the page (say, a poem is a line or two over), think twice before just decreasing the leading; you may be better off shrinking both the type size and the leading by a quarter or half point, resulting in smaller type but easy reading because the leading is still comfortable on the eye. And if you have to shrink the type on one page, do it for the whole book to keep your design consistent throughout.

CHOOSE A GOOD FONT

This may seem very basic, but picking out a font for poetry can be surprisingly difficult. There are many schools of thought on what makes a good poetry font—browse through a dozen chapbooks, and you'll probably see a dozen different text fonts. But if you look closely, you'll find that many fonts are too blocky, too narrow, or too rounded to make for smooth reading.

When in doubt, go with the old favorites—Garamond's a classic font for poetry, or something in the Times family may be a good choice. For a more modern look, try sans-serif fonts like Franklin Gothic or Helvetica. The most important thing is that the font should not be distracting—as your reader settles into her easy chair to enjoy your chapbook, you don't want her first thought to be, "What the heck font is that?"

The most important thing is that the font should not be distracting.

Bonus tip: When trying out a font, print out a poem or two in that font before deciding on it, and really scrutinize the printout—what looks good on your screen may look very different on the printed page, and your printer may render some fonts more crisply than others. Plan to use up some scrap paper while you experiment with printing out fonts.

FIND CENTER OF THE BOOK, AND PUT A GOOD POEM THERE

Most chapbooks are simply a stack of papers, folded in the middle and stapled along that fold. So when someone picks up your book to browse through it, it's likely to fall open to the center spot where the staples are. Because of this little chapbook phenomenon, that center spread is usually the third thing a reader will see, after the front cover and back cover, and the first poem he or she will read. So think of that center spot as prime real estate, and put a strong poem or two there that can be read without turning the page.

USE WHITE SPACE TO HELP YOUR READER

By its nature, poetry is a rich, dense reading experience. And as with a rich meal, it's wise to give your guest a little time to breathe between courses. Leaving some white space on the last page of a poem, or putting a blank left page before a new section (if you have sections) gives the reader a brief break to contemplate what he's just read and gear up for the next poem. One place where you should always have a blank page is on the left page before your first poem in the book.

That first poem should start on a right-hand page, and the blank page to its left serves as a little drumroll that lets the reader know the show's about to begin. And in the body of the book, it's fine to have the occasional poem spill over onto an extra page by five or six lines; again, the white space at the end of the poem gives the reader a mental resting spot.

PERFECT YOUR PUNCTUATION

Chapbooks, even ones from well-known publishers, seem to suffer more than their share of careless punctuation: double spaces, straight quote marks, two hyphens standing in for an em-dash, and other small glitches that a spell-check might not catch. Most typographers hate straight quotes (", ') and prefer curly ones (", '), but there's nothing really wrong with straight quotes; just make sure you choose one or the other and don't mix them. As for em-dashes (—), you can get a true one on a PC by typing ctrl-alt-<minus sign on the number pad>; on a Mac, it's shift-option-hyphen. Set aside some time at the end of your design process to do some search-and-replaces and root out these inconsistences. This seemingly simple step will make a big difference to your reader.

EMBRACE ODD SIZES

Most chapbooks are 5-1/2 x 8-1/2 inches—not surprisingly, that's what you get when you take a stack of standard 8-1/2 x 11 sheets and fold them in half. That's all very convenient, but with a $30 guillotine-style paper trimmer (or the fancy one at the office), you can experiment with all sorts of other sizes—tall, small, horizontal, square—and come up with something unusual that will really pique your reader's interest. One popular size is a book that fits nicely in one hand—about 4 x 5 inches. And square books have an alluring power at the book table.

The challenge, of course, is getting your poems to fit into the format; poems with long lines will have a hard time squeezing into a narrow book, for instance. But sometimes fitting the trim size to the poems is part of the fun. A sweet size—and an easy cheat, requiring only one cut on the paper trimmer—is 4-1/4 x 5-1/2, which you can get by taking 8-1/2 x 11 sheets, cutting them in half, and then folding the resulting sheets in half.

BEWARE THE HASTY BACK COVER

Back covers are where a lot of otherwise good chapbooks go bad. It's not unusual to see strong poems and a good interior design marred by a back cover that was obviously thrown together in a hurry. Some poets opt out and just leave the back cover blank.

That's okay, but it's a missed opportunity; the back cover is a big chunk of free advertising space, a chance to give your prospective reader a taste of what's inside—a snippet of a poem, a short bio, and maybe an author photo. But don't try to jam too much on there; crowded typography is a common malady in back covers, often because of our old nemesis, type size vs. leading (see tip #1).

> The back cover is a big chunk of free advertising space, a chance to give your prospective reader a taste of what's inside.

And if you do include an author photo, make it a good one. Whether it's serious or friendly, just make sure your photo isn't off-putting—a stiff grammar-school-type picture, or a badly lit mug shot that looks like it was ripped out of somebody's passport. If you can't find a good photo of yourself, leave it out; it is better to have no author photo than a bad one.

Bonus tip: Steal your back-cover design. A chapbook's back cover can look exactly like one on a full-length poetry collection, so grab a stack of poetry books from big publishers, study their back covers, and steal design elements that you like.

ENDPAPERS ADD ELEGANCE

Endpapers, also known as flyleaves, are the easiest way to add a hint of artistry to a chapbook. An endpaper is a single, blank sheet of paper just inside the cover of your book—a page that's there purely for decoration. These are fun to pick out, and the possibilities are almost limitless: a translucent vellum, textured stationery paper, a delicate sheet embedded with flower petals, or something bold and contrasting.

But there's some room for error—nothing says "cheap" like wrinkle-prone colored paper that you bought at the dollar store, and overly ornate endpapers may make your book look more like a tchotchke than a serious book of poetry.

BONUS TIP: When shopping for endpapers, take a sheet of your interior paper and cover stock (or, better yet, a printed cover) to the store with you to make sure the colors don't clash.

TRIM OFF THE OUTER EDGE

Any time you take a stack of papers and fold it in the middle, the outer edge—the right edge of your book, if you're looking at your front cover—will have a "peak" to it where the edges of the inner pages get pushed out beyond those of the outer pages. This isn't the worst thing in the world, but trimming off that outer edge so that it's flat, smooth, and flush with the edge of the cover will give the book a more finished, professional feel. A $40 rotary trimmer with a wheel-shaped blade, like the kind scrapbookers use, can do the trick with a little practice.

Or, if you have patience and a steady hand, you can trim off the edge with an X-Acto knife and a ruler. Another option is to take the books to a print shop and have them trim off the edges (for a few dollars) using one of their professional cutting machines.

BIND THE BOOK WITH STITCHING INSTEAD OF STAPLING

This one's an especially good trick because it looks hard to do, but it's actually very easy. All it takes to add this classic touch of elegance is a needle, an awl to make a few holes, some heavy thread in a color that complements or contrasts with your cover design, and a simple stitching diagram that you can find online (google "chapbook stitching").

This little upgrade will get an "ooh" out of almost everyone who picks up your book, making it that much more memorable—which is the whole point of having a chapbook in the first place.

AMY MILLER is the author of eight chapbooks of poetry and prose, and her writing has appeared in *Northwest Review, ZYZZYVA, Many Mountains Moving, Fine Gardening, The Writer's Journal,* and many other publications. During her 35-year career in publishing, she has worked as a layout artist, editor, and project manager for several magazines and book publishers. She blogs about writing, disaster movies, and life at writers-island.blogspot.com.

MISTAKES POETS MAKE

In putting together listings for *Poet's Market*, we ask editors for any words of advice they want to share with our readers. Often the editors' responses include comments about what poets should and shouldn't do when submitting work—the same comments, over and over. That means a lot of poets are repeating similar mistakes when they send out their poems for consideration.

The following list includes the most common of those mistakes—the ones poets should work hardest to avoid.

NOT READING A PUBLICATION BEFORE SUBMITTING WORK

Researching a publication is essential before submitting your poetry. Try to buy a sample copy of a magazine (by mail, if necessary) or at least see if an issue is available at the library. It may not be economically feasible for poets to purchase a copy of every magazine they target, especially if they send out a lot of poems. However, there are additional ways to familiarize yourself with a publication.

Read the market listing thoroughly. If guidelines are available, send for them by e-mail or regular mail, or check for them online. A publication's website often presents valuable information, including sample poems, magazine covers—and guidelines.

SUBMITTING INAPPROPRIATE WORK

Make good use of your research so you're sure you understand what a magazine publishes. Don't rationalize that a journal favoring free verse might jump at the chance to consider your long epic poem in heroic couplets. Don't convince yourself your experimental style will be a good fit for the traditional journal filled with rhyming poetry. Don't go into denial about whether a certain journal and your poetry are made for each other. It's counterproductive and ultimately wastes postage (not to mention time—yours and the editor's).

SUBMITTING AN UNREASONABLE NUMBER OF POEMS

If an editor recommends sending three to five poems (a typical range), don't send six. Don't send a dozen poems and tell the editor to pick the five she wants to consider. If the editor doesn't specify a number (or the listing says "no limit"), don't take that as an invitation to mail off 20 poems. The editors and staff of literary magazines are busy enough as it is, and they may decide they don't have time to cope with you. (When submitting book or chapbook manuscripts to publishers, make sure your page count falls within the range they state.)

Don't go to the other extreme and send only one poem, unless an editor says it's okay (which is rare). One poem doesn't give an editor much of a perspective on your work, and it doesn't give you very good odds on getting the piece accepted.

IGNORING THE EDITOR'S PREFERENCES REGARDING FORMATS

If an editor makes a point of describing a preferred manuscript format, follow it, even if that format seems to contradict the standard. (Standard format includes using 8½ × 11 white paper and conventional typeface and point size; avoid special graphics, colors or type flourishes; put your name and address on every page.) Don't devise your own format to make your submission stand out. Keep everything clean, crisp and easy to read (and professional).

Be alert to e-mail submission formats. Follow directions regarding what the editor wants printed in the subject line, how many poems to include in a single e-mail, whether to use attachments or paste work in the body of the message, and other elements. Editors have good reasons for outlining their preferences; ignoring them could mean having your e-mail deleted before your poems are even read.

OMITTING A SELF-ADDRESSED STAMPED ENVELOPE (SASE)

Why do editors continuously say "include an SASE with your submission?" Because so many poets don't do it. Here's a simple rule: Unless the editor gives alternate instructions, include a #10 SASE, whether submitting poems or sending an inquiry.

WRITING BAD COVER LETTERS (OR OMITTING THEM COMPLETELY)

Cover letters have become an established part of the submission process. There are editors who remain indifferent about the necessity of a cover letter, but many consider it rude to be sent a submission without any other communication from the poet.

Unless the editor says otherwise, send a cover letter. Keep it short and direct, a polite introduction of you and your work. (See "Frequently Asked Questions" for more tips on cover letters, and an example.)

Here are a few important don'ts:

- **DON'T** list all the magazines where your work has appeared; limit yourself to five magazine titles. The work you're submitting has to stand on its own.
- **DON'T** tell the editor what a good poet you are—or how good someone else thinks you are.
- **DON'T** tell the editor how to edit, lay out or print your poem. Some of those decisions are up to the editor, assuming she decides to accept your poem in the first place.
- **DON'T** point out the poem is copyrighted in your name or include the copyright symbol. All poems are automatically copyrighted in the poet's name as soon as they're "fixed" (i.e., written down), and editors know this.

NOT MAINTAINING GOOD EDITOR/POET RELATIONS

Most editors are hard-working poetry lovers dedicated to finding and promoting good work. They aspire to turn submissions around as quickly as possible and to treat all poets with respect. They don't want to steal your work. Often they aren't paid for their labor and may even have to dip into their own pockets just to keep their magazines going.

Poets should finesse their communications with editors regarding problems, especially in initial letters and e-mail. Editors (and their magazines and presses) aren't service-oriented businesses, like the phone company. Getting huffy with an editor as if arguing with your cable provider about an overcharge is inappropriate. Attitude isn't going to get you anywhere; in fact, it could create additional obstacles.

That's not to say poets shouldn't feel exasperated when they're inconvenienced or ill-treated. None of us likes to see our creations vanish, or to pay good money for something we're never going to receive (like a subscription or sample copy). However, exasperated is one thing; outraged is another. Too often poets go on the offensive with editors and make matters worse. Experts on how to complain effectively recommend you keep your cool and stay professional, no matter what kind of problem you're trying to work out.

For additional advice on editor/poet relations, see "Dealing With Problem Editors."

DEALING WITH PROBLEM EDITORS

There *are* problem editors out there, and we've all encountered them at one time or another. Some rip people off, prey on poets' desires to be published, or treat poets and their work with flagrant disregard. Fortunately, such editors are in the minority.

Now and then you may discover the disorganized editor or the overwhelmed editor; these two cause heartache (and heartburn) by closing up shop without returning manuscripts or failing to honor paid requests for subscriptions and sample copies. More often than not, their transgressions are rooted in chaos and irresponsibility, not malicious intent. Frustrating as such editors are, they're not out to get you.

There are many instances, too, where larger circumstances are beyond an editor's control. For example, a college-oriented journal may be student-staffed, with editors changing each academic year. Funds for the journal may be cut unexpectedly by administration belt-tightening, or a grant could be cancelled. The editorial office may be moved to another part of the university. An exam schedule could impact a publishing schedule. All of these things cause problems and delays.

Then again, a literary journal may be a one-person, home-based operation. The editor may get sick or have an illness in the family. Her regular job may suddenly demand lots of overtime. There may be divorce or death with which the editor has to cope. A computer could crash. Or the editor may need to scramble for money before the magazine can go to the printer. Emergencies happen, and they take their toll on deadlines. The last thing the editor wants is to inconvenience poets and readers, but sometimes life gets in the way.

Usually, difficulties with these kinds of "problem" editors can be resolved satisfactorily through communication and patience. There are always exceptions, though. Here are a few typical situations with problem editors and how to handle them.

AN EDITOR IS RUDE.

If it's a matter of bad attitude, take it with a grain of salt. Maybe he's having a rotten day. If there's abusive language and excessive profanity involved, let us know about it. (See the complaint procedure .)

COMPLAINT PROCEDURE

If you feel you have not been treated fairly by a market listed in *Poet's Market*, we advise you to take the following steps:

- First, try to contact the market. Sometimes one phone call, letter, or e-mail can quickly clear up the matter. Document all your communications with the market.
- When you contact us with a complaint, provide the details of your submission, the date of your first contact with the market and the nature of your subsequent communication.
- We will file a record of your complaint and further investigate the market.
- The number and severity of complaints will be considered when deciding whether or not to delete a market from the next edition of *Poet's Market*.

AN EDITOR HARSHLY CRITICIZES YOUR POEM.

If an editor takes time to comment on your poetry, even if the feedback seems overly critical, consider the suggestions with an open mind and try to find something valid and useful in them. If, after you've given the matter fair consideration, you think the editor was out of line, don't rush to defend your poetry or wave your bruised ego in the editor's face. Allow that the editor has a right to her opinion (which you're not obligated to take as the final word on the quality of your work), forget about it and move on.

AN EDITOR IS SLOW TO RESPOND TO A SUBMISSION.

As explained above, there may be many reasons why an editor's response takes longer than the time stated in the market listing or guidelines. Allow a few more weeks to pass beyond the deadline, then write a polite inquiry to the editor about the status of your manuscript. (Include an SASE if sending by regular mail.) Understand an editor may not be able to read your letter right away if deadlines are pressing or if he's embroiled in a personal crisis. Try to be patient. If you haven't received a reply to your inquiry after a month or so, however, it's time for further action.

AN EDITOR WON'T RETURN YOUR MANUSCRIPT.

Decide whether you want to invest any more time in this journal or publisher. If you conclude you've been patient long enough, write a firm but professional letter to the editor withdrawing your manuscript from consideration. Request that the manuscript be returned; but know, too, a truly indifferent editor probably won't bother to send it back or reply in any way. Keep a copy of your withdrawal letter for your files, make a new copy of your manuscript and look for a better market.

Also, contact *Poet's Market* by letter or e-mail with details of your experience. We always look into problems with editors, although we don't withdraw a listing on the basis of a single complaint unless we discover evidence of consistent misbehavior. We do, however, keep complaints on file and watch for patterns of unacceptable behavior from any specific market.

AN EDITOR TAKES YOUR MONEY.

If you sent a check for a subscription or sample copy and you haven't received anything, review your bank statement to see if the check has been cashed. If it has, send the editor a query. Politely point out the editor has cashed your check, but you haven't yet received the material you were expecting. Give the editor the benefit of the doubt: An upcoming issue of a magazine could be running late, your subscription could have been overlooked by mistake, or your copy could have been lost in transit or sent in error to the wrong address.

If your check has *not* been cashed, query the editor to see if your order was ever received. It may have been lost (in the mail or on the editor's desk), the editor may be holding several checks to cash at one time, or the editor may be waiting to cash checks until a tardy issue is finally published.

If you get an unsatisfactory response from the editor (or no response at all), wait a few weeks and try again. If the matter still isn't resolved, let us know about it. We're especially interested in publishers who take money from poets but don't deliver the goods. Be sure to send us all the details of the transaction, plus copies of any correspondence (yours and the editor's). We can't pursue your situation in any legal way or act as mediator, but we can ban an unscrupulous publisher from *Poet's Market* and keep the information as a resource in case we get later complaints.

Should you continue trying to get your money back from such editors? That's your decision. If your loss is under $10 (say, for a subscription or sample copy), it might cost you less in the long run to let the matter go. And the fee for a "stop payment" order on a check can be hefty—possibly more than the amount you sent the editor in the first place. Yes, it's infuriating to be cheated, but sometimes fighting on principle costs more than it's worth.

If your monetary loss is significant (for instance, you shelled out a couple hundred dollars in a subsidy publishing agreement), consider contacting your state attorney general's office for advice about small claims court, filing a complaint and other actions you can take.

HOW TO WRITE A SUCCESSFUL GRANT TO FUND YOUR WRITING

by Kris Bigalk

Whether it's applying for a $25,000 fellowship or applying for a $500 travel grant, writers have many opportunities to compete for money to fund their writing projects. The key to writing a successful grant lies in one general concept: writing the grant so that it meets the priorities and mission of the audience—in this case, the granting organization and/or the grant review committee.

Organizations offer grants for many reasons, but ultimately, their goals involve funding projects that line up with the organization's mission, values, and current initiatives. The first step in writing a successful grant is letting go of the focus on what the grant can do for you, and turning the focus around—what can you do with the grant that will reflect well on the granting organization? In other words, make the granting organization see how you will forward their mission, values, and initiatives.

FIND THE RIGHT GRANT

Writing a grant for a specific project is much more difficult than writing a grant with a general goal in mind. In other words, don't go into the search for a grant with a specific, inflexible schedule or plan. Never write or plan the grant before reading the guidelines. Most grants have limitations as to what they will and won't fund, and most also preference certain kinds of projects. Concentrate on moving your ideas toward the granting organization's preferences.

There are many lists and databases where writers can search for grant opportunities. A good place to begin is locally. Find the website of your city, county, regional, or state arts organizations and arts-oriented non-profits to search for grant opportunities. These grants are often a good bet, because the applicant pool is smaller and limited to a certain population. To search for national grant opportunities, check out the sidebar.

STUDY THE GUIDELINES

Once you've found a grant that interests you, print out the guidelines. These may be in one or two documents, so be sure to print everything related to the grant. The key to good grant writing is to be acutely aware of the audience—the people who will decide whether or not to fund your proposal.

In the guidelines you've printed out, locate the "Qualifications" or "Requirements" section. Highlight any prerequisites for application, such as a certain number of literary magazine publications, a published book, etc. If you don't meet the prerequisites, stop and find another grant. If you do meet the prerequisites, find the part of the application that outlines how you will prove that you have met those prerequisites (photocopies of magazines? links to online publications? a copy of the book?). Do you have the materials you need to prove you've met the prerequisite? If not, stop and find another grant. If so, gather them together.

Highlight any information on what the grant reviewers will be looking for, specifically.

Read through the grant guidelines again, with a highlighter. Highlight the main sections of the grant (usually bolded headings), and mark any instructions on how to write these sections. Also highlight any information on what the grant reviewers will be looking for, specifically. Often, the grant will include a list of desired characteristics of a proposal, for example, or even a list of characteristics that are more likely to be funded. Highlight keywords in those sections, as they will become keywords in your proposal.

IMAGINE YOUR "AUDIENCE"

Now that you have a general idea of what the organization is looking for in the grant, it's time to delve a little deeper into your audience's wants and needs. Go to the sponsoring organization's website, and collect any publications, podcasts, or other media generated by the organization. How does the organization present itself? What can you garner about the mission, values, and activities of the organization? Write a short paragraph that "profiles" the organization, again using any keywords you see repeated in the materials on the website.

Locate a list of past grants and projects the organization has funded. What do these projects have in common with one another? How do they connect with the mission and values of the organization? Write out the answers to these questions in another paragraph.

Sometimes sponsoring organizations will provide examples of past proposals that were funded. Another way to find these successful proposals is to ask your writer friends if they have examples. If you can locate an example of a successfully written grant for this specific opportunity, study it. Notice how it is formatted and what is emphasized by the grant writer. Highlight words or ideas you notice coming up more than once, especially if those words or ideas match what you've found in your highlighting and research.

GENERATE IDEAS/ROUGH DRAFTS

Now that you've done your research, write out the parameters of the grant on a separate sheet of paper, in your own words. What are the limitations of what the grant will fund/not fund? What projects will be preferenced? Refer to your paragraphs and analysis.

Make a list of ideas. What do you want to do that fits into these parameters? How could you do it so that it will be preferenced? Don't try to make a previous idea fit the parameters. Design a project that will definitely fit the parameters, even if it's different than the project you originally envisioned. Think about what your overall goals are, instead of a specific goal. So, for example, if a grant won't fund classes that count towards a degree, you could propose attending a series of writer's conferences or working with a writing mentor to achieve the goal of improving and honing your writing skills.

When an arts organization receives hundreds of grants and needs to cut them down to a manageable number, people need to be able to skim the proposals and find a reason to put yours in the "keeper" pile.

Before you begin drafting, keep in mind that it's very likely that your grant will not be read carefully, at least not in the first round. When an arts organization receives hundreds of grants and needs to cut them down to a manageable number, people need to be able to skim the proposals and find a reason to put yours in the "keeper" pile.

Additionally, many granting organizations serve people in all of the fine arts, and are not staffed by writers. The way to ensure your proposal will eventually make it to a final round and be read more carefully is to use headings, strategic bolds, underlines, and italics, and bulleted or numbered items, which tend to draw the eye to the criteria that will be important to the grant reviewers at all levels.

Begin writing out drafts of the sections of the grant. Use bolded headings that match the funding criteria; use exact keywords from the guidelines and the website to appeal to your audience. Make the proposal easy to read by using bulleted or numbered items and keeping the prose tight, succinct, and specific. Refer to the highlighted words that recurred in the guidelines, on the website, etc., and be sure to use these words and close synonyms to describe your project.

REVISE AND CHECK

Revise the sections of the grant application so that they flow well, make sense, and are proof-read perfectly. While you can't assume that any of the reviewers are writers, you can't assume that they aren't writers, either. You're a writer, so reviewers will expect more from you than from other artists when it comes to writing. Poorly written or sloppy grants rarely get funded.

As you finish revising, check your work against the guidelines again to make sure you haven't strayed from them. Grants that veer off of guidelines do not get funded, because there are always plenty of others with merit that have stayed within the guidelines.

Finally, have a friend read your grant application and compare it to the guidelines, and give you feedback. Make any changes you deem necessary, and compile all of the materials together in a packet. Many grant guidelines include a checklist to help with this.

SUBMIT THE GRANT

Read over the instructions on how to submit the grant. Submit the grant exactly as detailed in the instructions, by the deadline listed. Grants that are incomplete, submitted in different formats, or submitted late are not funded. Take your time. Read things twice. Don't wait until the last day to submit the grant to start on this.

If you don't receive a confirmation that your application has been received, it's usually okay to call or e-mail and ask for that confirmation, unless this is expressly forbidden in the guidelines.

WAIT. PATIENTLY.

Most grants will list a ballpark date by which a decision will be made. Don't contact them before that date. Check the website and your junk mail folder, and then wait a week after that date to contact them if you still haven't heard anything.

If your grant is not funded, resist any urge to complain to the funding organization, judges, or anyone associated with the grant. Do not complain on Facebook, Twitter, or in any public forum. This is a great way to burn bridges and tends to make the writer look bitter and cantankerous; it rarely has the desired effect of making the granting organization look bad. Complain to your friends if you must, in private.

Do not complain on Facebook, Twitter, or in any public forum. This is a great way to burn bridges.

Like rejections for creative work, rejections for grants can sting, but it's often not a reflection on the writer or the project. Grant reviewers have a set of priorities for funding, and try to choose the projects that best meet those priorities. If a grant isn't funded, it may still have merit as a proposal, and a grant writer should not take such rejections personally.

If your grant is funded, feel free thank the funding organization, judges, or anyone associated with the grant. Celebrate as publicly as you wish, both online and in the real world. Tell others about your project and about the grant itself on your webpage and in other public forums.

It's a win-win situation for both the writer and the granting organization, and focuses on the mutual benefit to both. Organizations that make grants to writers serve a vital purpose in the writing community, and any time we can celebrate their contribution to the arts, we should do so.

KRIS BIGALK'S poetry collection, *Repeat the Flesh in Numbers,* will be released by NYQ Books in 2012. Her poetry has recently appeared in *Silk Road, Water~Stone Review, cream city review,* and *Mead,* and is forthcoming in *Rougarou.* Bigalk was awarded a 2010 Minnesota State Arts Board Individual Artist Grant in poetry, and attended Bread Loaf Writer's Conference as a contributor in 2010 and 2011. She is the Director of Creative Writing at Normandale Community College, where she founded and now directs a successful AFA in Creative Writing program.

IS IT A 'CON'?

Think Before You Trust

What is a "con?" Con is short for "confidence," an adjective defined by *Webster's* as "of, relating to, or adept at swindling by false promise," as in "confidence man" or "confidence game." While the publishing world is full of legitimate opportunities for poets to gain honor and exposure for their work, there are also plenty of "cons." How can you tell the difference? The following are some of the most common situations that cost poets disappointment, frustration—and cash. Learn to spot them before submitting your work, and don't let your vanity be your guide.

ANTHOLOGIES

Has this happened to you? You see an ad in a perfectly respectable publication announcing a poetry contest with big cash prizes. You enter, and later you receive a glowing letter congratulating you on your exceptional poem, which the contest sponsor wants to include in his deluxe hardbound anthology of the best poetry submitted to the contest. The anthology costs only, say, $65. You don't have to buy it—they'll still publish your poem—but wouldn't you be proud to own one? And wouldn't it be nice to buy additional copies to give to family and friends? And for an extra charge you can include a biographical note. And so on . . .

Of course, when the anthology arrives, the quality of the poetry may not be what you were expecting, with several poems crammed unattractively onto a page. Apparently everyone who entered the contest was invited to be published; you basically paid cash to see your poem appear in a phone-book-like volume with no literary merit whatsoever.

Were you conned? Depends on how you look at it. If you bought into the flattery and believed you were being published in an exclusive, high-quality publication, no doubt you feel duped. On the other hand, if all you were after was seeing your poem in print, even knowing you'd have to pay for the privilege, then you got what you wanted. (Unless you've deceived yourself into believing you've truly won an honor and now have a worthy publishing credit; you don't.)

If you don't want to add insult to injury, resist additional spiels, like having your poem printed on coffee mugs and T-shirts (you can do this yourself through print shops or on-line services like www.cafepress.com) or spending large sums on awards banquets and conferences. And, before you submit a single line of poetry, find out what rights the contest sponsor acquires. You may be relinquishing all rights to your poem simply by mailing it in or submitting it through a website. If the poem no longer belongs to you, the publisher can do whatever he wishes with it. Don't let your vanity propel you into a situation you'll always regret.

READING AND CONTEST FEES

Suppose you notice a promising market for your poetry, but the editor requires a set fee just to consider your work. Or you see a contest that interests you, but you have to pay the sponsor a fee just to enter. Are you being conned?

In the case of reading fees, keep these points in mind: Is the market so exceptional that you feel it's worth risking the cost of the reading fee to have your work considered? What makes it so much better than markets that do not charge fees? Has the market been around awhile, with an established publishing schedule? What are you paid if your work is accepted? Are reasonably priced samples available so you can judge the production values and quality of the writing?

Reading fees don't necessarily signal a suspicious market. In fact, they're increasingly popular as editors struggle with the costs of publishing books and magazines, including the man-hours required to read loads of (often bad) submissions. However, fees represent an additional financial burden on poets, who often don't receive any monetary reward for their poems to begin with. It's really up to individual poets to decide whether paying a fee is beneficial to their publishing efforts. Think long and hard about fee-charging markets that are new and untried, don't pay poets for their work (at the very least a print publication should offer a contributor's copy), charge high prices for sample copies or set fees that seem unreasonable.

Entry fees for contests often fund prizes, judges' fees, honorariums and expenses of running and promoting the contest (including publishing a "prize" collection or issue of a magazine). Other kinds of contests charge entry fees, from Irish dancing competitions to bake-offs at a county fair. Why not poetry contests?

Watch out for contests that charge higher than average fees, especially if the fees are out of proportion to the amount of money being given.

That's not to say you shouldn't be cautious. Watch out for contests that charge higher-than-average fees, especially if the fees are out of proportion to the amount of prize money being given. (Look through the Contests & Awards section to get a sense of what most competitions charge.) Find out how long the contest has been around, and verify whether prizes have been awarded each year and to whom. In the case of book and chapbook contests, send for one of the winning publications to confirm that the publisher puts out a quality product. Regard with skepticism any contest that tells you you've won something, then demands payment for an anthology, trophy or other item. (It's okay if a group offers an anthology for a modest price without providing winners with free copies. Most state poetry societies have to do this; but they also present cash awards in each category of the contest, and their entry fees are low.)

SUBSIDY PUBLISHERS, PRINT-ON-DEMAND

Poetry books are a hard sell to the book-buying public. Few of the big publishers handle these books, and those that do feature the "name" poets (i.e., the major prize winners and contemporary masters with breathtaking reputations). Even the small presses publish only so many books per year—far less than the number of poets writing.

No wonder so many poets decide to pay to have their poetry collections published. While some may self-publish (i.e., take full control of their book, working directly with a printer), others turn to subsidy publishers (also called "vanity publishers") and print-on-demand (POD) publishers.

There are many differences between subsidy publishing and POD publishing, as well as similarities (having to pay to get published is a big one). Whether or not you get conned is entirely up to you. You have to take responsibility for asking questions, doing research on presses, and reading the fine print on the contract to make sure you know exactly what you're paying for. There are landmines in dealing with subsidy and POD publishers, and you have to investigate thoroughly and intelligently to avoid damage.

Some questions to keep in mind: Are fees inflated compared to the product and services you'll be receiving? Will you still own the rights to your book? Does the publisher put out a quality product that's attractive and cleanly printed? (Get a sample copy and find out.) How many copies of the book will you receive? How much will you have to pay for additional copies? How will your book be sold and distributed? (Don't count on seeing your volume in bookstores.)

Will you receive royalties? How much? Does the publisher offer any kind of promotional assistance or is it all up to you? Will those promotion efforts be realistic and results-oriented? (Sometimes "promotion" means sending out review copies, which is a waste—such volumes are rarely reviewed.) Don't wait until *after* you've signed a contract (and a check) to raise these issues. Do your homework first.

Obviously, poets who don't stay on their toes may find themselves preyed upon. And a questionable publishing opportunity doesn't have to be an out-and-out rip-off for you to feel cheated. In every situation, you have a choice *not* to participate. Exercise that choice, or at least develop a healthy sense of skepticism before you fling yourself and your poetry at the first smooth talker who compliments your work. Poets get burned because they're much too impatient to see their work in print. Calm your ego, slow down and devote that time, energy and money toward reading other poets and improving your own writing. You'll find that getting published will eventually take care of itself.

REVOLUTION ROAD

How to Start Your Own Poetry Journal

....

by Nate Pritts

A poet is someone who writes poems, true enough, but along with that comes a commitment to the overall art of poetry. If you believe in the art of poetry enough to write poems, then you probably find sustenance in reading them as well. Maybe, when you're feeling particularly evangelical, you feel moved to more generally promote the reading and writing of poetry. Getting to this point means you're in deep, that you're allowing yourself to become receptive to a higher calling–something that transcends your local dedication to your own poems and blossoms in universal scope.

I believe that to truly live as a poet means that you have to stop thinking exclusively about your own product and focus more on how you can help advance and further the art of poetry itself. Having a myopic and exclusive focus on only your own poems can shut you off from so many other types of good work you can do, exciting avenues open to any poet-in-the-world. Rather than delineate a whole crop of them here, I want to close in on one particular open channel – setting yourself up as founder and editor, as veritable captain, of your own poetry journal.

REVOLUTION ROAD

In a way, it's a revolution–not the kind that is armed and deadly, though there are always risks with any kind of endeavor worth undertaking. I'm talking about the road to a wider perspective, a full 360-degree view of the role of the poet.

Starting your own poetry journal provides a vast array of benefits for the larger community–for everyone around you, not just poets–and if the satisfaction of having that kind of seismic impact isn't enough, there are some small scale rumbles that go along with it, internal aftershocks that will leave you changed as a writer. I know that since starting my own poetry journal (*H_NGM_N*, in 2001, which has grown and grown to include chapbook and book publishing) my poetry and life have been enriched by the friendships and connections I've formed, through reading thousands of submissions every single year, by having a focus for my thoughts on this field which matters to me more than anything else.

GETTING STARTED

So Step One is to do it, to commit to it fully, to throw yourself against the wall even if your favorite football team is playing a pivotal game or your brother is in town and wants to meet for dinner. There's no other way. Submissions need to be responded to, a new issue needs to be formatted. There are plans to be hatched and schemes to be formed. You have a responsibility you can't dodge, a duty of the highest order. Because, consider this: any deviation of intent, any flagging of devotion, any swerve, and the entire project could collapse. You'll miss an opportunity to level up, or you'll be treading water in the pond as it drains. You need to be at the forefront of what's going on, out on the leading edge, not sitting back watching the horses and placing bets. If you don't have fanatic single-minded drive for your cause then there's no way that anyone else will ever sign on.

In this configuration, Step Two is to keep doing it, to never give up or surrender, to continue forever.

Any deviation of intent, any flagging of devotion, any swerve, and the entire project could collapse.

I realize these aren't steps so much as spiritual qualifications, a kind of intellectual and emotional summary of skills. It's difficult to follow dance steps when they're not movements you make with your feet, but ideals that live in your heart. So since these steps are a mishmash and all happen at once together, it might be more productive to consider the problem from a different angle. Though it is difficult to jot down a specific recipe for starting your own poetry journal, I do think there are some specific considerations of both a theoretical and practical nature that a prospective editor needs to take into account. By fully understanding what is at stake for any creative enterprise trying to exist in the real world, you will be better armed for the struggle.

While it is true that there is a complex and tidal overlap between these two aspects, thinking of them in different columns helps to make it easier to isolate and talk about. And before completely deflating your balloon by worrying about those things of a more practical nature, I'd like to focus on those considerations that are more theoretical or aesthetic in nature. I suspect this is where the initial desire to start a poetry journal is born for most people, where those primal intentions are nurtured. The journal I started was started to serve partly as a corrective. Talking about intention here is always going to be cloudy because thousands and millions of impulses coalesce like particles to form the essential course matter. But I remember clearly feeling excluded by the journals and presses that stomped around the literary landscape, behemoths that didn't seem to be responsive at all to me or the kinds of values I felt were important to a vibrant sense of poetry. They seemed more interested in showing you the door than setting another place at the table. Once I was able to articulate that to myself, once I was able to say "I have recognized and defined a lack in the contemporary poetry scene," I had no choice but to work to fill that gap in whatever way I could.

....

Here's the revelation that came like a bolt from the blue: Editors are people...I was (and still am) a person.

....

But right alongside this corrective motivation for starting a journal was the realization that I could start one. I didn't think the poems I saw being published were of a higher quality than mine, or inherently more worthy of an audience. There was no divine aura that proclaimed one poem or one poet "publishable." It was a matter of taste (I'm oversimplifying some here), specifically the editor's taste, or the established taste/focus of the journal in question. And, here's the revelation that came like a bolt from the blue: editors are people – albeit people with training and dedication and a refined sense of their own predilections and preferences. I was (and still am) also a person. At the time I had a kneejerk, elastic type of taste – it responded quickly and moved fluidly.

I suddenly realized that there was nothing stopping me from starting my own publishing project (a journal, a press) but I also recognized that to do so would carry with it a heavy responsibility that I could not lay down, could not shirk on. I would have to be serious and articulate, I would have to shine a light on various murky internal mechanisms, and I would have to become transparent – to myself most of all.

BUILDING TRUST

When you set yourself up as an editor of a journal, you're asking people to trust you with their poems. What does this mean? The editor is the one responsible for creating a context for your poem, an aesthetic landscape that consists of the other poems and writing sequenced around it as well as the overall design of the journal itself and also the look and feel of the brand itself. Just think of how you would feel if your poems finally come out in the world in a journal which disappears the next day, or with an unreadable font.

If you are not ready to think about all those issues, separately and together, with vigor and determination, then you are not ready to be an editor. You can stop reading now before the whole enterprise gets harder and infused with those practical real world problems.

TIME AND MONEY

Let's list the two biggest considerations and get them out of the way to remove some of the tension that surrounds the unspeakable: time and money. If you ask any editor, so many of them will give a name to their pain, and this is what that name looks like. "I wish I had more time to commit to this project" or "I wish I had more money to do all kinds of amazing things with." Since everyone is going to have different solutions to these problems, different ways around the roadblocks, I don't want to go much further than naming the hurdles right here. I will say that if you view these things are problems, then you're coming at it all wrong.

These are hurdles that help you to innovate and grow, these are realities that help dictate the shape of the world you're making. They are nothing more than two new areas to which you can apply your vast creativity and adaptability. When I started my poetry journal, time and money were two things I never had any of. But I found a way – there are so many ways. If you care, you find a way. If you're alive and still breathing, there is a way. So: find a way. Find your way.

PLAN OF ATTACK

Many people will preach the benefits of having a plan (a five-year plan, an agenda of some type) and this seems like good, clear-cut advice. I will counter that by saying that my own H_NGM_N did not start with a plan, but with a stapler. What I mean is that in the beginning was the verb, the action. If I had stopped to think about everything that went into starting a journal, all the pressures and all the necessities, then I might have been so overwhelmed in the lab with my notes that I might never have come out into the real light of the world. Certainly now, more than 12 years later, it is fair to say that H_NGM_N does have something resembling a plan (or at least an established mode of operation I can either adhere to or deviate from).

However, rather than spreadsheets and flowcharts, the most important attribute is the ability to adapt. A plan that covers every eventuality and whim would fill enough binders to bury your house, but a spirit that is saturated with an eternal drive to satisfy and fulfill the task at hand is so much more essential. None of us can predict what the landscape will look like in two years, or in five, and I'm sure many ships have sunk while the captain stared in vain at some printed out maps. An editor needs to have first and foremost an indomitable spirit, an immortal love, a huge fire in her chest.

JUST ONE THING

Before the end, it is probably best to insert a caveat. Though I do feel that anyone can start a poetry journal, I don't think everyone should. Certainly there are so many options open to us. A prospective editor can create an online journal (with a bare bones skeleton or professional pricey design) or a print journal (paper from their printer that gets stapled or snazzy trimmed pages and a big chunky spine). But without a thorough understanding of both the aesthetic and practical challenges that await you, this enterprise might fold and collapse. We need more suns to keep the universe bright, not a bunch of flickering and dying lights.

All of this may sound daunting. It is. It's actually much worse than I'm able to articulate. Starting a poetry journal requires stores of energy you didn't know you had, requires access to systems that were sleeping in your brain. It's also much better, much more enriching, much more essential. It will truly change your perceptions about what it means to be a poet; it will give you a better perspective on the culture of poetry publication. Here, now, more than a decade after my poetry journal kicked off, my life is fairly inextricable from it, my identity is melded with it.

I can't think of anything better.

NATE PRITTS is the author of five books of poetry, including *Sweet Nothing, Honorary Astronaut,* and *Big Bright Sun*. He is the founder and principal editor of *H_NGM_N*, an online journal and small press. Learn more at his website www.natepritts.com.

WHY POETS NEED PLATFORMS:

And How to Create One

....

by Sage Cohen

If you want your poetry to be read, people need to know who you are, what you write, and where to find it. A viable platform can take you there. The good news is that anyone who wants to establish a poetry platform can take the necessary steps to build one over time. No matter what your level of writing, publishing and social media savvy, you can have more fun end enjoy more success as you take small steps over time to cultivate your poetry platform. This article will tell you how.

WHAT A PLATFORM IS

Platform is the turf you name and claim as your area of writing expertise, and it's everything you do to make that expertise visible. Just as a thesis is the foundation of a term paper around which its argument is built, a platform is an organizing principle around which a poet's many expressions of work revolve. A platform says to both the poet and the world, "I am an expert in [fill in the blanks with your specialty]!"

Platform is both the destination and the path. Think of your platform as your portfolio of accomplishments (publications, leadership roles, Web presence, public appearances, classes) that demonstrate your authority on a given topic. You build it as you go. It keeps you moving forward, tells you where forward is, and is the measure against which you decide if you're getting there.

HOW A PLATFORM CAN HELP YOU

Every poet can benefit from having a platform—even you. Following are the primary advantages of platform consciousness:

- **POETIC PROWESS.** The more focused you are on taking your poetry forward, the more likely you will stay engaged in honing your craft, polishing drafts, completing poems and identifying organizing principles or themes in your growing collection of work.

- **PUBLISHING.** As you gain experience researching literary journals and sending out your work, your knowledge about the publications best suited (and most receptive) to your work will grow. Over time, you will develop relationships, insight and a publishing track record that may significantly increase your chances of publishing (both individual poems and collections of poems).

- **FUNDRAISING.** Platform gives success an opportunity to snowball. With each publication, award, recognition or other notch on your belt, you'll improve the odds of winning prizes and receiving grants and residencies if this is of interest to you.

- **AUTHORITY.** The more experience you have writing and publishing poetry (and potentially educating/exciting others about their own poetic process), the more you and others will trust in your authority.

- **OPPORTUNITY.** Once you have earned a reputable name among your poetic peers, requests for interviews, articles, speaking engagements, teaching, and more are likely to start rolling in. But more importantly, you will have paved the way to go after exactly what you want to create in your writing life, buoyed by the confidence that comes from proven expertise.

NAMING AND CLAIMING YOUR PLATFORM

Not sure what your platform is or what you want it to be? It may be as simple as "Poetry." Or you could name what you believe your poetry is serving or striving for—if this is relevant to your work. Several years ago I named my platform "Writing the Life Poetic," which quickly led to me authoring a nonfiction book by this name. One thing is certain: naming and claiming your area of expertise is going to give you a new sense of clarity and purpose. And you may be surprised at how quickly this clarity magnetizes new, relevant opportunities to you.

If you'd like to explore some of the possibilities for your poetic platform, the following exercise can help. I encourage you to map out your own Platform at a Glance using the example below as a starting place. It's OK if you don't have all the answers yet. Having a record of what you're aspiring to today can help you learn about where you're headed over time.

PLATFORM AT A GLANCE

PLATFORM BUILDING BLOCKS	INSIGHTS
Theme, topic, genre, or area of expertise	Poetry for the people: with a goal of encouraging writers of all levels to write, read, and enjoy poetry.
Audience(s) you serve	• People who feel afraid, unwelcome, or unsure of how to start writing poetry. • People already writing poetry who want to write more, improve their craft, and have more fun. • Writers of all stripes wanting to invigorate their relationship with language. • People who love poetry and read poems.
Needs, desires, and preferences of your audience(s)	• People who feel afraid: Want to be invited in to poetry and assured that they are welcome/can do it. • People already writing poetry: Seeking tools, techniques, and tips to help improve their craft. • Writers of all stripes: Seeking a poetic lens through which to better appreciate and apply language in anything and everything they write. • People who love reading poems: Want to find poems that connect, move them, reveal something new.
Value you bring to each different type of reader	• People who feel afraid: Friendly encouragement and useful information. • People already writing poetry: Vast selection of tips, tools, strategies, and examples. • Writers of all stripes: A way into—and an enjoyable exploration of—the life poetic. • People who love reading poems: Poems I've written that they can embrace and enjoy.

PLATFORM NAME	WRITING THE LIFE POETIC
Why you are the ideal person to develop this platform over time	I have more than 20 years of experience cultivating a poetic way of life. I have an advanced degree in creative writing, a great deal of teaching experience, and a well-established career of writing and publishing poetry.
Why you are passionate about doing so	Poetry matters—not just as a literary form, but as a way of life. I know from my own experience that a relationship with poetry can significantly expand a person's sense of possibility, delight, and camaraderie with one's self, universal human truths, and life itself. I want to make this gift available to anyone who's interested in receiving it—as a teacher, author and poet.

MULTIPLE PATHS TO PLATFORM DEVELOPMENT

Publishing is certainly a significant way to establish and build your platform. But it is one of many. The good news is that while you're waiting for your latest batch of poems to make a safe landing in just the right literary journal(s), there are many ways to grow your visibility as an expert in your field that are available to you right now. Let's consider a few:

- **GO PUBLIC.** Read your work publicly as much as possible—either as a featured reader through a reading series or special event or at an open mic reading. Open mics are far more widely accessible and encourage everyone to participate. They're a good way to establish a community of writers if you attend and share work regularly. Over time, people will start to recognize you and your work. This will help you learn who your audience is and what it is about your poems that appeals to them.

- **TEACH WHAT YOU KNOW.** If you are passionate about poetry and have been schooling yourself in the craft (either through formal education or self-study), chances are good that you have something to offer other poets. From tenured academic positions to workshops you've organized and publicized yourself, you can choose the forum that fits your experience and temperament—then bring people together to learn about what's possible in poetry.

- **GIVE SERVICE.** There are endless ways to give service to poets—both paid and volunteer. You could become active in an online community—or start your own—that writes or contemplates poetry. Depending on your level of expertise, you could offer coaching, consulting, or editing. If you enjoy working with people of certain ages or circumstances (such as students, prisoners, elders), you could find ways to share poetry in your community through religious, educational or civic organizations.

- **PUBLISH.** Most poets are likely to experience multiple types and stages of publishing throughout their career. Because publishing individual poems can be slow and full collections even slower, you may want to explore other ways of sharing your knowledge of poetry along the way by publishing how-to articles, interviews or essays about the life poetic. You can query print and online magazines, share free content with organizations or online communities that serve poets and writers and/or create Squidoo lenses on any number of craft or publishing issues. If self-publishing is of interest to you, you could write and sell instructional e-books or publish print-on-demand collections of your poems (only if you are not seeking "mainstream" publication for this work.)

- **GO SOCIAL.** Social media gives poets instantaneous access to a virtually limitless community that can help your poetry and your platform evolve over time. When you want to exchange ideas, inspiration, poems, encouragement, tips and resources, book reviews, links, or professional recommendations, you can do so using any number of social media outlets. Facebook, Twitter, GoodReads and LinkedIn are just a few of the most popular places to do so. Choose one or two online forums in which to start; spend some time investigating how others are using these; decide what kind of information exchange best reflects your platform; and then pace yourself as you become a relevant contributor to the online conversation.

- **BECOME YOUR OWN MEDIA CHANNEL.** With a wide range of simple and inexpensive interactive media available today, you have numerous options for getting your message out. First, consider your platform aspirations. Then, decide what kind of information you'd like to share—and whether your goal is to inspire, collaborate, teach, build community or some combination of these. Depending on your goals, you might consider employing interactive media such as: webinars, teleclasses, e-zines, podcasts, and specialized online communities such as Ning. Try one and commit to it for at least six months; then evaluate, refine and expand as you go.

COHERENCE AND YOUR POETIC SOUL

These days, readers expect to have a personal connection with the poets they enjoy through their websites, blogs, teaching and live appearances. Plus, with the widespread use of social media bridging the space between writer and reader, anyone who has admired your work can tap into your moment-by-moment publicized thinking through the social media communities you frequent.

Therefore, who you are (or more accurately, how you present yourself publicly) and what you write are often one continuous experience for readers. A writing life that grows out of and reflects who you authentically are is going to be the most grounded and sustainable path to success.

My friend Dan Raphael is an example of someone who has built a writing empire on the foundation of his wildly entertaining and unusual command of language and life. On the back of one of Dan's books is a quote that says:

She: Do you think he's ever taken acid?

He: Taken it? I think he wears a patch.

Dan delivers on this very engaging and entertaining promise. He is a transcendent force of nature and engaging linguistic acrobatics on stage when delivering his poems and behind the scenes, when sending e-mail to friends.

I have another friend who is a widely sought photographer who has recently been recognized in several national magazines. This photographer has a parallel platform as a poet; and a good number of her poems explore the socioeconomic dynamics of being a person providing a service for the elite and the wealthy. This presents a bit of a platform pretzel, as she has no desire to alienate valued clients with her poetry. The expert photographer/poet is very delicately navigating how to hold these two parts of her life with integrity and authenticity as she quickly becomes more visible and respected in both chosen fields.

How is your life in alignment or out of whack with your platform(s) today? Is there anything you need to reconcile to create a greater coherence between what you write and how you live?

HAVE PLATFORM, WILL PROSPER

With a clear platform as the organizing principle in your life poetic, you can take the steps that will make your poems and your life poetic more visible in the communities and publications that matter to you. As you become increasingly effective at creating the writing results you want, over time you will attract more readers, expand your sphere of influence and generate far more opportunities to share your love of poetry.

BLOGGING BASICS:

Get the Most Out of Your Blog

....

by Robert Lee Brewer

In these days of publishing and media change, writers have to build platforms and learn how to connect to audiences if they want to improve their chances of publication and over-all success. There are many methods of audience connection available to writers, but one of the most important is through blogging.

Since I've spent several years successfully blogging—both personally and professionally—I figure I've got a few nuggets of wisdom to pass on to writers who are curious about blogging or who already are.

Here's my quick list of tips:

1. **START BLOGGING TODAY.** If you don't have a blog, use Blogger, WordPress, or some other blogging software to start your blog today. It's free, and you can start off with your very personal "Here I am, world" post.

2. **START SMALL.** Blogs are essentially very simple, but they can get very complicated (for people who like complications). However, I advise bloggers to start small and evolve over time.

3. **USE YOUR NAME IN YOUR URL.** This will make it easier for search engines to find you when your audience eventually starts seeking you out by name. For instance, my url is http://robertleebrewer.blogspot.com. If you try Googling "Robert Lee Brewer," you'll notice that My Name Is Not Bob is one of the top 5 search results (behind my other blog: Poetic Asides).

4. **UNLESS YOU HAVE A REASON, USE YOUR NAME AS THE TITLE OF YOUR BLOG.** Again, this helps with search engine results. My Poetic Asides blog includes my name in

the title, and it ranks higher than My Name Is Not Bob. However, I felt the play on my name was worth the trade off.

5. **FIGURE OUT YOUR BLOGGING GOALS.** You should return to this step every couple months, because it's natural for your blogging goals to evolve over time. Initially, your blogging goals may be to make a post a week about what you have written, submitted, etc. Over time, you may incorporate guests posts, contests, tips, etc.

6. **BE YOURSELF.** I'm a big supporter of the idea that your image should match your identity. It gets too confusing trying to maintain a million personas. Know who you are and be that on your blog, whether that means you're sincere, funny, sarcastic, etc.

7. **POST AT LEAST ONCE A WEEK.** This is for starters. Eventually, you may find it better to post once a day or multiple times per day. But remember: Start small and evolve over time.

8. **POST RELEVANT CONTENT.** This means that you post things that your readers might actually care to know.

> Don't spend a week writing each post. Try to keep it to an hour or two tops and then post.

9. **USEFUL AND HELPFUL POSTS WILL ATTRACT MORE VISITORS.** Talking about yourself is all fine and great. I do it myself. But if you share truly helpful advice, your readers will share it with others, and visitors will find you on search engines.

10. **TITLE YOUR POSTS IN A WAY THAT GETS YOU FOUND IN SEARCH ENGINES.** The more specific you can get the better. For instance, the title "Blogging Tips" will most likely get lost in search results. However, the title "Blogging Tips for Writers" specifies which audience I'm targeting and increases the chances of being found on the first page of search results.

11. **LINK TO POSTS IN OTHER MEDIA.** If you have an e-mail newsletter, link to your blog posts in your newsletter. If you have social media accounts, link to your blog posts there. If you have a helpful post, link to it in relevant forums and on message boards.

12. **WRITE WELL, BUT BE CONCISE.** At the end of the day, you're writing blog posts, not literary manifestos. Don't spend a week writing each post. Try to keep it to an hour

or two tops and then post. Make sure your spelling and grammar are good, but don't stress yourself out too much.

13. **FIND LIKE-MINDED BLOGGERS.** Comment on their blogs regularly and link to them from yours. Eventually, they may do the same. Keep in mind that blogging is a form of social media, so the more you communicate with your peers the more you'll get out of the process.

14. **RESPOND TO COMMENTS ON YOUR BLOG.** Even if it's just a simple "Thanks," respond to your readers if they comment on your blog. After all, you want your readers to be engaged with your blog, and you want them to know that you care they took time to comment.

15. **EXPERIMENT.** Start small, but don't get complacent. Every so often, try something new. For instance, the biggest draw to my Poetic Asides blog are the poetry prompts and challenges I issue to poets. Initially, that was an experiment—one that worked very well. I've tried other experiments that haven't panned out, and that's fine. It's all part of a process.

SEO TIPS FOR WRITERS

Most writers may already know what SEO is. If not, SEO stands for *search engine optimization*. Basically, a site or blog that practices good SEO habits should improve its rankings in search engines, such as Google and Bing. Most huge corporations have realized the importance of SEO and spend enormous sums of time, energy and money on perfecting their SEO practices. However, writers can improve their SEO without going to those same extremes.

In this section, I will use the terms of *site pages* and *blog posts* interchangeably. In both cases, you should be practicing the same SEO strategies (when it makes sense).

Here are my top tips on ways to improve your SEO starting today:

1. **USE APPROPRIATE KEYWORDS.** Make sure that your page displays your main keyword(s) in the page title, content, URL, title tags, page header, image names and tags (if you're including images). All of this is easy to do, but if you feel overwhelmed, just remember to use your keyword(s) in your page title and content (especially in the first and last 50 words of your page).

2. **USE KEYWORDS NATURALLY.** Don't kill your content and make yourself look like a spammer to search engines by overloading your page with your keyword(s). You don't get SEO points for quantity but for quality. Plus, one of the main ways to improve your page rankings is when you...

3. **DELIVER QUALITY CONTENT.** The best way to improve your SEO is by providing content that readers want to share with others by linking to your pages. Some of the top results in search engines can be years old, because the content is so good that people keep coming back. So, incorporate your keywords in a smart way, but make sure it works organically with your content.

4. **UPDATE CONTENT REGULARLY.** If your site looks dead to visitors, then it'll appear that way to search engines too. So update your content regularly. This should be very easy for writers who have blogs. For writers who have sites, incorporate your blog into your site. This will make it easier for visitors to your blog to discover more about you on your site (through your site navigation tools).

....

If you interview someone on your blog, don't title your post with an interesting quotation. While that strategy may help get readers in the print world, it doesn't help with SEO at all.

....

5. **LINK BACK TO YOUR OWN CONTENT.** If I have a post on Blogging Tips for Writers, for instance, I'll link back to it if I have a Platform Building post, because the two complement each other. This also helps clicks on my blog, which helps SEO. The one caveat is that you don't go crazy with your linking and that you make sure your links are relevant. Otherwise, you'll kill your traffic, which is not good for your page rankings.

6. **LINK TO OTHERS YOU CONSIDER HELPFUL.** Back in 2000, I remember being ordered by my boss at the time (who didn't last too much longer afterward) to ignore any competitive or complementary websites—no matter how helpful their content—because they were our competitors. You can try basing your online strategy on these principles, but I'm nearly 100% confident you'll fail. It's helpful for other sites and your own to link to other great resources. I shine a light on others to help them out (if I find their content truly helpful) in the hopes that they'll do the same if ever they find my content truly helpful for their audience.

7. **GET SPECIFIC WITH YOUR HEADLINES.** If you interview someone on your blog, don't title your post with an interesting quotation. While that strategy may help get readers in the print world, it doesn't help with SEO at all. Instead, title your post as "Interview With (insert name here)." If you have a way to identify the person further, include that in the title too. For instance, when I interview poets on my Poetic Asides blog, I'll title those posts like this: Interview With Poet Erika Meitner. Erika's name is a keyword, but so are the terms *poet* and *interview*.

8. **USE IMAGES.** Many expert sources state that the use of images can improve SEO, because it shows search engines that the person creating the page is spending a little extra time and effort on the page than a common spammer. However, I'd caution anyone using images to make sure those images are somehow complementary to the content. Don't just throw up a lot of images that have no relevance to anything. At the same time...

9. **OPTIMIZE IMAGES THROUGH STRATEGIC LABELING.** Writers can do this by making sure the image file is labeled using your keyword(s) for the post. Using the Erika Meitner example above (which does include images), I would label the file "Erika Meitner headshot.jpg"—or whatever the image file type happens to be. Writers can also improve image SEO through the use of captions and ALT tagging. Of course, at the same time, writers should always ask themselves if it's worth going through all that trouble for each image or not. Each writer has to answer that question for him or herself.

10. **USE YOUR SOCIAL MEDIA PLATFORM TO SPREAD THE WORD.** Whenever you do something new on your site or blog, you should share that information on your other social media sites, such as Twitter, Facebook, LinkedIn, online forums, etc. This lets your social media connections know that something new is on your site/blog. If it's relevant and/or valuable, they'll let others know. And that's a great way to build your SEO.

Programmers and marketers could get even more involved in the dynamics of SEO optimization, but I think these tips will help most writers out immediately and effectively while still allowing plenty of time and energy for the actual work of writing.

BLOG DESIGN TIPS FOR WRITERS

Design is an important element to any blog's success. But how can you improve your blog's design if you're not a designer? I'm just an editor with an English Lit degree and no formal training in design. However, I've worked in media for more than a decade now and can share some very fundamental and easy tricks to improve the design of your blog.

Here are my seven blog design tips for writers:

1. **USE LISTS.** Whether they're numbered or bullet points, use lists when possible. Lists break up the text and make it easy for readers to follow what you're blogging.

2. **BOLD MAIN POINTS IN LISTS.** Again, this helps break up the text while also highlighting the important points of your post.

3. **USE HEADINGS.** If your posts are longer than 300 words and you don't use lists, then please break up the text by using basic headings.

4. **USE A READABLE FONT.** Avoid using fonts that are too large or too small. Avoid using cursive or weird fonts. Times New Roman or Arial works, but if you want to get "creative," use something similar to those.

5. **LEFT ALIGN.** English-speaking readers are trained to read left to right. If you want to make your blog easier to read, avoid centering or right aligning your text (unless you're purposefully calling out the text).

6. **USE SMALL PARAGRAPHS.** A good rule of thumb is to try and avoid paragraphs that drone on longer than five sentences. I usually try to keep paragraphs to around three sentences myself.

7. **ADD RELEVANT IMAGES.** Personally, I shy away from using too many images. My reason is that I only like to use them if they're relevant. However, images are very powerful on blogs, so please use them—just make sure they're relevant to your blog post.

If you're already doing everything on my list, keep it up! If you're not, then you might want to re-think your design strategy on your blog. Simply adding a header here and a list there can easily improve the design of a blog post.

GUEST POSTING TIPS FOR WRITERS

Recently, I've broken into guest posting as both a guest poster and as a host of guest posts (over at my Poetic Asides blog). So far, I'm pretty pleased with both sides of the guest posting process. As a writer, it gives me access to an engaged audience I may not usually reach. As a blogger, it provides me with fresh and valuable content I don't have to create. Guest blogging is a rare win-win scenario.

That said, writers could benefit from a few tips on the process of guest posting:

1. **PITCH GUEST POSTS LIKE ONE WOULD PITCH ARTICLES TO A MAGAZINE.** Include what your hook is for the post, what you plan to cover, and a little about who you are. Remember: Your post should somehow benefit the audience of the blog you'd like to guest post.

2. **OFFER PROMOTIONAL COPY OF BOOK (OR OTHER GIVEAWAYS) AS PART OF YOUR GUEST POST.** Having a random giveaway for people who comment on a blog post can help spur conversation and interest in your guest post, which is a great way to get the most mileage out of your guest appearance.

3. **CATER POSTS TO AUDIENCE.** As the editor of *Writer's Market* and *Poet's Market*, I have great range in the topics I can cover. However, if I'm writing a guest post for a fiction blog, I'll write about things of interest to a novelist—not a poet.

4. **MAKE IT PERSONAL, BUT PROVIDE NUGGET.** Guest posts are a great opportunity for you to really show your stuff to a new audience. You could write a very helpful and impersonal post, but that won't connect with readers the same way as if you write a very helpful and personal post that makes them want to learn more about you (and your blog, your book, your Twitter account, etc.). Speaking of which...

5. **SHARE LINKS TO YOUR WEBSITE, BLOG, AND SOCIAL NETWORKS.** After all, you need to make it easy for readers who enjoyed your guest post to learn more about you and your projects. Start the conversation in your guest post and keep it going on your own sites, and profiles. And related to that...

6. **PROMOTE YOUR GUEST POST THROUGH YOUR NORMAL CHANNELS ONCE THE POST GOES LIVE.** Your normal audience will want to know where you've been and what you've been doing. Plus, guest posts lend a little extra "street cred" to your projects. But don't stop there...

7. **CHECK FOR COMMENTS ON YOUR GUEST POST AND RESPOND IN A TIMELY MANNER.** Sometimes the comments are the most interesting part of a guest post (no offense). This is where readers can ask more in-depth or related questions, and it's also where you can show your expertise on the subject by being as helpful as possible. And guiding all seven of these tips is this one:

8. **PUT SOME EFFORT INTO YOUR GUEST POST.** Part of the benefit to guest posting is the opportunity to connect with a new audience. Make sure you bring your A-game, because you need to make a good impression if you want this exposure to actually help grow your audience. Don't stress yourself out, but put a little thought into what you submit.

ONE ADDITIONAL TIP: Have fun with it. Passion is what really drives the popularity of blogs. Share your passion and enthusiasm, and readers are sure to be impressed.

A YEAR IN THE LIFE OF A CITY POET LAUREATE

by Jeannine Hall Gailey

So, you're thinking of applying for your city's Poet Laureate position and you want to know what it's like, what it takes to succeed and want to know what kind of problems you might encounter? What kind of person does it take to be a successful city Poet Laureate, to rouse a community to the wonders of poetry?

In my past year as Redmond's Poet Laureate, I have found it's a job for someone part Don Quixote (fond of tilting at windmills,) part old-time evangelist (of poetry, of course), part professor, part salesperson and part arts administrator. It's also a once-in-a-lifetime chance to put your love of poetry into practice in your own backyard. There are Poet Laureates of towns, counties, cities and states, and all of them take the position out of a love for both poetry and people, and a desire to put themselves out there and actually make a difference.

THE MOTIVATION

When I first moved to the small-but-bustling tech center city of Redmond, Washington in 2000 for a job at the "world's biggest software company," as it was called then, I looked in vain for poetry workshop groups, poetry readings, or even coffee shops hosting open mics. I kept coming up empty-handed. I ended up driving the 45 minutes (sometimes an hour with traffic) to downtown Seattle to find poetry classes or even the 40-minutes-and-a-ferry-ride to attend poetry workshops on Bainbridge Island.

Because of this lack of poetry in my area, I was determined to help create a poetry community for myself and other poetry-hungry newcomers to my town when I became Redmond's second Poet Laureate. I also had a sneaking suspicion that a lot of the tech workers in my town were bright, secretly artistic types who would love poetry – once they heard or saw poetry that appealed to their interests. So I began to think about how to create a poetry program for those people – potential poetry lovers who just didn't know it yet.

WHAT EXACTLY DOES A CITY POET LAUREATE DO?

One of the things we were asked to do when we applied and interviewed for the position was talk about a slogan and our proposed activities. Since the town is made up largely of folk who work in technology, and our city – which boasts little in the way of bookstores and art galleries, but does have an excellent comic book store and anime shop – I decided on "Geeks for Poetry, Poetry for Geeks." I arranged to present workshops on geek-friendly topics like superheroes and anime, as well as a series of talks from poets who wrote about science or who were familiar with technologies that might be helpful to writers, like e-book publishing and social media. I brought in artists to illustrate poetry, worked with local musicians, and editors and publishers who could tell audiences about the opportunities for getting their work out into the world. I created social media entities for Redmond Poetry, like a blog, a twitter identity, and a Facebook identity, that I could pass on to the next Redmond Poet Laureate as a kind of high-tech legacy.

This approach might not work for every city, but my goal, and the goal of every Poet Laureate, was to figure out the people in my city, and their particular proclivities, and provide poetry activities for them. I learned a lot about my city in the process; I learned demographics, and the kind of parks and art projects the city had been participating in. It was a fascinating lesson in civics as well as learning more about the city I had moved to and made my home. And meeting everyone from accounts payable to deputy directors also increased my understanding of who was running our city and their values. I discussed with Redmond's Mayor, John Marchione, how we might bring an understanding and love of the arts to a city well-known for its high-tech brainpower. "Redmond needs a heart and soul as well as a brain," he said as he talked about his enthusiasm for the Poet Laureate position and why he and the City Council decided to create the position: "A Poet Laureate adds richness and texture to our community that allows us to see the world from many perspectives." I was inspired by his vision and moved by his enthusiasm for bringing more artistic presence to our city. The people in the City Council and Arts Commission were equally inspiring in their encouragement.

FINANCIAL CONSIDERATIONS

As far as finances: if you apply, expect to get paid very little, and for most Poet Laureates, budgets for poetry programming for the Poet Laureates I spoke to ranged from zero to very little. The new Poet Laureate of Los Angeles, California, for example, has the almost unheard-of programming budget of $10,000. Though I have found this work can take a lot of time and energy, it doesn't necessarily pay like it does, so make sure you have income from another job or freelance work.

THE BENEFITS AND CHALLENGES OF BEING REDMOND'S POET LAUREATE

What are the best parts of being Poet Laureate of my city? I love getting to know my community better. There have been comic moments – like judging a limerick contest for a local poetry group's party – and heartwarming moments – like answering questions from precocious 10-year-old children about how to publish poetry. Partnering with our wonderful local library has been a highlight (and King County's libraries have been rated some of the best in the country, no bragging, cough cough) and has brought me into contact with local readers and writers I would never have met without that opportunity, some of whom will be with me as friends long after the Poet Laureate gig is over. And nothing is quite as heartwarming, for me, as talking to a local high school class about poetry. Especially when they are nice enough to laugh at my jokes. I had the opportunity to work with a neighboring city's art museum, to open for an indie rock band at a coffee shop, and to talk about the finer details of haiku with a local group of Japanese language and culture experts. "The Best Part of Being Poet Laureate" below chronicles the best parts of the Poet Laureate job from some other Poet Laureates of cities and states.

THE BEST PART OF BEING POET LAUREATE

I talked with a few Poet Laureates to see what they thought of as the best part of the job.

MICHELLE BITTING: "The best thing about being Poet Laureate of the city of Pacific Palisades, California is the increased receptivity to and support for all things literary and poetic. It kind of ups the ante, makes the game, or the "taking of it" more serious. Also an increased sense of the longevity and importance of the art form. So this is true with the kids as well as the parents. I think people in the community feel a certain pride and fire about it, maybe a more forged intention as a group and openness to the place in us linked to the eternal, to the emotional. The downside is it's really hard to wear a laurel crown without looking like a reindeer. The most effective way to outreach the community, for me, has been my work as a California Poet in the Schools. I teach hundreds of kids in town and then I teach their siblings. The kids come home blabbering about how much they love poetry! Kids who sometimes hate writing otherwise! Then the parents talk it up and the teachers are ecstatic for the support and life-breathing force brought gleefully, charitably, to their classrooms. The local public library has been crucial in providing motivation and validation to the creation of the post."

KATHLEEN FLENNIKEN, Poet Laureate of Washington State: "I've loved being invited into those poetry microcosms flourishing all over the state. Seeing the way these so-called isolated poets take care of each other—with regular book clubs and writing groups, readings at the local coffee shop, publishing opportunities. Seeing poetry taught well in many small schools by teachers who actually read it. My role switches from advocate to admirer. And I carry that enthusiasm forward to the next stop where there might not be a thriving poetry community yet, but there could be.

And I love presenting to groups—picture a luncheon full of Rotarians, or a breakfast fundraiser—who are uneasy when they see poetry coming, and the feeling of the room as they realize en masse that maybe poetry can be kind of wonderful after all. Getting e-mails afterward, "Will you send me that poem by Casey Fuller that you read today?"

TAMMY ROBACKER: The best part of being Poet Laureate of Tacoma, Washington was getting invited to read poetry and teach writing classes to many folks in the community who I would have never met otherwise. I have been introduced to so many amazing and talented senior citizens, high school students, middle school students, artists and arts program leaders in this city whom I would have never met outside of my Poet Laureateship. It was a real honor to be invited to community centers, schools, classrooms and special events to share my poetry or to teach poetry to those who don't have access to it. It was definitely a scenario where the giver becomes the gift. By teaching and giving, I wound up receiving the greatest reward.

DIANE LOCKWARD: The best thing about being Poet Laureate of West Caldwell, New Jersey is bringing together several hundred people at the two annual events I run: 1) Girl Talk: A Poetry Reading in Celebration of Women's History Month, and 2) Poetry Festival: A Celebration of Literary Journals. Editors, poets, neophytes, and the uninitiated come to these events like pilgrims to Canterbury. Together we spend a day feasting on poetry.

The challenges of trying to bring poetry to the public – sometimes a public who isn't aware of needing or wanting poetry – have included knocking vainly at doors of possible sponsors, venues, trying to find those people-who-might-love-poetry-but-don't-know-it-yet and figuring out what this particular community wants. The other big challenges include the loss of time to write, the need to be out in public A LOT, and this may just be my city, but a surprising amount of detail-oriented documentation, scheduling and even accounting and budgets. Being a Poet Laureate means that sometimes, I have to put the needs of the poetry community above my own needs as a poet, which, for me, was worth the sacrifice. As Tammy Robacker, the former Poet Laureate of Tacoma, put it: "If you plan on applying for a Poet Laureateship in your city or state, be ready to take a bit of a break from that introverted, creative, solitary side of yourself that engages the 'writing' of poetry. To constantly take part in special events, poetry readings, literary and teaching engagements, and open mics, you won't always have those extra, quiet hours to write your deep, intense poems."

If you're an enthusiastic workaholic type-A person like I am, you might want to be careful and pace yourself – I felt I could put in 40-50 hours a week and still not accomplish everything I wanted to do. Growing a poetry community is an invisible, ever-expanding goal. There is a city event or meeting or arts community group almost every night, and sometimes I wish I could clone myself so I could attend them all. So one piece of advice I can pass on from my first year is to target your most important goals and priorities and focus on those audiences and projects that are really your passion.

IT'S NOT A JOB, IT'S AN ADVENTURE...

You wouldn't do this job for the money, but you might take it for the chance to get to know your community better, and the chance to spread the love of poetry. By taking this position, I got to meet the people who run my city, I learned the names of my neighbors, my librarians and local high school teachers, I learned which business owners were enthusiastic supporters of the arts (and decided to patronize their businesses more often!) I went to a City Council meeting at the Town Hall for the first time and discussed the need for the arts with our Mayor. I've worked with coffee shops, community theaters, art museums and wine bars, partnering with local publishers and even a local con (Thanks, Geek Girl Con!) to try to get the word out about poetry. The really interesting thing was that there are opportunities everywhere, and the more I talked about poetry to others, the more opportunities there were. After my time in the position, I feel braver and more empowered about approaching venues for readings, starting workshops, and talking to everyone from librarians to teachers to politicians about poetry.

Last note: If your city or state doesn't already have a Poet Laureate position, you might want to get a group together and approach your city council with the idea. It never hurts to encourage more poetic activity in your community!

JEANNINE HALL GAILEY is the Poet Laureate of Redmond, Washington and the author of three books of poetry, Becoming the Villainess, She Returns to the Floating World and Unexplained Fevers. Her website is www.webbish6.com.

POETRY READINGS

The Place Where Everyone Wins

....

by Scott Owens

As a graduate student at the University of North Carolina at Charlotte, I was greatly influenced by Tim Peeler's poem "Carolina Trailer Park, Take 6: Danny's Real Dad." This poem liberated me from a narrow perspective on the proper subject matter for poetry such that I finally felt free to explore my own experience, growing up father"less" and on the wrong side of the tracks, as fodder for poetry.

Over the next several years I encountered Peeler's work fairly regularly in various journals, and what I read always resonated meaningfully with my own experience and my budding understanding of what poetry could and should do. Years later, when I took a job at Catawba Valley Community College in Hickory, NC, I was surprised to discover that Peeler was already on staff there. I was even more surprised, given his work's impact on me and the fact that he had published more than 600 poems and a half dozen books by then, how few people in the community knew who he was.

I decided the proper thing to do was to improve the community's awareness of Peeler's work and of poetry in general and that the best and easiest way I could do that was to start a reading series for local and regional poets. That was nearly 6 years ago. Peeler was, of course, the first featured writer at Poetry Hickory, but 80 readings and more than 200 poets later, the series is still going strong, bringing an audience of 30 or more to Taste Full Beans Coffeehouse once a month (and for occasional special events) to listen to both new writers and such luminaries as NC Poet Laureate Joseph Bathanti, NEA Recipient David Rigsbee, Pulitzer Prize Nominee Tony Abbott, and other award-winning writers like Sandra Beasley, Joanna Catherine Scott, and Ronald Moran. One thing I've learned from facilitating these events is that poetry readings are one of the few places where everyone wins.

IF YOU BUILD IT, THEY WILL COME OR HOW BUSINESSES WIN

Before I begin to talk about why one should go to poetry readings, I want to make it clear that not having a reading to go to is simply not an excuse. Poetry readings are everywhere. Some are true open mics; others feature invited writers only; still others are a mix of featured writers and open mic. I have given readings in more than 50 different cities, and a quick review of the NC Writers' Network calendar reveals that there are about that many series in NC alone. If there isn't one in your hometown, start one. Coffee shops, bookstores, libraries, museums, art galleries, schools, community theaters, etc. are all more than willing to accommodate poetry reading series because such a series brings in traffic, increases awareness of the host organization, brings in business, makes them newsworthy, or just gives them the opportunity to expand their support of the arts. All one needs to start a series is the gumption to ask and the wherewithal to let writers and readers know they are welcome to participate. Poets want to be heard/read; poetry lovers want to hear/buy poetry; and others have other reasons to come.

HOW POETS WIN

Obviously, for the poet who is featured at a reading, the reasons to go include reaching potential readers, making a few sales, and networking with other poets and editors. Most generalizations about poets are as false as most generalizations in general. However, it is fairly safe to say that what most poets most want is to be read, perhaps considered, maybe even understood.

Presenting one's work "in the flesh" with the opportunity to discuss it helps make poets accessible, approachable, and appealing, which helps develop committed readers, which in turn helps with both immediate and word-of-mouth sales, and ultimately expands the poet's reputation, market, and potential influence. Most featured writers at Poetry Hickory, for example, sell between 5 and 10 copies of their books at the reading. Given that these are direct sales, the profit margin is typically three or four times higher than royalties. Those buyers then relay their reactions to the work to other prospective readers/buyers, so the potential rewards extend far beyond one night's connection with a handful of listeners.

The range of the featured writer's connections can also be expanded through the networking that takes place at a poetry reading. I have rarely given a reading that didn't result in another reading, or a review, or an interview, or the opportunity to lead a workshop or have a poem published in a journal or anthology. Predictably, poetry lovers attend poetry readings, and that group includes editors, teachers, publishers, arts activists, and the general busybodies who stay involved and get things done. Readers at Poetry Hickory, for example, have included the publishers from Main Street Rag, Rank Stranger Press, Jacar Press, and Future Cycle Press; the editors from *Iodine Poetry Journal, Asheville Review, The Dead*

Mule School of Southern Literature, Redheaded Stepchild, Writer's Market, and *The Pedestal Magazine*; organizers from the Lenoir-Rhyne Visiting Writers Series, the NC Poetry Society, the Poetry Council of NC, and The Writers Circle, and reviewers from *The Charlotte Observer, The Pilot, The Raleigh News & Observer,* and *Pirene's Fountain.*

Given such opportunities for networking, the "winning" poets are not just the ones who read, but also those who attend. I, for example, first met each of my four publishers at readings by other people. Nevertheless, the biggest reward for a poet attending a poetry reading, whether they are there to read or not, may not be the networking, the sales, or the audience.

The biggest reward may be the opportunity for what some might call inspiration. After years of struggling with antiquated concepts of poetic aesthetics, I came to recognize what I wanted to do with my own writing while listening to Galway Kinnell read at Ohio University, and I have modified that aesthetic under the influence of every reading I have attended. On a simpler, level, the one place I have begun more of my poems than any other is . . . well, actually, it's driving in my car (one hand on the wheel; the other writing, without looking, on the center console). But the place I have started the second largest number of poems is at poetry readings (my apologies to all those reading poets who have noticed that far away look in my eyes or seen me furiously scribbling in my notebook while they read).

....

Nevertheless, the biggest reward for a poet attending a poetry reading, whether they are there to read or not, may not be the networking, the sales, or the audience.

....

A naive view of this dynamic might refer to it as an opportunity to "steal ideas." Yes, all good poets are good thieves. We tend to thrive on an image, a word, a phrase, an idea that we pick up from the streets, the hallways, the things we read. Such "thievery" is more properly seen as collecting. Unfortunately, we are often kept too busy to focus on the language possibilities swirling around us, to collect the various impressions and make the associations that lead to poetry. A poetry reading, however, is that rare situation in which it is actually our task to focus on those possibilities, to gather all that we can and let our discursive minds delve more deeply into the connections between things. Thus, a more enlightened view will see this activity not as stealing, but, as Mary Oliver suggests, as paying attention.

HOW THE AUDIENCE WINS

Contrary to the preconceptions of the uninformed and uninitiated, poetry readings can be very entertaining. A speaker in Muriel Rukeyser's poem "Waiting for Icarus" says, "Inventors are like poets, a trashy lot." A speaker in Lucille Clifton's poem "Admonitions" says, "when they ask you / why is your mama so funny / say / she is a poet / she don't have no sense." However they are characterized, one thing is certain about poets: They tend to be an interesting collection of people. At one reading I attended, a male poet stripped off his clothes to reveal he was wearing a dress underneath. At another, a poet chanted feudalistic Japanese songs. At yet another, a poet recited his poems while doing one-armed push-ups and later threw his wadded up poems at members of the audience. Poets can be quite spectacular at times, and who doesn't love a spectacle? Of course, poetry lovers can be just as interesting as the poets themselves, so sometimes the spectacle is just as entertaining on the other side of the microphone.

More often than they are spectacular though, and more importantly, poetry readings can be cathartic, even mind or life-altering. Poetry is simultaneously emotional, intellectual, and spiritual. Poetry works through the imagistic recreation of complex experience. The poet finds just the right word, sound, combinations of words and sounds to conjure not just images in the reader's or listener's mind but images that resonate with our own associations, thoughts, feelings, and memories. Even the movement of poetry—the speaking in distilled fragments, making integral associative leaps, seeming always almost but not quite under control—is a lot like how we experience things in our own lives. In this way, poems both reflect and deepen our experience as human beings; they mine the timeless emotional undercurrents of perception, helping us to recognize our implicit involvement in each other and in all things human.

However they are characterized, one thing is certain about poets: They tend to be an interesting collection of people.

At virtually every poetry reading I've given or attended, many have laughed, and at least one has cried. I consider that a good thing. Thus, the audience wins by thinking and feeling in ways that we too often lack the time or the understanding of the need to do in our daily lives. William Carlos Williams said, "It is difficult to get the news from poetry, yet men die miserably every day for lack of what is found there." Edwin Honig added, "The poet's voice is needed now more than ever before—that voice which celebrates the difficult, joyous, imaginative process by which the individual discovers and enacts selfhood."

HOW TO GIVE A POETRY READING

The first step in giving a poetry reading is becoming familiar with poetry readings. Look for one in your hometown. Again, if there isn't one, start one. Once you're familiar with the format, sign up for an Open Mic. When you get comfortable with that audience, begin branching out by contacting the organizers of other reading series. Lists of regional readings are available through most writing and poetry organizations. In NC, for example, the NC Writers' Network does a weekly e-blast listing all of the upcoming literary events they are aware of. They also maintain a monthly calendar of events on their website.

Once you're on a schedule, a bit of preparation goes a long way. In some ways the most important part of the process is poem selection. Be kind to your audience. Remember that they are there in some part at least to be entertained. Don't expect them to pay attention to and understand your magnum opus when delivered verbally. Select shorter poems, funny poems, shocking poems, accessible poems, and the poems with the greatest emotional impact, the ones you will deliver with zeal, relish, or passion.

Practice your reading so that you know the poems well enough to establish some eye contact with your audience and so that your delivery assists your listeners in understanding the poem. Keep your comments about the poems brief and be yourself in those comments. People listen better when they like the person they're listening to. Always read too little rather than too much—leave them wanting more.

Arrange your poems to begin with a bang and to end with something that resonates, and alternate your selections to avoid seeming too dark or too glib. And never be afraid. Remember as much as you fear you won't be understood, they fear they won't understand. Most importantly, enjoy yourself, and your audience will enjoy you as well.

SCOTT OWENS tenth collection *Shadows Trail Them Home* is due out from Clemson University Press. His prior work has received awards from the Academy of American Poets, the Pushcart Prize, the NC Writers Network, and the Poetry Society of SC. He is the founder of Poetry Hickory, editor of *Wild Goose Poetry Review* and *234*, and vice president of the Poetry Council of NC and the NC Poetry Society.

HOW TO GIVE A GREAT POETRY READING

....

by Jeannine Hall Gailey

Everyone has a horror story about a bad poetry reading—one that went too long, where the reader droned on in a monotone, made the audience uncomfortable or wasn't prepared and spent lots of time shuffling papers around in a notebook or—let's face it, we've all seen it happen—was too drunk to be coherent.

But how about creating a wonderful poetry reading? How can we create as positive an experience as possible with our poetry readings, as inviting to strangers as it might be to poets, a reading that keeps the audience awake, entertained, and enlightened? If you've just published a chapbook or full-length book, you'll probably want to book several readings around your town to promote it. It's such an exciting time and you want your audience to have the best possible experience.

TIPS TO PREPARE A GREAT READING

Here are a few tips to help mitigate the nerves that most people feel before reading in front of an audience that have worked for me. These preparations will help your be as relaxed and ready as possible to give an energetic, interesting reading.

- Prepare your reading by organizing your poems ahead of time and practicing your "set list." Think about your audience; if you're reading in the evening in a wine bar, you can probably prepare a more rowdy set of poems that if you're performing at a high school or a coffee shop in the afternoon. Try to open with a poem that you've read before and has connected with an audience; I often start with a funny poem, to put the audience at ease before moving to more serious work. And if you can, end the reading with a high energy poem.

- Time yourself on one of your practice runs so you make sure you don't go over the allotted time. Maybe jot down some beginning remarks or thanks and include those when you practice. If you're reading with another reader, it is even more important that you keep to the assigned amount of time, whether that is five minutes or twenty minutes, because another reader staring you down, probably willing you to disappear, will not help you feel relaxed.

It's not about gimmicks, you don't need a funny hat or a guitar— you just need to bring yourself and your poetry.

- Though you want to stay conscious of time, it's also important to breathe and take your time when you read, rather than nervously rushing through your work. A tip from award-winning poet Dorianne Laux: "I've found the two most important things for me are to not read too long and to slow down... It shows a respect for your audience... Respect the poem, give it its due."
- Bring a "reading kit" with you, like a bottle of water or tea, lip balm, and cough drops, in case you have a scratchy throat or feel dry-mouthed when you get up at the podium. Avoid uncomfortable shoes, anything you might trip on, or too-fussy items that might get in your way. Wear something you feel comfortable in, not a costume. It's not about gimmicks, you don't need a funny hat or a guitar—you just need to bring yourself and your poetry.
- If you can, check out the venue ahead of time. Figure out things like parking and layout and find out if you'll have a microphone available. What's the atmosphere like? Is it a smoky and bohemian hangout, or a quiet bookstore with an elderly but faithful audience? If you're reading out of town, see if you can get in touch with someone nearby and find out a little about the place. If you're reading on the radio, make sure your poems are more accessible, since you probably won't have the audience's undivided attention.
- Bring along friends or family members to give you support—they can provide not only emotional support, but your "cheerleaders" can help you sell books, make change, chat to people who are in line, and of course, laugh and applaud at the right times.

LET YOUR WORK BE THE STAR OF THE SHOW

It's important to remember that focusing on the work rather than on your performance will help you stay centered. Laux gives this advice: "When I give a reading, I think of myself as a representative, an ambassador for poetry, all poetry, and so I want the audience to leave wanting more. I also will often begin a reading by reciting a poem by a poet I love. It's not about you. It's about the culture gathering around the light of language for a brief moment. The poet is not in the center, but in the circle. The fire of poetry is in the center."

'The most important thing is to be present with the language, to think, feel and speak simultaneously.'

Jericho Brown, award-winning poet and amazing reader, echoes that spirit in his tip: "I think the most important thing is for the poet put herself in the same emotional state she found herself while writing the poem. The key, for me, is enjoying the rhythms I wrote in the midst of writing and revising."

Elizabeth Austen, poet and public radio producer, who also teaches performance workshops for writers, recommends getting into the spirit of the work: "The most important thing is to be present with the language, to think, feel and speak simultaneously. You want to bring these words to life, not 'report' them. You don't have to put anything on the language; you just have to commit to it, to inhabit it."

REALLY, BE YOURSELF

Trust that your own talents and proclivities will shine through during the poetry reading. If you're funny, use that. If you're relaxed and casual, that will also come through. Laux encourages poets to use their own style: "Really, mostly try to have fun, and engage the audience in some way. It's hard to make hard and fast rules since everyone has their own style. Be the best of yourself."

The whole point of a reading is to introduce your work to people. If you like, and it's okay with the reading organizer, set some time aside after the reading for a Q&A session—people like to interact and ask questions, so let them! If you're adventurous, you can also introduce other art elements to your reading—I've done readings with musicians who put poems to music, readings with thematically-related art shows, and readings with video clips. I love the idea of making the whole experience more integrated and interactive for the audience.

WILL ANYONE BE AT YOUR READING?

A last point about making your reading a success is to try a little publicity—don't rely on the person or group that invited you to do the reading to do all the promotional work. Be sure you let your audiences know—via Facebook, Twitter, or e-mail—where and when you'll be reading. Don't assume everyone already knows. I miss friends' readings unintentionally all the time because they assume I know about their readings—and I forget to let people know about my readings all the time, and I'll hear "I didn't even know about it!"

So Remember...

Try to stay present, stay aware of your audience and other readers, and remember that the poetry should be the star of the reading. Take a deep breath, maybe a drink of hot water with lemon and honey, and of course, always leave them wanting more.

JEANNINE HALL GAILEY is the Poet Laureate of Redmond, Washington and the author of three books of poetry, Becoming the Villainess, She Returns to the Floating World, and Unexplained Fevers. Her website is www.webbish6.com.

SOCIAL MEDIA PRIMER FOR POETS

How to Use Social Media the Right Way

by Robert Lee Brewer

Beyond the actual writing, the most important thing writers can do for their writing careers is to build a writer platform. This writer platform can consist of any number of quantifiable information about your reach to your target audience, and one hot spot is social media.

Here's the thing: I think it's more important to chase quality connections than quantity connections on social media. More on that below.

So social media is one way to quantify your reach to your target audience. If you write poetry, your target audience is people who read poetry (often other folks who write poetry). If you write cookbooks, your target audience is people who like to cook.

And in both cases, you can drill down into more specifics. Maybe the target audience for the poetry book is actually people who read sonnets. For the cookbook, maybe it's directed at people who like to cook desserts.

4 SOCIAL MEDIA TIPS FOR WRITERS

Anyway, social media is one way to connect with your target audience and influencers (like agents, editors, book reviewers, other writers) who connect to your target audience. Sites like Facebook, Twitter, LinkedIn, YouTube, Pinterest, Goodreads, Red Room, and so many more–they're all sites dedicated to helping people (and in some cases specifically writers) make connections.

Here are my 4 social media tips for writers:

1. Start small. The worst thing writers can do with social media is jump on every social media site ever created immediately, post a bunch of stuff, and then quit because they're overwhelmed on the time commitment and underwhelmed by the lack of

response. Instead, pick one site, complete all the information about yourself, and start browsing around in that one neighborhood for a while.

2. **Look for connections.** Notice that I did not advise looking for leads or followers or whatever. Don't approach strangers online like a used car salesman. Be a potential friend and/or source of information. One meaningful connection is worth more than 5,000 disengaged "followers." Seriously.

3. **Communicate.** There's two ways to make a mistake here. One, never post or share anything on your social media account. Potential new connections will skip over your ghost town profile assuming your account is no longer active. Plus, you're missing an opportunity to really connect with others. The other mistake is to post a million (hopefully an exaggeration) things a day and never communicate with your connections. It's social media, after all; be social.

One meaningful connection is worth more than 5,000 disengaged 'followers.'

4. **Give more than you take.** So don't post a million things a day, but be sure to share calls for submissions, helpful information (for your target audience), fun quotes, great updates from your connections (which will endear you to them further). Share updates from your end of the world, but don't treat your social media accounts as a place to sell things nonstop. Remember: Don't be a used car salesman.

One final tip: Focus. Part of effective platform building is knowing your target audience and reaching them. So with every post, every status update, every Tweet, every connection, etc., keep focused on how you are bringing value to your target audience.

POPULAR SOCIAL NETWORKING SITES

The social media landscape is constantly shifting, but here are some that are currently popular:

- Bebo (http://bebo.com)
- Digg (http://digg.com)
- Facebook (http://facebook.com)
- Flickr (http://flickr.com)
- Google+ (http://plus.google.com)
- Habbo (http://habbo.com)
- Hi5 (http://hi5.com)
- Instagram (http://instagram.com)

- LinkedIn (http://linkedin.com)
- MeetUp (http://meetup.com)
- Ning (http://ning.com)
- Orkut (http://orkut.com)
- Pinterest (http://pinterest.com)
- Reddit (http://reddit.com)
- StumbleUpon (http://stumbleupon.com)
- Twitter (http://twitter.com)
- Yelp (http://yelp.com)
- YouTube (http://youtube.com)
- Zorpia (htttp://zorpia.com)

9 THINGS TO DO ON ANY SOCIAL MEDIA SITE

Not all social media sites are created the same. However, there are some things poets can do on any site to improve the quantity and quality of the connections they make online.

1. Use your real name. If the point of social media is to increase your visibility, then don't make the mistake of cloaking your identity behind some weird handle or nickname. Use your real name—or that is, use your real byline as it appears (or would appear) when published.
2. Use your headshot for an avatar. Again, avoid concealing your identity as a cartoon image or picture of a celebrity or pet. The rules of online networking are the same as face-to-face networking. Imagine how silly it would be to see someone holding up a picture of a pet cat while talking to you in person.
3. Complete your profile. Each site has different ways to complete this information. You don't have to include religious or political views, but you do want to make your site personal while still communicating your interest and experience in poetry. One tip: Give people a way to contact you that doesn't involve using the social networking site. For instance, an e-mail address.
4. Link to websites. If you have a blog and/or author website, link to these in your profile on all social media sites. After all, you want to make it as easy as possible for people to learn more about you. If applicable, link to your previously published books at points of purchase too.
5. Make everything public. As a poet, you are a public figure. Embrace that state of mind and make everything you do public on social media. This means you may have to sacrifice some privacy, but there are pre-Facebook ways of communicating private matters with friends and family.
6. Update regularly. Whether it's a status update or a tweet, regular updates accomplish two things: One, they keep you in the conversation; and two, they let people

you know (and people you don't know) see that you're actively using your account. Activity promotes more connections and conversations, which is what poets want on social media sites.

Give people a way to contact you that doesn't involve using the social networking site. For instance, an e-mail address.

7. Join and participate in relevant groups. One key to this tip is relevancy. There are lots of random groups out there, but the ones that will benefit you the most are ones relevant to your interests and goals. Another key is participation. Participate in your group when possible.

8. Be selective. Piggybacking on the previous tip, be selective about who you friend, who you follow, which groups you join, etc. Don't let people bully you into following them either. Only connect with and follow people or groups you think might bring you value—if not immediately, then eventually.

9. Evolve. When I started social media, MySpace was the top hangout. Eventually, I moved on to Facebook and Twitter (at the urging of other connections). Who knows which sites I'll prefer in 5 months, let alone 5 years, from now. Evolve as the landscape evolves. In fact, even my usage of specific sites has had to evolve as user behavior changes and the sites themselves change.

FINAL THOUGHT

If you have a blog, be sure to use it to feed your social media site profiles. Each new post should be a status update or tweet. This will serve the dual purpose of bringing traffic to your blog and providing value to your social media connections.

TRACI BRIMHALL

Poet Interview

....

by Robert Lee Brewer

I'm always excited to find a fresh voice, and that's the case with Traci Brimhall. I've had her collection *Our Lady of the Ruins* (Norton) next to my desk for months, but it was running across her on Facebook that prompted me to ask her for an interview and re-visit the poems. And they are brilliant poems.

In addition to *Our Lady of the Ruins*, Traci is the author of *Rookery*, which was a finalist for the ForeWord Book of the Year Award. Plus, she recently won the first ever Diode Editions chapbook contest for *Bright Power, Dark Peace*, which she co-wrote with Brynn Saito.

Here's a poem I especially enjoyed from *Our Lady of the Ruins*:

The Visitation, by Traci Brimhall

In the new dream, we search for a sacrifice,
put our fingers in our own wounds,

wake with our hands over each other's mouths.
Boys return from war as men who know

two languages. We learn three so we will know
the message when we hear it. The street prophet

says, *If God is your enemy, rejoice, for the darkness
remembers you.* In the old dream, we readied

our stainless altar, but a wolf stole our offering.
We were lucky enough to sing the song once,

but we couldn't bring the dead any joy. Men ask
to borrow our sadness so they won't have to feel

their own. *Yes*, we say and kissed their arms. Yes, trees
cover us with shadows. We give the prophet money

to save something we'll never see. In the first dream,
men accept a new ecstasy. Our breath shows itself

to us and disappears. As we enter the woods,
the astonished wolf lifts its mouth from the lamb.

What are you currently up to?

I'm currently working on a series of poems set in a small river town on the Amazon where mysterious things keep happening and everyone has a different explanation for the miracles and curses plaguing them.

The poems in *Our Lady of the Ruins* tell a larger story. Do you write poems as one-offs, or do you write with a collection in mind?

I feel like the poems cohered as I chose a final ordering for the book, though I didn't write the poems with a certain structure or overarching narrative in mind. I knew all my poems were about a mid-apocalyptic wandering, but the nature of the poems ranged really widely as I wrote. I cut over a couple dozen poems from the final draft because they didn't fit with the narrative that emerged through ordering.

I'm a hoarder in poems, and I need rules to keep from cluttering up what the poem is trying to say.

You play with form throughout *Our Lady of the Ruins*, whether it's "Hysteria: A Requiem" or the title poem. How much do you play with structure when writing and revising your poetry? Do you go through a similar process each time?

Most of my poems have some formal play, whether it's immediately evident or not. I often create some sort of formal restraint on my work (sometimes before beginning, sometimes after I've finished a draft), because it helps me decide what images and bits of language are essential to a poem and what I should probably cut. I'm a hoarder in poems, and I need rules to keep from cluttering up what the poem is trying to say.

Your chapbook *Bright Power, Dark Peace* recently won first place in Diode Editions chapbook competition. It's also co-authored with Brynn Saito. How did the collaborative process work on that chapbook?

Before we began writing together, we created a lot of rules. It was really important to me that we contribute equally and that one of us didn't feel unrepresented or drowned out in the poems. One person opened the poem and set the structure (couplets, tercets, etc.), and the next person wrote the next stanza and passed it back. The person who began the poem also ended it, and since that person had a greater amount of creative control in that way, the other person got to edit it once it was done. Working out a balance of powers between friends is not something I've ever had to do before, but having boundaries seemed even more important because we're such good friends.

I'm grateful for all the things poetry has brought to my life, from travel to good conversations to the greatest friends a person could hope for.

Your collections have won several awards. Do you submit exclusively to contests for your collections?

When I started submitting my first collection, I wasn't very aware of open reading periods and most of the books I read seemed to be contest winners. I submitted to a couple of open reading periods for my second book, but I heard back from a contest before I heard back from them.

Your best poetry moment—what is it?

There are lots of moments, I think. I'm grateful to the poems I've read by strangers and the dead that gave me clarity about myself and the world. I'm grateful to the poems I've been able to write that seemed to be smarter than I am. I'm grateful for all the things poetry has brought to my life, from travel to good conversations to the greatest friends a person could hope for.

Finish this statement: I think poetry should _____.

Be read aloud in bed.

Who (or what) are you currently reading?

Coming-of-age narratives in graphic novels—the last one I finished was called *Epileptic* by David B.

If you could only pass on one piece of advice to fellow poets, what would it be?

Just in case there are other poets like me out there who started writing because they loved it and then grew to judge themselves harshly every time they wrote because what they wrote wasn't as good as they wished it was, I would say that every time you want to get mad at yourself or give up on writing, love it harder. Poetry has always given me way more than I could give it, and I believe it can do that for everyone.

CARMEN CALATAYUD

Poet Interview

....

by Robert Lee Brewer

Carmen Calatayud's first poetry collection *In the Company of Spirits* was published in October 2012 as part of the Silver Concho Series by Press 53 and was a runner-up for the 2010 Walt Whitman Award from the Academy of American Poets. Her poetry has appeared in journals such as *Beltway Poetry Quarterly, Borderlands: Texas Poetry Review, Cutthroat: A Journal of the Arts, Gargoyle, La Bloga, Más Tequila Review, PALABRA: A Magazine of Chicano and Latino Literary Art, Red River Review* and *Slow Trains*. Her poems are anthologized in various collections, including *Mondo Barbie* (St. Martin's Press), *DC Poets Against the War: An Anthology* (Argonne House Press) and the upcoming *Poetry of Resistance: A Multicultural Response to Arizona SB 1070 and Other Xenophobic Laws*, to be published by University of Arizona Press in 2014. Carmen is a Larry Neal Poetry Award winner and recipient of a Virginia Center for the Creative Arts fellowship. She is a poet moderator for Poets Responding to SB 1070, a Facebook group founded by poet Francisco X. Alarcón that features poetry and news about Arizona's controversial immigration law that legalizes racial profiling, as well immigrant-related and human rights news. Born to a Spanish father and Irish mother in the U.S., Carmen works and writes in Washington, DC.

There are two things I especially enjoy about Carmen's poetry: one is the sort of spiritual/magical essence of her poems, and two is that her poems often feel very important—life and death important. Here is one of my favorites:

Losing the Ocean, by Carmen Calatayud

The sea is my religion that brings me
to the bottom and this is what I know:

The fear of suffocation and the fear of joy,
the selfishness that fills my throat
and tonsils too big to fossilize.

This face of scars from fishing with the mouth
and always dropping the catch.

I'm afraid of love that chews hips,
trespasses liver, runs after hurricanes.

Past oceans become present day beaches
and it's too late, mermaid,
lonely woman
without breast stroke maneuver,
without oxygen song.

You are the mineral washed away.
You are the salt that chokes a child
in August.

What are you currently up to?

On December 8, I returned from a two-week writing residency at the Virginia Center for the Creative Arts. My close friend and poet Niki Herd pushed me to apply, and I'm so grateful that I listened to her. It was my first writing residency experience and it was amazing to have that kind of time and space to write. I'm working on a memoir that focuses primarily on the years I spent living in Tucson in the 1990s.......and in between, I'm still writing poems. Poetry is a natural and necessary break from writing prose for me.

Your collection *In the Company of Spirits* includes enough Spanish that there are translations in the back of the book. Is it challenging to write in two tongues?

Well I can't say that it's challenging, in the sense that I'm just using words and phrases that come to me, and that I end up using them because I often like the sounds of Spanish words better than the sounds of English words. Sound is really important to me in my writing. I spoke Spanish with my father when I was very young, but when he began to travel for work for extended periods of time, we stopped speaking Spanish at home. My mother, who was born in Ireland and emigrated from London, didn't speak any Spanish. I'm by no means fluent in Spanish but I can get by in a simple conversation, and I understand more than I speak.

To address the translations in the back of the book, I spoke with several poets I deeply respect about using a glossary and received different answers. In the end, I was left with having to decide for myself what to do. I know some poets, including Latino poets, disagree with the use of a glossary. I thought about that a lot, and came to the conclusion that for poetry readers who dive deeply into the work, knowing the meaning of a word in Spanish might make reading the poem a more complete experience. With all the immigrant bashing, racism and English-only movements going on in this country, I wanted to honor the readers who care enough to understand some Spanish for the context of a poem.

Having said that, my preference in the future would be to let go of using a glossary and not italicize words just because they are in Spanish. I like to use italicization for emphasis in a poem, and prefer to be free to decide on italicization of Spanish or English words on case-by-case basis.

I rarely feel alone because I feel spirits around me much of the time.

In this collection, there's a world offered up in which spirits do seem to walk with the living. This leads me to wonder, what is your spiritual life like?

My spiritual life is hard to put into words…I feel as though I spend a lot of time in the world of spirits and communicating with them in some way. It's almost as natural as breathing. I rarely feel alone because I feel spirits around me much of the time. This isn't something I talk about often, and when I do, it's with people who I believe will understand. Yoga classes and meditation are part of my spiritual practice, as is reading spiritual texts. I feel most connected to Buddhism and indigenous spirituality. My husband Ricardo and I were married by a Mayan shaman in Mexico 10 years ago this October.

You're a psychotherapist. Does that part of your life ever bleed into your poetry or vice versa? Or are they two separate worlds?

You know, I thought that my psychotherapy work would influence my writing much more than it has. Moving into psychology was a mid-life change for me, and when I went to grad school from 2004 to 2006, I was quite passionate about mental health and the mind-body connection. What I've found so far is that my work world doesn't bleed into my poetry or prose. What motivates me to write, and what seems to arise as I write, is my spiritual and psychological life, my views on the human condition, and my own experiences. So without trying, my therapy work with clients and my writing are two separate worlds.

Do you have any poetry pet peeves when reading poetry? Are there things you try to avoid in your own poems?

Hmmmm......I suppose I have a small pet peeve about what appears to be and sounds like forced rhyme. I try to avoid clichés in my poems, but they pop up easily. Thankfully, we can edit and get feedback from others on our work.

Your best poetry experience to date. What is it and why?

Going to California in November 2012 included my best poetry experiences so far. There is a tie between three events: My reading in Sacramento for Día de los Muertos, reading a poem at the end of the two-mile Día de los Muertos procession in the Mission District in San Francisco, and my reading at Casita del Pueblo in Whittier, outside of LA.

In Sacramento, there was a small but warm, receptive crowd, and it was lovely to meet poets in person who I had connected with on Facebook. I read with poet Francisco X. Alarcón, which was a great privilege, and I could feel an understanding for my poetry in that room. In the Mission, after having the honor of walking near the front of the procession with Francisco and Starhawk for two miles, Francisco surprised me by pulling out my book, introducing me, and handing me the mic to read a poem to close the ceremony. It was my first Día de los Muertos procession in the Mission, and the love and exurberance from the large crowd along the entire route was palpable.

....

I suppose I have a small pet peeve about what appears to be and sounds like forced rhyme.

....

At Casita del Pueblo in Whittier, I read with two LA poets who I love and admire: Abel Salas and John Martinez. The event was also an art show that featured work by the artist whose painting is on the cover of my book, Aydee López Martínez. It was a joy to be with Abel, John and Aydee, and to feel the energy of a standing crowd that was so attentive and enthusiastic. I have to admit I didn't want to leave because I felt so at home there, in both Northern and Southern California. I can feel my heart expand just by writing about and remembering these events.

Your bio mentions moderating "Poets Responding to SB 1070," a group on Facebook. Could you share a little about what that is and what that experience has been like?

Poets Responding to SB 1070 is a Facebook page and a gathering place for poets, artists of all kinds, activists and the public to come together to respond to Arizona's SB 1070, a law that targets immigrants and legalizes racial profiling. The result of Arizona SB 1070 is that undocumented immigrant workers and legalized immigrants are harassed, jailed, and in some cases deported, based on their skin color or accent. Our page features poetry submitted by people across the U.S. and from other countries, and we post news stories related to Arizona, immigration and human rights violations of U.S. immigrants. We also feature news on other human rights issues around the globe to bring attention to and raise support for human rights-related causes.

....

Being involved with this group of poets, whose poetry, activism and generosity inspire me on a daily basis, has been life-changing.

....

Maricopa County, Arizona, in particular, is known for its civil rights abuses against legal and undocumented immigrants. Since the law passed in April 2010, another side of Arizona that gets little attention has risen up and taken a stand against the law and the constant abuses—the Latino population and the Anglos who support them and support human rights. Together, we're calling for humane immigration reform to stop the unjust deportations that split families apart and ruin lives.

The founder of Poets Responding to SB 1070 is poet, writer and University of California/Davis professor Francisco X. Alarcón. The other poet moderators include Odilia Galván Rodríguez, Elena Díaz Bjorkquist, Andrea Hernandez Holm, and Hedy Treviño. Our page has become a known presence in the poetry world, which is heartening, and an important part of the activist fabric that advocates for civil rights in Arizona.

Being involved with this group of poets, whose poetry, activism and generosity inspire me on a daily basis, has been life-changing. The overwhelming positive response and the poetry contributions to our page, which gets several thousands hits a week, continues to restore my faith in the American spirit of fairness and compassion, despite the loud, virulent voices of racism that garner so much attention. Many people *do* want to educate themselves. They are learning that the American economy runs on the backs of hard-working undocumented immigrants who pick the food that gets to our grocery stores, clean the offices and homes of millions, and provide child care. That's the reality. Historically, undocumented immigrants have always done the back-breaking work to help build this nation. My parents were immigrants and I grew up around their immigrant friends, so this human rights issue is personal for me.

Who (or what) are you currently reading?
I tend to read several books at a time, and use my subway commuting time to read, as well as squeezed-in time at home. Here's what I'm reading:

State Out of the Union, by Jeff Biggers: This book was chosen by *Publishers Weekly* at one of the Top 10 Social Science Books for Fall 2012, and chronicles the history—past and current—of the contentious debate around immigration in Arizona, and how it's affecting the rest of our country. Luis Alberto Urrea calls Biggers one of his American literary heroes, and I concur.

Please, by Jericho Brown: I'm a latecomer to Brown's work, as this first book came out in 2008 and won the American Book Award in 2009. Brown's poetry is fiery, gut-wrenching and beyond honest. He's a contemporary master poet.

Lorca: A Dream of Life, by Leslie Stainton: I still cry thinking about Lorca's execution by firing squad for being gay and for speaking out against Franco's Fascism. This beautiful yet candid biography chronicles the short, intense life of poet and playwright Federico García Lorca, whose literary and activist influence continues to vibrate around the world today.

Rilke's Book of Hours, by Rainer Maria Rilke (translated by Anita Barrows and Jo-anna Macy): Rilke's deep connection to the divine is explored and expressed in each of these poems, most no more than a page. This book is a treasure trove of spiritual poetry.

Bringing Yoga to Life: The Everyday Practice of Enlightened Living, by Donna Farhi: I'm only 32 pages into this book that brings the deeper meaning and philosophy of yoga alive, beyond the physical practice. Farhi's writing is gorgeous and potent.

If you could share only one piece of advice for other poets, what would it be?

Write for yourself—what you need to write and what you're scared to write—and stay true to your own voice. In the end, opinions are subjective.

BARTON SMOCK

Poet Interview

....

by Robert Lee Brewer

I first met Barton Smock years ago on MySpace—a fellow poet, a fellow buckeye—and immediately fell in love with his unique style of poeming. In fact, I chose him as my referral poet when I was published in *La Fovea*. Smock lives in Columbus, Ohio, with his wife and four children. His latest self-published poetry collection, *mating rituals of the responsibly poor*, is available at www.lulu.com/spotlight/acolyteroad. He can be found writing at king-softrain.wordpress.com and also at bartonsmock.com.

Most recently, I've been reading his collection *Angel Scene* (also available at Lulu). Here's one of my favorites from the collection:

your actual, your bad, heart

when late
in life
on a porch
7pm

you cannot hear
the sirens
going off
in the town
of your birth-

be patient
for what the hound
brings.

What are you currently up to?

I just finished my third 'actual' poetry collection, *mating rituals of the responsibly poor*. I've also been collecting baseball cards after a 20+ year hiatus as something logical to do with my 12- and 9-year-old sons.

Your collection *Angel Scene* is filled with poems told in the first person. Do you worry about truth vs. fiction in your poems?

Worry, no. I try not to pit them against each other. I think they should meet, as each has a hard time existing separately. In first person, I make the talking into a prayer, as I believe prayer whittles the truth down by way of addition, by way of creating another you're talking to, pleading with, which I think allows a more unabashed or local dialect to take hold in the voice without shackling said voice with inquiries as to who the narrator is, was, or wants to be.

I prefer the past, but feel history is sometimes overindulged. I could write 'my youngest son has a brain disorder and mitochondrial dysfunction' and it would be true and it would be sad but I don't think it would be honest until I curse for him in the presence of any maid tending the foreign house of his death.

....

It seems in many good, even great, poems there is a tendency to have the real last line of the poem be followed by the fake last line of the poem. I try to stop early.

....

One element of your poems that I've always enjoyed is that they often feel like little mysteries in which it's almost as important what you don't say as what you do. Is this something you consciously try to play with?

I do actively try to achieve rightness with the words I keep, as maybe later they'll take care of the ones I don't. It seems in many good, even great, poems there is a tendency to have the real last line of the poem be followed by the fake last line of the poem. I try to stop early. Also, I have always been fascinated by, and addicted to, movie previews.

As a Facebook friend, I know that you write poems daily. Do you have a set writing routine?

I write onscreen, mostly, at work. Up until recently, I worked two jobs Monday through Friday, and had to channel what I could. I rarely write at home because I'm already there. I post daily, I think, to reverse the damage.

Your best poetry moment—what is it?

I had a chance to read at a coffee shop in Annapolis, Maryland, and took it. I was invited by a Facebook friend, Cliff Lynn, who wasn't aware I lived in Ohio. I got to see my brother and some good friends who live around there, and made the trip from Ohio with my best friend. I have a voice that trails off in monotone when nervous, and the whole thing could've been disastrous. But it wasn't.

When I read, people were quiet, and listened, and were not only polite in doing so. There was a best moment in there somewhere. Otherwise, my best moment would be yesterday, when I finished my latest poem.

> I started self-publishing mostly so I would have something tangible in my hand that stood for the hundreds of Word documents that had been accumulating.

Angel Scene is not your first self-published collection. What do you like about the experience of self-publishing?

Control. And, I guess, safety. I started self-publishing mostly so I would have something tangible in my hand that stood for the hundreds of Word documents that had been accumulating from 2006-2011. I hardly ever print anything or write in longhand. From there, it became something of an exercise, of following themes, or stepping in front of them.

Have you learned anything new about self-publishing by going through the process multiple times?

Only that it's dismissed, ha. I really can't say I've learned anything, except maybe how to save a PDF correctly to retain formatting. Because I allow Lulu to facilitate the 'publishing,' it's clean and quick and I know the result will only be infused with what I began with. It's an angel and demon kind of thing…when I'm putting together a book I feel like I'm dying, but not dead, and after…just stuck with an illness.

Finish this statement: I think poetry should _____.

avoid, but not erase.

If you could share only one piece of advice with other poets, what would it be?

Even if you have to do it with others, quote yourself.

ERICA WRIGHT

Poet Interview

....

by Robert Lee Brewer

Erica Wright is the author of *Instructions for Killing the Jackal* (Black Lawrence Press) and the chapbook *Silt* (Dancing Girl Press). Her poems have appeared or are forthcoming in *Blackbird, Crazyhorse, Denver Quarterly, Drunken Boat, From the Fishouse, New Orleans Review,* and elsewhere. Plus, she's the Poetry Editor at *Guernica Magazine.*

Here's a personal favorite poem of mine from *Instructions for Killing the Jackal*:

After the Crocodile Cemetery at Kahun, by Erica Wright

On the train, the spitters and knock-kneed
start fights as the woman sneaks

her keys out, *just in case*, she doesn't say to me,
but we know each other in the teeth.

My tabby has taken up aggression
toward strangers, and who could blame her?

She was once a mummified crocodile.
I was once, too, can still feel the tightening

some dawns, still the paralysis. Big men
held our heads down with their knees, one by one.

What are you currently up to?
    Have you heard of rattlesnake roundups? Hunters capture hundreds, sometimes thousands, of rattlesnakes for skinning, eating, and selling of parts. I moved to Atlanta in

September, and one of my first conversations with a native Georgian was about these annual, fair-like events. For years, I've been haunted by the Richard Avedon photograph of a boy holding a gutted snake in Clearwater, Texas. I had no idea that round-ups still happened, though.

I don't think I can handle the real one in Whigham, but the one in Claxton has recently been turned into a wildlife appreciation festival, complete with not-there-to-be-slaughtered rattlers. I'm planning a series of essays on Georgia festivals, starting with either that one or the Groundhog Day celebration with celebrity critter General *Beauregard Lee.*

....

The war between formalists and non-formalists has always baffled me. Why would you ignore any of the tools available to you as an artist?

....

Your collection *Instructions for Killing the Jackal* seems filled with troubled people. Would you agree that many poems can be found in our problems?

I would. Your question makes me think about how difficult it is to find effective occasional poetry, say, for a friend's wedding or a graduation ceremony. Joy can certainly be complicated, but we don't analyze it the way we do depression or anger. We don't seek an explanation or balm for it. The most joyful poem I know is "I Feel Drunk All the Time" by Kenneth Patchen, which begins, "Jesus it's beautiful! / Great mother of big apples it is a pretty / World!" But you can hear the panic in the exclamation points even before you get to "You're a bastard Mr. Death."

Many of the poems in the collection employ couplets and tercets. What are your feelings about using form in poetry?

The war between formalists and non-formalists has always baffled me. Why would you ignore any of the tools available to you as an artist? Engaging with your roots does not mean rejecting the present. For me, it's the same as missing New York City while being excited about the New Year's Eve Possum Drop (not a live possum) in Tallapoosa, Georgia.

When you're in a poetry rut, what usually helps you break loose of it?

I can only slog through the muck. Sometimes I become obsessed with something—say, bridges or taxidermy—and I can't seem to stop writing the same poem over and over again. Five, ten, twenty. I have to get them all out. In my mind, there's a certain number. I don't know what the number is, but I know that when I reach it, the subject will finally be out of my system. And maybe one of those poems will be the one I needed to write.

Your best poetry moment—what was it?

In her essay "On Keeping a Notebook," Joan Didion talks about being on speaking terms with your younger selves. There are a few younger versions of myself that make me cringe, but the twenty-year-old one is okay, inexcusably lonely but easily awestruck. I remember going to hear Göran Sonnevi read with his translator Rika Lesser at Poet's House. It was a bilingual reading—a format that wearies me today, if I'm being honest—but at the time, I was enthralled. I think they were reading from *Mozart's Third Brain,* which was released by Yale University Press just this year. Can that be right? It took more than a decade for the translation to be released? Anyway, if an evening can be a moment, I choose that one.

Basically, if you like what the editors choose, you should feel comfortable submitting. If you don't like what the editors choose, why would you want to be included?

You're the poetry editor at *Guernica Magazine,* and I'm sure you've had to reject a fair share of poems in that position. Do you find common problems poets could avoid?

I love reading submissions, even the terrible ones. I received a poem in green font last week. Green font! What a hoot. Not printed, mind you, which I could sort of understand—we all run out of black ink—but e-mailed.

New submitters should take the time to present their work professionally. Beyond that, editorial decisions are a matter of taste, which is why editors so often recommend reading back issues before submitting. There's rarely an obvious connection between all of the poems, though, unless a journal only publishes sci-fi pantoums or some such niche. Basically, if you like what the editors choose, you should feel comfortable submitting. If you don't like what the editors choose, why would you want to be included?

Finish this statement: I think poetry should _____.

startle us, like rattlesnakes at a serpentarium.

Who (or what) are you currently reading?

I picked up Lily Ladewig's delightful collection *The Silhouettes* at a recent Atlanta reading. And keeping with the Atlanta theme, I'm reading Charles McNair's 1994 novel *Land O' Goshen,* which contains the most surprising, rich prose I've encountered in awhile. Also on my desk is Aimee Nezhukumatathil's *Lucky Fish*, and the latest issue of *The Dark Horse,* a Scottish journal.

If you could share only one piece of advice with other poets, what would it be?

My friend Ricardo Maldonado has been sending out his manuscript for a few years now with no bites. When I read his manuscript, I think this is a collection people will be talking about for years when it's finally published. And it will be. So while the advice "Don't get discouraged" sounds prosaic, it's personal. I don't want my friend to get discouraged, and neither should anyone else who loves this art as much as you must in order to become a poet.

HEATHER BELL

Poet Interview

....

by Robert Lee Brewer

//

Heather Bell is sort of a nomad poet in the sense that she's been published extensively in literary journals, but she's self-published two of her poetry collections, including her most recent (*Expletive Deleted*). Her first collection (*How to Make People Love You*) was also self-published, and then, she has two other collections *Nothing Unrequited Here* (Verve Bath Press) and *Facts of Combat* (Achilles Chapbooks).

Heather's work has been published in many publications, including *Rattle, Grasslimb, Barnwood, Poets/Artists,* and *Third Wednesday*. She was nominated for the 2009, 2010, and 2011 Pushcart Prize from *Rattle* and also won the New Letters 2009 Poetry Prize (judged by Kim Addonizio). More details can be found on her blog; http://hrbell.wordpress.com.

Here's a poem from her collection *Expletive Deleted*:

Interview

It has been two years, how am I to
explain the lack of work? Each morning:
the rhinoceros pajamas, the roots growing
from the ceiling, occasionally

the hallucinations. I dip my body slowly
into a suit coat and flatten my
hair. How to explain

that I spent the last two years as a mad
woman? Everyone suggests that I refer to
that time as a "personal matter," instead

of strange, or drowned,

or tailed by men with hound faces.

I slip my resume across the table
like a love note.

My shoes shriek when I get up because
the floor is made of people who watched
this and it made them shocked and sad
that I can still be so untruthful.

What are you currently up to?

I'm currently a stay-at-home mom to a wonderful 18-month-old daughter, Anna, and pregnant with my second. I try to write when I can, but we live in a 100-year-old house that we're doing a complete remodel on, so it can be quite hard to find the time. I did finish my fifth book and am in the process of searching for a home for it.

Your collection *Expletive Deleted* was self-published. What has that experience been like?

My first book, *How To Make People Love You*, was also self-published, so I knew the process at this point. Self-publishing is interesting and I have gotten a lot of writers asking me about it, thinking it's an easy way to "success." I generally tell them to publish in journals and magazines first, as self-publishing is pointless without "fans" of your work (AKA customers).

The best way for me to do it (and this is very different for other people) is to buy about 200 copies (my first book went through three reprints, so I thankfully knew my magic number). It will take me a year or more to sell them all, mostly through "advertising" through social media and word of mouth.

I prefer to use POD publishers in the same way you would make copies of a book you constructed at Kinko's: cut out the middle man (the POD publisher) and just do the work yourself, because at the end of the day, a self-publishing online marketplace really isn't helping you sell your work (I suppose there's exceptions to the rule, but I personally don't troll them looking for books, so I assume others also don't). The only thing you can do is be confident in your work, continue to publish in magazines and journals and let your writing speak for itself.

This isn't a knock at traditional publishing, because I have also gone that route and loved it, but self-publishing can be a good thing depending on how much you believe in your writing and how much other people want to see it.

I know recently you've been submitting work and many of your poems have found homes in literary publications. Do you have a submission process or routine?

My routine is to currently be looking for new magazines that jazz my socks off, through friends and fellow writers. That's really where I start. From there, you obviously have to know what you're submitting to (like using common sense, don't send a sci-fi poem to a magazine that only publishes horror, things like that). Know who are the "big guys" in the business and if you're ready to go there. And prepare yourself to make a three-piece suit out of all the rejections! Ha!

Just have a thick skin and press on.

....

When you're in love with someone, there are occasional winters where a wolf breaks into your garage and eats all of your emergency stored food.

....

This voice in your poems is often very immediate and confessional. Do you attempt to draw a line between truth and fiction in your poetry?

This is an interesting question because I get asked it often, specifically about my Klimt poem. The question usually is "is it true?"

Here's a fun writing exercise, go and find a poem that is really boring (feel free to start at any "big" magazine … haha … kidding, kind of!). Then, take their theme and make it into something that a person will walk away from and think about it all day and wonder, "Is it true?"

Here's my issue: I'm tired of love poems where people kiss and make up. When you're in love with someone, there are occasional winters where a wolf breaks into your garage and eats all of your emergency stored food. Can you write a poem about what is on the edges of subjects and then connect it TO your subject?

And no, "Love" is not true, just in case anyone is now wondering. I was actually doing a "Klimt-esque" sort of oil painting and I admit I am a terrible painter, so it looked like the top figure was pushing down on the female. It got me thinking about the original, and how people make assumptions about poems, paintings, every kind of art. If Klimt DID beat his wife, does HIS history make you look at every one of his paintings differently or does it matter?

If I write a therapy poem but I have never been in therapy, does it matter? Or maybe I'm writing now from a mental health clinic. The poem still sits as it does, truthful or not, the point is to make it stay rooted in your brain even when you walk away.

Do you have any pet peeves when reading poetry? Are there things you try to avoid in your own poems?

Boring poems, ha!

I think poets are kind of egomaniacs and we have a tendency to think all our poems are really super amazing and glorious. The trick is to write something and then come back to it as the reader, not the writer. How many poems have I read about the winter's beauty? How many do I remember lines from (not many!).

Modern poetry isn't read by most people simply because it's either flat or so abstract that you need the writer to explain what the heck is going on (at the point in which you are explaining, you have failed, sorry). Anne Carson is actually one of my favorite writers and she can get pretty abstract and yet, still make sense. You have to know what you're doing.

When I write my own poems, I am trying to connect with another human being. Is poetry boring to any person off the street? Yes. Does that person watch back-to-back episodes of *Jersey Shore* at home at night? Maybe. Does that mean we discount that person as someone who can never "get" our poetry? You know what's the true challenge? Writing the *Jersey Shore* of intellectual poems and getting that person to reflect, think about it, and want more.

> Modern poetry isn't read by most people simply because it's either flat or so abstract that you need the writer to explain what the heck is going on (at the point in which you are explaining, you have failed, sorry).

You aren't writing anything dumbed down, you're actually making someone dig deeper, but at the same time be entertained. This is such an issue with me with modern poetry, how it can really ignore a huge population of people and act like some people just aren't smart enough to understand. It's YOUR job to write a poem that makes people think, not the person's job to have to get a Master's Degree in Greek literature in order to understand whatever is in your poetry!

Best poetry experience to date. What is it and why?

Winning the New Letters Poetry Award in 2009! I was in the process of moving from Arizona to New York and we had broken down in a corn field in Indiana (sounds more romantic than it was–ha ha!). I have always thought I was hitting my head against a brick wall and winning made me feel like I had some relevance.

It shouldn't be about awards, but I'm a weak-hearted and scared writer just like anyone else, so it really blew me away. I don't think I ever thanked them enough or truly told them what it meant to me, but maybe someone from New Letters will read this!

Who (or what) are you currently reading?

I'm mostly reading *Green Eggs and Ham* these days. Ha! I actually have a backlog of books that haven't been touched, because I just can't find the time (I still have no ceiling in my dining room, if that's any excuse).

Because I now feel like a terrible person, I will list my all-time favorites: *The Beauty of the Husband*, by Anne Carson; *No One Belongs Here More Than You*, by Miranda July; and anything by Paul Celan, Amy Hempel, Alice Walker, and Sherman Alexie.

If you could share only one piece of advice for other poets, what would it be?

That you can do it. That the world needs you to be there and bright and amazing. I know a lot of writers who blow away anyone being published now, but are too afraid to publish or keep saying they just don't have the time. You do have the time. Because you watched TV today (could have submitted), you brushed your hair (could have submitted), you ate a sandwich (could have submitted) and you spent all afternoon researching new utensils on Amazon (could have submitted).

No excuses, guys. I'm tired of boring poetry, so you need to rise up like crazy apocalyptic looters with backpacks of poems and take over the literary magazines.

S. THOMAS SUMMERS

Poet Interview

....

by Robert Lee Brewer

S. Thomas Summers is a sort of specialist poet. His poetry tends to focus on history, specifically the American Civil War. His first book, *Private Hercules McGraw: Poems of the American Civil War* (Anaphora Literary Press, 2012), has been nominated for a Pushcart Prize. Summers' second book, *The Journals of Lt. Kendall Everly: a Story of the American Civil War*, will be released later in 2013.

When I caught up with Summers, he was busy transitioning from one book to the next: "I've been putting the finishing touches on my second manuscript and forthcoming book *The Journals of Lt. Kendal Everly: A Story of the American Civil War*. I'm also doing my best to market my first book. Marketing is a frustrating business. Slowly, I'm getting better at it."

Summers is a teacher of Writing and Literature at Wayne Hills High School in Wayne, NJ and an adjunct writing professor at Passaic County Community College in Wanaque, NJ. He's also a Civil War enthusiast who does a fine job of translating his passion into poetry. Here's one of his historical poems:

Shards of Night

Them Feds started pouring through
the wood like a river that run its banks.
My heart started thunking wilder than a cat's
heart after that cat scampered up a tree
cause a dog done breathed on its tail –

and sure enough, I was up a tree.
But, hell – my jaw almost clanked

the ground when I see that flood
a might closer. I was perched on top
a whole cluster of Yankee darkies.

Hell, I says, Abe sent them damn slaves
to fight. I first guessed they'd be whooping
and shucking like a gaggle of monkeys,
but they clutched their guns like soldiers
and their faces where all chiseled from stone

solid as Zion. Our boys started popping muskets
first and a few of them darkies fell,
but the others paid no mind to that. They ran
straight at those pickets like shards of night,
screaming hell and spitting lead.

I seen one take three bullets before
he toppled. Each time blood puffed
from his belly like a red cloud at sunset.
And the one swinging the flag made certain
them stripes never scraped the ground.

I swear them slaves be men.
By God, they be men.

Your collection Private Hercules McGraw is comprised of poems about the American Civil War. Did you have to do an extra bit of research for these poems?

I did. My book is a narrative. Poem by poem, Private McGraw tells his story. As he treks through the war, he takes place in many important historical events: the Battle of Shiloh, the Battle of Gettysburg. I needed to research those battles. Who commanded who to charge where? Casualties. Outcomes. Locations. Battlefields. Etc.

Additionally, McGraw is from Tennessee so I did a bit of research on the Southern dialect. I think it all came together pretty good.

Your best poetry moment—what is it?

Once it was published, holding a copy of my first book. It was…thrilling.

In setting up this interview, you mentioned you're a poet, but your primary roles are dad and husband. How do you go about working writing in with your primary duties?

I'm married to a very lovely lady. Her name is Laura. We have two kids, Reanna, 19, and Garrett, 9. Together, we are a mighty army. That army is my first priority. Therefore, I write when I can: at karate lessons, at basketball practice, before I leave for work.

It's funny. When I have all kinds of time, I don't write. I write better, far better when time is short. I guess a writer needs to adapt.

Also, I believe you're an educator. Does this phase of your life influence your writing?

I'm a literature teacher at Wayne Hills High School in Wayne, NJ. I'm also an adjunct writing professor at Passaic County Community College in Wanaque, NJ. I love what I teach. I love a story and all the nuances of a story: novels, dramas, poems, etc.

I love the words that build a story. Because I love those words, I wanted to create my own so I started to write. Besides, I've convinced my students that their kids will be doing research papers on me.

Finish this statement: I think poetry should _____.

I think poetry should hush for a day or two. It keeps screaming, "Write, Scott. Write!"

It's funny. When I have all kinds of time, I don't write. I write better, far better when time is short.

What or who are you currently reading?

Jeff Shaara, Ted Kooser, Jane Hirshfield, Jim Berkheiser, Bill Flewelling, Linda Pastan, … I could list a hundred names and still fail to mention everyone I'm reading. I also read the Bible every day. Couldn't stay sane without it and my faith.

If you could pass on only one piece of advice to fellow poets, what would it be?

Find your passion and write about it: It all gets easier after that.

KAREN RIGBY

Poet Interview

....

by Robert Lee Brewer

Karen Rigby is the author of *Chinoiserie* (Ahsahta Press, 2012), winner of the 2011 Sawtooth Poetry Prize, and of the chapbooks *Savage Machinery* and *Festival Bone*. She has received a literature fellowship from the National Endowment for the Arts, a residency at the Vermont Studio Center, and a grant from the Greater Pittsburgh Arts Council. A graduate of the University of Minnesota's MFA program, she currently resides in Arizona. Her work has appeared in *Quarterly West, Meridian, Washington Square, failbetter.com, New England Review*, and other journals.

In other words, Rigby keeps herself busy. In fact, this is what she had to say about her current projects when I caught up with her: "At the time of this writing (May 2013), I'm at work on a longer poem as part of the 2013 Flying House project, in collaboration with artist CJ Hungerman. Though I can't elaborate until the work is shown in October, drafting this poem is proving to be a real shift."

For readers new to Rigby, her writing already makes big shifts and takes big chances—often with big results. Here's a poem I really enjoyed from *Chinoiserie*:

Dear Reader,

The mink shouldered out of its cage,
paced four meters square.
I admired the indexed spine. The guard hairs
slick. The mouth
suspect.

The black eye trained against the water pump, the white magnolia–

what could I bring to the dooryard?
He wanted nothing of torn bread.
Nothing to drink.

One night the mink climbed my throat
and out of bone and grasping
a demon was born
to haunt the city of steeples.

It blessed the pedestals worn
by thumbprints. Leather Bibles. Rivers bruising
in their beds. Its jaw hung like a petal
darkening by the hour.

Dear reader: What I started to tell you
had something to do with hunger
but the mink was demon
turned bodiless terror.

It led me closer to the firs
where the dead wait for an answer.
All night the mink appeared
and disappeared. The demon wept.

Bodies lined up like blonde guitars
without their necks. Faces I loved thorned
in the trees. A tanager shone
like a pitcher of blood.

Your collection Chinoiserie includes epigraphs for each of its three main sections—all three of them translations. Especially with the title of the collection, could you explain how much non-English language poems have influenced your poetry—if at all?

I was born in Panama City, Panama, in a household with both English and Spanish. I found my way toward the work of several authors—in their original language—through excellent teachers. Ana María Matute, Gabriela Mistral, Juan Ramón Jiménez, Rubén Darío, and Miguel de Unamuno come to mind. Fiction, mostly. Then Lorca's plays. Poetry didn't enter my imagination until later.

The line from reading in adolescence to writing Chinoiserie, however, is a spider thread. I'm not sure which, if any, influences remain. I do think, though, that everything absorbed eventually manifests in other ways.

In this collection, the poems often seem to use space as an asset. What are your thoughts on using white space as a poetic device?

White space is like breathing, always present. Consider a line break—is it a decision arising from meaning or music? A desire for emphasis or pause? Or is the line sculpting, interrogating, articulating the white space surrounding it? Or is it the other way—does the white space define the words? If an image is framed in white, deliberately made to stand apart, why?

Questions happen in the background, but when I write, the decisions are instinctive. Even as the words fill one side, I'm looking at the margin on the other side.

Before Chinoiserie, you authored two chapbooks: Festival Bone and Savage Machinery. Do you have a process for assembling a poetry collection?

All of these gathered poems on various topics —they were not written as part of an intentional series (a thematic project, for instance). Sometimes I went by the images, excluding poems that repeated too many of the same ones. Sometimes I arranged according to the last lines of one poem and the first lines of another.

....

> White space is like breathing, always present. Consider a line break—is it a decision arising from meaning or music? A desire for emphasis or pause? Or is the line sculpting, interrogating, articulating the white space surrounding it? Or is it the other way—does the white space define the words?

....

Regardless of the choices made, in all three cases I printed everything and arranged the pages on the floor. I stood back to take in the different shapes. Lengths of poems, line-lengths, variety in the forms. Then I considered opening and closing poems, second and second-to-the-last poems, and so on, working back to the center. It is sometimes surprising what can stand out just from the visual survey.

Do you have any poetry pet peeves when reading poetry? Are there things you try to avoid in your own poems?

I don't know. What I find myself drawn to changes over time—I also hesitate to set parameters. I can say, though, that more and more the poetry I like is poetry I remember, which has nothing to do with whether the work is actually memorable (in a larger canonical or historical sense, or more simply, to other readers, and has nothing to do with the complexity of the work). It takes a lot for certain lines to adhere, let alone haunt me, and not many poems do.

Lowell's "a savage servility / slides by on grease" is one line that has stayed with me. In my own work, Pope's "sound must seem an echo to the sense" is admittedly seductive. I try to avoid the larger clunkers, if I can.

Your best poetry experience to date. What is it and why?

The poem I'm writing now. What is currently on the table is what is best (even if time reveals it as otherwise), because that space is the active one.

Who (or what) are you currently reading?

Prose poems by Paige Ackerson-Kiely and Andrew Grace.

If you could share only one piece of advice for other poets, what would it be?

Words. Wonderment. Waiting.

DEBORAH HAUSER

Poet Interview

....

by Robert Lee Brewer

///

Deborah Hauser, author of *Ennui: From the Diagnostic and Statistical Field Guide of Feminine Disorders* (Finishing Line Press, 2011), has some unique advice for poets getting started, "Find your poetry doppelgänger; a special person you trust to be your first reader. Someone who understands your poetry spirit, is supportive and encouraging, believes in you, and is also capable of giving you an honest critique."

Hauser graduated from Stony Brook University with a Masters in English Literature and has taught at Stony Brook University and Suffolk County Community College. Her award-winning poetry has appeared in journals such as *Dogwood, Dash, The Found Poetry Review, The Pedestal Magazine, Mobius,* and *Stony Brook University Press Women's Studies Department Literary Journal.* Learn more at http://deborahhauser.com.

Hauser's chapbook *Ennui* is a long poem that digs deeper into the meaning of the word and the condition of ennui. Here's an excerpt:

XV

METAPHOR

damp wood that won't spark

XVI

SIMILE

as lifeless as a warm flat glass of diet ginger ale used to treat nausea

XVII

SYMBOLISM

housewife trapped
beneath heavy furniture
that requires constant dust-
ing polishing cleaning

What are you currently up to?

I'm simultaneously working on two projects for full length poetry collections. One is a collection of modern fairy tales with a recurring riot grrrl theme titled *(dis)Enchanted: A Grrrls' Guide to Surviving Happily Ever After.* The other is a collection of longer *Enuui* style poems tentatively titled *Asking For It.*

Your chapbook Ennui is essentially a long poem that looks at the condition of a bored housewife. What sparked this poem/chapbook?

I was taking a workshop at NYU SCPS with Erica Wright, and she gave me a writing assignment to write a poem that defined a word and provided Les Murray's poem "The Quality of Sprawl" as an example. After several false starts, I hit on the word "ennui" and the first draft just poured out of me.

....

I think the breaks serve to set the pace and encourage the reader to contemplate each section as its own poem before turning the page.

....

"Ennui" is a word that had been stuck in my mind since reading Kate Chopin's *The Awakening.* I have vivid memories of writing the first draft while riding the train to New York City.

In this chapbook, the sections are clinical and—at times—hilarious; most sections also take up less than half of each page. What are your thoughts on using white space as a poetic device?

In *Ennui* I think of the white space as the reader's space. Placing each short section on its own page surrounded by blank space makes room for the reader to enter the poem. *Ennui* would be a rather long poem if presented without the section breaks.

I think the breaks serve to set the pace and encourage the reader to contemplate each section as its own poem before turning the page. It signals the reader that each section is an important statement on its own as well as an integral part of the whole poem.

Your poetry has appeared in numerous journals, including Crab Creek Review and The Pedestal Magazine. Do you have a submission routine?

In theory, I have my current "best" poems in circulation at all times. I keep a list of places I'd like to submit to and send out submissions weekly or monthly.

In current practice, I scramble to get a submission out in response to some deadline.

Also, do you have a writing routine?

In theory, I free write for 10 minutes every day, just as an exercise with no expectation of producing a poem. Usually once a week a free write does develop into a poem. I did this regularly for several years.

....

I go to a lot of poetry readings in New York City. What I'm reading is often inspired by who I'm going to see or have recently seen give a reading.

....

In current practice, I write in response to a workshop prompt or when "lightning strikes" and something moves me to put paper to pen (or more likely fingers to keyboard). I also write in response to what I'm reading. After reading a collection of poetry, I'll write an imitation or tribute poem in the style of the author or put together a found poem using some of my favorite lines from the collection.

Do you have any poetry pet peeves when reading poetry? Are there things you try to avoid in your own poems?

When reading poetry, I'm aware of the weaknesses I've worked to overcome in my own writing. For example, weak line breaks are something I'm always on the lookout for in my own work, so I'm hyperaware of that when reading poetry.

Your best poetry experience to date. What is it and why?

Being invited to read at NYU SCPS' 75th Anniversary event in April 2010. It was a magical evening. I read poems from *(dis)Enchanted* and felt like Cinderella at the ball. It was an honor to read in that hallowed space in the company of distinguished faculty and fellow students.

At the reception after the reading, I met many talented writers and made some special friends with whom I'm still in contact.

Who (or what) are you currently reading?

In general I'm always reading poetry journals, a book of poetry, a novel, feminist theory, and literary criticism. Currently, I'm reading *The Anxiety of Influence* by Harold Bloom, *The Immoralist* by Andre Gide, and the latest issue of *American Poetry Review*. I recently read Sharon Olds, Marie Howe, and Alex Dimitrov. Allison Benis White's new book is next on my reading list.

I go to a lot of poetry readings in New York City. What I'm reading is often inspired by who I'm going to see or have recently seen give a reading. I get together with a friend once a month to read and discuss a book of poetry, and I've belonged to a fiction book club for seven years.

POETIC FORMS

....

by Robert Lee Brewer

Not every poet likes the idea of writing in poetic forms, but for many poets—including myself—poetic forms are a sort of fun challenge. Whether playing with a sestina or working haiku, I find that attempting poetic forms often forces me into corners that make me think differently than if I'm just writing in free verse.

If you don't have any—or much—experience with poetic forms, I encourage you to peruse the following list and try them. If you are very familiar with poetic forms, I hope the following list can act as a reference for when you're unsure of the rhyme scheme for a triolet versus a kyrielle—or shadorma.

Have fun poeming!

Abstract poetry

Apparently, *abstract* was a term used by Dame Edith Sitwell to describe poems in her book *Facade*. Abstract (or sound) poetry is more about how sounds, rhythms, and textures evoke emotions than about the actual meanings of words.

Acrostic poetry

Acrostic poetry is very easy and fun. The most basic form spells words out on the left-hand side of the page using the first letter of each line. For instance,

> *I like to write*
> *Acrostic poems*
> *Mostly because*
> *Reading them*
> *Out loud is*
> *Bound to be fun.*

If you notice, the first letter of every line makes the simple sentence, "I am Rob." It's very simple, and you can make it as difficult as you want—where the fun part begins.

The brave at heart can even try double acrostics—that is, spelling things out using the first and last letter of each line.

Alphabet poetry

There are many different ways to write an alphabet poem. You can write a poem in which the first letter of each word is a different letter of the alphabet. A tactic for writing this poem is to write out the alphabet ahead of time so that you can pay attention to which letters have been used and which letters are still up for grabs. Of course, you can also do this consecutively through the alphabet.

Another method for alphabet poems is to go through the alphabet using the first letter of the first word for each line.

Poets can always flip the alphabet, too. That is, instead of going A to Z, write alphabet poems from Z to A. It's all about having fun and stretching your mind. Kind of like school.

Anagrammatic Poetry

In Christian Bok's comments about his poem "Vowels" in *The Best American Poetry 2007*, he writes, "'Vowels' is an anagrammatic text, permuting the fixed array of letters found only in the title. 'Vowels' appears in my book *Eunoia*, a lipogrammatic suite of stories, in which each vowel appears by itself in its own chapter." So an anagrammatic poem uses only the letters used in the title.

For instance, if I titled a poem "Spread," it could use only words like red, dresses, drape, spare, pear, pressed, etc.

The real challenge with this kind of poem is first picking a word that has at least a couple vowels and a good mix of consonants. Then, brainstorm all the words you can think of using only those letters (as many times as you wish, of course).

The Blitz Poem

The blitz poem was created by Robert Keim and is a 50-line poem of short phrases and images. Here are the rules:

- Line 1 should be one short phrase or image (like "build a boat")
- Line 2 should be another short phrase or image using the same first word as the first word in Line 1 (something like "build a house")
- Lines 3 and 4 should be short phrases or images using the last word of Line 2 as their first words (so Line 3 might be "house for sale" and Line 4 might be "house for rent")

- Lines 5 and 6 should be short phrases or images using the last word of Line 4 as their first words, and so on until you've made it through 48 lines
- Line 49 should be the last word of Line 48
- Line 50 should be the last word of Line 47
- The title of the poem should be three words long and follow this format: (first word of Line 3) (preposition or conjunction) (first word of line 47)
- There should be no punctuation

There are a lot of rules, but it's a pretty simple and fun poem to write once you get the hang of it.

The Bop

The Bop is a poetic form that was developed by poet Afaa Michael Weaver at a Cave Canem summer retreat. Here are the basic rules:

- 3 stanzas
- Each stanza is followed by a refrain
- First stanza is 6 lines long and presents a problem
- Second stanza is 8 lines long and explores or expands the problem
- Third stanza is 6 lines long and either presents a solution or documents the failed attempt to resolve the problem

Cascade Poem

The cascade poem was a form invented by Udit Bhatia. For the cascade poem, a poet takes each line from the first stanza of a poem and makes those the final lines of each stanza afterward. Beyond that, there are no additional rules for rhyming, meter, etc.

So to help this make sense, here's what a cascade poem with a tercet would look like:

A
B
C

a
b
A

c
d
B

e
f
C

A quatrain cascade would look so:

A
B
C
D

a
b
c
A

d
e
f
B

g
h
i
C

j
k
l
D

And, of course, you can make this even more involved if you want.

Concrete poetry

Concrete poetry is one of the more experimental poetic forms available to poets. Concrete poems use space and sound to communicate the meanings of the words. Words can cover other words; and the poem has trouble standing without the structure. Concrete poetry is more visual than other poetic forms.

Of course, concrete poetry has plenty of detractors because of the weight structure has on the words, but as much thought goes into concrete poetry as any other form.

Elegy

An elegy is a song of sorrow or mourning—often for someone who has died. However, poets being an especially creative and contrary group have also written elegies for the ends of things, whether a life, a love affair, a great era, a football season, etc.

While there are such things as elegiac couplets and elegiac stanzas, form does not rule an elegy; content *is* king (or queen) when writing elegies.

Epitaphs

The epitaph is a note meant to appear on a tombstone. From the Greek, epitaph means "upon a tomb." Since it has to fit on a tombstone, this note is usually brief and often rhymes. Some epitaphs are funny; most are serious. Most try to get the reader thinking about the subject of the tombstone.

The Fib

Fibonacci poetry was founded by Gregory K. Pincus as a 6-line poem that follows the Fibonacci sequence for syllable count per line.

For the 6-line poem that means:

- 1 syllable for first line
- 1 syllable for second line
- 2 syllables for third
- 3 syllables for fourth
- 5 syllables for fifth
- 8 syllables for sixth

There are variations where the Fibonacci expands even further with each line, but to understand how to accomplish this, you need to understand the Fibonacci math sequence of starting with 0 and 1 and then adding the last two numbers together to add to infinity.

$$0+1=1$$
$$1+1=2$$
$$1+2=3$$
$$2+3=5$$
$$3+5=8$$
$$5+8=13$$
$$8+13=21$$
$$13+21=34$$
and so on and so forth...

Anyway, those lines can easily get more and more unwieldy the more you let them expand. So, there's another variation that has taken flight in making Fibonacci poems that ascend and descend in syllables. For poets who also like mathematics, this is definitely an interesting form to get your mind working.

Found Poems

Found poetry is all about taking words not originally meant to be a poem (as they originally appeared) and turning those words into a poem anyway. You can use newspaper articles, bits of conversation, instructions, recipes, letters, e-mails, direct mail and even spam e-mail.

With found poetry, you do not alter the original words, but you can make line breaks and cut out excess before and/or after the poem you've "found." The power of found poetry is how words not intended as poetry can take on new and profound meanings as found poems.

Ghazal

The ghazal (pronounced "guzzle") is a Persian poetic form. The original form was very simple: five to 15 couplets using the same rhyme with the poet's name in the final couplet. The main themes were usually love or drinking wine.

Contemporary ghazals have abandoned the rhymes and insertion of the poet's name in the final couplet. In fact, even the themes of love and drinking wine are no longer mandatory—as the poem now just needs the couplets which are complete thoughts on their own but also all work together to explore a common theme (whatever that might be).

If you wish to stay traditional though, here's the rhyme scheme you would follow:

a

a

b

a

c

a

and so on to the final stanza (depending upon how many you include).

Many traditional ghazals will also incorporate a refrain at the end of each couplet that could be one word or a phrase.

Haiku

Haiku is descended from the Japanese *renga* form, which was often a collaborative poem comprised of many short stanzas. The opening stanza of the renga was called *hokku*. Eventually, haiku evolved from the leftover and most interesting hokku that were not used in renga.

Most haiku deal with natural topics. They avoid metaphor and simile. While most poets agree that haiku have three short lines, there is some disagreement on how long those lines are. For instance, some traditional haiku poets insist on 17 syllables in lines of 5/7/5. Other contemporary haiku poets feel that the first and third lines can be any length as long as they're shorter than the middle line.

Haiku do not have to include complete sentences or thoughts. They do not have titles. The best haiku contain some shift in the final line.

Hay(na)ku

Hay(na)ku is a very simple poetic form created in 2003 by poet Eileen Tabios. Hay(na)ku is a 3-line poem with one word in the first line, two words in the second, and three in the third. There are no restrictions beyond this.

There are already some variations of this new poetic form. For instance, a reverse hay(na)ku has lines of three, two, and one word(s) for lines one, two, and three respectively. Also, multiple hay(na)ku can be chained together to form longer poems.

Insult poetry

There are no hard and fast rules to the insult poem, but it's usually done in a joking (all in good fun) fashion as opposed to seriously trying to annoy anyone. Many insult poems also have a repetitive form or recurring method of delivering the insults. The insult poem is a good way to show just how clever you are (or think you are). But beware writing them! Once you attack someone (even in jest), you are suddenly fair game to receive an insult poem in retaliation.

Kyrielle

The kyrielle is a French four-line stanza form—with 8 syllables per line—that has a refrain in the fourth line. Often, there is a rhyme scheme in the poem consisting of the following possibilities:

- aabb
- abab
- aaab
- abcb

The poem can be as long as you wish and as short as two stanzas (otherwise, the refrain is not really a refrain, is it?), and, as with many French forms, it is very nice for stretching your poetic muscles.

Limericks

The origin of the limerick is shrouded in some mystery, but most sources seem to point to the early 18th century—one theory being that soldiers returning from France to the Irish town of Limerick started the form, the other theory pointing to the 1719 publication of *Mother Goose Melodies for Children*. Either way, Edward Lear popularized the form in the mid-19th century.

Basically, the limerick is a five-line poem consisting of a tercet split by a couplet. That is, lines 1, 2, and 5 are a bit longer and rhyme, while the shorter lines of 3 and 4 rhyme. After studying many effective limericks, there is not a precise syllable count per line, but the norm is about 8-10 syllables in the longer lines and around 6 syllables in the shorter lines.

List Poems

A list poem (also known as a catalog poem) is a poem that lists things, whether names, places, actions, thoughts, images, etc. Even a grocery list could turn into a poem with this form.

Lune

The lune is also known as the American Haiku. It was first created by the poet Robert Kelly and was a result of Kelly's frustration with English haiku. After much experimentation, he settled on a 13-syllable, self-contained poem that has 5 syllables in the first line, 3 syllables in the second line and 5 syllables in the final line.

Unlike haiku, there are no other rules. No need for a cutting word. Rhymes are fine; subject matter is open. While there are fewer syllables to use, this form has a little more freedom.

There is also a variant lune created by the poet Jack Collom. His form is also a self-contained tercet, but it's word-based (not syllable-based) and has the structure of 3 words in the first line, 5 words in the second line and 3 words in the final line.

Monotetra

The monotetra is a poetic form developed by Michael Walker. Here are the basic rules:

- Comprised of quatrains (four-line stanzas) in tetrameter (four metrical feet) for a total of 8 syllables per line
- Each quatrain consists of mono-rhymed lines (so each line in the first stanza has the same type of rhyme, as does each line in the second stanza, etc.)
- The final line of each stanza repeats the same four syllables
- This poem can be as short as one quatrain and as long as a poet wishes

Personally, I like the rhyme scheme and the repetitive final line of each stanza. I also appreciate the flexibility of this form in terms of how long or short the poem can be.

Occasional Poems

There are no specific guidelines for occasional poems except that they mark a specific occasion. The poems can be long or short, serious or humorous, good or bad—just as long as they mark the occasion. Good occasions for poems include birthdays, weddings and holidays.

Odes

The ode is a poetic form formed for flattery. There are three types of odes: the Horation; the Pindaric; and the Irregular.

The Horation ode (named for the Latin poet, Horace) contains one stanza pattern that repeats throughout the poem—usually 2 or 4 lines in length.

The Pindaric ode (named for the Greek poet, Pindar) is made up of a pattern of three stanzas called triads. This type of ode can be composed of several triads, but the first (the strophe) and the second (antistrophe) should be identical metrically with the third (epode) wandering off on its own metrical path.

The irregular ode (named for no one in particular) does away with formalities and focuses on the praising aspect of the ode.

Palindrome poetry

The palindrome seems like a simple enough form—until you actually try to write a good one. The rules are simple enough:

1. You must use the same words in the first half of the poem as the second half, but
2. Reverse the order for the second half, and
3. Use a word in the middle as a bridge from the first half to the second half of the poem.

At first, the simplicity of the rules made me feel like this would be easy enough to do, but I ran into problems almost immediately. For instance, you can't start the poem with the word "the" unless you plan to end the poem on the word "the." And just because something makes sense in the first half doesn't guarantee it'll pass the same test on the way back.

Pantoum

The **pantoum** is a poetic form originating in Malay where poets write quatrains (4-line stanzas) with an *abab* rhyme scheme and repeat lines 2 and 4 in the previous stanza as lines 1 and 3 in the next stanza.

Poets differ on how to treat the final quatrain: Some poets repeat lines 1 and 3 of the original quatrain as lines 2 and 4 in the final quatrain; other poets invert lines 1 and 3 so that the beginning line of the poem is also the final line of the poem.

Also, the pantoum can be as long or as short as you wish it to be, though mathematically it does require at least 4 lines.

Paradelle

The paradelle is a poetic form that Billy Collins originally introduced as "one of the more demanding French forms," though eventually Collins fessed up that he created it as a joke.

However, Collins was not kidding about the demanding rules of the paradelle. Here they are:

- The paradelle is a 4-stanza poem.
- Each stanza consists of 6 lines.

- For the first 3 stanzas, the 1st and 2nd lines should be the same; the 3rd and 4th lines should also be the same; and the 5th and 6th lines should be composed of all the words from the 1st and 3rd lines and only the words from the 1st and 3rd lines.
- The final stanza should be composed of all the words in the 5th and 6th lines of the first three stanzas and only the words from the 5th and 6th lines of the first three stanzas.

Parody Poems

A parody poem is one that pokes fun at another poem or poet. For instance, I recently read a parody of "We Real Cool," by Gwendolyn Brooks, in an online version of *Coe Review* called "We Real White." The best parodies are those that are easily recognizable—and funny, of course.

Rondeau

The rondeau is a form that has a refrain and rhymes—two elements I love in many French poems. The traditional rondeau is a poem consisting of 3 stanzas, 13 original lines, and 2 refrains (of the first line of the poem) with 8 to 10 syllables per line and an A/B rhyme scheme.

The skeleton of the traditional rondeau looks like this:

A(R)
A
B
B
A

A
A
B
A(R)

A
A
B
B
A
A(R)

There are variations of the rondeau, including the rondeau redouble, rondel, rondel double, rondelet, roundel, and roundelay. Of course, poets tend to break the rules on each of these as well, which is what poets like to do.

Sestina

The sestina is one of my favorite forms. You pick 6 words, rotate them as the end words in 6 stanzas and then include 2 of the end words per line in your final stanza.

Let's pick 6 random words: bears, carving, dynamite, hunters, mothers, blessing. Here's how the end words would go:

Stanza 1

Line 1-bears (A)
Line 2-carving (B)
Line 3-dynamite (C)
Line 4-hunters (D)
Line 5-mothers (E)
Line 6-blessing (F)

Stanza 2

Line 7-blessing (F)
Line 8-bears (A)
Line 9-mothers (E)
Line 10-carving (B)
Line 11-hunters (D)
Line 12-dynamite (C)

Stanza 3

Line 13-dynamite (C)
Line 14-blessing (F)
Line 15-hunters (D)
Line 16-bears (A)
Line 17-carving (B)
Line 18-mothers (E)

Stanza 4

Line 19-mothers (E)
Line 20-dynamite (C)
Line 21-carving (B)
Line 22-blessing (F)
Line 23-bears (A)
Line 24-hunters (D)

Stanza 5

Line 25-hunters (D)

Line 26-mothers (E)
Line 27-bears (A)
Line 28-dynamite (C)
Line 29-blessing (F)
Line 30-carving (B)

Stanza 6

Line 31-carving (B)
Line 32-hunters (D)
Line 33-blessing (F)
Line 34-mothers (E)
Line 35-dynamite (C)
Line 36-bears (A)

Stanza 7

Line 37-bears (A), carving (B)
Line 38-dynamite (C), hunters (D)
Line 39-mothers (E), blessing (F)

While many poets try to write sestinas in iambic pentameter, that is not a requirement. Also, when choosing your six end words, it does help to choose words that can be altered if needed to help keep the flow of the poem going.

Sevenling

The sevenling was created by Roddy Lumsden. Here are the rules:

- The sevenling is a 7-line poem (clever, huh?) split into three stanzas.
- The first three lines should contain an element of three. It could be three connected or contrasting statements, a list of three details or names, or something else along these lines. The three things can take up all three lines or be contained anywhere within the stanza.
- The second three lines should also contain an element of three. Same deal as the first stanza, but the two stanzas do not need to relate to each other directly.
- The final line/stanza should act as either narrative summary, punchline, or unusual juxtaposition.
- Titles are not required. But when titles are present, they should be titled Sevenling followed by the first few words in parentheses.
- Tone should be mysterious, offbeat or disturbing.
- Poem should have ambience which invites guesswork from the reader.

Shadorma

Shadorma is a Spanish 6-line syllabic poem of 3/5/3/3/7/5 syllable lines respectively.

Skeltonic poetry

Skeltonic verse is named after the poet John Skelton (1460-1529), who wrote short rhyming lines that just sort of go on from one rhyme to the next for however long a poet wishes to take it. Most skeltonic poems average less than six words a line, but keeping the short rhymes moving down the page is the real key to this form.

Sonnet

The sonnet is a 14-line poem that usually rhymes and is often written in iambic pentameter, though not always. Over time, this Italian poem has been pushed to its limits and some contemporary sonnets abandon many of the general guidelines.

The two most famous forms of the sonnet are the *Shakespearean Sonnet* (named after William Shakespeare) and the *Petrarcan Sonnet* (named after Francesco Petrarca).

The rhyme scheme for a Shakespearean Sonnet is:

a
b
a
b

c
d
c
d

e
f
e
f

g
g

The rhyme scheme for the Petrarcan Sonnet is a little more complicated. The first eight lines (or octave) are always rhymed abbaabba. But the final six lines (or sestet) can be rhymed any number of ways: cdcdcd, cdedce, ccdccd, cdecde, or cddcee. Of course, this offers a little more flexibility near the end of the poem.

But sonnets don't necessarily need to be Shakespearean or Petrarcan to be considered sonnets. In fact, there are any number of other sonnet varieties.

A few extra notes about the sonnet:

- A crown of sonnets is made by seven sonnets. The last line of each sonnet must be used as the first line of the next until the seventh sonnet. The last line of that seventh sonnet must be the first line of the first sonnet.
- A sonnet redouble is a sequence of 15 sonnets. Each line from the first sonnet is used (in order) as the the last line of the following 14 sonnets.

Tanka

If a haiku is usually (mistakenly) thought of as a 3-line, 5-7-5 syllable poem, then the tanka would be a 5-line, 5-7-5-7-7 syllable poem. However, as with haiku, it's better to think of a tanka as a 5-line poem with 3 short lines (lines 2, 4, 5) and 2 very short lines (lines 1 and 3).

While imagery is still important in tanka, the form is a little more conversational than haiku at times. It also allows for the use of poetic devices such as metaphor and personification (2 big haiku no-no's).

Like haiku, tanka is a Japanese poetic form.

Triolet

The triolet (TREE-o-LAY) has 13th-century French roots linked to the rondeau or "round" poem. Like other French forms, the triolet is great for repetition, because the first line of the poem is used three times and the second line is used twice. If you do the math on this 8-line poem, you'll realize there are only three other lines to write: two of those lines rhyme with the first line, the other rhymes with the second line.

A diagram of the triolet would look like this:

> A *(first line)*
> B *(second line)*
> a *(rhymes with first line)*
> A *(repeat first line)*
> a *(rhymes with first line)*
> b *(rhymes with second line)*
> A *(repeat first line)*
> B *(repeat second line)*

Villanelle

The villanelle, like the other French forms, does have many of the same properties: plenty of rhyme and repetition. This French form was actually adapted from Italian folk songs (villanella) about rural life. One of the more famous contemporary villanelles is "Do Not Go Gentle Into That Good Night," by Dylan Thomas.

The villanelle consists of five tercets and a quatrain with line lengths of 8-10 syllables. The first and third lines of the first stanza become refrains that repeat throughout the poem. It looks like this:

A(1)
b
A(2)

a
b
A(1)

a
b
A(2)

a
b
A(1)

a
b
A(2)

a
b
A(1)
A(2)

HOW TO FOCUS ON REVISION

Everybody's Trying to Tell Me What Is Right for Me

by Nate Pritts

When we think about revising a poem, we often have a very specific action in mind. Step one is to pull a poem out of the drawer (or out of the desktop folder) and step two is to look at it with fresh critical eyes, removed from the unsteady ecstasies of creation, in an effort to improve or enhance the writing. While this is obviously partly what happens, I think this severely limits the possibilities in the necessary work.

Because I think, on a larger scale, revision is the process whereby we explore the difference between the work of art we are creating and the life experience which led to that creation. In revision, we pull and stretch at the fabric of our sensibility, our identity, and in this process we learn what it is to be human. We deepen and enrich meaning through word choice, we complicate and explore through decisions we make regarding the deployment of information and logic. We come to a deeper understanding through the process of making choices and revisions, rather than through one specific result. We test ourselves, we confirm ourselves, we explore the implications of action and sensation, of feeling and thought. The result of all this experimental work? A poem. But, also, if we have done it right and with every ounce of our heart, the result is also a poet, one more fully equipped than ever for what comes next.

What's at stake isn't just one line or one stanza, or even just one poem. It is much grander than that, much more far-reaching. The act of revision should embody the same artistic effort that sparked the original act of composition. It's not work relegated to some other editor. It's not a different hat. Revision is part of the poet's work.

ART OF REVISION

While the act of revision is something we are mostly familiar with, the art of revision is something bigger altogether. Through identifying the principle aims of revision, we can understand the broader methods we have at our disposal. From there, we can come to a better sense of what is really at stake in the process of revision.

Revision sometimes carries with it an unfair stigma – the implication that something is wrong, that something needs to be fixed and made better. It makes people think that emergency work needs to be done in order to get the words on the page closer (ever closer!) to the original impulse and hence more responsive to the reason the piece of writing exists, its cloudy intentions.

> His poems weren't documents to him, something that is in existence as a record of something so much as they were a constant happening, something that actually exists.

Certainly some of the revision that any writer does is a kind of necessary house cleaning, more grammatical and mechanical in nature. It is a way to deal with the myriad potentials of word choice that are available, the arrangement of clauses and commas, an examination of the fundamental configurations for sentence or line or paragraph or stanza construction.

But of course there is the other side of revision, the fuzzy side: the apparatus of meaning, the actual content. This aspect of revision gets harder to talk about since it's not the result of codified processes or a checklist of qualities. It is purely personal, it's located in the soul of the writer herself, and it probably never ends – this process of bringing something to a full realization of the life it needs to live.

Juan Ramon Jimenez was said to rip the cover off his copy of any new edition of his poems so that he wouldn't feel as if they were finished, so that he could open up his head to the process of going back in, pen in hand, to make things new and to make things now. His poems weren't documents to him, something that is in existence as a record of something, so much as they were a constant happening, something that actually exists.

To me, this seems a good index for revision. Is the poem flat, a piece of stone? Then jump back in. Revise. Make it live.

AIMS OF REVISION

The aims of revision are twofold: the more cosmetic level of linguistic deployment as well as the more foundational level of a hoped for spiritual communion / realization / activation. Everyone is going to have a different sense of when these two aims are satisfied in their own work, of when they've achieved what they've aimed at. Though many people will try, no one else can really tell you what is right for you.

As you work to achieve these aims of revision, you have many methods of revision waiting to try out. Though there are literally thousands of ways to jump in and begin the messy work of change, of estrangement and arrangement, I believe there are two main methodologies, two main categories for how the surgery can proceed. You can work at an intuitive level, responding to the mystery that lies in your own heart, or you can work at the intentional level, embarking on a series of strategies and practices.

Intuitive Side of Revision

If you've ever written anything, then you know about the intuitive side of revision. It's that impulse you can't quite explain that causes you to change one word for another in an email you're working on, that whispered suggestion to backspace a whole clause and thus rewrite the trajectory of your sentence, the high frequency that only you can hear that forces you to scratch out a line, a title, a whole stanza.

....

You can work at an intuitive level, responding to the mystery that lies in your own heart, or you can work at the intentional level, embarking on a series of strategies and practices.

....

For many writers, after you've been at it a while and if you're lucky enough to be sensitive to your own impulses, this type of revision becomes embedded in the writing process itself. A complex series of choices are constantly running as a background hum in your head (or your heart, or wherever the spirit of your creativity thrums) and you're making determinations about the direction of what you write with these outcomes in mind.

Intentional Side of Revision

But there is also the intentional side, and I think this is worth exploring and explaining, worth pulling out of the closet and trying on. I suspect that much of our internal apparatus for intuitive revision starts as a roster of intentional strategies – things we have to think about, things we do on purpose – that slowly works its way into muscle memory.

Once we truly learn all the possibilities inherent, those purposeful actions become part of the ingrained toolbox we pull from as we write. Revision equals possibility in this equation, and the possibility here has to do with word choice and sentence structure (two things that are easy to tweak and change through intentional revision) but also with more foundational considerations (what if the setting is winter instead of summer, what if the person referenced is unhappy instead of happy).

PROMISE OF REVISION

To me revision has an altogether higher promise, a new kind of consequence. Revision can be made a part of the process, an energetic exploration that leads to wholly unknown continents, a generative and dynamic method for getting somewhere new every time.

Perhaps, the most important aspect of revision–the overriding concern, the umbrella under which you can shove the aims and methodologies I just discussed–is that it is a personal journey.

Each stanza, each line, each word in your poem is like the tumbler mechanism behind the lock, clicking through the possibilities that eventually spring it all wide open. But instead of imagining that there's one right slot for each of the dials, only one right word or phrase which unlocks the poem, consider that each click could be an entirely different lock that you're springing! Instead of worrying/workshopping one poem to death, you're making many many new poems!

Perhaps, the most important aspect of revision – the overriding concern, the umbrella under which you can shove the aims and methodologies I just discussed – is that it is a personal journey. And I use the word journey on purpose, though I know it smacks of new age empowerment. Still, consider this: the process of revision, of working harder and better to always be more authentic, to communicate with ever richer fields of empathy and feeling, is a human process. Hopefully, this is the same path we're all on as human beings! Only an individual knows what an individual is capable of, only you know what your best version looks like. In poetry, when we embark on revision as a way of pleasing other people (a trusted reader, an editor, a workshop full of peers) we hinder any chance we have of creating a poem that is truly a vehicle for our own unique blend of sensibilities. Sure, sometimes other people are incredibly perceptive. Sometimes advice from outside can help us to see ourselves from a fresh perspective.

This is valuable. But what I'm saying is that to make changes simply because someone else told you to, in an effort to win their accolades or commendations, leaves you with a poem that doesn't embody all the necessary possibilities you sought to imbue it with. You've severed that direct connection to your own soul, created some kind of public document. When you revise, look first inside. If something comes from outside, think it over. Consider it.

This work you're doing, the work of revision, isn't secondary in importance. It comes after the initial burst of inspiration and composition, true. There are those who think your first word is your best word, those who would say that revising a poem takes it further and further away from that best prime version. But I would suggest that the work of a poet isn't primarily concerned with generating a finished poem. The poet is someone who risks re-flection, a person who plunges again and again into dangerous waters in the hopes of find-ing some insight or linguistic configuration that can transform us. So if you write down a string of words and then leave them, you're not allowing yourself to fully explore the diffi-cult emotions and meanings embodied therein. You've left a mark but you haven't under-stood it, you haven't learned from it.

If you don't throw yourself fully into the process of revision you're not opening your-self up to the possibilities inherent in that process and you're not testing your insights and passions against a field that matters – there's no pressure, there's no strength. If you, as writer, can learn the lessons that the revision process is trying to teach you, then you'll have succeeded.

FRESHEN YOUR POETRY BY REVISING STALE LANGUAGE

by Nancy Susanna Breen

During a recent stint of poetry judging, I decided to keep a running list of the words and phrases that turned up again and again in entries. What I discovered is that too many poets, especially new or developing poets, depend on clichés in their writing. Others simply don't stretch enough for originality when crafting their lines. Instead, they invoke wording and images that have become exhausted with use.

You can freshen your poetry and increase your individuality by targeting stale language during the revising process. Like mold on bread, instances of exhausted images and overused words act as alerts once you know what you're looking for.

CLICHÉS

A cliché is any trite phrase or expression; that is, a phrase or expression that has been run into the ground. Avoid clichés like the plague. (See how easy it is to work clichés into your writing? There are two in those two sentences.) Because of their familiarity, clichés are comfortable and seemingly add a conversational touch to a line of poetry. They seem to guarantee clarity as well, because readers know what the clichés mean.

However, when poets turn to the same tired phrases and overused words, their poems all sound alike. Cliché-ridden lines have a cookie cutter effect. They result in poems that seem prefabricated, assembled of standard parts.

Here's a brief list of clichés that turned up more than three times in the batch of poems I was judging:

> lips are/were sealed
> blood, sweat, and tears

into thin air
heart and soul
thick and thin
bitter end
on a silver platter
life is precious
time stands still
as far as the eye can see
tore like a knife
sands in an hourglass
sun, moon, and stars

If you need help recognizing clichés, the Internet offers some valuable sites. For example, ClicheList.net provides an alphabetized list of clichés, each example linked to an explanation of its meaning. Cliché Finder (www.westegg.com/cliche) allows you to search its 3,000-plus cliché bank by keyword; "cat" turned up over 50 examples, such as "cat has your tongue," "cat's meow," and "raining cats and dogs." There's also a cliché generator that provides 10 random clichés at a time. Make a practice of reading through those 10 random clichés daily for a month and you'll find it much easier to spot clichés in your poems.

OH, NO! NOT ANOTHER [BLANK] POEM

Clichés include dull, stereotypical ideas and situations. Consequently, entire poems can be clichés. Gather a large enough sample of poems, such as entries in a poetry contest or submissions to a magazine, and you'll probably see several examples of the same clichéd poem, sometimes with surprisingly little variation. Below are types of poems poets can't seem to resist writing. Exercise heightened originality if attempting these poems.

Butterflies

I have nothing against butterflies, and I appreciate how symbolic they are. However, they turn up constantly as poem subjects, accompanied by all the typical verbs: flit, flutter, and so on. Describing or referring to butterflies emerging from cocoons is also popular. Understand how commonplace butterflies are before writing an entire poem about them if you really want to set your work apart. For that matter, restrain yourself from using them as images or symbols without plenty of careful thought.

Sea and sand

Poets simply must write about the ocean. (I certainly have.) They stroll through the tide, meditate on the coming and going of the tide, study what the tide leaves behind, and compare life to the movements of the tide.

There's nothing wrong with writing about strolling on the beach, watching the waves, or examining the shells and driftwood at low tide. However, because they're so popular with poets, the ocean and beach are hard to write about in an original way, especially if the physical descriptions basically make up the poem.

Poets consistently choose the same words to describe the sea and shore, and the ring of familiarity isn't a virtue. Even a touching account of a dying person visiting the seaside for the last time or a broken-hearted lover examining a ruined relationship fades into sameness when the speakers' actions are similar and they seem to be viewing the scene through the same pair of eyes.

Seasonal

The most uninspired, and uninspiring, poetry I see usually focuses on one of the seasons or on all four at once. This is primarily because poets pull out all the standard images, as if putting up those colored cardboard cutouts in a classroom: colored leaves and pumpkins for fall, snowflakes for winter, buds and robins for spring, a big, smiling sun for summer. Such images are beloved and iconic; and because of this, you need to move past them when writing about a season. Read enough poems that cite "the golden leaves drift lazily to ground" and you'll wince at the mere thought of autumn.

I'm going to go a step farther and suggest that freshening the seasonal imagery you use isn't enough—you should avoid the seasons as the sole subjects of poems. Instead, use the season as a background. That way your poem develops into sometime more than a laundry list of the same old spring showers, hot July noons, and shimmering blankets of snow on a rolling landscape.

Love

It's a shame so many love poems come across as time-creased valentines. I've rarely read a clichéd love poem that made me doubt the sincerity of the writer's feelings. When such verse seems cribbed from the most mundane greeting card, though, especially when expressed in *oo-aa* rhymes, the poem appears mass-produced rather than the true expression of an individual. Poems about unrequited love or rejection are especially painful, not because of the sadness involved but because a kind of injured, righteous indignation overrides the poet's artistic common sense. And, of course, the same images are evoked and the same flowery language applied as though squeezed out of a tube of frosting.

When writing a poem that addresses a romantic partner or someone who has cast you aside, consider sending it only to the intended recipient or keeping it strictly to yourself. Otherwise, be sure you can treat the work as a piece of literary art, not a love letter. Even then, make it your own. Don't resort to gooey valentine verses or resentful poison notes.

A subset of the love poem is the "love is" poem. If you insist on defining love, have something new to say. "Love is" poems range from a list of clichéd comparisons, both positive and negative (a delicate rose, a knife to the heart, a blanket against the cold) to a series of unsurprising adjectives (kind, understanding, forgiving, harsh, demoralizing, etc.). Throw out the cookie cutter images and the threadbare language or don't bother at all, at least not if you're writing for a general readership. The same goes for "my love is like" poems.

OTHER CLICHÉ PITFALLS

Hearts

In poetry, hearts aren't mere organs that pump blood. Poets have them doing more tricks than a trained poodle in a one-ring circus: pounding, shrieking, weeping, dancing, swelling, bleeding, exploding, freezing, or stopping dead (without killing the poet). Poets assist their hearts in hyperactivity by opening them, shutting them, writing on them, exploring them, hiding things in them, and nursing them. Other people do things to poets' hearts as well: stomp on them, warm them, break them, steal them, stab them, fill them with joy or sadness, play with them, heal them, and reawaken them when they're dead (figuratively speaking).

"Heart" is one of those words you have to handle carefully, if at all. Despite its versatility, in most cases you can leave "heart" out of your poem. It's a cliché that can do more harm than good; and the more animated the heart is in your poem, the more danger of giving the reader a mental image that resembles a Wile E. Coyote cartoon.

Obviously, if you're writing about someone's cardiac event, *heart* is a necessary clinical term, not a cliché. Where emotions are concerned, though, don't go breaking, teasing, or exposing anyone's heart in your poems.

Despair

It's astonishing how many poets "plunge into the abyss" or "descend into oblivion" at some point in their poetry. Sometimes they hurtle their entire beings into the black pit of nothingness; in other instances, their minds or hearts take the dive of despair.

Sadly, it's hard for readers to take you seriously when you're melodramatic. Write with even more finesse when addressing such intense emotional conditions as grief and depression. Imagine an over-the-top actor in 19th-century theater wailing to the balcony, writhing on the stage, or whirling his cape around him like a shroud. This shouldn't be the effect you want your lines to convey.

Read the confessional poetry of Sylvia Plath, Robert Lowell, Anne Sexton, John Berryman, and others to learn how to calibrate your language so you express the most emotion with the least hyperbole.

Tears

Too many poets turn the human face into a Niagara Falls of tears. These tears run, cascade, course, drip, trickle, and flow. Or poets turn to clichés to describe weeping, such as "cried like a baby," "cried a river," or "cried her eyes out."

When you write skillfully, showing rather than telling, you can convey sorrow without using tears at all. Uncontrolled waterworks are just overkill; they don't make the scene more convincing. Think of a movie where an actor cries. It's usually an extreme situation when a character dissolves into heaving sobs; otherwise, the viewers don't buy it. Often a character struggling *not* to cry is more affecting than drenched cheeks. Remember that the next time you're inclined to flood someone's face with tears in your poem.

Colors

Although simply putting "green," "blue," or "red" into your descriptions is pretty mundane, it's almost worse to employ clichéd colors. If you notice "ruby red," "golden yellow," "baby pink," "sky blue," and similar color clichés in your poems, revise them to more specific colors or create original similes—in other words, don't just substitute "red as a ruby" or "blue as a summer sky." Come up with something vivid and new. If your color phrase turns up in the lyrics of pop songs or standards, it's too worn-out to use in your poetry. For inspiration, review some paint company Internet sites for the creative ways they name various colors, then work on original examples of your own.

While I'm discussing colors, I want to mention red, white, and blue. This combination is a favorite of poets writing about the military, patriotism, or the United States in general. Unfortunately, those colors used together have become cliché, detracting from verse that may otherwise make valid statements. There's plenty to say about a soldier's sacrifice, love of one's country, or the esteem for U.S. liberty and democracy without tying everything up in red, white, and blue bunting. Make your poem stirring enough and readers will see the stars and stripes without a specific reference.

A WORD ABOUT DEAD METAPHORS

When people repeat a metaphor so often its original imagery gives way to a new, literal meaning, the result is a *dead metaphor*. I once heard a talk at the Geraldine R. Dodge Poetry Festival by poet Donald Hall in which he cited the use of dead metaphors as one of the most common reasons he rejects poems. One of his examples was *sea of wheat*, which now means an expanse of wheat rather than an ocean-like view of the grain field.

Determining what constitutes a dead metaphor and when to delete it can be confusing. For instance, *eye of the needle* is considered a dead metaphor, yet it's also what we call that opening in the top of a needle. On the other hand, in the phrase *he plowed through the stacks of paper*, "plowed" at first glance seems a vigorous verb choice rather than a dead metaphor. However, consider how many times you hear this metaphor in televised news reports. "The robbery suspect plowed through the festival crowd." "The car plowed into the front porch of the home." *Plow* doesn't conjure up its original imagery of a blade digging through dirt; it's taken on a meaning of its own through heavy repetition as a popular term.

If you're unsure about dead metaphors, apply the yardstick of frequency: If the term in question gets repeated a lot, especially in the media, revise the term whether it's a dead metaphor or not.

BE ALERT, NOT OBSESSIVE

Don't inhibit your writing by being overly conscious about stale language as you're putting the words down. First or even second and third drafts aren't a time for self-editing. When you revise, watch carefully for overused words and tired imagery. They're tricky little devils to catch because we're so used to them. Reread this article and I'm sure you'll target some clichés or dead metaphors that slipped right by me. The point is to be aware of them as you hone your skills. Over time you'll become more astute about when you need to cast them aside to freshen up the lines of your poems.

NANCY SUSANNA BREEN is a poet, freelance writer, and editor. Her poetry is available in e-chapbook form at www.Smashwords.com as is an e-book of writing prompts, *Nudged by Quotes—20 Writing Prompts Inspired by The World's Great Poetry, Volume 10: Poetical Quotations*. She's the former editor of *Poet's Market* and judges poetry contests at the state and national levels.

THE IMPORTANCE OF READING POETRY

Even Poetry You Hate

···

by Nancy Susanna Breen

In his guide to poetry writing, *The Ode Less Travelled* (Gotham Books, 2005), British author Stephen Fry lists 10 habits of successful poets. Number four on his list is "Read poetry."

I agree. I firmly believe every poet should read poetry, even poets who simply write for a select circle in a critique group or in an online forum. Such poets often protest, "You don't *have* to read other poets to write poetry." Technically, they're right, but I admit I don't understand their reasoning or their aversion to reading a literary genre in which they're enthusiastic participants. I'm even more astonished by poets who say, "I'm intimidated by poetry" or "I don't like to read poetry because I usually don't understand it." I've even heard a few poets say, "I don't like to read other poets because I'm afraid they'll influence my style."

Those of you who write only for yourselves or for your coterie of fellow poets can get by with such an outlook. Your objective is self-expression, getting your feelings into words and nothing more. If you can share your poems with people you trust in a group or online forum, you're good with that. And you may be happier with your literary life than more ambitious poets. However, I can't fathom doing anything creative in a vacuum. Even knitters like to see what others are making, and cooks love to sample recipes, even if they wind up changing them. Plus you're missing out on so much great poetry that you may well understand if you just search it out. You might even learn to like it.

Those of you, though, who are concerned with craft and hope to gain a wide readership for your poems have no excuse. You *must* read others' poetry. After all, how can you justify ignoring the work of other poets while hoping others will read *your* poems? Poetry in modern society needs all the support, and all the readers, it can get. A golden rule for poets could be, "Read other poets as you would have them read you."

Beyond supporting your art form, there are many benefits to gain from reading poetry—even bad poetry or poetry you hate.

DEVELOPING AN EAR

Reading a variety of poems helps you develop an ear for the necessary music, rhythm, and flow of verse. This applies to free verse poems as well as rhymed, metered poetry. So much free verse falls flat because poets haven't learned how much sound variance and texture free verse actually can contain. This is why reading poems aloud can be even more effective than reading them silently to yourself. Read the same poem aloud more than once, tasting the shape of the vowels and consonants, playing with pauses and breathing according to punctuation, and exploring how lines flow into each other rather than ending where the lines break. You'll learn how naturally conversational a poem can be even when it plays with meter; eventually your own work will reflect such lessons.

Reading rhymed, metered poetry is also important, whether you write only formal poetry or stick strictly to free verse. However, those who write in rhyme and meter definitely need plenty of exposure to such poetry from all eras. Poets who never get past Shakespeare or the Romantic poets show it in their writing. Their metered lines sound like stiff imitations of the old masters, they think it's okay (or even required) to use "thee" and "'twere," and employ they such stale tricks as the order of their words inverting. Read modern formalist poets for contemporary approaches to this kind of verse to purge yourself of outmoded techniques.

Absolutely read poetry with meter and rhyme aloud. Study what the poet does to avoid a sing-song effect and how he or she chooses rhymes. Note the impact of repeated one-syllable end rhymes and the probably-unintended comic effect of multiple-syllable rhymes. In addition, reading (and listening) to structured verse will help you distance yourself from the "greeting card" taint that afflicts so many attempts at rhymed, metered poetry.

READING WHAT YOU DON'T LIKE

In *The Ode Less Travelled*, Fry notes, "Variety is important or you end up an imitative shadow of your favourites." Often poets stay in their comfort zones when reading poetry; that is, they gravitate toward poems they like and/or understand. The best way to stretch your writing muscles, though, is to read fine examples of work you do *not* enjoy. Yes, the experience isn't as satisfactory, but think of it as a kind of literary workout challenge. As you're reading, observe and even record all the things you don't like about the poem, including subject matter, style, voice, and sound. Bravely admit it when a line or even an entire poem leaves you clueless, but take a shot at deciding what you think it means. If you meet such a poem head-on and don't let it deflect you, you may find the struggle illuminating. The point is not to force yourself to like a certain style or poem but to encourage you to open your mind to poetry's many possibilities.

Adventurous reading may lead you to discover a poet, work, or style you never encountered before, one that may intrigue you into examining it further. Remember, you shouldn't write every poem with publication as your goal. Experimentation is vital to your artistic development, so try some of these alien forms and styles, doing it in secret, if necessary, to relieve your inhibitions. You may surprise yourself, and you'll certainly expand your abilities as a poet.

POETRY AS A HOW-TO REFERENCE

If you're unsure when to break the lines of your poems or you stumble over how to begin or end each work, reading the poetry of others can provide useful demonstrations of best practices. Don't assume only the renowned poets have something to teach you. An unknown, little-published poet may have a fresh arsenal of approaches for you to observe and imitate. Again, don't hesitate to experiment. It will help you understand what works for you and what doesn't; and even if you don't employ certain techniques in your own poems, you may begin to appreciate them in the work of others.

POETRY FROM VARIOUS CULTURES

Poets benefit not only from exposure to different forms of poetry but also to poetry from different cultures. If you know a second language, by all means read verse in a poet's native tongue. However, translations offer you access to the whole world of poetry going back to ancient times. Some poets and critics argue that too much is lost in translation to make the reading of translated poetry worthwhile. However, weigh the loss of never having read a given poem to the boon of being exposed to it in even a flawed translation. You may find yourself less hesitant about delving into translated poetry.

If a poem especially intrigues you, seek out alternate translations of the same piece to get a feel for the different ways translators interpret the words literally and stylistically. Go a step further and write your own version of the poem based on the translations you've reviewed. This is another of those don't-have-to-share exercises that can produce interesting results and beckon you down new paths in your own poetry writing.

Don't think solely in terms of language and foreign countries when seeking out poetry from other cultures. Your own background and experience determine what cultures may seem "foreign" to you. If you're straight, read gay, lesbian, bi-gender, and transgender (GLBT) poets. If you live in a small Midwestern town or a highly rural area, read poetry inspired by gritty urban life. If you were born and raised in the United States, read what immigrants have to say about venturing into American life and society. If you've never been a soldier or a member of a military family, read poems that capture the battlefield, the army base, experiences aboard ships or jets, or what it's like to watch a loved one leave for a tour of duty.

WHAT ABOUT BAD POETRY?

Naturally, you don't want to pick up poor writing habits. However, reading bad or simply mediocre poetry can be a strangely productive motivator.

Sometimes reading wonderful poetry makes me swoon; other times it makes me want to curl up in a ball of diminished self-confidence because I'm sure I'll never write anything that good. That's when I delve into some poetry I don't admire, whether in print or online. I'm not fishing for reasons to feel superior, but an inadequate poem can make my inner artist rear up and shout, "Hey, even *I* can write something better than that!"

It's also a great tonic for feeling flat and uninspired. I may prime the pump by rewriting someone else's poem in ways I think would improve it (an exercise only). Or that aforementioned inner artist squirms over the dull work I'm reading and whines, "I'm bored! Let's write something interesting."

I can't promise reading bad poetry will work for everyone. You may recoil from a terrible poem feeling more deflated than inspired. Sometimes a bad poem is simply a bad poem, and all I can do is wince and move on. Also, if you're suggestible or mimic work easily, reading lousy poetry may be exactly what you *don't* need.

There's another benefit of reading bad poetry, though, that you ought to consider. Read enough consistently poor work and you'll begin to pick up on the mistakes poets make again and again: overused words and phrases; wordy, flaccid poems that cry out for trimming and tension; trite scenes and perspectives that seemed so original when you thought only *you* were writing about them. Familiarity does breed contempt; and once you start spotting such flaws in your own work, you'll avoid the pitfalls of bad poetry writing and self-edit your own poems more diligently.

NURTURE THE HABIT

In *The Poetry Home Repair Manual* (University of Nebraska Press, 2005), former U.S. Poet Laureate Ted Kooser observes that imitation is how poets learn to write, "just as every painter learns to paint by looking at paintings" or composers learn from the work of other composers. The great thing about poetry is your art gallery or symphonic hall is as close as your bookshelf, e-reader, or computer screen.

If you're not a regular poetry reader, start out with a poem a day. Keep a volume of work by a single poet, a literary magazine, or an anthology where you're sure to pick it up and open it. Select daily readings randomly or move through the publication from cover to cover. Don't regard it as an assignment or a chore you have to complete. Stay relaxed and open as you read, and don't read too much at a time.

Another way to make regular poetry reading easier to achieve is to subscribe to daily poems by e-mail. Soon reading poems will become a basic part of checking your inbox; just make sure you do read them and don't let them build up over days and days.

Some of the most popular subscription sites include:

- Poem-a-Day at the Academy of American Poets (www.poets.org/poemADay.php)
- Poetry Daily (www.poems.com/about_newsletter.php)
- The Poetry Foundation, which offers RSS feeds for Poem of the Day and Audio Poem of the Day as well as a free mobile app for iPhone and Android (www.poetryfoundation.org/mobile/; links for the RSS feeds are at the bottom of the page)
- The Writer's Almanac with Garrison Keillor (http://mail.publicradio.org/content/506927/forms/twa_signup.htm)
- Poetry 180, with daily poems intended for American high school students, but the selections are excellent for poets of any age (http://www.loc.gov/poetry/180/)

In addition, Ted Kooser's "American Life in Poetry," a weekly newspaper feature, also offers a poem with accompanying comment by e-mail subscription (http://www.americanlifeinpoetry.org/email.html).

However you do it and whatever method you use, add reading poetry to your daily regimen. Once developed, it's a habit you won't want to break.

INVENTION OF EVERYTHING ELSE

by Susan Rich

Once a man offered me his heart like a glass of water
how to accept or decline?

Sometimes all I speak is doubt

delineated by double lines
of railroad tracks; sometimes

I'm an incomplete bridge, crayon red Xs extending

across a world map.
A man offers me his bed like an emergency

exit, a forklift, a raft.

The easy-to-read instructions
sequestered in the arms of his leather jacket.

Sometimes a woman needs

small habits, homegrown salad, good sex.
Instead, I cultivate two cats and a gramophone

attempt enlightenment

scrubbing winter's brine from the deck.

The woman and the man say yes –

then no, say maybe, perhaps.

They don't yet apprehend what they'll find
in the other.

Perhaps it's acorns falling

on the roof, a Sunday paper, this all-embracing
ocean view.

Once a man offered his fortune
in drumbeats and song

in tune with some internal window; something buried in blue.

BREAKING MORNING

....

by Scott Owens

This ritual of coffee is an ancient gesture.
One half of a couple rises early,
prepares the beans, the filtered water,
remembers exactly how much sugar
or cream, even the preferred size
or style of the cup. The other is moved
by the sound of the spoon tapped against
the rim, an articulation of aroma.
The presentation: cup in up-turned palm,
steam rising as if to announce *This*
was made especially for you.
Odysseus approached Penelope this way,
half in apology, half to say
you're still the one I want to see at first light.

IF TESLA HAD AIMED HIS DEATH RAY AT VORTEX, KENTUCKY

by Shaindel Beers

There wouldn't be a girl at Target in her red polo shirt
and khakis, waiting for a boy in a Ford Ranger
who will drive up, steady as an assembly line,
singing Garth Brooks' "Friends in Low Places,"
to pick her up from work. She would not stretch
like a lily on a stem, straining for the sun, to see if he is there,
in the indigo pick-up to rescue her from shoppers
too good for Wal-Mart who will let you know it
by unleashing a storm of insults the way Wal-Mart shoppers
are too meek to. When she gets in, he will change
from Garth Brooks to The Beatles out of respect,
and they will sing off-key about the octopus's garden.
They will joke about getting a van and painting it
like a yellow submarine. You are happy for them,
Dear Reader, because you know that death is stalking them
like a panther. Time does not stretch like Turkish Delight,
and you are glad that Tesla did not aim his death ray
at Vortex, Kentucky, because these are your parents.
The quiet trailer park girl, the burly boy in the pick-up.

FIVE WAYS OF LOOKING AT A MUSHROOM CLOUD

by Chris Haven

I

The white and orange hot heat
of the explosion, melted filmstrips,
faces and flappy projectors,
the five times you vomited at school,
the one face that teacher and student,
frozen every time, made.

II

The blue of it
the sky of it
the yes of it
the too bad of it
the gay of it
the pilot of it
the why not of it

III

It's the little punching bag in the back
of everyone's mouth.

It's a tiny little boxer

in an Old Testament minor prophet cave.

It's a speed bag, bippity bippity bip,
reverse, negative exposure.

It's a mouthpiece boiled in water and sweat.
We're all training for something.

IV

Once the Ancient Grecian ruins weren't ruined and they weren't actually white but polka-dotted, and there was one that was not multi-columnar but uni-columnar and they made it of smoke and split pebbles and they wore robes around it and engaged it in dialogue about its nature and teased it and chortled with knowing looks and their laughs laughed the smoke away and all the pebbles fell straightaway and buried those sons of bitches.

V

A few steps from a wooded trail, buried
in a crackle of leaves, a fungus top
orange as an encyclopedia frog,
a wonder uncaring and unbidden,
never ridden a train or been to France,
stanched bleeding or looked into a canyon
or stuck seed in the crevice of a tooth,
or published a scholarly article,
uploaded a video demonstration,
or cried for the want of a color
it never knew existed outside itself,
for a small dirt-borne tragedy, buried,
memorialized, with no witnesses.

VI

the dark of it

INTRODUCTION TO DISASTER PREPAREDNESS

or How to Go Into the Dark

by Jeannine Hall Gailey

While you told me about the bee colony collapse
caused by cell phones or maybe Monsanto and their magic poisons

I was thinking about a friend who said "they found a lump"
and another friend finishing chemo and waiting for a scan

and a third who said "my hair is a disaster" and she meant the layers
would take forever to grow out. My house is a disaster, she says, my yard, my outfit.

When you told me "my son is autistic" I thought of his bright eyes
and beautiful tears. It's not the life you planned. How our minds

and bodies spin apart, like hives of bees confused about whom to follow,
flying further and further out to discover – what – that they'd flown

too far and now are frozen, flightless. How many hives abandoned.
We cannot sleep too far from disaster zones. I saw a tornado blacken the sky,

slept through hurricanes, knelt during earthquakes. How to face the dark?
Did I pray, did I ask for something then? I only held my breath

and later asked, are you okay? I said, everything is temporary.

TROUBLE IN MIND

....

by Nancy Posey

I can't shake these blues, this haunting
trouble in mind. Surrounded by brick and concrete,
I dream of trains and cries of lonesome doves.
Even the buskers rapping in the subway tunnel
sound like they're singing sad old blues songs,
lyrics their grannies crooned over their cradles.
The soundtrack plays, running through my head,
accompanied by the soft whine of harmonica
untucked from some hobo's jacket pocket
unwrapped from his worn bandana.

Trouble smells like pine trees, whispers like wind
along a mountain ridge, cries like Janis
before she dies. It tastes a bit like moonshine
sipped right out of the jug. I can't look trouble
straight in the eye. Instead, he slinks around
behind my back, muttering in my ear,
telling me why, why I too should be blue,
his breath so hot, his fingers cold
on the back of my neck. Trouble knows
where to find me, even when I leave without
a forwarding address. He has my number.

THE OFFERING OF HIS EYE

by J. P. Dancing Bear

Across the dinner table
He offers his eye
She pulls a magnifying glass
As he holds her hair
And dreams pillows of her scent
The curtains ghost and flap
Lightning in the distance
Drops stick figures to the ground
—Rigid and stiff
He can feel static air building in the room
Three rain drops fill his palm
A partial answer to a farm prayers
He listens to her steady breathing
Like counting thunder
Their shadows grow from the raw bulb above
Blending on the swirling eddies of wood grain
Her skin was smooth
He can sense this through her movements
The rustle of her clothes
He holds onto her hair long after
She's done looking into his eye

ALONE IN FADING LIGHT

....

by Helen Losse

The natural clean of pine
perfumes the air. A breeze

stirs leaves, vacated from deciduous
trees in the woods. Near the property line,

Queen Anne's Lace
& flowering goldenrod gently

sway. I pass the tobacco shed, pause
by the seldom-painted barn, watch

the last rays of sunset. I settle
on a blanket of pink clover,

hear music from a nearby club:
saxophones, horns, & guitars.

Guttural beckoning from an alto
harmonizes with the throbbing beat

of a bluesman singing of hard times.
No longer aware of cows in adjacent

fields nor the bull's horns and firm
erection, I myself burn hot

with invisible flames. I close my eyes,
content to let words prick my heart.

About midnight, just as my loneliness
reaches its climax, the singing stops.

When I open my eyes, the darkness is deep.
Someone turned off the moonlight.

Wild air movement: frosty & cold.
Then flashes of lightning. Thunder slaps

like a bell-clapper. The sky is missing
millions of stars. Even the soft glow

from the nearest planet—
once inviting as a trembling virgin—

mocks me from behind a cloud.

THE ARTISTS' HONEYMOON

by Daniel Ari

after "In Bed The Kiss" by Henri de Toulouse-Lautrec

We rest, rung. On everything, a slight
blur. Parisian. Post-coital.
Like Sleeping Beauty in reverse,
we kiss, then fall into deep sleep.
Next day, we eat the city. Then
we rest, run. Gone. Very thin gaslight
makes cities of our bodies.
We're natives and we're newcomers.
One morning, we kiss, and the sun
goes down. In the dark parlor where
we restrung one very thin gaslight,
we conjoin at the window...
The world seemed underwater then:
the night supporting our wet weight
while our living souls, wild as thoughts,
were strung on everything as light.

ORIFICE

....

by Terry Wolverton

Mothers disappear
in a forgotten language,
follow distraction,
a war of bright chords
flood of tin vowels.

We tongue the endings,
become the memory,
fly blind toward some
lost source, clumsy
with caution and faith.

It's a longshot, but
we're not circumspect;
we follow the light and heat
of our small hunches, burning
toward the long sound of her.

TRESPASS WITH HORSEFLY

by Kevin McLellan

Triangular-winged: you hone in on
his transitioning: his practicing
being pond-side in lieu of the dirt
road: the two drainage pipes turn
pond water into stream and here
like language in the born current
he considers the shadow of his head
beside the shapeshifting minnows:
he says to himself one and part
of the whole and then two small frogs
confirm this: the event and the welt
on one of his pale arms as you now
lead the ankle high swarming:

RECIPE

....

by Martha Silano

Begins with a dash of giant impact, a sprinkling
of moon-lets, pinch of heavy bombardment.
Sift in crusty iron sulfide, fricasseed stromatolites,
one level teaspoon cyanobacteria. Slowly
dribble in ammonia, methane, hydrogen,
custard; a dollop of ocean. Chill
this velvety soup, cream congealing
in a Proterozic freezer. Mix well
your deep hypothermal marine. Let go
your nucleus, embrace your blue-green,
equal parts cointreau and cran-raz (let's call it
sunset). After the foaming, beat in trilobites
highly spiny, highly spiffy. After the rising,
serve on a bed of rock salt 488 million years
in the sand where a horseshoe crab
still lays her 60,000 eggs. Take your baster,
tickle its telson, its pedipalps. Brush
with pineapple mud glaze. Reserve.
Go kolacky, go goo-goo for Siphusactum
gregarium goulash, bonkers for sponge.
Do that thing you do with disambiguation,
with cartilage and dip, with molting.
Give it that ol' placoderm shaping

till it's time to roll out the lobe-fins,
to pack this floating island brachiopodishly,
to get this gin fizz fizzing, this volcano revolting.
Hurry up and make that Hurry-up Gravy,
decorate Pangea with gingko dainties.
Then headlong into the dark, dark fast-
fudge Black Gold Betty, which is always
nipping at the heels of the collembola
crepes, the fairy shrimp consommé.
Beat in the hexapods! (Goodbye, gill branches!)
Fire up that grill; make way for metamorphosis,
for 10,000 blooming delphiniums, for Liopleurodon
and Megatherium—for the nimble Hagerman Horse,
for the leg of lamb in a wire basket, spitting and hissing.

ELEGY

....

by Amorak Huey

Train slides & slices through summer heat—wind in oak leaves,

small rustle of a thing in the midst of being forgotten.

Raucous grope & stretch of a Saturday night. If we cry out

in the darkness who hears? Press against the flesh

of the first woman who remembers your name. Wrap your arms

around emptiness, spaces where notes join like wood into wood:

dovetail. Warp & wrap & weave & womb. Linger. Leave.

Look up. Sharp-shinned hawks circle & rise

& praise the wind. As if the wind. As if harmony.

Sun edges pink & amber over cotton field. The babble & tongue

of the big rivers. The heft & fall. The fingers, the hands, the flight. The highways. Those who came before. The dust & swamp

& the holy holy holy sounds of love.

NINE GULLS

....

by Maril Crabtree

There is no place that does not see you.
    -Rainer Marie Rilke

the sea carves itself
into sunlit spines
that lift and curl
spirals of sound
lift and lower
damp twine marks
a fisherman's footprint
eight gulls taste air together
a ninth flies above
in the opposite direction
impossible to tell
who's leading whom

wrapping arms
in defense against sky
sharp bones of blue
echo down the shore
rise and fall
a rough outline
hidden in wet sand
spurred by wind
gliding and flapping
a startle of white over blue
or blue against white
as the day shudders on

POET BIOS

DANIEL ARI has written and published extensively since devoting himself to the practice in 1985. His work has appeared in *Writer's Digest, McSweeney's Internet Tendency, 42 Magazine, Pif Magazine,* and *Ceramics Now*; and his poems have frequently earned top spots in the Poetic Forms Challenges hosted by *Writer's Digest*. Daniel leads poetry groups, events, and performances throughout the Pacific Northwest. His blogs are imunuri.blogspot.com and fightswithpoems.blogspot.com.

SHAINDEL BEERS recently had her second collection of poetry, *The Children's War*, published by Salt Publishing. In fact, her poem in this edition comes from that collection. Beers' poetry, fiction, and creative nonfiction have appeared in numerous journals and anthologies. She is currently an instructor of English at Blue Mountain Community College in Pendleton, Oregon, in Eastern Oregon's high desert and serves as Poetry Editor of *Contrary*.

J. P. DANCING BEAR is editor for the American Poetry Journal and Dream Horse Press. Bear also hosts the weekly hour-long poetry show, Out of Our Minds, on public station, KKUP and available as podcasts. His latest book of poetry is *Family of Marsupial Centaurs and other birthday poems* (Iris Press, 2012). His twelfth collection of poetry, *The Abandoned Eye*, will be published in 2013 by FutureCycle Press.

MARIL CRABTREE lives in the Central Midwest, also known as The Heartland. A Pushcart prize nominee, her award-winning poetry has appeared in numerous anthologies and literary journals including *Kalliope, The DMQ Review, Steam Ticket, Coal City Review, Mid-America Poetry Review, Third Wednesday,* and *New Works Review*. Her chapbook, *Dancing* *with Elvis*, was published in 2005 and her second chapbook, *Moving On*, in 2010. She is Poetry Co-Editor for *Kansas City Voices*, a visual and literary arts magazine.

JEANNINE HALL GAILEY is the Poet Laureate of Redmond, Washington and the author of *Becoming the Villainess* (Steel Toe Books, 2006) and *She Returns to the Floating World* (Kitsune Books, 2011,) which was a finalist for the Eric Hoffer Montaigne Medal. Her poems have appeared in *The American Poetry Review, The Iowa Review,* and *Prairie Schooner*. She volunteers for *Crab Creek Review* and teaches part-time at the National University MFA program.

CHRIS HAVEN'S poetry has appeared or is forthcoming in many journals including *Blackbird, Slice, Crab Orchard Review, Sentence, Sycamore Review, Fugue,* and *Seneca Review*. He teaches creative writing at Grand Valley State University in Michigan, where he edits *Wake: Great Lakes Thought & Culture*.

AMORAK HUEY is a longtime newspaper reporter and editor who now teaches writing at Grand Valley State University in Michigan. His poems can be found in *The Best American Poetry 2012, The Southern Review, Oxford American, The Journal,* and other print and online journals.

HELEN LOSSE is the author of two full-length books, *Seriously Dangerous* (Main Street Rag, 2011) and *Better With Friends* (Rank Stranger Press, 2009) and three chapbooks. Her poems have been nominated twice for a Pushcart Prize and three times for a Best of the Net award, one of which was a finalist. Her book *Seriously Dangerous* was on the long list for a 2012 SIBA Book Award.

KEVIN MCLELLAN is the author of the chapbook *Round Trip* (Seven Kitchens, 2010), a collaborative series of poems with numerous women poets. His poems have recently appeared in: *Barrow Street, Colorado Review, failbetter, Horse Less Review, Kenyon Review Online, Western Humanities Review, Witness* and numerous others. Kevin lives in Cambridge MA, and sometimes teaches poetry workshops at the University of Rhode Island.

SCOTT OWENS' tenth collection of poetry, *Shadows Trail Them Home*, is due out from Clemson University Press this fall. His prior work has received awards from the Academy of American Poets, the Pushcart Prize Anthology, the NC Writers Network, the NC Poetry Society, and the Poetry Society of SC. His poems have been in *Georgia Review, North American Review, Chattahoochee Review, Southern Poetry Review,* and *Poetry East* among others. He is the founder of Poetry Hickory, editor of *Wild Goose Poetry Review* and *234*, and vice president of the Poetry Council of NC and the NC Poetry Society. Born and raised in Greenwood, SC, he teaches at Catawba Valley Community College in Hickory, NC.

NANCY POSEY of Hickory. North Carolina, is an English instructor, as well as a poet and voracious reader. Her first chapbook *Let the Ladies Speak* was published in January 2011.

Rescuing Libraries, her second chapbook was published by Dead Mule School of Southern Literature. She had published poems in *Referential Magazine, Wild Goose Poetry Review, Branches, Writer's Digest, First Light, Prompted* and other print and online publications. She serves on the board of the Poetry Council of North Carolina. Posey writes book reviews and blogs regularly at www.discriminatingreader.com.

SUSAN RICH is the author of three collections of poetry, *The Alchemist's Kitchen*, named a finalist for the Foreword Prize and the Washington State Book Award, *Cures Include Travel*, and *The Cartographer's Tongue*, winner of the PEN USA Award for Poetry. *Cloud Pharmacy*, her fourth collection, will be published by White Pine Press in 2014. Along with Jared Hawkley and Brian Turner, Susan is co-editor of *The Strangest Theatres: Poets Crossing Borders* (2013) a selection of essays on poets who travel published by McSweeney's and the Poetry Foundation.

MARTHA SILANO is the author of three books of poetry: *What the Truth Tastes Like, Blue Positive,* and *The Little Office of the Immaculate Conception*, winner of the 2010 Saturnalia Books Poetry Prize, and a bronze metal winner in *Foreword Magazine*'s 2011 Book of the Year Awards. Her poems have appeared or are forthcoming in *North American Review, Paris Review, Kenyon Review,* and *American Poetry Review*, among others. Martha blogs at Blue Positive and teaches at Bellevue College.

TERRY WOLVERTON is the author of nine books of poetry, fiction and creative nonfiction. Her current project, *Wounded World*, is a linked collection of lyric essays about our spiritual disquietl she has been publishing these serially on a blog (www.woundedworldproject.com) in advance of print publication later this year. She is Affiliate Faculty in the MFA Writing Program at Antioch University Los Angeles.

MAGAZINES/ JOURNALS

Literary magazines and journals usually provide a poet's first publishing success. In fact, you shouldn't be thinking about book/chapbook publication until your poems have appeared in a variety of magazines, journals and zines (both print and online). This is the preferred way to develop an audience, build publishing credits and learn the ins and outs of the publishing process.

In this section you'll find hundreds of magazines and journals that publish poetry. They range from small black-and-white booklets produced on home computers to major periodicals with high production values and important reputations. To help you sort through these markets and direct your submissions most effectively, we've organized information in each listing according to a basic format.

GETTING STARTED, FINDING MARKETS

If you don't have a certain magazine or journal in mind, read randomly through the listings, making notes as you go. (Don't hesitate to write in the margins, underline, use highlighters; it also helps to flag markets that interest you with Post-It Notes). Browsing the listings is an effective way to familiarize yourself with the kind of information presented and the publishing opportunities that are available at various skill levels. If you have a specific market in mind, however, begin with the General Index.

THE NEXT STEP

Once you know how to interpret the listings in this section and identify markets for your work, the next step is to start submitting your poems.

2RIVER VIEW

7474 Drexel Dr., University City MO 63130. **E-mail:** long@2River.org. **E-mail:** su3m1t@2river.org. **Website:** www.2River.org. **Contact:** Richard Long. *2River View*, published quarterly online, restricts each issue to ten poets. Claims first electronic rights and first North American rights, "meaning that publications here at 2River must be the first publication to feature the work online and/or in print." Publishes ms 3 months after acceptance. Guidelines on website. **MAGAZINE'S NEEDS** Submit up to 5 poems once per reading period. Paste in body of an e-mail. "We prefer poems with these qualities: image, subtlety, and point of view; a surface of worldly exactitude, as well as a depth of semantic ambiguity; and a voice that negotiates with its body of predecessors."

AASRA PUNJABI ENGLISH MAGAZINE

22619 97th Ave. S, Kent WA 98031. **E-mail:** aasra@q.com. **Contact:** Sarab Singh, editor. *"Aasra Punjabi English Magazine*, published bimonthly, features current events mainly Indian, but have featured others, too, of interest. Also features interviews, yoga, and other articles, and poetry." Acquires one-time rights. Rights revert to poet upon publication. Time between acceptance and publication is 2 months. Sometimes comments on rejected poems. Guidelines in magazine.

Magazine: Measures approximately 8.5x11, press printed, staple bound, includes ads. Single copy cost $3 (postage); subscription: $20/year. Page count varies. "The magazine is distributed free in the Seattle area and available through other libraries. We charge $3 per copy for postage and handling or $2 per copy if purchased more than 10 copies. Please send $3 for each poem. We will print 1 poem per issue. Back issue is $2 per copy." Best Poem of the Year is awarded one-year free subscription. Has published poetry by Joan Robers, Elizabeth Tallmadge, Carmen Arhiveleta.
MAGAZINE'S NEEDS Submit 1-2 small poems at a time. Cover letter is required. Include SASE, name, address, telephone number, and e-mail address with age and sex on cover letter. Include a short bio. "If interested we can print 'About the Poet' also along with the poem." Reads submissions year round. Sometimes publishes theme issues.

CONTEST/AWARD OFFERINGS Best Poem of the Year is awarded one-year free subscription.

ABLE MUSE

467 Saratoga Ave., #602, San Jose CA 95129-1326. **Website:** www.ablemuse.com. **Contact:** Alex Pepple, editor. *"Able Muse: A Review of Poetry, Prose & Art* published twice/year, predominantly publishes metrical poetry complemented by art and photography, fiction and nonfiction including essays, book reviews, and interviews with a focus on metrical and formal poetry. We are looking for well-crafted poems of any length or subject that employ skillful and imaginative use of meter and rhyme, executed in a contemporary idiom, that reads as naturally as your free verse poems." Acquires first rights. Time between acceptance and publication is 3 months. Sometimes comments on rejected poems. Responds in 4 months. Sometimes sends prepublication galleys.

Considers poetry by teens. "High levels of craft still required even for teen writers." Has published poetry by Mark Jarman, A.E. Stallings, Annie Finch, Rhina P. Espaillat, Rachel Hadas, and R.S. Gwynn. Receives about 1,500 poems/year, accepts about 5%. Subscription: $22 for 1 year. Also sponsors 2 annual contests: The Able Muse Write Prize for Poetry & Fiction, and The Able Muse Book Award for Poetry (in collaboration with Able Muse Press at www.ablemusepress.com). See website for details.
MAGAZINE'S NEEDS Submit 1-5 poems and short bio. No previously published poems or simultaneous submissions. Electronic submissions only welcome through the online form at www.ablemuse.com/submit, or by e-mail to editor@ablemuse.com. "The e-mail submission method is being phased out. We strongly encourage using the online submission method." Will not accept postal submissions. Reviews books of poetry. Send materials for review consideration.

ABRAXAS

P.O. Box 260113, Madison WI 53726-0113. **E-mail:** abraxaspress@hotmail.com. **Website:** www.abraxaspressinc.com/Welcome.html. **Contact:** Ingrid Swanberg, editor-in-chief. *ABRAXAS*, published "irregularly; 9- to 12-month intervals or much longer," is interested in poetry that's "contemporary lyric, experimental, and poetry in translation. When submitting translations, please include poems in the original language. *ABRAXAS'* new format features longer selections of fewer contributors." Does not want "political posing; academic regurgitations." Has published poetry by Ivan Argüelles, Denise Levertov, Ceésar Vallejo, d.a. levy, T.L. Kryss, and Andrea Moorhead. *ABRAXAS* is up to 80 pages, digest-sized, litho-offset-printed, flat-spined, with matte or glossy card cover with original art and photography. Press run is 700. Subscription: $16 (4 issues). Sample: $4 USD plus $1.90 s&h. Guidelines online.

MAGAZINE'S NEEDS Submit 7-10 poems along with SASE. No electronic submissions. Payment is contributer's copy and 40% discount on additional copies.

ABZ

P.O. Box 2746, Huntington WV 25727. **E-mail:** editor@abzpress.onmicrosoft.com. **Website:** http://abzpress.sharepoint.com/Pages/default.aspx. Sample copy for $8. Guidelines online.

MAGAZINE'S NEEDS *ABZ*, published annually, wants poetry using interesting and exciting language. Submit 1 to 6 poems at a time with SASE. Does not consider e-mail submissions. Pays in contributor's copies.

TIPS "We want to read your best poems."

ACM (ANOTHER CHICAGO MAGAZINE)

P.O. Box 408439, Chicago IL 60640. **E-mail:** editors@anotherchicagomagazine.net. **Website:** www.anotherchicagomagazine.net. **Contact:** Jacob S. Knabb, editor-in-chief; Caroline Eick Kasner, managing editor. "*Another Chicago Magazine* is a biannual literary magazine that publishes work by both new and established writers. We look for work that goes beyond the artistic and academic to include and address the larger world. The editors read submissions in fiction, poetry, creative nonfiction, etc. year round. We often publish special theme issues and sections. We will post upcoming themes on our website. Fiction: Short stories and novel excerpts of 15-20 pages or less. Poetry: Usually no more than 4 pages. Creative Nonfiction: Usually no more than 20 pages. Et Al.: Work that doesn't quite fit into the other genres such as Word & Image Texts, Satire, and Interviews." Responds in 3 months to queries; 6 months to mss. Sample copy available for $8.

Work published in *ACM* has been included frequently in *The Best American Poetry* and *The Pushcart Prize*.

MAGAZINE'S NEEDS Submit 3-4 typed poems at a time, usually no more than 4 pages. Considers simultaneous submissions with notification; no previously published poems. Reads submissions year-round. Guidelines available on website; however, "The best way to know what we publish is to read what we publish. If you haven't read *ACM* before, order a sample copy to know if your work is appropriate." Responds in 3 months. Sends prepublication galleys. Pays monetary amount "if funds permit," and/or one contributor's copy and one-year subscription. Acquires first serial rights. Reviews books of poetry in 250-800 words. Send materials for review consideration. No more than 4 pages.

TIPS "Support literary publishing by subscribing to at least one literary journal—if not ours, another. Get used to rejection slips, and don't get discouraged. Keep introductory letters short. Make sure manuscript has name and address on every page, and that it is clean, neat and proofread. We are looking for stories with freshness and originality in subject angle and style, and work that encounters the world."

ACORN

OutOfPocket Press, 115 Conifer Lane, Walnut Creek CA 94598. **E-mail:** acornhaiku@gmail.com. **Website:** www.acornhaiku.com. **Contact:** Susan Antolin, editor. "Biannual magazine dedicated to publishing the best of contemporary English language haiku, and in particular to showcasing individual poems that reveal the extraordinary moments found in everyday life." Buys first rights, buys one-time rights. Publishes ms an average of 1-3 months after acceptance. Reads submissions in January-February and July-August only. Responds in 3 weeks to mss. Guidelines and sample poems available online at www.acornhaiku.com.

MAGAZINE'S NEEDS "Decisions made by editor on a rolling basis. Poems judged purely on merit." Sometimes acceptance conditional on minor edits. Often comments on rejected poems. Accepts submissions via mail or e-mail, however e-mail is preferred. "Does *not* want epigrams, musings, and overt emotion poured into 17 syllables; surreal, science fiction, or political commentary 'ku;' strong puns or raunchy humor. A 5-7-5 syllable count is not necessary or encouraged." Length: 1-5 lines; 17 or fewer syllables.

TIPS "This is primarily a journal for those with a focused interest in haiku. It is a much richer genre than one might surmise from many of the recreational websites that claim to promote 'haiku.'"

ACUMEN MAGAZINE

Ember Press, 6 The Mount, Higher Furzeham, Brixham, South Devon TQ5 8QY, United Kingdom. **E-mail:** patriciaoxley6@gmail.com. **Website:** www.acumen-poetry.co.uk. **Contact:** Patricia Oxley, general editor. *Acumen*, published 3 times/year in January, May, and September, is "a general literary magazine with emphasis on good poetry." Wants "well-crafted, high-quality, imaginative poems showing a sense of form." Does not want "experimental verse of an obscene type." Has published poetry by Ruth Padel, William Oxley, Hugo Williams, Peter Porter, Danielle Hope, and Leah Fritz. *Acumen* is 120 pages, A5, perfect-bound. Responds in 3 months. Submission guidelines online at website.

MAGAZINE'S NEEDS Submit 5-6 poems at a time. All submissions should be accompanied by SASE. Include name and address on each separate sheet. Doesn't accept e-mail submissions, but will send rejections, acceptances, proofs and other communications via e-mail overseas to dispense with IRCs and other international postage. Any poem that may have chance of publication is shortlisted and from list final poems are chosen. All other poems returned within 2 months. "If a reply is required, please send IRCs. One IRC for a decision, 3 IRCs if work is to be returned." Willing to reply by e-mail to save IRCs. Pays "by negotiation" and 1 contributor's copy.

TIPS "Read *Acumen* carefully to see what kind of poetry we publish. Also, read widely in many poetry magazines, and don't forget the poets of the past— they can still teach us a great deal."

THE ADIRONDACK REVIEW

Black Lawrence Press, 8405 Bay Parkway, Apt C8, Brooklyn NY 11214. **E-mail:** editors@theadirondackreview.com. **Website:** www.adirondackreview.homestead.com. **Contact:** Angela Leroux-Lindsey, editor; Kara Christenson, senior fiction editor; Nicholas Samaras, poetry editor. *The Adirondack Review*, published quarterly online, is a literary journal dedicated to quality free verse poetry and short fiction as well as book and film reviews, art, photography, and interviews. "We are open to both new and established writers. Our only requirement is excellence. We would like to publish more French and German poetry translations as well as original poems in these languages. We publish an eclectic mix of voices and styles, but all poems should show attention to craft. We are open to beginners who demonstrate talent, as well as established voices. The work should speak for itself." Responds to queries in 1-2 months. Responds to mss in 2-4 months.

Uses online submissions manager.

MAGAZINE'S NEEDS Submit 2-7 poems at a time. Submit via online submissions manager. Cover letter is preferred. Does not want "religious, overly sentimental, horror/gothic, rhyming, greeting card, pet-related, humor, or science fiction poetry."

TIPS "*The Adirondack Review* accepts submissions all year long, so send us your poetry, fiction, nonfiction, translation, reviews, interviews, and art and photography. Please note that we've recently shifted our submission management to Submittable."

ADVOCATE, PKA'S PUBLICATION

1881 Little Westkill Rd., Prattsville NY 12468. (518)299-3103. **Website:** Advocatepka.weebly.com; www.facebook.com/Advocate/PKAPublications; www.facebook.com/GaitedHorseAssociation. advoad@localnet.com. **Contact:** Patricia Keller, publisher. *Advocate, PKA's Publication*, published bimonthly, is an advertiser-supported tabloid using "original, previously unpublished works, such as feature stories, essays, 'think' pieces, letters to the editor, profiles, humor, fiction, poetry, puzzles, cartoons, or line drawings. Advocates for good writers and quality writings. We publish art, fiction, photos and poetry. *Advocate*'s submitters are talented people of all ages who do not earn their livings as writers. We wish to promote the arts and to give those we publish the opportunity to be published." Acquires first rights for mss, artwork, and photographs. Pays on publication with contributor's copies. Publishes ms 2-18 months after acceptance. Responds to queries in 6 weeks; mss in 2 months. Sample copy: $5 (includes guidelines). Subscription: $18.50 (6 issues). Previous three issues are on our website.

"This publication has a strong horse orientation." Includes Gaited Horse Association newsletter. Horse-oriented stories, poetry, art and photos are currently needed.

MAGAZINE'S NEEDS Wants "nearly any kind of poetry, any length." Occasionally comments on rejected poems. No religious or pornographic poetry. Pays 2 contributor copies.

TIPS "Please, no simultaneous submissions, work that has appeared on the Internet, pornography, overt religiosity, anti-environmentalism or gratuitous violence. Artists and photographers should keep in mind that we are a b&w paper. Please do not send postcards. Use envelope with SASE."

AFRICAN VOICES

African Voices Communications, Inc., 270 W. 96th St., New York NY 10025. (212)865-2982. **Fax:** (212)316-3335. **E-mail:** africanvoicesmag@gmail.com. **Website:** www.africanvoices.com. *African Voices*, published quarterly, is an "art and literary magazine that highlights the work of people of color. We publish ethnic literature and poetry on any subject. We also consider all themes and styles: avant-garde, free verse, haiku, light verse, and traditional. We do not wish to limit the reader or author." Buys first North American serial rights. Pays on publication. Publishes ms an average of 3-6 months after acceptance. Responds in 3 months to queries. Editorial lead time 3 months. Sample copy for $5.

Considers poetry written by children. Has published poetry by Reg E. Gaines, Maya Angelou, Jessica Care Moore, Asha Bandele, Tony Medina, and Louis Reyes Rivera. *African Voices* is about 48 pages, magazine-sized, professionally printed, saddle-stapled, with paper cover. Receives about 100 submissions/year, accepts about 30%. Press run is 20,000. Single copy: $4; subscription: $12.

MAGAZINE'S NEEDS Submit no more than 2 poems at any 1 time. Accepts previously published poems and simultaneous submissions. Accepts submissions by e-mail (in text box), by fax, and by postal mail. Cover letter and SASE required. Seldom comments on rejected poems. Responds in 3 months. Pays 2 copies. Acquires first or one-time rights. Reviews books of poetry in 500-1,000 words. Send materials for review consideration to Layding Kaliba. Sponsors periodic poetry contests and readings. Send SASE for details. Length: 5-100 lines. Pays in contributor copies.

TIPS "A ms stands out if it is neatly typed with a well-written and interesting story line or plot. Originality is encouraged. We are interested in more horror, erotic, and drama pieces. *AV* wants to highlight the diversity in our culture. Stories must touch the hu-

manity in us all. We strongly encourage new writers/poets to send in their work. Accepted contributors are encouraged to subscribe."

A GATHERING OF THE TRIBES

P.O. Box 20693, Tompkins Square Station, New York NY 10009. (212)674-3778. **Fax:** (212)388-9813. **E-mail:** info@tribes.org. **Website:** www.tribes.org. **Contact:** Steve Cannon. *A Gathering of the Trees* is a multicultural and multigenerational publication featuring poetry, fiction, interviews, essays, visual art, musical scores. Audience is anyone interested in the arts from a diverse perspective." Publishes ms 3-6 months after acceptance. Sample copy for $15. Guidelines on website.

Magazine: 8 1/2x10; 130 pages; glossy paper and cover; illustrations; photos. Receives 20 unsolicited mss/month. Publishes 40% new writers/year. Has published work by Carl Watson, Ishle Park, Wang Pang, and Hanif Kureishi. Sponsors awards/contests.

MAGAZINE'S NEEDS Submit 5 poems maximum. Send SASE for reply, return of poetry or send a disposable copy of ms. Accepts simultaneous submissions. No metrical or rhyming poetry, "unless it is exceedingly contemporary/experimental."

TIPS "Make sure your work has substance."

AGNI

Creative Writing Program, Boston University, 236 Bay State Rd., Boston MA 02215. (617)353-7135. **Fax:** (617)353-7134. **E-mail:** agni@bu.edu. **Website:** www.agnimagazine.org. **Contact:** Sven Birkerts, editor. "Eclectic literary magazine publishing first-rate poems, essays, translations, and stories." Buys serial rights. Rights to reprint in *AGNI* anthology (with author's consent). Pays on publication. Publishes ms an average of 6 months after acceptance. Responds in 2 weeks to queries. Responds in 4 months to mss. Editorial lead time 1 year. Sample copy for $10 or online. Guidelines available online.

Reading period is September 1-May 31 only. Online magazine carries original content not found in print edition. All submissions are considered for both. Founding editor Askold Melnyczuk won the 2001 Nora Magid Award for Magazine Editing. Work from *AGNI* has been included and cited regularly in the *Pushcart Prize* and *Best American* anthologies.

MAGAZINE'S NEEDS Submit no more than 5 poems at a time. Considers simultaneous submissions; no previously published poems. No e-mail submissions. Cover letter is required ("brief, sincere"). "No fancy fonts, gimmicks. Include SASE or e-mail address; no preformatted reply cards." Pays $20/page up to $150.

TIPS "We're also looking for extraordinary translations from little-translated languages. It is important to read work published in *AGNI* before submitting, to see if your own might be compatible."

● AGNIESZKA'S DOWRY (AGD)

A Small Garlic Press (ASGP), 5445 Sheridan Rd., #3003, Chicago IL 60640. **E-mail:** marek@enteract.com; ketzle@ketzle.net. **Website:** http://asgp.org. **Contact:** Marek Lugowski and Katrina Grace Craig, co-editors. *"Agnieszka's Dowry (AgD)* is an innovative installation of mostly contemporary and mostly not yet famous literary texts (poems, letters to Agnieszka, occasional short short stories), computer and freehand art, photography and more. The magazine ispublished both in print and online. The print version consists of professionally crafted chapbooks. The online version comprises fast-loading pages employing an intuitive, if uncanny, navigation in an interesting space, all conducive to fast and comfortable reading. No restrictions on form or type. We use contextual and juxtapositional tie-ins with other material in making choices, so visiting the online *AgD* or reading a chapbook of an *AgD* issue is required of anyone making a submission." S Acquires one-time rights where applicable. Responds by e-mail or SASE, usually within 2 months.

〇 Sized 5.5 inch by 8.5 inch, stapled, 20-60 pages. "We use heavy opaque white laser paper, covered with appropriate card stock for cover, saddle-stitched (stapled), with cover art and often with internal art, in grayscale." ingle copy: $3 plus $5 shipping, if ordered from website. Make checks payable to A Small Garlic Press.

MAGAZINE'S NEEDS Submit 5-10 poems at a time. Accepts e-mail submissions only (NOTE: pasted into body of message in plain text, sent to both editors simultaneously; no attachments). "We ask you to read well into *Agnieszka's Dowry*, and to fit your submissions to the partially filled content of its open issues." Pays 1 contributor's copy.

ADDITIONAL INFORMATION A Small Garlic Press (ASGP) publishes up to 3 chapbooks of poetry/year. Query with a full online ms, ASCII (plain text) only.

〇 THE AGUILAR EXPRESSION

1329 Gilmore Ave., Donora PA 15033. (724)379-8019. **E-mail:** xyz0@access995.com. **Website:** www.word-runner.com/xfaguilar. **Contact:** Xavier F. Aguilar, editor/publisher. *The Aguilar Expression*, published annually in October, encourages "poetics that deal with now, which our readers can relate to. Has published poetry by Martin Kich and Gail Ghai. *The Aguilar Expression* is 4-20 pages, 8x11, typeset, printed on 20 lb. paper. Receives about 10-15 poems/month, accepts about 10-15/year. Circulation is 150. Sample: $5. Make checks payable to Xavier Aguilar. Submit up to 5 poems at a time. Lines/poem: 30 maximum. No e-mail submissions. Cover letter is required (include writing background). SASE (for contact purposes) is required. Manuscripts should be submitted in clear, camera-ready copy. Submit copies, not originals; mss will not be returned. "We encourage all writers to send a SASE for writer's guidelines before submitting." Responds in 2 months.

〇 "In publishing poetry, I try to exhibit the unique reality that we too often take for granted and acquaint as mediocre."

MAGAZINE'S NEEDS Submit up to 5 poems at a time. Lines/poem: 30 maximum. No e-mail submissions. Cover letter is required (include writing background). SASE (for contact purposes) is required. Mss should be submitted in clear, camera-ready copy. Submit copies, not originals; mss will not be returned. "We encourage all writers to send a SASE for writer's guidelines before submitting." Pays 2 contributor's copies.

❶ ALBATROSS

The Anabiosis Press, 2 South New St., Bradford MA 01835. (978)469-7085. **E-mail:** rsmyth@anabiosispress.org. **Website:** www.anabiosispress.org. **Contact:** Richard Smyth, editor. *Albatross*, published "as soon as we have accepted enough quality poems to publish an issue—about 1 per year," considers the albatross "to be a metaphor for the environment. The journal's title is drawn from Coleridge's *The Rime of the Ancient Mariner* and is intended to invoke the allegorical implications of that poem. This is not to say that we publish only environmental or nature poetry, but that we are biased toward such subject matter. We publish mostly free verse, and we prefer a narrative style." Acquires all rights. Returns rights provided that "previous publication in *Albatross* is mentioned in all subsequent reprintings." Time between acceptance and publication is up to 6 months to a year. Responds in 2-3 months to poems. Sample copy for $5. Guidelines available online.

○ *Albatross* is 28 pages, digest-sized, laser-typeset, with linen cover. Subscription: $8 for 2 issues. Has published poetry by Jody Azzouni, Joseph Bruchac, Don Russ, Adam Penna, and George Looney.

MAGAZINE'S NEEDS Submit 3-5 poems at a time. No simultaneous submissions. Accepts e-mail submissions if included in body of message (but is "often quicker at returning mailed submissions"). Name and address must accompany e-mail submissions. Cover letter is not required. "We do, however, need bio notes and SASE for return or response. Poems should be typed single-spaced, with name, address, and phone number in upper left corner." Wants "poetry written in a strong, mature voice that conveys a deeply felt experience or makes a powerful statement." Does not want "rhyming poetry, prose poetry, or haiku." Lines/poem: 200 maximum. Pays 1 contributor's copy.

◑ ALIMENTUM, THE LITERATURE OF FOOD

P.O. Box 210028, Nashville TN 37221. **E-mail:** editor@alimentumjournal.com. **Website:** www.alimentumjournal.com. **Contact:** Paulette Licitra, publisher/editor-in-chief; Peter Selgin, fiction & nonfiction editor; Cortney Davis, poetry editor. *Alimentum* is 128 pages, perfect-bound, with matte coated cover with 4-color art, interior b&w illustration includes ads. Contains illustrations. "All of our stories, poems and essays have food or drink as a theme." Semiannual. "We do not read year-round. Check website for reading periods." Acquires First North American Serial rights. Rights revert to poets upon publication. Responds in 1-3 months to mss. Sample copy $10. Guidelines available online.

MAGAZINE'S NEEDS *Alimentum, The Literature of Food*, published semiannually in winter and summer, is "the only literary journal all about food." Has published poetry by Dick Allen, Stephen Gibson, Carly Sachs, Jen Karetnik, Virginia Chase Sutton. Publishes an annual broadside of "menu poems" for restaurants during National Poetry Month in April. Pays contributor copy.

TIPS "No e-mail submissions, only snail mail. Mark outside envelope to the attention of Poetry, Fiction, or Nonfiction Editor."

◑◉ ALIVE NOW

1908 Grand Ave., P.O. Box 340004, Nashville TN 37203. (615)340-7254. **Fax:** (615)340-7267. **E-mail:** alivenow@upperroom.org. **Website:** www.alivenow.org; www.upperroom.org. **Contact:** Beth A. Richardson, editor. *Alive Now*, published bimonthly, is a devotional magazine that invites readers to enter an ever-deepening relationship with God. "*Alive Now* seeks to nourish people who are hungry for a sacred way of living. Submissions should invite readers to see God in the midst of daily life by exploring how contemporary issues impact their faith lives. Each word must be vivid and dynamic and contribute to the whole. We make selections based on a list of upcoming themes. Manuscripts which do not fit a theme will be returned." Considers avant-garde and free verse. *Alive Now* is 64 pages. Accepts 20 poems/year. Circulation is 70,000. Subscription: $17.95/year (6 issues); $26.95 for 2 years (12 issues). Additional subscription information, including foreign rates, available on website. Pays on acceptance. Guidelines online at website.

MAGAZINE'S NEEDS Submissions should invite readers to seek God in the midst of daily life by exploring how contemporary issues impact their faith lives. If ms does not fit a theme, it will not be considered. Themes can be found on website. Prefers electronic submissions, pasted into body of e-mail or attached as Word document. Postal submissions should include SASE. Include name, address, theme on each sheet. Payment will be made at the time of acceptance for publication. "We will notify contributors of manuscript status when we make final decisions for an issue, approximately two months before the issue date." Pays $35 or more on acceptance.

⊕ ALL GENRES LITERARY MAGAZINE

E-mail: editor@allgenres24.com. **Website:** www.mikesharlowwritercom.fatcow.com/allgenres24. **Contact:** Michael Miller, managing editor; Elizabeth Miller. "*All Genres* means we accept any writing as long as we like it. We are very open to new and emerging writers. Your chances of publication in *All Genres* is presently about 50/50. So send us your work! *All Genres Literary Magazine* is an independent online periodical not affiliated with or sponsored by any educational system's creative writing program. It is funded by donations and small fees." Buys first North American serial and electronic rights. Publishes ms 3 months after acceptance. Responds to queries in 1 month; mss in 3 months. Editorial lead time 1 month. Sample copy and guidelines available online at website.

MAGAZINE'S NEEDS Submit no more than 5 poems at a time. Length: no more than 1,000 words.

TIPS "We are seeking anything that trips our triggers. It can be literary, fantasy, science fiction, speculative fiction, erotic, Western. . . We believe that good writing is not genre specific. Accepted pieces will be published on the website and may be published in an annual hard-copy issue."

◐◉ AMAZE: THE CINQUAIN JOURNAL

10529 Olive St., Temple City CA 91780. **E-mail:** cinquains@hotmail.com. **Website:** www.amaze-cinquain.com. **Contact:** Deborah P. Kolodji, editor. *AMAZE: The Cinquain Journal*, published bi-anually online, is a literary webzine devoted to the cinquain poetry form. Wants American cinquains as invented by Adelaide Crapsey (5 lines with a 2-4-6-8-2 syllable pattern) and cinquain variations (mirror cinquains, crown cinquains, cinquain sequences, etc.). Has published poetry by an'ya, Ann K. Schwader, Michael McClintock, naia, and Denis Garrison. Receives about 1,500 poems/year, accepts about 100. Acquires one-time rights. Rsponds in 6 weeks. Guidelines available for SASE or on website.

MAGAZINE'S NEEDS Submit 1-5 poems at a time. "E-mail submissions preferred, with poems in the body of the e-mail. Do not send attachments." Include SASE with postal mail submissions. "Poems are evaluated on quality, form, and content." Often comments on rejected poems.

◑◐◉ AMBIT

17 Priory Gardens, Highgate, London N6 5QY, United Kingdom. **E-mail:** info@ambitmagazine.co.uk. **Website:** www.ambitmagazine.co.uk. **Contact:** Edwin Brock, Carol Ann Duffy, and Henry Graham, Poetry Editors. *Ambit* magazine is a literary and artwork quarterly created in London, published in the UK, and read internationally. *Ambit* is put together entirely from unsolicited, previously unpublished poetry and short fiction submissions. Responds in

3-4 months. Sample copy £9. Guidelines available in magazine or online.

MAGAZINE'S NEEDS No previously published poems or simultaneous submissions. Poems should be typed, double-spaced. Never comments on rejected poems. Staff reviews books of poetry. Send materials for review consideration to review editor. Does not accept e-mail submissions. Does not want "indiscriminately centre-justified poems; jazzy fonts; poems all in italics for the sake of it." Pays small token plus 2 contributor copies.

TIPS "Read a copy of the magazine before submitting!"

◑ THE AMERICAN DISSIDENT: A JOURNAL OF LITERATURE, DEMOCRACY & DISSIDENCE

217 Commerce Rd., Barnstable MA 02630. **E-mail:** todslone@hotmail.com. **Website:** www.theamericandissident.org. **Contact:** G. Tod Slone, editor. Journal, published 2 times/year, provides "a forum for, amongst other things, criticism of the academic/literary established order, which clearly discourages vigorous debate, cornerstone of democracy, to the evident detriment of American Literature. The Journal seeks rare poets daring to risk going against that established-order grain." Wants "poetry, reviews, artwork, and short (1,000 words) essays in English, French, or Spanish, written on the edge with a dash of personal risk and stemming from personal experience, conflict with power, and/or involvement." Submissions should be "iconoclastic and parrhesiastic in nature." Acquires First North American serial rights. Publishes ms 2 months after acceptance. Responds in 1 month. Guidelines available for SASE.

◗ Magazine: 56-64 pages, digest-sized, offset-printed, perfect-bound, with card cover. Press run is 200. Single copy: $9; subscriptions: individuals, $18; institutions $20. Almost always comments on rejected poems. Pays 1 contributor's copy. Reviews books/chapbooks of poetry and other magazines in 250 words, single-book format. Send materials for review consideration.

MAGAZINE'S NEEDS Submit 3 poems at a time. Considers simultaneous submissions; no previously published poems. E-mail submissions from subscribers only. "Far too many poets submit without even reading the guidelines. Include SASE and cover letter containing not credits, but rather personal dissident information, as well as incidents that provoked you to 'go upright and vital, and speak the rude truth in all ways' (Emerson)." Acquires first North American serial rights. Reviews books/chapbooks of poetry and other magazines in 250 words, single-book format. Send materials for review consideration. Pays 1 contributor's copy.

AMERICAN LETTERS AND COMMENTARY

Department of English, University of Texas at San Antonio, One UTSA Circle, San Antonio TX 78249. **E-mail:** amerletters@satx.rr.com. **Website:** www. amletters.org. "Only previously unpublished work is considered. We publish creative nonfiction essays and critical essays with experimental slant/subject matter." Publishes ms an average of 1 year after acceptance. Guidelines available on website.

MAGAZINE'S NEEDS Length: 10 pages. Pays 1 contributor's copy.

TIPS "Our reading period is October 1-March 1. A brief cover letter is always welcome. Read a recent issue before submitting—75% of submissions are rejected because they don't fit the journal's aesthetic or don't comply with our guidelines. No e-mailed submissions. We will make contact via e-mail by September 1 for forthcoming issue inclusions. Include an e-mail address in your contact info. All rights are returned to author upon publication."

ⓞ AMERICAN LITERARY REVIEW

University of North Texas, P.O. Box 311307, Denton TX 76203-1307. (940)565-2755. **Fax:** (940)565-4355. **E-mail:** americanliteraryreview@gmail.com; bond@ unt.edu. **Website:** www.engl.unt.edu/alr. "The *American Literary Review* welcomes submissions of previously unpublished poems, short stories, and creative nonfiction. We also accept submissions for cover art. Please include an SASE and cover letter with your submission. Also include enough postage to return your work. Please mark envelopes and cover letters 'Fiction,' 'Poetry,' or 'Nonfiction.' Simultaneous submissions are acceptable if noted in your cover letter. For any questions not covered in this section, please refer to our 'Frequently Asked Questions' page. Our reading period extends from October 1 to May 1. Unsolicited manuscripts received outside this reading period will be returned unread. Online submissions areaccepted via the website. Submissions should be directed to the appropriate editor (Fiction, Poetry, Nonfiction, or Art)." Responds in 2-4 months to mss. Sample copy for $8. Writer's guidelines for #10 SASE.

MAGAZINE'S NEEDS *American Literary Review*, published semi-annually, considers all forms and modes of poetry, creative nonfiction, and fiction. "We are especially interested in originality, substance, imaginative power, and lyric intensity." Has published poetry by Kathleen Pierce, Mark Irwin, Stephen Dunn, William Olsen, David St. John, and Cate Marvin. *American Literary Review* is about 120 pages, digest-sized, attractively printed, perfect-bound, with color card cover with photo. Subscription: $14/year, $26 for 2 years. Sample: $8.

HOW TO CONTACT No fax submissions. Online submissions welcomed. Cover letter is required. Include author's name, address, phone number, and poem titles. Reads mss October 1-May 1. Guidelines available on website. Responds in up to 3 months. Pays 2 contributor's copies. Considers simultaneous submissions.

CONTEST/AWARD OFFERINGS Check website for contest details.

TIPS "We encourage writers and artists to examine our journal. The *American Literary Review* publishes semi-annually. If you would like to subscribe to our journal, subscription rates run $14 for a 1-year subscription, $26 for a 2-year subscription, and $36 for a 3-year subscription. You may also obtain a sample copy of the *American Literary Review* for $7 plus $1 per issue for shipping and handling in the U.S. and Canada ($2 for postage elsewhere)."

ⓞ THE AMERICAN POETRY JOURNAL

P. O. Box 2080, Aptos CA 95001-2080. **E-mail:** editor@americanpoetryjournal.com. **Website:** www. americanpoetryjournal.com. **Contact:** J.P. Dancing Bear, senior editor. *The American Poetry Journal*, published annually (July), seeks "to publish work using poetic device, favoring image, metaphor, and good sound. We like alliteration, extended metaphors, image, movement, and poems that can pass the 'so what' test. *The American Poetry Journal* has in mind the reader who delights in discovering what a poem can do to the tongue and what the poem paints on the cave of the mind." Wants poems "that exhibit strong, fresh imagery, metaphor, and good sound." Does not want "narratives about family, simplistic verse, annoying word hodge-podges." Acquires first rights. Publishes ms 2-6 months after acceptance. Responds in 3 months. Guidelines available on website.

◐ Accepts submissions through online submission form only.

MAGAZINE'S NEEDS Submit 3-5 poems at a time. Electronic submissions only. Cover letter is preferred. Considers unsolicited submissions February 1-May 31—All decisions made no later than June 30. (Poets may submit no more than twice during the reading period). "Poems are read first for clarity and technique, then read aloud for sound quality." Pays 1 contributor's copy.

TIPS "Know the magazine you are submitting to, before you commit your work and yourself. It's not that difficult, but it helps your odds when the editor can tell that you get what the magazine is about. Reading an issue is the easiest way to do this."

THE AMERICAN POETRY REVIEW

1700 Sansom St., Suite 800, Philadelphia PA 19103. **E-mail:** sberg@aprweb.org. **Website:** www.aprweb. org. **Contact:** Stephen Berg, editor. Acquires first serial rights. Responds in 3 months.

◐ Accepts mss via postal mail only.

MAGAZINE'S NEEDS Submit with SASE.

CONTEST/AWARD OFFERINGS "The Jerome J. Shestack Poetry Prizes of $1,000 are awarded annually to each of 2 poets whose work has appeared in APR during the preceding calendar year."

⬤ AMERICAN TANKA

E-mail: laura@lauramaffei.com. **Website:** www. americantanka.com. "*American Tanka* seeks to present the best and most well-crafted English-language tanka being written today, in a visually calm space that allows the reader's eye to focus on the single poem and linger in the moment it evokes." Acquires first North American serial rights. Responds in 3 months.

MAGAZINE'S NEEDS *American Tanka* is devoted to single English-language tanka. Wants "concise and vivid language, good crafting, and echo of the original Japanese form, but with unique and contemporary content." Does not want "anything that's not tanka. No sequences or titled groupings." Has published poetry by Sanford Goldstein, Marianne Bluger, Jeanne Emrich, Tom Hartman, Larry Kimmel, Pamela Miller Ness, and George Swede. Submit up to 5 poems. No previously published poems or simultaneous submissions. Accepts submissions by online submission form found on website or by e-mail (pasted into body). Welcomes submissions

from anyone who has been writing tanka: experienced tanka poets, experienced poets in other forms, and novices. Seeks concise, well-crafted, 5-line tanka that evoke a specific moment in time.

⬤ⓢ ANCIENT PATHS

P.O. Box 7505, Fairfax Station VA 22039. **E-mail:** sklyarburris@yahoo.com. **Website:** www.editor-skylar.com. **Contact:** Skylar H. Burris, Editor. *Ancient Paths*, published biennially in odd-numbered years, provides "a forum for quality Christian poetry." Acquires one-time or reprint rights. Responds in 3-4 weeks "if rejected; longer if being seriously considered." Single copy: $5 for new e-book format; $10 for hard copy back issues. Make checks payable to Skylar Burris. Guidelines available for SASE or on website.

MAGAZINE'S NEEDS E-mail all submissions. Paste poems in e-mail message. Use the subject heading "AP Online Submission (title of your work)." Include your name and e-mail address at the top of your e-mail. Poems may be rhymed, unrhymed, free verse, or formal. Does not want 'preachy' poetry, inconsistent meter, or forced rhyme; no stream of conscious or avant-garde work; no esoteric academic poetry. Length: no more than 40 lines. "Payment for online publication will be $1.25 for the first work and $0.75 for each additional work accepted."

TIPS "Read the great religious poets: John Donne, George Herbert, T.S. Eliot, Lord Tennyson. Remember not to preach. This is a literary magazine, not a pulpit. This does not mean you do not communicate morals or celebrate God. It means you are not overbearing or simplistic when you do so."

⬤ⓒ ANDERBO.COM

Anderbo Publishing, 270 Lafayette St., Suite 705, New York NY 10012-3364. **E-mail:** editors@anderbo.com. **Website:** www.anderbo.com. **Contact:** Rick Rofihe, editor-in-chief. Online literary magazine/journal. "Quality fiction, poetry, 'fact' and photography on a website with 'print-feel' design." Member CLMP. Acquires first rights, first North American serial rights, one-time rights, electronic rights. Publication is copyrighted. Publishes ms 1 month after acceptance. Responds to queries in 2 weeks. Responds to mss in 1-4 weeks. Considers simultaneous submissions. Editorial lead time 1-2 months. Guidelines available on website.

○ Received the Best New Online Magazine or Journal, *storySouth* Million Writers Award in 2005.

MAGAZINE'S NEEDS "We are looking for serious, affecting work." Publishes 40 poems/year. Send complete ms. "We prefer your poems to be in the e-mail or together as a single attachment." Length: 6-60 lines. Does not pay.

TIPS "We are looking for fiction that is unique, urgent, accessible and involving. Look at our site and read what we've already published."

○⑤ THE ANTIGONISH REVIEW

St. Francis Xavier University, P.O. Box 5000, Antigonish NS B2G 2W5, Canada. (902)867-3962. **Fax:** (902)867-5563. **E-mail:** tar@stfx.ca. **Website:** www.antigonishreview.com. **Contact:** Bonnie McIsaac, office manager. Rights retained by author. Pays on publication. Publishes ms an average of 8 months after acceptance. Responds in 1 month to queries; 6 months to mss. Editorial lead time 4 months. Sample copy for $7 or online. Guidelines for #10 SASE or online.

MAGAZINE'S NEEDS *The Antigonish Review*, published quarterly, tries "to produce the kind of literary and visual mosaic that the modern sensibility requires or would respond to." Open to poetry on any subject written from any point of view and in any form. However, writers should expect their work to be considered within the full context of old and new poetry in English and other languages. No more than 6-8 poems should be submitted at any one time. A preferable submission would be from 3-4 poems. No previously published poems or simultaneous submissions. Has published poetry by Andy Wainwright, W.J. Keith, Michael Hulse, Jean McNeil, M. Travis Lane, and Douglas Lochhead. Submit 6-8 poems at a time. Lines/poem: not over 80, i.e., 2 pages. Pays $10/page to a maximum of $50 and 2 contributor's copies. Acquires first North American serial rights.

TIPS "Send for guidelines and/or sample copy. Send ms with cover letter and SASE with submission."

○⑤ ANTIOCH REVIEW

P.O. Box 148, Yellow Springs OH 45387-0148. **E-mail:** mkeyes@antiochreview.org. **Website:** www.antiochreview.org. **Contact:** Robert S. Fogarty, editor; Judith Hall, poetry editor. Literary and cultural review of contemporary issues, and literature for general readership. *The Antioch Review* "is an independent quarterly of critical and creative thought. For well

over 70 years, creative authors, poets, and thinkers have found a friendly reception—regardless of formal reputation. We get far more poetry than we can possibly accept, and the competition is keen. Here, where form and content are so inseparable and reaction is so personal, it is difficult to state requirements or limitations. Studying recent issues of *The Antioch Review* should be helpful." Has published poetry by Richard Howard, Jacqueline Osherow, Alice Fulton, Richard Kenney, and others. Receives about 3,000 submissions/year. Pays on publication. Publishes ms an average of 10 months after acceptance. Responds in 3-6 months to mss. Sample copy for $7. Guidelines available online.

○ Work published in the *Antioch Review* has been included frequently in *The Best American Stories, Best American Essays,* and *The Best American Poetry.* Finalist for National Magazine Award for essays in 2009 and 2011, and for fiction in 2010.

MAGAZINE'S NEEDS Submit 3-6 poems at a time. No previously published poems or simultaneous submissions. Include SASE with all submissions. No light or inspirational verse. Poetry submissions are not accepted between between May 1 and September 1. Pays $20/printed page, plus 2 contributor's copies.

○⑤ AOIFE'S KISS

The Speculative Fiction Foundation, P.O. Box 782, Cedar Rapids IA 52406. **E-mail:** aoifeskiss@yahoo.com. **Website:** www.samsdotpublishing.com. **Contact:** Tyree Campbell, managing editor. "*Aoife's Kiss* is a print and online magazine of fantasy, science fiction, horror, sword & sorcery, and slipstream, published quarterly in March, June, September, and December. *Aoife's Kiss* publishes short stories, poems, illustrations, articles, and movie/book/chapbook reviews, and interviews with noted individuals in those genres." Responds in 2 weeks to queries. Editorial lead time is 2 months.

MAGAZINE'S NEEDS Submit up to 5 poems at a time. E-mail submissions accepted with submission pasted into body of message. Length: less than 100 lines.

○ APALACHEE REVIEW

Apalachee Press, P.O. Box 10469, Tallahassee FL 32302. (850)644-9114. **E-mail:** arsubmissions@gmail.com (for queries outside of the U.S.). **Website:** apalacheereview.org. **Contact:** Michael Trammell, editor; Mary Jane Ryals, fiction editor. "At *Apalachee Review*, we are interested in outstanding literary fiction, but we especially like poetry, fiction, and nonfiction that addresses intercultural issues in a domestic or international setting/context." Annual. Acquires one-time rights, electronic rights. Publication is copyrighted. Pays on publication. Publishes mss 1 year after acceptance. Responds to queries in 4-6 weeks. Responds to mss in 3-14 months. Sometimes comments on/critiques rejected mss. Sample copy available for $8 for current issue; $5 for back issue. Guidelines available for SASE or on website.

○ *Apalachee Review* is 120 pages, digest-sized, professionally printed, perfect-bound, with card cover. Press run is 700. Subscription: $15 for 2 issues ($30 foreign). Includes photographs. Receives 60-100 mss/month. Accepts 5-10 mss/issue. Agented fiction: 0.5%. Publishes 1-2 new writers/year. Sample: $5. Has published Lu Vickers, Joe Clark, Joe Taylor, Jane Arrowsmith Edwards, Vivian Lawry, Linda Frysh, Charles Harper Webb, Reno Raymond Gwaltney. Member CLMP.

MAGAZINE'S NEEDS Submit 3-5 poems at a time. Considers simultaneous submissions. Accepts submissions by postal mail only. "Submit clear copies, with name and address on each." SASE required. Reads submissions year round. Staff reviews books of poetry. Send materials for review consideration. Has published poetry by Rita Mae Reese and Charles Harper Webb. Pays 2 contributor's copies.

● APPALACHIAN HERITAGE

CPO 2166, Berea KY 40404. (859)985-3699. **Fax:** (859)985-3903. **E-mail:** george_brosi@berea.edu; appalachianheritage@berea.edu. **Website:** http://community.berea.edu/appalachianheritage. **Contact:** George Brosi. "We are seeking poetry, short fiction, literary criticism and biography, book reviews, and creative nonfiction, including memoirs, opinion pieces, and historical sketches. Unless you request not to be considered, all poems, stories, and articles published in *Appalachian Heritage* are eligible for our annual Plattner Award. All honorees are rewarded with a sliding bookrack with an attached commemorative plaque from Berea College Crafts and First Place winners receive an additional stipend of $200." Author retains all rights. Responds in 1 month to queries; 6 months to mss. Guidelines available online at website.

MAGAZINE'S NEEDS Submit up to 8 short poems at one time. Length: up to 42 lines. "One-page poems cannot exceed 42 lines, and two-page poems cannot exceed 84 lines." Pays 3 contributor's copies.

TIPS "Sure, we are *Appalachian Heritage* and we do appreciate the past, but we are a forward-looking contemporary literary quarterly, and, frankly, we receive too many nostalgic submissions. Please spare us the "Papaw Was Perfect" poetry and the "Mamaw Moved Mountains" manuscripts and give us some hard-hitting prose, some innovative poetry, some inventive photography, and some original art. Help us be the ground-breaking, stimulating kind of quarterly we aspire to be."

●● APPLE VALLEY REVIEW: A JOURNAL OF CONTEMPORARY LITERATURE

88 South 3rd St., Suite 336, San Jose CA 95113. **E-mail:** editor@leahbrowning.net. **Website:** www.applevalleyreview.com. **Contact:** Leah Browning, editor. *Apple Valley Review: A Journal of Contemporary Literature*, published semiannually online, features "beautifully crafted poetry, short fiction, and essays." Wants "work that has both mainstream and literary appeal. All work must be original, previously unpublished, and in English. Translations are welcome if permission has been granted. Preference is given to short (under 2 pages), non-rhyming poetry." Does not want "erotica, work containing explicit language or violence, or work that is scholarly, critical, inspirational, or intended for children." Acquires first rights and first serial rights and retains the right to archive the work online for an indefinite period of time. "As appropriate, we may also choose to nominate published work for awards or recognition. Author retains all other rights." Time between acceptance and publication is 1-6 months. Sometimes comments on rejected poems and mss. Responds to mss in 1 week-2 months. Guidelines available on website.

○ Considers poetry by children and teens: "Our audience includes teens and adults of all ages." Has published poetry by Vince Corvaia, Michael Lauchlan, Jin Cordaro, Gregory Lawless, Anna Evans, and Keetje Kuipers. Receives about 5,000+ poems/year, accepts less than 1%.

MAGAZINE'S NEEDS Submit 1-6 poems at a time. Lines/poem: "no limit, though we prefer short poems (under 2 pages)." No previously published poems. Accepts e-mail submissions (pasted into body of message, with "poetry" in subject line); no disk submissions. Reads submissions year round. Offers the annual *Apple Valley Review* Editor's Prize. Award varies. "From 2006-2011, the prize was $100 and a book of poetry or fiction." Submit 1-6 poems. **Entry fee:** none. **Deadline:** rolling; all submissions to the *Apple Valley Review*, and all work published during a given calendar year will be considered for the prize.

CONTEST/AWARD OFFERINGS Offers the annual *Apple Valley Review* Editor's Prize. Award varies. "From 2006-2011, the prize was $100 and a book of poetry or fiction." Submit 2-6 poems. **Entry fee:** none. **Deadline:** rolling; all submissions to the *Apple Valley Review*, and all work published during a given calendar year will be considered for the prize.

☺ ARC

Arc Poetry Society, P.O. Box 81060, Ottawa ON K1P 1B1, Canada. **E-mail:** managingeditor@arcpoetry.ca; coordinatingeditor@arcpoetry.ca. **Website:** www.arcpoetry.ca. **Contact:** Monty Reid, managing editor; Robyn Jeffrey, coordinating editor. "Our focus is poetry, and Canadian poetry in general, although we do publish writers from elsewhere. We are looking for the best poetry from new and established writers. We often have special issues. Send a SASE for upcoming special issues and contests." Buys one-time rights. Pays on publication. Publishes ms an average of 6 months after acceptance. Responds in 4 months. Guidelines for #10 SASE.

○ Only accepts submissions via online submissions manager.

MAGAZINE'S NEEDS E-mail submissions not accepted. Pays $40/printed page (Canadian).

TIPS Please include brief biographical note with submission.

☺◑◔ ARC POETRY MAGAZINE

P.O. Box 81060, Ottawa ON K1P 1B1, Canada. **E-mail:** arc@arcpoetry.ca. **Website:** www.arcpoetry.ca. **Contact:** Monty Reid, managing editor. "*Arc Poetry Magazine* has been publishing the best in contemporary Canadian and international poetry and criticism for over 30 years." Press run is 1,500. Subscriptions: 1 year—$35 CDN; 2 years—$60 CND (in Canada). US subscriptions: 1 year—$45 CAD; 2 years—$80 CAD. International subscriptions: 1 year—$55 CDN; 2 year—$90 CDN. Online ordering available for subscriptions and single copies (with occasional promotions). Acquires first Canadian serial rights. Pays $40

CAD/page, plus contributor's copy. Responds in 4-6 months.

○ *Arc* is published 3 times a year, including an annual themed issue each fall. Canada's poetry magazine publishes poetry, poetry-related articles, interviews, and book reviews, and occasionally publishes on its website; *Arc* also runs a Poet-in-Residence program. Has published poetry by Don Coles, Karen Solie, Carmine Starnino, David O'Meara, Elizabeth Bachinsky, George Elliott Clarke, Daryl Hine, Michael Ondaatje, Stephanie Bolster, and Don Domanski. *Arc* is 130-160 pages, perfect-bound, printed on matte white stock "with a crisp, engaging design and a striking visual art portfolio in each issue." Receives over 2,500 submissions/year; accepts about 40-50 poems.

MAGAZINE'S NEEDS *Arc* accepts unsolicited submissions of previously unpublished poems from September 1 to May 31; maximum of 5 poems, 1 submission per year per person. "Please see www.arcpoetry.ca for full guidelines and to use our online submission manager. For reviews, interviews, and articles, please query first."

CONTEST/AWARD OFFERINGS Poem of the Year Contest—deadline: February 1; $5,000 grand prize; entry fee includes 1-year subscription. Confederation Poets Prize and Critic's Desk Award for best poem and reviews published in *Arc* in the preceding year. Other awards include the Archibald Lampman Award and the Diana Brebner Prize.

ARDENT!

Poetry in the Arts, Inc., 302 Cripple Creek, Cedar Park TX 78613. **E-mail:** rimer777@gmail.com. **Website:** www.poetryinarts.org/publishing/ardent.html. **Contact:** Dillon McKinsey, executive editor. *Ardent!*, published semiannually, is a journal of poetry and art. All forms and styles are considered. *Ardent!* is perfect-bound.

MAGAZINE'S NEEDS E-mail up to 3 poems (pasted in body of e-mail). "Include a statement giving Poetry in the Arts, Inc. your permission to use your work." Provide brief bio. Accepts attachments in e-mails; no snail mail. See website for guidelines.

◑ ARIES: A JOURNAL OF CREATIVE EXPRESSION

Dept. of Languages and Literature, 1201 Wesleyan St., Fort Worth TX 76105. (817)531-4900. **E-mail:**

pmcmurray@txwes.edu. **Website:** www.txwes.edu. **Contact:** Dr. Price McMurray, general editor. *Aries: A Journal of Creative Expression*, published annually in summer. Accepting poetry, short fiction, creative nonfiction, short plays, and b&w photography. Deadline: December 1 for publication, notification by May.

⬤ ARKANSAS REVIEW

A Journal of Delta Studies, Department of English and Philosophy, P.O. Box 1890, Office: Wilson Hall, State University AR 72467-1890. (870) 972-3043; (870)972-2210. **Fax:** (870)972-3045. **E-mail:** arkansasreview@astate.edu. **E-mail:** jcollins@astate.edu; arkansasreview@astate.edu. **Website:** http://altweb.astate.edu/arkreview. Tom Williams. **Contact:** Dr. Janelle Collins, general editor/associate professor of English. "All material, creative and scholarly, published in the *Arkansas Review*, must evoke or respond to the natural and/or cultural experience of the Mississippi River Delta region." Buys first North American serial rights. Time between acceptance and publication is about 6 months. Occasionally publishes theme issues. Responds in 2 weeks to queries. Responds in 4 months to mss. Sometimes comments on rejected mss. Editorial lead time 4 months. Sample copy for $7.50. Guidelines available online.

⬤ *Arkansas Review* is 92 pages, magazine-sized, photo offset-printed, saddle-stapled, with 4-color cover. Press run is 600; 50 distributed free to contributors. Receives 30-50 unsolicited mss/month. Accepts 2-3 mss/issue; 5-7 mss/year. Receives about 500 poems/year; accepts about 5%. Publishes ms 6-12 months after acceptance. Agented fiction 1%. Publishes 3-4 new writers/year. Has published work by Susan Henderson, George Singleton, Scott Ely and Pia Erhart. Subscription: $20. Make checks payable to ASU Foundation.

MAGAZINE'S NEEDS Accepts e-mail and disk submissions. Cover letter is preferred. Include SASE. Staff reviews books/chapbooks of poetry "that are relevant to the Delta" in 500 words, single- and multi-book format. Send materials for review consideration to Janelle Collins. ("inquire in advance"). Has published poetry by Greg Fraser, Jo McDougall, and Catherine Savage Brosman. Length: 1-100 lines. Pays 3 contributor's copies.

TIPS "Submit via mail. E-mails are more likely to be overlooked or lost. Submit a cover letter, but don't try to impress us with credentials or explanations of the submission. Immerse yourself in the literature of the Delta, but provide us with a fresh and original take on its land, its people, its culture. Surprise us. Amuse us. Recognize what makes this region particular as well as universal, and take risks. Help us shape a new Delta literature."

ARSENIC LOBSTER

E-mail: lobster@magere.com. **Website:** http://arseniclobster.magere.com. Guidelines available at http://arseniclobster.magere.com/1submission.html.

MAGAZINE'S NEEDS E-mail submissions to lobster@magere.com; submit 3-5 poems. "Poems should be timeless, rich in imagery, and edgy; seeking elegant emotion, articulate experiment. Be compelled to write." "We do not want political rants or Hallmark poetry."

TIPS "All works must be previously unpublished. Include a lively, short biography. Poetry topics, reviews and criticism, and art/photographs (.pdf or .jpg attachment only) are also welcome."

ARTFUL DODGE

Dept. of English, College of Wooster, Wooster OH 44691. (330)263-2577. **E-mail:** artfuldodge@wooster.edu. **Website:** www.wooster.edu/artfuldodge. **Contact:** Daniel Bourne, editor-in-chief; Karin Lin-Greenberg, fiction editor; Marcy Campbell, associate fiction editor; Carolyne Wright, translation editor. There is no theme in this magazine, except literary power. We also have an ongoing interest in translations from Central/Eastern Europe and elsewhere. Buys first North American serial rights. Responds in 1-6 months to mss. Sample copy for $7. Guidelines for #10 SASE.

MAGAZINE'S NEEDS We are interested in poems that utilize stylistic persuasions both old and new to good effect. We are not afraid of poems which try to deal with large social, political, historical, and even philosophical questions—especially if the poem emerges from one's own life experience and is not the result of armchair pontificating. We don't want cute, rococo surrealism, someone's warmed-up, left-over notion of an avant-garde that existed 10-100 years ago, or any last bastions of rhymed verse in the civilized world. Pays $5/page honorarium and 2 contributor's copies.

TIPS Poets may send books for review consideration; however, there is no guarantee we can review them.

⚫❖ ARTS & LETTERS JOURNAL OF CONTEMPORARY CULTURE

Campus Box 89, Georgia College & State University, Milledgeville GA 31061. **E-mail:** al.journal@gcsu.edu. **Website:** http://al.gcsu.edu. *Arts & Letters Journal of Contemporary Culture*, published semiannually, is devoted to contemporary arts and literature, featuring ongoing series such as The World Poetry Translation Series and The Mentors Interview Series. Wants work that is of the highest literary and artistic quality. Acquires one-time rights. Pays on publication. Responds in 1-2 months. Guidelines online or for SASE.

○ Work published in *Arts & Letters Journal* has received the Pushcart Prize.

MAGAZINE'S NEEDS Has published poetry by Margaret Gibson, Marilyn Nelson, Stuart Lishan, R.T. Smith, Laurie Lamon, and Miller Williams. Query first. Submit 4-6 poems at a time with SASE or using online submission manager. Include cover letter. "Poems are screened, discussed by group of readers, then if approved, submitted to poetry editor for final approval." No light verse. Pays $10 per printed age, 1 contributor's copy, and 1-year subscription.

CONTEST/AWARD OFFERINGS Offers the annual Arts & Letters/Rumi Prize for Poets (see separate listing in Contests & Awards).

⚫❖ ART TIMES

A Literary Journal and Resource for All the Arts, P.O. Box 730, Mount Marion NY 12456. (845)246-6944. **Fax:** (845)246-6944. **E-mail:** info@ArtTimesJournal. com. **Website:** www.arttimesjournal.com. **Contact:** Raymond J. Steiner, editor. *"Art Times* covers the art fields and is distributed in locations most frequented by those enjoying the arts. Our copies are distributed throughout the lower part of the northeast as well as metropolitan New York area; locations include theaters, galleries, museums, schools, art clubs, cultural centers and the like. Our readers are mostly over 40, affluent, art-conscious and sophisticated. Subscribers are located across US and abroad (Italy, France, Germany, Greece, Russia, etc.)." Buys first North American serial rights, buys first rights. Pays on publication. Publishes ms an average of 3 years after acceptance. Responds in 6 months to queries. Responds in 6 months to mss. Sample copy for sae with 9x12 envelope and 6 first-class stamps. Writer's guidelines for #10 SASE or online.

MAGAZINE'S NEEDS Wants "poetry that strives to express genuine observation in unique language. All topics, all forms. We prefer well-crafted 'literary' poems. No excessively sentimental poetry." Publishes 2-3 poems each issue. Length: no more than 20 lines. Offers contributor copies and 1 year's free subscription

TIPS "Competition is greater (more submissions received), but keep trying. We print new as well as published writers. Be advised that we are presently on an approximate 3-year lead for short stories, 2-year lead for poetry. We are now receiving 300-400 poems and 40-50 short stories per month. Be familiar with *Art Times* and its special audience."

❖○ ASCENT ASPIRATIONS

1560 Arbutus Dr., Nanoose Bay BC C9P 9C8, Canada. **E-mail:** ascentaspirations@shaw.ca. **Website:** www. ascentaspirations.ca. **Contact:** David Fraser, editor. *"Ascent Aspirations* magazine publishes monthly online and once in print. The print issues are operated as contests. Please refer to current guidelines before submitting. *Ascent Aspirations* is a quality electronic publication dedicated to the promotion and encouragement of aspiring writers of any genre. The focus however is toward interesting experimental writing in dark mainstream, literary, science fiction, fantasy and horror. Poetry can be on any theme. Essays need to be unique, current and have social, philosophical commentary." Rights remain with author. Accepts simultaneous, multiple submissions, and reprints. Responds in 1 week to queries; 3 months to mss. Sometimes comments on rejected mss. Guidelines by e-mail or on website.

○ Magazine: 40 electronic pages; illustrations; photos. Receives 100-200 unsolicited mss/month. Accepts 40 mss/issue; 240 mss/year. Publishes ms 3 months after acceptance. Publishes 10-50 new writers/year. Has published work by Taylor Graham, Janet Buck, Jim Manton, Steve Cartwright, Don Stockard, Penn Kemp, Sam Vargo, Vernon Waring, Margaret Karmazin, Bill Hughes; and recently spoken word artists Sheri-D Wilson, Missy Peters, Ian Ferrier, Cathy Petch, and Bob Holdman.

MAGAZINE'S NEEDS Submit 1-5 poems at a time. Considers previously published poems and simultaneous submissions. Prefers e-mail submissions (pasted into body of message or as attachment in Word);

no disk submissions. "If you must submit by postal mail because it is your only avenue, provide a SASE with IRCs or Canadian stamps." Reads submissions on a regular basis year round. "We accept all forms of poetry on any theme. Poetry needs to be unique and touch the reader emotionally with relevant human, social, and philosophical imagery." Considers poetry by children and teens. Does not want poetry "that focuses on mainstream overtly religious verse." "No payment at this time."

TIPS "Short fiction should, first of all tell, a good story, take the reader to new and interesting imaginary or real places. Short fiction should use language lyrically and effectively, be experimental in either form or content and take the reader into realms where they can analyze and think about the human condition. Write with passion for your material, be concise and economical and let the reader work to unravel your story. In terms of editing, always proofread to the point where what you submit is the best it possibly can be. Never be discouraged if your work is not accepted; it may just not be the right fit for a current publication."

ASHEVILLE POETRY REVIEW

P.O. Box 7086, Asheville NC 28802. (828)450-0357. **Website:** www.ashevillereview.com. **Contact:** Keith Flynn, founder/managing editor. *Asheville Poetry Review*, published annually, prints "the best regional, national, and international poems we can find. We publish translations, interviews, essays, historical perspectives, and book reviews as well." Wants "quality work with well-crafted ideas married to a dynamic style. Any subject matter is fit to be considered so long as the language is vivid with a clear sense of rhythm. We subscribe to the Borges dictum that great poetry is a combination of 'algebra and fire." Rights revert back to author upon publication. Up to 1 year from acceptance to publishing time. Responds in up to 4 months. Sample: $13. **"We prefer poets purchase a sample copy prior to submitting."** Guidelines available for SASE or on website.

Asheville Poetry Review is 160-300 pages, digest-sized, perfect-bound, laminated, with full-color cover. Receives about 8,000 submissions/year, accepts about 5%. Press run is 3,000. Subscription: $22.50 for 2 years, $43.50 for 4 years. Occasionally publishes theme issues. Reviews books/chapbooks of poetry. Send materials for review consideration. Has published po-

etry by Sherman Alexie, Eavan Boland, Gary Snyder, Colette Inez, Robert Bly, and Fred Chappell.

MAGAZINE'S NEEDS Submit 3-5 poems at a time. No previously published poems or simultaneous submissions. No e-mail submissions. Cover letter is required. Include comprehensive bio, recent publishing credits, and SASE. Reads submissions January 15-July 15. Poems are circulated to an editorial board. Seldom comments on rejected poems. **Sponsors the William Matthews Poetry Prize: $1,000 awarded for a single poem, reads submissions September 15-January 15. See website for complete guidelines.** Pays 1 contributor's copy.

ASININE POETRY

E-mail: editor@asininepoetry.com. **Website:** www.asininepoetry.com. **Contact:** R. Narvaez, editor. *asinine poetry and prose*, published monthly online, "features 10-12 new works each month. We specialize in poetry that does not take itself too seriously." Wants "any form of poetry, but for us the poetry must be in a humorous, parodic, or satirical style. We prefer well-crafted poems that may contain serious elements or cover serious subjects—but which are also amusing, absurd, or hilarious." Does not want serious, straightforward poems. Has published poetry by Hal Sirowitz, William Trowbridge, Elizabeth Swados, Daniel Thomas Moran, and Colonel Drunky Bob. Receives about 1,000 poems/year, accepts about 10%.

MAGAZINE'S NEEDS Submit 3-4 poems at a time. Lines/poem: 50 maximum. Considers previously published poems and simultaneous submissions. Accepts e-mail (pasted into body of message).

CONTEST/AWARD OFFERINGS Sponsors 1 contest/year. Guidelines available on website.

ASSENT

Assent c/o Tracey Roberts, Room E701, Kedelston Rd., University of Derby, Derby DE22 1GB, England. **E-mail:** t.roberts@derby.ac.uk. **Website:** http://nottinghampoetrysociety.co.uk. **Contact:** Adrian Buckner, editor; Tracey Roberts, editorial assistant. Subscription Rates: £12.00 UK; £18.00 Sterling overseas (3 issues). Current issue: £4.00 + 80p p&p. Back issues: £1.50 inc p&p. Cheques payable to Derby University. Subscribers who wish to pay in $US: Please send cheque to 1036 Menlo Avenue, Apt. 301, Los Angeles, California 90006 USA. Subscription: $25 inc p&p.

Current issue $7.00. Back issue $4.00. US Cheque payable to Karen Crosbie.

CONTEST/AWARD OFFERINGS The Nottingham Open Poetry Competition offers cash prizes, annual subscriptions, and publication in *Assent*. Open to all. Guidelines available on website.

ATLANTA REVIEW

P.O. Box 8248, Atlanta GA 31106. **E-mail:** atlanta.review@yahoo.com. **Website:** www.atlantareview.com. **Contact:** Dan Veach, editor/publisher. *Atlanta Review*, published semiannually, is devoted primarily to poetry, but occasionally features interviews and b&w artwork. Wants "quality poetry of genuine human appeal." Has published poetry by Seamus Heaney, Billy Collins, Derek Walcott, Maxine Kumin, Alicia Stallings, Gunter Grass, Eugenio Montale, and Thomas Lux. *Atlanta Review* is 128 pages, digest-sized, professionally printed on acid-free paper, flat-spined, with glossy color cover. Receives about 10,000 poems/year, accepts about 1%. Press run is 2,500. Single copy: $6; subscription: $10. Sample: $5. Publishes ms 6 months after acceptance. Responds in 1 month. Guidelines available online at website.

Work published in *Atlanta Review* has been included in *The Best American Poetry* and *The Pushcart Prize*.

MAGAZINE'S NEEDS Submit no more than 5 poems at a time. No previously published poems. No e-mail submissions from within the U.S.; postal submissions only. Include SASE for reply. "Authors living outside the United States and Canada may submit work via e-mail." Cover letter is preferred. Include brief bio. Put name and address on each poem. Reads submissions according to the following deadlines: June 1 for Fall; December 1 for Spring. "While we do read year round, response time may be slower during summer and the winter holidays." Pays in contributor's copies.

THE ATLANTIC MONTHLY

The Watergate, 600 New Hampshire Ave., NW, Washington DC 20037. (202)266-6000. **Website:** www.theatlantic.com. **Contact:** James Bennet, editor; C. Michael Curtis, fiction editor; David Barber, poetry editor. General magazine for an educated readership with broad cultural and public-affairs interests. "*The Atlantic* considers unsolicited manuscripts, either fiction or nonfiction. A general familiarity with what we have published in the past is the best guide to our needs and preferences. Manuscripts must be typewritten and double-spaced. Receipt of manuscripts will be acknowledged if accompanied by a self-addressed stamped envelope. Manuscripts will not be returned. **At this time, the print magazine does not read submissions sent via fax or e-mail.** TheAtlantic.com no longer accepts unsolicited submissions." Buys first North American serial rights. Guidelines available onine.

MAGAZINE'S NEEDS "Interest is in the broadest possible range of work: traditional forms and free verse, the meditative lyric and the 'light' or comic poem, the work of the famous and the work of the unknown. We have long been committed to the discovery of new poets. Our one limitation is length; we are unable to publish very long poems." Wants "the broadest possible range of work: traditional forms and free verse, the meditative lyric and the 'light' or comic poem, the work of the famous and the work of the unknown." *The Atlantic Monthly* publishes some of the most distinguished poetry in American literature. "We read with interest and attention every poem submitted to the magazine and, quite simply, we publish those that seem to us to be the best." Has published poetry by Maxine Kumin, Stanley Plumly, Linda Gregerson, Philip Levine, Ellen Bryant Voigt, and W.S. Merwin. Receives about 60,000 poems/year. Subscription: $24.50 for 10 issues. Sample: $7.50 (back issue).

HOW TO CONTACT Submit 2-6 poems at a time. No previously published poems or simultaneous submissions. No e-mail or disk submissions; postal submissions only. SASE required. Responds in 4-6 weeks. Pays upon acceptance. Always sends prepublication galleys. Acquires first North American serial rights only.

TIPS "Writers should be aware that this is not a market for beginner's work (nonfiction and fiction), nor is it truly for intermediate work. Study this magazine before sending only your best, most professional work. When making first contact, cover letters are sometimes helpful, particularly if they cite prior publications or involvement in writing programs. Common mistakes: melodrama, inconclusiveness, lack of development, unpersuasive characters and/or dialogue."

THE AVALON LITERARY REVIEW

CCI Publishing, P.O. Box 780696, Orlando FL 32878. (407)574-7355. **E-mail:** submissions@avalonliteraryreview.com. **Website:** www.avalonliteraryre-view.com. **Contact:** Valerie Rubino, managing editor. Quarterly magazine. "*The Avalon Literary Review* welcomes work from both published and unpublished writers and poets. We accept submissions of poetry, short fiction, and personal essays. The author's voice and point of view should be unique and clear. We seek pieces which spring from the author's life and experiences. Submissions which explore both the sweet and bitter of life, with a touch of humor, are a good fit for our *Review*. While we appreciate the genres of fantasy, science fiction and horror, our magazine is not the forum for such work." Buys one-time rights. Pays on publication. Publishes ms an average of 3 months after acceptance. Editorial lead time is 3-6 months. Sample copy available for $10, by e-mail, or on website. Writer's guidelines available online at website or by e-mail.

MAGAZINE'S NEEDS Accepts 40-60 poems/year. Electronic submissions only. Submit maximum 3 poems. No rhyming verse. Length: no more than 50 lines. Pays 5 contributor's copies.

TIPS "We seek work that is carefully structured. We like vivid descriptions, striking characters, and realistic dialogue. A humorous but not ridiculous point of view is a plus."

AVOCET, A JOURNAL OF NATURE POEMS

P.O. Box 19186, Fountain Hills AZ 85269. **E-mail:** cportolano@hotmail.com. **Website:** www.avocetreview.com. **Contact:** Charles Portolano, editor. *Avocet, A Journal of Nature Poems*, published quarterly, is "devoted to poets who find meaning in their lives from the natural world." Wants "imagist/transcendental poetry that explores the beauty and divinity in nature." Does not want "poems that have rhyme, cliché, or abstraction."

Has published poetry by Greg Gregory, Charles H. Harper, Michael Keshigian, Cynthia Chadwick Linkas, Georgia Ressmeyer, and Dennis Saleh. *Avocet* is 60 pages, 4 1/4x5 1/2, professionally printed, saddle-stapled, with card cover. Single copy: $6; subscription: $24. Make checks payable to Charles Portolano.

MAGAZINE'S NEEDS Submit 3-5 poems at a time. Considers previously published poems, if acknowledged. Cover letter with e-mail address is helpful.

Include SASE for reply only; mss will not be returned. Time between acceptance and publication is up to 3 months. Responds in up to 2 months.

THE AWAKENINGS REVIEW

P.O. Box 177, Wheaton IL 60187. **E-mail:** info@awakeningsproject.org. **Website:** www.awakeningsproject.org. **Contact:** Robert Lundin, director. *The Awakenings Review* is published by the Awakenings Project. Begun in cooperation with the University of Chicago Center for Psychiatric Rehabilitation in 2000, *The Awakenings Review* has been acclaimed internationally and draws writers from all over the United States and from several other countries including Israel, South Africa, Australia, Finland, Switzerland, the United Kingdom, and Canada. Acquires first rights. Publishes ms 8 months after acceptance. Responds in 1 month. Guidelines available in magazine, for SASE, by e-mail, or on website.

MAGAZINE'S NEEDS Submit 5 poems at a time. No previously published poems or simultaneous submissions. No e-mail submissions. Cover letter is preferred. Include SASE and short bio. Poems are read by a board of editors. Often comments on rejected poems. Occasionally publishes theme issue. Pays 1 contributor's copy, plus discount on additional copies.

BABEL: THE MULTILINGUAL, MULTICULTURAL ONLINE JOURNAL AND COMMUNITY OF ARTS AND IDEAS

E-mail: submissions@towerofbabel.com. **Website:** http://towerofbabel.com. **Contact:** Malcolm Lawrence, editor-in-chief. "*Babel* is an electronic zine recognized by the UN as one of the most important social and human sciences online periodicals. Writers whose work discriminates against the opposite sex, different cultures, or belief systems will not be considered." Time between acceptance and publication vis usually no more than 2 months. Seldom comments on rejected poems. Guidelines available on website. Responds in 2-4 weeks. Reviews books/chapbooks of poetry and other magazines, single- and multi-book format. Open to unsolicited reviews. Publishes regional reports from international stringers all over the planet, as well as features, round table discussions, fiction, columns, poetry, erotica, travelogues, and reviews of all the arts and editorials. We're interested in fiction, nonfiction and poetry from all over the world, including multicultural or multilingual work, as well as poetry that has been translated from or into another language, as long as it is also in English. We also appreciate gay/lesbian and bisexual poetry. Cover letter is required. Reviews books/chapbooks of poetry and other magazines, single- and multi-book format. Open to unsolicited reviews. Send materials for review consideration. Accepts ms 1-2 months after acceptance. Responds in 2-4 weeks. Guidelines available on website.

- *Babel* is recognized by the U.N. as one of the most important social and human sciences online periodicals.

MAGAZINE'S NEEDS WordPress bloggers in the following languages: Arabic, Bulgarian, Bengali, Catalan, Czech, Welsh, Danish, German, English, Esperanto, Spanish, Persian, Finnish, Faroese, French, Hebrew, Croatian, Indonesian, Italian, Japanese, Korean, Latvian, Malay, Dutch, Polish, Portuguese, Russian, Albanian, Serbian, Swedish, Tamil, Thai, Ukrainian, Urdu, Uzbek, Vietnamese and Chinese.

HOW TO CONTACT Submit no more than 10 poems at a time. Considers previously published poems and simultaneous submissions. Accepts e-mail submissions only. Cover letter is required. "Please send submissions with a résumé or bio as a Microsoft Word or RTF document attached to e-mail."

ADDITIONAL INFORMATION Our bloggers include James Schwartz, the first out gay poet raised in the Old Order Amish community in Southwestern Michigan and author of the book *The Literary Party*; Susanna Zaraysky, author of the book *Language Is Music: Making People Multilingual*; James Rovira, Assistant Professor of English and Program Chair of Humanities at Tiffin University and author of the book *Blake & Kierkegaard: Creation and Anxiety*; and Paul B. Miller, Assistant Professor Department of French and Italian at Vanderbilt University.

TIPS "We would like to see more fiction with first-person male characters written by female authors, as well as more fiction first-person female characters written by male authors. We would also like to see that dynamic in action when it comes to other languages, cultures, races, classes, sexual orientations and ages. Know what you are writing about and write passionately about it."

BABYSUE®

babysue ATTN: LMNOP aka dONW7, P.O. Box 15749, Chattanooga TN 373415. **E-mail:** LMNOP@babysue.com. **Website:** www.babysue.com; www. LMNOP.com. **Contact:** Don W. Seven, editor/publisher. *babysue* is an ongoing online magazine featuring continually updated cartoons, poems, literature, and reviews. It is also published twice/year and offers obtuse humor for the extremely open-minded. "We are open to all styles, but prefer short poems." No restrictions. Has published poetry by Edward Mycue, Susan Andrews, and Barry Bishop. "We print prose, poems, and cartoons. We usually accept about 5% of what we receive." Pays 1 contributor's copy. Responds "immediately, if we are interested." Seldom comments on rejected poems. Sample: $7; cash only (no checks or money orders).

TIPS "We do occasionally review other magazines."

THE BALTIMORE REVIEW

E-mail: editor@baltimorereview.org. **Website:** www.baltimorereview.org. **Contact:** Barbara Westwood Diehl, senior editor; Kathleen Hellen, senior editor. "*The Baltimore Review* publishes poetry, fiction, and creative nonfiction from Baltimore and beyond." Submission periods are August 1 through November 30 and February 1 through May 31. Buys first North American serial rights. Publishes ms an average of 6 months after acceptance. Responds in 3 months. Sample copy for $10. Guidelines available online.

- In 2012, *The Baltimore Review* began its new life as a quarterly, online literary.

MAGAZINE'S NEEDS Submit 1-4 poems at a time. Does not want "sentimental-mushy, loud, or very abstract poetry; corny humor; poorly crafted or preachy poetry." Length: no more than 4 pages. Pays 2 contributor's copies, reduced rate for additional copies.

CONTEST/AWARD OFFERINGS Sponsors an annual poetry contest. Offers 1st Prize: $300 plus publication in *The Baltimore Review*; 2nd Prize: $150; 3rd Prize: $50. Submit 1-4 poems (no more than 5 pages total). All forms and styles accepted, including prose poems. Guidelines available on website. **Entry fee:** $12 (includes copy of issue in which 1st-Prize winner is published) or $20 (includes one-year subscription).

TIPS "Please read what is being published in other literary journals, including our own. As in any other profession, writers must know what the trends and the major issues are in the field. We look for compelling stories and a masterful use of the English language. We want to feel that we have never heard this story, or this voice, before. Read the kinds of publications you want your work to appear in. Make your reader believe and care."

BARBARIC YAWP

BoneWorld Publishing, 3700 County Rt. 24, Russell NY 13684-3198. (315)347-2609. **Website:** www.boneworldpublishing.com. Acquires one-time rights. Responds in 2 weeks to queries; 4 months to mss. Sample copy for $4. Guidelines for #10 SASE.

TIPS "Don't give up. Read much, write much, submit much. Observe closely the world around you. Don't borrow ideas from TV or films. Revision is often necessary—grit your teeth and do it. Never fear rejection."

BARN OWL REVIEW

Olin Hall 342, The University of Akron, Akron OH 44325. **E-mail:** info@barnowlreview.com. **Website:** www.barnowlreview.com. **Contact:** Mary Biddinger and Jay Robinson, editors-in-chief. "We are a handsomely designed print journal looking for work that takes risks while still connecting with readers. We aim to publish the highest quality poetry from both emerging and established writers."

Uses online submissions manager.

MAGAZINE'S NEEDS Barn Owl Review favors no particular poetic school or style; "however, we look for innovation and risk-taking in the poems that we publish." Submit 3-5 poems (in single attachment) via Submishmash between June 1-November 1. Contributors receive 2 copies of the issue.

BARROW STREET

71 First Ave., Suite 12, New York NY 10003. **E-mail:** infobarrow@gmail.com. **Website:** www.barrowstreet. org. **Contact:** Lorna Blake, Patricia Carlin, Peter Covino, and Melissa Hotchkiss, editors. *Barrow Street*, published annually, "is dedicated to publishing new and established poets." Wants "poetry of the highest quality; open to all styles and forms." Has published poetry by Molly Peacock, Lyn Hejinian, Carl Phillips, Marie Ponsot, Charles Bernstein, and Stephen Burt. *Barrow Street* is 96-120 pages, digest-sized, professionally printed, perfect-bound, with glossy cardstock cover with color or b&w photography. Receives about 3,000 poems/year, accepts about 3%. Press run is 1,000. Subscription: $18 for 2 years, $25 for 3 years. Acquires first rights. Responds in 3-6 months. Sample copy for $10. Guidelines available on website.

Poetry published in *Barrow Street* is often selected for *The Best American Poetry*.

MAGAZINE'S NEEDS Submit up to 5 poems at a time. Please always check our website to confirm submission guidelines. Online only-does not accept hard copy submissions. Considers simultaneous submissions (but poets must read guidelines and withdraw and resubmit, not e-mail us to tell us about poems accepted elsewhere); no previously published poems. Cover letter is preferred. Include brief bio. Must have name, address, e-mail, and phone on each page submitted or submission will not be considered. Reads submissions October 1-March 31. Poems circulated to an editorial board. Does not return or respond to submissions made outside the reading period or any hard copy submissions sent via mail. Always sends prepublication galleys. Pays 2 contributor's copies.

BATEAU

P.O. Box 1584, Northampton MA 01061. (413)586-2494. **E-mail:** info@bateaupress.org. **Website:** www.bateaupress.org. **Contact:** James Grinwis, editor. "*Bateau*, published semiannually, subscribes to no trend but serves to represent as wide a cross-section of contemporary writing as possible. For this reason, readers will most likely love and hate at least something in each issue. We consider this a good thing. To us, it means *Bateau* is eclectic, open-ended, and not mired in a particular strain." Has published poetry by Tomaz Salamun, John Olsen, Michael Burkhardt, Joshua Marie Wilkinson, Allison Titus, Allan Peterson, Dean Young. *Bateau* is around 80 pages, digest-sized, offset print, perfect-bound, with a 100% recycled letterpress cover. Receives about 5,000 poems/year, accepts about 60. Press run is 250. Single copy: $12; subscription $24. Make checks payable to Bateau Press. Acquires first North American serial rights, electronic rights. Publishes ms 3-8 months after acceptance. Responds in 1-6 months. Guidelines for SASE or on website.

MAGAZINE'S NEEDS Submit up to 5 pages by mail or online submission form. Cover letter not necessary. Submissions are closed in June, July, and August. Pays in contributor's copies.

BAYOU

English Dept. University of New Orleans, 2000 Lakeshore Dr., New Orleans LA 70148. (504)280-5423. **E-mail:** bayou@uno.edu. **Website:** www.uno.edu/bayou. **Contact:** Joanna Leake, editor. "A non-profit journal for the arts, each issue of *Bayou Magazine* contains beautiful fiction, nonfiction and poetry. From quirky shorts to more traditional stories, we are committed to publishing solid work. Regardless of style, at *Bayou* we are always interested first in a well-told tale. Our poetry and prose are filled with memorable characters observing their world, acknowledging both the mundane and the sublime, often at once, and always with an eye toward beauty. *Bayou* is packed with a range of material from established, award-winning authors as well as new voices on the rise. Recent contributors include Eric Trethewey, Virgil Suarez, Marilyn Hacker, Sean Beaudoin, Tom Whalen, Mark Doty, Philip Cioffari, Lyn Lifshin, Timothy Liu and Gaylord Brewer. And in one issue every year, *Bayou* features the winner of the annual Tennessee Williams/New Orleans Literary Festival One-Act Play Competition." Responds in 4-6 months. Guidelines available online at website.

○ Does not accept e-mail submissions. Reads submissions from September 1 to June 1.

MAGAZINE'S NEEDS "Our poetry and prose are filled with memorable characters observing their world, acknowledging both the mundane and the sublime, often at once, and always with an eye toward beauty. Contains a range of material from established, award-winning authors as well as new voices on the rise." Length: "We have no strict length restrictions, though obviously it is harder to fit in very long poems." Pays 2 contributor's copies.

TIPS "Do not submit in more than one genre at a time. Don't send a second submission until you receive a response to the first."

◑ BEAR CREEK HAIKU

P.O. Box 3787, Boulder CO 80307. **Website:** www.coloradopoetscenter.org/links/bearCreek.html. **Contact:** Ayaz Daryl Nielsen, editor. Acquires first rights. Acceptance to publication time varies. Response time varies. Sample copy for SASE.

○ Reads submissions year round.

MAGAZINE'S NEEDS Lenth: 11 lines or less or haiku. Pays two contributor's copies.

◐◯ THE BEAR DELUXE MAGAZINE

Orlo, 810 SE Belmont, Studio 5, Portland OR 97214. (503)242-1047. **E-mail:** bear@orlo.org. **Website:** www.orlo.org. **Contact:** Tom Webb, editor-in-chief; Kristin Rogers Brown, art director. "*The Bear Deluxe Magazine* is a national independent environmental arts magazine publishing significant works of reporting, creative nonfiction, literature, visual art and design. Based in the Pacific Northwest, it reaches across cultural and political divides to engage readers on vital issues effecting the environment. Published twice per year, *The Bear Deluxe* includes a wider array and a higher-percentage of visual art work and design than many other publications. Artwork is included both as editorial support and as stand alone or independent art. It has included nationally recognized artists as well as emerging artists. As with any publication, artists are encouraged to review a sample copy for a clearer understanding of the magazine's approach. Unsolicited submissions and samples are accepted and encouraged." Buys first rights, buys one-time rights. Pays on publication. Publishes ms an average of 6 months after acceptance. Responds in 3-6 months to mail queries. Only responds to e-mail queries if interested. Editorial lead time 6 months. Sample copy for $3. Guidelines for #10 SASE or on website.

MAGAZINE'S NEEDS Submit 3-5 poems at a time. Considers previously published poems and simultaneous submissions "so long as noted." Poems are reviewed by a committee of 3-5 people. Publishes 1 theme issue/year. Acquires first or one-time rights. Length: 50 lines maximum. Pays $20, subscription, and copies.

TIPS "Offer to be a stringer for future ideas. Get a copy of the magazine and guidelines, and query us with specific nonfiction ideas and clips. We're looking for original, magazine-style stories, not fluff or PR. Fiction, essay, and poetry writers should know we have an open and blind review policy and should keep sending their best work even if rejected once. Be as specific as possible in queries."

◐◯ BELLEVUE LITERARY REVIEW

NYU Langone Medical Center, Department of Medicine, 550 First Ave., OBV-A612, New York NY 10016. (212)263-3973. **E-mail:** info@BLReview.org. **E-mail:** stacy.bodziak@nyumc.org. **Website:** www.blreview.org. **Contact:** Stacy Bodziak, managing editor. *Bellevue Literary Review,* published semiannually, prints "works of fiction, nonfiction, and poetry that touch upon relationships to the human body, illness, health, and healing." Aquires first North American serial rights. Pays on publication. Sends galleys to author. Publishes ms 3-6 months after acceptance. Responds in 3-6 months to mss. Sample copy for $7. Guidelines for SASE or on website.

○ *Bellevue Literary Review* is 160 pages, digest-sized, perfect-bound; includes ads. Press run is 5,000; distributed free to literary magazine conferences, promotions, and other contacts. Single copy: $9; subscription: $15/year, $35 for 3 years (plus $5/year postage to Canada, $8/year postage foreign). Make checks payable to *Bellevue Literary Review*. Work published in *Bellevue Literary Review* has appeared in *The Pushcart Prize*. Recently published work by Rafael Campo, Paul Harding, Tom Sleigh.

MAGAZINE'S NEEDS Submit up to 3 poems at a time. Prefers poems of 1 page or less. Considers simultaneous submissions. No previously published poems; work published on personal blogs or Web sites will be considered on a case-by-case basis. No e-mail or disk submissions. "We accept poems via regular mail and through our website; when submitting via regular mail, please include SASE." Cover letter is preferred. Reads submissions year round. Time between acceptance and publication is about 6-7 months. "Poems are reviewed by 2 independent readers, then sent to an editor." Sometimes comments on rejected poems. Sometimes publishes theme issues. Upcoming themes available on website. Receives about 1,800 poetry mss/year; accepts about 3%. Has published poetry by Edward Hirsch, Naomi Shihab Nye, Cornellius Eady, and David Wagoner. Pays 2 contributor's copies and 1-year subscription for author, plus 1-year gift subscription for friend. Acquires first North American serial rights. Rights revert to poet upon publication.

BELLINGHAM REVIEW

Mail Stop 9053, Western Washington University, Bellingham WA 98225. (360)650-4863. **E-mail:** bhreview@wwu.edu. **Website:** wwww.bhreview.org. Brenda Miller, editor-in-chief. **Contact:** Tyler Koshakow, managing editor. Annual nonprofit magazine published once a year in the spring. Seeks "literature of palpable quality: poems stories and essays so beguiling they invite us to touch their essence. The *Bellingham Review* hungers for a kind of writing that nudges the limits of form, or executes traditional forms exquisitely." Buys first North American serial rights. Pays on publication when funding allows. Publishes ms an average of 6 months after acceptance. Responds in 1-6 months. Editorial lead time 6 months. Sample copy for $12. Guidelines available online.

○ The editors are actively seeking submissions of creative nonfiction, as well as stories that push the boundaries of the form. The Tobias

Wolff Award in Fiction Contest runs December 1-March 15; see website for guidelines or send SASE.

MAGAZINE'S NEEDS *Bellingham Review*, published twice/year, has no specific preferences as to form. Wants "well-crafted poetry, but are open to all styles." Has published poetry by David Shields, Tess Gallagher, Gary Soto, Jane Hirshfield, Albert Goldbarth, and Rebecca McClanahan. Accepts submissions by postal mail and e-mail. Include SASE. Reads submissions September 15-December 1 only (submissions must be postmarked within this reading period). Responds in 2 months. Will not use light verse. Indicate approximate word count on prose pieces. Pays contributor's copies, a year's subscription, plus monetary payment (if funding allows).

TIPS "Open submission period is from Sept. 15-Dec. 1. Manuscripts arriving between December 2 and September 14 will be returned unread. The *Bellingham Review* holds 3 annual contests: the 49th Parallel Award for poetry, the Annie Dillard Award for Nonfiction, and the Tobias Wolff Award for Fiction. Submissions: December 1-March 15. See the individual listings for these contests under Contests & Awards for full details."

BELL'S LETTERS POET

P.O. Box 14319 N. Swan Rd., Gulfport MS 39503. **E-mail:** jimbelpoet@aol.com. **Contact:** Jim Bell, editor/publisher. *Bell's Letters Poet*, published quarterly, **must be purchased by contributors before they can be published.** Wants "clean writing in good taste; no vulgarity, no artsy vulgarity." Guidelines available online or for SASE.

○ Has published poetry by Betty Wallace, C. David Hay, Mary L. Ports, and Tgrai Warden. *Bell's Letters Poet* is about 60 pages, digest-sized, photocopied on plain bond paper (including cover), saddle-stapled. Single copy: $7; subscription: $28. Sample: $5. "Send a poem (20 lines or under, in good taste) with your sample order, and we will publish it in our next issue."

MAGAZINE'S NEEDS Submit 4 poems at a time. Lines/poem: 4-20. Considers previously published poems "if cleared by author with prior publisher"; no simultaneous submissions. Accepts submissions by postal mail or e-mail. Submission deadline is 2 months prior to publication. Accepted poems by subscribers are published immediately in the next issue. Reviews chapbooks of poetry by subscribers. No payment for accepted poetry, but "many patrons send cash awards to the poets whose work they especially like."

TIPS "The Ratings" is a competition in each issue. Readers are asked to vote on their favorite poems, and the "Top 40" are announced in the next issue, along with awards sent to the poets by patrons. News releases are then sent to subscriber's hometown newspaper. *Bell's Letters Poet* also features a telephone and e-mail exchange among poets, a birth-date listing, and a profile of its poets."Tired of seeing no bylines this year? Subscription guarantees a byline in each issue."

◑ BELOIT POETRY JOURNAL

Beloit Poetry Journal, P.O. Box 151, Farmington ME 04938. (207)778-0020. **E-mail:** bpj@bpj.org. **Website:** www.bpj.org. *Beloit Poetry Journal*, published quarterly, prints "the most outstanding poems we receive, without bias as to length, school, subject, or form. For more than 60 years of continuous publication, we have been distinguished for the extraordinary range of our poetry and our discovery of strong new poets." Wants "visions broader than the merely personal; language that makes us laugh and weep, recoil, resist—and pay attention. We're drawn to poetry that grabs hold of the whole body, not just the head." Responds in 1-16 weeks to queries. Sample copy for $5. Guidelines available on website.

◐ Has published poetry by Sherman Alexie, Mark Doty, Albert Goldbarth, Sonia Sanchez, A.E. Stallings, Janice Harrington, Douglas Kearney, Susan Tichy, and Eduardo Corral.

MAGAZINE'S NEEDS Limit submissions to 5 pages or a single long poem. Pays 3 contributor's copies.

TIPS "We seek only unpublished poems or translations of poems not already available in English. Poems may be submitted electronically on our website Submission Manager, or by postal mail. Before submitting, please buy a sample issue or browse our website archive."

◎ BELTWAY POETRY QUARTERLY

E-mail: info@beltwaypoetry.com. **Website:** www.beltwaypoetry.com. **Contact:** Kim Roberts, editor. *Beltway Poetry Quarterly,* published online, "features poets who live or work in the greater Washington, D.C., metro region. *Beltway* showcases the richness and diversity of Washington, D.C., authors, with poets from different backgrounds, races, ethnicities, ages, and sexual orientations represented. We have included Pulitzer Prize-winners and those who have never previously published. We publish academic, spoken word, and experimental authors—and those whose work defies categorization." Themes change annually; check website for details.

MAGAZINE'S NEEDS "Other than annual themed issue, we consider poems by invitation only. Theme issues have included poetic responses to Walt Whitman, the war in Iraq, and D.C. Places. 2 issues per year feature 5 poets from the greater-D.C. region, and these issues are open only by invitation. 1 issue per year is guest-edited." Never comments on rejected poems. Guidelines available on website. "Monthly Poetry News section has information on new publications, calls for entries, workshops, readings, and performances. Extensive links also include the most complete listing anywhere of artist residency programs in the U.S." Has published poetry by Cornelius Eady, Anthony Hecht, E. Ethelbert Miller, Jane Shore, Sharan Strange, and Hilary Tham.

◐◎ BEYOND CENTAURI

Website: www.samsdotpublishing.com. *Beyond Centauri*, published quarterly, contains "fantasy, science fiction, sword and sorcery, very mild horror short stories, poetry, and illustrations for readers ages 10 and up. " Wants "fantasy, science fiction, spooky horror, and speculative poetry for younger readers." Does not want "horror with excessive blood and gore." Considers poetry by children and teens. Has published poetry by Bruce Boston, Bobbi Sinha-Morey, Debbie Feo, Dorothy Imm, Cythera, and Terrie Leigh Relf. *Beyond Centauri* is 44 pages, magazine-sized, offset printed, perfect bound, with paper cover for color art, includes ads. Receives about 200 poems/year, accepts about 50 (25%). Press run is 100; 5 distributed free to reviewers. Single copy: $6; subscription: $20/year, $37 for 2 years. Make checks payable to Tyree Campbell/Sam's Dot Publishing. Publishes ms 1-2 months after acceptance. Responds in 4-6 weeks.

MAGAZINE'S NEEDS Submit up to 5 poems at a time. Lines/poem: prefers less than 50. Considers previously published poems; no simultaneous submissions. Accepts e-mail submissions (pasted into body of message); no disk submissions. "Submission should include snail mail address and a short (1-2 lines) bio." Reads submissions year round. Often comments on rejected poems. Guidelines available on website. Acquires first North American serial rights. Reviews books/chapbooks of poetry. Send materials for review consideration to Tyree Campbell. Pays $2/original poem, plus 1 contributor's copy.

BIBLE ADVOCATE

Bible Advocate, Church of God (Seventh Day), P.O. Box 33677, Denver CO 80233. (303)452-7973. **E-mail:** bibleadvocate@cog7.org. **Website:** http://baonline. org/. **Contact:** Sherri Langton, associate editor. "Our purpose is to advocate the Bible and represent the Church of God (Seventh Day) to a Christian audience." Buys first rights, buys second serial (reprint) rights, buys electronic rights. Pays on publication. Publishes ms an average of 9 months after acceptance. Responds in 2 months to queries. Editorial lead time 3 months. Sample copy for sae with 9x12 envelope and 3 first-class stamps. Guidelines available online.

MAGAZINE'S NEEDS Prefers e-mail submissions. Cover letter is preferred. "No handwritten submissions, please." Time between acceptance and publication is up to 1 year. "I read them first and reject those that won't work for us. I send good ones to editor for approval." Seldom comments on rejected poems. No avant-garde. Length: 5-20 lines. Pays $20 and 2 contributor's copies.

TIPS "Be fresh, not preachy! Articles must be in keeping with the doctrinal understanding of the Church of God (Seventh Day). Therefore, the writer should become familiar with what the Church generally accepts as truth as set forth in its doctrinal beliefs. We reserve the right to edit manuscripts to fit our space requirements, doctrinal stands and church terminology. Significant changes are referred to writers for approval. No fax or handwritten submissions, please."

BIG MUDDY: A JOURNAL OF THE MISSISSIPPI RIVER VALLEY

Southeast Missouri State University Press, One University Plaza, MS 2650, Cape Girardeau MO 63701. (573)651-2044. **Website:** www6.semo.edu/universitypress/bigmuddy. **Contact:** Susan Swartwout, publisher/editor. "*Big Muddy* explores multidisciplinary, multicultural issues, people, and events mainly concerning, but not limited to, the 10-state area that borders the Mississippi River. We publish fiction, poetry, historical essays, creative nonfiction, environmental essays, biography, regional events, photography, art, etc." Acquires first North American serial rights. Publishes ms 6-12 months after acceptance. Responds in 12 weeks to mss. Send SASE for return of ms or send a disposable copy of ms and #10 SASE for reply only. Sample copy for $6. Guidelines for SASE, e-mail, fax, or on website.

○ Magazine: perfect-bound; 150 pages; acid-free paper; color cover stock; layflat lamination; illustrations; photos.

MAGAZINE'S NEEDS Receives 50 unsolicited mss/month. Accepts 20-25 mss/issue. Accepts multiple submissions. Pays 2 contributor's copies; additional copies $5.

TIPS "We look for clear language, avoidance of clichés except in necessary dialogue, a fresh vision of the theme or issue. Find some excellent and honest readers to comment on your work-in-progress and final draft. Consider their viewpoints carefully. Revise if needed."

BIG PULP

Exter Press, P.O. Box 92, Cumberland MD 21501. E-mail: editors@bigpulp.com. **E-mail:** editors@bigpulp. com. **Website:** www.bigpulp.com. **Contact:** Bill Olver, editor. "We define 'pulp fiction' very broadly—it's lively, challenging, thought-provoking, thrilling and fun, regardless of how many or how few genre elements are packed in. We don't subscribe to the theory that genre fiction is disposable; in our opinion, a great deal of literary fiction could easily fall under one of our general categories. We place a higher value on character and story than genre elements." Acquires one-time and electronic rights. Pays on publication. Publishes ms 1 year after acceptance. Responds in 2 months to mss. Sample copy available for $10; excerpts available online at no cost. Guidelines available online at website.

○ Currently accepting submissions for themed collections only. See website for details on current needs.

MAGAZINE'S NEEDS "All types of poetry are considered, but poems should have a genre connection." Length: 100 lines maximum. Pays $5/poem.

TIPS "We like to be surprised, and have few boundaries. Fantasy writers may focus on the mundane aspects of a fantastical creature's life, or the magic that can happen in everyday life. Romances do not have to requited, or have happy endings, and the object of one's obsession may not be a person. Mysteries need not focus on 'whodunit?' We're always interested in science or speculative fiction focusing on societal issues, but writers should avoid being partisan or shrill. We also like fiction that crosses genre—for example, a science fiction romance, or fantasy crime story. We have an online archive or fiction and poetry and encourage writers to check it out. That said, *Big Pulp* has a strong editorial bias in favor of stories with monkeys. Especially talking monkeys."

THE BITTER OLEANDER

4983 Tall Oaks Dr., Fayetteville NY 13066. **Fax:** (315)637-5056. **E-mail:** info@bitteroleander.com. **Website:** www.bitteroleander.com. **Contact:** Paul B. Roth, editor and publisher. Publishes ms an average of 1-6 months after acceptance. Editorial lead time is 6 months. Sample copy for $10. Guidelines available online.

MAGAZINE'S NEEDS *The Bitter Oleander*, published semiannually in April and October, seeks "highly imaginative poetry whose language is serious. Particularly interested in translations." Has published poetry by Alan Britt, George Kalamaras, Duane Locke, Silvia Scheibli, ShawnFawson, Anthony Seidman, and Christine Boyka Kluge. Does not want rhyme and meter or most traditional forms. Submit maximum 8 poems. Length: 1-60 lines. Pays contributor's copies.

TIPS "If you are writing poems or short fiction in the tradition of 95% of all journals publishing in this country, then your work will usually not fit for us. If within the first 100 words my mind drifts, the rest rarely makes it. Be yourself and listen to no one but yourself."

⬤ BLACKBIRD

Virginia Commonwealth University Department of English, P.O. Box 843082, Richmond VA 23284. (804)827-4729. **E-mail:** blackbird@vcu.edu. **Website:** www.blackbird.vcu.edu. *Blackbird* is published twice a year. Responds in 6 months. Guidelines online at website.

MAGAZINE'S NEEDS Submit 2-6 poems at a time. "If submitting online, put all poems into one document."

TIPS "We like a story that invites us into its world, that engages our senses, soul and mind. We are able to publish long works in all genres, but query *Blackbird* before you send a prose piece over 8,000 words or a poem exceeding 10 pages."

⬤⬤⬤ BLACK WARRIOR REVIEW

P.O. Box 862936, Tuscaloosa AL 35486. (205)348-4518. **E-mail:** interns.bwr@gmail.com. **Website:** www.bwr.ua.edu. **Contact:** Jenny Gropp Hess, editor. "We publish contemporary fiction, poetry, reviews, essays, and art for a literary audience. We publish the freshest work we can find." Buys first rights. Pays on publication. Publishes ms 6 months after acceptance. Responds in 3-6 months. Sample copy for $10. Guidelines available online.

⬤   Work that appeared in the *Black Warrior Review* has been included in the *Pushcart Prize* anthology, *Harper's Magazine, Best American Short Stories, Best American Poetry* and *New Stories from the South*.

MAGAZINE'S NEEDS "We welcome most styles and forms, and we favor poems that take risks-whether they are quiet or audacious." Submit poems in one document. Accepts up to 5 poems per submission at a maximum of 10 pages. "BWR pays a one-year subscription and a nominal lump-sum fee for all works published."

TIPS "We look for attention to language, freshness, honesty, a convincing and sharp voice. Send us a clean, well-printed, proofread manuscript. Become familiar with the magazine prior to submission."

⬤ BLOOD LOTUS

E-mail: bloodlotusjournal@gmail.com; bloodlotusfiction@gmail.com. **Website:** www.bloodlotusjournal.com. **Contact:** Stacia M. Fleegal, managing editor. *Blood Lotus*, published quarterly online, publishes "poetry, fiction, and anything in between!" Wants "fresh language, memorable characters, strong images, and vivid artwork." Will not open attachments. Reads submissions year round. Acquires first North American rights, electronic archival rights. Guidelines on website.

MAGAZINE'S NEEDS "To us, excellent poems are well-crafted, image-heavy, and don't sound like something we've already read."

TIPS "Don't be boring."

⬤ BLOOD ORANGE REVIEW

E-mail: hkhummel@bloodorangereview.com. **Website:** www.bloodorangereview.com. **Contact:** H.K. Hummel; Stephanie Lenox; Bryan Fry. *Blood Orange Review* publishes fiction, poetry, and nonfiction in an online quarterly. The *Review* is committed to cultivating an audience for exciting literary voices and promoting its writers. *Blood Orange Review*, published online quarterly, is "looking for more than an interesting story or a descriptive image. The pieces we publish are the ones that we remember days or even weeks afterward for their compelling characters, believable voices, or sharp revelations. We're not afraid of anything, but if we bristle or stop having fun, we figure there is a good chance our readers will too. In a word, write deftly. Leave us desiring more." Buys first North American serial rights. Publishes mss 3 months after acceptance. Responds in 8-10 weeks. Editorial lead time 2 months. Sample copy online. Guidelines on website.

MAGAZINE'S NEEDS Submit 3-5 poems at a time in a single file with a .doc, .docx, or .pdf extension. "Don't send just one poem unless it's a long poem (more than three pages). We want to get a sense of your style as a writer, and one poem is not enough to do this." Submit via online submissions manager.

THE BLOOMSBURY REVIEW

1553 Platte St., Suite 206, Denver CO 80202. (303)455-3123. **Fax:** (303)455-7039. **E-mail:** info@bloomsburyreview.com. **E-mail:** editors@bloomsburyreview.com. **Website:** www.bloomsburyreview.com. **Contact:** Marilyn Auer, editor-in-chief/publisher. "We publish book reviews, interviews with writers and poets, literary essays, and original poetry. Our audience consists of educated, literate, nonspecialized readers." Buys first rights, asks for non-exclusive electronic rights. Pays on publication. Publishes ms an average of 4-6 months after acceptance. Responds in 4 months to queries. Sample copy for $5 and 9x12 SASE. Guidelines for #10 SASE.

MAGAZINE'S NEEDS Pays $5-10.

TIPS "We appreciate receiving published clips and/or completed mss. Please—no rough drafts. Book reviews should be of new books (within 6 months of publication)."

BLUE COLLAR REVIEW

Partisan Press, P.O. Box 11417, Norfolk VA 23517. **E-mail:** red-ink@earthlink.net. **Website:** www.partisanpress.org. **Contact:** A. Markowitz, editor; Mary Franke, co-editor. *Blue Collar Review (Journal of Progressive Working Class Literature)*, published quarterly, contains poetry, short stories, and illustrations "reflecting the working class experience—a broad range from the personal to the societal. Our purpose is to promote and expand working class literature and an awareness of the connections between workers of all occupations and the social context in which we live. Also to inspire the creativity and latent talent in 'common' working people."

Has published poetry by Simon Perchik, Jim Daniels, Mary McAnally, Marge Piercy, Alan Catlin, and Rob Whitbeck. *Blue Collar Review* is 60 pages, digest-sized, offset-printed, saddle-stapled, with colored card cover, includes ads. Receives hundreds of poems/year, accepts about 15%. Press run is 500. Subscription is $15/year; $25 for 2 years. Sample copy for $7. Make checks payable to Partisan Press.

MAGAZINE'S NEEDS Send no more than 5 poems. Include name and address on each page. Cover letter is helpful, though not required. Include SASE for response. Does not accept simultaneous submissions. Partisan Press looks for "poetry of power that reflects a working class consciousness and moves us forward as a society. Must be good writing reflecting social realism including but not limited to political issues." Publishes about 3 chapbooks/year; not presently open to unsolicited submissions. "Submissions are requested from among the poets published in the *Blue Collar Review*." Has published *A Possible Explanation* by Peggy Safire and *American Sounds* by Robert Edwards. Chapbooks are usually 20-60 pages, digest-sized, offset-printed, saddle-stapled or flat-spined, with card or glossy covers. Sample chapbooks are $7 and listed on website.

BLUELINE

120 Morey Hall, Department of English and Communication, Postdam NY 13676. (315)267-2043. **E-mail:** blueline@potsdam.edu. **Website:** www2.potsdam.edu/blueline. **Contact:** Donald McNutt, editor; Caroline Downing, art editor. *Blueline* is 200 pages, digest-sized. Press run is 600. "*Blueline* seeks poems, stories, and essays relating to the Adirondacks and regions similar in geography and spirit, or focusing on the shaping influence of nature. Payment in copies. Submission period is July through November. *Blueline* welcomes electronic submissions, either in the body of an e-mail message or in Word or html formatted files. Please avoid using compression software." Acquires first North American serial rights. Publishes ms 3-6 months after acceptance. Responds in up to 3 months to mss. "Decisions in early February." Occa-

sionally comments on rejected mss. Sample copy: $7. Guidelines available for SASE or by e-mail.

🖰 Magazine: 6×9; 200 pages; 70 lb. white stock paper; 65 lb. smooth cover stock; illustrations; photos. "Proofread all submissions. It is difficult for our editors to get excited about work containing typographical and syntactic errors."

MAGAZINE'S NEEDS Has published poetry by L.M. Rosenberg, John Unterecker, Lloyd Van Brunt, Laurence Josephs, Maurice Kenny, and Nancy L. Nielsen. Reviews books of poetry in 500-750 words, single- or multi-book format. "We are interested in both beginning and established poets whose poems evoke universal themes in nature and show human interaction with the natural world. We look for thoughtful craftsmanship rather than stylistic trickery." Does not want "sentimental or extremely experimental poetry." Submit 3 poems at a time. Lines/poem: 75 maximum; "occasionally we publish longer poems." Submit September 1-November 30 only. Include short bio. Poems are circulated to an editorial board. Sometimes comments on rejected poems. Pays 1 contributor's copy.

ADDITIONAL INFORMATION "We are interested in both beginning and established poets whose poems evoke universal themes in nature and show human interaction with the natural world. We look for thoughtful craftsmanship rather than stylistic trickery."

TIPS "We look for concise, clear, concrete prose that tells a story and touches upon a universal theme or situation. We prefer realism to romanticism but will consider nostalgia if well done. Pay attention to grammar and syntax. Avoid murky language, sentimentality, cuteness or folkiness. We would like to see more good fiction related to the Adirondacks and more literary fiction and prose poems. If manuscript has potential, we work with author to improve and reconsider for publication. Our readers prefer fiction to poetry (in general) or reviews. Write from your own experience, be specific and factual (within the bounds of your story) and if you write about universal features such as love, death, change, etc., write about them in a fresh way. Triteness and mediocrity are the hallmarks of the majority of stories seen today."

BLUE MESA REVIEW

E-mail: bmreditr@unm.edu. **Website:** www.unm. edu/~bluemesa/index.htm. **Contact:** Suzanne Richarson, editor; Bonnie Arning, managing editor. "Originally founded by Rudolfo Anaya, Gene Frumkin, Da-

vid Johnson, Patricia Clark Smith, and Lee Bartlette in 1989, the *Blue Mesa Review* emerged as a source of innovative writing produced in the Southwest. Over the years the magazine's nuance has changed, sometimes shifting towards more craft-oriented work, other times re-aligning with its original roots." "We purchase first North American serial rights for print and non-exclusive electronic rights for our website." Responds in 2-6 months.

🖰 Open for submissions from September 1 to May 31. Only accepts submissions through online submissions manager.

MAGAZINE'S NEEDS Submit 3-5 poems.

BLUESTEM

E-mail: info@bluestemmagazine.com. **Website:** www. bluestemmagazine.com. **Contact:** Olga Abella, editor. "*Bluestem*, formerly known as *Karamu*, produces a quarterly online issue (December, March, June, September) and an annual print issue. Submissions are accepted year-round. Print contributors receive a complimentary copy of the issue containing their work, and may purchase extra copies at a discounted price. There is no compensation for online contributors but we will promote your work enthusiastically and widely. Past issues have included themes such as: The Humor Issue, The Music Issue, The Millennium." Responds in 6-8 weeks. "Response times will be significantly longer in the summer. The wait will be longer if we are seriously considering your work." "Sample back issues of *Bluestem (Karamu)* are available for $4 for each issue you would like."

🖰 Only accepts submissions through online submissions manager.

MAGAZINE'S NEEDS Submit using online submissions manager. Include bio (less than 100 words) with submission.

🖰🟢 BOMB MAGAZINE

New Arts Publications, 80 Hanson Place, Suite 703, Brooklyn NY 11217. (718)636-9100. **Fax:** (718)636-9200. **E-mail:** firstproof@bombsite.com; generalinquiries@bombsite.com. **Website:** www.bombsite.com. **Contact:** Monica de la Torre, senior editor. "Written, edited and produced by industry professionals and funded by those interested in the arts. Publishes work which is unconventional and contains an edge, whether it be in style or subject matter." Buys first rights, buys one-time rights. Pays on publication. Publishes ms an average of 3-6 months after acceptance. Responds in 3-5 months to mss. Editorial lead time 3-4 months. Sample copy for $10. Guidelines by e-mail.

MAGAZINE'S NEEDS *BOMB Magazine* accepts unsolicited poetry and prose submissions for our literary pull-out *First Proof* by mail from January 1-August 31. Submissions sent outside these dates will be returned unread. Pays $100, and contributor's copies. Sends galleys to author.

TIPS "Manuscripts should be typed, double-spaced, proofread and should be final drafts. Purchase a sample issue before submitting work."

◐ BORDERLANDS: TEXAS POETRY REVIEW

P.O. Box 33096, Austin TX 78764. **E-mail:** borderlandspoetry@hotmail.com. **Website:** www.borderlands.org. *Borderlands: Texas Poetry Review*, published semiannually, prints "high-quality, outward-looking poetry by new and established poets, as well as brief reviews of poetry books and critical essays. Cosmopolitan in content, but particularly welcomes Texas and Southwest writers." Wants "outward-looking poems that exhibit social, political, geographical, historical, feminist, or spiritual awareness coupled with concise artistry. Does not want "introspective work about the speaker's psyche, childhood, or intimate relationships." Has published poetry by Walter McDonald, Naomi Shihab Nye, Mario Susko, Wendy Barker, Larry D. Thomas, Reza Shirazi, and Scott Hightower. *Borderlands* is 100-150 pages, digest-sized, offset-printed, perfect-bound, with 4-color cover. Receives about 2,000 poems/year, accepts about 120. Press run is 1,000. Sample: $12. Guidelines available online.

MAGAZINE'S NEEDS Submit 4 typed poems at a time. Include cover letter. Include SASE with sufficient return postage. "Please submit outwardly directed poetry that exhibits social, political, geographical, historical, or spiritual awareness. We are open to traditional and experimental forms."

TIPS "Editors read year round in two cycles. Submissions postmarked by June 15 will be considered for the Fall/Winter issue, and submissions postmarked by December 15 will be considered for the Spring/Summer issue. Occasionally, work may be held for publication in the following issue. Note that response times may be slower for work received immediately after a

deadline. Do not submit work while we are considering a previous submission."

◐◉⑤ BOSTON REVIEW

PO Box 425786, Cambridge MA 02142. (617)324-1360. **Fax:** (617)452-3356. **E-mail:** review@bostonreview.net. **Website:** www.bostonreview.net. "The editors are committed to a society and culture that foster human diversity and a democracy in which we seek common grounds of principle amidst our many differences. In the hope of advancing these ideals, the *Review* acts as a forum that seeks to enrich the language of public debate." Buys first North American serial rights, buys first rights. Publishes ms an average of 4 months after acceptance. Responds in 4 months to queries. Sample copy for $5 or online. Guidelines available online.

◒ *Boston Review* is a recipient of the Pushcart Prize in Poetry.

MAGAZINE'S NEEDS "We are open to both traditional and experimental forms. What we value most is originality and a strong sense of voice." Send materials for review consideration. Reads poetry between September 15 and May 15 each year. Payment varies.

TIPS "The best way to get a sense of the kind of material *Boston Review* is looking for is to read the magazine. (Sample copies are available for $6.95 plus shipping.) We do not consider previously published material. Simultaneous submissions are fine as long as we are notified of the fact. We accept submissions through our **online submissions system**."

◐◉⑤ BOULEVARD

Opojaz, Inc., 6614 Clayton Rd., Box 325, Richmond Heights MO 63117. (314)862-2643. **Fax:** (314)862-2982. **E-mail:** richardburgin@att.net; jessicarogen@boulevardmagazine.org; kellyleavitt@boulevardmagazine.com. **Website:** www.boulevardmagazine.org. **Contact:** Richard Burgin, editor; Jessica Rogen, managing editor; Kelly Leavitt, associate editor. "*Boulevard* is a diverse literary magazine presenting original creative work by well-known authors, as well as by writers of exciting promise." Buys first North American serial rights. Rights revert to author upon publication. Pays on publication. Publishes ms an average of 9 months after acceptance. Responds in 2 weeks to queries. Responds in 3 months to mss. Sample copy for $10 Guidelines available online.

◒ "*Boulevard* has been called 'one of the half-dozen best literary journals' by Poet Laureate Daniel Hoffman in *The Philadelphia Inquirer*.

We strive to publish the finest in poetry, fiction and nonfiction."

MAGAZINE'S NEEDS *Boulevard*, published 3 times/year, strives "to publish only the finest in fiction, poetry, and nonfiction (essays and interviews). While we frequently publish writers with previous credits, we are very interested in publishing less experienced or unpublished writers with exceptional promise. We've published everything from John Ashbery to Donald Hall to a wide variety of styles from new or lesser known poets. We're eclectic. We are interested in original, moving poetry written from the head as well as the heart. It can be about any topic." Has published poetry by Albert Goldbarth, Molly Peacock, Bob Hicok, Alice Friman, Dick Allen, and Tom Disch. *Boulevard* is 175-250 pages, digest-sized, professionally printed, flat-spined, with glossy card cover. Subscription: $15 for 3 issues, $22 for 6 issues, $25 for 9 issues. "Foreign subscribers, please add $6." Sample: $8 plus 5 first-class stamps and SASE. Make checks payable to Opojaz, Inc. Considers simultaneous submissions with notification; no previously published poems. Guidelines available for SASE, by e-mail, or on website. Responds in less than 2 months. Acquires first-time publication and anthology rights. Does not consider book reviews. "Do not send us light verse." Does not want "poetry that is uninspired, formulaic, self-conscious, unoriginal, insipid." Length: 200/max lines. Pays $25-300 (sometimes higher) depending on length, plus one contributor's copy.

HOW TO CONTACT No e-mail submissions. All submissions must include SASE. Author's name and address must appear on each submission, with author's first and last name on each page. Cover letter is encouraged ("but not required"). Reads submissions October 1-April 30 only. Sometimes comments on rejected poems.

TIPS "Read the magazine first. The work *Boulevard* publishes is generally recognized as among the finest in the country. We continue to seek more good literary or cultural essays. Send only your best work."

THE BREAKTHROUGH INTERCESSOR

Breakthrough, Inc., P.O. Box 121, Lincoln VA 20160. **E-mail:** breakthrough@intercessors.org. **Website:** http://intercessors.org. *The Breakthrough Intercessor*, published quarterly, focuses on "encouraging people in prayer and faith; preparing and equipping those who pray." Accepts multiple articles per issue: 300-1,000 word true stories on prayer. Time between acceptance and publication varies. Guidelines available on website.

- *The Breakthrough Intercessor* is 36 pages, magazine-sized, professionally printed, saddle-stapled with self cover, includes art/graphics. Press run is 4,000. Subscription: $18. Make checks payable to Breakthrough, Inc.

THE BRIAR CLIFF REVIEW

3303 Rebecca St., Sioux City IA 51104. (712)279-5477. **E-mail:** tricia.currans-sheehan@briarcliff.edu (editor); jeanne.emmons@briarcliff.edu (poetry). **Website:** www.briarcliff.edu/bcreview. **Contact:** Tricia Currans-Sheehan, Jeanne Emmons, Phil Hey, Paul Weber, editors. *The Briar Cliff Review*, published annually in April, is "an attractive, eclectic literary/art magazine." The *Briar Cliff Review* focuses on (but is not limited to) "Siouxland writers and subjects. We are happy to proclaim ourselves a regional publication. It doesn't diminish us; it enhances us." Acquires first serial rights. Sample copy available for $15 and 9x12 SAE. Guidelines available on website or for #10 SASE.

- Magazine: 125 pages; 70 lb. 100# Altima Satin Text; illustrations; photos; perfect-bound, with 4-color cover on dull stock. Member: CLMP; Humanities International Complete.

MAGAZINE'S NEEDS Wants "quality poetry with strong imagery and tight, well-wrought language; especially interested in, but not limited to, regional, Midwestern content." Receives about 1,000 poems/year; accepts about 30. Considers simultaneous submissions, but expects prompt notification of acceptance elsewhere. No e-mail submissions, unless from overseas. Cover letter is required. "Include short bio. Submissions should be typewritten or letter quality, with author's name and address on each page. No mss returned without SASE." Reads submissions August 1-November 1 only. Time between acceptance and publication is up to 6 months. Seldom comments on rejected poems. Responds in 6-8 months. Pays with 2 contributor's copies.

TIPS "So many stories are just telling. We want some action. It has to move. We prefer stories in which there is no gimmick, no mechanical turn of events, no moral except the one we would draw privately."

BRILLIANT CORNERS: A JOURNAL OF JAZZ & LITERATURE

Lycoming College, 700 College Place, Williamsport PA 17701. **Website:** www.lycoming.edu/brilliantcorners. **Contact:** Sascha Feinstein. "We publish jazz-related literature—fiction, poetry, and nonfiction. We are open as to length and form." Semiannual. Acquires first North American serial rights. Publishes ms 4-12 months after acceptance. Responds in 2 weeks to queries; 1-2 months to mss. Sample Copy $7. Guidelines available online.

Journal: 6×9; 90 pages; 70 lb. Cougar opaque, vellum, natural paper; photographs. Does not read mss May 15-September 1. Receives 10-15 unsolicited mss/month. Accepts 1-2 mss/issue; 2-3 mss/year. Rarely comments on rejected mss.

MAGAZINE'S NEEDS Submit 3-5 poems at a time. No previously published poems or simultaneous submissions. No e-mail or fax submissions. Cover letter is preferred. Staff reviews books of poetry. Send materials for review consideration. Wants "work that is both passionate and well crafted—work worthy of our recent contributors." Has published poetry by Amiri Baraka, Jayne Cortez, Yusef Komunyakaa, Philip Levine, Sonia Sanchez, and Al Young. Does not want "sloppy hipster jargon or improvisatory nonsense."

TIPS "We look for clear, moving prose that demostrates a love of both writing and jazz. We primarily publish established writers, but we read all submissions carefully and welcome work by outstanding young writers."

BRYANT LITERARY REVIEW

Faculty Suite F, Bryant University, 1150 Douglas Pike, Smithfield RI 02917. **E-mail:** blr@bryant.edu. **Website:** http://bryantliteraryreview.org. **Contact:** Tom Chandler, editor; Stasia Walmsley, managing editor; Lucie Koretsky, associate editor. *Bryant Literary Review* is an international magazine of poetry and fiction published annually in May. Features poetry, fiction, photography, and art. "Our only standard is quality." Has published poetry by Michael S. Harper, Mary Crow, Denise Duhamel, and Baron Wormser. *Bryant Literary Review* is 125 pages, digest-sized, offset-printed, perfect-bound, with 4-color cover with art or photo. Single copy: $8; subscription: $8. To submit work, please review the submission guidelines on our website. Acquires one-time rights. Publishes ms 5 months after acceptance. Responds in 3 months. Guidelines available online and in magazine.

MAGAZINE'S NEEDS Submit 3-5 poems at a time. Cover letter is required. "Include SASE; please submit only once each reading period." Reads submissions September 1-December 31. Pays 2 contributor's copies.

TIPS "We expect readers of the *Bryant Literary Review* to be sophisticated, educated, and familiar with the conventions of contemporary literature. We see our purpose to be the cultivation of an active and growing connection between our community and the larger literary culture. Our production values are of the highest caliber, and our roster of published authors includes major award and fellowship winners. The *BLR* provides a respected venue for creative writing of every kind from around the world. Our only standard is quality. No abstract expressionist poems, please. We prefer accessible work of depth and quality."

BURNSIDE REVIEW

P.O. Box 1782, Portland OR 97207. **Website:** www.burnsidereview.org. *Burnside Review* is 80 pages, 6x6, professionally printed, perfect-bound. *Burnside Review*, published every 9 months, prints "the best poetry and short fiction we can get our hands on." Each issue includes one featured poet with an interview and new poems. "We tend to publish writing that finds beauty in truly unexpected places; that combines urban and natural imagery; that breaks the heart." Acquires first rights. Pays on publication. Publishes ms 9 months after acceptance. Responds in 1-4 months. Submit seasonal poems 3-6 months in advance. Single copy: $8; subscription: $13. Make checks payable to Burnside Review or order online.

MAGAZINE'S NEEDS Has published poetry by Linda Bierds, Dorianne Laux, Ed Skoog, Campbell McGrath, Paul Guest, and Larissa Szporluk. Reads submissions year-round. "Editors read all work submitted." Seldom comments on rejected work. Submit electronically on website. Pays $50 plus 1 contributor's copy.

TIPS "*Burnside Review* accepts submissions of poetry and fiction. If you have something else that you think would be a perfect fit for our journal, please query the editor before submitting. We like work that breaks the heart. That leaves us in a place that we don't expect to be. We like the lyric. We like the narrative. We like when the two merge. We like whiskey. We like hourglass figures. We like crying over past mistakes. We like to be surprised. Surprise us. Read a past issue and try to to understand our tastes. At the least, please read the sample poems that we have linked from our prior issues."

●●⑤ BUTTON

P.O. Box 77, Westminster MA 01473. **E-mail:** sally@moonsigns.net. **Website:** www.moonsigns.net. *"Button* is New England's tiniest magazine of poetry, fiction, and gracious living, published once a year. As 'gracious living' is on the cover, we like wit, brevity, cleverly-conceived essay/recipe, poetry that isn't sentimental, or song lyrics. I started *Button* so that a century from now, when people read it in landfills or, preferably, libraries, they'll say, 'Gee, what a great time to have lived. I wish I lived back then.'" Buys first North American serial rights. Pays on publication. Publishes ms 3-9 months after acceptance. Responds in 1 month to queries. Responds in 2 months to mss. Sometimes comments on rejected mss. Editorial lead time 6 months. Sample copy for $2.50. Guidelines available online.

○ Receives 20-40 unsolicited mss/month. Accepts 3-6 mss/issue; 3-6mss/year. *Button* is 16-24 pages, saddle-stapled, with cardstock offset cover with illustrations that incorporate 1 or more buttons. Press run is 500. Subscription: $5 for 3 issues. "We don'ttake e-mail submissions, unless you're living overseas, in which case we respond electronically. But we strongly suggest you request writers' guidelines (send an SASE). Better still, look over our online issue or order a sample copy for $2.50, which includes postage." Has published poetryby Amanda Powell, Brendan Galvin, Jean Monahan, Mary Campbell, KevinMcGrath, and Ed Conti.

MAGAZINE'S NEEDS Wants quality poetry; "poetry that incises a perfect figure 8 on the ice, but also cuts beneath that mirrored surface. Minimal use of vertical pronoun. Do not submit more than twice in 1 year." No previously published poems. Cover letter is required. Does not want "sentiment; no 'musing' on who or what done ya wrong." Pays honorarium and at least 2 contributor's copies.

TIPS *"Button* writers have been widely published elsewhere, in virtually all the major national magazines. They include Ralph Lombreglia, Lawrence Millman,

They Might Be Giants, Combustible Edison, Sven Birkerts, Stephen McCauley, Amanda Powell, Wayne Wilson, David Barber, Romayne Dawnay, Brendan Galvin, and Diana DerHovanessian. It's $2.50 for a sample, which seems reasonable. Follow the guidelines, make sure you read your work aloud, and don't inflate or deflate your publications and experience. We've published plenty of new folks, but on the merits of the work."

CAKETRAIN

P.O. Box 82588, Pittsburgh PA 15218. **E-mail:** editors@caketrain.org. **Website:** www.caketrain.org. **Contact:** Amanda Raczkowski and Joseph Reed, editors. "Please submit up to seven poems, works of fiction or creative nonfiction (no book reviews), works of visual art, or any combination therein, to editors@caketrain.org only; do not send work by mail. Submissions should include a cover letter with titles of pieces and a brief biographical statement. *Caketrain* does not accept previously published pieces. Simultaneous submissions are permitted; please notify immediately if a piece is chosen for publication elsewhere. Response time can take up to 6 months, but is often much shorter. Please do not submit additional work until a decision has been made regarding your current submission. Contributors receive 1 complimentary copy. All rights revert to authors upon publication." Price: $9.

● CALYX

Calyx, Inc., P.O. Box B, Corvallis OR 97339. (541)753-9384. **Fax:** (541)753-0515. **E-mail:** info@calyxpress.org; editor@calyxpress.org. **Website:** www.calyxpress.org. **Contact:** Rebecca Olson, senior editor. *"Calyx* exists to publish fine literature and art by women and is committed to publishing the work of all women, including women of color, older women, working class women and other voices that need to be heard. We are committed to discovering and nurturing developing writers." Publishes ms an average of 6-12 months after acceptance. Responds in 4-8 months to mss. Sample copy for $10 plus $4 postage and handling.

○ Annual open submission period is October 1-December 31.

MAGAZINE'S NEEDS "When submitting through our online submissions manager, please put all poems in the same document." Wants "excellently crafted poetry that also has excellent content." "A contributor's payment for publication in *CALYX* journal includes copies of the issue (re pages published in Journal) and a one-volume subscription following that issue."

TIPS "A forum for women's creative work—including work by women of color, lesbian and queer women, young women, old women—*CALYX* journal breaks new ground. Each issue is packed with new poetry, short stories, full-color artwork, photography, essays, and reviews."

☺ CANADIAN WRITER'S JOURNAL

Box 1178, New Liskeard ON P0J 1P0, Canada. (705)647-5424. **Fax:** (705)647-8366. **E-mail:** editor@ cwj.ca. **Website:** www.cwj.ca. **Contact:** Deborah Ranchuk, editor. "Digest-size magazine for writers emphasizing short 'how-to' articles, which convey easily understood information useful to both apprentice and professional writers. General policy and postal subsidies require that the magazine must carry a substantial Canadian content. We try for about 90% Canadian content, but prefer good material over country of origin, or how well you're known. Writers may query, but unsolicited mss are welcome." Buys one-time rights. Pays on publication. Publishes ms an average of 2-9 months after acceptance. Responds in 2 months to queries. Sample copy for $8, including postage. Guidelines available online.

MAGAZINE'S NEEDS Poetry must be unpublished elsewhere; short poems or extracts used as part of articles on the writing of poetry. Submit up to 5 poems at a time. No previously published poems. Accepts e-mail submissions (pasted into body of message, with 'Submission' in the subject line). Include SASE with postal submissions. "U.S. postage accepted; do not affix to envelope. Poems should be titled." Responds in 3-6 months. Pays $2-5 per poem published (depending on length) and 1 contributor's copy. SASE required for response and payment.

TIPS "We prefer short, tightly written, informative how-to articles. US writers: note that US postage cannot be used to mail from Canada. Obtain Canadian stamps, use IRCs, or send small amounts in cash."

☺❶❸ THE CAPILANO REVIEW

2055 Purcell Way, North Vancouver BC V7J 3H5, Canada. (604)984-1712. **E-mail:** tcr@capilanou.ca. **Website:** www.thecapilanoreview.ca. **Contact:** Tamara Lee, managing editor. Tri-annual visual and literary arts magazine that "publishes only what the editors consider to be the very best fiction, poetry, drama, or visual art being produced. *TCR* editors

are interested in fresh, original work that stimulates and challenges readers. Over the years, the magazine has developed a reputation for pushing beyond the boundaries of traditional art and writing. We are interested in work that is new in concept and in execution." Buys first North American serial rights. Pays on publication. Publishes ms an average of within 1 year after acceptance. Responds in 4-6 months to mss. Sample copy for $10 (outside of Canada, USD). Guidelines with #10 SASE with IRC or Canadian stamps.

MAGAZINE'S NEEDS Submit up to 8 pages of poetry. Pays $50-300.

◯ THE CARIBBEAN WRITER

University of the Virgin Islands, RR 1, P.O. Box 10,000, Kingshill, St. Croix USVI 00850. (340)692-4152. **Fax:** (340)692-4026. **E-mail:** info@thecaribbeanwriter.org. **E-mail:** submit@thecaribbeanwriter.org. **Website:** www.thecaribbeanwriter.org. **Contact:** Erika J. Waters, founding editor. "*The Caribbean Writer* features new and exciting voices from the region, and beyond that explore the diverse and multi-ethnic culture in poetry, short fiction, personal essays, creative nonfiction, and plays. Social, cultural, economic and sometimes controversial issues are also explored, employing a wide array of literary devices."

◯ Poetry published in *The Caribbean Writer* has appeared in The Pushcart Prize. Has published poetry by Edwidge Danticat, Geoffrey Philp, and Thomas Reiter. *The Caribbean Writer* is 300+ pages, digest-sized, handsomely printed on heavy stock, perfect-bound, with glossy card cover. Press run is 1,200. Single copy: $10; subscription: $25/2 years.

HOW TO CONTACT Submit up to 5 poems at a time. Considers simultaneous submissions; no previously published poems. Accepts e-mail as attachment; no fax submissions. Name, address, phone number, e-mail address, and title of ms should appear in cover letter along with brief bio. Title only on ms. Guidelines available in magazine, for SASE, by e-mail, or on website. Pays 2 contributor's copies. Acquires first North American serial rights. Reviews books of poetry and fiction in 1,000 words. Send materials for review consideration.

CONTEST/AWARD OFFERINGS All submissions are eligible for the Daily News Prize ($300) for poetry, The Marguerite Cobb McKay Prize to a Virgin Island author ($200), the David Hough Literary Prize to a

Caribbean author ($500), the Canute A. Brodhurst Prize for Fiction ($400), and the Charlotte and Isidor Paiewonsky Prize ($200) for first-time publication.

◑ THE CAROLINA QUARTERLY

CB #3520 Greenlaw Hall, University of North Carolina, Chapel Hill NC 27599-3520. (919)962-0244. **E-mail:** carolina.quarterly@gmail.com. **Website:** www.thecarolinaquarterly.com. *The Carolina Quarterly*, published 3 times/year, prints fiction, poetry, reviews, nonfiction, and visual art. No specifications regarding form, length, subject matter, or style of poetry. Considers translations of work originally written in languages other than English. Acquires first rights. Responds in 4-6 months. Sample copy: $9.

○   Has published poetry by Denise Levertov, Richard Wilbur, Robert Morgan, Ha Jin, and Charles Wright. *The Carolina Quarterly* is about 100 pages, digest-sized, professionally printed, perfect-bound, with glossy cover, includes ads. Receives about 6,000 poems/year, accepts about 1%. Press run is 1,000. Subscription: $24 for individuals, $30 for institutions.

MAGAZINE'S NEEDS Submit 1-6 poems at a time. No previously published poems. (Simultaneous submissions welcome with nonficton.) No e-mail submissions. SASE required. Electronic submissions accepted, see website for details. "All mss are read by an editor. Poems that make it to the meeting of the full poetry staff are discussed by all. Poems are accepted by majority consensus informed by the poetry editor's advice." Seldom comments on rejected poems. "Poets are welcome to write or e-mail regarding their submission's status, but please wait about four months before doing so." Reviews books of poetry. Send materials for review consideration (attn: Editor). Pays 2 contributor's copies.

CONTEST/AWARD OFFERINGS The Charles B. Wood Award for Distinguished Writing is given to the author of the best poem or short story published in each volume of *The Carolina Quarterly*. Only those writers without major publications are considered, and the winner receives a cash award.

CARUS PUBLISHING COMPANY

30 Grove St., Suite C, Peterborough NH 03458. **Website:** www.cricketmag.com. "We do not accept e-mailed submissions. Mss must be typed and accompanied by an SASE so that we may respond to your submission. Mss without an accompanying SASE

will not be considered. Unfortunately, we are unable to return mss. Please do not send us your only copy. When submitting poetry, please send us no more than 6 poems at a time. Be sure to include phone and e-mail contact information. Please allow us up to 8 months for careful consideration of your submission. No phone calls, please."

○   See listings for *Babybug*, *Cicada*, *Click*, *Cricket*, *Ladybug*, *Muse*, *Spider* and *ASK*. Carus Publishing owns Cobblestone Publishing, publisher of *AppleSeeds*, *Calliope*, *Cobblestone*, *Dig*, *Faces* and *Odyssey*.

◑ CAVEAT LECTOR

400 Hyde St., Apt. 606, San Francisco CA 94109. (415)928-7431. **Fax:** (415)928-7431. **E-mail:** editors@caveat-lector.org. **Website:** www.caveat-lector.org. **Contact:** Christopher Bernard, co-editor. *Caveat Lector*, published 2 times/year, "is devoted to the arts and cultural and philosophical commentary. As well as literary work, we publish art, photography, music, streaming audio of selected literary pieces, and short films. Poetry, fiction, artwork, music, and short films are posted on our website. Visit www.caveat_lector.org to see examples of the kind of work we are interested in. But don't let those examples limit your submissions. Please send us what you feel is your strongest work, in any style and on any subject." Acquires first rights.

MAGAZINE'S NEEDS Wants poems "on any subject, in any style, as long as the work is authentic in feeling and appropriately crafted. We are looking for accomplished poems, something that resonates in the mind long after the reader has laid the poem aside. We want work that has authenticity of emotion and high craft; poems that, whether raw or polished, ring true—and if humorous, are actually funny, or at least witty. Classical to experimental. Note: We sometimes request authors for audio of work we publish to post on our website." Has published poetry by Joanne Lowery, Simon Perchik, Les Murray, Alfred Robinson, and Ernest Hilbert. Submit poetry through postal mail only. Send brief bio and SASE with submission. Accepts submissions between February 1 and June 30. Pays contributor's copies.

CAVE WALL

P.O. Box 29546, Greensboro NC 27429. **E-mail:** editor@cavewallpress.com. **Website:** www.cavewallpress.com. "*Cave Wall*, published twice a year, is a national literary magazine dedicated to publishing the best in contemporary poetry. We are interested in poems of any length and style from both established and emerging poets. Each issue includes black & white art, as well. Poems first published in *Cave Wall* have been featured on *Poetry Daily, Verse Daily, The Writer's Almanac*, and in the *Best New Poets* awards anthology." Buys first North American serial rights. Responds in 1-5 months to mss. Guidelines on website.

MAGAZINE'S NEEDS Submit 3-6 poems at a time with SASE. *Cave Wall* reads unsolicited poetry submissions twice a year. Check the website for our fall open reading period. Pays 2 contributor's copies.

TIPS "We encourage you to read an issue of *Cave Wall* before you submit. Find out what kind of poetry we like. Please note that we read blind. Your name should not appear on your poems."

CC&D: CHILDREN, CHURCHES & DADDIES: THE UNRELIGIOUS, NON-FAMILY-ORIENTED LITERARY AND ART MAGAZINE

Scars Publications and Design, 829 Brian Court, Gurnee IL 60031. (847)281-9070. **E-mail:** ccandd96@scars.tv. **Website:** http://scars.tv/ccd. **Contact:** Janet Kuypers. "Our biases are works that relate to issues such as politics, sexism, society, and the like, but are definitely not limited to such. We publish good work that makes you think, that makes you feel like you've lived through a scene instead of merely reading it. If it relates to how the world fits into a person's life (political story, a day in the life, coping with issues people face), it will probably win us over faster. We have received comments from readers and other editors saying that they thought some of our stories really happened. They didn't, but it was nice to know they were so concrete, so believable people thought they were nonfiction. Do that to our readers." Publishes short shorts, essays and stories. Also publishes poetry. Always comments on/critiques rejected mss if asked. Ms published 1 year after acceptance. Responds to queries in 2 weeks; mss in 2 weeks. "Responds much faster to e-mail submissions and queries." Sample copy available of issues before 2010 for $6. Guidelines available for SASE, via e-mail, on website.

Monthly literary magazine/journal: 5.5x8.5 perfect-bound, 84-page book. Contains illustrations and photographs as well as short stories, essays, and poetry. Has published Mel Waldman, Kenneth DiMaggio, Linda Webb Aceto, Brian Looney, Joseph Hart, Fritz Hamilton, G.A. Scheinoha, Ken Dean.

CELLAR DOOR POETRY JOURNAL

Dreamland Books, Inc., P.O. Box 1714, Minnetonka MN 55345. **E-mail:** dreamlandbooks@inbox.com. **Website:** www.cellardoorpoetry.com; www.dreamlandbooksinc.com. Acquires one-time rights. Rights revert to poet upon publication. Publishes ms 1 year after acceptance. Guidelines available on website.

MAGAZINE'S NEEDS Does not want poetry promoting pornography, violence, racism, sexism, or any form of hate.

CONTEST/AWARD OFFERINGS Sponsors annual contest. See web page for guidelines. Prize: publication plus royalty.

CEREMONY, A JOURNAL OF POETRY AND OTHER ARTS

Dance of My Hands Publishing, 120 Vista Dr., Warminster PA 18974. **Website:** www.danceofmyhands.com. *Ceremony, a Journal of Poetry and Other Arts*, published biannually, encourages "all expression and articism. Beginning poets are especially encouraged." Wants poetry, short pieces of prose, photography and other printable arts. Considers poetry by teens. *Ceremony* is small, home-printed on 20 lb. recycled paper, and single staple-bound. Receives about 200 submissions/year, accepts 50%. Single copy: $3. Publishes ms 1-2 years after acceptance. Guidelines available on website under 'Contact.'

MAGAZINE'S NEEDS Submit up to 6 poems at a time. Poems of shorter length preferred. Considers previously published poems and simultaneous submissions. Accepts e-mail submissions only. Reads submissions year round. Sometimes comments on rejected poems. Sometimes publishes theme issues. Pays 1 contributor's copy.

CERISE PRESS

P.O. Box 241187, Omaha NE 68124. **E-mail:** editors@cerisepress.com. **E-mail:** submissions@cerisepress.com. **Website:** www.cerisepress.com. *Cerise Press*, published 3 times/year, is an "international, online journal of literature, arts, and culture (with a forthcoming print anthology) based in the US and France, offering poetry, nonfiction, translations, fiction, artwork, and photography." Has published Mahmoud Darwish, Auxeméry, Tess Gallagher, Yusef Komunyakaa, EleanorWilner, Pierre-Albert Jourdan, Abdelwahab Meddeb, Pura López-Colomé, Dorianne

Laux, Ray Gonzalez, Victoria Chang. Responds in 2-3 months. Guidelines available online.

MAGAZINE'S NEEDS Submit via e-mail. Considers simultaneous submissions. Cover letter is required. "Please let us know if work is accepted elsewhere. Do not query until 3 months from the date of submission." Reads submissions year round. Reviews books and chapbooks of poetry, fiction, critical essays, biographies, photography, and more.

◑ CHAFFIN JOURNAL

English Department, Eastern Kentucky University, C, Richmond KY 40475-3102. (859)622-3080. **E-mail:** robert.witt@eku.edu. **Website:** www.english.eku. edu/chaffin_journal. **Contact:** Robert Witt, editor. *The Chaffin Journal*, published annually in December, prints quality short fiction and poetry by new and established writers/poets. "We publish fiction on any subject; our only consideration is the quality." Pays on publication for one-time rights. Publishes 6 months after acceptance. Send SASE for return of ms. Responds in 1 week to queries; responds in 3 months to mss. Sample copy for $6.

○ Receives 20 unsolicited mss/month. Accepts 6-8 mss/year. Does not read mss October 1 through May 31. Publishes 2-3 new writers/ year. Has published work by Meridith Sue Willis, Marie Manilla, Raymond Abbott, Marjorie Bixler, Chris Helvey.

MAGAZINE'S NEEDS Submit 5 poems per submission period. Considers simultaneous submissions (although not preferred); no previously published poems. No e-mail or disk submissions. Cover letter is preferred. "Submit typed pages with only 1 poem per page. Enclose SASE." Wants any form, subject matter, or style of poetry. Has published poetry by Taylor Graham, Diane Glancy, Judith Montgomery, Simon Perchik, Philip St. Clair, and Virgil Suárez. Does not want "poor quality." Pays 1 contributor's copy.

TIPS "All mss submitted are considered."

◐◑ CHALLENGER INTERNATIONAL

E-mail: lukivdan@hotmail.com. **Website:** http:// challengerinternational.20m.com/index.html. *Challenger international*, published annually, contains "poetry and (on occasion) short fiction." Wants "any type of work, especially by teenagers (our mandate: to encourage young writers, and to publish their work alongside established writers), providing it is not pornographic, profane, or overly abstract." Has published

poetry from Canada, the continental U.S., Hawaii, Switzerland, Russia, Malta, Italy, Slovenia, Ireland, England, Korea, Pakistan, Australia, Zimbabwe, Argentina, and Columbia. *Challenger international* is generally 20-50 pages, magazine-sized, laser-printed, side-stapled. Press run is 50. *Challenger international* is distributed free to McNaughton Centre Secondary Alternate School sudents.

MAGAZINE'S NEEDS Considers previously published poems and simultaneous submissions. Cover letter is required. Include list of credits, if any. Accepts e-mail submissions only; no postal submissions. "Sometimes we edit to save the poet rejection." Responds in 6 months. Payment is 1 e-copy (sent as an e-mail attachment) of the issue in which the author's work appears. Poet retains rights.

ADDITIONAL INFORMATION Island Scholastic Press publishes chapbooks by authors featured in *Challenger international*. Pays 3 author's copies. Copyright remains with author. Distribution of free copies through McNaughton Centre.

○ CHANTARELLE'S NOTEBOOK

E-mail: chantarellesnotebook@yahoo.com. **Website:** www.chantarellesnotebook.com. **Contact:** Kendall A. Bell and Christinia Bell, editors. *Chantarelle's Notebook*, published quarterly online, seeks "quality work from undiscovered poets. We enjoy poems that speak to us—poems with great sonics and visuals. *Chantarelle's Notebook* will publish a 'best of' print journal that will cull poems from each of the previous 4 quarterly issues in the past year. The authors of the poems chosen will receive 1 contributor's copy and can buy additional copies at half price." Acquires one-time rights. Rights revert to poets upon publication. Responds in 6-8 weeks. Never comments on rejected poems. Sample: see website for latest issue. Guidelines available on website. "Please follow the guidelines— all the information is there!"

○ Has published poetry by Emily Brogan, Heather Cadenhead, Taylor Copeland, Amber Decker, Taylor Graham, and Donna Vorreyer.

MAGAZINE'S NEEDS Receives about 500 poems/ year, accepts about 20%. Submit 3-5 poems at a time. Lines/poem: "shorter poems have a better chance, but long poems are fine." Accepts e-mail submissions (pasted into body of message; "we will not open any attachments—they will be deleted"). Cover letter is required. "Please include a short bio of no more than 75 words, should we decide to accept your work." Reads submissions year round. "The editors will review all submissions and make a decision within a week's time." Does not want "infantile rants, juvenile confessionals, greeting card-styled verse, political posturing, or religious outpourings." Considers poetry by children and teens. "There are no age restrictions, but submissions from younger people will be held to the same guidelines and standards as those from adults."

◉◑ CHAPMAN

Chapman Publishing, 4 Broughton Place, Edinburgh EH1 3RX Scotland. (44)(131)557-2207. **E-mail:** chapman-pub@blueyounder.co.uk. **Website:** www.chapman-pub.co.uk. **Contact:** Joy Hendry, editor. Magazine published 3 times/year covering poetry, fiction, articles, and reviews. *Chapman*, Scotland's quality literary magazine, is a dynamic force in Scotland, publishing poetry, fiction, criticism, reviews, and articles on theatre, politics, language, and the arts. Our philosophy is to publish new work, from known and unknown writers—mainly Scottish, but also worldwide. Buys first rights. Pays on publication. Publishes ms an average of 3 months after acceptance. Guidelines by e-mail.

◑ Does not accept e-mail submissions.

MAGAZINE'S NEEDS "Submit 4-10 poems laid out so that the shape and structure of the work is shown to best advantage (12 font/15-16 line space ideal). One poem to each sheet."

TIPS "Keep your stories for six months and edit carefully. We seek challenging work which attempts to explore difficult/new territory in content and form, but lighter work, if original enough, is welcome. We have no plans at present to publish longer fiction or novels. - Plays: We do not publish plays that have not been performed. If you would like to get a better impression of Chapman, individual copies of the magazine are available from us. Sample issue costs £3.45 inc p&p."

CHARACTER I

443 W. Hight St., Suite D, Peoria IL 61606. **E-mail:** editor@characteri.com. **Website:** www.characteri.com. **Contact:** Edward Maximilian, editor. "*character i* is focused on publishing works that embody and explore the first-person narrative." Purchases worldwide print and electronic first rights. Responds in 1 week for queries and 2 weeks for mss. Editorial lead time 2 months. Writer's guidelines are available online at website.

MAGAZINE'S NEEDS Send complete ms.

TIPS "Please be sure to proofread your work prior to submission."

◐ THE CHARITON REVIEW

Truman State University Press, 100 E Normal Ave., Kirksville MO 63501. (800)916-6802. **E-mail:** chariton@truman.edu. **Website:** http://tsup.truman.edu/aboutChariton.asp. **Contact:** Barbara Smith-Mandell, managing editor. "Truman State University Press (TSUP) publishes peer-reviewed research in the humanities for the scholarly community and the broader public, and publishes creative literary works. TSUP is a resource to the Truman campus community, where students explore their publishing interests and scholars seek publishing advice." TSUP is now publishing *The Chariton Review*, an international literary journal. Guidelines available on website

◑ James D'Agostino became editor in July 2010. He teaches at Truman State University and is the author of *Nude with Anything*. See also The Chariton Review Short Fiction Prize at http://tsup.truman.edu/prizes.asp.

MAGAZINE'S NEEDS *TSUP is currently not accepting unsolicited poetry manuscripts.* Poetry mss are published through TSUP's annual T.S. Eliot Prize for Poetry. Deadline is October 31 of each year. See competition guidelines at http://tsup.truman.edu/prizes.asp.

◐ CHAUTAUQUA LITERARY JOURNAL

Department of Creative Writing, University of North Carolina at Wilmington, 601 S. College Rd., Wilmington NC 28403. **E-mail:** clj@uncw.edu. **Website:** http://writers.ciweb.org. **Contact:** Jill Gerard, editor; Philip Gerard, editor. *Chautauqua*, published annually in June, prints poetry, short fiction, and creative nonfiction. "The editors actively solicit writing that expresses the values of Chautauqua Institution broadly construed: A sense of inquiry into questions of personal, social, political, spiritual, and aesthetic importance, regardless of genre. We consider the work of any writer, whether or not affiliated with Chautauqua institution. The qualities we seek include a mastery of craft, attention to vivid and accurate language, a true lyric 'ear,' an original and compelling vision, and strong narrative instinct. Above all, we value work that is intensely personal, yet somehow implicitly comments on larger public concerns—work that answers every reader's most urgent question: Why are you telling me this?" Acquires first rights "plus one-time non-exclusive rights to reprint accepted work in an anniversary issue." Publishes ms 1 year after acceptance. Responds in 3 months.

🖸 Poetry published in *Chautauqua* has been included in *The Pushcart Prize* anthology.

MAGAZINE'S NEEDS Submit 3 poems maximum at a time. Considers simultaneous submissions (if notified); no previously published poems. Prefers writers submit via Submishmash. Cover letter is preferred. "We prefer single-spaced manuscripts in 12 pt. font. Cover letters should be brief and mention recent publications (if any). SASE is mandatory." Reads submissions February 15-April 15 and August 15-November 15. "The editor is the sole arbiter, but we do have advisory editors who make recommendations." Sometimes comments on rejected poems. Pays 2 contributor's copies.

🖸 CHEST

3300 Dundee Rd., Northbrook IL 60062. 800-343-2222. **E-mail:** poetrychest@aol.com. **Website:** www.chestjournal.org. **Contact:** Michael Zack, M.D., poetry editor. *CHEST*, published monthly, "is the official medical journal of the American College of Chest Physicians, the world's largest medical journal for pulmonologists, sleep, and critical care specialists, with over 30,000 subscribers." Wants "poetry with themes of medical relevance." *CHEST* is approximately 300 pages, magazine-sized, perfect-bound, with a glossy cover, and includes ads. Press run is 22,000. Number of unique visitors: 400,000 to website. Subscription: $276. Make checks payable to American College Chest Physicians.

MAGAZINE'S NEEDS Submit up to 2 poems at a time, between 10 and 80 lines. Only accepts e-mail submissions (as attachment or in body of e-mail); no fax or disk submissions. Brief cover letter preferred. Reads submissions year round. Poems are circulated to an editorial board. Sometimes comments on rejected poems. Never publishes theme issues. Guidelines available in magazine and on website. Responds in 2 months; always sends prepublication galleys. Retains all rights.

CHICKEN SOUP FOR THE SOUL PUBLISHING, LLC

Fax: (203)861-7194. **E-mail:** webmaster@chickensoupforthesoul.com (for all inquires). **Website:** www.chickensoup.com. Buys one-time rights. Pays on pub-

lication. Responds upon consideration. Guidelines available online.

🖸 "Stories must be written in the first person."

MAGAZINE'S NEEDS No controversial poetry.

TIPS "We no longer accept submissions by mail or fax. Stories and poems can only be submitted on our website. Select the 'Submit Your Story' tab on the left toolbar. The submission form can be found there."

🌀🅞🅠🆂 CHIZINE: TREATMENT OF LIGHT AND SHADE IN WORDS

"Subtle, sophisticated dark fiction with a literary bent." Quarterly. Responds in 3 months to mss. Guidelines on website.

🖸 Received Bram Stoker Award for Other Media in 2000.

MAGAZINE'S NEEDS "Subtle, sophisticated dark fiction with a literary bent." Quarterly. Experimental, fantasy, horror (dark fantasy, futuristic, psychological, supernatural), literary, mystery, science fiction (soft/sociological). Does not want "tropes of vampires, werewolves, mummies, monsters, or anything that's been done to death."

CHRISTIAN COMMUNICATOR

9118 W. Elmwood Dr., Suite 1G, Niles IL 60714-5820. (847)296-3964. **Fax:** (847)296-0754. **E-mail:** ljohnson@wordprocommunications.com. **Website:** acwriters.com. **Contact:** Lin Johnson, managing editor. Buys first rights, buys second serial (reprint) rights. Pays on publication. Publishes ms an average of 6-12 months after acceptance. Responds in 6-8 weeks to queries. Responds in 8-12 weeks to mss. Editorial lead time 3 months. Sample copy for SAE and 5 first-class stamps. Writer's guidelines by e-mail or on website.

MAGAZINE'S NEEDS Length: 4-20 lines. Pays $5.

TIPS "We primarily use how-to articles and profiles of editors. However, we're willing to look at any other pieces geared to the writing life."

🖸🆂 THE CHRISTIAN SCIENCE MONITOR

The Home Forum Page, 210 Massachussetts Ave., P02-30, Boston MA 02115. **E-mail:** homeforum@csmonitor.com. **Website:** www.csmonitor.com; http://www.csmonitor.com/About/Contributor-guidelines#homeforum. **Contact:** Susan Leach, Marjorie Kehe, editors. *The Christian Science Monitor*, an international daily newspaper, regularly features poetry in The Home Forum section. Wants "finely crafted poems that explore and celebrate daily life; that provide a respite from daily news and from the bleakness that appears in so much contemporary verse." Considers free verse and fixed forms. Has published poetry by Diana Der-Hovanessian, Marilyn Krysl, and Michael Glaser. Publishes 1-2 poems/week.

MAGAZINE'S NEEDS Submit up to 5 poems at a time. Lines/poem: Prefers short poems under 20 lines. No previously published poems or simultaneous submissions. Accepts e-mail submissions only (by attachment in MS Word, 1 poem/e-mail). Pays $20/haiku; $40/poem. Does not want "work that presents people in helpless or hopeless states; poetry about death, aging, or illness; or dark, violent, sensual poems. No poems that are overtly religious or falsely sweet."

CICADA MAGAZINE

Cricket Magazine Group, 70 E. Lake St., Suite 300, Chicago IL 60601. (312)701-1720. **Fax:** (312)701-1728. **E-mail:** cicada@cicadamag.com. **Website:** www.cicadamag.com. **Contact:** Marianne Carus, editor-in-chief; Deborah Vetter, executive editor; John Sandford, art director. Bimonthly literary magazine for ages 14 and up. Publishes original short stories, poems, and first-person essays written for teens and young adults. *Cicada* publishes fiction and poetry with a genuine teen sensibility, aimed at the high school and college-age market. The editors are looking for stories and poems that are thought-provoking but entertaining. Pays on publication. Responds in 4-6 months to mss. Guidelines available online at www.cricketmag.com (adults) and www.cicadamag.com (young adults 14-23)

MAGAZINE'S NEEDS Reviews serious, humorous, free verse, rhyming (if done well) poetry. Limit submissions to 5 poems. Length: 25 lines maximum. Pays up to $3/line on publication.

TIPS "Quality writing, good literary style, genuine teen sensibility, depth, humor, good character development, avoidance of stereotypes. Read several issues to familiarize yourself with our style."

◑ CIDER PRESS REVIEW

P.O. Box 33384, San Diego CA 92163. **E-mail:** editor@ ciderpressreview.com. **Website:** http://ciderpressreview.com. **Contact:** Caron Andregg, editor-in-chief; Ruth Foley, managing editor. "*Cider Press Review*, quarterly online, features 'the best new work from contemporary poets.' It was founded by Co-Publisher/Editors Caron Andregg and Robert Wynne. Since its inception, *CPR* has published thousands of poems

by over 500 authors. Each year, Cider Press publishes an annual journal of poetry and the winning manuscript from the *Cider Press Review* Book Award. Our reading period is from Apr. 1-Aug. 31 each year, and full mss. (in conjunction with the CPR Annual Book Award) between Sept. 1-Nov. 30 each year." Submit up to 5 poems at a time. No previously published poems or simultaneous submissions. "International authors or special needs, please query via e-mail. Do not send unsolicited disk or e-mail submissions." Cover letter is preferred. Include short bio (25 words maximum). SASE or valid e-mail address required for reply. Reads submissions September 1-June 30 only. Poems are circulated to an editorial board. Always sends prepublication galleys. Pays 1 contributor's copy. *Cider Press Review* also published two winning mss from their book awards: The *Cider Press Review* Book Award and The Editor's Prize. Our reading period for the online journal is from September 1 to May 31 each year. We accept submissions of full mss between April 1 and June 20, and September 1 through November 20. Mss entries must be accompanied by a require entry fee. Prize is $1,000 or $1,500 and publication for a full length book of poetry and 25 copies. Acquires first North American serial rights. Publishes ms 3-9 months after acceptance. Responds in 1-4 months. Guidelines available by SASE or on website.

◑ Press run for print edition is 500. Single copy: $14.95; subscription: $24 for 2 issues (1 journal, 1 book from the *Cider Press Review* Book Award). Sample: $12 (journal).

MAGAZINE'S NEEDS *Cider Press Review*, published annually, features "the best new work from contemporary poets." Wants "thoughtful, well-crafted poems with vivid language and strong images. We prefer poems that have something to say. We would like to see more well-written humor. We also encourage translations." Does not want "didactic, inspirational, greeting card verse, empty word play, therapy, or religious doggerel." Also welcomes reviews in not more than 500 words of current full-length books of poetry. Has published poetry by Robert Arroyo, Jr., Virgil Suárez, Linda Pastan, Kathleen Flenniken, Tim Seibles, Joanne Lowery, Thomas Lux, and Mark Cox. *Cider Press Review* is 128 pages, digest-sized, offset-printed, perfect-bound, with 4-color coated card cover. Receives about 2,500 poems/year, accepts about 3%.

CIMARRON REVIEW

205 Morrill Hall, English Department, Oklahoma State University, Stillwater OK 74078. **E-mail:** cimarronreview@okstate.edu. **Website:** http://cimarronreview.com. **Contact:** Toni Graham, editor. "We want strong literary writing. We are partial to fiction in the modern realist tradition and distinctive poetry—lyrical, narrative, etc." Buys first North American serial rights. Publishes ms 2-6 months after acceptance. Responds in 3-6 months to mss. Sample copy for $7. Guidelines available on website.

Magazine: 6×9; 110 pages. Accepts 3-5 mss/issue; 12-15 mss/year. Publishes 2-4 new writers/year. Eager to receive mss from both established and less experienced writers "who intrigue us with their unusual perspective, language, imagery and character." Has published work by Molly Giles, Gary Fincke, David Galef, Nona Caspers, Robin Beeman, Edward J. Delaney, William Stafford, John Ashbery, Grace Schulman, Barbara Hamby, Patricia Fargnoli, Phillip Dacey, Holly Prado, and Kim Addonizio.

MAGAZINE'S NEEDS Submit 3-6 poems at a time with SASE; include cover letter. No restrictions as to subject matter." Wants "poems whose surfaces and structures risk uncertainty and which display energy, texture, intelligence, and intense investment." Pays 2 contributor's copies.

TIPS "All work must come with SASE. A cover letter is encouraged. No e-mail submissions from authors living in North America. Query first and follow guidelines. In order to get a feel for the kind of work we publish, please read an issue or 2 before submitting."

THE CLAREMONT REVIEW

4980 Wesley Rd., Victoria V8Y 1Y9, B.C. (250)658-5221. **Fax:** (250)658-5387. **E-mail:** lmoran@telus.net. **Website:** www.theclaremontreview.ca. **Contact:** Linda Moran, managing editor. "We publish anything from traditional to post modern, but with a preference for works that reveal something of the human condition. By this we mean stories that explore real characters in modern settings. Who are we, what are we doing to the planet, what is our relationship to one another, the earth, or God. Also, reading samples on this website or from past issues will give you a clearer indication of what we are looking for." Responds in 1-2 months. Guidelines available on website.

MAGAZINE'S NEEDS Submit complete poems on separate pages. Include SASE. Does not want rhyming poetry.

TIPS "Read guidelines before submitting."

CLARK STREET REVIEW

P.O. Box 1377, Berthoud CO 80513. **E-mail:** clarkreview@earthlink.net. **Contact:** Ray Foreman, editor. *Clark Street Review*, published 6 times/year, uses narrative poetry and short shorts. Tries "to give writers and poets cause to keep writing by publishing their best work." Wants "narrative poetry under 100 lines that reaches readers who are mostly published poets and writers. Subjects are open." Does not want "obscure or formalist work." Acquires one-time rights. Publishes ms 2 months after acceptance. Responds in 3 weeks. Guidelines for SASE or by e-mail.

"Editor reads everything with a critical eye of 30 years of experience in writing and publishing small press work." *Clark Street Review* is 20 pages, digest-sized, photocopied, saddle-stapled, with paper cover. Receives about 1,000 poems/year, accepts about 10%. Press run is 200. Single copy: $2; subscription: $10 for 10 issues postpaid for writers only. Make checks payable to R. Foreman. Has published poetry by Charles Ries, Anselm Brocki, Ed Galling, Ellaraine Lockie, and J. Glenn Evans.

MAGAZINE'S NEEDS Submit narrative poems (human condition poetry only). Maximum 55 characters in width. Flush left. Considers previously published poems and simultaneous submissions. Send disposable sharp hard copies. Include SASE for reply. No cover letter. No limit on submissions.

CLOUDBANK: JOURNAL OF CONTEMPORARY WRITING

P.O. Box 610, Corvallis OR 97339. **Website:** www.cloudbankbooks.com. **Contact:** Michael Malan, editor. Acquires one-time rights. Rights revert to poets upon publication. Responds in 4 months to poems. Guidelines available in magazine, for SASE, by e-mail, or on website.

Digest-sized, 84 pages of print, perfect bound; color artwork on cover, includes ads. Press run is 400. Subscribers: 300; shelf sales: 100 distributed free. Single copy $8; subscription: $15. Make checks payable to Cloudbank. Has published poetry by Dennis Schmitz, Christopher Buckley, Stuart Friebert, Dore Kiessel-bach, Karen Holmberg, Vern Rutsala.

MAGAZINE'S NEEDS Submit 5 poems or less at a time by mail with SASE. Cover letter is preferred. Does not accept fax, e-mail, or disk submissions. Reads year round. Rarely sends prepublication galleys. Receives 1,600 poems/year; accepts about 8%. Pays $200 prize for 1 poem or flash fiction piece per issue.

CONTEST/AWARD OFFERINGS Cloudbank Contest for $200 prize. $15 entry fee. See website for guidelines.

TIPS "Please consider reading a copy of *Cloudbank* before submitting."

○ COAL CITY REVIEW

Coal City Press, University of Kansas, English Department, Lawrence KS 66045. **E-mail:** coalcity@ sunflower.com. **E-mail:** briandal@ku.edu. **Website:** www.coalcityreview.com. **Contact:** Brian Daldorph, founder and editor. Responds in 3 months. Guidelines for SASE and online.

○ Only accepts submissions by postal mail.

MAGAZINE'S NEEDS *Coal City Review*, published annually in the fall, prints poetry, short stories, reviews, and interviews—"the best material I can find. As Pound said, 'Make it new.' Has published poetry by Gary Lechliter, Phil Miller, Cheela Chilala, Maggie Sawkins, and Denise Low. Submit up to 6 poems through postal mail. Does not accept e-mail submissions. Does not want "experimental poetry, doggerel, five-finger exercises, or beginner's verse." Pays 1 contributor's copy.

TIPS "We are looking for artful stories—with great language and great heart. Please do not send work that has not been thoughtfully and carefully revised or edited."

○ C/OASIS

E-mail: eide491@earthlink.net. **Website:** www.sunoasis.com/oasis.html. **Contact:** David Eide, Editor. "*C/Oasis* has been dedicated to bringing, to the Net, the best short story writing and poetry writing available." Usually buys one-time rights.

MAGAZINE'S NEEDS Wants "mostly poems and stories since those are the appropriate forms for the web. Any work sent to *Oasis* will be respected. The editors respond to artful poems that have some consciousness of the poetry written in the 20th century."

TIPS "Note: Sunoasis.com has set up a new Network called Sunoasis Writers Network. If you want to sub-

mit poetry or story go to sunoasis.ning.com and sign up. It is free. Then you can do one of several things:Put your poem or story or essay in a blog and load it onto the networkJoin a group, submit it there and let others read itPut a notice on the Forum you have stories and poems and then give a link.The Network has over 850 members at this time and is growing so take advantage of it. It was set up to provide writing and career opportunities for the writing crowd but there are plenty of fiction and poetry writers on it. I've always been impressed by the level of talent *C/Oasis* was able to draw to it and hope that talent hops on the Network!"

COBBLESTONE

Carus Publishing, 30 Grove St., Suite C, Peterborough NH 03458. (800)821-0115. **Fax:** (603)924-7380. **E-mail:** customerservice@caruspub.com. **Website:** www.cobblestonepub.com. "We are interested in articles of historical accuracy and lively, original approaches to the subject at hand. Writers are encouraged to study recent *Cobblestone* back issues for content and style. All material must relate to the theme of a specific upcoming issue in order to be considered. To be considered, a query must accompany each individual idea (however, you can mail them all together) and must include the following: a brief cover letter stating the subject and word length of the proposed article, a detailed one-page outline explaining the information to be presented in the article, an extensive bibliography of materials the author intends to use in preparing the article, a SASE. Authors are urged to use primary resources and up-to-date scholarly resources in their bibliography. Writers new to COBBLESTONE° should send a writing sample with the query. If you would like to know if your query has been received, please also include a stamped postcard that requests acknowledgment of receipt. In all correspondence, please include your complete address as well as a telephone number where you can be reached. A writer may send as many queries for one issue as he or she wishes, but each query must have a separate cover letter, outline, bibliography, and SASE. All queries must be typed. Please do not send unsolicited manuscripts—queries only! Prefers to work with published/established writers. Each issue presents a particular theme, making it exciting as well as informative. Half of all subscriptions are for schools. All material must relate to monthly theme." Buys all rights. Pays on publication. Guidelines available on website or with SASE; sample copy for $6.95, $2 shipping/handling, 10x13 SASE.

○ *"Cobblestone* stands apart from other children's magazines by offering a solid look at one subject and stressing strong editorial content, color photographs throughout, and original illustrations." *Cobblestone* themes and deadline are available on website or with SASE.

MAGAZINE'S NEEDS Serious and light verse considered. Must have clear, objective imagery. Length: 100 lines maximum. Pays on an individual basis. Acquires all rights.

TIPS "Review theme lists and past issues to see what we're looking for."

○ COLD MOUNTAIN REVIEW

Department of English, Appalachian State University, ASU Box 32052, Boone NC 28608. **E-mail:** coldmountain@appstate.edu. **Website:** www.coldmountain.appstate.edu. **Contact:** Betty Miller Conway, managing editor. *Cold Mountain Review*, published twice/year (Spring and Fall), features poetry, interviews with poets, poetry book reviews, and b&w graphic art. Has published poetry by Sarah Kennedy, Robert Morgan, Susan Ludvigson, Aleida Rodríguez, R.T. Smith, and Virgil Suaárez. *Cold Mountain Review* is about 72 pages, digest-sized, neatly printed with one poem/page (or 2-page spread), perfect-bound, with light cardstock cover. Publishes only 10-12 poems/issue; "hence, we are extremely competitive: send only your best." Responds in 3 months. Guidelines for SASE.

MAGAZINE'S NEEDS Submit up to 5 poems at a time. Include short bio and SASE. "Please include name, address, phone number, and (if available) e-mail address on each poem. Poems should be single-spaced on one side of the page. Pays in contributor's copies.

COLORADO REVIEW

Center for Literary Publishing, Colorado State University, 9105 Campus Delivery, Fort Collins CO 80523. (970)491-5449. **E-mail:** creview@colostate.edu. **Website:** http://coloradoreview.colostate.edu. **Contact:** Stephanie G'Schwind, editor-in-chief and nonfiction editor. Literary magazine published 3 times/year. Buys first North Americans erial rights. Rights revert to author upon publication. Pays on publication. Publishes ms an average of 6 months after acceptance. Responds in 2 months to mss. Editorial lead time 1 year. Sample copy for $10. Guidelines available online.

○ Work published in *Colorado Review* has been included in *Best American Poetry*, *Best New American Voices*, *Best Travel Writing*, *Best Food Writing*, and the *Pushcart Prize Anthology*.

MAGAZINE'S NEEDS Considers poetry of any style. Poetry mss are read August 1-April 30. Mss received May 1-July 31 will be returned unread. Has published poetry by Sherman Alexie, Laynie Browne, John Gallaher, Kevin Prufer, Craig Morgan Teicher, Susan Tichy, Elizabeth Robinson, Elizabeth Willis, and Keith Waldrop. Pays minimum of $25 or $5/page.

○ COLUMBIA: A JOURNAL OF LITERATURE AND ART

Website: http://columbiajournal.org. **Contact:** Binnie Kirshenbaum and William Wadsworth, faculty board. *"Columbia: A Journal of Literature and Art* is an annual publication that features the very best in poetry, fiction, nonfiction, and art. We were founded in 1977 and continue to be one of the few national literary journals entirely edited, designed, and produced by students. You'll find that our minds are open, our interests diverse. We solicit manuscripts from writers we love and select the most exciting finds from our virtual submission box. Above all, our commitment is to our readers—to producing a collection that informs, surprises, challenges, and inspires."

MAGAZINE'S NEEDS Submit using online submissions manager.

CONTEST/AWARD OFFERINGS Sponsors annual contest with an award of $500. Submit no more than 5 poems/entry or 20 double-spaced pages for fiction and nonfiction submissions. **Entry fee:** $12. **Deadline:** see website or recent journal issue. All entrants receive a copy of the issue publishing the winners.

○ COMMON GROUND REVIEW

Western New England College, H-5132, Western New England College, 1215 Wilbraham Rd., Springfield MA 01119. **E-mail:** editors@cgreview.org. **Website:** http://cgreview.org. **Contact:** Janet Bowdan, editor. *Common Ground Review*, published semiannually (Spring/Summer, Fall/Winter), prints poetry and 1 short nonfiction piece in the Fall issue, 1 short fiction piece in Spring issue. Has published poetry by James Doyle, B.Z. Nidith, Ann Lauinger, Kathryn Howd Machan, and Sheryl L. Nelms. "We want poems with strong imagery, a love of language, a fresh message, that evoke a sense of wonder. This is the official literary journal of Western New England College."

Acquires one-time rights. Publishes ms 4-6 months after acceptance. Responds in 2 months to mss. Submit seasonal poems 6 months in advance. Guidelines available on website.

MAGAZINE'S NEEDS Poetry with strong imagery; well-written free or traditional forms. Submit up to 3 poems under 61 lines. No previously published poems. Simultaneous submissions are allowed; see website for details. Cover letter and biography are required. "Poems should be single-spaced indicating stanza breaks; include name, address, phone number, e-mail address, brief bio, and SASE (submissions without SASE will not be notified)." Reads submissions year round, but deadlines for non-contest submissions are August 31 and March 1. "Editor reads and culls submissions. Final decisions made by editorial board." Seldom comments on rejected poems. Does not want "greeting card verse, overly sentimental or stridently political poetry." Length: 60 lines/max. Pays 1 contributor's copy.

CONTEST/AWARD OFFERINGS Sponsors an annual poetry contest. Offers 1st Prize: $500; 2nd Prize: $200; 3rd Prize: $100; Honorable Mentions. **Entry fee:** $15 for 1-3 unpublished poems. **Deadline:** March 1 for contest submissions only. All contest submissions are considered for publication in *Common Ground Review*.

TIPS "For poems, use a few good images to convey ideas. Poems should be condensed and concise, free from words that do not contribute. The subject matter should be worthy of the reader's time and appeal to a wide range of readers. Sometimes the editors may suggest possible revisions."

⭕ COMMON THREADS

Mail submissions to: 3520 St. Rt. 56, Mechanicsburg OH 43044. (419)512-7675. **E-mail:** team@ohiopoetryassn.org. **Website:** http://ohiopoetryassn.com. **Contact:** Mark Hersman, OPA president. *Common Threads*, published annually, is the Ohio Poetry Association's member poetry magazine. **Only members of OPA may submit poems.** "We accept poems from both beginners and accomplished writers. We like poems to make us think as well as feel something. We do not want to see poetry that is highly sentimental, overly morbid, religiously coercive, or pornographic. Poetry by students will also be considered and prioritized if the student is a high school contest winner."

Has published poetry by Bill Reyer, Michael Bugeja, Timothy Russell, Yvonne Hardenbrook, Dalene Stull and other well-known published artists. *Common Threads* is devoted primarily to members' poetry, but will also include book reviews, essays on craft, interviews, and other articles related to poetry as an art. Subscription: annual OPA membership dues to OPA treasurer; includes annual issue of *Common Threads* ($18; $15 for seniors over age 65). Single copy: $5.

MAGAZINE'S NEEDS Previously published poems are considered, if author notes when and where the work was previously published. Submissions are accepted by postal mail only and are accepted and read year round. Guidelines available for SASE. All rights revert to poet after publication. Lines/poem: 40 lines.

TIPS "Please visit www.ohiopoetryassn.com for membership applications and additional information on submissions."

COMMONWEAL

Commonweal Foundation, 475 Riverside Dr., Room 405, New York NY 10115. (212)662-4200. **Fax:** (212)662-4183. **E-mail:** editors@commonwealmagazine.org. **Website:** www.commonwealmagazine.org. **Contact:** Paul Baumann, editor; Tiina Aleman, production editor. Buys all rights. Pays on publication. Responds in 2 months to queries. Sample copy free. Guidelines available online.

MAGAZINE'S NEEDS *Commonweal*, published every 2 weeks, is a Catholic general interest magazine for college-educated readers. Does not publish inspirational poems. Length: no more than 75 lines. Pays 75¢/line plus 2 contributor's copies. Acquires all rights. Returns rights when requested by the author.

TIPS "Articles should be written for a general but well-educated audience. While religious articles are always topical, we are less interested in devotional and churchy pieces than in articles which examine the links between 'worldly' concerns and religious beliefs."

◐ THE COMSTOCK REVIEW

4956 St. John Dr., Syracuse NY 13215. **E-mail:** poetry@comstockreview.org. **Website:** www.comstockreview.org. **Contact:** Georgia A. Popoff, managing editor. Responds in 3 months.

MAGAZINE'S NEEDS Accepts submissions of 3-5 poems, with SASE, for the Open Reading Period postmarked from January 1 to March 15, yearly. Single poem contest yearly. Chapbook contest every other year (held in 2013). No previously published poems.

CONFRONTATION

English Department, LIU Post, Brookville NY 11548. (516)299-2720. **E-mail:** confrontationmag@gmail. com. **Website:** www.confrontationmagazine.org. **Contact:** Jonna Semeiks, editor-in-chief. *Confrontation* has been in continuous publication since 1968. Our taste and our magazine is eclectic, but we always look for excellence in style, an important theme, a memorable voice. We enjoy discovering and fostering new talent. Each issue contains work by both well-established and new writers. In addition, *Confrontation* often features a thematic special section that "confronts" a topic. The ensuing confrontation is an attempt to see the many sides of an issue or theme, rather than to present a formed conclusion. "We prefer single submissions. Clear copy. No e-mail submissions unless writer resides outside the U.S. Mail submissions with a SASE. We read August 16-May 15. Do not send mss or e-mail submissions between May 16 and August 15. We publish theme issues. Upcoming themes are announced on our website and Facebook page and in our magazine." Buys first North American serial rights; electronic rights; first rights; one-time rights; all rights. Pays on publication. Publishes work in the first or second issue after acceptance. Responds in 3 weeks to queries; 8-10 weeks to mss.

- *Confrontation* has garnered a long list of awards and honors, including the Editor's Award for Distinguished Achievement from CLMP (given to Martin Tucker, the founding editor of the magazine) and NEA grants. Work from the magazine has appeared in numerous anthologies, including the Pushcart Prize, Best Short Stories and The O. Henry Prize Stories.

MAGAZINE'S NEEDS *Confrontation* is interested in all poetic forms. Our only criterion is high literary merit. We think of our audience as an educated, lay group of intelligent readers. Has published poetry by David Ray, T. Alan Broughton, David Ignatow, Philip Appleman, Jane Mayhall, and Joseph Brodsky. Submit no more than 10 pages at a time (up to 6 poems). Buys 60 poems per year. *Confrontation* also offers the biennial Confrontation Poetry Prize.

No sentimental verse. No previously published poems. Lines/poem: Length should generally be kept to 2 pages. Pays $25-75; more for commissioned work. **TIPS** "We look for literary merit. Keep honing your skills and keep trying."

CONGRUENT SPACES

P.O. Box 91, Talent OR 97540. **E-mail:** info@congruentspaces.com. **Website:** www.congruentspaces.com. **Contact:** Michael Camarata, managing editor. *"Congruent Spaces* was developed as a common ground for a diverse variety of voices and writing styles within the writing community. In keeping with this sense of community, all submissions are posted directly to the slush pile in our Writer's Lair, where our community of writers and readers come together to read and rate these submissions. Each issue we then select from the top rated submissions which stories and poems appear within the pages of our magazine." Purchases one-time rights.

- *Congruent Spaces* (ISSN 2163-7601) is published quarterly, by Michael Camarata. Individual issues for $1.99, US. Subscription price, 1 year online membership (includes previously published issues) for $9.99, US. Subscriptions available online only. Submissions are currently accepted online only. For current guidelines, visit http://congruentspaces.com/home/submission/ For general inquiries, contact info@ congruentspaces.com.

MAGAZINE'S NEEDS Submit complete ms. No erotic or pornographic poetry. Length: less than 120 lines. Pays contributor's copies.

TIPS "As a brand new magazine, now is the best opportunity for getting published. Competition will grow stronger as awareness of our magazine grows. Having said that, don't submit your work unless you truly believe it is ready for publication. Be sure to proof your formatting for readbility before posting the manuscript for our ratings process. The most common error is failing to adequately separate paragraphs after copying and pasting the submission in the submission form. Either indent your paragraphs or leave a line space between the paragraphs with 2 line spaces for additional breaks. The easier it is to read your ms, the better your chances of receiving a quality rating."

CONNECTICUT REVIEW

Southern Connecticut State University, English Department, 501 Crescent St., New Haven CT 06515. E-

mail: ctreview@southernct.edu. **Website:** www.ctstateu.edu/ctreview/index.html. **Contact:** Vivian Shipley, editor (Southern); Jian-Zhong Lin, editor (Eastern); Lisa Siedlarz, managing editor. "*Connecticut Review* is a high-quality literary magazine. We take both traditional literary pieces and those on the cutting edge of their genres. We are looking for poetry, fiction, short-shorts, creative essays, and scholarly articles accessible to a general audience. Each issue features an 8-page color fine art section with statements from the painters or photographers featured." Buys first rights, buys first electronic rights. Publishes ms an average of 18 months after acceptance. Responds in 6 weeks to queries. Responds in 4 months to mss Sample copy for $12 and 3 first-class stamps Guidelines for #10 SASE

○ Poetry published in *Connecticut Review* has been included in *The Best American Poetry* and *The Pushcart Prize* anthologies; has received special recognition for Literary Excellence from Public Radio's series *The Poet and the Poem*; and has won the Phoenix Award for Significant Editorial Achievement from the Council of Editors of Learned Journals (CELJ).

MAGAZINE'S NEEDS Submit 3-5 typed poems at a time. No doggerel poetry.

TIPS "We read manuscripts blind—stripping off the cover letter—but the biographical information should be there. Be patient. Our editors are spread over 4 campuses and it takes a while to move the manuscripts around."

◐ THE CONNECTICUT RIVER REVIEW

P.O. Box 516, Cheshire CT 06410. **E-mail:** patricia-mottola@yahoo.com. **Website:** www.ct-poetry-society.org/publications.htm. **Contact:** Pat Mottola, editor. *Connecticut River Review,* published annually in July or August by the Connecticut Poetry Society, prints "original, honest, diverse, vital, well-crafted poetry." Wants "any form, any subject. Translations and long poems welcome." Has published poetry by Marilyn Nelson, Jack Bedell, Maria Mazziotti Gillan, and Vivian Shipley. *Connecticut River Review* is digest-sized, attractively printed, perfect-bound. Receives about 2,000 submissions/year, accepts about 100. Press run is about 300. Membership in the Connecticut Poetry Society is $30 per year and includes *Connecticut River Review* and *Long River Run*, a members-only magazine. "Poet retains copyright."

Responds in up to 8 weeks. Guidelines available for SASE or on website.

MAGAZINE'S NEEDS Submit no more than 3-5 poems at a time. Considers simultaneous submissions if notified of acceptance elsewhere; no previously published poems. Cover letter is preferred. Include bio. "Complete contact information typed in upper right corner; SASE required." Reads submissions January 1-April 15. Pays 1 contributor's copy.

●⊚ CONTEMPORARY HAIBUN

P.O. Box 2461, Winchester VA 22604-1661. (540)722-2156. **E-mail:** jim.kacian@comcast.net; ray@raysweb.net. **Website:** www.contemporaryhaibunonline.com; www.redmoonpress.com. **Contact:** Jim Kacian, editor/publisher. *contemporary haibun,* published annually in April, is the first Western journal dedicated to haibun. Considers poetry by children and teens. Acquires first North American serial rights. Time between acceptance and publication varies according to time of submission. Sample available for SASE or by e-mail.

○ *contemporary haibun* is 128 pages, digest-sized, offset-printed on quality paper, with 4-color heavy-stock cover. Receives several hundred submissions/year, accepts about 5%. Print run is 1,000. Subscription: $17 plus $5 p&h. Has published poetry by Steven Carter, Penny Harter, Ce Rosenow, and Jeffrey Woodward.

MAGAZINE'S NEEDS Submit up to 3 haibun at a time. Considers previously published poems. Accepts e-mail submissions. Include SASE for postal submissions. Poems are circulated to an editorial board.

●⊚ CONTRARY

3133 S. Emerald Ave., Chicago IL 60616-3299. **E-mail:** chicago@contrarymagazine.com (no submissions). **Website:** www.contrarymagazine.com. **Contact:** Jeff McMahon, editor. "*Contrary* publishes fiction, poetry, literary commentary, and prefers work that combines the virtues of all those categories. Founded at the University of Chicago, it now operates independently and not-for-profit on the South Side of Chicago. We like work that is not only contrary in content, but contrary in its evasion of the expectations established by its genre. Our fiction defies traditional story form. For example, a story may bring us to closure without ever delivering an ending. We don't insist on the ending, but we do insist on the closure. And we value fiction as poetic as any poem." Quarterly. Member CLMP.

Acquires first rights and perpetual archive and anthology rights. Publication is copyrighted. Pays on publication. Mss published no more than 21 days after acceptance. Responds to queries in 2 weeks; 3 months to mss. Rarely comments on/critiques rejected mss. Guidelines available on website.

Online literary magazine/journal. Contains illustrations. Receives 650 mss/month. Accepts 6 mss/issue; 24 mss/year. Publishes 1 new writer/year. Has published Sherman Alexie, Andrew Coburn, Amy Reed, Clare Kirwan, Stephanie Johnson, Laurence Davies, and Edward McWhinney.

MAGAZINE'S NEEDS No mail or e-mail submissions; submit work via the website. Considers simultaneous submissions; no previously published poems. Accepts submissions through online form only. Often comments on rejected poems. $20 per byline, $60 for featured work."Upon acceptance, *Contrary* acquires the following rights: 1) exclusive rights for the three-month period that the accepted work appears in the current issue of *Contrary* magazine, 2) the right to permanent inclusion of the work in *Contrary's* electronic archive, and 3) the right to reproduce the work in print and electronic collections of our content. After the current issue expires, the author is free to seek republication elsewhere, but *Contrary* must be credited upon republication."

ADDITIONAL INFORMATION "We like work that is not only contrary in content, but contrary in its evasion of the expectations established by its genre. Our fiction defies traditional story form. For example, a story may bring us to closure without ever delivering an ending. And we value fiction as poetic as any poem. We look especially for plurality or meaning, for dual reverberation or beauty and concern. *Contrary's* poetry in particular often mimics the effects of fiction or commentary. We find ourselves enamored of prose poems because they are naturally ambiguous about form — they tug overtly on the forces of narrative — but prose poems remain the minority of all the poetic forms we publish."

TIPS "Beautiful writing catches our eye first. If we realize we're in the presence of unanticipated meaning, that's what clinches the deal. Also, we're not fond of expository fiction. We prefer to be seduced by beauty, profundity and mystery than to be presented with the obvious. We look for fiction that entrances, that stays the reader's finger above the mouse button. That is,

in part, why we favor microfiction, flash fiction and short-shorts. Also, we hope writers will remember that most editors are looking for very particular species of work. We try to describe our particular species in our mission statement and our submission guidelines, but those descriptions don't always convey nuance. That's why many editors urge writers to read the publication itself; in the hope that they will intuit an understanding of its particularities. If you happen to write that particular species of work we favor, your submission may find a happy home with us. If you don't, it does not necessarily reflect on your quality or your ability. It usually just means that your work has a happier home somewhere else."

CONVERGENCE: AN ONLINE JOURNAL OF POETRY AND ART

E-mail: clinville@csus.edu. **E-mail:** clinville@csus.edu. **Website:** www.convergence-journal.com. **Contact:** Cynthia Linville, managing editor. "We look for well-crafted work with fresh images and a strong voice. Work from a series or with a common theme has a greater chance of being accepted. Seasonally-themed work is appreciated (spring and summer for the January deadline, fall and winter for the June deadline). Please include a 75-word bio with your work (bios may be edited for length and clarity). A cover letter is not needed. Absolutely no simultaneous or previously published submissions."

Deadlines are January 5 and June 5.

MAGAZINE'S NEEDS New interpretations of the written word by pairing poems and flash fiction with complementary art. "We are open to many different styles, but we do not often publish formal verse. Read a couple of issues to get a sense of what we like; namely, well-crafted work with fresh images and a strong voice." *Convergence* is published quarterly online, Has published poetry by Oliver Rice, Simon Perchik, Mary Ocher. Receives about 800 poems/year, accepts about 10 per issue plus monthly selections for "Editor's Choice." Has about 200 online subscribers. Guidelines available on website. Does not often publish formal verse. Does not want "poetry with trite, unoriginal language or unfinished work." Length: 60 max. No payment.

HOW TO CONTACT No simultaneous or previously published submissions. Accepts e-mail submissions only. Reads submissions year round. Time between acceptance and publication is 1-2 months. Poems are circulated to an editorial board. Responds in 6 months. Acquires first rights.

TIPS "We look for freshness and originality and a mastery of the craft of flash fiction. Working with a common theme has a greater chance of being accepted."

◖ COTTONWOOD

Room 400 Kansas Union, 1301 Jayhawk Blvd., University of Kansas, Lawrence KS 66045. **E-mail:** tlorenz@ ku.edu. **Website:** www2.ku.edu/~englishmfa/cottonwood. **Contact:** Tom Lorenz, fiction editor. "Established in the 1960s, *Cottonwood* is the nationally circulated literary review of the University of Kansas. We publish high quality literary work in poetry, fiction, and creative nonfiction. Over the years authors such as William Stafford, Rita Dove, Connie May Fowler, Virgil Suarez, and Cris Mazza have appeared in the pages of *Cottonwood*, and recent issues have featured the work of Kim Chinquee, Quinn Dalton, Carol Lee Lorenzo, Jesse Kercheval, Joanne Lowery, and Oliver Rice. We welcome submissions from new and established writers. New issues appear once yearly, in the fall." Acquires one-time rights. Responds in 6 months. Guidelines available online at website.

MAGAZINE'S NEEDS Submit 4-6 poems. Pays in contributor's copies.

TIPS "We're looking for depth and/or originality of subject matter, engaging voice and style, emotional honesty, command of the material and the structure. *Cottonwood* publishes high quality literary fiction, but we are very open to the work of talented new writers. Write something honest and that you care about and write it as well as you can. Don't hesitate to keep trying us. We sometimes take a piece from a writer we've rejected a number of times. We generally don't like clever, gimmicky writing. The style should be engaging but not claim all the the attention itself."

● THE COUNTRY DOG REVIEW

P.O. Box 1476, Oxford MS 38655. **E-mail:** countrydogreview@gmail.com. **Website:** www.countrydogreview.org. **Contact:** Danielle Sellers, editor. *The Country Dog Review*, published semiannually online, publishes "poetry, book reviews, and interviews with poets. "Wants "poetry of the highest quality, not limited to style or region. Also accepts book reviews and interviews. Query first." Does not want "translations, fiction, nonfiction." Receives about 400 poems/year, accepts about 10%.

MAGAZINE'S NEEDS Submit 3-5 poems at a time. No previously published poems or simultaneous submissions. Only accepts e-mail submissions with attachment; no fax or disk submissions. Subject of e-mail should read: last name, date, poetry. Bio is required. Reads submissions year round. Submit seasonal poems 6 months in advance. "Please submit no more than twice a submission period." Time between acceptance and publication is 1-4 months. Never comments on rejected poems. Sometimes publishes theme issues. Upcoming themes and guidelines available by e-mail and on website. Responds in 1-2 months. Sometimes sends prepublication galleys. Acquires first North American serial rights. Reviews books of poetry in 500 words, single-book format.

CRAB CREEK REVIEW

7315 34th Ave. NW, Seattle WA 98117. **E-mail:** crabcreekreview@gmail.com. **Website:** www.crabcreekreview.org. *Crab Creek Review* is an 80- to 120-page, perfect-bound paperback. Subscription: $15/year, $28/2 year. Buys first North American rights. Responds in 3-5 months to mss. Sample copy: $6. Guidelines available online.

◖   Nominates for the Pushcart Prize and offers annual Crab Creek Review Editors' Prize of $100 for the best poem, essay, or short story published in the previous year.

MAGAZINE'S NEEDS Has published poetry by Oliver de la Paz, Dorianne Laux, Denise Duhamel, and translations by Ilya Kaminsky and Matthew Zapruder. Fiction by Shann Ray and Daniel Homan. Pays 1 copy.

CONTEST/AWARD OFFERINGS Offers annual poetry contest with deadline of May 31. Entry fee: $10. Submit up to 5 poems. All entries will be considered for publication. See website for more information.

TIPS "We currently welcome submissions of poetry, short fiction, and creative nonfiction. Shorter pieces in all genres preferred. We are an international journal based in the Pacific Northwest that is looking for poems, stories, and essays that pay attention to craft while still surprising us in positive ways with detail and content. We publish well-known and emerging writers."

CRAB ORCHARD REVIEW

Department of English, Southern Illinois University at Carbondale, Faner Hall 2380, Mail Code 4503, 1000 Faner Dr., Carbondale IL 62901. (618)453-6833. **Fax:** (618)453-8224. **Website:** www.craborchardreview.

siuc.edu. "We are a general interest literary journal published twice/year. We strive to be a journal that writers admire and readers enjoy. We publish fiction, poetry, creative nonfiction, fiction translations, interviews and reviews." Buys first North American serial rights. Publishes ms an average of 9-12 months after acceptance. Responds in 3 weeks to queries. Responds in 9 months to mss. Sample copy for $8. Guidelines for #10 SASE.

MAGAZINE'S NEEDS Wants all styles and forms from traditional to experimental. Does not want greeting card verse; literary poetry only. Has published poetry by Luisa A. Igloria, Erinn Batykefer, Jim Daniels, Bryan Tso Jones. Submit up to 5 poems at a time. Considers simultaneous submissions with notification; no previously published poems. Postal submissions only. Cover letter is preferred. "Indicate stanza breaks on poems of more than 1 page." Reads submissions April-November for Summer/Fall special theme issue, February-April for regular, non-thematic Winter/Spring issue. Time between acceptance and publication is 6 months to a year. "Poems that are under serious consideration are discussed and decided on by the managing editor and poetry editor."

TIPS "We publish 2 issues per volume—1 has a theme (we read from May to November for the theme issue); the other doesn't (we read from January through April for the non-thematic issue). Consult our website for information about our upcoming themes."

CRAZYHORSE

College of Charleston, Department of English, 66 George St., Charleston SC 29424. (843)953-4470. **E-mail:** crazyhorse@cofc.edu. **Website:** http://crazyhorse.cofc.edu. "We like to print a mix of writing regardless of its form, genre, school, or politics. We're especially on the lookout for original writing that doesn't fit the categories and that engages in the work of honest communication." Buys first North American serial rights. Publishes ms an average of 6-12 months after acceptance. Responds in 1 week to queries. Responds in 3-5 months to mss. Sample copy for $5. Guidelines for SASE or by e-mail.

MAGAZINE'S NEEDS Submit 3-5 poems at a time. Considers simultaneous submissions. No previously published poems. No fax, e-mail or disk submissions. Cover letter is preferred. Reads submissions year round, but slows down during the summer. Pays $20-35/page and 2 contributor's copies.

TIPS "Write to explore subjects you care about. The subject should be one in which something is at stake. Before sending, ask, 'What's reckoned with that's important for other people to read?'"

CREAM CITY REVIEW

E-mail: info@creamcityreview.org. **Website:** www.creamcityreview.org. **Contact:** Ching-In Chen, editor-in-chief; Shanae Aurora Martinez, managing editor. Memorable and energetic fiction, poetry and creative nonfiction. Features reviews of contemporary literature and criticism as well as author interviews and artwork. We are interested in camera-ready art depicting themes appropriate to each issue. Responds in 2-8 months to mss. Sample back issues for $7. Guidelines available online at www.creamcityreview.org/submit.

CONTEST/AWARD OFFERINGS Sponsors an annual poetry contest, The Beau Boudreaux Prize. Awards $1000 plus publication. **Entry fee:** $15 for 3-5 poems. For now, because of the entry fee, all competition submissions must be made by regular mail. All entries are considered for publication. Guidelines available on website.

TIPS Please include a few lines about your publication history. CCR seeks to publish a braod range of writings and a broad range of writers with diverse backgrounds. We accept submissions for our annual theme issue from Aug. 1 - Nov. 1, and general submissions from Dec. 1 - Apr. 1. No e-mail submissions, please.

CREATIVE WITH WORDS PUBLICATIONS

P.O. Box 223226, Carmel CA 93922. **Fax:** (831)655-8627. **E-mail:** geltrich@mbay.net. **Website:** creativewithwords.tripod.com. **Contact:** Brigitta Gisella Geltrich-Ludgate, publisher and editor. Publishes ms 1-2 months after acceptance. Responds in 2 weeks. Guideline available online.

MAGAZINE'S NEEDS Submit using online form or by postal mail. Always include SASE. Cover letter preferred.

TIPS "We offer a great variety of themes. We look for clean family-type fiction/poetry. Also, we ask the writer to look at the world from a different perspective, research topic thoroughly, be creative, apply brevity, tell the story from a character's viewpoint, tighten dialogue, be less descriptive, proofread before submitting and be patient. We will not publish every manuscript we receive. It has to be in standard English, well written, proofread. We do not appreciate receiving manuscripts where we have to do the proofreading and the correcting of grammar."

CRUCIBLE

Barton College, College Station, Wilson NC 27893. (252)399-6343. **E-mail:** crucible@barton.edu. **Website:** www.barton.edu/academics/english/crucible.htm. **Contact:** Terrence L. Grimes, editor. *Crucible*, published annually in November, uses "poetry that demonstrates originality and integrity of craftsmanship as well as thought. Traditional metrical and rhyming poems are difficult to bring off in modern poetry. The best poetry is written out of deeply felt experience which has been crafted into pleasing form." Wants "free verse with attention paid particularly to image, line, stanza, and voice." Does not want "very long narratives, poetry that is forced." Has published poetry by Robert Grey, R.T. Smith, and Anthony S. Abbott. *Crucible* is under 100 pages, digest-sized, professionally printed on high-quality paper, with matte card cover. Press run is 500. Sample: $8. Acquires first rights. Responds in 6 weeks to queries; 4 months to mss. Writer's guidelines free.

MAGAZINE'S NEEDS Submit no more than 5 poems at a time. No previously published poems or simultaneous submissions. "We require electronic submission of work and a short biography including a list of publications." Receives submissions between Christmas and mid-April only. Pays contributor's copies.

CONTEST/AWARD OFFERINGS The Sam Ragan Prize ($150), in honor of the former Poet Laureate of North Carolina, and other contests (prizes of $150 and $100). Guidelines available on website.

CURA: A LITERARY MAGAZINE OF ART AND ACTION

441 E. Fordham Rd., English Department, Dealy 541W, Bronx NY 10548. **E-mail:** curamag@fordham.edu. **Website:** www.curamag.com. **Contact:** Sarah Gambito, managing editor. "*CURA: A Literary Magazine of Art and Action* is a multi-media initiative based at Fordham University committed to integrating the arts and social justice. Featuring creative writing, visual art, new media and video in response to current news, we seek to enable an artistic process that is rigorously engaged with the world at the present moment. *CURA* is taken from the Ignatian educational principle of "cura personalis," care for the

whole person. On its own, the word "cura" is defined as guardianship, solicitude, and significantly, written work. Each year, *CURA* will feature a sustaining theme in dialogue with a non-profit organization that reflects the vision of "care for the whole person." Our aim is to provide support for and to raise awareness of the critical work these organizations are undertaking. For information on this year's theme, please check out our website at curamag.com. All publication proceeds will directly benefit the featured non-profit organization. We seek to foster a movement of creative response guided by concrete and meaningful action— to celebrate informed and active citizenship where a republic of writers, filmmakers, visual and digital artists converge. What Martín Espada has written about the social responsibility of the "Republic of Poetry" we believe applies to a Republic of all the Arts. It is "a place where creativity meets community, where the imagination serves humanity. It is a republic of justice because the practice of justice is the highest form of human expression." Content is published in print and in online and Kindle editions. *CURA* holds first serial rights on featured material." Acquires first rights. Publishes ms 5 months after acceptance. Editorial lead time is 5 months. Sample copy available online at website. Guidelines available online at website.

MAGAZINE'S NEEDS Pays 1 contributor's copy.

CURRENT ACCOUNTS

Current Accounts, Apt. 2D, Bradshaw Hall, Hardcastle Gardens, Bolton BL2 4NZ, UK. **E-mail:** fjameshartnell@aol.com. **Website:** http://bankstreetwriters.webs.com/currentaccounts.htm. **Contact:** FJ Hartnell. *Current Accounts*, published semiannually, prints poetry, fiction, and nonfiction by members of Bank Street Writers, and other contributors. Open to all types of poetry. "No requirements, although some space is reserved for members." Considers poetry by children and teens. Has published poetry by Pat Winslow, M.R. Peacocke, and Gerald England. *Current Accounts* is 52 pages, A5, photocopied, saddle-stapled, with card cover with b&w or color photo or artwork. Receives about 300 poems/year, accepts about 5%. Press run is 80; 8 distributed free to competition winners. Subscription: £6. Sample: £3. Make checks payable to Bank Street Writers (sterling checks only). Acquires first rights. Publishes ms 6 months after acceptance. Responds in 3 months. Guidelines available for SASE, by fax, by e-mail or on website.

MAGAZINE'S NEEDS Submit up to 6 poems at a time. Lines/poem: 100 maximum. No previously published poems (unpublished poems preferred) or simultaneous submissions. Prefers e-mail submissions (pasted into body of message). Cover letter is required. SAE or IRC essential for postal submissions. Published semiannually. Doesn't mind rhyming poetry. "Travel or tourist poetry needs to be more than just exotic names and places. Titles need care. Poetry should be poetic in some form. Experimental work is welcome. As a writer you are expected to be able to spell." Welcomes submissions from any writers or any age. Subscription: $15/3 issues. Pays 1 contributor's copy.

TIPS Bank Street Writers meets once/month and offers workshops, guest speakers, and other activities. Write for details."We like originality of ideas, images, and use of language. No inspirational or religious verse unless it's also good in poetic terms."

○ CURRICULUM VITAE

Simpson Publications, 342 Aiken Rd., Trumansburg NY 14886. **E-mail:** simpub@hotmail.com. **Contact:** Amy Dittman, managing editor. *Curriculum Vitae*, published semiannually in January and July, is "a zine where quality work is always welcome." Time between acceptance and publication is 8 months. Responds within 1 month. Guidelines available for SASE or by e-mail.

○ *Curriculum Vitae* is 40 pages, digest-sized, photocopied, saddle-stapled, with 2-color cardstock cover. Receives about 500 poems/year, accepts about 75. Press run is 1,000. Subscription: $6 for 4 issues. Sample: $4. Submit 3 poems at a time. Considers previously published poems and simultaneous submissions. Cover letter is preferred ("to give us an idea of who you are"). "Submissions without a SASE cannot be acknowledged due to postage costs." Poetry is circulated among 3 board members. Often comments on rejected poems. Publishes theme issues. Pays 2 contributor's copies plus one-year subscription. "We're also interested in expanding our list of innovative side projects, books, graphic novels, chapbooks like *The Iowa Monster*, and the CV Poetry Postcard Project." Simpson Publications publishes about 5 chapbooks/year. Query with full manuscripts or well-thought-out plans with clips. Include SASE. "We are currently looking for poets who would like to be part of our Poetry Postcard series."

MAGAZINE'S NEEDS *Curriculum Vitae*, published semiannually in January and July, is "a zine where quality work is always welcome. We'd like to see more metrical work, especially more translations, and well-crafted narrative free verse is always welcome. We do not want to see rambling Bukowski-esque free verse or poetry that overly relies on sentimentality." *Curriculum Vitae* is 40 pages, digest-sized, photocopied, saddle-stapled, with 2-color cardstock cover. Receives about 500 poems/year, accepts about 75. Press run is 1,000. Subscription: $6 for 4 issues. Sample: $4. Submit 3 poems at a time. Considers previously published poems and simultaneous submissions. Cover letter is preferred ("to give us an idea of who you are"). "Submissions without a SASE cannot be acknowledged due to postage costs." Poetry is circulated among 3 board members. Often comments on rejected poems. Publishes theme issues. "We're also interested in expanding our list of innovative side projects, books, graphic novels, chapbooks like *The Iowa Monster*, and the CV Poetry Postcard Project." Simpson Publications publishes about 5 chapbooks/year. Query with full mss or well-thought-out plans with clips. Include SASE. "We are currently looking for poets who would like to be part of our Poetry Postcard series." Pays 2 contributor's copies plus one-year subscription.

HOW TO CONTACT Submit 3 poems at a time. Considers previously published poems and simultaneous submissions. Cover letter is preferred ("to give us an idea of who you are"). "Submissions without a SASE cannot be acknowledged due to postage costs." Time between acceptance and publication is 8 months. Poetry is circulated among 3 board members. Often comments on rejected poems. Publishes theme issues. Guidelines available for SASE or by e-mail. Responds within 1 month. Pays 2 contributor's copies plus one-year subscription.

ADDITIONAL INFORMATION "We're also interested in expanding our list of innovative side projects, books, graphic novels, chapbooks like *The Iowa Monster*, and the CV Poetry Postcard Project." Simpson Publications publishes about 5 chapbooks/year. Query with full mss or well-thought-out plans with clips. Include SASE.

ALSO OFFERS "We are currently looking for poets who would like to be part of our Poetry Postcard series."

CUTBANK

English Dept., University of Montana, LA 133, Missoula MT 59812. **E-mail:** cutbank@umontana.edu. **Website:** www.cutbankonline.org. **Contact:** Andrew Martin, editor-in-chief. Publishes ms 6 months after acceptance.

MAGAZINE'S NEEDS Submit up to 5 poems at a time. Considers simultaneous submissions ("discouraged, but accepted with notification").

TIPS "Familiarity with the magazine is essential. *Cutbank* is very open to new voices—we have a legacy of publishing acclaimed writers early in their careers—but we will consider only your best work. *Cutbank* only accepts online submissions."

DALHOUSIE REVIEW

E-mail: dalhousie.review@dal.ca. **Website:** http://dalhousiereview.dal.ca. Anthony Stewart, editor. **Contact:** Poetry editor. *Dalhousie Review*, published 3 times/year, is a journal of criticism publishing poetry and fiction. Considers poetry from both new and established writers. *Dalhousie Review* is 144 pages, digest-sized. Accepts about 5% of poems received. Press run is 500. Single copy: $15 CAD; subscription: $22.50 CAD, $28 USD. Make checks payable to *Dalhousie Review*. Responds in 3-9 months.

MAGAZINE'S NEEDS Submit up to 5 poems, no more than 40 lines each. Does not accept simultaneous submissions or previously published submissions. Accepts postal submissions only, include e-mail address on submission. Reads year round. Pays 2 contributor's copies and 10 offprints.

DARKLING MAGAZINE

Darkling Publications, 28780 318th Avenue, Colome SD 57528. (605)455-2892. **E-mail:** darkling@mitchelltelecom.net. **Contact:** James C. Van Oort, editor-in-chief. *Darkling Magazine*, published annually in late summer, is "primarily interested in poetry. All submissions should be dark in nature and should help expose the darker side of man. Dark nature does not mean whiny or overly murderous, and being depressed does not make an artist's work dark. Pornography will not be considered and will merit no response. Profanity that is meritless or does not support the subject of any piece is unacceptable. Has published poems by Robert Cooperman, Kenneth DiMaggio, Arthur Gottlieb, Simon Perchik, Cathy Porter and Susanna Rich, among others. Subscription: $10 with s&h. Sample copies are $10.00. Make checks payable to Darkling Publications.

MAGAZINE'S NEEDS Submit up to 8 poems at a time. Lines/poem: any length is acceptable, but "Epic poems must be of exceptional quality. Considers simultaneous submissions but please no previously published poems. Will accept e-mail submissions; no disk submissions. Cover letter is required. Reads submissions June or July. Time between acceptance and publication is varies. Poems are circulated to an editorial board. Sometimes comments on rejected poems. Guidelines available in magazine. Announces rejections and acceptance in May or June. Pays 1 contributor's copy. All rights revert to author upon publication.

THE DEAD MULE SCHOOL OF SOUTHERN LITERATURE

E-mail: deadmule@gmail.com. **E-mail:** submit.mule@gmail.com. **Website:** www.deadmule.com. **Contact:** Valerie MacEwan, publisher and editor; Helen Losse, poetry editor. "No good southern fiction is complete without a dead mule." Celebrating over 15 years online means *The Dead Mule* is one of the oldest, if not *the* oldest continuously published online literary journals alive today. Publisher and editor Valerie MacEwan welcomes submissions. *The Dead Mule School of Southern Literature* wants flash fiction, poetry, visual poetry, essays, and creative nonfiction. We usually publish new work on the 1st and 15th of the month, depending on whims, obligations, and mule jumping contest dates. Helen Losse, poetry; Phoebe Kate Foster, fiction; Valerie MacEwan editor/publisher; Robert MacEwan, technical and design; and other volunteers who graciously donate their time and love to this fine journal." Acquires first electronic rights and indefinite archival rights. All other rights revert to author upon publication.

"The Dead Mule School of Southern Literature Institutional Alumni Association recruits year round. Want to join the freshman class of 2015? Submit today."

MAGAZINE'S NEEDS Submissions: see the instruction page at www.deadmule.com/submissions. Follow the guidelines.

TIPS "Read the site to get a feel for what we're looking to publish. Limit stories and essays to 1,000 words. All submissions must be accompanied by a "southern legitimacy statement," details of which can be seen within each page on *The Dead Mule* and within the submishmash entrypage. We've been around for over 15 years, send us something original. Chapbooks published by invitation, also short fiction compilations. Sporadic payment to writers whenever cafepress/deadmule sales reach an agreeable amount and then we share!"

●◍ DENVER QUARTERLY

University of Denver, 2000 E. Asbury, Denver CO 80208. (303)871-2892. **Website:** www.denverquarterly.com. **Contact:** Bill Ramke. "We publish fiction, articles and poetry for a generally well-educated audience, primarily interested in literature and the literary experience. They read *DQ* to find something a little different from a stictly academic quarterly or a creative writing outlet." Quarterly. Reads between September 15 and May 15. Acquires first North American serial rights. Publishes ms 1 year after acceptance. Responds in 3 months.

○ *Denver Quarterly* received an Honorable Mention for Content from the American Literary Magazine Awards and selections have been anthologized in the *Pushcart Prize* anthologies. *Denver Quarterly.* received an Honorable Mention for Content from the American Literary Magazine Awards and selections have been anthologized in the *Pushcart Prize* anthologies.

MAGAZINE'S NEEDS Poetry submissions should be comprised of 3-5 poems. Submit ms by mail, include SASE. Accepts simultaneous submissions. Sample copy for $10. Pays $5/page for fiction and poetry and 2 contributor's copies.

TIPS "We look for serious, realistic and experimental fiction; stories which appeal to intelligent, demanding readers who are not themselves fiction writers. Nothing so quickly disqualifies a manuscript as sloppy proofreading and mechanics. Read the magazine before submitting to it. We try to remain eclectic, but the odds for beginners are bound to be small considering the fact that we receive nearly 10,000 mss per year and publish only about ten short stories."

◐ THE DERONDA REVIEW

P.O. Box 5531, Madison WI 53705. **E-mail:** derondareview@att.net. **Website:** www.derondareview.org; www.pointandcircumference.com. Mindy Aber Barad, co-editor for Israel, P.O.B. 1299, Efrat 90435, Israel. **E-mail:** maber4kids@yahoo.com. **Contact:**

Esther Cameron, editor-in-chief; Mindy Aber Barad (Israel only). Semiannual literary journal publishing poetry and seeking to "promote a literature of introspection, dialogue, and social concern. Acquires first rights. Publishes ms 1 year after acceptance. Responds in up to 4 months; "if longer, please query via the website."

○ Now mainly a digital publication, with print copies for libraries.

MAGAZINE'S NEEDS Cover letter is unnecessary. "Do include SASE with sufficient postage to return all manuscripts or with 'Reply Only" clearly indicated. First-time contributors in the U.S. are requested to submit by surface mail. Poets whose work is accepted will be asked for URLS and titles of books available to be published in the online contributors exchange.

TIPS "Longer selections of poets frequently published in the magazine are posted on www.pointandcircumference.com."

♡ DESCANT

P.O. Box 314, Station P, Toronto ON M5S 2S8, Canada. (416)593-2557. **Fax:** (416)593-9362. **E-mail:** info@descant.ca. **E-mail:** submit@descant.ca. **Website:** www.descant.ca. Pays on publication. Publishes ms an average of 16 months after acceptance. Editorial lead time 1 year. Sample copy for $8.50 plus postage. Guidelines available online.

○ Pays $100 honorarium, plus 1-year's subscription for accepted submissions of any kind.

MAGAZINE'S NEEDS "*Descant* seeks high quality poems and stories in both traditional and innovative form." Annual. Circ. 500-750. Member CLMP. Literary. Pays $100.

CONTEST/AWARD OFFERINGS Sponsors the $500 Betsy Colquitt Award for the best poem in an issue; the $250 Baskerville Publishers Award for outstanding poem in an issue. Several stories first published by *descant* have appeared in *Best American Short Stories.*

TIPS "Familiarize yourself with our magazine before submitting."

◐◍ DESCANT: FORT WORTH'S JOURNAL OF POETRY AND FICTION

TCU Box 297270, Ft. Worth TX 76129. (817)257-6537. **Fax:** (817)257-6239. **E-mail:** descant@tcu.edu. **Website:** www.descant.tcu.edu. **Contact:** David Kuhne, editor. Magazine: 6×9; 120-150 pages; acid-free paper; paper cover. "*Descant* seeks high quality poems and stories in both traditional and innovative form."

Member CLMP. Pays on publication for one-time rights. Pays 2 contributor's copies; additional copies $6. Responds in 6-8 weeks to mss. Sample copy for $10. SASE, e-mail, or fax.

○ Offers 4 cash awards: The $500 Frank O'Connor Award for the best story in an issue; the $250 Gary Wilson Award for an outstanding story in an issue; the $500 Betsy Colquitt Award for the best poem in an issue; the $250 Baskerville Publishers Award for outstanding poem in an issue. Several stories first published by *Descant* have appeared in *Best American Short Stories*.

TIPS "We look for character and quality of prose. Send your best short work."

○ ⑤ DEVOZINE

1908 Grand Ave., P.O. Box 340004, Nashville TN 37203-0004. **E-mail:** smiller@upperroom.org. **Website:** www.devozine.org. **Contact:** Sandi Miller, Editor. *devozine,* published bimonthly, is a 64-page devotional magazine for youth (ages 12-19) and adults who care about youth. Offers meditations, scripture, prayers, poems, stories, songs, and feature articles to "aid youth in their prayer life, introduce them to spiritual disciplines, help them shape their concept of God, and encourage them in the life of discipleship." Considers poetry by teens. Lines/poem: 10-20. No e-mail submissions; submit by regular mail with SASE or use online submmission form. Include name, age/birth date (if younger than 25), mailing address, e-mail address, phone number, and fax number (if available). Always publishes theme issues (focuses on nine themes/issue, one for each week). Indicate theme you are writing for. Guidelines available for SASE or on website. Pays $25.

DIAGRAM

Department of English, University of Arizona, P.O. Box 210067, Tucson AZ 85721-0067. **E-mail:** editor@thediagram.com. **Website:** www.thediagram. com. "*DIAGRAM* is an electronic journal of text and art, found and created. We're interested in representations, naming, indicating, schematics, labelling and taxonomy of things; in poems that masquerade as stories; in stories that disguise themselves as indices or obituaries. We specialize in work that pushes the boundaries of traditional genre or work that is in some way schematic. We do publish traditional fiction and poetry, too, but hybrid forms (short stories, prose poems, indexes, tables of contents, etc.) are particularly welcome! We also publish diagrams and schematics (original and found)." Buys first North American serial rights. Time between acceptance and publication is 1-10 months. Responds in 2 weeks to queries; 1-2 months to mss. Often comments on rejected mss. Sample copy for $12 for print version. Writer's guidelines online.

○ Receives 100 unsolicited mss/month. Accepts 2-3 mss/issue; 15 mss/year. Receives about 1,000 poems/year, accepts about 5%. Publishes 6 new writers/year. Bimonthly. Member CLMP. "We sponsor yearly contests for unpublished hybrid essays and innovative fiction. Guidelines on website."

MAGAZINE'S NEEDS Submit 3-6 poems at a time. Considers simultaneous submissions; no previously published poems. Electronic submissions accepted through submissions manager; no e-mail, disk, or fax submissions. Electronic submissions much preferred; print submissions must include SASE if response is expected. Cover letter is preferred. Reads submissions year round. Poems are circulated to an editorial board. Sometimes comments on rejected poems. Sometimes publishes theme issues. Does not want light verse. Lines/poem: no limit.

ADDITIONAL INFORMATION *DIAGRAM* also publishes periodic perfect-bound print anthologies.

TIPS "Submit interesting text, images, sound and new media. We value the insides of things, vivisection, urgency, risk, elegance, flamboyance, work that moves us, language that does something new, or does something old—well. We like iteration and reiteration. Ruins and ghosts. Mechanical, moving parts, balloons, and frenzy. We want art and writing that demonstrates/interaction; the processes of things; how functions are accomplished; how things become or expire, move or stand. We'll consider anything. We do not consider e-mail submissions, but encourage electronic submissions via our submissions manager software. Look at the journal and submissions guidelines before submitting."

DIG MAGAZINE

Carus Publishing Co., 30 Grove St., Suite C, Peterborough NH 03458. (603)924-7209. **Fax:** (603)924-7380. **Website:** www.digonsite.com. **Contact:** Rosalie Baker, editor. Buys all rights. Pays on publication. Publishes ms an average of 1 year after acceptance. Responds in several months. Editorial lead time 1 year. Sample copy for $5.95 with 8x11 SASE or $10 without SASE. Guidelines available online.

MAGAZINE'S NEEDS Query. Length: up to 100 lines.

TIPS "Please remember that this is a children's magazine for kids ages 9-14 so the tone is as kid-friendly as possible given the scholarship involved in researching and describing a site or a find."

⊙⊙ DIODE POETRY JOURNAL

Virginia Commonwealth University in Qatar, Doha , Qatar. +9744134812. **Fax:** +9744920332. **Website:** www.diodepoetry.com. **Contact:** Patty Paine, editor. "*Diode* is looking for 'electropositive' poetry. What is electropositive poetry? It's poetry that excites and energizes. It's poetry that uses language that crackles and sparks. We're looking for poetry from all points on the arc, from formal to experimental." Acquires one-time rights. Rights revert to poet upon publication. Responds in 3-5 weeks. Always sends prepublication galleys. Guidelines available on website, by e-mail, in magazine.

> ⊙ Does not want "light verse, erotic." Has published poetry by Bob Hicok, Beckian Fritz Golberg, G.C. Waldrep, Dorianne Laux, Ada Limon, Joshua Maries Wilkinson. Receives about 6,000 poems/year; accepts about 3%.

MAGAZINE'S NEEDS Submit 3-5 poems at a time. Considers simultaneous submissions, no previously published poetry. Accepts submissions by e-mail; attach document. Cover letter is required. Reads submissions year round. Time between acceptance and publication is 3-5 weeks. Sometimes comments on rejected poems. Considers reviews books and chapbooks of poetry of 1,500-4,000 words, single and multi-book format.

⊙ THE DIRTY NAPKIN

E-mail: thedirtynapkin@thedirtynapkin.com. **Website:** thedirtynapkin.com. **Contact:** J. Argyl Plath, managing director/co-creator. Acquires first North American Serial rights. Guidelines online at website.

MAGAZINE'S NEEDS "Please submit no more than three poems at a time. We accept any length and style—although if you can cripple us with your brilliance in a short amount of time it is all the better. Please include something juicy and revealing about yourself in your cover letter."

TIPS "Oh, and one last thing: instead of listing your contact information and previous publications in the

cover letter, tell us something intriguing about yourself. We've made some good friends this way."

⊙ DISLOCATE

University of Minnesota English Department, the Edelstein-Keller Endowment, and Adam Lerner of the Lerner Publishing Group., Dept. of English, University of Minnesota, 1 Lind Hall, 207 Church St. SE, Minneapolis MN 55455. **E-mail:** dislocate.magazine@gmail.com. **Website:** http://dislocate.umn.edu. *dislocate* is a print and online literary journal dedicated to publishing Minnesota art that pushes the traditional boundaries of form and genre. "We like work that operates in the gray areas, that resists categorization, that ignores the limits; we like work that plays with the relationship between form and content. We publish fiction, nonfiction, poetry, and art, but we don't mind (or even prefer) that we can't tell which one we're dealing with." Guidelines available online.

MAGAZINE'S NEEDS Submit 3-5 poems.

TIPS "We are primarily looking for work from Minnesotan writers and artist, but submissions are also open to artists from (or with a connection to) Wisconsin, Michigan, Iowa, Illinois, Indiana, and North/South Dakota."

DMQ REVIEW

E-mail: editors@dmqreview.com. **Website:** www.dmqreview.com. **Contact:** Sally Ashton, editor-in-chief; Marjorie Manwaring, editor. "We seek work that represents the diversity of contemporary poetry and demonstrates literary excellence, whether it be lyric, free verse, prose, or experimental form." Buys first North American serial rights. Publishes ms 1-3 months after acceptance. Responds in 3 months. Guidelines available online.

MAGAZINE'S NEEDS Has published poetry by David Lehman, Ellen Bass, Amy Gerstler, Bob Hicok, Ilya Kaminsky, and Jane Hirshfield. Receives about 3,000-5,000 poems/year, accepts about 1%. E-mail submissions only; no attachments. Include a brief bio, 50 words/max. Type "Poetry Submission," followed by your name, in the subject line of your e-mail.

ADDITIONAL INFORMATION Nominates for the Pushcart Prize. "We also consider submissions of visual art, which we publish with the poems in the magazine, with links to the artists' Web sites."

TIPS "Check our current and past issues and read and follow submission guidelines closely. Important: Copy and include the permission statement with your submission (it's in our guidelines online). For Visual Art submissions: Type 'Art Submission' followed by your name in your e-mail. Send a working URL where we may view samples of your work."

○ DOWN IN THE DIRT

829 Brian Court, Gurnee IL 60031-3155. (847)281-9070. **E-mail:** dirt@scars.tv. **Website:** www.scars.tv. **Contact:** Janet Kuypers, editor. *Down in the Dirt*, published monthly online, prints "good work that makes you think, that makes you feel like you've lived through a scene instead of merely read it." Also can consider poems. *Down in the Dirt* is published "electronically as well as in print, either as printed magazines sold through our printer over the Internet, on the Web (Internet web pages) or sold through our printer in e-book form (PDF file)." Publishes ms within 1 year after acceptance. Responds in 1 month to queries; 1 month to mss. Always, if asked, comments on rejected mss. Sample copy for issues before 2010 are $6. "Samples 2010+ do not exist; you can just directly purchase the issues online any time." Guidelines for SASE, e-mail, or on website.

○ Literary magazine/journal: 5.5x8.5 perfect-bound, 84-page book. Contains illustrations and photographs as well as short stories, essays, and poetry." Has published work by Pat Dixon, Mel Waldman, Ken Dean Aeon Logan, Helena Wolfe.

MAGAZINE'S NEEDS Considers previously published poems and simultaneous submissions. Accepts e-mail submissions (vastly preferred to snail mail; pasted into body of message or as Microsoft Word .doc file attachment) and disk submissions (formatted for Macintosh). "Currently, accepted writings get their own Web page in the 'writings' section at http://scars.tv, and samples of accepted writings are placed into an annual collection book Scars Publications produces." Has published work by I.B. Rad, Pat Dixon, Mel Waldman, and Brian Looney. Does not want smut, rhyming poetry, or religious writing. Lines/poem: any length is appreciated. No payment.

TIPS Scars Publications sponsors a contest "where accepted writing appears in a collection book. Write or e-mail (dirt@scars.tv) for information." Also able to publish electronic chapbooks. Write for more information.

● DROWN IN MY OWN FEARS

E-mail: drowninmyownfears@yahoo.com. **Website:** http://drowninmyownfears.angelfire.com. **Contact:** Kaia Braeburn and Alla Kozak, editors. *Drown In My Own Fears*, published quarterly online, "is a poetry journal about the human condition, therefore, we want poems reflecting that. Poems submitted should be about love, hate, pain, sorrow, etc. We don't want maudlin sentimentality, we want the depths of your very being. We want well-written, deeply conceived pieces of work. Anything that isn't about the human condition really isn't for us." Acquires first rights. Rights revert to poets upon publication. Publishes ms 1-2 months after acceptance. Responds in 8-10 weeks. Never comments on rejected poems.

MAGAZINE'S NEEDS Wants "all styles of poetry, as long as it's your best work." Does not want "syrupy sweet, gooey nonsense, religious rants, political grandstandings." Considers poetry by teens. Has published poetry by Kendall A. Bell, April Michelle Bratten, Natalie Carpentieri, MK Chavez, James H. Duncan, and Taylor Graham. Receives about 300 poems/year, accepts about 10%. Submit 3-5 poems at a time. "We prefer short poems, but long ones are okay." Considers previously published poems; no simultaneous submissions. Accepts e-mail submissions (pasted into body of e-mail message); no fax or disk submissions. Cover letter is rquired. Include a brief bio. Reads submissions year round. Sometimes publishes theme issues. Upcoming themes and guidelines available on website.

DRUNKEN BOAT

119 Main St., Chester CT 06412. **E-mail:** editor@drunkenboat.com. **Website:** www.drunkenboat.com. *Drunken Boat*, published twice yearly online, is a multimedia publication reaching an international audience with an extremely broad aesthetic. Considers poetry by teens. "We judge by quality, not age. However, most poetry we publish is written by published poets with training in creative writing. "Has published more than 500 poets, including Heather McHugh, Jane Hirshfield, Alfred Corn, Alice Fulton, Ron Silliman, and Roseanna Warren. Received about 3,000 poems/year, accepts about 5%. Responds in 3 months to mss. Guidelines available online.

MAGAZINE'S NEEDS "Submit no more than 3 poems, in a single document. Our aesthetic is very broad. We welcome work ranging from received form to the cutting edge avant-garde, from one line to the multi-page, from collaborations to hybridizations & cut-ups as well as works that use other media in their composition, originality & in translation (with the writer's permission), American, & from around the globe." Length: 1 lines.

TIPS "Submissions should be submitted in Word & rtf format only. (This does not apply to audio, visual & web work.) Accepts chapbooks. See our submissions manager system."

⬤ DUCTS

P.O. Box 3203, Grand Central Station, New York NY 10163. **E-mail:** vents@ducts.org. **Website:** www.ducts.org. **Contact:** Jonathan Kravetz, editor-in-chief. *DUCTS* is a webzine of personal stories, fiction, essays, memoirs, poetry, humor, profiles, reviews and art. "*DUCTS* was founded in 1999 with the intent of giving emerging writers a venue to regularly publish their compelling, personal stories. The site has been expanded to include art and creative works of all genres. We believe that these genres must and do overlap. *DUCTS* publishes the best, most compelling stories and we hope to attract readers who are drawn to work that rises above." Semi-annual. Pays on publication. Responds in 1-6 months. Guidelines available on website.

MAGAZINE'S NEEDS Submit 3-5 poems to poetry@ducts.org.

TIPS "We prefer writing that tells a compelling story with a strong narrative drive."

⬤ EARTHSHINE

P.O. Box 245, Hummelstown PA 17036. **E-mail:** poetry@ruminations.us. **Website:** www.ruminations.us. **Contact:** Sally Zaino and Julie Moffitt, poetry editors. *Earthshine*, published irregularly in print, and constantly online, features poetry and 1-2 pieces of cover art per volume. "When the online journal is full, a printed volume is produced and offered for sale. Subscriptions will be available as the publication becomes regular. The voice of *Earthshine* is one of illumination, compassion, humanity, and reason. Please see submission guidelines Web page for updated information. Poems are the ultimate rumination, and if the world is to be saved, the poets will be needed; they are who see the connections between all things, and the patterns shared. We seek poetry of high literary quality which will generate its own light for our readers." Acquires first rights and requests ongoing electronic rights. Responds in 1-2 months. Guidelines available in magazine, for SASE, and on website.

○ Has published poetry by Richard Schiffman, Anne Pierson Wiese, Steven Keletar, Mario Susko, Daniel J. Langton.

MAGAZINE'S NEEDS Considers previously published poems; no simultaneous submissions. Accepts e-mail submissions (pasted into body of message); no fax or disk submissions. Cover letter is preferred. "Please let us know where you heard about *Earthshine*. If submitting by mail, please include a SASE for reply only. Please do not send the only copy of your work." Reads submissions year round. Time between acceptance and publication is: "online publication is almost immediate, printed publication TBD." Sometimes comments on rejected poems. Never publishes theme issues. Pays 2 contributor's copies.

ALSO OFFERS "The parent of *Earthshine* is also at Ruminations.us, and offers full editing and review services for a fee."

ECLECTICA

E-mail: editors@eclectica.org. **Website:** www.eclectica.org. **Contact:** Tom Dooley, managing editor. "A sterling quality literary magazine on the World Wide Web. Not bound by formula or genre, harnessing technology to further the reading experience and dynamic and interesting in content. *Eclectica* is a quarterly World Wide Web journal devoted to showcasing the best writing on the Web, regardless of genre. 'Literary' and 'genre' work appear side-by-side in each issue, along with pieces that blur the distinctions between such categories. Pushcart Prize, National Poetry Series, and Pulitzer Prize winners, as well as Nebula Award nominees, have shared issues with previously unpublished authors." Buys first North American serial rights, buys one-time, nonexclusive use of electronic rights rights. Guidelines available online at website.

MAGAZINE'S NEEDS Seeks "outstanding poetry." Submit using online submissions manager.

TIPS "We pride ourselves on giving everyone (high schoolers, convicts, movie executives, etc.) an equal shot at publication, based solely on the quality of their work. Because we like eclecticism, we tend to favor the varied perspectives that often characterize the work of international authors, people of color, women, alternative lifestylists—but others who don't fit into these categories often surprise us."

❂❶ THE ECLECTIC MUSE

Suite 307, 6311 Gilbert Rd., Richmond BC V7C 3V7, Canada. (778)822-3864. **E-mail:** jrmbooks@hotmail.com. **Website:** mbooksofbc.com; thehypertexts.com. **Contact:** Joe M. Ruggier, publisher. *The Eclectic Muse*, published annually at Christmas, is devoted "to publishing all kinds of poetry (eclectic in style and taste) but specializing in rhyme- and neo-classicist revival." Does not want "bad work (stylistically bad or thematically offensive)." Time between acceptance and publication is 1 year. Single copy: $15 includes shipping and handling; subscription: $25. Make checks payable to Joe M. Ruggier. Guidelines available in magazine or on website.

❍ Has published poetry by Mary Keelan Meisel, John Laycock, Philip Higson, Roy Harrison, Michael Burch, and Ralph O. Cunningham. *The Eclectic Muse* is magazine-sized, digitally copied, saddle-stapled, with paper cover. The number of pages varies from year to year (32 minimum to 56 maximum). Receives about 300 poems/year, accepts about 15%. Press run is 200; distributed free to all contributing authors plus selected gift subscription recipients. Reads submissions year round. Sometimes comments on rejected poems. "If authors wish to have a manuscript carefully assessed and edited, the fee is $250 USD; will respond within 8 weeks." Responds in 2 months. Pays 2 contributor's copies. Reviews books/chapbooks of poetry and other magazines/journals at varying length. Send materials for review consideration to Joe M. Ruggier, managing editor.

MAGAZINE'S NEEDS Submit no more than 5 poems at a time. Lines/poem: 60 maximum; "please consult if longer." Accepts e-mail submissions (as 1 .doc or .rtf attachment containing all 5 poems) and disk submissions. "Send your submission by regular mail only if you have no access to a computer or you are computer illiterate. Typeset everything in Times New Roman 12 point. If your poetry features indents and special line spacing, please make sure you reproduce these features yourself in your data entry since it will not be possible for the editor to determine your intentions." Cover letter is preferred. "Include brief bio (100 words maximum) with your name, credentials (degrees, etc.), occupation and marital status, your most major publication credits only, and any hobbies or interests." Provide SASE plus clear e-mail and postal addresses for communication and for sending contributor's copy.

ECOTONE

Department of Creative Writing, University of North Carolina Wilmington, 601 S. College Rd., Wilmington NC 28403. (910)962-2547. **Fax:** (910)962-7461. **E-mail:** info@ecotonejournal.com. **Website:** www.ecotonejournal.com. **Contact:** Sally J. Johnson, managing editor. "*Ecotone* is a literary journal of place that seeks to publish creative works about the environment and the natural world while avoiding the hushed tones and cliches of much of so-called nature writing. Reading period is August 15-April 15." Responds in 3-6 months to mss.

❶ EKPHRASIS

Frith Press, P.O. Box 161236, Sacramento CA 95816-1236. **E-mail:** frithpress@aol.com. **Website:** ekphrasisjournal.com. **Contact:** Laverne Frith and Carol Frith, editors. *Ekphrasis*, published semiannually in March and September, is an "outlet for the growing body of poetry focusing on individual works from any artistic genre. Poetry should transcend mere description. Open to all forms." Acquires first North American serial rights or one-time rights. Publishes ms 1 year after acceptance. Responds in 4 months. Seldom comments on rejected poems. Sample copy for $6. Guidelines available for SASE or on website.

❍ Has published poetry by Jeffrey Levine, Peter Meinke, David Hamilton, Barbara Lefcowitz, Molly McQuade, Alice Friman, and Annie Boutelle. *Ekphrasis* is 32-50 pages, digest-sized, photocopied, saddle-stapled. Subscription: $12/year. Make checks payable, in U.S. funds, to Laverne Frith. Poems from *Ekphrasis* have been featured on *Poetry Daily*. Nominates for Pushcart Prize.

MAGAZINE'S NEEDS Submit 3-5 poems at a time. Considers previously published poems "infrequently, must be credited." Cover letter is required, including short bio with representative credits and phone number. Include SASE. Until further notice, Frith Press will publish **occasional chapbooks by invitation only**. Does not want "poetry without ekphrastic focus. No poorly crafted work. No archaic language." Pays 1 contributor's copy.

⊙ ⊕ ⑤ ELLERY QUEEN'S MYSTERY MAGAZINE

Dell Magazines, 267 Broadway, 4th Floor, New York NY 10017. (212)686-7188. **Fax:** (212)686-7414. **E-mail:** elleryqueenmm@dellmagazines.com. **Website:** www.themysteryplace.com/eqmm. **Contact:** Jackie Sherbow, assistant editor. "*Ellery Queen's Mystery Magazine* welcomes submissions from both new and established writers. We publish every kind of mystery short story: the psychological suspense tale, the deductive puzzle, the private eye case—the gamut of crime and detection from the realistic (including the policeman's lot and stories of police procedure) to the more imaginative (including 'locked rooms' and 'impossible crimes'). We look for strong writing, an original and exciting plot, and professional craftsmanship. We encourage writers whose work meets these general criteria to read an issue of *EQMM* before making a submission." Buys first North American serial rights. Pays on acceptance. Publishes ms an average of 6-12 months after acceptance. Responds in 3 months to mss. Sample copy for $5.50. Guidelines for SASE or online.

MAGAZINE'S NEEDS *Ellery Queen's Mystery Magazine*, published 10 times/year, uses primarily short stories of mystery, crime, or suspense—little poetry. *Ellery Queen's Mystery Magazine* is 112 pages (double-issue, published twice/year, is 192 pages), digest-sized, professionally printed on newsprint, flat-spined, with glossy paper cover. Single copy: $5.50 by check to publisher, available for $4.99 on newsstands; subscription: $55.90. Short mystery verses, limericks. Length: 1 page, double spaced maximum.

HOW TO CONTACT Considers simultaneous submissions; no previously published poems. Guidelines available on website. Responds in 3 months. Pays $15-65 and 3 contributor's copies. "*EQMM* uses an online submission system (http://eqmm.magazinesubmissions.com) that has been designed to streamline our process and improve communication with authors. We ask that all submissions be made electronically, using this system, rather than on paper. All stories should be in standard ms format and submitted in .DOC format. We cannot accept .DOCX, .RTF, or .TXT files at this time. For detailed submission instructions, see http://eqmm.magazinesubmissions.com or our writers guidelines page (http://www.themysteryplace.com/eqmm/guidelines)."

TIPS "We have a Department of First Stories to encourage writers whose fiction has never before been in print. We publish an average of 10 first stories every year. Mark subject line Attn: Dept. of First Stories."

⊙ ⑤ ELLIPSIS MAGAZINE

(801)832-2321. **E-mail:** ellipsis@westminstercollege.edu. **Website:** www.westminstercollege.edu/ellipsis. **Contact:** Mikki Whitworth, managing editor; Lauren Johnson, editor-in-chief. Buys first North American serial rights. Pays on publication. Publishes ms an average of 3 months after acceptance. Responds in 6 months to mss. Sample copy for $7.50. Guidelines available online.

○ Reads submissions August 1 to November 1.

MAGAZINE'S NEEDS Reads submissions August 1-November 1. No fax or e-mail submissions. One poem per page, with name and contact information on every page. Include SASE and brief bio No previously published poems. Pays $10/poem, plus 2 contributor's copies.

CONTEST/AWARD OFFERINGS All accepted poems are eligible for the *Ellipsis* Award which includes a $100 prize. Past judges have included Jorie Graham, Sandra Cisneros, and Stanley Plumly.

⊙ EPICENTER: A LITERARY MAGAZINE

P.O. Box 367, Riverside CA 92502. **E-mail:** submissions@epicentermagazine.org. **Website:** www.epicentermagazine.org. **Contact:** Jeff Green, Cali Linfor, Rowena Silver, editors. *Epicenter: A Literary Magazine* published semiannually, is open to all styles. "*Epicenter* is looking for poetry, essays, short stories, creative nonfiction, and artwork. We publish new and established writers." Considers translations. Does not want "angst-ridden, sentimental, or earthquake poetry. We are not adverse to graphic images as long as the work contains literary merit." Has published poetry by Virgil Suarez, Alba Cruz-Hacher, B.Z. Niditch, Egon Lass, and Zdravka Evtimova. *Epicenter* is 100 pages, perfect-bound. Receives about 2,000 submissions/year, accepts about 5%. Press run is 800. Single copy: $9. Make checks payable to *Epicenter: A Literary Magazine*. Acquires one-time and electronic rights. Guidelines in magazine, by e-mail or for SASE.

MAGAZINE'S NEEDS Submit up to 5 poems at a time. Send poetry with vivid imagery and fresh ideas. Accepts any style of poetry. Submit through postal mail or e-mail. "Due to the volume of e-mail submissions, we do not respond unless we wish to use a piece."

Include SASE with postal mail. Pays 1 contributor's copy.

EPIPHANY—WHERE CREATIVITY AND INSPIRATION EVOLVE!

E-mail: contact@epiphmag.com. **E-mail:** submissions@epiphmag.com. **Website:** www.epiphmag.com. **Contact:** JW Smith, editor. *Epiphany* was started in 2010, solely to be an online venue in which writers and artists can display their works. "*Epiphany*'s dynamic formatting sets our publication apart from other online magazines. We strive to bring poetry, prose, fiction, nonfiction, artwork, and photography together to form a visually and creatively stimulating experience for our readers." Six issues/year in February, April, June, August, October, and December. Contributors retain their rights. Publishes ms an average of 3-4 months after acceptance. Responds in 1-4 weeks to queries; 1-4 months to mss. Sample copy available on website.

○ "*Epiphany* is a non-paying market at this time."

MAGAZINE'S NEEDS "Please write 'Poetry' in the subject line of your e-mail."

TIPS "We are open to a variety of writing styles and content subject matter. Our audience includes writers, artists, students, teachers, and all who enjoy reading short fiction, poetry, and creative nonfiction. We will not publish any works which we feel have a derogatory nature. Please visit our submission guidelines page at www.epiphmag.com/guide.html for more details. "Please write the type of submission you are sending in the subject line of your e-mail."

EPOCH

251 Goldwin Smith Hall, Cornell University, Ithaca NY 14853. (607)255-3385. **Fax:** (607)255-6661. **Website:** http://english.arts.cornell.edu/publications/epoch. "Well-written literary fiction, poetry, personal essays. Newcomers always welcome. Open to mainstream and avant-garde writing." Buys first North American serial rights. Pays on publication. Publishes ms an average of 6 months after acceptance. Responds in 2 weeks to queries. Responds in 6 weeks to mss. Sometimes comments on rejected mss. Editorial lead time 6 months. Sample copy for $5. Guidelines online and for #10 SASE.

○ Magazine: 6×9; 128 pages; good quality paper; good cover stock. Receives 500 unsolicited mss/month. Accepts 15-20 mss/issue. **Reads submissions September 15-April 15.** Publish-

es 3-4 new writers/year. Has published work by Antonya Nelson, Doris Betts, Heidi Jon Schmidt.

MAGAZINE'S NEEDS No simultaneous submissions. Mss not accompanied by SASE will be discarded unread. Occasionally provides criticism on poems. Pays $5 up/printed page.

TIPS "Tell your story, speak your poem, straight from the heart. We are attracted to language and to good writing, but we are most interested in what the good writing leads us to, or where."

◑ EUREKA LITERARY MAGAZINE

300 E. College Ave., Eureka College, Eureka IL 61530. **E-mail:** elm@eureka.edu. **Website:** www.eureka.edu/arts/literary/literary.htm. Responds to queries in 2 weeks, mss in 4 months. Sample copy for $7.50.

MAGAZINE'S NEEDS Submit via e-mail. See website for examples.

TIPS "Do something that hasn't been done a thousand times already. Give us unusual but believable characters in unusual but believable conflicts—clear resolution isn't always necessary, but it's nice. We don't hold to hard and fast rules about length, but most stories could do with some cutting. Make sure your title is relevant and eye-catching. Please do not send personal gifts or hate mail. We're a college-operated magazine, so we do not actually exist in summer. If we don't take a submission, that doesn't automatically mean we don't like it—we try to encourage authors who show promise to revise and resubmit. Order a copy if you can."

◑◑ EUROPEAN JUDAISM

LBC, The Sternberg Centre, 80 East End Rd., London N3 2SY, England. **E-mail:** european.judaism@lbc.ac.uk. **Website:** www.berghahnbooks.com/journals/ej. *European Judaism*, published twice/year, is a "glossy, elegant magazine with emphasis on European Jewish theology/philosophy/literature/history, with some poetry in every issue. Poems should (preferably) be short and have some relevance to matters of Jewish interest." Has published poetry by Linda Pastan, Elaine Feinstein, Daniel Weissbort, and Dannie Abse. *European Judaism* is 110 pages, digest-sized, flat-spined. Press run is 950 (about 500 subscribers, over 100 libraries). Subscription: $45 individual, $20 student, $162 institution.

MAGAZINE'S NEEDS Submit 3-4 poems at a time. Lines/poem: short poems preferred. "I prefer unpublished poems, but poems from published books are acceptable." Cover letter is required. "No material is read or returned if not accompanied by SASE (or SAE with IRCs). We cannot use American stamps." Pays 1 contributor's copy.

◐ ⑤ EVANGEL

Light and Life Communications, 770 N. High School Rd., Indianapolis IN 46214. (317)244-3660. **Contact:** Julie Innes, editor. *Evangel,* published quarterly, is an adult Sunday School paper. "Devotional in nature, it lifts up Christ as the source of salvation and hope. The mission of *Evangel* is to increase the reader's understanding of the nature and character of God and the nature of a life lived for Christ. Material that fits this mission and isn't longer than 1 page will be considered." Buys second serial (reprint) or one-time rights. Pays on publication. Publishes ms 18-36 months after acceptance. Responds in 4-6 weeks to queries. Responds in up to 2 months to poems. Seldom comments on rejected poems. Sample copy and writer's guidelines for #10 SASE. "Write 'guidelines request' on your envelope so we can sort it from the submissions."

○　*Evangel* is 8 pages, 5.5 x 8.5, printed in 4-color, unbound, color and b&w photos. Does not want rhyming work. Accepts about 5% of poetry received. Fiction involves people coping with everday crises, making decisions that show spiritual growth. Weekly distribution. Recently published work by Kelli Wise and Hope Byler. Press run is about 10,000. Subscription: $2.59/quarter (13 weeks).

MAGAZINE'S NEEDS Submit no more than 5 poems at a time. Considers simultaneous submissions. Cover letter is preferred. "Poetry must be typed on 8.5 x 11 white paper. In the upper left-hand corner of each page, include your name, address, phone number, and social security number. In the upper right-hand corner of cover page, specify what rights you are offering. One-eighth of the way down the page, give the title. All subsequent material must be double-spaced, with 1-inch margins." Pays $10 plus 2 contributor's copies.

TIPS "Desire, concise, tight writing that supports a solid thesis and fits the mission expressed in the guidelines."

◐ EVANSVILLE REVIEW

University of Evansville Creative Writing Department, 1800 Lincoln Ave., Evansville IN 47722.

(812)488-1402. **E-mail:** evansvillereview@evansville. edu. **Website:** http://evansvillereview.evansville.edu. Acquires one-time rights. Pays on publication. Responds in 3 months. Sample copy for $5. Guidelines available online at website.

MAGAZINE'S NEEDS Submit 3-5 poems at a time. Considers previously published poems and simultaneous submissions. No fax or e-mail submissions; postal submissions only. Cover letter is required. Include brief bio. Pays in contributor's copies.

TIPS "Because editorial staff rolls over every 1-2 years, the journal always has a new flavor."

EXIT 13 MAGAZINE, "THE CROSSROADS OF POETRY SINCE 1988"

P.O. Box 423, Fanwood NJ 07023-1162. **E-mail:** exit13magazine@yahoo.com. **Contact:** Tom Plante, editor. *Exit 13*, published annually, uses poetry that is "short, to the point, with a sense of geography. It features poets of all ages, writing styles and degrees of experience, focusing on where and how we live and what's going on around us. The emphasis is on geography, travel, adventure, and the fertile ground of the imagination. It's a travelogue in poetry, a reflection of the world we see, and a chronicle of the people we meet along the way." Acquires one-time and possible anthology rights. Pays 1 contributor's copy. Responds in 4 months. Guidelines available in magazine or for SASE.

○　Has published poetry by Paul Brooke, Ruth Moon Kempher, Sandy McCord, Sander Zulauf, Paul Sohar, and Charles Rammelkamp. *Exit 13* is about 76 pages. Press run is 300. Sample: $8.

MAGAZINE'S NEEDS Submit through postal mail or e-mail. Paste in body of e-mail. Considers simultaneous submissions and previously published poems.

◐ EYE ON LIFE ONLINE MAGAZINE

P.O. Box 534, Brookline MA 02445. **E-mail:** eyeonlife.ezine@gmail.com. **Website:** http://eyeonlifemag.com. **Contact:** Tom Rubenoff, senior poetry editor. Poets keep all rights. Responds in 4-6 weeks.

MAGAZINE'S NEEDS Publishes up to 5 poems/week. Submissions through online submission form only. Seeking poetry with vivid imagery that either works well within its form or transcends it in less than 400 words. Does not pay for poetry at this time.

CONTEST/AWARD OFFERINGS Eyes on Life Poetry Contest first prize $100, second prize $50. E-mail tomr@rubecome.us for details.

⑤ FACES MAGAZINE

Cobblestone Publishing, Editorial Dept., 30 Grove St., Suite C, Peterborough NH 03458. (603)924-7209. **E-mail:** facesmag@yahoo.com. **Website:** www.cricket-mag.com. *FACES Magazine*, published 9 times/year, features cultures from around the globe for children ages 9-14. "Readers learn how other kids live around the world and about the important inventions and ideas that a particular culture has given to the world. All material must relate to the theme of a specific upcoming issue in order to be considered." Wants "clear, objective imagery. Serious and light verse considered. Must relate to theme." Subscription: $33.95/year (9 issues). Sample pages available on website. Acquires all rights.

MAGAZINE'S NEEDS Query first. Accepts e-mail queries. Include SASE for postal submissions and queries. Reads submissions according to deadlines for queries (see website for schedule and details). Always publishes theme issue. Themes and guidelines available on website. Length: up to 100 lines. Pay varies.

FAULTLINE

University of California at Irvine, Department of English, 435 Humanities Instructional Building, Irvine CA 92697. (949)824-1573. **E-mail:** faultline@uci.edu. **Website:** http://faultline.sites.uci.edu. Buys first North American serial rights. Pays on publication. Publishes ms an average of 5 months after acceptance. Responds in 4 weeks to queries. Responds in 4 months to mss. Editorial lead time 4 months. Sample copy for $5 or online. Writer's guidelines for #10 SASE or online.

○ Reading period is September 15-February 15. Submissions sent at any other time will not be read.

MAGAZINE'S NEEDS Submit up to 5 poems. Include SASE with submissions. Pays in contributor copies.

TIPS "Our commitment is to publish the best work possible from well-known and emerging authors with vivid and varied voices."

① FICKLE MUSES

E-mail: editor@ficklemuses.com. **Website:** www.ficklemuses.com. "*Fickle Muses* is an online journal of poetry and fiction engaged with myth and legend. A poet or fiction writer is featured each week, with new selections posted on Sundays. Art is updated monthly." Nonpaying market. Publishes ms 3 months after acceptance. Responds in 3 weeks. Guidelines available online at website.

MAGAZINE'S NEEDS Open to all kinds of poetry. No limits on length.

TIPS "Originality. An innovative look at an old story. I'm looking to be swept away. Get a feel for our website."

☼❶⑤ THE FIDDLEHEAD

University of New Brunswick, Campus House, 11 Garland Court, Box 4400, Fredericton NB E3B 5A3, Canada. (506)453-3501. **Fax:** (506) 453-5069. **E-mail:** fiddlehd@unb.ca. **Website:** www.thefiddlehead.ca. Mark Anthony Jarman and Gerard Beirne, fiction editors; Sarah Bernstein, Phillip Crymble, Claire Kelly, and Ian LeTourneau, poetry editors. **Contact:** Kathryn Taglia, managing editor. "Canada's longest living literary journal, *The Fiddlehead* is published 4 times a year at the University of New Brunswick, with the generous assistance of the University of New Brunswick, the Canada Council for the Arts, and the Province of New Brunswick. It is experienced; wise enough to recognize excellence; always looking for freshness and surprise. *The Fiddlehead* publishes short stories, poems, book reviews, and a small number of personal essays. Our full-colour covers have become collectors' items, and feature work by New Brunswick artists and from New Brunswick museums and art galleries. *The Fiddlehead* also sponsors an annual writing contest. The journal is open to good writing in English from all over the world, looking always for freshness and surprise. Our editors are always happy to see new unsolicited works in fiction and poetry. Work is read on an ongoing basis; the acceptance rate is around 1-2%. Apart from our annual contest, we have no deadlines for submissions." Pays on publication for first or one-time serial rights. Responds in 3-9 months to mss. Occasionally comments on rejected mss. Sample copy for $15 (U.S.).

○ Magazine: 6×9; 128-180 pages; ink illustrations; photos. "No criteria for publication except quality. For a general audience, including many poets and writers." Has published work by Marjorie Celona, Wasela Hiyate, Alexander MacLeod, and Erika Van Winden.

MAGAZINE'S NEEDS Send SASE and *Canadian* stamps or IRCs for return of mss. No e-mail submissions. Simultaneous submissions only if stated on cover letter; must contact immediately if accepted elsewhere. Pays up to $40 (Canadian)/published page and 2 contributor's copies.

CONTEST/AWARD OFFERINGS Sponsors poetry contest.

TIPS "If you are serious about submitting to *The Fiddlehead*, you should subscribe or read an issue or 2 to get a sense of the journal. Contact us if you would to order sample back issues ($10-15 plus postage)."

FIELD: CONTEMPORARY POETRY & POETICS

Oberlin College Press, 50 N. Professor St., Oberlin OH 44074-1091. (440)775-8408. **Fax:** (440)775-8124. **E-mail:** oc.press@oberlin.edu. **Website:** www.oberlin.edu/ocpress. **Contact:** managing editor. *FIELD: Contemporary Poetry and Poetics*, published semiannually in April and October, is a literary journal with "emphasis on poetry, translations, and essays by poets. See electronic submission guidelines." Buys first rights. Pays on publication. Responds in 6-8 weeks to mss. Editorial lead time 4 months. Sample copy for $8. Guidelines available online and for #10 SASE.

○ *FIELD* is 100 pages, digest-sized, printed on rag stock, flat-spined, with glossy color card cover. Subscription: $16/year, $28 for 2 years. Sample: $8 postpaid. Has published poetry by Michelle Glazer, Tom Lux, Carl Phillips, Betsy Sholl, Charles Simic, Jean Valentine and translations by Marilyn Hacker and Stuart Friebert.

MAGAZINE'S NEEDS Submissions are read August 1 through May 31. Submit 3-5 of your best poems. No previously published poems or simultaneous submissions. No e-mail submissions. Include cover letter and SASE. Submit using submission manager: www.oberlin.edu/ocpress/submissions.html. Pays $15/page and 2 contributor's copies.

TIPS "Keep trying!"

○ ⑤ THE FIFTH DI...

Tyree Campbell, attn: Sam's Dot Publishing, PO Box 782, Cedar Rapids IO 52406-0782. **Website:** www.samsdotpublishing.com/fifth/fifth.htm. *The Fifth Di..*, published quarterly online, features fiction and poetry from the science fiction and fantasy genres. Open to most forms, but all poems must be science fiction or fantasy. Does not want horror, or anything that is not science fiction or fantasy. Considers poetry by children and teens. Has published poetry by Bruce Boston, Cathy Buburuz, Marge Simon, Aurelio Rico Lopez III, Terrie Relf, and John Bushore. Receives about 200 poems/year, accepts about 20. Acquires first rights. Publishes ms 3 months after acceptance. Responds in 1 month. Guidelines online.

MAGAZINE'S NEEDS Submit 1 poem at a time. Lines/poem: no limit. No previously published poems or simultaneous submissions. Accepts e-mail submissions only (as attachment); no disk submissions. Cover letter is preferred. Reads submissions year round.

○ ❶ FILLING STATION

P.O. Box 22135, Bankers Hall, Calgary AB T2P 4J5, Canada. **E-mail:** mgmt@fillingstation.ca; poetry@fillingstation.ca; fiction@fillingstation.ca; nonfiction@fillingstation.ca. **Website:** www.fillingstation.ca. **Contact:** Caitlynn Cummings, managing editor. *filling Station*, published 3 times/year, prints contemporary poetry, fiction, visual art, interviews, reviews, and articles. "We are looking for all forms of contemporary writing. but especially that which is original and/or experimental." Responds in 3-4 months. "After your work is reviewed by our Collective, you will receive an e-mail from an editor to let you know if your work has been selected for publication. If selected, you will later receive a second e-mail to let you know which issue your piece has been selected to appear in. Note that during the design phase, we sometimes discover the need to shuffle a piece to a future issue instead. In the event your piece is pushed back, we will inform you."

○ Has published poetry by Fred Wah, Larissa Lai, Margaret Christakos, Robert Kroetsch, Ron Silliman, Susan Holbrook, and many more. *filling Station* is 64 pages, perfect-bound, with card cover, includes photos and artwork. Receives about 100 submissions for each issue, accepts approximately 10%. Press run is 700. Subscription: $20/3 issues; $36 for 6 issues. Sample: $8.

MAGAZINE'S NEEDS Up to 6 pages of poetry may be sent to poetry@fillingstation.ca. A submission lacking mailing address and/or bio will be considered incomplete.

TIPS "*filling Station* accepts singular or simultaneous submissions of previously unpublished poetry, fiction, creative nonfiction, nonfiction, or art. We are always on the hunt for great writing!"

⭕ FIRST CLASS

P.O. Box 86, Friendship IN 47021. **E-mail:** christopherm@four-sep.com. **Website:** www.four-sep.com. **Contact:** Christopher M, editor. Acquires one-time rights. Responds in 1-2 months. Guidelines for #10 SASE or on website.

MAGAZINE'S NEEDS Does not want traditional work.

ADDITIONAL INFORMATION Chapbook production available.

TIPS "Don't bore me with puppy dogs and the morose/sappy feeling you have about death. Belt out a good, short, thought-provoking, graphic, uncommon piece."

⭕ 5 AM

P.O. Box 205, Spring Church PA 15686. (715)284-0328. **Website:** www.5ampoetry.com. **Contact:** Ed Ochester and Judith Vollmer. "*5 AM*, published twice/year, is a poetry publication open in regard to form, length, subject matter, and style. Does not want religious poetry or "naive rhymers." Has published poetry by Virgil Suaárez, Nin Andrews, Alicia Ostriker, Edward Field, Billy Collins, and Denise Duhamel. *5 AM* is 24-pages, tabloid size, offset-printed. Receives about 5,000 poems/year, accepts about 2%. Press run is 1,200. Subscription: $12 for 2 issues (one year), $20 for 4 issues (two years)." Responds in 4-6 weeks to mss.

TIPS "We read all year. Manuscripts cannot be returned without SASE with sufficient postage."

⭕ FLINT HILLS REVIEW

Dept. of English, Box 4019, Emporia State University, Emporia KS 66801. **Website:** www.emporia.edu/fhr/. **Contact:** Kevin Rabas. *Flint Hills Review*, published annually in late summer, is "a regionally focused journal presenting writers of national distinction alongside new authors." Magazine: 9×6; 115 pages; 60 lb. paper; glossy cover; illustrations; photos. "*FHR* seeks work informed by a strong sense of place or region, especially Kansas and the Great Plains region. We seek to provide a publishing venue for writers of the Great Plains and Kansas while also publishing authors whose work evidences a strong sense of place, writing of literary quality, and accomplished use of language and depth of character development." Acquires one-time rights. Publishes ms 4-12 months af-

ter acceptance. Sample copy $5.50 Writer's guidelines for SASE, by e-mail, fax, or on website.

MAGAZINE'S NEEDS Wants all forms of poetry except rhyming. Does not want sentimental or gratuitous verse. Has published poetry by E. Ethelbert Miller, Elizabeth Dodd, Walt McDonald, and Gwendolyn Brooks. Submit 3-5 poems at a time. Considers simultaneous submissions; no previously published poems. Accepts submissions by fax or e-mail (pasted into body of message). Cover letter is required. Include SASE. Reads submissions January-March only.

CONTEST/AWARD OFFERINGS *FHR* hosts an annual nonfiction contest. **Entry Fee**: $10. **Deadline:** March 15.

TIPS "Strong imagery and voice, writing that is informed by place or region, writing of literary quality with depth of character development. Hone the language down to the most literary depiction that is possible in the shortest space that still provides depth of development without excess length."

⭕ THE FLORIDA REVIEW

Deptartment of English, University of Central Florida, P.O. Box 161346, Orlando FL 32816. (407)823-5329. **E-mail:** flreview@mail.ucf.edu. **Website:** http://floridareview.cah.ucf.edu/. **Contact:** Jocelyn Bartkevicius, editor. Responds in 2-4 weeks to queries about reviews or interviews; 3-8 months to mss. Sample copy for $8. Writer's guidelines for #10 SASE or online.

⭕ Magazine: 6×9; 185 pages; semi-gloss full color cover, perfect bound. "We publish fiction of high 'literary' quality—stories that delight, instruct and take risks. Our audience consists of avid readers of fiction, poetry and creative nonfiction." Recently published work by Gerald Vizenor, Billy Collins, Sherwin Bitsui, Kelly Clancy, Denise Duhamel, Tony Hoagland, Baron Wormser, Marcia Aldrich, and Patricia Foster.

MAGAZINE'S NEEDS "We look for clear, strong poems, filled with real people, emotions and objects. Any style will be considered."

TIPS "We're looking for writers with fresh voices and original stories. We like risk."

FLOYD COUNTY MOONSHINE

720 Christiansburg Pike, Floyd VA 24091. (540)745-5150. **E-mail:** floydshine@gmail.com. **Contact:** Aaron Moore, editor-in-chief. *Floyd County Moonshine*, published biannually, is a "literary and arts magazine

in Floyd, Virginia, and the New River Valley. We accept poetry, short stories, and essays addressing all manner of themes; however, preference is given to those works of a rural or Southern/Appalachian nature. We welcome cutting-edge and innovative fiction and poetry in particular."

Wants "literature addressing rural or Appalachian themes." Has published poetry by Steve Kistulentz, Louis Gallo, Ernie Wormwood, R.T. Smith, Chelsea Adams, and Justin Askins. Single copy: $8; subscription: $16/1 year, $30/2 years.

MAGAZINE'S NEEDS Accepts e-mail submissions only. Submit a Word document as attachment. Accepts previously published poems and simultaneous submissions. Cover letter is unnecessary. Include brief bio. Reads submissions year round.

FLYWAY

Department of English, 206 Ross Hall, Iowa State University, Ames IA 50011-1201. **E-mail:** flywayjournal@gmail.com; flyway@iastate.edu. **Website:** www.flyway.org. "Based out of Iowa State University, *Flyway: Journal of Writing and Environment* publishes poetry, fiction, nonfiction, and visual art exploring the many complicated facets of the word environment – at once rural, urban, and suburban –and its social and political implications. We are also open to all different interpretations of 'environment.'" Acquires first North American serial rights, electronic rights, and future anthology rights. Publishes ms 4 months after acceptance. Often comments on rejected mss. Sample copy and guidelines on website.

Has published work by Rick Bass, Jacob M. Appel, Madison Smartt Bell, Jane Smiley. Also sponsors the annual fall "Notes from the Field" nonfiction contest, and the spring "Sweet Corn Prize in Fiction" short story contest. Details on website.

MAGAZINE'S NEEDS Submit up to 5 poems (combined in 1 document) only via online submission manager at https://flyway.submittable.com/submit. Submissions are closed May 1-August. Pays one-year subscription to *Flyway*.

TIPS "For *Flyway*, there should be tension between the environment or setting of the story and the characters in it. A well-known place should appear new, even alien and strange through the eyes and actions of the characters. We want to see an active environment, too—a setting that influences actions, triggers it's one events."

FOGGED CLARITY

(231)670-7033. **E-mail:** editor@foggedclarity.com. **E-mail:** submissions@foggedclarity.com. **Website:** www.foggedclarity.com. Ryan Daly, managing editor. **Contact:** Ben Evans, executive editor/managing editor. "*Fogged Clarity* is an arts review that accepts submissions of poetry, fiction, nonfiction, music, visual art and reviews of work in all mediums. We seek art that is stabbingly eloquent. Our print edition will be released once every year, while new issues of our online journal will come out the beginning of every month. Artists maintain the copyrights to their work until they are monetarily compensated for said work. If your work is selected for our print edition and you consent to its publication, you will be compensated." All work selected for print is purchased. Averages 1-2 months from acceptance to publishing. Accepts queries by e-mail only. Sample copy available on website. Guidelines available at www.foggedclarity.com/submissions.

"By incorporating music and the visual arts and releasing a new issue monthly, *Fogged Clarity* aims to transcend the conventions of a typical literary journal. Our network is extensive and our scope is as broad as thought itself; we are, you are, unconstrained. With that spirit in mind *Fogged Clarity* examines the work of authors, artists, scholars, and musicians, providing a home for exceptional art and thought that warrants exposure."

MAGAZINE'S NEEDS Send no more than 6 poems, with short bio and complete contact information. Does not accept simultaneous submissions. Averages 1-2 months from acceptance to publishing. Does not accept previously published work. Responds in 2 weeks to queries; 1-2 months on mss. Editorial lead time is 2 months. Sample copy and guidelines available on website. Payment varies

TIPS "The editors appreciate artists communicating the intention of their submitted work and the influences behind it, in a brief cover letter. Any artists with proposals for features or special projects should feel free to contact our editors directly at editor@foggedclarity.com."

FOLIATE OAK LITERARY MAGAZINE

University of Arkansas-Monticello, Arts & Humanities, 562 University Dr., Monticello AR 71656. **Website:** www.foliateoak.uamont.edu. **Contact:** Diane Payne. "We are a general literary magazine for adults." Acquires one-time, nonexclusive rights. Publishes ms an average of 1 month after acceptance. Responds in 1 week to queries. Responds in 1 month to mss. Editorial lead time 1 month. Sample copy for #10 SASE. Guidelines available online at http://foliateoak.weebly.com/guidelines.html.

○ "After you receive a rejection/acceptance notice, please wait 1 month before submitting new work. **Submission Period: August 1 -April 24**. We do not read submissions during summer break. If you need to contact us for anything other than submitting your work, please write to: foliateoak@uamont.edu."

MAGAZINE'S NEEDS "Submit poems via online submission manager. We enjoy poems that we understand, preferably not rhyming poems, unless you make the rhyme so fascinating we'll wonder why we ever said anything about avoiding rhymes. Give us something fresh, unexpected, and will make us say, 'Wow!'" "No homophobic, religious rants, or pornographic, violent stories. Please avoid using offensive language."

ADDITIONAL INFORMATION "At the end of the year, we'll use selected works from our website for the annual print anthology. **Snail mail submissions will not be returned**. Paste all your poems into one attachment. Always include a short (less than 50 words) third person bio. Please send no more than two prose selections and no more than 5 poems. Wait until your hear from us before you send more work. If your work is accepted by another publication, please notify us immediately."

TIPS "Please submit all material via our online submission manager. Read our guidelines before submitting. We are eager to include multi-media submissions of videos, music, and collages. Please read guidelines and submit your best work."

❶ FOLIO, A LITERARY JOURNAL AT AMERICAN UNIVERSITY

Department of Literature, American University, Washington DC 20016. (202)885-2971. **Fax:** (202)885-2938. **E-mail:** folio.editors@gmail.com. **Website:** www.american.edu/cas/literature/folio. "*Folio* is a nationally recognized literary journal sponsored by the College of Arts and Sciences at American University in Washington, DC. Since 1984, we have published original creative work by both new and established authors. Past issues have included work by Michael Reid Busk, Billy Collins, William Stafford, and Bruce Weigl, and interviews with Michael Cunningham, Charles Baxter, Amy Bloom, Ann Beattie, and Walter Kirn. We look for well-crafted poetry and prose that is bold and memorable." Acquires first North American serial rights. Publishes ms 2 months after acceptance. Guidelines available on website.

○ Poems and prose are reviewed by editorial staff and senior editors. *Folio* is 80 pages, digest-sized, with matte cover with graphic art. Receives about 1,000 poems/year, accepts about 25. Press run is 400; 50-60 distributed free to the American University community and contributors. Single copy: $6; subscription: $12/year. Make checks payable to *Folio* at American University.

MAGAZINE'S NEEDS Submit up to 4 poems at a time via the online submission form at https://folio-litjournal.submittable.com/submit. Considers simultaneous submissions "with notice." No fax, e-mail, or disk submissions. Cover letter is preferred. Include name, address, e-mail address, brief brio, and phone number. "SASE required for notification only; mss are not returned." Reads submissions September 1-March 1. Pays 2 contributor's copies.

FOOTHILL: A JOURNAL OF POETRY

165 E. 10th St., Claremont CA 91711. (909)607-3962. **Fax:** (909)621-8029. **E-mail:** foothill@cgu.edu. **Website:** www.cgu.edu/foothill. **Contact:** Kevin Riel; editor-in-chief. Directed by students at Claremont Graduate University, *Foothill: a journal of poetry*, a biannual journal, is the only literary journal devoted exclusively to poetry written by graduate students who are based in the United States. It is published online quarterly, with one print edition each year. Digest-sized, 72 pages, digital press, perfect bound. Press run is 500. No ads. Never publishes theme issues. Sometimes comments on rejected poems. Single copy, $25; subscription, $25. Make checks payable to CGU. *Foothill* acquires electronic rights as well as right to print poem in year-end print journal. Rights revert to poets upon publication. Responds in 5 weeks. Guidelines available in magazine, by e-mail, and on website.

MAGAZINE'S NEEDS Will accept "any poetry by graduate students [currently enrolled or recently graduated, from anywhere in the world. Students do not need to be enrolled in an MFA or writing program. We welcome poetry submissions from those in other disciplines." Submit via e-mail. Include document as attachment in e-mail. Cover letter preferred. Poems are circulated to an editorial board. Accepts submissions year round. Welcomes submissions from beginning poets. Does not consider poetry by children or teens. Does not consider poetry by children or teens. No limit for poem length.

⬤ FORPOETRY.COM

E-mail: sub@ForPoetry.com. **Website:** www.forpoetry.com. **Contact:** Jackie Marcus, editor. *ForPoetry.Com*, published online with daily updates, wants "lyric poetry, vivid imagery, open form, natural landscape, philosophical themes—but not at the expense of honesty and passion." Does not want "city punk, corny sentimental fluff, or academic workshop imitations." Has published poetry by Sherod Santos, John Koethe, Robert Hass, Kim Addonizio, and Brenda Hillman.

💬   Not currently accepting unsolicited poems.

MAGAZINE'S NEEDS Submit no more than 2 poems at a time. Considers simultaneous submissions; no previously published poems. Accepts e-mail submissions only (pasted into body of message; no attachments). Cover letter is preferred. Reads submissions September-May only. Guidelines available on website. Responds in 2 weeks. "If you do not hear back from us within two weeks, then your poems were not accepted. Rejection of poems may have more to do with a backlog; i.e., there are periods when we cannot read new submissions." Reviews books/chapbooks of poetry and other magazines in 800 words.

⬤ FOURTEEN HILLS

Department of Creative Writing, San Francisco State University, 1600 Holloway Ave., San Francisco CA 94132-1722. **E-mail:** hills@sfsu.edu. **Website:** www.14hills.net. "*Fourteen Hills* publishes the highest quality innovative fiction and poetry for a literary audience." Editors change each year. Acquires one-time rights. Responds in 5 months to mss. Sometimes comments on rejected mss. SASE for return of ms. Sample copy for $9. Guidelines available on website.

💬   Magazine: 6×9; 200 pages; 60 lb. paper; 10-point C15 cover.

MAGAZINE'S NEEDS Always sends prepublication galleys. Submit 3-5 unpublished, unsolicited poems. Writers may submit once per submission period. The submission periods are: Sept. 1-Jan. 1 for inclusion in the spring issue (released in May); March 1-July 1 for inclusion in the winter issue (released in Dec.). Response times vary from 4-9 months, "depending on where your submission falls in the reading period, but we will usually respond within 5 months. Mss and artwork may be mailed and addressed to the proper genre editor, and *must* be accompanied by an SASE for notification, in addition to an e-mail and telephone contact. Due to the volume of submissions, mss cannot be returned, so please, do not send any originals. We accept simultaneous submissions; however, please be sure to notify us immediately by e-mail should you need to withdraw submissions due to publication elsewhere. Please note that we accept electronic submissions at this time via our website: www.14hills.net. However, we do not accept submissions by e-mail. Please check website for changes in submission policies." Pays 2 contributor copies.

TIPS "Please read an issue of *Fourteen Hills* before submitting."

THE FOURTH RIVER

Chatham College, Woodland Rd., Pittsburgh PA 15232. **E-mail:** 4thriver@gmail.com. **Website:** http://fourthriver.chatham.edu. **Contact:** Sheryl St. Germain, executive editor; Peter Oresick, editor-in-chief. "*The Fourth River*, an annual publication of Chatham University's MFA in Creative Writing Programs, features "literature that engages and explores the relationship between humans and their environments." Wants "writings that are richly situated at the confluence of place, space, and identity, or that reflect upon or make use of landscape and place in new ways." Buys first North American serial rights. Pays with contributor copies only. Responds in 3 months to mss. Sample copy for $10. Guidelines available online.

💬   *The Fourth River* is digest-sized, perfect-bound, with full-color cover by various artists. Accepts about 30-40 poems/year. Press run is 500. Single copy: $10; subscription: $16 for 2 years. Back issues: $5. Make checks payable to Chatham University."

MAGAZINE'S NEEDS Submit 7 poems at a time. Lines/poem: submit 25 pages maximum. No previously published poems. Submit by post or through

Submittable (https://4thriver.submittable.com/submit). Cover letter is preferred. SASE is required for response. Reads submissions September 1-March 15. Time between acceptance and publication is 5-8 months. Poems are circulated to an editorial board. Sometimes comments on rejected poems. Sometimes publishes theme issues. Guidelines available on website. Responds in 3-5 months. Length: 7 poems maximum.

☉◐ FREEFALL MAGAZINE

Freefall Literary Society of Calgary, 922 Ninth Ave. SE, Calgary AB T2G 0S4, Canada. **E-mail:** freefallmagazine@yahoo.com. **Website:** www.freefallmagazine.ca. **Contact:** Lynn S. Fraser, managing editor. "Magazine published biannually containing fiction, poetry, creative nonfiction, essays on writing, interviews, and reviews. Submit up to 5 poems at once. Pays $25 per poem and one copy of the issue poems appeaer in. Wants prose of all types, up to 3,000 words; pays $10/page to a maximum of $100 per piece and one copy of issue piece appears in. We are looking for exquisite writing with a strong narrative." Buys first North American serial rights (ownership reverts to author after one-time publication). Pays on publication. Guidelines online.

MAGAZINE'S NEEDS Submit 2-5 poems via e-mail. E-mail subject line should include your name and type of submission (poetry, fiction, nonfiction, creative nonfiction, flash fiction, short fiction, photo, art work, etc.) Include name, contact information, description, title, and 50 word bio in body of e-mail. Attach submission titled with your name and submission title. Accepts any style of poetry. Length: no more than 6 pages. Pays $25 per poem and 1 contributor's copy.

TIPS "Our mission is to encourage the voices of new, emerging, and experienced Canadian writers and provide a platform for their quality work. Although we accept work from all over the world we maintain a commitment to 85% Canadian content."

☉◐ FREEXPRESSION

P.O. Box 4, West Hoxton NSW 2171, Australia. **E-mail:** editor@freexpression.com.au. **Website:** www. freexpression.com.au. **Contact:** Peter F. Pike, managing editor. *FreeXpresSion*, published monthly, contains "creative writing, how-to articles, short stories, and poetry including cinquain, haiku, etc., and bush verse." Open to all forms. "Christian themes OK.

Humorous material welcome. No gratuitous sex; bad language OK. We don't want to see anything degrading." Has published poetry by Ron Stevens, Ellis Campbell, John Ryan, and Ken Dean. *FreeXpresSion* is 28 pages, magazine-sized, offset-printed, saddle-stapled, with paper cover. Receives about 2,500 poems/year, accepts about 30%. Subscription: $15 AUS/3 months, $25 AUS/6 months, $42 AUS/1 year. Purchases first Australian rights. Publishes ms 2 months after acceptance. Responds in 2 months. Guidelines available in magazine, for SAE and IRC, or by fax or e-mail.

○ *FreeXpresSion* also publishes books up to 200 pages **through subsidy arrangements with authors**. Some poems published throughout the year are used in *Yearbooks* (annual anthologies).

MAGAZINE'S NEEDS Submit 3-4 poems at a time. Accepts e-mail (pasted into body of message) and disk submissions. Cover letter is preferred. Lines/poem: "very long poems are not desired but would be considered."

CONTEST/AWARD OFFERINGS Sponsors an annual contest with 3 categories for poetry: blank verse (up to 60 lines); traditional verse (up to 80 lines), and haiku. 1st Prize in blank verse: $200 AUS; 2nd Prize: $100 AUS; 1st Prize in traditional rhyming poetry: $250 AUS; 2nd Prize: $150 AUS; 3rd Prize: $100 AUS. Haiku, one prize $100 AUS. Guidelines and entry form available by e-mail.

☉ THE FRIEND

The Friend Publications Ltd, 173 Euston Rd., London England NW1 2BJ, United Kingdom. (44)(207)663-1010. **Fax:** (44)(207)663-1182. **E-mail:** editorial@thefriend.org. **Website:** www.thefriend.org. **Contact:** Ian Kirk Smith. Completely independent, *The Friend* brings readers news and views from a Quaker perspective, as well as from a wide range of authors whose writings are of interest to Quakers and non-Quakers alike. There are articles on issues such as peace, spirituality, Quaker belief, and ecumenism, as well as news of Friends from Britain and abroad. Guidelines available online.

○ Prefers queries, but sometimes accepts unsolicited mss.

MAGAZINE'S NEEDS There are no rules regarding poetry, but doesn't want particularly long poems.

🐸● THE FROGMORE PAPERS

21 Mildmay Rd., Lewes, East Sussex BN7 1PJ, England. **Website:** www.frogmorepress.co.uk. **Contact:** Jeremy Page, editor. *The Frogmore Papers*, published semiannually, is a literary magazine with emphasis on new poetry and short stories. "Quality is generally the only criterion, although pressure of space means very long work (over 100 lines) is unlikely to be published." Has published poetry by Marita Over, Brian Aldiss, Carole Satyamurti, John Mole, Linda France, and Tobias Hill. *The Frogmore Papers* is 46 pages, photocopied in photo-reduced typescript, saddle-stapled, with matte card cover. Accepts 2% of poetry received. Press run is 500. Subscription: £10/1 year (2 issues); £15/2 years (4 issues). Responds in 6 months.

MAGAZINE'S NEEDS Submit 4-6 poems at a time. "Poems where the form drives the meaning are unlikely to find favour. Poems written by people who clearly haven't read any poetry since Wordsworth will not find favour. Prose may be experimental or traditional, but is unlikely to be accepted if it's either very experimental or very traditional." Length: up to 80 lines. Pays 1 contributor's copy.

CONTEST/AWARD OFFERINGS Sponsors the annual Frogmore Poetry Prize. Write for information.

FROGPOND: JOURNAL OF THE HAIKU SOCIETY OF AMERICA

Haiku Society of America, 985 S. Grandview Ave., Dubuque IA 52003. **E-mail:** fnbanwarth@yahoo.com. **Website:** www.hsa-haiku.org/frogpond. **Contact:** Francine Banwarth, editor. *Frogpond*, published triannually, is the international journal of the Haiku Society of America, an affiliate of the American Literature Association. Its primary function is to "publish the best in contemporary English-language haiku and senryu, linked forms including sequences, renku, rengay, and haibun, essays and articles on these forms, and book reviews." Subscription: $33/year. Single issue: $14. Responds at the end of each submission period (June 1-August 1; September 15-November 15; February 15-April 15). Guidelines available for SASE or on website. Detailed instructions on website.

MAGAZINE'S NEEDS Submissions to *Frogpond* by e-mail are preferred. "Postal submissions should be accompanied by SASE with sufficient U.S. postage to reach your location. Submit to fnbanwarth@yahoo.com or 985 S. Grandview, Dubuque, IA." No simultaneous submissions. Reviews books of poetry, usually in 1,000 words or less. Also accepts articles, 1,000-4,000 words, that are properly referenced according to 1 of the 3 style guides: MLA, APA, Chicago Manual.

CONTEST/AWARD OFFERINGS The "Best of Issue" prize is awarded to a poem from each issue of *Frogpond* through a gift from the Museum of Haiku Literature, located in Tokyo. The Haiku Society of America also sponsors a number of other contests, most of which have cash prizes: The Harold G. Henderson Haiku Award Contest, the Gerald Brady Senryu Award Contest, the Bernard Lionel Einbond Memorial Renku Contest, the Nicholas A. Virgilio Memorial Haiku Competition for High School Students, the Mildred Kanterman Merit Book Awards for outstanding books in the haiku field. Guidelines available on website.

●●⑤ FUGUE LITERARY MAGAZINE

200 Brink Hall, University of Idaho, P.O. Box 44110, Moscow ID 83844. **E-mail:** fugue@uidaho.edu. **Website:** www.fuguejournal.org. **Contact:** Alexandra Teague, faculty advisor. Biannual literary magazine. "Submissions are accepted online only. Poetry, Nonfiction, and Experiment submissions are accepted September 1 through May 1. Fiction Submissions are accepted September 1 to April 1. All material received outside of this period will not be read." See website for submission instructions. Sample copies available for $8.00. Guidelines available online.

○ Work published in *Fugue* has won the Pushcart Prize and has been cited in *Best American Essays*.

MAGAZINE'S NEEDS Submit a set of up to 3 poems using online submissions manager. All contributors receive payment and 2 complimentary copies of the journal.

CONTEST/AWARD OFFERINGS "For information regarding our annual spring poetry contest, please visit our website."

TIPS "The best way, of course, to determine what we're looking for is to read the journal. As the name *Fugue* indicates, our goal is to present a wide range of literary perspectives. We like stories that satisfy us both intellectually and emotionally, with fresh language and characters so captivating that they stick with us and invite a second reading. We are also seeking creative literary criticism which illuminates a piece of literature or a specific writer by examining that writer's personal experience."

⬤ GARGOYLE

Paycock Press, 3819 N. 13th St., Arlington VA 22201. (703)525-9296. **E-mail:** hedgehog2@erols.com. **Website:** www.gargoylemagazine.com. **Contact:** Richard Peabody, editor, Lucinda Ebersole, co-editor. "*Gargoyle Magazine* has always been a scallywag magazine, a maverick magazine, a bit too academic for the underground and way too underground for the academics. We are a writer's magazine in that we are read by other writers and have never worried about reaching the masses." Annual. Wants "edgy realism or experimental works. We run both." Wants to see more Canadian, British, Australian, and Third World fiction. Receives 50-200 unsolicited mss/month. Accepts 10-15 mss/issue. Accepts submissions during June, July, and Aug. Agented fiction 5%. **Publishes 2-3 new writers/year.** Recently published work by Stephanie Allen, Tom Carson, Michael Casey, Kim Chinquee, Susan Cokal, Ramola D., Janice Eidus, Thaisa Frank, James Grady, Colette Inez, Susan Smith Nash, Zena Polin, Wena Poon, Pilar Quintana, Kris Saknussem, Tomaz Salamun, Lynda Sexson, Elisabeth Sheffield, Barry Silesky, Curtis Smith, Patricia Smith, Marilyn Stablein, Ronald Wallace. Length: 30 pages maximum; average length: 5-10 pages. Publishes short shorts. Also publishes literary essays, literary criticism, poetry. Sometimes comments on rejected mss. "We prefer electronic submissions. Please use submission engine online." Acquires first North American serial, and first British rights. Publishes ms 1 year after acceptance. Responds in 1 month to queries, proposals, and to mss. Sample copy for $12.95. Catalog available online at FAQ link. "We don't have guidelines; we have never believed in them."

MAGAZINE'S NEEDS Submit electronically. Query. Pays contributor's copies.

TIPS "We have to fall in love with a particular fiction."

⬤ GEORGETOWN REVIEW

Box 227, 400 East College St., Georgetown KY 40324. (502)863-8308. **Fax:** (502)868-8888. **E-mail:** gtownreview@georgetowncollege.edu. **Website:** http://georgetownreview.georgetowncollege.edu. **Contact:** Steven Carter, editor. *Georgetown Review*, published annually in May, is a literary journal of poetry, fiction, and creative nonfiction. " Does not want "work that is merely sentimental, political, or inspirational." Acquires first North American serial rights. Publication is copyrighted. Pays on publication. Publishes ms 1 year after acceptance. Responds to mss in 1-3 months. Sample copy $7. Guidelines available on website.

⬤ *Georgetown Review* is 192 pages, digest-sized, offset-printed, perfect-bound, with 60 lb. glossy 4-color cover with art/graphics, includes ads. Press run is 1,000. Single copy: $7. Make checks payable to *Georgetown Review.*

MAGAZINE'S NEEDS "We have no specific guidelines concerning form or content of poetry, but are always eager to see poetry that is insightful, rooted in reality, and human." Has published poetry by Denise Duhamel, X.J. Kennedy, Fred Chappell, Frederick Smock, Mark Halperin, David Citino, William Greenway, James Harms, and Margarita Engle. Submit 1-10 poems at a time. Lines/poem: open. Considers simultaneous submissions; no previously published poems. No fax, e-mail, or disk submissions. Cover letter is preferred. "In cover letter, please include short bio and a list of publications. Also, must include SASE for reply." Reads submissions September 1-March 15. Pays 2 contributor's copies.

CONTEST/AWARD OFFERINGS Sponsors annual contest, offering $1,000 prize and publication; runners-up also receive publication. Guidelines available for SASE, by e-mail, or on website. **Entry fee:** $10/poem, $5 for each additional poem.

TIPS "We look for fiction that is well written and that has a story line that keeps our interest. Don't send a first draft, and even if we don't take your first, second, or third submission, keep trying."

THE GEORGIA REVIEW

The University of Georgia, Athens GA 30602. (706)542-3481. **Fax:** (706)542-0047. **E-mail:** garev@uga.edu. **Website:** www.uga.edu/garev. **Contact:** Stephen Corey, editor. Our readers are educated, inquisitive people who read a lot of work in the areas we feature, so they expect only the best in our pages. All work submitted should show evidence that the writer is at least as well-educated and well-read as our readers. Essays should be authoritative but accessible to a range of readers. Buys first North American serial rights. Pays on publication. Publishes ms an average of 6 months after acceptance. Responds in 2 weeks to queries. Responds in 2-3 months to mss. Sample copy for $10 Guidelines available online.

⬤ No simultaneous or electronic submissions.

MAGAZINE'S NEEDS "We seek original, excellent poetry. Submit 3-5 poems at a time." Pays $4/line.

TIPS "Unsolicited manuscripts will not be considered from May 15-August 15 (annually); all such submissions received during that period will be returned unread. Check website for submission guidelines."

THE GETTYSBURG REVIEW

Gettysburg College, Gettysburg PA 17325. (717)337-6770. **Fax:** (717)337-6775. **Website:** www.gettysburgreview.com. **Contact:** Peter Stitt, editor. "Our concern is quality. Manuscripts submitted here should be extremely well written. Reading period September-May." Buys first North American serial rights. Pays on publication. Publishes ms an average of 6 months after acceptance. Responds in 1 month to queries. Responds in 3-6 months to mss. Editorial lead time 1 year. Sample copy for $11. Guidelines available online.

MAGAZINE'S NEEDS Considers "well-written poems of all kinds." Has published poetry by Rita Dove, Alice Friman, Philip Schultz, Michelle, Boisseau, Bob Hicok, Linda Pastan, and G.C. Waldrep. Submit 3-5 poems at a time. Pays $2.50 per line and 1 contributor's copy.

GINOSKO

P.O. Box 246, Fairfax CA 94978. **E-mail:** ginoskoeditor@aol.com. **Website:** www.ginoskoliteraryjournal.com. **Contact:** Robert Paul Cesaretti, editor. "*Ginosko* (ghin-océ-koe): To perceive, understand, realize, come to know; knowledge that has an inception, a progress, an attainment. The recognition of truth by experience." Accepting short fiction and poetry, creative nonfiction, interviews, social justice concerns, and spiritual insights for www.GinoskoLiteraryJournal.com. Member CLMP. Copyright reverts to author. Editorial lead time 1-2 months. Guidelines available online at website.

○ Reads year round. Length of articles flexible; accepts excerpts. Publishing as semiannual ezine. Check downloadable issues on website for tone and style. Downloads free; accepts donations. Also looking for books, art, and music to post on website, and links to exchange.

GLASS: A JOURNAL OF POETRY

E-mail: glasspoetry@yahoo.com. **Website:** www.glass-poetry.com. **Contact:** Holly Burnside, editor. "We are not bound by any specific aesthetic; our mission is to present high quality writing. Easy rhyme and 'light' verse are less likely to inspire us. We want to see poetry that enacts the artistic and creative purity of glass." Buys first North American serial rights.

Responds in 4 months to queries. Guidelines online at website.

○ Submissions must follow our guidelines.

TIPS "Accepts submissions from September 1 to May 31. We like poems that show a careful understanding of language, sound, passion and creativity and poems that surprise us. Include brief cover letter and biography. Include your e-mail address."

○○○ GRAIN

P.O. Box 67, Saskatoon SK S7K 3K1, Canada. (306)244-2828. **Fax:** (306)244-0255. **E-mail:** grainmag@sasktel.net. **Website:** www.grainmagazine.ca. **Contact:** Rilla Friesen, editor. "*Grain, The Journal Of Eclectic Writing*, is a literary quarterly that publishes engaging, diverse, and challenging writing and art by some of the best Canadian and international writers and artists. Every issue features superb new writing from both developing and established writers. Each issue also highlights the unique artwork of a different visual artist. *Grain* has garnered national and international recognition for its distinctive, cutting-edge content and design." Pays on publication for first Canadian serial rights. Typically responds in 3-6 months. Guidelines available by SASE (or SAE and IRC), e-mail, or on website.

○ *Grain* is 112-128 pages, digest-sized, professionally printed. Press run is 1,100. Receives about 3,000 submissions/year. Subscription: $35 CAD/year, $55 CAD for 2 years. Sample: $13 CAD. (See website for U.S. and foreign postage fees.) Has published poetry by Lorna Crozier, Don Domanski, Cornelia Haeussler, Patrick Lane, Karen Solie, and Monty Reid.

MAGAZINE'S NEEDS Wants "High quality, imaginative, well-crafted poetry." Submit up to 12 pages of poetry, typed in readable font on 1 side only. No previously published poems or simultaneous submissions. No fax or e-mail submissions; postal submissions only. Cover letter with all contact information, title(s), and genre of work is required. "No staples. Your name and address must be on every page. Pieces of more than 1 page must be numbered. Please only submit work in one genre at one time." Pays $50-225 CAD (depending on number of pages) and 2 contributor's copies.

TIPS "Submissions read September-May only. Mss postmarked between June 1 and August 31 will not be read. Only work of the highest literary quality is accepted. Read several back issues."

THE GREAT AMERICAN POETRY SHOW

P.O. Box 691197, West Hollywood CA 90069. (323)424-4943. **E-mail:** info@tgaps.net. **Website:** www.tgaps.net. **Contact:** Larry Ziman, editor/publisher. *The Great American Poetry Show*, published about every 3-5 years, is an 812x11 hardcover serial poetry anthology. Wants poems on any subject, in any style, of any length. "For Volume 1, we read over 8,000 poems from about 1,400 poets and accepted only 113 poems from 83 poets. For Volume 2, we read over 15,000 poems and accepted 134 poems from 92 poets." Press run is 1,000. Single copy: $35 (print), $.99 (e-book, download only). Responds usually within 1-2 weeks ("depends on how busy we are").

The Great American Poetry Show is 150 pages, sheet-fed offset-printed, perfect-bound, with cloth cover with art/graphics. Has published poetry by Carol Carpenter, Philip Wexler, Fredrick Zydek, Patrick Polak, Steve de Frances, Lois Swann, Alan Catlin, and Julie M. Tate.

MAGAZINE'S NEEDS Submit any number of poems at a time. Considers previously published poems and simultaneous submissions. Accepts e-mail submissions in body of e-mail or as attachment. Cover letter is optional. Include SASE. "If we reject a submission of your work, please send us another group to go through." Pays 1 contributor's copy.

TIPS "Please visit our website where anyone can have us post poetry news, reviews, essays, articles, and recommended books, and where you can link to over 10,000 literary subjects such as articles, essays, interviews, reviews, magazines, publishers, and blogs."

GREEN HILLS LITERARY LANTERN

McClain Hall, Truman State University, Kirksville MO 63501. (660)785-4513. **E-mail:** jbeneven@truman.edu. **Website:** http://ll.truman.edu/ghllweb/. **Contact:** Joe Benevento, poetry editor. "The mission of *GHLL* is to provide a literary market for quality fiction writers, both established and beginners, and to provide quality literature for readers from diverse backgrounds. We also see ourselves as a cultural resource for North Missouri. Our publication works to publish the highest quality fiction—dense, layered, subtle—and, at the same time, fiction which grabs the ordinary reader. We tend to publish traditional short stories, but we are open to experimental forms." Annual. The *GHLL* is now an online, open-access journal.

Acquires one-time rights. Publishes ms up to 1 year after acceptance. Responds in 4 months. Sample: $7 (back issue). Guidelines for SASE, by e-mail, or online.

MAGAZINE'S NEEDS Submit 3-7 poems at a time. Considers simultaneous submissions, "but not preferred"; no previously published poems. No e-mail submissions. Cover letter is preferred. Include list of publication credits. Type poems one per page. Often comments on rejected poems. Wants "the best poetry, in any style, preferably understandable. There are no restrictions on subject matter. Both free and formal verse forms are fine, though we publish more free verse overall." Has published poetry by Jim Thomas, David Lawrence, Mark Belair, Louis Philips, Francine Tolf, and Julie Lechevsky. Does not want "haiku, limericks, or anything over 2 pages. Pornography and gratuitous violence will not be accepted. Obscurity for its own sake is also frowned upon."

GREEN MOUNTAINS REVIEW

Johnson State College, 337 College Hill, Johnson VT 05656. (802)635.1350. **E-mail:** gmr@jsc.vsc.edu; Jacob. White@jsc.edu. **Website:** http://greenmountainsreview.com/. **Contact:** Elizabeth Powell, poetry editor; Jacob White, fiction editor. The editors are open to a wide rane of styles and subject matter. Acquires first North American serial rights. Rights revert to author upon request. Publishes ms 6-12 months after acceptance. Responds in 1 month to queries; 6 months to mss. Sample copy for $7. Guidelines available free.

"Manuscripts received between March 1 and September 1 will not be read and will be returned."

MAGAZINE'S NEEDS Has published poetry by Carol Frost, Sharon Olds, Carl Phillips, David St. John, and David Wojahn. Submit no more than 5 poems at a time.

TIPS "We encourage you to order some of our back issues to acquaint yourself with what has been accepted in the past. Unsolicited mss are read from September 1 to March 1."

THE GREENSBORO REVIEW

MFA Writing Program, 3302 HHRA Building, UNC-Greensboro, Greensboro NC 27402. (336)334-5459. **E-mail:** jlclark@uncg.edu. **Website:** www.greensbororeview.org. **Contact:** Jim Clark, editor. Acquires first North American serial rights. Responds in about 4 months.

Stories for *the Greensboro Review* have been included in *Best American Short Stories*, *The O. Henry Awards Prize Stories*, *New Stories from The South* and *Pushcart Prize*. Does not accept e-mail submissions.

MAGAZINE'S NEEDS Submit 5-7 poems per submission. Length: no length limit. Pays in contributor's copies.

TIPS "We want to see the best being written regardless of theme, subject or style."

🔲🎧 GUERNICA MAGAZINE

112 W. 27th St., Suite 600, New York NY 10001. **E-mail:** editors@guernicamag.com; art@guernicamag.com; publisher@guernicamag.com. **Website:** www.guernicamag.com. **Contact:** Erica Wright, poetry; Dan Eckstein, art/photography. *"Guernica* is called a "great online literary magazine" by *Esquire*. *Guernica* contributors come from dozens of countries and write in nearly as many languages." Publishes mss 3-4 months from acceptance. Responds in 4 months. Guidelines available online.

Received Caine Prize for African Writing, Best of the Net, cited by *Esquire* as a "great literary magazine."

MAGAZINE'S NEEDS Please send 3-5 poems to poetry@guernicamag.com. Attn: Erica Wright. Translations welcome (with rights to publish). Accepts 15-20 poems/year. Has published James Galvin, Barbara Hamby, Terrance Hayes, Richard Howard.

TIPS "Please read the magazine first before submitting. Most stories that are rejected simply do not fit our approach. Submission guidelines available online."

🎧 GULF COAST: A JOURNAL OF LITERATURE AND FINE ARTS

University of Houston, Department of English, University of Houston, Houston TX 77204-3013. (713)743-3223. **E-mail:** editors@gulfcoastmag.org. **Website:** www.gulfcoastmag.org. **Contact:** Zachary Martin, editor; Karyna McGlynn, managing editor; Michelle Oakes, Justine Post, Kimberly Bruss, poetry editors; Aja Gabel, D'Lynn Barham, Ashley Wurzbacher, fiction editors; Jameelah Lang, Beth Lyons, nonfiction editors. Buys one-time rights. Publishes ms 6 months-1 year after acceptance. Responds in 4-6 months to mss. Sometimes comments on rejected mss. Back issue for $8, 7x10 SASE with 4 first-class stamps. Writer's guidelines for #10 SASE or on website.

Magazine: 7×9; approximately 300 pages; stock paper, gloss cover; illustrations; photos. Receives 350 unsolicited mss/month. Accepts 6-8 mss/issue; 12-16 mss/year. Agented fiction: 5%. Publishes 2-8 new writers/year. Recently published work by Maggie Shipstead, Norman Dubie, Mary Biddinger, Bret Anthony Johnston, G.C. Waldrep, Clancy Martin, Steve Almond, Sam Lipsyte, Dean Young, Eula Biss, Sarah Manguso. Publishes short shorts.

MAGAZINE'S NEEDS Submit up to 5 poems at a time. Considers simultaneous submissions with notification; no previously published poems. Cover letter is required. List previous publications and include a brief bio. Reads submissions September-April. Pays $30/poem.

TIPS "Submit only previously unpublished works. Include a cover letter. Online submissions are strongly preferred. Stories or essays should be typed, double-spaced, and paginated with your name, address, and phone number on the first page, title on subsequent pages. Poems should have your name, address, and phone number on the first page of each." The Annual Gulf Coast Prizes awards publication and $1,500 each in poetry, fiction, and nonfiction; opens in January of each year. Honorable mentions in each category will receive a $250 second prize. Postmark/online entry deadline: March 15 of each year. Winners and honorable mentions will be announced in May. **Entry fee:** $20 (includes one-year subscription). Make checks payable to *Gulf Coast*. Guidelines available on website.

🔲 GULF STREAM MAGAZINE

English Department, FIU, Biscayne Bay Campus, 3000 NE 151 St., North Miami FL 33181. **E-mail:** gulfstreamfiu@yahoo.com. **Website:** www.gulfstreamlitmag.com. **Contact:** Jason Jones, editor. *"Gulf Stream Magazine* has been publishing emerging and established writers of exceptional fiction, nonfiction and poetry since 1989. We also publish interviews and book reviews. Past contributors include Sherman Alexie, Steve Almond, Jan Beatty, Lee Martin, Robert Wrigley, Dennis Lehane, Liz Robbins, Stuart Dybek, David Kirby, Ann Hood, Ha Jin, B.H. Fairchild, Naomi Shihab Nye, F. Daniel Rzicznek, and Connie May Fowler. *Gulf Stream Magazine* is supported by the Creative Writing Program at Florida International University in Miami, Florida. Each year we publish

2 online issues." Responds in 6 months. Guidelines online.

MAGAZINE'S NEEDS Submit no more than 5 poems at a time. Cover letter is required. Wants "poetry of any style and subject matter as long as it's of high literary quality." Has published poetry by Robert Wrigley, Jan Beatty, Jill Bialosky, and Catherine Bowman.

TIPS "Looks for fresh, original writing—well plotted stories with unforgettable characters, fresh poetry and experimental writing. Usually longer stories do not get accepted. There are exceptions, however."

THE G.W. REVIEW

The George Washington University, 800 21st St. NW, Marvin Center Box 20, Washington DC 20052. (202)994-7779. **E-mail:** gwreview@gwu.edu. **Website:** http://thegwreview.weebly.com. **Contact:** Linda Cui, editor-in-chief. "*The G.W. Review* seeks to expose readers to new and emerging writers from both the United States and abroad. New, innovative writing—both in style and subject—is valued above the author's previous publishing history." Reserves first rights. Publishes ms an average of 3-6 months after acceptance. Responds in 2 months to queries. Responds in 3-6 months to mss. Editorial lead time 3 months. Sample copy for $7. Writer's guidelines on website or by e-mail.

MAGAZINE'S NEEDS Publishes 20 poems a year.

TIPS "We enjoy work that is thought-provoking and challenging in its subject matter and style."

HAIGHT ASHBURY LITERARY JOURNAL

558 Joost Ave., San Francisco CA 94127. (415)584-8264. **E-mail:** haljeditor@gmail.com. **Website:** http://haightashburyliteraryjournal.wordpress.com/; www.facebook.com/pages/Haight-Ashbury-Literary-Journal/365542018331. **Contact:** Alice Rogoff, Indigo Hotchkiss, Alice Rogoff, and Cesar Love, editors. *Haight Ashbury Literary Journal*, publishes "well-written poetry and fiction. HALJ's voices are often of people who have been marginalized, oppressed, or abused. HALJ strives to bring literary arts to the general public, to the San Francisco community of writers, to the Haight Ashbury neighborhood, and to people of varying ages, genders, ethnicities, and sexual preferences. The Journal is produced as a tabloid to maintain an accessible price for low-income people." Rights revert to author. Responds in 4 months. Guidelines available for SASE.

Haight Ashbury is 16 pages, includes ads. Includes fiction under 20 pages, 1 story/issue, and b&w drawings. Press run is 1,500. Subscription: $10/ 2 issues, $20 for 4 issues; $50 for a lifetime subscription. Sample: $4. Has published poetry by Dan O'Connell, Diane Frank, Dancing Bear, Lee Herrick, Al Young, and Laura Beausoleil.

MAGAZINE'S NEEDS Submit up to 6 poems at a time. Submit only once/6 months. No e-mail submissions (unless overseas); postal submissions only. "Please type 1 poem to a page, put name and address on every page, and include SASE. No bio." Sometimes publishes theme issues (each issue changes its theme and emphasis).

ADDITIONAL INFORMATION An anthology of past issues, *This Far Together*, is available for $12.

HANGING LOOSE

Hanging Loose Press, 231 Wyckoff St., Brooklyn NY 11217. **E-mail:** editor@hangingloosepress.com. **Website:** www.hangingloosepress.com. **Contact:** Robert Hershon, Dick Lourie, and Mark Pawlak, poetry editors. *Hanging Loose*, published in April and October, "concentrates on the work of new writers." Wants "excellent, energetic" poems. Responds in 3 months. Sample: $12.

Hanging Loose is 120 pages, offset-printed on heavy stock, flat-spined, with 4-color glossy card cover. Considers poetry by teens ("one section contains poems by high-school-age poets"). Has published poetry by Sherman Alexie, Paul Violi, Donna Brook, Kimiko Hahn, Harvey Shapiro, and Ha Jin.

MAGAZINE'S NEEDS Submit up to 6 poems at a time. No fax or e-mail submissions; postal submissions only. No simultaneous submissions. "Would-be contributors should read the magazine first." Pays small fee and 2 contributor's copies.

ADDITIONAL INFORMATION Hanging Loose Press does not consider unsolicited book mss or artwork.

HARPUR PALATE

English Department, P.O. Box 6000, Binghamton University, Binghamton NY 13902-6000. **E-mail:** harpur.palate@gmail.com. **Website:** http://harpurpalate.blogspot.com. **Contact:** Sara Erdmann and Jennie Case, editors. *Harpur Palate*, published biannually, is "dedicated to publishing the best poetry and prose, regardless of style, form, or genre. We have no restrictions on subject matter or form. Quite simply, send us your highest-quality fiction and poetry." Buys first North American serial rights, buys electronic rights. Pays on publication. Publishes ms an average of 1-2 months after acceptance. Responds in 1-3 week to queries; 4- 8 months to mss. No response without SASE. Sometimes comments on rejected mss. Accepts simultaneous submissions if stated in the cover letter. Sample copy for $8. Guidelines available online.

○ Magazine: 6×9; 180-200 pages; coated or uncoated paper; 100 lb. coated cover; 4-color art portfolio insert. Single copy: $10; subscription: $16/year (2 issues). Sample: $5. Make checks payable to *Harpur Palate*.

MAGAZINE'S NEEDS Considers simultaneous submissions, "but we must be notified immediately if the piece is taken somewhere else"; no previously published poems. Submissions can be made via submittable.com, or by post. No e-mail submissions. Cover letter and SASE is required. Reads submissions year round. Time between acceptance and publication is 2 months. Poems are circulated to an editorial board. Seldom comments on rejected poems. Has published poetry by Sherman Alexie, Tess Gallagher, Alex Lemon, Marvin Bell, Ryan G. Van Cleave, Sascha Feinstein, Allison Joseph, Neil Shepard, and Ruth Stone No more than 10 pages total. No response without SASE. Pays 2 contributor copies.

TIPS "*Harpur Palate* now accepts submissions all year; deadline for Winter issue is November 15, for Summer issue is April 15. We also sponsor a fiction contest for the Summer issue and a poetry and nonfiction contest for the Winter issue. We do not accept submissions via e-mail. We are interested in high quality writing of all genres, but especially literary poetry and fiction."

HARTWORKS

D.C. Creative Writing Workshop, 601 Mississippi Ave. SE, Washington DC 20032. (202)445-4280. **E-mail:** nschwalb@dccww.org; info@dccww.org. **Website:** www.dccww.org. **Contact:** Nancy Schwalb, artistic director. *hArtworks* appears 3 times/year. "We publish the poetry of Hart Middle School students (as far as we know, Hart may be the only public middle school in the U.S. with its own poetry magazine) and the writing of guest writers such as Nikki Giovanni, Alan Cheuse, Arnost Lustig, Henry Taylor, Mark Craver,

and Cornelius Eady, along with interviews between the kids and the grown-up pros. We also publish work by our writers-in-residence, who teach workshops at Hart, and provide trips to readings, slams, museums, and plays." Wants "vivid, precise, imaginative language that communicates from the heart as well as the head." Does not want "poetry that only 'sounds' good; it also needs to say something meaningful." Has published poetry by Maryum Abdullah, Myron Jones, Nichell Kee, Kiana Murphy, James Tindle, and Sequan Wilson. *hArtworks* is 92 pages, magazine-sized, professionally printed, perfect bound, with card cover. Receives about 1,000 poems/year, accepts about 20%. Press run is 500; 100 distributed free to writers, teachers. Single copy: $12; subscription: $30. Make checks payable to D.C. Creative Writing Workshop.

○ Although this journal doesn't accept submissions from the general public, it's included here as an outstanding example of what a literary journal can be (for anyone of any age).

MAGAZINE'S NEEDS "Writers-in-residence solicit most submissions from their classes, and then a committee of student editors makes the final selections. Each year, our second issue is devoted to responses to the Holocaust."

HAWAII REVIEW

University of Hawaii Board of Publications, 2445 Campus Rd., Hemenway Hall 107, Honolulu HI 96822. (808)956-3030. **Fax:** (808)956-3083. **E-mail:** hawaiireview@gmail.com. **Website:** www.kaleo.org/hawaii_review. Buys first North American serial rights, first electronic rights. Publishes ms an average of 3 months after acceptance. Responds in approximately 3 months to mss. Sample copy for $10. Guidelines available online.

○ Offers yearly award with $500 prizes in poetry and fiction.

TIPS "Make it new."

HAYDEN'S FERRY REVIEW

c/o Virginia G. Piper Center for Creative Writing, Arizona State University, P.O. Box 875002, Tempe AZ 85287. (480)965-1337. **E-mail:** HFR@asu.edu. **Website:** www.haydensferryreview.org. **Contact:** Beth Staples, managing editor. "*Hayden's Ferry Review* publishes the best quality fiction, poetry, and creative nonfiction from new, emerging, and established writers." Buys first North American serial rights. Pays on publication. Publishes ms an average of 6 months after acceptance. Responds in 1 week or less to e-mail queries. Responds in 3-4 months to mss. Editorial lead time 5 months. Sample copy for $7.50. Guidelines available online.

○   Work from *Hayden's Ferry Review* has been selected for inclusion in *Pushcart Prize* anthologies and *Best Creative Nonfiction*.

MAGAZINE'S NEEDS Word length open. Pays $50.

HIGHLIGHTS FOR CHILDREN

803 Church St., Honesdale PA 18431. (570)253-1080. **Fax:** (570)251-7847. **Website:** www.highlights.com. **Contact:** Christine French Cully, editor-in-chief; Drew Hires, art director. "This book of wholesome fun is dedicated to helping children grow in basic skills and knowledge, in creativeness, in ability to think and reason, in sensitivity to others, in high ideals, and worthy ways of living—for children are the world's most important people. We publish stories for beginning and advanced readers. Up to 500 words for beginners (ages 3-7), up to 800 words for advanced (ages 8-12)." Buys all rights. Pays on acceptance. Responds in 2 months to queries. Sample copy free. Guidelines on website in "About Us" area.

MAGAZINE'S NEEDS Lines/poem: 16 maximum ("most poems are shorter"). Considers simultaneous submissions ("please indicate"); no previously published poetry. No e-mail submissions. "Submit typed manuscript with very brief cover letter." Occasionally comments on submissions "if manuscript has merit or author seems to have potential for our market." Guidelines available for SASE. Responds "generally within one month." Always sends prepublication galleys. Pays 2 contributor's copies; "money varies." Acquires all rights.

TIPS "Know the magazine's style before submitting. Send for guidelines and sample issue if necessary." Writers: "At *Highlights* we're paying closer attention to acquiring more nonfiction for young readers than we have in the past." Illustrators: "Fresh, imaginative work encouraged. Flexibility in working relationships a plus. Illustrators presenting their work need not confine themselves to just children's illustrations as long as work can translate to our needs. We also use animal illustrations, real and imaginary. We need crafts, puzzles and any activity that will stimulate children mentally and creatively. We are always looking for imaginative cover subjects. Know our publication's standards and content by reading sample issues, not just the guidelines. Avoid tired themes, or put a fresh twist on an old theme so that its style is fun and lively. We'd like to see stories with subtle messages, but the fun of the story should come first. Write what inspires you, not what you think the market needs. We are pleased that many authors of children's literature report that their first published work was in the pages of *Highlights*. It is not our policy to consider fiction on the strength of the reputation of the author. We judge each submission on its own merits. With factual material, however, we do prefer that writers be authorities in their field or people with first-hand experience. In this manner we can avoid the encyclopedic article that merely restates information readily available elsewhere. We don't make assignments. Query with simple letter to establish whether the nonfiction subject is likely to be of interest. A beginning writer should first become familiar with the type of material that *Highlights* publishes. Include special qualifications, if any, of author. Write for the child, not the editor. Write in a voice that children understand and relate to. Speak to today's kids, avoiding didactic, overt messages. Even though our general principles haven't changed over the years, we are contemporary in our approach to issues. Avoid worn themes."

◑ HIRAM POETRY REVIEW

P.O. Box 162, Hiram OH 44234. (330)569-5331. **E-mail:** poetryreview@hiram.edu. **Website:** http://hirampoetryreview.wordpress.com/. **Contact:** Willard Greenwood, poetry editor. *Hiram Poetry Review*, published annually in spring, features "distinctive, beautiful, and heroic poetry." Wants "works of high and low art. We tend to favor poems that are pockets of resistance in the undeclared war against 'plain speech,' but we're interested in any work of high quality." Press run is 400 (300 subscribers, 150 libraries). Subscription: $9/year; $23/3 years. Acquires first North American serial rights. Rights return to poets upon publication. Responds in 6 months.

MAGAZINE'S NEEDS Send 3-5 poems at a time. Considers simultaneous submissions. No e-mail submissions unless international. Cover letter is required. Include brief bio. Reads submissions year round. Length: no more than 50 lines. Pays 2 contributor's copies.

◉ HOLINESS TODAY

Nazarene Global Ministry Center, 17001 Prairie Star Pkwy., Lenexa KS 66220. (913)577-0500. **E-mail:**

holinesstoday@nazarene.org. **Website:** www.holinesstoday.org. **Contact:** Carmen J. Ringhiser, managing editor; Devid J. Felter, editor-in-chief. *Holiness Today*, published bimonthly online and in print, is "the primary print voice of the Church of the Nazarene, with articles geared to enhance holiness living by connecting Nazarenes with our heritage, vision, and mission through real life stories of God at work in the world." Holiness Today (print) is 40 pages. Subscription: $12/year U.S.

THE HOLLINS CRITIC

P.O. Box 9538, Hollins University, Roanoke VA 24020-1538. **E-mail:** acockrell@hollins.edu. **Website:** www.hollins.edu/academics/critic. **Contact:** Cathryn Hankla. Buys first North American serial rights. Pays on publication. Publishes ms an average of 1 year after acceptance. Responds in 2 months to mss. Sample copy for $3. Guidelines for #10 SASE.

Ⓠ Uses a few short poems in each issue, interesting in form, content, or both. *The Hollins Critic* is 24 pages, magazine-sized. Press run is 500. Subscription: $10/year ($15 outside US). No postal or e-mail submissions. Has published poetry by Natasha Trethewey, Carol Moldaw, David Huddle, Margaret Gibson, and Julia Johnson.

MAGAZINE'S NEEDS Submit up to 5 poems at a time using the online submission form at www.hollinscriticsubmissions.com, available September 15-December 1. Submissions received at other times will be returned unread. Responds in 6 weeks. "We read poetry only from September 1-December 15." Publishes 16-20 poems/year. Pays $25/poem plus 5 contributor's copies.

TIPS "We accept unsolicited poetry submissions; all other content is by prearrangement."

Ⓞ Ⓞ HOME PLANET NEWS

P.O. Box 455, High Falls NY 12440. (845)687-4084. **E-mail:** homeplanetnews@yahoo.com. **Website:** www.homeplanetnews.org. **Contact:** Donald Lev, editor. Triannual. "*Home Planet News* publishes mainly poetry along with some fiction, as well as reviews (books, theater and art) and articles of literary interest. We see *HPN* as a quality literary journal in an eminently readable format and with content that is urban, urbane and politically aware." Acquires one-time rights. Publishes ms 1 year after acceptance. Responds in 6 months to mss. Sample copy for $4. Guidelines available for SASE or on website; "however, it is usually best to simply send work."

Ⓠ *HPN* has received a small grant from the Puffin Foundation for its focus on AIDS issues. Tabloid: 1112×16; 24 pages; newsprint; illustrations; photos. Receives 12 unsolicited mss/month. Accepts 1 mss/issue; 3 mss/year. Has published work by Hugh Fox, Walter Jackman, Jim Story.

MAGAZINE'S NEEDS Submit 3-6 poems at a time. No previously published poems or simultaneous submissions. Cover letter is preferred. "SASE is a must." Time between acceptance and publication is 1 year. Seldom comments on rejected poems. Occasionally publishes theme issues. Upcoming themes available in magazine. Reviews books/chapbooks of poetry and other magazines in 1,200 words, single- and multi-book format. Send materials for review consideration to Donald Lev. "Note: we do have guidelines for book reviewers; please write for them or check website. Magazines are reviewed by a staff member." Lines/poem: no limit on length, "but shorter poems (under 30 lines) stand a better chance." Pays one-year gift subscription plus 3 contributor's copies.

TIPS "We use very little fiction, and a story we accept just has to grab us. We need short pieces of some complexity, stories about complex people facing situations which resist simple resolutions."

Ⓞ HOMESTEAD REVIEW

Box A-5, 156 Homestead Ave., Hartnell College, Salinas CA 93901. (831)755-6943. **Website:** www.hartnell.edu/homestead_review. *Homestead Review*, published annually in April, seeks "avant-garde poetry as well as fixed form styles of remarkable quality and originality." Does not want "Hallmark-style writing or first drafts." Considers poetry written by children and teens. Has published poetry by Sally Van Doren, Kathryn Kirkpatrick, Laura Le Hew, Allison Joseph, and Hal Sirowitz. Receives about 1,000 poems/year, accepts about 15%. Press run is 500 (300 subscribers/libraries); 200 are distributed free to poets, writers, bookstores. Single copy: $10; subscription: $10/year. Make checks payable to *Homestead Review*. Acquires one-time rights. Publishes ms 6 months after acceptance. Responds in 5 months. Guidelines for SASE.

Ⓠ Manuscripts are read by the staff and discussed. Poems/fiction accepted by majority consensus."

MAGAZINE'S NEEDS Submit 3 poems at a time. No previously published poems or simultaneous submissions. Postal submissions preferred. Cover letter is required. "A brief bio should be included in the cover letter." Pays 1 contributor's copy.

CONTEST/AWARD OFFERINGS Contest with categories for poetry and fiction. Offers 1st Prize: $250 plus publication in *Homestead Review*. All entries will be considered for publication in *Homestead Review*. Guidelines available on website. **Entry fee:** $15 for 3 poems. **Deadline:** see website for current dates.

⊛ HOOT

A postcard review of {mini} poetry and prose, 1413 Academy Lane, Elkins Park PA 19027. **E-mail:** info@hootreview.com. **E-mail:** onlinesubmissions@hootreview.com. **Website:** www.hootreview.com. **Contact:** Amanda Vacharat and Dorian Geisler, editors. "*HOOT* publishes 1 piece of writing, designed with original art/photographs, on the front of a postcard every month. The postcards are intended for sharing, to be hung on the wall, etc. Therefore, we look for very brief, surprising-yet-gimmick-free writing that can stand on its own, that also follows 'The Refrigerator Rule'—something that you would hang on your refrigerator and would want to read and look at for a whole month. This 'rule' applies to our online content as well." Buys first North American serial rights and electronic rights. Pays on publication. Publishes ms 2 months after acceptance. Sample copy available for $2. Writer's guidelines available on website.

MAGAZINE'S NEEDS Length: 10 lines. Pays $10-100 for print publication.

TIPS "We look for writing with audacity and zest, from authors who are not afraid to take risks. We appreciate work that is able to go beyond mere description in its 150 words. We offer free online workshops every Wednesday for authors who would like feedback on their work from the *HOOT* editors. We also often give feedback with our rejections. We publish roughly 6-10 new writers each year."

HORIZONS

100 Witherspoon St., Louisville KY 40202-1396. (502)569-5897. **Fax:** (502)569-8085. **E-mail:** yvonne.hileman@pcusa.org. **Website:** www.pcusa.org/horizons/. **Contact:** Yvonne Hileman, assistant editor. "Magazine owned and operated by Presbyterian women offering information and inspiration for Presbyterian women by addressing current issues facing the church and the world." Buys all rights. Pays on publication. Publishes ms an average of 4 months after acceptance. Sample copy for $4 and 9x12 SAE. Guidelines for #10 SASE or online at website.

MAGAZINE'S NEEDS Submit by mail, e-mail, or fax. Include contact information. Accepts various themes and topics. Pays "an honorarium of no less than $50 per page printed in the magazine—amount will vary depending on time and research required for writing the article."

⊙ HOSPITAL DRIVE

Hospital Drive, P.O. Box 800761, Charlottesville VA 22908-0761. **E-mail:** hospitaldrive@virginia.edu. **Website:** http://hospitaldrive.med.virginia.edu. **Contact:** Dr. Daniel Becker, editor. *Hospital Drive* "encourages original creative work that examines themes of health, illness, and healing. Submissions will be accepted from anyone, but preference is given to those involved in providing, teaching, studying, or researching patient care. All work will be judged anonymously by reviewers and the editorial board. Poems, short fiction, personal essays, reviews, photography, and visual art (painting, drawing, sculpture, mixed media) will be considered. Issues will be released at least twice a year, and may include invited work. Please review our web site thoroughly and direct any additional questions to query@hospitaldrive.med.virginia.edu." Time between acceptance and publication is 3-6 months. Guidelines available on website.

MAGAZINE'S NEEDS Submit up to 5 poems. Accepts e-mail submissions as attachment; no fax or disk submissions. Cover letter is unnecessary. All works must be submitted by e-mail (mailed, printed submissions cannot be accepted for review), accompanied by basic contact information and the titles of each piece. Attach each poem as a separate document to 1 e-mail. Put "poetry submission" in the e-mail subject line. "All submissions will be reviewed anonymously by the editorial board, and only the highest quality work will be published." Never comments on rejected poems.

⊙ HOTEL AMERIKA

Columbia College, English Department, 600 S. Michigan Ave., Chicago IL 60605. (312)369-8175. **E-mail:** editors@hotelamerika.net. **Website:** www.hotelamerika.net. **Contact:** David Lazar, editor; Adam McOmber, managing editor. "Manuscripts will be considered between September 1 and May 1. Materials received after May 1 and before September 1 will be returned unread." Guidelines online.

○ Work published in *Hotel Amerika* has been included in *The Pushcart Prize* and *The Best American Poetry* and featured on *Poetry Daily*.

● HUBBUB

5344 SE 38th Ave., Portland OR 97202. **E-mail:** lisa. steinman@reed.edu. **Website:** www.reed.edu/hubbub/. J. Shugrue and Lisa M. Steinman, co-editors. *Hubbub*, published once/year in the spring, is designed "to feature a multitude of voices from interesting contemporary American poets." Wants "poems that are well-crafted, with something to say. We have no single style, subject, or length requirement and, in particular, will consider long poems." Acquires first North American serial rights. Responds in 4 months. Guidelines available for SASE.

○ *Hubbub* is 50-70 pages, digest-sized, offset-printed, perfect-bound, with cover art. Receives about 1,200 submissions/year, accepts up to 2%. Press run is 350. Subscription: $7/year. Sample: $3.35 (back issues), $7 (current issue). Has published poetry by Madeline DeFrees, Cecil Giscombe, Carolyn Kizer, Primus St. John, Shara McCallum, and Alice Fulton.

MAGAZINE'S NEEDS Submit 3-6 typed poems at a time. No previously published poems or simultaneous submissions. Include SASE. "We review 2-4 poetry books/year in short (3-page) reviews; all reviews are solicited. We do, however, list books received/recommended." Send materials for review consideration. Does not want light verse. Pays $20/poem.

TIPS Outside judges choose poems from each volume for 3 awards: Vi Gale Award ($500), Stout Award ($75), and Kenneth O. Hanson Award ($100). There are no special submission procedures or entry fees involved.

THE HUDSON REVIEW

The Hudson Review, Inc., 684 Park Ave., New York NY 10065. **E-mail:** info@hudsonreview.com. **Website:** www.hudsonreview.com. **Contact:** Paula Deitz, editor. Pays on publication. Publishes ms an average of 6 months after acceptance. Responds in 6 months. Editorial lead time 3 months. Sample copy for $10. Guidelines for #10 SASE or online.

○ Send with SASE. Mss sent outside accepted reading period will be returned unread if SASE contains sufficient postage.

MAGAZINE'S NEEDS Reads poems only between April 1 and June 30. Pays 50¢/line.

TIPS "We do not specialize in publishing any particular 'type' of writing; our sole criterion for accepting unsolicited work is literary quality. The best way for you to get an idea of the range of work we publish is to read a current issue. We do not consider simultaneous submissions. Unsolicited manuscripts submitted outside of specified reading times will be returned unread. Do not send submissions via e-mail."

●$ HUNGER MOUNTAIN

Vermont College of Fine Arts, 36 College St., Montpelier VT 05602. (802)828-8517. **E-mail:** hungermtn@vcfa.edu. **Website:** www.hungermtn.org. Accepts high quality work from unknown, emerging, or successful writers. No genre fiction, drama, or academic articles, please. *Hunger Mountain* is about 200 pages, 7x10, professionally printed, perfect-bound, with full-bleed color artwork on cover. Press run is 1,000; 10,000 visits online monthly. Single copy: $10; subscription: $12/year, $22 for 2 years. Make checks payable to Vermont College of Fine Arts. Member: CLMP. Buys first worldwide serial rights. Pays on publication. Publishes ms an average of 1 year after acceptance. Responds in 4 months to mss. Sample copy for $10. Writer's guidelines online.

○ Uses online submissions manager.

MAGAZINE'S NEEDS Submit 3-10 poems at a time. All poems should be in ONE file. "We look for poetry that is as much about the world as about the self, that's an invitation, an opening out, a hand beckoning. We like poems that name or identify something essential that we may have overlooked. We like poetry with acute, precise attention to both content and diction." Submit using online submissions manager. No light verse, humor/quirky/catchy verse, greeting card verse.

CONTEST/AWARD OFFERINGS Annual contests: Ruth Stone Poetry Prize; The Howard Frank Mosher Short Fiction Prize; the Katherine Paterson Prize for Young Adult and Children's Writing; The Hunger Mountain Creative Nonfiction Prize. Visit www.hungermtn.org for information about prizes.

TIPS "Mss must be typed, prose double-spaced. Poets submit at least 3 poems. No multiple genre submissions. Fresh viewpoints and human interest are very important, as is originality. We are committed to publishing an outstanding journal of the arts. Do not send entire novels, mss, or short story collections. Do not send previously published work."

⊙ ⑤ HUNGUR MAGAZINE

P.O. Box 782, Cedar Rapids IA 52406-0782. **E-mail:** hungurmagazine@yahoo.com. **Website:** www.samsdotpublishing.com. **Contact:** Terrie Leigh Relf, editor. *Hungur Magazine*, published biannually, features "stories and poems about vampires, and especially about vampires on other worlds." Prefers a "decadent literary style." Pays on publication. Publishes ms 4-6 months after acceptance. Responds in 2-3 weeks. Guidelines online at www.samsdotpublishing.com/HungurGL.htm.

⊙ *Hungur Magazine* is 32 pages, magazine-sized, offset-printed, saddle-stapled, with paper cover with color art, includes ads. Press run is 100/issue. Subscription: $13/year. $23/2 years. Make checks payable to Tyree Campbell/Sam's Dot Publishing. Member: The Speculative Literature Foundation (http://SpeculativeLiterature.org).

MAGAZINE'S NEEDS Submit up to 5 poems at a time. No simultaneous submissions. Accepts e-mail submissions (pasted into body of message); no disk submissions. Reads submissions year round. Reviews books and chapbooks of poetry. Send materials for review consideration to Tyree Campbell. Lines/poem: prefers less than 100. Pays $4/poem and 1 contributor's copy.

⊙ IBBETSON ST. PRESS

25 School St., Somerville MA 02143-1721. **E-mail:** dougholder@post.harvard.edu. **Website:** http://ibbetsonpress.com. *Ibbetson St. Press*, published semiannually in June and November, prints "'down to earth' poetry that is well-written; has clean, crisp images; with a sense of irony and humor." Wants "mostly free verse, but are open to rhyme." Does not want "maudlin, trite, overly political, vulgar for vulgar's sake work." Acquires one-time rights. Time between acceptance and publication is up to 8 months. Responds in 2 months. Guidelines available for SASE.

⊙ *Ibbetson St. Press* is 50 pages, magazine-sized, desktop-published, with glossy white cover, includes ads. Receives about 1,000 poems/year, accepts up to 10%. Press run is 200. Also archived at Harvard, Brown, University of Wisconsin, Poets House-NYC, Endicott College and Buffalo University Libraries. Has pub-

lished poetry by Marge Piercy, X.J. Kennedy, Ted Kooser, Elizabeth Swados, Sarah Hannah, Gloria Mindock, Harris Gardner, Diana-der Hovanessian, Robert K. Johnson, Gary Metras. Single copy: $8; subscription: $13. Make checks payable to *Ibbetson St. Press*.

MAGAZINE'S NEEDS Submit 3-5 poems at a time. Considers previously published poems; no simultaneous submissions. No e-mail submissions; postal submissions only. Cover letter is required. "3 editors comment on submissions." Reviews books/chapbooks of poetry and other magazines in 250-500 words. Send materials for review consideration. Does not accept unsolicited chapbook mss. Has published *Dead Beats*, by Sam Cornish; *King of the Jungle*, by Zvi A. Sesling; *Steerage*, by Bert Stern; *From the Paris of New England*, by Doug Holder; *Ti and Blood Soaked*; *East of the Moon*, by Ruth Kramer Baden; and *Lousia Solano: The Grolier Poetry Book Shop*, edited by Steve Glines and Doug Holder. Pays 1 contributor's copy.

IDEAGEMS

IdeaGems Publications, P.O. Box 4748, Portland ME 04112. (202)746-5160. **E-mail:** ideagems@aol.com. **Website:** www.ideagems.com. **Contact:** Laurie Notch, managing editor. "Bimonthly magazine with 2 tracks: *IdeaGems Magazine*, with seasonal/holiday themes, and *Tough Lit*, devoted to crime/mystery, edge, fantasy, and sci-fi. Both issues seek short fiction, flash fiction, essay, anecdotal memoir, poetry, photography, artwork, and illustrations. Acquires one-time rights. Publishes ms an average of 1-3 months after acceptance. Editorial lead time 1-3 months. Free sample PDF copy upon request. Guidelines by e-mail and on website.

⊙ "Due to economic downturn and radical reduction in sales, we are sad to say that we cannot pay for accepted work. However, we do our very best to give writers the platform they need in print, electronic, and online formats to showcase their work and get publishing credentials. We accept pretty much anything in the way of fiction, nonfiction, poetry, photography, and artwork. We reserve the right to refuse to publish material that we deem unsuitable for our publication. We ask all writers to format their submissions accordingly: Electronic formats please! If you send us a print copy, then we have to retype it in its entirety, which is quite labor intensive for us. Please use a single space with a paragraph indentation of no more than 4 spaces. Use font size Calibri 10, if possible (but not critical). All digital photography, authors' head shots, and scanned artwork should be sized at a minimum of 200 dpi. 300 dpi is preferred."

MAGAZINE'S NEEDS Length: 3-50 lines.

TIPS "As is true with any publication, check us out online and/or order a sample issue to understand the nature of our material. Check out our contests, and above all, be patient."

◗◯ IDIOM 23

Central Queensland University, Idiom 23 Literary Magazine, Rockhampton QLD 4702, Australia. **E-mail:** idiom@cqu.edu.au; l.hawryluk@cqu.edu.au. **Website:** www.cqu.edu.au/faculties/faculty-of-arts,-business,-informatics-and-education/schools/humanities-and-communication/idiom-23-literary-magazine. **Contact:** *Idiom 23* editorial board. *Idiom 23*, published annually, is "named for the Tropic of Capricorn and is dedicated to developing the literary arts throughout the Central Queensland region. Submissions of original short stories, poems, articles, and black-and-white drawings and photographs are welcomed by the editorial collective. *Idiom 23* is not limited to a particular viewpoint but, on the contrary, hopes to encourage and publish a broad spectrum of writing. The collective seeks out creative work from community groups with as varied backgrounds as possible." Single copy: $20, available at http://bookshop.cqu.edu.au.

MAGAZINE'S NEEDS Poems are circulated to an editorial board. Send materials for review consideration to idiom@cqu.edu.au. Electronic submissions only. Considers poetry written by children and teens.

ILLUMEN

Sam's Dot Publishing, P.O. Box 782, Cedar Rapids IA 52406-0782. **E-mail:** illumensdp@yahoo.com. **Website:** www.samsdotpublishing.com/aoife/cover.htm. **Contact:** Karen L. Newman, editor. "*Illumen* publishes speculative poetry and articles about speculative poetry, and reviews of poetry and collections." Buys first North American serial rights, buys one-time rights, buys second serial (reprint) rights. Responds in 2 weeks to queries. Responds in 3-4 months to mss. Editorial lead time 2 months. Sample copy for $8. Guidelines available online.

MAGAZINE'S NEEDS *Illumen*, published biannually, contains speculative poetry and articles about speculative poetry. "Speculative poetry includes, but is not limited to, fantasy, science fiction, sword and sorcery, alternate history, and horror." Wants "fantasy, science fiction, spooky horror, and speculative poetry with minimal angst." Does not want "horror with excessive blood and gore." Considers poetry by children and teens. Has published poetry by Ian Watson, Bruce Boston, Sonya Taaffe, Mike Allen, Marge B. Simon, and David C. Kopaska-Merkel. *Illumen* is 50 pages, digest-sized, offset-printed, perfect-bound, with color cover with color art, includes ads. Receives about 200 poems/year, accepts about 50 (25%). Press run is 100/issue (20 subscribers, 50 shelf sales); 5 distributed free to reviewers. Single copy: $9; subscription: $15/year. Make checks payable to Tyree Campbell/Sam's Dot Publishing. "Scifaiku is a difficult sell with us because we also publish a specialty magazine—*Scifaikuest*—for scifaiku and related forms." Length: 200 lines. Pays 1-2¢/word

HOW TO CONTACT Submit up to 5 poems at a time. Lines/poem: prefers less than 200. Considers previously published poems; no simultaneous submissions. Accepts e-mail submissions (pasted into body of message); no disk submissions. "Submission should include snail mail address and a short (1-2 lines) bio." Reads submissions year round. Submit seasonal poems 6 months in advance. Time between acceptance and publication is 1-2 months. Often comments on rejected poems. Guidelines available on website. Responds in 4-6 weeks. Pays 2 cents/word (minimum: $3) for original poems and 1 contributor's copy. Acquires first North American serial rights. Reviews books/chapbooks of poetry. Send materials for review consideration to Tyree Campbell.

TIPS "*Illumen* publishes beginning writers, as well as seasoned veterans. Be sure to read and follow the guidelines before submitting your work. The best advice for beginning writers is to send your best effort, not your first draft."

◑ ILLUMINATIONS

Dept. of English, College of Charleston, 26 Gleb St., Charleston SC 29424. (843)953-4972. **E-mail:** scottcopsesm@cofc.edu. **Website:** www.cofc.edu/illuminations. **Contact:** Meg Scott-Copses, editor. Returns rights on request. Sample copy $10.

MAGAZINE'S NEEDS Open as to form and style, and to translations. Does not want to see anything "bland or formally clunky." Has published poetry by Brenda Marie Osbey, Geri Doran, Dennis Brutus, and Carole Satyamurti. Submit upto 6 poems at a time.

IMAGE: ART, FAITH, MYSTERY

3307 Third Ave. W., Seattle WA 98119. **E-mail:** image@imagejournal.org. **Website:** www.imagejournal. org. *Image: Art, Faith, Mystery*, published quarterly, "explores and illustrates the relationship between faith and art through world-class fiction, poetry, essays, visual art, and other arts." Acquires first North American serial rights. Publishes ms 1 year after acceptance. Responds in 3 months.

MAGAZINE'S NEEDS Submit up to 4 poems at a time. No previously published poems. No e-mail submissions. Cover letter is preferred. Wants "poems that grapple with religious faith, usually Judeo-Christian." Pays 4 contributor's copies plus $2/line ($150 maximum).

INDEFINITE SPACE

P.O. Box 40101, Pasadena CA 91114. **E-mail:** indefinitespace@yahoo.com. **Website:** www.indefinitespace.net. "Published annually. From minimalist to avant-garde—open to innovative, imagistic, philosophical, experimental creations—poetry, drawings, collage, photography; reads year round." Poet retains copyright. Responds in 3 months. Seldom comments on rejected poems.

Has published poetry by Peter J. Grieco, Lauren Hilger, Guy R. Being, Kristina Marie Darling, Dan Raphael, and Marton Koppany. *Indefinite Space* is 48 pages, digest-sized. Single copy: $7; subscription: $12 for 2 issues. Make checks payable to Marcia Arrieta.

MAGAZINE'S NEEDS No rhyming poetry. No previously published poems. Pays 1 contributor's copy.

INDIANA REVIEW

Ballantine Hall 465, 1020 E. Kirkwood, Indiana University, Bloomington IN 47405. (812)855-3439. **E-mail:** inreview@indiana.edu. **Website:** www.indiana.edu/~inreview. **Contact:** Jennifer Luebbers, editor. "*Indiana Review*, a nonprofit organization run by IU graduate students, is a journal of previously unpublished poetry and fiction. Literary interviews and essays are also considered. We publish innovative fiction, nonfiction, and poetry. We're interested in energy, originality, and careful attention to craft. While we publish many well-known writers, we also welcome new and emerging poets and fiction writers." Buys first North American serial rights. Pays on publication. Publishes ms an average of 3-6 months after acceptance. Responds in 2 or more weeks to queries. Responds in 4 or more months to mss. Sample copy for $9. Guidelines available online.

MAGAZINE'S NEEDS "We look for poems that are skillful and bold, exhibiting an inventiveness of language with attention to voice and sonics. Experimental, free verse, prose poem, traditional form, lyrical, narrative." 5 lines minimum. Pays $5/page ($10 minimum), plus 2 contributor's copies.

CONTEST/AWARD OFFERINGS Holds yearly poetry and prose-poem contests.

TIPS "We're always looking for nonfiction essays that go beyond merely autobiographical revelation and utilize sophisticated organization and slightly radical narrative strategies. We want essays that are both lyrical and analytical where confession does not mean nostalgia. Read us before you submit. Often reading is slower in summer and holiday months. Only submit work to journals you would proudly subscribe to, then subscribe to a few. Take care to read the latest 2 issues and specifically mention work you identify with and why. Submit work that `stacks up' with the work we've published. Offers annual poetry, fiction, short-short/prose-poem prizes. See website for full guidelines."

INNISFREE POETRY JOURNAL

E-mail: editor@innisfreepoetry.org. **Website:** www. innisfreepoetry.org. **Contact:** Greg McBride, editor. Buys first North American serial rights. "Acquires first publication rights, including the right to publish it online and maintain it there as part of the issue in which it appears, to make it available in a printer-friendly format, to make the issue of *Innisfree* in which it appears downloadable as a PDF document and available as a printed volume. All other rights revert to the poet after online publication of the poem in *The Innisfree Poetry Journal*." Guidelines available on website.

MAGAZINE'S NEEDS Submit up to 5 poems by e-mail; single Word attachment. "Include your name, as you would like it to appear in *Innisfree*, in the subject line of your submission. Format all poems flush with the left margin—no indents other than any within the poem itself. Simultaneous submissions are welcome.

If a poem is accepted elsewhere, however, please be sure to notify us immediately." Does not accept previously published poetry.

TIPS "Welcomes original previously unpublished poems year round. We accept poems only via e-mail from both established and new writers whose work is excellent. We publish well-crafted poems, poems grounded in the specific which speak in fresh language and telling images. And we admire musicality. We welcome those who, like the late Lorenzo Thomas, 'write poems because I can't sing.'"

INTERPRETER'S HOUSE

9 Glenhurst Rd., Mannamead, Plymouth PL3 5LT, England. **Website:** www.interpretershouse.org.uk. **Contact:** Simon Curtis, editor. *Interpreter's House*, published 3 times/year in February, June, and October, prints short stories and poetry. Wants "good poetry, not too long." Does not want "Christmas-card verse or incomprehensible poetry." Has published poetry by Dannie Abse, Tony Curtis, Pauline Stainer, Alan Brownjohn, Peter Redgrove, and R.S. Thomas. *Interpreter's House* is 74 pages, A5, with attractive cover design. Receives about 1,000 poems/year, accepts up to 5%. Press run is 300 (200 subscribers). Single copy: £3 plus 55p. postage; subscription: £12 for 3 issues. Sample: £3.50. Responds in 3 months. Guidelines for SASE.

MAGAZINE'S NEEDS "All work is dealt with swiftly. Usually no more than one poem is accepted, and writers who have already appeared in the magazine are asked to wait for at least a year before submitting again. Submit 5 poems at a time." Pays in contributor's copies.

IODINE POETRY JOURNAL

P.O. Box 18548, Charlotte NC 28218. (704)595-9526. **E-mail:** iodineopencut@aol.com. **Website:** www.iodinepoetryjournal.com. **Contact:** Jonathan K. Rice, editor/publisher. *Iodine Poetry Journal*, published semiannually, provides "a venue for both emerging and established poets." Wants "good poetry of almost any style, including form (e.g., pantoum and sestina) and experimental." Does not want rhyme, religion, or pornography. Has published poetry by Fred Chappell, Colette Inez, Ron Koertge, Dorianne Laux, and R.T. Smith. *Iodine Poetry Journal* is 84 pages, digest-sized, perfect-bound, with full-color laminated cover, includes ads. Receives about 2,000 poems/year, accepts about 75 poems/issue. Press run is 350. Single copy:

$8; subscription: $14/year (2 issues) $26 for 2 years (4 issues). Sample: "Back issues vary in price." Make checks payable to *Iodine Poetry Journal*. Acquires first North American serial rights. Time between acceptance and publication is 6 months to 1 year. Responds in 2-3 months. Guidelines available in magazine, for SASE, or on website.

Poetry published in *Iodine Poetry Journal* has been selected for inclusion in *The Best American Poetry*.

MAGAZINE'S NEEDS Submit 3-5 poems at a time. Lines/poem: 40 or less preferred, "but not totally averse to longer poems." No previously published poems or simultaneous submissions. Accepts e-mail submissions from international poets only; no disk submissions. Cover letter is preferred. "Always include SASE, and specify if SASE is for return of manuscript or reply only. I like a brief introduction of yourself in the cover letter." Reads submissions year round. Poems are circulated to an editorial board. Associate editors assist in the selection process. Sometimes comments on rejected poems. Sometimes sends prepublication galleys. Pays 1 contributor's copy and discounts extra copies of the issue in which work appears.

TIPS "We no longer publish our broadside, *Open Cut*."

IOTA

P.O. Box 7721, Matlock, Derbyshire DE4 9DD, England. (44)01629 582500. **E-mail:** info@iotamagazine.co.uk. **Website:** www.iotamagazine.co.uk. *iota* considers "any style and subject; no specific limitations as to length." Has published poetry by Jane Kinninmont, John Robinson, Tony Petch, Chris Kinsey, Christopher James, and Michael Kriesel. Responds in 3 months (unless production of the next issue takes precedence).

iota is 120 or more pages, professionally printed, litho stitched, with full-color cover. Receives 6,000 poems/year, accepts about 300. Press run is around 1,000. Single copy: £6.99 UK; subscription: £18 UK, £25 outside UK.

MAGAZINE'S NEEDS Submit up to 6 poems at a time. No previously published poems or simultaneous submissions. Cover letter is required. Prefers name and address on each poem, typed. "No SAE, no reply." Online submissions now accepted; see details at www.iotamagazine.co.uk/submissions." Reviews books of poetry. Send materials for review consideration. Pays 1 contributor's copy.

ADDITIONAL INFORMATION The editors also publish Templar Poetry (www.templarpoetry.co.uk), sponsor the annual Derwent Poetry Festival, and host an online poetry bookshop of their titles at www.templarpoetry.com. "Templar Poetry is a major UK poetry publisher and publishes poetry collections, nonfiction, and an annual anthology of poetry linked to international pamphlet and collection awards. Details at www.templarpoetry.co.uk/awards.

CONTEST/AWARD OFFERINGS Sponsors an annual poetry Pamphlet/Chapbook-Iota Shot Award, offering 2-3 awards of £100, plus publication of *ishot* chapbook. Submission fee: £15.50 online. Worldwide submissions in English welcome. **Deadline:** November 19, 2012.

ⓞⓢ THE IOWA REVIEW

308 EPB, The University of Iowa, Iowa City IA 52242. (319)335-0462. **Website:** www.iowareview.org. **Contact:** Russell Scott Valentino, editor. *The Iowa Review*, published 3 times/year, prints fiction, poetry, essays, reviews, and, occasionally, interviews. *The Iowa Review* is 5½ ×8½, approximately 200 pages, professionally printed, flat-spined, first-grade offset paper, Carolina CS1 10-point cover stock. Receives about 5,000 submissions/year, accepts up to 100. Press run is 2,900; 1,500 distributed to stores. Subscription: $25. Stories, essays, and poems for a general readership interested in contemporary literature. Buys first North American serial rights, buys nonexclusive anthology, classroom, and online serial rights. Pays on publication. Publishes ms an average of 12-18 months after acceptance. Responds in 4 months to mss. Sample copy for $9.95 and online. Guidelines available online.

💬 "This magazine uses the help of colleagues and graduate assistants. Its reading period for unsolicited work is September 1-December 1. From January through April, we read entries to our annual Iowa Awards competition. Check our website for further information."

MAGAZINE'S NEEDS Submit up to 8 poems at a time. Online submissions accepted, but no e-mail submissions. Cover letter (with title of work and genre) is encouraged. SASE required. Reads submissions "only during the fall semester, September through November, and then contest entries in the spring." Time between acceptance and publication is "around a year." Occasionally comments on rejected poems or offers suggestions on accepted poems. Pays $1.50/line of poetry, $40 minimum. "We simply look for poems that, at the time we read and choose, we find we admire. No specifications as to form, length, style, subject matter, or purpose. Though we print work from established writers, we're always delighted when we discover new talent."

TIPS "We publish essays, reviews, novel excerpts, stories, poems, and photography. We have no set guidelines as to content or length, but strongly recommend that writers read a sample issue before submitting. Buys 65-80 unsolicited ms/year. Submit complete ms with SASE."

ⓢ ISLAND

P.O. Box 210, Sandy Bay Tasmania 7006, Australia. (61)(3)6226-2325. **E-mail:** island.magazine@utas.edu.au. **Website:** www.islandmag.com. "*Island* seeks quality fiction, poetry, essays, and articles. A literary magazine with an environmental heart." Buys one-time rights. Subscriptions and sample copies available for purchase online. Guidelines available online.

MAGAZINE'S NEEDS Pays $100.

ⓞ ITALIAN AMERICANA

80 Washington St., Providence RI 02903. **E-mail:** it.americana@yahoo.com. **Website:** www.italianamericana.com. **Contact:** C.B. Albright, editor-in-chief. Responds in 1-2 months.

MAGAZINE'S NEEDS Submit up to 3 poems at a time. Length: no more than 3 pages.

CONTEST/AWARD OFFERINGS Along with the National Italian American Foundation, *Italian Americana* co-sponsors the annual $1,000 John Ciardi Award for Lifetime Contribution to Poetry. *Italian Americana* also presents $250 fiction or memoir award annually; and $1,500 in history prizes.

TIPS "Check out our new website supplement to the journal at www.italianamericana.com. Read *Wild Dreams: The Best of Italian Americana* (Fordham University Press), the best stories, poems and memoirs in the journal's 35-year history."

ⓞ JABBERWOCK REVIEW

Department of English, Mississippi State University, Drawer E, Mississippi State MS 39762. **E-mail:** jabberwockreview@english.msstate.edu. **Website:** www.msstate.edu/org/jabberwock. **Contact:** Michael Kardos, editor. Submissions will be accepted from August 15-October 20 and January 15-March 15. Rights revert to author upon publication. Responds in 3-5 months. "If you have not heard from us in 5 months, feel free to contact us about the status of your submission." Guidelines available online at website.

MAGAZINE'S NEEDS Submit no more than 5 poems at a time. Submit with SASE. "Poems of multiple pages should indicate whether or not stanza breaks accompany page breaks."

TIPS "It might take a few months to get a response from us, but your manuscript will be read with care. Our editors enjoy reading submissions (really!) and will remember writers who are persistent and commited to getting a story 'right' through revision."

JACK AND JILL

U.S. Kids, 1100 Waterway Blvd., Indianapolis IN 46206-0567. (317)634-1100. **E-mail:** editor@saturdayeveningpost.com. **Website:** www.jackandjillmag. org. Buys all rights. Pays on publication. Publishes ms an average of 8 months after acceptance. Responds to mss in 3 months. Guidelines available online.

○ "Please do not send artwork. We prefer to work with professional illustrators of our own choosing."

MAGAZINE'S NEEDS Wants light-hearted poetry appropriate for the age group. Mss must be typewritten with poet's contact information in upper right-hand corner of each poem's page. SASE required. Pays $25-50.

TIPS "We are constantly looking for new writers who can tell good stories with interesting slants—stories that are not full of outdated and time-worn expressions. We like to see stories about kids who are smart and capable, but not sarcastic or smug. Problem-solving skills, personal responsibility, and integrity are good topics for us. Obtain current issues of the magazine and study them to determine our present needs and editorial style."

JERRY JAZZ MUSICIAN

2207 NE Broadway, Portland OR 97232. (503)287-5570. **Fax:** (801)749-9896. **E-mail:** jm@jerryjazz.com. **Website:** www.jerryjazz.com.

MAGAZINE'S NEEDS Submit 1-2 poems at a time. Length: 6-100.

JEWISH CURRENTS

P.O. Box 111, Accord NY 12404. (845)626-2427. **E-mail:** editor@jewishcurrents.org. **Website:** www.jewishcurrents.org. **Contact:** Lawrence Bush, editor. *Jewish Currents*, published 4 times/year, is a progressive

Jewish bimonthly magazine that carries on the insurgent tradition of the Jewish left through independent journalism, political commentary, and a 'countercultural' approach to Jewish arts and literature. *Jewish Currents* is 48 pages, magazine-sized, offset-printed, saddle-stapled with a full-color arts section, "Jcultcha & Funny Pages." Press run is 700. Subscription: $25/year. Publishes ms 2 years after acceptance. Responds in 3 months.

MAGAZINE'S NEEDS Submit 4 poems at a time with a cover letter. No previously published poems or simultaneous submissions. Cover letter is required. "Include brief bio with author's publishing history." Poems should be typed, double-spaced; include SASE. Pays 3 contributor's copies.

JEWISH WOMEN'S LITERARY ANNUAL

NCJW New York Section, 820 2nd Ave., New York NY 10017. (212)687-5030. **E-mail:** info@ncjwny.org. **Website:** www.ncjwny.org/services_annual.htm. *Jewish Women's Literary Annual*, published in April, prints poetry and fiction by Jewish women.

○ *Jewish Women's Literary Annual* is 230 pages, digest-sized, perfect-bound, with laminated card cover. Receives about 1,500 poems/year, accepts about 10%. Press run is 1,500. Subscription: $18 for 3 issues. Sample: $7.50. Has published poetry by Linda Zisquit, Merle Feld, Helen Papell, Enid Dame, Marge Piercy, and Lesleéa Newman.

MAGAZINE'S NEEDS Submit previously unpublished poetry and prose written by Jewish women. Accepts any topic. Submit through postal mail only.

TIPS "Send only your very best. We are looking for humor, as well as other things, but nothing cutesy or smart-aleck. We do no politics; prefer topics other than 'Holocaust'."

J JOURNAL: NEW WRITING ON JUSTICE

524 West 59th St., 7th Floor, New York NY 10019. (212) 327-8697. **E-mail:** jjournal@jjay.cuny.edu. **Website:** www.jjournal.org. **Contact:** Adam Berlin and Jeffrey Heiman, editors. "*J Journal* publishes literary fiction, creative nonfiction and poetry on the subjects of crime, criminal justice, law and law enforcement. While the themes are specific, they need not dominate the work. We're interested in questions of justice from all perspectives." Acquires first rights. Publication is

copyrighted. Pays on publication. Responds to queries in 4 weeks; mss in 12 weeks. Sometimes comments on/critiques rejected mss. Send recyclable copy of ms and e-mail for reply. Sample copy available for $10. Guidelines available online.

○ Literary magazine/journal: 6x9; 120 pages; 60 lb paper; 80 lb cover.

MAGAZINE'S NEEDS Submit up to 3 poems. Include brief bio and list of publications. Writers receive 2 contributor's copies. Additional copies $10.

TIPS "We're looking for literary fiction/memoir/personal narrative poetry with a connection, direct or tangential, to the theme of justice."

⑤ JOURNAL OF ASIAN MARTIAL ARTS

Via Media Publishing Co., 941 Calle Mejia, #822, Santa Fe NM 87501. (505)983-1919. **E-mail:** info@goviamedia.com. **Website:** www.goviamedia.com. Buys first rights, buys second serial (reprint) rights. Pays on publication. Publishes ms an average of 1 year after acceptance. Responds in 1 month to queries. Responds in 2 months to mss. Sample copy for $10. Guidelines with #10 SASE or online.

MAGAZINE'S NEEDS No poetry that does not focus on martial arts culture. Pays $10-100, or copies.

TIPS "Always query before sending a manuscript. We are open to varied types of articles; most however require a strong academic grasp of Asian culture. For those not having this background, we suggest trying a museum review, or interview, where authorities can be questioned, quoted, and provide supportive illustrations. We especially desire articles/reports from Asia, with photo illustrations, particularly of a martial art style, so readers can visually understand the unique attributes of that style, its applications, evolution, etc. Location and media reports are special areas that writers may consider, especially if they live in a location of martial art significance."

① JOURNAL OF NEW JERSEY POETS

English Department, County College of Morris, 214 Center Grove Rd., Randolph NJ 07869-2086. (973)328-5467. **Fax:** (973)328-5425. **E-mail:** mayres1@ccm.edu. **Contact:** Matthew Ayres, editor; Debra Demattio, Emily Birx, Matthew Jones, Philip Chase, associate editors. *Journal of New Jersey Poets*, published annually in April, is "not necessarily about New Jersey—but of, by, and for poets from New Jersey." Wants "serious work that conveys the essential, real, whole emotional moment of the poem to the reader without

sentimentality." Acquires first North American serial rights. Time between acceptance and publication is within 1 year. Responds in up to 1 year. Guidelines available for SASE or by e-mail.

○ *Journal of New Jersey Poets* is about 90 pages, perfect-bound, offset-printed on recycled stock. Press run is 600. Single copy: $10; subscription: $16 for 2 issues ($16/issue for institutions). Sample: $5. Has published poetry by Joe Weil, X.J. Kennedy, Marvin Silbersher, Tina Kelley, Gerald Stern, Kenneth Burke, and Catherine Doty.

MAGAZINE'S NEEDS Poets who live or work in New Jersey (or who formerly lived or worked here) are invited to submit up to 3 poems with their New Jersey bio data mentioned in the cover letter. Accepts fax and e-mail submissions, "but they will not be acknowledged nor returned. Include SASE with sufficient postage for return of manuscript, or provide instructions to recycle." Annual deadline for submissions: September 1. All reviews are solicited. Send 2 copies of books for review consideration. Pays 2 contributor's copies and a one-year subscription.

ADDITIONAL INFORMATION Awarded first New Jersey poets prize to Stephen Dobyns in 2010. For prize guidelines, e-mail editor Matthew Ayres.

① JOURNAL OF THE AMERICAN MEDICAL ASSOCIATION (JAMA)

(312)464-4444. **E-mail:** jamams@jama-archives.org. **Website:** www.jama.com.

MAGAZINE'S NEEDS *Journal of the American Medical Association (JAMA)*, published weekly, includes a poetry and medicine column and publishes poetry "in some way related to a medical experience, whether from the point of view of a health care worker or patient, or simply an observer. No unskilled poetry." Has published poetry by Jack Coulehan, Floyd Skloot, and Walt McDonald. *JAMA* is magazine-sized, flat-spined, with glossy paper cover. Receives about 750 poems/year, accepts about 7%. Has 360,000 subscribers (369 libraries).

①⑤ THE JOURNAL

(614)292-4076. **Fax:** (614)292-7816. **E-mail:** managingeditor@thejournalmag.org. **Website:** http://thejournalmag.org. "We're open to all forms; we tend to favor work that gives evidence of a mature and sophisticated sense of the language." Buys first North American serial rights. Pays on publication. Publishes ms an average of 1 year after acceptance. Responds in 2 months to mss. Sample copy for $7 or online. Guidelines available online.

○ "We are interested in quality fiction, poetry, nonfiction, art, and reviews of new books of poetry, fiction, and nonfiction. We impose no restrictions on category, type, or length of submission for Fiction, Poetry, and Nonfiction. We are happy to consider long stories and self-contained excerpts of novels. Please double-space all prose submissions. Please send 3-6 poems in 1 submission. We only accept online submissions and will not respond to mailed submissions."

MAGAZINE'S NEEDS "However else poets train or educate themselves, they must do what they can to know our language. Too much of the writing we see indicates poets do not, in many cases, develop a feel for the possibilities of language, and do not pay attention to craft. Poets should not be in a rush to publish—until they are ready." Pays 2 contributor's copies and one-year subscription.

TIPS "Mss are rejected because of lack of understanding of the short story form, shallow plots, undeveloped characters. Cure: Read as much well-written fiction as possible. Our readers prefer 'psychological' fiction rather than stories with intricate plots. Take care to present a clean, well-typed submission."

🌓 ◑ THE JOURNAL

Original Plus Press, 17 High St., Maryport Cumbria CA15 6BQ, United Kingdom. 01900 812194. **E-mail:** smithsssj@aol.com. **Website:** http://thesamsmith. webs.com. *The Journal*, published 3 times a year, features English poetry/translations, reviews, and articles. Wants "new poetry howsoever it comes; translations and original English-language poems." Does not want "staid, generalized, all form/no content." Buys all rights. Pays on publication. Publishes ms an average of 6 months after acceptance. Responds in 4 weeks to queries. Often comments on rejected poems. Editorial lead time 6 months. Guidelines free.

○ Since 1997, Original Plus Press has been publishing collections of poetry. Has recently published books by Chris Hardy, Brian Daldorph, Siobhan Logan, Alice Lenkiewics and Helen Bunkingham. But from now will be publishing only chapbooks. Send SASE (or SAE and IRC) or e-mail for details.

MAGAZINE'S NEEDS Submit up to 6 poems at a time. Considers previously published poems and simultaneous submissions. Accepts e-mail submissions. Cover letter is preferred. "Please send 2 IRCs with hard-copy submissions." Always sends prepublication galleys. Pays 1 contributor's copy "only to U.K. contributors. Contributors outside of the U.K. receive PDF copy of that issue."

TIPS "Send 6 poems; I'll soon let you know if it's not *Journal* material."

● KAIMANA: LITERARY ARTS HAWAI'I

Hawai'i Literary Arts Council, P.O. Box 11213, Honolulu HI 96828. **E-mail:** reimersa001@hawaii.rr.com. **Website:** www.hawaii.edu/hlac. *Kaimana: Literary Arts Hawai'i*, published annually, is the magazine of the Hawai'i Literary Arts Council. Wants poems with "some Pacific reference—Asia, Polynesia, Hawai'i—but not exclusively." Has published poetry by Kathryn Takara, Howard Nemerov, Anne Waldman, Reuel Denney, Haunani-Kay Trask, and Simon Perchik. *Kaimana* is 64-76 pages, 7½x10, saddle-stapled, with high-quality printing. Press run is 1,000. Subscription: $15, includes membership in HLAC. Sample: $10.

MAGAZINE'S NEEDS Cover letter is preferred. Sometimes comments on rejected poems. Guidelines available in magazine or on website. Responds with "reasonable dispatch." Pays 2 contributor's copies. "Hawai'i gets a lot of 'travelling regionalists,' visiting writers with inevitably superficial observations. We also get superb visiting observers who are careful craftsmen anywhere. *Kaimana* is interested in the latter, to complement our own best Hawai'i writers."

TIPS "Poets published in Kaimana have received the Pushcart Prize, the Hawaii Award for Literature, the Stefan Baciu Award, the Cades Award, and the John Unterecker Award."

●◑⑤ KALEIDOSCOPE

Kaleidoscope Press, 701 S. Main St., Akron OH 44311-1019. (330)762-9755. **Fax:** (330)762-0912. **E-mail:** kaleidoscope@udsakron.org. **Website:** www.udsakron.org/services/kaleidoscope/index.asp. **Contact:** Gail Willmott, editor-in-chief. "*Kaleidoscope* magazine creatively focuses on the experiences of disability through literature and the fine arts. Unique to the field of disability studies, this award-winning publication expresses the experiences of disability from the perspective of individuals, families, healthcare professionals, and society as a whole." Buys first rights.

Rights return to author upon publication. Pays on publication. Responds within 6 months. Sample copy for $6 prepaid. Guidelines available online.

○ *Kaleidoscope* has received awards from the American Heart Association, the Great Lakes Awards Competition and Ohio Public Images.

MAGAZINE'S NEEDS Wants poems that have strong imagery, evocative language. Submit up to 6 poems. "Do not get caught up in rhyme scheme. High quality with strong imagery and evocative language. Reviews any style."

TIPS "The material chosen for *Kaleidoscope* challenges and overcomes stereotypical, patronizing, and sentimental attitudes about disability. We accept the work of writers with and without disabilities, however the work of a writer without a disability must focus on some aspect of disability. The criteria for good writing apply: effective technique, thought-provoking subject matter, and in general, a mature grasp of the art of story-telling. Writers should avoid using offensive language and always put the person before the disability."

● ◎ **KELSEY REVIEW**

P.O. Box B, Liberal Arts Division, Trenton NJ 08690. **E-mail:** kelsey.review@mccc.edu. **Website:** www.mccc.edu/community_kelsey-review.shtml. **Contact:** Ed Carmien. *Kelsey Review*, published annually in September by Mercer County Community College, serves as "an outlet for literary talent of people living and working in Mercer County, New Jersey only." Rights revert to author on publication. Responds no later than September 1 to mss. SASE for return of ms. Sample copy free. Guidelines online.

○ *Kelsey Review* is about 90 glossy pages, 7x11, with paper cover. Receives 100+ submissions/year; accepts 10. Press run is 2,000; all distributed free to contributors, area libraries, bookstores, and schools. Black and white art. Has published poetry by Vida Chu, Carolyn Foote Edelmann, and Mary Mallery.

MAGAZINE'S NEEDS Deadline is May 15. Submissions are limited to people who live, work, or give literary readings in Mercer County, New Jersey. Decisions on which material will be published are made by the 4-person editorial board in June and July. Contributors will be notified of submission acceptance determination(s) by the second week of August. Has no specifications as to form, subject matter,

or style. Does not want to see poetry "about kittens and puppies." Pays 3 contributor's copies.

HOW TO CONTACT Submit up to 6 poems at a time. No previously published poems or simultaneous submissions. No fax or e-mail submissions. Manuscripts must be typed. Submit poems by May 15 deadline. Send SASE for returns. Guidelines available by e-mail. Responds in August of each year. Pays 3 contributor's copies. All rights revert to authors.

TIPS "See the *Kelsey Review* website for current guidelines. Note: we only accept submissions from the Mercer County, New Jersey, area."

● ◎ ⑤ **THE KENYON REVIEW**

Finn House, 102 W. Wiggin, Gambier OH 43022. (740)427-5208. **Fax:** (740)427-5417. **E-mail:** kenyonreview@kenyon.edu. **Website:** www.kenyonreview.org. **Contact:** Marlene Landefeld. "An international journal of literature, culture, and the arts, dedicated to an inclusive representation of the best in new writing (fiction, poetry, essays, interviews, criticism) from established and emerging writers." Buys first rights. Pays on publication. Publishes ms an average of 1 year after acceptance. Responds in 4 months to mss. Editorial lead time 1 year. Sample copy $10, includes postage and handling. Call or e-mail to order. Guidelines available online.

○ *The Kenyon Review* is 180 pages, digest-sized, flat-spined. Receives about 6,000 submissions/year. Also now publishes *KR Online*, a separate and complementary literary magazine.

MAGAZINE'S NEEDS Features all styles, forms, lengths, and subject matters. Considers translations. Has published poetry by Billy Collins, Diane Ackerman, John Kinsella, Carol Muske-Dukes, Diane di Prima, and Seamus Heaney. Submit up to 6 poems at a time. No previously published poems or simultaneous submissions. Accepts submissions through online registration only at www.kenyon-review.org/submissions (group poems in a single document; do not submit poems individually). Reads submissions September 15-January 15.

TIPS "We no longer accept mailed or e-mailed submissions. Work will only be read if it is submitted through our online program on our website. Reading period is September 15-January 15. We look for strong voice, unusual perspective, and power in the writing."

THE KERF

College of the Redwoods, 883 W. Washington Blvd., Crescent City CA 95531. **E-mail:** david-holper@redwoods.edu. **Website:** www.redwoods.edu/Departments/english/poets&writers/clm.htm. **Contact:** David Holper. *The Kerf*, published annually in fall, features "poetry that speaks to the environment and humanity." Wants "poetry that exhibits an environmental consciousness." Considers poetry by children and teens.

The Kerf is 54 pages, digest-sized, printed via Docutech, saddle-stapled, with CS2 coverstock. Receives about 1,000 poems/year, accepts up to 3%. Press run is 400 (150 shelf sales); 100 distributed free to contributors and writing centers. Sample: $5. Make checks payable to College of the Redwoods. Has published poetry by Ruth Daigon, Alice D'Alessio, James Grabill, George Keithley, and Paul Willis.

MAGAZINE'S NEEDS Submit up to 5 poems (7 pages maximum) at a time. No previously published poems or simultaneous submissions. Reads submissions January 15-March 31 only.

KOTAPRESS LOSS JOURNAL

(928)225-5416. **E-mail:** editor@kotapress.com. **Website:** www.kotapress.com; www.kotapress.blogspot.com. **Contact:** Kara L.C. Jones, editor. *KotaPress Loss Journal*, published quarterly online with blogs almost daily, provides support "of the grief and healing process after the death of a child. We publish *only* nonfictional poetry that somehow relates to grief and healing in relation to the death of a child. Please do not make up poems about this kind of loss and send them just to get in the magazine; it is insulting to many of our readers who are living this reality. As always, our interest is more in the content and story rather than one's ability to write in form; more in the ideas of poetry therapy rather than the academic, critique, competitive ideas normally fostered in universities." Has published poetry by John Fox, Poppy Hullings, Patricia Wellingham-Jones, Carol Jo Horn, and Sarah Bain. Responds in 2-6 months.

MAGAZINE'S NEEDS "Please read the *Loss Journal* site and blog before sending anything. Then send a letter explaining your interest in contributing. We are interested in knowing how your personal experiences with death, dying, grief, and healing are playing out in the specific poems you are submitting. Include a bio. Send your letter, poems, and bio as text all in one e-mail. Submissions without letter explaining your interest will be ignored. Make sure the subject line of your e-mail says 'Loss Journal Submission'"

LADYBUG

Carus Publishing Co., 700 E. Lake St., Suite 300, Chicago IL 60601. (312)701-1720. **Website:** www.cricketmag.com. **Contact:** Marianne Carus, editor-in-chief; Suzanne Beck, managing art director. *LADYBUG Magazine*, published monthly, is a reading and listening magazine for young children (ages 2-6). "We look for quality literature and nonfiction." Subscription: $35.97/year (12 issues). Sample: $5; sample pages available on website. Pays on publication. Responds in 6 months to mss. Guidelines available online.

MAGAZINE'S NEEDS Wants poetry that is "rhythmic, rhyming; serious, humorous, active." Length: 20 lines maximum. Pays $3/line ($25 minimum).

TIPS "Reread manuscript before sending. Keep within specified word limits. Study back issues before submitting to learn about the types of material we're looking for. Writing style is paramount. We look for rich, evocative language and a sense of joy or wonder. Remember that you're writing for preschoolers—be age-appropriate, but not condescending or preachy. A story must hold enjoyment for both parent and child through repeated read-aloud sessions. Remember that people come in all colors, sizes, physical conditions, and have special needs. Be inclusive!"

LA FOVEA

E-mail: editors@lafovea.org. **Website:** www.lafovea.org. **Contact:** Frank Giampietro, creator and senior editor. Published 20 times/year online. "Each Nerve editor (found on the main page of www.lafovea.org) is in charge of a nerve. The nerves are made up of poets who are invited to submit to *La Fovea*. Click on the editors name to see all the poets and poems in his or her nerve. The nerve editor asks a poet to submit two poems. After that poet has had his or her poems on *La Fovea*, he or she will ask another poet to submit poems. If the last poet on the nerve does not find a poet to submit poems for whatever reason, the nerve is dead. It's okay to have a dead nerve. The most important thing is for the never editor to notice a nerve has died and begin a new nerve from their first page of poems."

MAGAZINE'S NEEDS Wants any poetry. "If a poet wants to submit to *La Fovea* but has not been invited, he or she may submit to *La Fovea* and choose the editor whom the poet believes most matches his or her family of aesthetic style. The editor of the never may choose to send these poems to the current nerve editor and ask if he or she wishes to publish the poet's work. If the poet does not wish to publish the work, than the work will be returned to the submitter." Has published poetry by Denise Duhamel, Campbell McGrath, Julianna Baggott. Submit 2 poems at a time and short bio.

◑ LAKE EFFECT: A JOURNAL OF THE LITERARY ARTS

School of Humanities & Social Sciences, Penn State Erie, 4951 College Dr., Erie PA 16563-1501. (814)898-6281. **Fax:** (814)898-6032. **E-mail:** gol1@psu.edu. **Website:** www.pserie.psu.edu/lakeeffect. **Contact:** George Looney, editor-in-chief. Sample copy for $6. Guidelines online at website.

MAGAZINE'S NEEDS "*Lake Effect* is looking for poems that demonstrate an original voice and that use multilayered, evocative images presented in a language shaped by an awareness of how words sound and mean. Each line should help to carry the poem. There is no length limit per poem, but send no more than four poems at a time. *Lake Effect* seeks poems from both established poets and from new and emerging voices."

◐ LANDFALL/OTAGO UNIVERSITY PRESS

P.O. Box 56, Dunedin , New Zealand. **E-mail:** landfall@otago.ac.nz. **Website:** www.otago.ac.nz/press/landfall. "*Landfall* is published six-monthly. Submissions may be made at any time and will be considered for the next issue. We send acceptance/rejection letters once all submissions have been considered and the issue's contents list has been completely finalised (this is usually the month before or of publication). Submissions will not be held over for future issues unless you have been contacted and agree to this."

MAGAZINE'S NEEDS Submit no more than 10 poems per issue. Submit via e-mail or postal mail with cover letter.

TIPS "*Landfall* is open to work by New Zealand and Pacific writers or by writers whose work has a connection to the region in subject matter or location. Work from Australian writers is occasionally included as a special feature. The editor is interested in new work that has not been published before. While many es-

tablished names appear in *Landfall*'s pages, the editor and *Landfall*'s readers are always on the lookout for exciting work from new writers and artists. If you are a new writer, find copies of *Landfall* in bookshops and libraries to get a sense of what is published."

◑ LANGUAGEANDCULTURE.NET

4000 Pimlico Dr., Suite 114-192, Pleasanton CA 94588. **E-mail:** review@languageandculture.net. **Website:** www.languageandculture.net. **Contact:** Liz Fortini, editor.

MAGAZINE'S NEEDS *Languageandculture.net*, published twice/year online, prints contemporary poetry in English. Also accepts translations of Spanish, French, German, Italian, and Russian; "other languages under review." No restrictions on form. Considers poetry by teens. Publishes 20-40 poems/issue. Submit 3-5 poems at a time. Lines/poem: 70 maximum. Considers previously published poems and simultaneous submissions. Accepts e-mail submissions; no disk submissions. "Return e-mail address must be included." Cover letter is preferred. Include brief bio. Reads submissions "yearly." Time between acceptance and publication "varies; no longer than 6-8 months." Poems are circulated to an editorial board. Rarely comments on rejected poems. No payment. Acquires one-time electronic rights.

◑ LA PETITE ZINE

E-mail: lapetitezine@gmail.com. **Website:** www.lapetitezine.org. **Contact:** Melissa Broder, chief editor; D.W. Lichtenberg, managing editor. Member: CLMP. *La Petite Zine*, an online literary magazine founded in 1999, which currently publishes fierce poetry and petite prose pieces of 1000 words or less. LPZ is not affiliated with a particular literary school or movement; we like what we like. Above all else, LPZ seeks to be unboring, a panacea for your emotional hangover. Has published work by Anne Boyer, Arielle Greenberg, Johannes Goransson, Joyelle McSweeney, Joshua Marie Wilkinson, and Jonah Winter. Receives about 3,000 poems/year, accepts about 150 (5%). Sample: free online; there is no subscription, but readers are invited to sign up for e-mail notification of new issues at the submission address. *La Petite Zine*'s home page "indexes all authors for each specific issue and offers links to past issues, as well as information about the journal, its interests and editors, and links to other sites. Art and graphics are supplied by Web del Sol. Additionally, we publish graphic poems, excerpts from graphic novels, and the like." Acquires one-time rights. Publishes ms 6 months after acceptance. Responds in 2 weeks to 6 months.

🔾 Work published in *La Petite Zine* has appeared in *The Best American Poetry*. "Any deviation from our guidelines will result in the disposal of your submission."

MAGAZINE'S NEEDS Submit up to 5 poems at a time ("please adhere to this guideline"). Considers simultaneous submissions, "but please notify us immediately if poems are accepted elsewhere"; no previously published poems. Only accepts submissions using submission manager on website. Cover letter is required. Include brief bio listing previous publications. Wait four months before submitting again. Reads year round.

◎❸ LEADING EDGE

4087 JKB, Provo UT 84602. **E-mail:** editor@leadingedgemagazine.com; fiction@leadingedgemagazine.com; art@leadingedgemagazine.com. **Website:** www.leadingedgemagazine.com. **Contact:** Nyssa Silvester, senior editor. "We strive to encourage developing and established talent and provide high quality speculative fiction to our readers." Does not accept mss with sex, excessive violence, or profanity. "*Leading Edge* is a magazine dedicated to new and upcoming talent in the field of science fiction and fantasy." Buys first North American serial rights. Pays on publication. Publishes ms an average of 2-4 months after acceptance. Responds in 2-4 months to mss. Single copy: $5.95; subscription: $10 (2 issues), $20 (4 issues), $27.50 (6 issues). Guidelines available online at website.

🔾 Accepts unsolicited submissions.

MAGAZINE'S NEEDS "Publishes 2-4 poems per issue. Poetry should reflect both literary value and popular appeal and should deal with science fiction- or fantasy-related themes." Submit 1 or more poems at a time. No e-mail submissions. Cover letter is preferred. Include name, address, phone number, length of poem, title, and type of poem at the top of each page. Please include SASE with every submission." Pays $10 for first 4 pages; $1.50/each subsequent page.

TIPS "Buy a sample issue to know what is currently selling in our magazine. Also, make sure to follow the writer's guidelines when submitting."

◑ THE LEDGE MAGAZINE

40 Maple Ave., Bellport NY 11713. (631)286-5252. **E-mail:** info@theledgemagazine.com. **Website:** www.theledgemagazine.com. **Contact:** Tim Monaghan, editor-in-chief and publisher. "*The Ledge Magazine* publishes cutting-edge contemporary fiction by emerging and established writers." Annual. Receives 120 mss/month. Accepts 9 mss/issue. Manuscript published 6 months after acceptance. Published Pia Chatterjee, Xujun Eberlein, Clifford Garstang, Richard Jespers, William Luvaas, Michael Thompson. Also publishes poetry. Rarely comments on/critiques rejected mss. Send complete ms with cover letter. Include estimated word count, brief bio. Send SASE (or IRC) for return of ms. Sample copy available for $10. Subscription: $20 (2 issues), $36 (4 issues). Guidelines available for SASE. Writers receive 1 contributor's copy. Additional copies $6. Sends galleys to author. Publication is copyrighted. Acquires first North American serial rights Pays on publication. Responds in 6-8 months.

🔾 Does not accept e-mail submissions.

MAGAZINE'S NEEDS "Excellence is the ultimate criterion." Has published poetry by Philip Dacey, Moira Egan, Tony Gloeggler, Melody Lacina, Rick Lott, and Jennifer Perrine. Submit 3-5 poems with SASE. Pays in contributor's copies.

CONTEST/AWARD OFFERINGS *The Ledge* Poetry Awards Competition and *The Ledge* Poetry Chapbook Contest.

TIPS "We seek compelling stories that employ innovative language and complex characterization. We especially enjoy poignant stories with a sense of purpose. We dislike careless or hackneyed writing."

◑ LEFT CURVE

P.O. Box 472, Oakland CA 94604-0472. (510)763-7193. **E-mail:** editor@leftcurve.org. **Website:** www.leftcurve.org. **Contact:** Csaba Polony, editor. "*Left Curve* is an artist-produced journal addressing the problem(s) of cultural forms emerging from the crises of modernity that strive to be independent from the control of dominant institutions, based on the recognition of the destructiveness of commodity (capitalist) systems to all life." Published irregularly. Rights revert to author. Publishes ms 6-12 months after acceptance. Responds in 6 months to mss and poems. Sometimes comments on rejected mss. Sample copy for $12; back copies $10. Guidelines available for SASE, by e-mail, or on website.

Magazine: 144 pages; 60 lb. paper; 100 pt. C1S gloss layflat lamination cover; illustrations; photos. Receives 50 unsolicited mss/month. Accepts 3-4 mss/issue. Has published work by Mike Standaert, Ilan Pappe, Terrence Cannon, John Gist.

MAGAZINE'S NEEDS Submit up to 5 poems at a time. Accepts e-mail or disk submissions. Cover letter is required. "Explain why you are submitting." Publishes theme issues. Lines/poem: "most of our published poetry is 1 page in length, though we have published longer poems of up to 8 pages." Pays 2-3 contributor's copies.

TIPS "We look for continuity, adequate descriptive passages, endings that are not simply abandoned (in both meanings). Dig deep; no superficial personalisms, no corny satire. Be honest, realistic and gouge out the truth you wish to say. Understand yourself and the world. Have writing be a means to achieve or realize what is real."

LILITH MAGAZINE: INDEPENDENT, JEWISH & FRANKLY FEMINIST

250 W. 57th St., Suite 2432, New York NY 10107. (212)757-0818. **Fax:** (212)757-5705. **E-mail:** info@lilith.org. **Website:** www.lilith.org. **Contact:** Susan Weidman Schneider, editor-in-chief. *Lilith Magazine: Independent, Jewish & Frankly Feminist*, published quarterly, has published poetry by Irena Klepfisz, Lyn Lifshin, Marcia Falk, Adrienne Rich, and Muriel Rukeyser. *Lilith Magazine* is 48 pages, magazine-sized, with glossy color cover. Publishes about 4 poems/year. Press run is about 10,000 (about 6,000 subscribers). Subscription: $26/year. Sample: $7. Responds in 3 months. Guidelines online.

MAGAZINE'S NEEDS Send up to 3 poems at a time. No simultaneous submissions or e-mail submissions. "Please put name and contact info on each sheet submitted. Copy should be neatly typed and proofread for typos and spelling errors." Uses poetry by Jewish women "about the Jewish woman's experience." Does not want poetry on other subjects.

TIPS "Read a copy of the publication before you submit your work. Please be patient."

LINEBREAK

333 Kimpel Hall, University of Arkansas, Fayetteville AR 72701. **E-mail:** editors@linebreak.org. **Website:** http://linebreak.org. **Contact:** Johnathon Williams, founding editor; Ash Bowen. "*Linebreak* is a weekly online magazine of original poetry. Each poem we publish is read and recorded by another working poet selected by the editors." Has published Dorianne Laux, Bob Hicok, D.A. Powell, C. Dale Young, Richard Siken, Sandra Beasley. Publishes ms 4 months after acceptance. Responds in 6 weeks. Guidelines available on website.

Poems published on *Linebreak* have been selected for the Best New Poets anthology and nominated for the Pushcart Prize.

MAGAZINE'S NEEDS Submit up to 5 poems at a time through upload form on website. Considers simultaneous submissions. Reads submissions year round. Poems are circulated to an editorial board. Sometimes comments on rejected poems. Guidelines available on website. Sometimes sends prepublication galleys. Acquires electronic rights: "We require the rights to publish and archive the work indefinitely on our website, and the right to create an audio recording of each poem, which is also archived indefinitely. Copyright remains with the author."

LIPS

7002 Blvd. East, #2-26G, Guttenberg NJ 07093. (201)662-1303. **E-mail:** LBoss79270@aol.com. **Contact:** Laura Boss, poetry editor. *Lips*, published twice/year, takes pleasure "in publishing previously unpublished poets as well as the most established voices in contemporary poetry. We look for quality work: the strongest work of a poet; work that moves the reader; poems that take risks that work. We prefer clarity in the work rather than the abstract. Poems longer than 6 pages present a space problem." Acquires first rights. Responds in 1 month (but has gotten backlogged at times). Sometimes sends prepublication galleys. Sample: $10, plus $2.50 for postage. Guidelines available for SASE.

Lips is about 150 pages, digest-sized, flat-spined. Has published poetry by Robert Bly, Allen Ginsberg, Michael Benedikt, Maria Gillan, Ruth Stone, Maria Mazziotti Gillan, Stanley Barkan, Lyn Lifshin, and Ishmael Reed.

MAGAZINE'S NEEDS Submit 6 pages maximum at a time. Poems should be typed. Reads submissions September-March only. Receives about 16,000 submissions/year, accepts about 1%. Pays 1 contributor's copy.

LISSETTE'S TALES OF THE IMAGINATION

Lissette's Publishing LLC., P.O. Box 144, Danville IN 46112. **E-mail:** lissette@lissettespublishing.com. **Website:** www.lissettespublishing.com. **Contact:** Kristin Roahrig, editor. "*Lissette* is dedicated to presenting the finest works of historical fiction with a twist, be it fantasy, horror, science fiction, or any other genre we haven't mentioned. We are not interested in world creation or invented cultures, but established mythologies and legendary realms (Olympus, Asgard, Camelot, etc.) are welcomed."

MAGAZINE'S NEEDS "Our interest in poetry is limited, but we hope to include at least one poem per issue. Atmosphere is paramount, and we would prefer something that tells a story, even in a few short stanzas. For these reasons, haiku is not a good fit for *Lissette's*." Pays $4/poem.

LITERAL LATTE

200 E. 10th St., Suite 240, New York NY 10003. (212)260-5532. **E-mail:** litlatte@aol.com. **Website:** www.literal-latte.com. **Contact:** Jenine Gordon Bockman. Bimonthly online publication with an annual print anthology featuring the best of the website. "We want great writing in all styles and subjects. A feast is made of a variety of flavors." Buys first rights and requests permission for use in anthology. Responds in 6 months to mss. Editorial lead time 3 months. Writer's guidelines online, via e-mail, or for #10 SASE

MAGAZINE'S NEEDS "We want any poem that captures the magic of the form." Length: no more than 4,000 words.

ADDITIONAL INFORMATION "We will publish an anthology in book form at the end of each year, featuring the best of our Web magazine."

TIPS "Keeping free thought free and challenging entertainment are not mutually exclusive. Words make a manuscript stand out, words beautifully woven together in striking and memorable patterns."

LITERARY JUICE

Mishawaka IN 46545. **E-mail:** info@literaryjuice.com. **E-mail:** srajan@literaryjuice.com. **Website:** www.literaryjuice.com. **Contact:** Sara Rajan, editor-in-chief; Andrea O'Connor and Dinesh Rajan, managing editors. Bimonthly online literary magazine. "*Literary Juice* publishes original works of short fiction, flash fiction, and poetry. We do not publish nonfiction material, essays, or interviews, nor do we accept previously published works." Acquires electronic rights.

Responds in 1-3 months to mss. Guidelines available on website.

MAGAZINE'S NEEDS Length: 2-20 lines.

TIPS "It is crucial that writers read our submission guidelines, which can be found on our website. Most importantly, send us your very best writing. We are looking for works that are not only thought-provoking, but venture into unconventional territory as well. For instance, avoid sending mainstream stories and poems (stories about wizards or vampires fall into this category). Instead, take the reader to a new realm that has yet to be explored."

LITERARY MAMA

E-mail: lminfo@literarymama.com. **Website:** www.literarymama.com. **Contact:** Caroline M. Grant, editor-in-chief. Departments include columns, creative nonfiction, fiction, Literary Reflections, poetry, Profiles & Reviews. We are interested in reading pieces that are long, complex, ambiguous, deep, raw, irreverent, ironic, body conscious. Responds in 3 weeks to 3 months to mss. "We correspond via e-mail only." Guidelines available at www.literarymama.com/submissions.

TIPS "We seek top-notch creative writing. We also look for quality literary criticism about mother-centric literature and profiles of mother writers. We publish writing with fresh voices, superior craft, vivid imagery. Please send submission (copied into e-mail) to appropriate departmental editors. Include a brief cover letter. We tend to like stark revelation (pathos, humor, and joy), clarity, concrete details, strong narrative development; ambiguity, thoughtfulness, delicacy, irreverence, lyricism, sincerity; the elegant. We need the submissions 3 months before the following months: October (Desiring Motherhood); May (Mother's Day Month); and June (Father's Day Month)."

THE LITERARY REVIEW: AN INTERNATIONAL JOURNAL OF CONTEMPORARY WRITING

Fairleigh Dickinson University, 285 Madison Ave., Madison NJ 07940. (973)443-8564. **Fax:** (973)443-8364. **E-mail:** info@theliteraryreview.org. **Website:** www.theliteraryreview.org. **Contact:** Minna Proctor, editor. *The Literary Review*, published quarterly, seeks "work by new and established poets that reflects a sensitivity to literary standards and the poetic form." No specifications as to form, length, style, subject matter, or purpose. Acquires first rights. Responds in 6-9 months.

○ *TLR Online*, available on the website, features original work not published in the print edition. *The Literary Review* is about 200 pages, digest-sized, professionally printed, flat-spined, with glossy color cover. Receives about 1,200 submissions/year, accepts 100-150. Press run is 2,000 (800 subscribers, one-third are overseas). Sample: $8 domestic, $8 + $3.99 shipping outside U.S.; request a "general issue." Has published poetry by Albert Goldbarth, Mary Jo Bang, David Citino, Rick Mulkey, Virgil Suárez and Gary Fincke.

MAGAZINE'S NEEDS Submit up to 5 typed poems at a time. Accepts only online submissions at www.theliteraryreview.org/submit.html. No mail, fax, or e-mail submissions. Considers simultaneous submissions. **Read-time September 1 through May 31.** Publishes theme issues. Reviews books of poetry in 500 words, single-book format. Send materials for review consideration. Pays 2 contributor's copies plus 1 year free subscription.

LITTLE PATUXENT REVIEW

6012 Jamina Downs, Columbia MD 21045. (443)255-5740. **E-mail:** editor@littlepatuxentreview.org. **Website:** www.littlepatuxentreview.org. **Contact:** Laura Shovan, editor. "*The Little Patuxent Review (LPR)* is a biannual print journal devoted to literature and the arts. We are a community-based publication with a focus on poets, writers and artists, primarily from the Mid-Atlantic region. We profile the work of a major poet or fiction writer in each issue. We celebrate the launch of each issue with a series of readings. Highlights are broadcast on *LPR*'s YouTube channel." Buys first rights. Responds in 3-5 months to mss. Sample copy $10 . Make checks payable to *Little Patuxent Review*. Guidelines available in magazine and on website.

○ *LPR* is about 120 pages, digest-sized, 100# Finch Cover/Artwork (varies depending on featured artist). Has published poetry by Lucille Clifton, Martín Espada, Donald Hall, Joy Harjo, Clarinda Harriss, Alan King. 2011 Pushcart Prize for "Patronized" by Tara Hart.

MAGAZINE'S NEEDS Submit up to 3 poems via online submission manager. "Poetry and prose must be typed using a standard, legible font (i.e, the equivalent of 12-point Times New Roman) with flush-left margins and submitted as a .doc, .docx, .pdf, .rtf, or .txt electronic file. Please include a biographical note of 60-75 words in cover letter. Let us know if you now live or have lived in the Mid-Atlantic area. We prefer submissions through the Submittable website via www.littlepatuxentreview.org/submissions." Unsolicited submissions cannot be previously published elsewhere. Does not accept multiple submissions. Submission period for the winter 2014 issue is August 1-November 1, 2013. Submission period for summer 2014 is December 1, 2013-March 1, 2014. No more than 100 lines/poem. Pays 1 contributor's copy.

ALSO OFFERS "*LPR* co-sponsors monthly arts Salon events in conjunction with the Columbia Art Center featuring literary readings, art presentations, and musical performances. Events are free and open to the public. Contributors are invited to participate in reading series and literary festivals, such as the Baltimore Book Festival. As part of our outreach effort, the *LPR* in the Classroom Program provides *LPR* issues to high schools and colleges at a discounted rate."

TIPS "Please see our website for the current theme. Poetry and prose must exhibit the highest quality to be considered. Please read a sample issue before submitting, or visit the 'Concerning Craft' section of *Little Patuxent Review*'s website."

⚫○ LIVING POETS MAGAZINE

Dragonheart Press, 11 Menin Rd., Allestree, Derby DE22 2NL, England. **Website:** www.dragonheartpress.com. *Living Poets Magazine*, published irregularly online, provides a showcase for poetry. Wants "crafted poetry with strong imagery." Does not want "constrained rhyming structures." Publishes ms 1-2 months after acceptance. Responds in 3 months.

MAGAZINE'S NEEDS Considers previously published poems and simultaneous submissions. Prefers e-mail submissions. Cover letter is preferred. Include bio and publication credits. Often comments on rejected poems. Publishes theme issues. Reviews books/chapbooks of poetry or other magazines in single-book format. Send materials for review consideration to Review Editor, Dragonheart Press. Length: no more than 40 lines. Pays 1 contributor's copy.

CONTEST/AWARD OFFERINGS Sponsors Dragonheart Press Annual Poetry Competition. **Deadline:** December 31. Guidelines available for SASE (or SAE and IRC) or by e-mail (competition@dragonheartpress.com).

🌐💲 THE LONDON MAGAZINE

11 Queen's Gate, London En SW7 5ELU, UK. +44 (0)20 7584 5977. **E-mail:** admin@thelondonmagazine.org. **Website:** www.thelondonmagazine.org. Buys first rights. Pays on publication. Published ms an average of 4 months after acceptance. Responds in 1 month to queries. Responds in 3 months to mss. Editorial lead time 3 months. Sample copy for £7.50. Guidelines available online.

MAGAZINE'S NEEDS "Abstraction is the enemy of good poetry. Poetry should display a commitment to the ultra specificities of language, and show a refined sense of simile and metaphor. The structure should be tight and exact." Submit via e-mail, both as an attachment and in the body of the e-mail. Enclose SASE if submitting through postal mail. "We do not publish long, loose poems." Length: no longer than 40 lines. Pays minimum £15; maximum rate is negotiable.

TIPS "We look for poetry and short fiction that startles and entertains us. We are obviously interested in writing that has a London focus, but not exclusively so, since London is a world city with international concerns. Reviews, essays, memoir pieces and features should be erudite, lucid and incisive. Please look at *The London Magazine* before you submit work, so that you can see the type of material we publish."

🌐 LONE STARS MAGAZINE

4219 Flint Hill St., San Antonio TX 78230-1619. **E-mail:** lonestarsmagazine@yahoo.com. **Website:** www.lonestarsmagazine.net. **Contact:** Milo Rosebud, Editor/Publisher. *Lone Stars*, published 3 times/year, features contemporary poetry. Wants poetry "that holds a continuous line of thought." Does not want profanity. Considers poetry by children and teens. Acquires one-time publication rights. Authors retain all rights. Time between acceptance and publication is 3-6 months. Responds within 3 months. Guidelines available for SASE.

💿 *Lone Stars* is 25+ pages, magazine-sized, photocopied, saddle-stapled, bound with tape. Press run is 200. Single copy: $6; subscription: $20 for 4 issues. Sample: $5.50 past issues. Has published poetry by Terry Lee, Eve J. Blohm, Linda Amos, and many more.

MAGAZINE'S NEEDS Submit 3-5 poems at a time. Considers previously published poems and simultaneous submissions. Cover letter is preferred. Submit poems on any subject, formatted and "typed the way you want them in print." **Charges reading fee of $1 per poem**.

CONTEST/AWARD OFFERINGS Sponsors Annual Songbook Lyric Poetry Contest. Annual Light of the Stars Poetry Contest. Details available for SASE.

TIPS "Submit poetry that expresses a reasonable train of thought."

LONG LIFE

Longevity through technology, The Immortalist Society, 1437 Pineapple Ave., Melbourne FL 32935. **E-mail:** 1cryoguy@gmail.com. **Website:** www.cryonics.org/immortalist/index.htm. **Contact:** John Bull, Editor. "*Long Life* magazine is a publication for people who are particularly interested in cryonic suspension: the theory, practice, legal problems, etc. associated with being frozen when you die in the hope of eventual restoration to life and health. Many people who receive the publication have relatives who have undergone cryonic preparation or have made such arrangements for themselves or are seriously considering this option. Readers are also interested in other aspects of life extension such as anti-aging research and food supplements that may slow aging. Articles we publish include speculation on what the future will be like; problems of living in a future world and science in general, particularly as it may apply to cryonics and life extension." Copyrighted. Responds in 1 month to queries and mss. Sample copy is free for SASE.

MAGAZINE'S NEEDS "Poems are welcomed, especially short, humorous poems with a cryonics or life extension theme." Pays with contributor's copy.

TIPS "We are a small magazine but with a highly intelligent and educated readership which is socially and economically diverse. We currently don't pay for material, but are seeking new authors and provide contributors with copies of the magazine with the contributor's published works. Look over a copy of *Long Life*, or talk with the editor to get the tone of the publication. There is an excellent chance that your ms will be accepted if it is well written and 'on theme.' Pictures to accompany the article are always welcome, and we like to publish photos of the authors with their first ms."

🌐 LONG STORY SHORT, AN E-ZINE FOR WRITERS

P.O. Box 475, Lewistown MT 59457. **E-mail:** dencassino@gmail.com. **Website:** www.alongstoryshort.net. **Contact:** Denise Cassino; Linda Barnett-Johnson, editors; Marie Delgado Travis, poetry editor. *Long Story Short, An E-zine for Writers*, published monthly online, is "eclectic—open to all forms and styles" of poetry. Does not want "profanity; overly explicit sex." Considers poetry by children (ages 10 and up) and teens. Has published poetry by Michael Lee Johnson, Maria Ercilla, Shonda Buchanan, Patricia Wellingham-Jones, Floriana Hall, and Russell Bittner. Time between acceptance and publication is up to 6 months, depending on theme. Guidelines available on website. "Read them!"

Free newsletter with poetry of the month chosen by poetry editor; includes author's bio and Web page listed in the e-zine. Also provides resource page on website. Offers light critique of submissions upon request, and a free writing forum.

MAGAZINE'S NEEDS Submit up to 3 poems at a time. Short, concise poems are preferred. Considers previously published poems and simultaneous submissions. Accepts e-mail submissions only ("paste poems in the body of your e-mail; no attachments will be opened"). Include a brief bio and permission to use e-mail address for reader contact. Reads submissions year round. "Poems are reviewed and chosen by the poetry editor." Often comments on rejected poems. All rights reserved by author.

● LOS

150 N. Catalina St., No. 2, Los Angeles CA 90004. **E-mail:** lospoesy@earthlink.net. **Website:** http://home.earthlink.net/~lospoesy. *Los*, published 4 times/year, features poetry. Has published poetry by John P. Campbell, Mark Cunningham, Jean Esteve, George J. Farrah, Bill Knott, Paul Lowe, and Charles Wuest. *Los* is digest-sized and saddle-stapled. Press run is 100. Publishes ms 1 month after acceptance. Responds in 3 months. Guidelines available online.

MAGAZINE'S NEEDS Accepts e-mail submissions (pasted into body of message or as attachment).

① LOUISIANA LITERATURE

SLU Box 10792, Southeastern Louisiana University, Hammond LA 70402. **E-mail:** lalit@selu.edu. **Website:** www.louisianaliterature.org. **Contact:** Jack B. Bedell, editor. Semiannual. "Essays should be about Louisiana material; preference is given to fiction and poetry with Louisiana and Southern themes, but creative work can be set anywhere." Acquires one-time rights. Responds in 3 months to mss. Sometimes com-

ments on rejected mss. Sample copy for $8. Guidelines available for SASE or on website.

Magazine: 6×9; 150 pages; 70 lb. paper; card cover; illustrations. Receives 100 unsolicited mss/month. May not read mss June-July. Publishes ms 6-12 after acceptance. Publishes 4 new writers/year. Publishes theme issues. Has published work by Anthony Bukowski, Aaron Gwyn, Robert Phillips, R.T. Smith.

MAGAZINE'S NEEDS Submit 3-5 poems at a time. No simultaneous submissions. No fax or e-mail submissions. "Send cover letter, including bio, to use in the event of acceptance. Enclose SASE and specify whether work is to be returned or discarded." Reads submissions year round, "although we work more slowly in summer." Sometimes sends prepublication galleys. Send materials for review consideration; include cover letter." Pays 2 contributor's copies.

TIPS "Cut out everything that is not a functioning part of the story. Make sure your ms is professionally presented. Use relevant specific detail in every scene. We love detail, local color, voice and craft. Any professional manuscript stands out."

● THE LOUISIANA REVIEW

Division of Liberal Arts, Louisiana State University Eunice, P.O. Box 1129, Eunice LA 70535. (337)550-1315. **E-mail:** bfonteno@lsue.edu. **Website:** web.lsue.edu/la-review. Dr. Michael Alleman, poetry editor; Dr. Diane Langlois, art editor. **Contact:** Dr. Billy Fontenot, fiction editor. *The Louisiana Review*, published annually during the fall or spring semester, offers "Louisiana poets, writers, and artists a place to showcase their most beautiful pieces. Others may submit Louisiana- or Southern-related poetry, stories, and b&w art, as well as interviews with Louisiana writers. We want to publish the highest-quality poetry, fiction, and art." Wants "strong imagery, metaphor, and evidence of craft." Pays on publication for one-time rights. Not copyrighted, but has an ISSN number. Publishes ms 6-12 months after acceptance. Responds in 5 weeks to queries; 10 weeks to mss. Sometimes comments on rejected mss.

The Louisiana Review is 100 pages, digest-sized, professionally printed, perfect-bound. Receives up to 2,000 poems/year, accepts 30-50. Press run is 300-600. Single copy: $5

MAGAZINE'S NEEDS Submit up to 5 poems at a time. No previously published poems. No fax or e-mail submissions. "Include cover letter indicating your association with Louisiana, if any. Name and address. Poets retain all rights. Has published poetry by Gary Snyder, Antler, David Cope, and Catfish McDaris. Does not want "sing-song rhymes, abstract, religious, or overly sentimental work." Pays 1 contributor's copy.

TIPS "We do like to have fiction play out visually as a film would rather than static and undramatized. Louisiana or Gulf Coast settings and themes preferred."

ⓞ THE LOUISVILLE REVIEW

Spalding University, 851 S. Fourth St., Louisville KY 40203. (502)585-9911, ext. 2777. **Fax:** (502)992-2409. **E-mail:** louisvillereview@spalding.edu. **Website:** www.louisvillereview.org. **Contact:** Kathleen Driskell, associate editor. *The Louisville Review*, published twice/year, prints all kinds of poetry. Has a section devoted to poetry by children and teens (grades K-12) called The Children's Corner. Has published poetry by Wendy Bishop, Gary Fincke, Michael Burkard, and Sandra Kohler. *The Louisville Review* is 150 pages, digest-sized, flat-spined. Receives about 700 submissions/year, accepts about 10%. Single copy: $8; subscription: $14/year, $27/2 years, $40/3 years (foreign subscribers add $6/year for s&h). Sample: $5.

MAGAZINE'S NEEDS Considers simultaneous submissions; no previously published poems. Accepts submissions via online manager; please see website for more information. "Poetry by children must include permission of parent to publish if accepted. Address those submissions to The Children's Corner." Reads submissions year round. Pays in contributor's copies.

LULLWATER REVIEW

Emory University, P.O. Box 122036, Atlanta GA 30322. **E-mail:** lullwater@lullwaterreview.com. **Website:** www.lullwaterreview.com. **Contact:** Laura Kochman, editor-in-chief; Tonia Davis, managing editor. "We're a small, student-run literary magazine published out of Emory University in Atlanta, GA with two issues yearly—once in the fall and once in the spring. You can find us in the *Index of American Periodical Verse*, the *American Humanities Index* and as a member of the Council of Literary Magazines and Presses. We welcome work that brings a fresh perspective, whether through language or the visual arts." Buys first North American serial rights. Pays on publication. Publishes ms an average of 1-2 months after acceptance. Responds in 1-3 months to queries;

3-6 months to mss. Sample copy for $5. Guidelines with #10 SASE.

MAGAZINE'S NEEDS *Lullwater Review*, published in May and December, prints poetry, short fiction, and artwork. Wants poetry of any genre with strong imagery, original voice, on any subject. Has published poetry by Amy Greenfield, Peter Serchuk, Katherine McCord, and Ha Jin. Submit 6 or fewer poems at a time. Considers simultaneous submissions; no previously published poems. Cover letter is preferred. Prefers poems single-spaced with name and contact info on each page. "Poems longer than 1 page should include page numbers. We must have a SASE with which to reply." Reads submissions September 1-May 15 only. Poems are circulated to an editorial board. Seldom comments on rejected poems. No profanity or pornographic material. Pays 3 contributor's copies.

TIPS "We at the *Lullwater Review* look for clear cogent writing, strong character development and an engaging approach to the story in our fiction submissions. Stories with particularly strong voices and well-developed central themes are especially encouraged. Be sure that your manuscript is ready before mailing it off to us. Revise, revise, revise! Be original, honest, and of course, keep trying."

ⓞ LUNGFULL!MAGAZINE

316 23rd St., Brooklyn NY 11215. **E-mail:** customerservice@lungfull.org. **E-mail:** lungfull@rcn.com. **Website:** http://lungfull.org. **Contact:** Brendan Lorber, editor/publisher.

○ *LUNGFULL!* was the recipient of a grant from the New York State Council for the Arts. Prefers postal mail submissions.

MAGAZINE'S NEEDS Submit by postal mail. Include SASE. If sending by e-mail (not preferred) do NOT send attachments. Submit up to 6 poems or 10 pages of prose. Include cover letter.

ⓞ THE LUTHERAN DIGEST

The Lutheran Digest, Inc., 6160 Carmen Ave. E, Inver Grove Heights MN 55076. (952)933-2820. **Fax:** (952)933-5708. **E-mail:** editor@lutherandigest.com. **Website:** www.lutherandigest.com. **Contact:** Nicholas A. Skapyak, editor. "Articles frequently reflect a Lutheran Christian perspective, but are not intended to be sermonettes. Popular stories show how God has intervened in a person's life to help solve a problem." Buys first rights, buys second serial (reprint) rights. Pays on publication. Publishes ms an average of 6 months after acceptance. Responds in 1 month to queries. Responds in 4 months to mss. No response to e-mailed mss unless selected for publication. Editorial lead time 9 months. Sample copy for $3.50. Guidelines available online.

○ *The Lutheran Digest* is 64 pages, digest-sized, offset-printed, saddle-stapled, with 4-color paper cover, includes local ads. Receives about 200 poems/year, accepts 10-20%. Press run is 60,000-65,000; most distributed free to Lutheran churches. Subscription: $16/year, $22/2 years.

MAGAZINE'S NEEDS Submit 3 poems at a time. Lines/poem: 25 maximum. Considers previously published poems and simultaneous submissions. Accepts fax and e-mail (as attachment) submissions. Cover letter is preferred. "Include SASE if return is desired." Time between acceptance and publication is up to 9 months. "Poems are selected by editor and reviewed by publication panel." Guidelines available for SASE or on website. Responds in 3 months. Pays credit and 1 contributor's copy. Acquires one-time rights.

TIPS "Reading our writers' guidelines and sample articles online is encouraged and is the best way to get a 'feel' of the type of material we publish."

◑ THE LYRIC

P.O. Box 110, Jericho Corners VT 05465. **E-mail:** themuse@thelyricmagazine.com. **Website:** www.thelyricmagazine.com. *The Lyric*, published quarterly, is "the oldest magazine in North America in continuous publication devoted to traditional poetry." Prints about 55 poems/issue. Seeks "rhymed verse in traditional forms, for the most part, with an occasional piece of blank or free verse; no translations, please. Most of our poems are accessible on first or second reading. Frost wrote: 'Don't hide too far away.'" Responds in 3 months to poems ("average; inquire after 6 months"). Sample for $5, available in Europe through the Rom office for 18 euros/year sent to Nancy Mellichamp-Savo, via Lola Montez, #14, Rome, Italy 00135; sample: 5 euros. Guidelines available for SASE or by e-mail.

○ *The Lyric* is 32 pages, digest-sized, professionally printed with varied typography, with matte card cover. Receives about 3,000 submissions/year, accepts 5%. Subscription: $15/year, $28/2 years, $38/3 years (U.S.), $17/year for Canada and other countries (in U.S. funds

only). Has published poetry by Michael Burch, Gail White, Constance Rowell Mastores, Ruth Harrison, Barbara Loots, and Glenna Holloway.

MAGAZINE'S NEEDS Submit up to 6 poems at a time by postal service; out of country poems may be submitted by e-mail. Considers simultaneous submissions (although "not preferred"); no previously published poems. Cover letter is "often helpful, but not required. Subscription will not affect publication of submitted poetry." "Our themes are varied, ranging from religious ecstasy to humor to raw grief, but we feel no compulsion to shock, embitter, or confound our readers. We also avoid poems about contemporary political or social problems—'grief but not grievances,' as Frost put it. Frost is helpful in other ways: If yours is more than a lover's quarrel with life, we are not your best market. And most of our poems are accessible on first or second reading." Lines/poem: 40 maximum. Pays 1 contributor's copy

TIPS All contributors are eligible for quarterly and annual prizes totaling $650. Also offers *The Lyric* College Contest, open to undergraduate students in the US. Awards prize of $500; 2nd Place: $100. **Deadline:** December 15. Send entries by e-mail: tanycim@aol.com, or to Tanya Cimonetti, 1393 Spear St., S, Burlington, VT 05403."Our *raison d'etre* has been the encouragement of form, music, rhyme, and accessibility in poetry. As we witness the growing tide of appreciation for traditional/lyric poetry, we are proud to have stayed the course for 91 years, helping keep the roots of poetry alive."

⊕●⑤ LYRICAL PASSION POETRY E-ZINE

P.O. Box 17331, Arlington VA 22216. **Website:** http://lyricalpassionpoetry.yolasite.com. **Contact:** Raquel D. Bailey, founding editor. Founded by award-winning poet Raquel D. Bailey, Lyrical Passion Poetry E-Zine is an attractive monthly online literary magazine specializing in Japanese short form poetry. Publishes quality artwork, well-crafted short fiction and poetry in English by emerging and established writers. Literature of lasting literary value will be considered. Welcomes the traditional to the experimental. Poetry works written in German will be considered if accompanied by translations. Offers annual short fiction and poetry contests. Acquires first-time rights, electronic rights (must be the first literary venue to publish online or in any electronic format). Rights revert to poets upon publication. Publishes ms 1 month after acceptance. Responds in 2 months. Guidelines and upcoming themes available on website.

MAGAZINE'S NEEDS Multiple submissions are permitted, but no more than 3 submissions in a 6-month period. Submissions from minors should be accompanied by a cover letter from parent with written consent for their child's submission to be published on the website with their child's first initial and last name accompanied by their age at the time of submission. Does not want: dark, cliché, limerick, erotica, extremely explicit, violent, or depressing literature. Free verse poetry length: between 1 and 40/lines.

◐ THE MACGUFFIN

18600 Haggerty Rd., Livonia MI 48152. (734)462-4400, ext 5327. **E-mail:** macguffin@schoolcraft.edu. **Website:** www.macguffin.org. **Contact:** Steven A. Dolgin, editor; Nicholle Cormier, managing editor; Elizabeth Kircos, fiction editor. "Our purpose is to encourage, support and enhance the literary arts in the Schoolcraft College community, the region, the state, and the nation. We also sponsor annual literary events and give voice to deserving new writers as well as established writers." Acquires first rights. Once published, rights revert back to author. Responds in 2-4 months to mss. Guidelines available online.

MAGAZINE'S NEEDS Poetry should be typed, single-spaced, only one poem per page. There are no subject biases. Length: no more than 400 lines.

CONTEST/AWARD OFFERINGS "Also sponsors the National Poet Hunt Contest. See contest rules online. For mail submissions: do not staple work. Include name, e-mail, address, and the page no. on each page. Include SASE for reply only. Submit each work (single story or five-poem submission) as a Word .doc attachment."

TIPS "We strive to give promising new writers the opportunity to publish alongside recognized writers. Follow the submission guidelines, proofread your work, and be persistent. When we reject a story, we may accept the next one you send. When we make suggestions for a rewrite, we may accept the revision. Make your characters come to life. Even the most ordinary people become fascinating if they live for your readers."

◐ THE MADISON REVIEW

University of Wisconsin, 600 N, Park St., 6193 Helen C. White Hall, Madison WI 53706. **E-mail:** madison-review@gmail.com. **Website:** www.english.wisc.edu/madisonreview/madisonReviewHome.htm. **Contact:** Joe Malone and Anna Wehrwein, fiction editors; Joyce Edwards, poetry editor. *The Madison Review* is a student-run literary magazine that looks to publish the best available fiction and poetry. Buys one-time rights. Publishes ms an average of 9 months after acceptance. Responds in 4 weeks to queries. Responds in 6 months to mss. Editorial lead time 6 months. Sample copy for $3. Guidelines free.

◯ Does not publish unsolicited interviews or genre ficion.

MAGAZINE'S NEEDS Submit up to 5 poems at a time. No simultaneous submissions. No e-mail submissions. Cover letter is preferred. Include SASE. Submissions must be typed. Does not want "religious or patriotic dogma and light verse." Pays 2 contributor's copies.

TIPS "Our editors have very ecclectic tastes, so don't specifically try to cater to us. Above all, we look for original, high-quality work."

◐◉⑨ THE MAGAZINE OF FANTASY & SCIENCE FICTION

P.O. Box 3447, Hoboken NJ 07030. (201) 876-2551. **E-mail:** fandsf@aol.com. **Website:** www.fandsf.com. **Contact:** Gordon Van Gelder, editor. "*The Magazine of Fantasy and Science Fiction* publishes various types of science fiction and fantasy short stories and novellas, making up about 80% of each issue. The balance of each issue is devoted to articles about science fiction, a science column, book and film reviews, cartoons, and competitions." Bimonthly. Buys first North American serial rights, buys foreign serial rights. Pays on acceptance. Publishes ms an average of 9-12 months after acceptance. Responds in 2 months to queries. Sample copy for $6. Guidelines for SASE, by e-mail or website.

◯ The *Magazine of Fantasy and Science Fiction* won a Nebula Award for Best Novelet for *What We Found*, by Geoff Ryman in 2012. Also won the 2012 World Fantasy Award for Best Short Story for *The Paper Menagerie*, by Ken Liu. Editor Van Gelder won the Hugo Award for Best Editor (short form), 2007 and 2008.

MAGAZINE'S NEEDS *The Magazine of Fantasy & Science Fiction*, published bimonthy, is "one of the longest-running magazines devoted to the literature of the fantastic." Wants only poetry that deals with the fantastic or the science-fictional. Has published poetry by Rebecca Kavaler, Elizabeth Bear, Sophie M. White, and Robert Frazier. "I buy poems very infrequently—just when one hits me right." Pays $50/poem and 2 contributor's copies. Acquires first North American serial rights.

TIPS "Good storytelling makes a submission stand out. Regarding manuscripts, a well-prepared manuscript (i.e., one that follows the traditional format, like that describted here: www.sfwa.org/writing/vonda/vonda.htm) stands out more than any gimmicks. Read an issue of the magazine before submitting. New writers should keep their submissions under 15,000 words—we rarely publish novellas by new writers."

MAGMA POETRY

23 Pine Walk, Carshalton Surrey SM5 4ES, United Kingdom. **E-mail:** contributions@magmapoetry.com. **Website:** www.magmapoetry.com. info@magmapoetry.com for general questions. *Magma* appears 3 times/year and contains "modern poetry, reviews and interviews with poets." Wants poetry that is "modern in idiom and shortish (2 pages maximum). Nothing sentimental or old fashioned." Has published poetry by Thomas Lynch, Thom Gunn, Michael Donaghy, John Burnside, Vicki Feaver, and Roddy Lumsden. *Magma* is 64 pages, 8×8, photocopied and stapled, includes b&w illustrations. Receives about 3,000 poems/year, accepts 4-5%. Press run is about 500. Single copy: £5.70 UK and Ireland, £6.15 rest of Europe, £7.50 airmail ROW. Subscription: £14.50 UK and Ireland, £18 rest of Europe, £20.50 airmail ROW. Make checks payable to *Magma*. For subscriptions, contact Helen Nicholson, distribution secretary, Flat 2, 86 St. James's Dr., London SW17 7RR England.

Only accepts contributions from the UK.

MAGAZINE'S NEEDS Submit up to 6 poems at a time. Accepts submissions by post (with SAE and IRCs). Cover letter is preferred. Deadlines for submissions: end of February, mid-July, end of October. "Poems are considered for one issue only. Each issue has an editor who submits his/her selections to a board for final approval. Editor's selection very rarely changed." Occasionally publishes theme issues. Pays 1 contributor's copy.

ALSO OFFERS "We hold a public reading in London three times/year, to coincide with each new issue, and poets in the issue are invited to read."

TIPS "See 'About Magma' and the contents of our website to gain an idea of the type of work we accept." Keep up with the latest news and comment from *Magma Poetry* by receiving free updates via e-mail. Sign up online to receive the Magma Blog and/or the *Magma* newsletter.

THE MAGNOLIA QUARTERLY

P.O. Box 10294, Gulfport MS 39505. **E-mail:** writerpllevin@gmail.com. **Website:** www.gcwriters.org. **Contact:** Phil Levin, editor. *The Magnolia Quarterly* publishes poetry, fiction, nonfiction, and reviews. **For members of GCWA only.** Returns rights to author upon publication. Time between acceptance and publication varies. Guidelines available in magazine or on website.

The Magnolia Quarterly is 40 pages, pocket-sized, stapled, with glossy cover, includes ads. Single copy: $3; subscription: included in $30 GCWA annual dues. Make checks payable to Gulf Coast Writers Assocation. Editing service offered on all prose. Has published poetry by Leonard Cirino, Catharine Savage Brosman, Angela Ball, Jack Bedell, and Larry Johnson.

MAGAZINE'S NEEDS Submit 1-3 poems at a time. Considers previously published poems and simultaneous submissions. Prefers e-mail submissions. Reads submissions year round. Will consider all styles of poetry. Does not want "pornography, racial or sexist bigotry, far-left or far-right political poems." Lines/poem: 40 lines maximum. No payment.

CONTEST/AWARD OFFERINGS "Let's Write" contest, with cash prizes for poetry and prose. Additional information available on website.

ALSO OFFERS The Gulf Coast Writers Association, "a nationally recognized organization dedicated to encouraging all writers."

THE MAIN STREET RAG

P.O. Box 690100, Charlotte NC 28227-7001. (704)573-2516. **E-mail:** editor@mainstreetrag.com. **Website:** www.mainstreetrag.com. **Contact:** M. Scott Douglass, editor/publisher. *The Main Street Rag*, published quarterly, prints "poetry, short fiction, essays, interviews, reviews, photos, art. We like publishing good material from people who are interested in more than notching another publishing credit, people who support small independent publishers like ourselves." Will consider "almost anything," but prefers "writing with an edge—either gritty or bitingly humorous. Contributors are advised to visit our website prior to submission to confirm current needs." Acquires first North American print rights. Time between acceptance and publication is up to 1 year. Responds within 6 weeks. Guidelines available for SASE, by e-mail, or on website.

○ *The Main Street Rag* is about 130 pages, digest-sized, perfect-bound, with 12-point laminated color cover. Receives about 5,000 submissions/year; publishes 50+ poems and 3-5 short stories per issue, a featured interview, photos, and an occasional nonfiction piece. Press run is about 500 (250 subscribers, 15 libraries). Single copy: $8; subscription: $24/year, $45 for 2 years.

MAGAZINE'S NEEDS Submit 6 pages of poetry at a time; no more than 1 poem per page. No previously published poems or simultaneous submissions. Cover letter is preferred. "No bios or credits—let the work speak for itself." Pays 1 contributor's copy.

THE MALAHAT REVIEW

The University of Victoria, P.O. Box 1700, STN CSC, Victoria BC V8W 2Y2, Canada. (250)721-8524. **E-mail:** malahat@uvic.ca (for queries only). **Website:** www.malahatreview.ca. **Contact:** John Barton, editor. "We try to achieve a balance of views and styles in each issue. We strive for a mix of the best writing by both established and new writers." Buys first world rights. Pays on acceptance. Publishes ms an average of 6 months after acceptance. Responds in 2 weeks to queries. Responds in 3-10 months to mss. Sample copy for $16.95 (US). Guidelines available online.

MAGAZINE'S NEEDS Length: 5-10 pages Pays $35/magazine page.

CONTEST/AWARD OFFERINGS Presents the P.K. Page Founders' Award for Poetry, a $1,000 prize to the author of the best poem or sequence of poems to be published in *The Malahat Review*'s quarterly issues during the previous calendar year. Also offers the Open Season Awards, biennial Long Poem Prize, and Far Horizons Award for Poetry.

TIPS "Please do not send more than 1 submission at a time: 4-8 poems, 1 piece of creative nonfiction, or 1 short story (do not mix poetry and prose in the same submission). See *The Malahat Review*'s Open Season Awards for poetry and short fiction, creative nonfiction, long poem, and novella contests in the Awards section of our website."

THE MANHATTAN REVIEW

440 Riverside Dr., #38, New York NY 10027. **E-mail:** phfried@gmail.com. **Website:** http://themanhattanreview.com. **Contact:** Philip Fried. *The Manhattan Review* publishes only poetry, reviews of poetry books, and poetry-related essays. The editor reads unsolicited submissions at all times of the year but requests that you observe the guidelines. "*The Manhattan Review* has first North American serial rights only for the work it publishes." Responds in 3 months, if possible. Guidelines online.

MAGAZINE'S NEEDS Send 3-5 poems with SASE and brief bio. Read magazine before submitting. Pays contributor's copies.

MANOA

English Dept., University of Hawaii, Honolulu HI 96822. (808)956-3070. **Fax:** (808)956-3083. **E-mail:** mjournal-l@listserv.hawaii.edu. **Website:** http://manoajournal.hawaii.edu. **Contact:** Frank Stewart, poetry editor. "High quality literary fiction, poetry, essays, personal narrative. In general, each issue is devoted to new work from Pacific and Asian nations. Our audience is international. US writing need not be confined to Pacific settings or subjects. Please note that we seldom publish unsolicited work." Buys first North American serial rights, buys non-exclusive, one-time print rights. Pays on publication. Responds in 3 weeks to queries; 1 month to poetry mss; 6 months to fiction. Editorial lead time 9 months. Sample copy for $15 (US). Guidelines available online.

○ *Manoa* has received numerous awards, and work published in the magazine has been selected for prize anthologies. *Manoa* has received numerous awards, and work published in the magazine has been selected for prize anthologies. See website for recently published issues.

MAGAZINE'S NEEDS No light verse. Pays $25 per poem.

TIPS "Not accepting unsolicited manuscripts at this time because of commitments to special projects. See website for more information."

⊙⊙⊜ THE MASSACHUSETTS REVIEW

South College, University of Massachusetts, Amherst MA 01003. (413)545-2689. **Fax:** (413)577-0740. **E-mail:** massrev@external.umass.edu. **Website:** www.massreview.org. **Contact:** Jim Hicks, editor. Buys first North American serial rights. Pays on publication. Publishes ms an average of 18 months after acceptance. Responds in 3 months to mss. Sample copy for $8. Guidelines available online.

⊙   Does not respond to mss without SASE.

MAGAZINE'S NEEDS Has published poetry by Catherine Barnett, Billy Collins, and Dara Wier. "A poetry submission may consist of up to 6 poems. Please include your name and contact on every page." Length: "There are no restrictions for length, but generally our poems are less than 100 lines." Pays 50¢/line to $25 maximum.

TIPS "No manuscripts are considered May-September. Electronic submission process on website. No fax or e-mail submissions. No simultaneous submissions. Shorter rather than longer stories preferred (up to 28-30 pages)." Looks for works that "stop us in our tracks." Manuscripts that stand out use "unexpected language, idiosyncrasy of outlook and are the opposite of ordinary."

⊙⊜ MATURE YEARS

The United Methodist Publishing House, 201 Eighth Ave. S., P.O. Box 801, Nashville TN 37202-0801. (615)749-6292. **Fax:** (615)749-6512. **E-mail:** matureyears@umpublishing.org. Buys first North American serial rights. Pays on acceptance. Publishes ms an average of 1 year after acceptance. Responds in 2 weeks to queries. Responds in 2 months to mss. Sample copy for $6 and 9x12 SAE. Writer's guidelines for #10 SASE or by e-mail.

MAGAZINE'S NEEDS Submit seasonal and nature poems for spring from December through February; for summer, March through May; for fall, June through August; and for winter, September through November. Accepts fax and e-mail submissions (e-mail preferred). Length: 3-16 lines of up to 50 characters maximum. Pays $5-20.

TIPS "Practice writing dialogue! Listen to people talk; take notes; master dialogue writing! Not easy, but well worth it! Most inquiry letters are far too long. If you can't sell me an idea in a brief paragraph, you're not going to sell the reader on reading your finished article or story."

⊙ MEASURE: A REVIEW OF FORMAL POETRY

526 S. Linkoln Park Dr., Evansville IN 47714. (812)488-2963. **E-mail:** editors@measurepress.com. **Website:** www.measurepress.com/measure. "While *Measure*, our international journal of formal poetry, was begun in 2005 in conjunction with the University of Evansville, Measure Press is a new enterprise by editors Rob Griffith and Paul Bone. Our goal is to continue bringing our readers the best new poetry from both established and emerging writers through our biannual journal. *Measure*, as a biannual journal, has a mission not only to publish the best new poetry from both established and emerging writers, but also to reprint a small sampling of poems from books of metrical poetry published the previous year. Likewise, each issue includes interviews with some of our most important contemporary poets and also offers short critical essays on the poetry that has helped to shape the craft." Responds in 3 months. Guidelines online at website.

MAGAZINE'S NEEDS "Send no more than 3 to 5 poems at a time. Poems must be metrical. Include poet's name and phone number." Submit electronically on website.

THE MENNONITE

718 N. Main St., Newton KS 67114-1703. (866)866-2872 ext. 34398. **Fax:** (316)283-0454. **E-mail:** gordonh@themennonite.org. **Website:** www.themennonite.org. **Contact:** Gordon Houser, associate editor. *The Mennonite*, published monthly, seeks "to help readers glorify God, grow in faith and become agents of healing and hope in the world. Our readers are primarily people in Mennonite churches." Single copy: $3; subscription: $46 U.S. Acquires first or one-time rights. Publishes ms up to 1 year after acceptance. Responds in 2 weeks. Guidelines online.

TIPS "Writing should be concise, accessible to the general reader, and with strong lead paragraphs. This last point cannot be overemphasized. The lead paragraph is the foundation of a good article. It should provide a summary of the article. We are especially interested in personal stories of Mennonites exercising their faith."

MENSBOOK JOURNAL

CQS Media, Inc., P.O. Box 418, Sturbridge MA 01566. **Fax:** (508)347-8150. **E-mail:** features@mensbook. com. **Website:** www.mensbook.com. **Contact:** P.C.

Carr, editor/publisher. "We target bright, inquisitive, discerning gay men who want more non-commercial substance from gay media. We seek primarily first-person autobiographical pieces—then: biographies, political and social analysis, cartoons, short fiction, commentary, travel, and humor." Buys first rights. Pays on publication. Responds in 8 weeks to queries. Editorial lead time 4 months. Sample copy sent free by PDF. Guidelines online at www.mensbook.com/writersguidelines.htm.

TIPS "Be a tight writer with a cogent, potent message. Structure your work with well-organized progressive sequencing. Edit everything down before you send it over so we know it is the best you can do, and we'll work together from there."

◐ MERIDIAN

University of Virginia, P.O. Box 400145, Charlottesville VA 22904-4145. (434)982-5798. **Fax:** (434)924-1478. **E-mail:** MeridianUVA@gmail.com; meridianpoetry@gmail.com; meridianfiction@gmail.com. **Website:** www.readmeridian.org. *Meridian*, published semiannually, prints poetry, fiction, nonfiction, interviews, and reviews. Time between acceptance and publication is 1-2 months. Seldom comments on rejected poems and mss. Responds in 1-4 months. Always sends prepublication galleys and author contracts. Guidelines available on website.

○ Has published poetry by Joelle Biele, David Kirby, Larissa Szporluk, and Charles Wright. *Meridian* is 190 pages, digest-sized, offset-printed, perfect-bound, with color cover. Receives about 2,500 poems/year, accepts about 30 (less than 1%). Press run is 1,000 (750 subscribers, 15 libraries, 200 shelf sales); 150 distributed free to writing programs. Single copy: $7; subscription: $12/year. Make checks payable to *Meridian*. Work published in *Meridian* has appeared in *The Best American Poetry* and *The Pushcart Prize*.

MAGAZINE'S NEEDS Submit up to 4 poems at a time. Considers simultaneous submissions (with notification of acceptance elsewhere); no previously published poems. No e-mail or disk submissions; accepts postal and online submissions (**$2 upload fee for up to 4 poems**; no fee for postal submissions). Cover letter is preferred. Reads submissions September-May primarily (do not send submissions April 15-August 15; accepts online submissions year round). *Merid-*

ian Editors' Prize Contest offers annual $1,000 award. Submit online only; see website for formatting details. Entry fee: $8, includes 1-year electronic subscription to *Meridian* for all U.S. entries or 1 copy of the prize issue for all international entries. Deadline: December or January; see website for current deadline. Reviews books of poetry.

CONTEST/AWARD OFFERINGS *Meridian* Editors' Prize Contest offers annual $1,000 award. Submit online only; see website for formatting details. **Entry fee:** $8, includes 1-year subscription to *Meridian* for all US entries or 1 copy of the prize issue for all international entries. **Deadline:** December or January; see website for current deadline.

●☺⑤ MICHIGAN QUARTERLY REVIEW

0576 Rackham Bldg., 915 E. Washington, University of Michigan, Ann Arbor MI 48109-1070. (734)764-9265. **E-mail:** mqr@umich.edu. **Website:** www.michiganquarterlyreview.com. **Contact:** Jonathan Freedman, editor; Vicki Lawrence, managing editor. "*MQR* is an eclectic interdisciplinary journal of arts and culture that seeks to combine the best of poetry, fiction, and creative nonfiction with outstanding critical essays on literary, cultural, social, and political matters. The flagship journal of the University of Michigan, *MQR* draws on lively minds here and elsewhere, seeking to present accessible work of all varieties for sophisticated readers from within and without the academy." Buys first serial rights. Pays on publication. Publishes ms an average of 1 year after acceptance. Responds in 2 months to queries. Responds in 2 months to mss. Sample copy for $4. Guidelines available online.

○ The Laurence Goldstein Award is a $500 annual award to the best poem published in *MQR* during the previous year. The Lawrence Foundation Award is a $1,000 annual award to the best short story published in *MQR* during the previous year. The Page Davidson Clayton Award for Emerging Poets is a $500 annual award given to the best poet appearing in *MQR* during the previous year who has not yet published a book.

MAGAZINE'S NEEDS No previously published poems or simultaneous submissions. No e-mail submissions. Cover letter is preferred. "It puts a human face on the ms. A few sentences of biography is all I want, nothing lengthy or defensive." Prefers typed mss. Reviews books of poetry. "All reviews are commissioned." Pays $8-12/published page.

TIPS "Read the journal and assess the range of contents and the level of writing. We have no guidelines to offer or set expectations; every manuscript is judged on its unique qualities. On essays—query with a very thorough description of the argument and a copy of the first page. Watch for announcements of special issues which are usually expanded issues and draw upon a lot of freelance writing. Be aware that this is a university quarterly that publishes a limited amount of fiction and poetry and that it is directed at an educated audience, one that has done a great deal of reading in all types of literature."

◑◔ MID-AMERICAN REVIEW

Bowling Green State University, Department of English, Bowling Green OH 43403. (419)372-2725. **E-mail:** mar@bgsu.edu. **Website:** www.bgsu.edu/midamericanreview. **Contact:** Abigail Cloud, editor-in-chief. "We aim to put the best possible work in front of the biggest possible audience. We publish contemporary fiction, poetry, creative nonfiction, translations and book reviews." Buys first North American serial rights. Pays on publication when funding is available. Publishes mss an average of 6 months after acceptance. Responds in 5 months to mss. Sample copy for $9 (current issue); $5 (back issue); $10 (rare back issues). Guidelines available online.

◗ Magazine: 6×9; 232 pages; 60 lb. bond paper; coated cover stock. Contests: The Fineline Competition for Prose Poems, Short Shorts, and Everything In Between (June 1 deadline, $10 per 3 pieces, limit 500 words each); The Sherwood Anderson Fiction Award (November 1 deadline, $10 per piece); and the James Wright Poetry Award (November 1 deadline, $10 per 3 pieces). "Visit our website!"

MAGAZINE'S NEEDS Submit by mail with SASE or through online submissions form at website. Publishes poems with "textured, evocative images, an awareness of how words sound and mean, and a definite sense of voice. Each line should help carry the poem, and an individual vision must be evident." Send 1-6 poems. Recently published work by Mary Ann Samyn, Sydney Lea, Bob Hicok, and Amy Newman. Pays $10/page up to $50, pending funding.

TIPS "We are seeking translations of contemporary authors from all languages into English; submissions must include the original and proof of permission to translate. We would also like to see more creative nonfiction."

◐ THE MIDWEST QUARTERLY

406b Russ Hall, Pittsburg State University, Pittsburg KS 66762. (620)235-4369; (620)235-4317. **E-mail:** midwestq@pittstate.edu; smeats@pittstate.edu. **Website:** www.pittstate.edu/department/english/midwestquarterly. **Contact:** James B. M. Schick. *The Midwest Quarterly* publishes "articles on any subject of contemporary interest, particularly literary criticism, political science, philosophy, education, biography, and sociology. Each issue contains a section of poetry usually 12 poems in length. We seek discussions of an analytical and speculative nature and well-crafted poems. Poems of interest to us use intense, vivid, concrete and/or surrealistic images to explore the mysterious and surprising interactions of the nature and inner human worlds." For publication in MQ and eligibility for the annual Emmett Memorial Prize competition, the Editors invite submission of articles on any literary topic, but preferably on Victorian or Modern British Literature, Literary Criticism, or the Teaching of Literature. The winner receives an honorarium and invitation to deliver the annual Emmett Memorial Lecture. Contact Dr. Stephen Meats, English Department, Pittsburg State University, Pittsburg, KS 66762 Acquires first serial rights. Responds in 2 months to mss. Guidelines available on website.

◗ *The Midwest Quarterly* is 130 pages, digest-sized, professionally printed, flat-spined, with matte cover. Press run is 650 (600 subscribers, 500 are libraries). Receives about 3,500-4,000 poems/year, accepts about 50. Has published poetry by Peter Cooley, Lyn Lifshin, Judith Skillman, Naomi Shihab Nye, Jonathan Holden and William Kloefkorn. Subscription: $15. Sample: $5.

MAGAZINE'S NEEDS Submit no more than 5 poems at a time. Considers simultaneous submissions; no previously published poems. No fax or e-mail submissions. "Mss should be typed with poet's name on each page. Include e-mail address for notification of decision. SASE only for return of poem." Comments on rejected poems "if the poet or poem seems particularly promising." Occasionally publishes theme issues or issues devoted to the work of a single poet. Wants "well-crafted poems, traditional or untraditional, that use intense, vivid, concrete, and/or surrealistic images to explore the mysterious and surprising interactions of the natural and inner human worlds." Does not want "'nature poems,' per se, but if a poem doesn't engage nature in a significant way, as an integral part of the experience it is offering, I am unlikely to be interested in publishing it." Lines/poem: 60 maximum ("occasionally longer if exceptional"). Pays 2 contributor's copies.

MIDWIFERY TODAY

P.O Box 2672, Eugene OR 97402. (541)344-7438. **Fax:** (541)344-1422. **E-mail:** editorial@midwiferytoday. com and jan@midwiferytoday.com (editorial only); layout@midwiferytoday.com (photography). **Website:** www.midwiferytoday.com. **Contact:** Jan Tritten, editor-in-chief and publisher. Publishes ms an average of 5 months after acceptance. Responds in 2 weeks to queries. Responds in 1 month to mss. Editorial lead time 3-9 months. Sample copy and guidelines available online.

○ "Through networking and education, *Midwifery Today*'s mission is to return midwifery to its rightful position in the family; to make midwifery care the norm throughout the world; and to redefine midwifery as a vital partnership with women."

MAGAZINE'S NEEDS Accepts e-mail submissions (pasted into body of message or as attachment). Cover letter is required. Does not want poetry unrelated to pregnancy or birth. Does not want poetry that is "off subject or puts down the subject." Maximum line length: 25. Pays 2 contributor's copies. Acquires first rights.

TIPS "Use Chicago Manual of Style formatting."

○ ❸ MILLER'S POND

E-mail: mail@handhpress.com (C.J. Houghtaling); mpwebeditor@yahoo.com (Julie Damerell). **Website:** www. millerspondpoetry.com. **Contact:** C.J. Houghtaling, publisher; Julie Damerell, editor. *miller's pond* is exclusively an e-zine and does not publish in hard copy format. "All submissions must be sent electronically from our website. Mail sent through the post office will be returned. No payment for accepted poems or reviews." Web version is published three times each year. Submissions accepted year round but read in December, April, and August. Responds within 3 months. "Current guidelines, updates, and

changes are always available on our website. Check there first before submitting anything."

TIPS "Follow submission guidelines on the website. Submissions that do not fulfill the guidelines are deleted without comment. Read the website to see the kind of poetry we like."

◐ THE MINNESOTA REVIEW

Virginia Tech, ASPECT, 202 Major Williams Hall (0192), Blacksburg VA 24061. **E-mail:** editors@theminnesotareview.org; submissions@theminnesotareview.org. **Website:** www.theminnesotareview. org. **Contact:** Janell Watson, editor. *The Minnesota Review*, published biannually, features quality poetry, short fiction, and critical essays. Each issue is about 200 pages, digest-sized, flat-spined, with glossy card cover. Press run is 1,000 (400 subscribers). Also available online. Subscription: $30/2 years for individuals, $60/year for institutions. Sample: $15.

MAGAZINE'S NEEDS Submit up to 5 poems every 3 months online. Reads poetry August 1-November 1 and January 1-April 1. Pays 2 contributor's copies.

M.I.P. COMPANY

P.O. Box 27484, Minneapolis MN 55427. (763)544-5915. **Website:** www.mipco.com. **Contact:** Michael Peltsman, editor. "The publisher of controversial Russian literature (erotic poetry)." Responds to queries in 1 month. Seldom comments on rejected poems.

MAGAZINE'S NEEDS Considers simultaneous submissions; no previously published poems.

● MISSISSIPPI REVIEW

University of Southern Mississippi, 118 College Dr., #5144, Hattiesburg MS 39406-0001. (601)266-4321. **Fax:** (601)266-5757. **E-mail:** andrew.milward@usm. edu; msreview@usm.edu. **Website:** www.mississippireview.com. Buys first North American serial rights. Sample copy for $10. Writer's guidelines online.

○ Publishes 25-30 new writers/year. "We do not accept unsolicited manuscripts except under the rules and guidelines of the *Mississippi Review* Prize Competition. See website for guidelines." Annual fiction and poetry competition: $1,000 awarded in each category, plus publication of all winners and finalists. Fiction entries 5,000 words or less. Poetry entry equals 1-3 poems; page limit is 10; $15 entry fee includes copy of prize issue. No limit on number of entries. Deadline October 1. No mss returned.

MAGAZINE'S NEEDS "We do not accept unsolicited manuscripts except under the rules and guidelines of the *Mississippi Review* Prize Competition. See website for guidelines.

○🐦💲 THE MISSOURI REVIEW

357 McReynolds Hall, University of Missouri, Columbia MO 65211. (573)882-4474. **Fax:** (573)884-4671. **E-mail:** question@moreview.com. **Website:** www.missourireview.com. **Contact:** Speer Morgan, editor. Offers signed contract. Responds in 2 weeks to queries. Responds in 10 weeks to mss. Editorial lead time 6 months. Sample copy for $8.95 or online Guidelines available online.

○ "We publish contemporary fiction, poetry, interviews, personal essays, cartoons, special features—such as History as Literature series and Found Text series—for the literary and the general reader interested in a wide range of subjects."

MAGAZINE'S NEEDS Submit 6-12 poems at a time. Pays $30/printed page and 3 contributor's copies.

ADDITIONAL INFORMATION The Tom McAfee Discovery Feature is awarded at least once/year to showcase an outstanding young poet who has not yet published a book; poets are selected from regular submissions at the discretion of the editors.

TIPS "Send your best work."

○ MOBIUS

505 Christianson St., Madison WI 53714. (608)242-1009. **E-mail:** fmschep@charter.net. **Website:** www.mobiusmagazine.com. **Contact:** Fred Schepartz, publisher and executive editor. *Mobius: The Journal of Social Change* became an online-only journal, published quarterly in March, June, September, and December, in 2009. Publishes ms 3-6 months after acceptance. Responds in 1 month. Guidelines available online.

MAGAZINE'S NEEDS Submit poetry dealing with themes of social change. Accepts e-mailed poetry submissions only. "We have a marked distaste for prosaic didacticism (but a weakness for prose poems)." Do not submit poems by postal mail.

TIPS "Note that fiction and poetry may be simultaneously published in e-version of Mobius. Due to space constraints of print version, some works may be accepted in e-version, but not print version. We like high impact, we like plot and character-driven stories that function like theater of the mind. Looks for first and foremost, good writing. Prose must be crisp and pol-

ished; the story must pique my interest and make me care due to a certain intellectual, emotional aspect. Second, *Mobius* is about social change. We want stories that make some statement about the society we live in, either on a macro or micro level. Not that your story needs to preach from a soapbox (actually, we prefer that it doesn't), but your story needs to have *something* to say."

MOBIUS: THE JOURNAL OF SOCIAL CHANGE

E-mail: fmschep@charter.net. **Website:** http://mobiusmagazine.com. **Contact:** Fred Schepartz, publisher and executive editor; F.J. Bergmann, poetry and art editor. *Mobius: The Journal of Social Change*, published quarterly, prints socially and politically relevant poetry and fiction and is distributed free in Madison, WI, and to libraries and subscribers. Wants any form of poetry on themes of social change. Does not want heavy-handed, transparent didacticism. Considers poetry by teens; however, the publication is not directed at children. Acquires one-time electronic rights; rights revert to poets upon publication. Publishes ms 6 months after acceptance. "Usually responds in 3 days; query if no response within 1 week." Guidelines on website.

○ *Mobius* is published quarterly online. Receives about 700 poems/year, accepts less than 30. Has published poetry by Rob Carney, Wade German, Michael Kriesel, Simon Perchik, Wendy Vardaman.

MAGAZINE'S NEEDS Submit 5 poems at a time. No multiple or simultaneous submissions. Accepts e-mail submissions (pasted into body of message); no fax or disk submissions. Cover letter is unnecessary. Include short bio and mailing address; postal submissions must include e-mail address or SASE. Reads submissions year round. Sometimes comments on rejected poems. Never publishes theme issues. Pays 2 contributor's copies.

○ THE MOCCASIN

The League of Minnesota Poets, 427 N. Gorman St., Blue Earth MN 56013. (507)526-5321. **Website:** www.mnpoets.org. *The Moccasin*, published annually in October, is the literary magazine of The League of Minnesota Poets. **Membership is required to submit work.** *The Moccasin* is 40 pages, digest-sized, offset-printed, stapled, with 80 lb. linen-finish text cover with drawing and poem. Receives about 190 poems/

year, accepts about 170. Press run is 200. Single copy: $5.25; subscription: free with LOMP membership.

MAGAZINE'S NEEDS Wants "all forms of poetry. Prefer strong short poems." Considers poetry by children and teens who are student members of The League of Minnesota Poets (write grade level on poems submitted). Has published poetry by Diane Glancy, Laurel Winter, Susan Stevens Chambers, Doris Stengel, Jeanette Hinds, and Charmaine Donovan. Does not want profanity or obscenity.

TIPS To become a member of The League of Minnesota Poets, send $20 ($10 if high school student or younger) to Angela Foster, LOMP Treasurer, 30036 St. Croix Rd, Pine City MN 55063. Make checks payable to LOMP. You do not have to live in Minnesota to become a member of LOMP. "Membership in LOMP automatically makes you a member of the National Federation of State Poetry Societies, which makes you eligible to enter its contests at a cheaper (members') rate."

THE MOCHILA REVIEW

Missouri Western State University, 4525 Downs Dr., St. Joseph MO 64507. **E-mail:** themochilareview@gmail.com. **Website:** www.missouriwestern.edu/orgs/mochila/homepage.htm. **Contact:** Bill Church, editor. "We are looking for writing that has a respect for the sound of language. We value poems that have to be read aloud so your mouth can feel the shape of the words. Send us writing that conveys a sense of urgency, writing that the writer can't *not* write. We crave fresh and daring work." Responds in 3-4 months to mss. Guidelines available online.

MAGAZINE'S NEEDS Submit no more than 5 poems at a time by postal mail. Include cover letter, contact information, SASE. Pays in contributor's copies.

TIPS "Manuscripts with fresh language, energy, passion and intelligence stand out. Study the craft and be entertaining and engaging."

MODERN HAIKU

P.O. Box 33077, Santa Fe NM 87594-3077. **E-mail:** modernhaiku@gmail.com. **Website:** http://modernhaiku.org. "*Modern Haiku* "the foremost international journal o fEnglish-language haiku and criticism, and publishes high quality material only. Haiku and related genres, articles on haiku, haiku book reviews, and translations comprise its contents. It has an international circulation; subscribers include many university, school, and public libraries." Buys first North American serial rights. Acquires first international se-

rial rights. Pays on acceptance. Publishes ms an average of 6 months after acceptance. Responds in 1 week to queries. Responds in 6-8 weeks to mss. Editorial lead time 4 months. Sample copy for $15 in North America, $16 in Canada, $20 in Mexico, $22 overseas. Subscription: $35 ppd by regular mail in the U.S. Payment possible by PayPal on the *Modern Haiku* website. Guidelines available for SASE or on website.

Has published haiku by Roberta Beary, Billy Collins, LawrenceFerlinghetti, Carolyn Hall, Sharon Olds, Gary Snyder, John Stevenson,George Swede, and Cor van den Heuvel. *Modern Haiku* is 140 pages (average), digest-sized, printed on heavy quality stock, with full-color cover illustrations 4-page full-color art sections. Receives about 15,000 submissions/year, accepts about 1,000. Press run is 700.

MAGAZINE'S NEEDS Postal submissions: "Send 5-15 haiku on 1 or 2 letter-sized sheets. Put name and address at the top of each sheet. Include SASE." E-mail submissions: "May be attachments (recommended) or pasted in body of message. Subject line must read: MH Submission. Adhere to guidelines on the website. No payment for haiki sent/accepted by e-mail." Reviews of books of haiku by staff and freelancers by invitation in 350-1,000 words, usually single-book format. Send materials for review consideration with complete ordering information. Does not want "general poetry, tanka, renku, linked verse forms. No special consideration given to work by children and teens." Pays $1 per haiku by postal mail only (not for e-mail).

CONTEST/AWARD OFFERINGS Sponsors the annual Robert Spiess Memorial Haiku Competition. Guidelines available for SASE or on website.

TIPS "Study the history of haiku, read books about haiku, learn the aesthetics of haiku and methods of composition. Write about your sense perceptions of the suchness of entities; avoid ego-centered interpretations. Be sure the work you send us conforms to the definitions on our website."

MOONSHOT MAGAZINE

E-mail: info@moonshotmagazine.org. **Website:** www.moonshotmagazine.org. **Contact:** JD Scott, editor. "*Moonshot*, a magazine of the literary and fine arts, was conceived in 2009 to provide an equal opportunity space for writers and artists based solely on the merits of their work. *Moonshot*'s mission is to eliminate the social challenges of publishing—encouraging all types of writers and artists to submit their work in the pursuit of exposing their creations to a wider range of audiences. It is our goal to utilize traditional printing techniques as well as new technologies and media arts to feature voices from all over the globe. *Moonshot* celebrates storytelling of all forms, embraces the dissemination of media, and champions diverse creators to construct an innovative and original literary magazine." Buys First North American serial rights, electronic rights. Pays on publication. Sample copy online at website, $10. Guidelines available on website.

⃝ MUDFISH

Box Turtle Press, 184 Franklin St., New York NY 10013. (212)219-9278. **E-mail:** mudfishmag@aol.com. **Website:** www.mudfish.org. **Contact:** Jill Hoffman, editor. Responds in 3 months.

MAGAZINE'S NEEDS *Mudfish*, published annually by Box Turtle Press, is an annual journal of poetry and art. Wants "free verse with energy, intensity, and originality of voice, mastery of style, the presence of passion." Has published poetry by Charles Simic, Jennifer Belle, Stephanie Dickinson, Ronald Wardall, Doug Dorph, and John Ashbery. Submit 4-6 poems at a time. No e-mail submissions; postal submissions only. Pays 1 contributor's copy.

CONTEST/AWARD OFFERINGS Sponsors the Mudfish Poetry Prize Award of $1,000. **Entry fee:** $15 for up to 3 poems, $3 for each additional poem. **Deadline:** varies. Guidelines available for SASE.

⃝ MUDLARK: AN ELECTRONIC JOURNAL OF POETRY & POETICS

Department of English, University of North Florida, Jacksonville FL 32224-2645. (904)620-2273. **Fax:** (904)620-3940. **E-mail:** mudlark@unf.edu. **Website:** www.unf.edu/mudlark. **Contact:** William Slaughter, editor and publisher. *Mudlark: An Electronic Journal of Poetry & Poetics*, published online "irregularly, but frequently," offers 3 formats: issues of *Mudlark* "are the electronic equivalent of print chapbooks; posters are the electronic equivalent of print broadsides; and flash poems are poems that have news in them, poems that feel like current events."

MAGAZINE'S NEEDS The poem is the thing at *Mudlark*, and the essay about it. As our full name suggests, we will consider accomplished work that locates itself

anywhere on the spectrum of contemporary practice. We want poems, of course, but we want essays, too, that make us read poems (and write them?) differently somehow. Although we are not innocent, we do imagine ourselves capable of surprise. The work of hobbyists is not for *Mudlark*." Has published poetry by Sherman Alexie, Denise Duhamel, T. R. Hummer, Kurt Brown, Susan Kelly-DeWitt, and Michael Hettich. *Mudlark* is archived and permanently on view at www.unf.edu/mudlark. Submit any number of poems at a time. "Prefers not to receive multiple submissions but will consider them if informed of the fact, up front, and if notified immediately when poems are accepted elsewhere. Considers previously published work only as part of a *Mudlark* issue, the electronic equivalent of a print chapbook, and only if the previous publication is acknowledged in a note that covers the submission. Only poems that have not been previously published will be considered for *Mudlark* posters, the electronic equivalent of print broadsides, or for *Mudlark* flashes."

HOW TO CONTACT Accepts e-mail or USPS submissions with SASE; no fax submissions. Cover letter is optional. Seldom comments on rejected poems. Always sends prepublication galleys "in the form of inviting the author to proof the work on a private website that *Mudlark* maintains for that purpose." Acquires one-time rights. No payment; however, "one of the things we can do at *Mudlark* to 'pay' our authors for their work is point to it here and there. We can tell our readers how to find it, how to subscribe to it, and how to buy it—if it is for sale. Toward that end, we maintain A-Notes on the authors we publish. We call attention to their work." Publishes ms no more than 3 months after acceptance. Responds in "1 day to 1 month, depending." Guidelines for SASE, by e-mail or on website.

⃝ ⑤ MYTHIC DELIRIUM

3514 Signal Hill Ave. NW, Roanoke VA 24017-5148. **E-mail:** mythicdelirium@gmail.com. **Website:** www.mythicdelirium.com. **Contact:** Mike Allen, editor. Reading periods: March 1-May 1 for the Summer/Fall issue and Aug. 1-Oct. 1 for the Winter/Spring issue. Publishes ms 2 months after acceptance. Responds in 5 weeks.

⃝   Accepts electronic submissions only.

MAGAZINE'S NEEDS "While any style of poem is fair game, Mythic Delirium is unusual in that we are not adverse to well-done rhyme and meter. When considering sending a rhyming poem to us, keep in mind that the best rhyme does not call attention to itself and that properly done traditional poems possess consistent rhythm; lines don't just end in words that sound similar. We are interested in work that demonstrates ambition, that casts new light on genre tropes, that introduces readers to the legends of other cultures, that re-evaluates the myths of old from a modern perspective, that twists reality in unexpected ways." Does not want "forced rhyme, corny humor, jarringly gross sexual material, gratuitous obscenity, handwritten manuscripts." Pays $5/poem, plus 1 contributor's copy. **TIPS** "*Mythic Delirium* isn't easy to get into, but we publish newcomers in every issue. Show us how ambitious you can be, and don't give up."

◐ NASSAU REVIEW

Nassau Community College, State University of New York, English Dept. Y9, 1 Education Dr., Garden City NY 11530. **E-mail:** nassaureview@ncc.edu. **Website:** www.ncc.edu/nassaureview. **Contact:** Christina Rau, editor. "The Nassau Review welcomes submissions of many genres via our online system only. Please read all guidelines and details on the website: www.ncc.edu/nassaureview. All open submissions are under consideration for the Writer Awards."

●⑤ THE NATION

33 Irving Place, 8th Floor, New York NY 10003. **E-mail:** submissions@thenation.com. **Website:** www.thenation.com. Steven Brower, art director. **Contact:** Jordan Davis, poetry editor. *The Nation*, published weekly, is a journal of left/liberal opinion, with arts coverage that includes poetry. The only requirement for poetry is "excellence." Guidelines available online.

�‿ Poetry published by *The Nation* has been included in *The Best American Poetry*. Has published poetry by W.S. Merwin, Maxine Kumin, James Merrill, May Swenson, Edward Hirsch, and Charles Simic.

MAGAZINE'S NEEDS Submit up to 3 poems at a time, no more than 8 poems within the calendar year. No simultaneous submissions. No fax, e-mail disk submissions. Doesn't reply to or return poems sent by fax or e-mail or submitted without an SASE.

HOW TO CONTACT *The Nation* welcomes unsolicited poetry submissions. You may send up to three poems at a time, and no more than eight poems during a calendar year. Send poems by first-class mail, accompanied by a SASE. Does not reply to or return

poems sent by fax or e-mail or submitted without an SASE. Submissions are not accepted from June 1 to September 15. Manuscripts may be mailed to: Jordan Davis, poetry editor.

● THE NATIONAL POETRY REVIEW

P.O. Box 2080, Aptos CA 95001-2080. **E-mail:** editor@nationalpoetryreview.com; nationalpoetryreview@yahoo.com. **Website:** www.nationalpoetryreview.com. **Contact:** C.J. Sage, editor. *The National Poetry Review* seeks "distinction, innovation, and *joie de vivre*. We agree with Frost about delight and wisdom. We believe in rich sound. We believe in the beautiful—even if that beauty is not in the situation of the poem but simply the sounds of the poem, the images, or (and, ideally) the way the poem stays in the reader's mind long after it's been read." *TNPR* considers both experimental and 'mainstream' work." Does not want "overly self-centered or confessional poetry." Acquires first rights. Time between acceptance and publication is no more than 1 year. "The editor makes all publishing decisions." Sometimes comments on rejected poems. Usually responds in about 1-12 weeks. Guidelines available in magazine or on website.

◯ *The National Poetry Review* is 80 pages, perfect-bound, with full-color cover. Accepts less than 1% of submissions received. Single copy: $15; subscription: $15/year. Make checks payable to *TNPR* only. Poetry appearing in *The National Poetry Review* has also appeared in *The Pushcart Prize*. Has published poetry by Bob Hicok, Jennifer Michael Hecht, Larissa Szplorluk, Martha Zweig, Nance Van Winkel, William Waltz, and Ted Kooser.

MAGAZINE'S NEEDS Submit 3-5 poems at a time by e-mail only to address below; postal submissions will be recycled unread. Considers simultaneous submissions "with notification only. Submit only between December 1 and February 28 unless you are a subscriber or benefactor. Put your name in the subject line of your e-mail and send to tnprsubmissions@yahoo.com." Bio is required. Subscribers and benefactors may submit any time during the year ("please write 'subscriber' or 'benefactor' in the subject line"). See website before submitting. Pays 1 contributor's copy and small honorarium when funds are available.

◐ NATURAL BRIDGE

Dept. of English, University of Missouri-St. Louis, One University Blvd., St. Louis MO 63121. (314)516-

7327. **E-mail:** natural@umsl.edu. **Website:** www.umsl.edu/~natural. *Natural Bridge*, published biannually, seeks "fresh, innovative poetry, both free and formal, on any subject. We want poems that work on first and subsequent readings—poems that entertain and resonate and challenge our readers. *Natural Bridge* also publishes fiction, essays, and translations." Has published poetry by Ross Gay, Beckian Fritz Goldberg, Joy Harjo, Bob Hicok, Sandra Kohler, and Timothy Liu. Acquire first North American rights. Publishes ms 9 months after acceptance. Responds in 4-8 months. Guidelines available online at website.

○ No longer accepts submissions via e-mail. Accepts submissions through online submission form and postal mail only.

MAGAZINE'S NEEDS Submit 4-6 poems at a time. "Submissions should be typewritten, with name and address on each page. Do not staple manuscripts. Send SASE." Reads submissions July 1-August 31 and November 1-December 31. "Work is read and selected by the guest-editor and editor, along with editorial assistants made up of graduate students in our MFA program. We publish work by both established and new writers." Length: no limit. Pays 2 contributor's copies.

TIPS "The editors invite submissions of poetry, fiction, personal essays, and translations year-round. Because we are tied to the academic calendar, we will not read between May 1 and August 1."

NATURALLY

Internaturally, Inc., P.O. Box 317, Newfoundland NJ 07435. (973)697-3552. **Fax:** (973)697-8313. **E-mail:** naturally@internaturally.com. **Website:** www.internaturally.com. "A full color, glossy magazine with online editions, and the foremost naturist/nudist magazine in the US with international distribution. *Naturally* focuses on the clothes-free lifestyle, publishing articles about worldwide destinations, first-time nudist experiences, with news information pertaining to the clothes-free lifestyle. Our mission is to demystify the human form, and allow each human to feel comfortable in their own skin, in a non-sexual environment. We offer a range of books, DVDs, magazines, and other products useful to naturists/nudists in their daily lives, and for the education of non-naturists. Travel DVDs featuring resorts to visit; books on Christianity and nudity,

nudist plays, memoirs, cartoons, and novellas; and also towels, sandals, calendars, and more." Buys first North American serial rights, buys first rights, buys one-time rights, buys second serial (reprint) rights, buys simultaneous rights, buys electronic rights. Makes work-for-hire assignments. Pays on publication. Publishes ms an average of 3 months after acceptance. Responds in 2 weeks to queries. Responds in 3 months to mss. Editorial lead time 3-6 months. Sample copy available online.

○ Write about nudists and naturists. More people stories than travel.

TIPS "Become a nudist/naturist. Appreciate human beings in their natural state."

NAUGATUCK RIVER REVIEW

P.O. Box 368, Westfield MA 01085. **E-mail:** naugatuckriver@aol.com. **Website:** http://naugatuckriverreview.wordpress.com/. **Contact:** Lori Desrosiers, publisher. The *Naugatuck River Review*, published semiannually, "is a literary journal for great narrative poetry looking for narrative poetry of high caliber, where the narrative is compressed with a strong emotional core." Acquires first North American serial rights. Responds in 2-12 weeks. Always sends prepublication galleys. Guidelines available in magazine and on website.

○ Accepts submissions through online submission form.

MAGAZINE'S NEEDS Submit 3 poems at a time. Prefers unpublished poems but will consider simultaneous submissions. Accepts online submissions through submission manager only; no fax or disk. Include a brief bio and mailing information. Reads submissions January 1-March 1 and July 1-September 1 for contest. Length: no more than 50 lines.

TIPS "What is narrative poetry? We get this question quite often. What *NRR* is looking for are poems that tell a story, or have a strong sense of story. They can be stories of a moment or an experience, and can be personal or historical. A good narrative poem that would work for our journal has a compressed narrative, and we prefer poems that take up two pages or less of the journal (50 lines max). We are looking above all for poems that are well-crafted, have an excellent lyric quality and contain a strong emotional core. Any style of poem is considered, including prose poems. Poems with very long lines don't fit well in the format. Hope this helps."

◯ NECROLOGY SHORTS: TALES OF MACABRE AND HORROR

Isis International, P.O. Box 510232, St. Louis MO 63151. **E-mail:** editor@necrologyshorts.com; submit@necrologyshorts.com. **Website:** www.necrologyshorts.com. **Contact:** John Ferguson, editor. Consumer publication published online daily and through Amazon Kindle. Also offers an annual collection. "*Necrology Shorts* is an online publication which publishes fiction, articles, cartoons, artwork, and poetry daily. Embracing the Internet, e-book readers, and new technology, we aim to go beyond the long time standard of a regular publication to bringing our readers a daily flow of entertainment. We will also be publishing an annual collection for each year in print, e-book reader, and Adobe PDF format. Our main genre is suspense horror similar to H.P. Lovecraft and/or Robert E. Howard. We also publish science fiction and fantasy. We would love to see work continuing the Cthulhu Mythos, but we accept all horror. We also hold contests, judged by our readers, to select the top stories and artwork. Winners of contests receive various prizes, including cash." Acquires one-time rights, anthology rights. *Does not currently pay for submissions.* Acceptance to publication is 1 month. Responds in 1 month to ms. Editorial lead time is 1 month. Sample copy online. Guidelines available on website.

MAGAZINE'S NEEDS Submit up to 5 poems at one time. Length: 4-100 lines.

TIPS "*Necrology Shorts* is looking to break out of the traditional publication types to use the Internet, e-book readers, and other technology. We not only publish works of authors and artists, we let them use their published works to brand themselves and further their profits of their hard work. We love to see traditional short fiction and artwork, but we also look forward to those that go beyond that to create multimedia works. The best way to get to us is to let your creative side run wild and not send us the typical fare. Don't forget that we publish horror, sci-fi, and fantasy. We expect deranged, warped, twisted, strange, sadistic, and things that question sanity and reality."

◑ NERVE COWBOY

Liquid Paper Press, P.O. Box 4973, Austin TX 78765. **Website:** www.jwhagins.com/nervecowboy.html. **Contact:** Joseph Shields or Jerry Hagins. "*Nerve Cowboy* publishes adventurous, comical, disturbing, thought-provoking, accessible poetry and fiction. We

like to see work sensitive enough to make the hardest hard-ass cry, funny enough to make the most hopeless brooder laugh and disturbing enough to make us all glad we're not the author of the piece." Buys one-time rights. Publishes ms an average of 6-12 months after acceptance. Responds in 2-3 months. Sample copy for $6. Guidelines available online.

MAGAZINE'S NEEDS Submit poems with SASE. Does not accept e-mail submissions. "Open to all forms, styles, and subject matter, preferring writing that speaks directly and minimizes literary devices." Wants "poetry of experience and passion which can find that raw nerve and ride it. We are always looking for that rare writer who inherently knows what word comes next."

TIPS "We look for writing which is very direct and elicits a visceral reaction in the reader. Read magazines you submit to in order to get a feel for what the editors are looking for. Write simply and from the gut."

◐◉ NEW ENGLAND REVIEW

Middlebury College, Middlebury VT 05753. (802)443-5075. **E-mail:** nereview@middlebury.edu. **E-mail:** Carolyn Kuebler, editor. **Website:** www.nereview.com. *New England Review* is a prestigious, nationally distributed literary journal. Reads September 1-May 31 (postmarked dates). Buys first North American serial rights, buys first rights, buys second serial (reprint) rights. Sends galleys to author. Pays on publication. Publishes ms an average of 6 months after acceptance. Responds in 2 weeks to queries. Responds in 3 months to mss. Sometimes comments on rejected mss. Sample copy for $10 (add $5 for overseas). Guidelines available online.

◯ Literary only. *New England Review* is 200+ pages, 7x10, printed on heavy stock, flat-spined, with glossy cover with art. Receives 3,000-4,000 poetry submissions/year, accepts about 70-80 poems/year. Receives 550 unsolicited mss/month. Accepts 6 mss/issue; 24 fiction mss/year. Does not accept mss June-August. Agented fiction less than 5%. Publishes approximately 10 new writers/year. Subscription: $30. Overseas shipping fees add $25 for subscription, $12 for Canada; international shipping $5 for single issues. Has published work by Steve Almond, Christine Sneed, Roy Kesey, Thomas Gough, Norman

Lock, Brock Clarke, Carl Phillips, Lucia Perillo, Linda Gregerson, and Natasha Trethewey.

MAGAZINE'S NEEDS Submit up to 6 poems at a time. No previously published poems or simultaneous submissions. Accepts submissions by postal mail or online submission manager only; accepts questions by e-mail. "Cover letters are useful." Address submissions to "Poetry Editor." Reads submissions postmarked September 1-May 31 only. Pays $10/page ($20 minimum), and 2 contributor's copies.

TIPS "We consider short fiction, including short-shorts, novellas, and self-contained extracts from novels in both traditional and experimental forms. In nonfiction, we consider a variety of general and literary, but not narrowly scholarly essays; we also publish long and short poems; screenplays; graphics; translations; critical reassessments; statements by artists working in various media; testimonies; and letters from abroad. We are committed to exploration of all forms of contemporary cultural expression in the US and abroad. With few exceptions, we print only work not published previously elsewhere."

◐ THE NEW LAUREL REVIEW

828 Lesseps St., New Orleans LA 70117. **Fax:** (504)948-3834. **Website:** www.nathanielturner.com/newlaurelreview.htm. **Contact:** Lewis Schmidt, managing editor. *The New Laurel Review*, published annually, is "an independent nonprofit literary magazine dedicated to fine art. The magazine is meant to be eclectic, and we try to publish the best we receive, whether the submission is poem, translation, short story, essay, review, or interview. We have no domineering preferences regarding style, and we do consult with invited readers and writers for their opinions. We are seeking original work without hackneyed phrases, indulgent voices, or tired thinking. We love surprises and to see a writer or artist enliven our too often dull, editorial worlds." *The New Laurel Review* is about 115-130 pages, 6×9, laser-printed, perfect-bound, with original art on laminated cover. Receives 400-600 submissions/year, accepts about 30-40 poems. Press run is about 500. Single copy: $12 for individuals, $14 for institutions. Sample (back issue): $5.

MAGAZINE'S NEEDS Submit 3-5 poems at a time. No simultaneous submissions. "Poems should be typed; no handwritten submissions will be read. Name and address should appear on each poem submitted. Include a brief biography of three or four

typed lines, including previous publications. Do not send cover letters, which may or may not distract from the submission. Be sure to include SASE; manuscripts will not be returned otherwise. If you are submitting from outside the U.S., provide International Reply Coupons. Because we are totally independent from various funding agencies, we sometimes take an inordinate time to reply." Has published poetry by Gerald Locklin, Roland John (British), Joyce Odam, Ryan G. Van Cleave, Robert Cooperman, and Jared Carter.

TIPS "READ, READ, READ. And it is wise to obtain a copy of any magazine to which you plan to submit work. Also, you might remember that you cannot be cummings, Eliot, Faulkner, or Hemingway. One of the most disheartening aspects of editing is to receive a submission of poems with low caps, no punctuation, or words sprawled all over the page, under the pretense that the work is original and not pseudo-cummings or Yawping Whitman. Find your own voice and techniques."

◐ ◔ ⑤ NEW LETTERS

University of Missouri-Kansas City, 5101 Rockhill Rd., Kansas City MO 64110. (816)235-1168. **Fax:** (816)235-2611. **E-mail:** newletters@umkc.edu. **Website:** www.newletters.org. **Contact:** Robert Stewart, editor-in-chief. Buys first North American serial rights. Pays on publication. Publishes ms an average of 6 months after acceptance. Responds in 1 month to queries; 5 months to mss. Editorial lead time 6 months. Sample copy for $10 or sample articles on website. Guidelines available online.

◐   Submissions are not read between May 1 and October 1.

MAGAZINE'S NEEDS No light verse. Open. Pays $10-25.

TIPS "We aren't interested in essays that are footnoted, or essays usually described as scholarly or critical. Our preference is for creative nonfiction or personal essays. We prefer shorter stories and essays to longer ones (an average length is 3,500-4,000 words). We have no rigid preferences as to subject, style, or genre, although commercial efforts tend to put us off. Even so, our only fixed requirement is on good writing."

◐ ⑤ NEW MILLENNIUM WRITINGS

New Messenger Writing and Publishing, P.O. Box 2463, Knoxville TN 37901. (865)428-0389. **E-mail:** alexis.williams@hotmail.com. **Website:** http://newmillenniumwritings.com. **Contact:** Alexis Williams, editor. "While we only accept general submissions January-March, we hold 4 contests twice each year for all types of fiction, nonfiction, short-short fiction, and poetry." Publishes mss 6 months to 1 year after acceptance. Rarely comments on/critiques rejected mss.

Annual anthology. 6x9, 204 pages, 50 lb. white paper, glossy 4-color cover. Contains illustrations. Includes photographs. "Superior writing is the sole criterion. We have launched careers."

MAGAZINE'S NEEDS Accepts mss through biannual *New Millennium Writing* Awards for Fiction, Poetry, and Nonfiction; also accepts general submissions January-March.

TIPS "Looks for originality, accessibility, musicality of language, psychological insight, mythic resonance. E-mail for list of writing tips or send SASE. No charge."

NEW OHIO REVIEW

English Department, 360 Ellis Hall, Ohio University, Athens OH 45701. (740)597-1360. **E-mail:** noreditors@ohio.edu. **Website:** www.ohiou.edu/nor. **Contact:** Jill Allyn Rosser, editor. *NOR*, published biannually in spring and fall, publishes fiction, nonfiction, and poetry. Single: $9; Subscription: $16. Member: CLMP. Reading period is September 15th to December 15th and January 15th to April 1st. Responds in 2-4 months. Guidelines available online.

MAGAZINE'S NEEDS Submit up to 6 poems at a time. "Do not submit more than once every six months.

NEW ORLEANS REVIEW

Box 195, Loyola University, New Orleans LA 70118. (504)865-2295. **E-mail:** noreview@loyno.edu. **Website:** http://neworleansreview.org. **Contact:** Amberly Fox, managing editor. Biannual magazine publishing poetry, fiction, translations, photographs, and nonfiction on literature, art and film. Readership: those interested in contemporary literature and culture. New Orleans Review is a journal of contemporary literature and culture, publishing new poetry, fiction, nonfiction, art, photography, film and book reviews. The journal was founded in 1968 and has since published an eclectic variety of work by established and emerging writers including Walker Percy, Pablo Neruda, Ellen Gilchrist, Nelson Algren, Hunter S. Thompson, John Kennedy Toole, Richard Brautigan, Barry Spacks, James Sallis, Jack Gilbert, Paul Hoover, Rodney Jones, Annie Dillard, Everette Maddox, Julio Cortazar, Gordon Lish, Robert Walser, Mark Halliday, Jack Butler, Robert Olen Butler, Michael Harper, Angela Ball, Joyce Carol Oates, Diane Wakoski, Dermot Bolger, Roddy Doyle, William Kotzwinkle, Alain Robbe-Grillet, Arnost Lustig, Raymond Queneau, Yusef Komunyakaa, Michael Martone, Tess Gallagher, Matthea Harvey, D. A. Powell, Rikki Ducornet, and Ed Skoog. Buys first North American serial rights. Pays on publication. Responds in 4 months to mss. Sample copy for $5.

TIPS "We're looking for dynamic writing that demonstrates attention to the language, and a sense of the medium, writing that engages, surprises, moves us. We're not looking for genre fiction, or academic articles. We subscribe to the belief that in order to truly write well, one must first master the rudiments: grammar and syntax, punctuation, the sentence, the paragraph, the line, the stanza. We receive about 3,000 manuscripts a year, and publish about 3% of them. Check out a recent issue, send us your best, proofread your work, be patient, be persistent."

NEW SOUTH

Campus Box 1894, Georgia State University, MSC 8R0322 Unit 8, Atlanta GA 30303-3083. (404)413-5874. **E-mail:** newsouth@gsu.edu. **Website:** www.review.gsu.edu. Semiannual magazine dedicated to finding and publishing the best work from artists around the world. Wants "original voices searching to rise above the ordinary." Seeks to publish high quality work, regardless of genre, form, or regional ties. *New South* is 160+ pages. Press run is 2,000; 500 distributed free to students. Single copy: $5; subscription: $8/year; $14 for 2 years. Single issue: $5. Sample:$3 (back issue). Acquires one-time rights. Time between acceptance and publication is 3-5 months. Responds in 3-5 months. Sample copy for $5. Guidelines available online.

The *New South* Annual Writing Contest offers $1,000 for the best poem and $1,000 for the best story or essay; one-year subscription to all who submit. Submissions must be unpublished. Submit up to 3 poems, 1 story, or 1 essay on any subject or in any form. Specify "poetry" or "fiction" on outside envelope." Guidelines available by e-mail or on website. **Deadline:** March 4. Competition receives 300 entries. Past judges include Sharon Olds, Jane Hirschfield, Anthony Hecht, Phillip Levine and Jake Adam

York. Winner will be announced in the Fall issue.

MAGAZINE'S NEEDS Submit up to 3 poems at a time. Considers simultaneous submissions (with notification in cover letter); no previously published poems. No e-mail submissions. Seldom comments on rejected poems. Rights revert to poets upon publication. Pays 2 contributor's copies.

TIPS "*New South* is now accepting submissions through Tell It Slant, an online submission manager. For a small fee that's roughly the cost of printing and posting paper submissions, Tell it Slant will save time, reduce paper waste, and increase our efficiency."

THE NEW VERSE NEWS

Tangerang, Indonesia. **E-mail:** nvneditor@yahoo.com; nvneditor@gmail.com. **Website:** www.newversenews.com. **Contact:** James Penha, editor. *The New Verse News*, published online and updated "every day or two," has "a clear liberal bias, but will consider various visions and views." Wants "poems, both serious and satirical, on current events and topical issues; will also consider prose poems and short-short stories and plays." Does not want "work unrelated to the news." Receives about 1,200 poems/year; accepts about 300. Acquires first rights. Rights revert to poet upon publication. "Normally, poems are published immediately upon acceptance." Responds in 1-3 weeks. Sometimes comments on rejected poems. Guidelines available on website.

MAGAZINE'S NEEDS Submit 1-5 poems at a time. No previously published poems or simultaneous submissions. Accepts only e-mail submissions (pasted into body of message); use "Verse News Submission" as the subject line; no disk or postal submissions. Send brief bio. Reads submissions year-round. Poems are circulated to an editorial board. Lines/poem: no length restrictions. No payment.

NEW WELSH REVIEW

P.O. Box 170, Aberystwyth, Ceredigion Wa SY23 1 WZ, United Kingdom. 01970-626230. **E-mail:** editor@newwelshreview.com. **E-mail:** submissions@newwelshreview.com. **Website:** www.newwelshreview.com. **Contact:** Gwen Davies, editor. "*NWR*, a literary quarterly ranked in the top five of British literary magazines, publishes stories, poems and critical essays. The best of Welsh writing in English, past and present, is celebrated, discussed and debated. We seek poems, short stories, reviews, special features/articles and commentary." Quarterly.

THE NEW WRITER

(44)(158)021-2626. **E-mail:** editor@thenewwriter.com. **Website:** www.thenewwriter.com. **Contact:** Abegail Morley, poetry editor. "Contemporary writing magazine which publishes the best in fact, fiction and poetry." Buys one-time rights. Pays on publication. Publishes ms an average of 1 year after acceptance. Responds in 2 months to queries. Responds in 4 months to mss. Sample copy for SASE and A4 SAE with IRCs only. Guidelines for SASE.

MAGAZINE'S NEEDS Length: 40 lines maximum. Pays £5/poem.

CONTEST/AWARD OFFERINGS Sponsors *The New Writer* Prose & Poetry Prizes annually. "All poets writing in the English language are invited to submit an original, previously unpublished poem or a collection of 6-10 poems. Up to 25 prizes will be presented, as well as publication for the prize-winning poets in an anthology, plus the chance for a further 10 shortlisted poets to see their work published in *The New Writer* during the year." Guidelines available by e-mail or on website.

TIPS "Hone it—always be prepared to improve the story. It's a competitive market."

THE NEW YORKER

4 Times Square, New York NY 10036. (212) 286-5900. **E-mail:** beth_lusko@newyorker.com; toon@cartoonbank.com. **Website:** www.newyorker.com; www.cartoonbank.com. **Contact:** Bob Mankoff, cartoon; David Remnick, editor-in-chief. A quality weekly magazine of distinct news stories, articles, essays, and poems for a literate audience. Pays on acceptance. Responds in 3 months to mss.

The New Yorker receives approximately 4,000 submissions per month. Subscription: $59.99/year (47 issues), $29.99 for 6 months (23 issues).

MAGAZINE'S NEEDS Send poetry to Poetry Department. Submit no more than 6 poems at a time. No previously published poems or simultaneous submissions. Use online e-mail source and upload as pdf attachment. Include poet's name in the subject line and as the title of attached document. "We prefer to receive no more than 2 submissions per writer per year." Pays top rates.

TIPS "Be lively, original, not overly literary. Write what you want to write, not what you think the editor would like."

NIMROD: INTERNATIONAL JOURNAL OF POETRY AND PROSE

University of Tulsa, 800 S. Tucker Dr., Tulsa OK 74104-3189. (918)631-3080. **Fax:** (918)631-3033. **E-mail:** nimrod@utulsa.edu. **Website:** www.utulsa.edu/nimrod. **Contact:** Francine Ringold, editor-in-chief; Elis O'Neal, managing editor. Magazine: 6x9; 192 pages; 60 lb. white paper; illustrations; photos. "We publish 1 thematic issue and 1 awards issue each year. A recent theme was 'Growing Season,' a compilation of poetry and prose from all over the world. We seek vigorous, imaginative, quality writing. Our mission is to discover new writers and publish experimental writers who have not yet found a 'home' for their work." Responds in 3 months to mss. Sample copy: $11. Guidelines available for SASE, by e-mail, or on website.

Semiannual. Receives 120 unsolicited mss/month. **Publishes 5-10 new writers/year.** Recently published work by Terry Blackhawk, Kellie Wells, Judith Hutchinson Clark, Tomaz Salamun. SASE for return of ms. Accepts queries by e-mail. Does not accept submissions by e-mail unless the writer is living outside the US. Subscription: $18.50/year U.S., $20 foreign. Poetry published in *Nimrod* has been included in *The Best American Poetry.*

MAGAZINE'S NEEDS Submit 5-10 poems at a time. No fax or e-mail submissions. Open to general submissions from January 1-November 30. Sponsors the annual *Nimrod* Literary Awards, including The Pablo Neruda Prize for Poetry (see separate listing in Contests & Awards). "During the months that the *Nimrod* Literary Awards competition is being conducted, reporting time on non-contest mss will be longer." Also sponsors the *Nimrod* workshop for readers and writers, a 1-day workshop held annually in October. Cost is about $50. Send SASE for brochure and registration form. Pays 2 contributor's copies, plus reduced cost on additional copies.

NINTH LETTER

Department of English, University of Illinois, 608 S. Wright St., Urbana IL 61801. (217)244-3145. **E-mail:** info@ninthletter.com; editor@ninthletter.com. **Website:** www.ninthletter.com. **Contact:** Jodee Stanley, editor. Member: CLMP; CELJ. "*Ninth Letter* accepts submissions of fiction, poetry, and essays from September 1 to February 28 (postmark dates). *Ninth Letter* is published semi-annually at the University of Illinois, Urbana-Champaign. We are interested in prose and poetry that experiment with form, narrative, and nontraditional subject matter, as well as more traditional literary work." Pays on publication.

Ninth Letter won Best New Literary Journal 2005 from the Council of Editors of Learned Journals (CELJ) and has had poetry selected for *The Pushcart Prize, Best New Poets,* and *The Year's Best Fantasy and Horror.*

MAGAZINE'S NEEDS Submit 3-6 poems (no more than 10 pages) at a time. "All mailed submissions must include an SASE for reply." Pays $25 per printed page and 2 contributor's copies.

NITE-WRITER'S INTERNATIONAL LITERARY ARTS JOURNAL

158 Spencer Ave., Suite 100, Pittsburgh PA 15227. (412)668-0691. **E-mail:** nitewritersliteraryarts@gmail.com. **Website:** http://nitewritersinternational.webs.com. **Contact:** John Thompson. *Nite-Writer's International Literary Arts Journal* is an online literary arts journal. "We are 'dedicated to the emotional intellectual' with a creative perception of life." Retains first North American serial rights. Copyright reverts to author upon publication. Guidelines available on website.

Journal is open to beginners as well as professionals. Receives about 1,000 poems/year, accepts about 10-15%. Has published poetry by Lyn Lifshin, Rose Marie Hunold, Peter Vetrano, Carol Frances Brown, and Richard King Perkins II.

MAGAZINE'S NEEDS Wants strong imagery and accepts free verse, avant-garde poetry, haiku, and senryu. Considers previously published poems and simultaneous submissions. Cover letter is preferred. "Give brief bio, state where you heard of us, state if material has been previously published and where." Does not want porn or violence. Open to length.

TIPS "Read a lot of what you write—study the market. Don't fear rejection, but use it as learning tool to strengthen your work before resubmitting."

THE NORMAL SCHOOL

The Press at the California State University - Fresno, 5245 North Backer Ave., M/S PB 98, Fresno CA 93740-

8001. **E-mail:** editors@thenormalschool.com. **E-mail:** submissions@thenormalschool.com. **Website:** http://thenormalschool.com. **Contact:** Steven Church, editor. Semiannual magazine that accepts "outstanding work by beginning and established writers." Acquires first North American serial rights. Publication is copyrighted. Publishes ms 3-6 months after acceptance. Responds to stories in 2 months. Sample copy available for $7 on website or via e-mail. For guidelines, send check and address or visit website.

MAGAZINE'S NEEDS Considers poetry of any style. Submit no more than 5 poems. "Please limit the number of cat poems."

TIPS "Manuscripts are read from September 1 to December 1 and from January 15 to April 15. Unsolicited manuscripts received outside of the designated reading periods will be printed out, sculpted into a political effigy, and burned ceremoniously in front of an unruly mob. Please address your submissions to the appropriate editor (i.e. Nonfiction Editor, Recipe Editor, Miscellaneous Editor, etc.). Please do not include pictures of yourself unless it is an extraordinarily funny picture of you wearing ridiculous glasses or unnecessarily tight pants with a large gravy stain. With any mailed submission, please tuck a SASE in along with your work. The trees would like you to submit online, but paper submissions are still welcome and there is no processing charge."

NORTH AMERICAN REVIEW

University of Northern Iowa, 1222 W. 27th St., Cedar Falls IA 50614. (319)273-6455. **Fax:** (319)273-4326. **E-mail:** nar@uni.edu. **Website:** northamericanreview.org. **Contact:** Kim Groninga, nonfiction editor. "The *NAR* is the oldest literary magazine in America and one of the most respected; though we have no prejudices about the subject matter of material sent to us, our first concern is quality." Buys first North American serial rights, buys first rights. Pays on publication. Publishes ms an average of 1 year after acceptance. Responds in 4 months to mss. Sample copy for $7. Guidelines available online.

⊙ This is the oldest literary magazine in the country and one of the most prestigious. Also one of the most entertaining—and a tough market for the young writer.

MAGAZINE'S NEEDS No restrictions; highest quality only. Pays $1/line; $20 minimum, $100 maximum

TIPS "We like stories that start quickly and have a strong narrative arc. Poems that are passionate about subject, language, and image are welcome, whether they are traditional or experimental, whether in formal or free verse (closed or open form). Nonfiction should combine art and fact with the finest writing. We do not accept simultaneous submissions; these will be returned unread. We read poetry, fiction, and nonfiction year-round."

NORTH CAROLINA LITERARY REVIEW

East Carolina University, ECU Mailstop 555 English, Greenville NC 27858-4353. (252)328-1537. **Fax:** (252)328-4889. **E-mail:** nclrsubmissions@ecu.edu. **Website:** www.nclr.ecu.edu. **Contact:** Gabrielle Freeman. "Articles should have a North Carolina slant. First consideration is always for quality of work. Although we treat academic and scholarly subjects, we do not wish to see jargon-laden prose; our readers, we hope, are found as often in bookstores and libraries as in academia. We seek to combine the best elements of magazine for serious readers with best of scholarly journal." Buys first North American serial rights. Rights returned to writer on request. Pays on publication. Publishes ms an average of 1 year after acceptance. Responds in 1 month to queries. Responds in 6 months to mss. Editorial lead time 6 months. Sample copy for $10-25. Guidelines available online.

⊙ Uses online submission form.

MAGAZINE'S NEEDS *North Carolina poets only.* Submit 3-5 poems at a time. Include cover letter. Length: 30-150 lines. Pays $50-100 honorarium, extra copies, back issues or subscription (negotiable).

TIPS "By far the easiest way to break in is with special issue sections. We are especially interested in reports on conferences, readings, meetings that involve North Carolina writers, and personal essays or short narratives with a strong sense of place. See back issues for other departments. Interviews are probably the other easiest place to break in; no discussions of poetics/theory, etc., except in reader-friendly (accessible) language; interviews should be personal, more like conversations, that explore connections between a writer's life and his/her work."

NORTH CENTRAL REVIEW

North Central College, CM #235, 30 N. Brainard St., Naperville IL 60540. (630)637-5291. **E-mail:** nccreview@noctrl.edu. **Website:** http://orgs.noctrl.edu/review. **Contact:** Drew Smith, Kelly Rasmussen. *North*

Central Review, published semiannually, considers "work in all literary genres, including occasional interviews, from undergraduate writers globally. The journal's goal is for college-level, emerging creative writers to share their work publicly and create a conversation with each other. ALL styles and forms are welcome as submissions. The readers tend to value attention to form (but not necessarily fixed form), voice, and detail. Very long poems or sequences (running more than 4 or 5 pages) may require particular excellence because of the journal's space and budget constraints." Does not want "overly sentimental language and hackneyed imagery. These are all-too-common weaknesses that readers see in submissions; we recommend revision and polishing before sending work." Considers poetry by teens (undergraduate writers only). *North Central Review* is 120 pages, digest-sized, perfect-bound, with cardstock cover with 4-color design. Press run is about 750, distributed free to contributors and publication reception attendees. Single copy: $5; subscription: $10. Make checks payable to North Central College. Acquires first rights. Publishes ms 1-4 months after acceptance. Responds in 1-4 months. Guidelines for SASE, by e-mail, online and in magazine.

MAGAZINE'S NEEDS Submit up to 5 poems at a time. Lines/poem: "no limit, but poems running more than 4-5 pages may undergo particular scrutiny." No previously published poems or simultaneous submissions. Accepts e-mail submissions (as Word attachments only); no fax submissions. Cover letter is preferred. Include name, postal address, phone number, and e-mail address (.edu address as proof of student status). If necessary (i.e., .edu address not available), include a photocopy of student ID with number marked out as proof of undergraduate status. Reads submissions September-March, with deadlines of February 15 and October 15. Poems are circulated to an editorial board. "All submissions are read by at least 3 staff members, including an editor." Rarely comments on rejected poems. Pays 2 contributor's copies.

TIPS "Don't send anything you just finished moments ago—rethink, revise, and polish. Avoid sentimentality and abstraction. That said, the *North Central Review* publishes beginners, so don't hesitate to submit and, if rejected, submit again."

NORTH DAKOTA QUARTERLY

276 Centennial Dr. Stop 7209, Merrifield Hall Room 15, Grand Forks ND 58202. (701)777-3322. **E-mail:** und.ndq@email.und.edu. **Website:** www.und.nodak.edu/org/ndq. Only reads fiction and poetry between September 1 and May 1. Requires first serial rights. Guidelines available online.

Work published in *North Dakota Quarterly* was selected for inclusion in *The O. Henry Prize Stories*, *The Pushcart Prize Series* and *Best American Essays*.

MAGAZINE'S NEEDS Simultaneous submissions NOT OK for poetry. Submit up to 5 poems as hard copy. No length restrictions.

NORTHWIND

Chain Bridge Press, LLC., 4201 Wilson Blvd., #110, Arlington VA 22203. **E-mail:** info@northwindmagazine.com. **Website:** www.northwindmagazine.com. **Contact:** Tom Howard, managing editor. "Our focus is originality and provocative, compulsively readable prose and poetry, in any style or genre. We look for smart, lyrical writing that will appeal to an intelligent and culturally sophisticated audience." Acquires first serial rights, both print and electronic. Pays on publication. Publishes ms 2 months after acceptance. Responds in 8-10 weeks. "If you haven't received a notification e-mail from us after 10 weeks, please feel free to contact us at submissions@northwindmagazine.com." Sample copy available online at website. Guidelines available online at website.

MAGAZINE'S NEEDS "We accept poetry submissions on any subject and in any style, although we tend to avoid rhyming poetry and prose poems. Read the magazine for excellent examples of what we're seeking. We want compelling ideas, unforced language, and genuine meaning over sentimentality." Submit up to 5 poems at a time, with all pieces in a single file. "*Northwind* pays $150 for the issue's featured story only. All contributors, however, will be provided with a dedicated page on the site for biographical information (including photo), any relevant web site links, and an optional feedback form for readers."

NOTES ON THE STATE OF NEW JERSEY

37 Chelsea Ct., Franklin Park NJ 08823. **E-mail:** editor@notesonnj.com. **Website:** www.notesonnj.com. **Contact:** Melissa Morris, editor. Notes on the State of New Jersey publishes material from a variety of perspectives and voices to give an authentic repre-

sentation of what is happening in New Jersey. Buys simultaneous rights. Responds in 2-4 weeks on queries. Editorial lead time 1-2 months. Sample copy available on website. Guidelines available on website.

MAGAZINE'S NEEDS Poetry must be about New Jersey or be written by a New Jersey poet to be considered.

TIPS "If you love to write about New Jersey, then we would love to hear from you."

⊕ ⊕ ⊕ NOTRE DAME REVIEW

University of Notre Dame, 840 Flanner Hall, Notre Dame IN 46556. (574)631-6952. **Fax:** (574)631-4795. **E-mail:** english.ndreview.1@nd.edu. **Website:** www. nd.edu/~ndr/review.htm. The *Notre Dame Review* is an indepenent, noncommercial magazine of contemporary American and international fiction, poetry, criticism, and art. We are especially interested in work that takes on big issues by making the invisible seen, that gives voice to the voiceless. In addition to showcasing celebrated authors like Seamus Heaney and Czelaw Milosz, the *Notre Dame Review* introduces readers to authors they may have never encountered before, but who are doing innovative and important work. In conjunction with the *Notre Dame Review*, the online companion to the printed magazine, the *Notre Dame Re-view* engages readers as a community centered in literary rather than commercial concerns, a community we reach out to through critique and commentary as well as aesthetic experience. Buys first North American serial rights. Pays on publication. Publishes ms an average of 6 months after acceptance. Responds in 4 or more months to mss. Sample copy for $6. Guidelines available online.

MAGAZINE'S NEEDS Submit 3-5 poems at a time.

TIPS "We're looking for high quality work that takes on big issues in a literary way. Please read our back issues before submitting."

NOW & THEN; THE APPALACHIAN MAGAZINE

East Tennessee State University, Box 70556, Johnson City TN 37614-1707. (423)439-5348. **Fax:** (423)439-6340. **E-mail:** nowandthen@etsu.edu. **E-mail:** wardenc@etsu.edu. **Website:** www.etsu.edu/cass/nowandthen. **Contact:** Jane Woodside, editor. Literary magazine published twice/year. "*Now & Then* accepts a variety of writing genres: fiction, poetry, non-fiction, essays, interviews, memoirs, and book reviews. All submissions must relate to Appalachia and to the issue's specific theme. Our readership is educated and interested in the region." Buys first North American serial rights. Rights revert back to author after publication. Sample copy available for $8 plus $3 shipping. Guidelines and upcoming themes available on website.

○ Magazine: 8½×11; 44-48 pages; coated paper and cover stock; illustrations; photos. *Now & Then* tells the stories of Appalachia and presents a fresh, revealing picture of life in Appalachia, past and present, with engaging articles, personal essays, fiction, poetry, and photography.

MAGAZINE'S NEEDS Submit up to 5 poems, with SASE and cover letter including "a few lines about yourself for a contributor's note and whether the work has been published or accepted elsewhere." Will consider simultaneous submissions; occasionally accepts previously published poems. Put name, address and phone number on every poem. Deadlines: March 31 (spring/summer issue) and August 31 (fall/winter issues). Publishes theme issues. Responds within 6 months. Sends prepublication galleys. Pays $20/poem plus 2 contributor's copies.

TIPS "Keep in mind that *Now & Then* only publishes material related to the Appalachian region. Plus we only publish fiction that has some plausible connection to a specific issue's themes. Get the guidelines. We like to offer first-time publication to promising writers."

⊕ NTH DEGREE

E-mail: submissions@nthzine.com. **Website:** www. nthzine.com. **Contact:** Michael Pederson. Acquires one-time rights. Pays on publication. Responds in 2 weeks to queries; 2 months to mss. Guidelines online.

○ No longer accepts hard copy submissions.

MAGAZINE'S NEEDS Submit through e-mail. Wants poetry about science fiction, fantasy, horror, alternate history, well-crafted mystery, and humor. Pays in contributor's copies.

TIPS "Don't submit anything that you may be ashamed of ten years later."

⊕ ⊕ NTHPOSITION

E-mail: val@nthposition.com; laurapoetry2012@ gmail.com. **Website:** www.nthposition.com. **Contact:** Laura Bottomley, poetry editor; Val Stevenson, managing editor. *nthposition*, published monthly online, is "an eclectic, London-based journal with politics and opinion, travel writing, fiction and poetry, art reviews and interviews, and some high weirdness." Does not request rights but expects proper acknowledgement if poems are reprinted later. Time between acceptance and publication is 4 months. Responds in 6 weeks. Never comments on rejected poems. Guidelines available online.

- Rufo Quintavalle, poetry editor, wants "all kinds of poetry, from post modern to mainstream." Receives about 2,000 poems/year; accepts about 10%. "We can only notify people whose work we accept." Val Stevenson, managing editor, wants clear, vivid prose. Receives about 1,500 articles/year, accepts about 10%.

MAGAZINE'S NEEDS Accepts e-mail submissions only (pasted into body of message; no attachments). Cover letter is required. "Please include a brief (2 sentences) biographical note." Reads submissions throughout the year. "Poems are read and selected by the poetry editor, who uses his own sense of what makes a poem work online to select." Occasionally publishes theme issues. Publishes special theme e-books from time to time, such as *100 Poets Against the War*. "No racism, nastiness, silkworm farming, or diabetes articles." No payment.

TIPS "Submit as text in the body of an e-mail, along with a brief bio note (2-3 sentences). If your work is accepted, it will be archived into the British Library's permanent collection."

NUTHOUSE

Website: www.nuthousemagazine.com. *Nuthouse*, published every 3 months, uses humor of all kinds, including homespun and political. Wants "humorous verse; virtually all genres considered." Has published poetry by Holly Day, Daveed Garstenstein-Ross, and Don Webb. *Nuthouse* is 12 pages, digest-sized, photocopied from desktop-published originals. Receives about 500 poems/year, accepts about 100. Press run is 100. Subscription: $5 for 4 issues. Sample: $1.50. Make checks payable to Twin Rivers Press. Acquires one-time rights. Publishes ms 6-12 months after acceptance. Responds in 1 month. Sample copy for $1.50. Guidelines for #10 SASE.

MAGAZINE'S NEEDS Pays 1 contributor's copy per poem.

OBSIDIAN

North Carolina State University, Department of English, Box 8105, Raleigh NC 27695. (919)515-4153. E-mail: obsidian@gw.ncsu.edu. **Website:** www.ncsu.edu/chass/obsidian/. **Contact:** Sheila Smith McKoy, editor. Acquires one-time rights. Responds in 4 months.

- Accepts submissions through online submission form ONLY. Accepts submissions from September 1 to April 30.

MAGAZINE'S NEEDS Submit single-spaced poems using online submission form. Submit no more than 5 poems. Should not exceed 8 pages. Include all poetry submissions in a single file.

TIPS "Following proper format is essential. Your title must be intriguing and text clean. Never give up. Some of the writers we publish were rejected many times before we published them."

OCEAN MAGAZINE

P.O. Box 84, Rodanthe NC 27968-0084. (252)256-2296. **E-mail:** diane@oceanmagazine.org. **Website:** www.oceanmagazine.org. *"OCEAN* magazine serves to celebrate and protect the greatest, most comprehensive resource for life on earth, our world's ocean. *OCEAN* publishes articles, stories, poems, essays, and photography about the ocean—observations, experiences, scientific and environmental discussions—written with fact and feeling, illustrated with images from nature." Buys one-time rights. Pays on publication. Publishes ms an average of 2-4 months after acceptance. Responds in 1 day to 2 months. Editorial lead time 3-6 months. Sample copy available for $3 digital, $8.45 print. Guidelines available online.

MAGAZINE'S NEEDS Pays $25-75.

TIPS "Submit with a genuine love and concern for the ocean and its creatures."

OFF THE COAST

Resolute Bear Press, P.O. Box 14, Robbinston ME 04671. (207)454-8026. **E-mail:** poetrylane2@gmail.com. **Website:** www.off-the-coast.com. **Contact:** Valerie Lawson, editor/publisher. Quarterly journal with deadlines of March, June, September and December 15. *Off the Coast* is accepting submissions of poetry (any subject or style, e-mail submissions preferred, postal submissions OK with SASE), photography, graphics, and books for review (books only, no chapbooks). Subscriptions are $35 for 1 year, $60 for 2 years. Single issue: $10. *Off the Coast* prints all styles and forms of poetry. Considers poetry by children and teens. Has published poetry by Wes McNair, Kate Barnes, Henry Braun, Baron Wormser, Betsy Sholl,

David Wagoner, Diana DerHovanessian, Simon Perchik, and Rhina Espaillat. *Off the Coast* is 80-100+ pages, perfect-bound, with stock cover with original art. Receives about 2,500 poems/year, accepts about 200. Press run is 300; occasional complimentary copies offered. Make checks payable to *Off the Coast*. Editorial decisions are not made until after the deadline for each issue. Notifications go out the first two weeks of the month following the deadline date eg: early April for March 15 deadline. **For samples of poetry, art and reviews, visit our website**. "The mission of *Off the Coast* is to become recognized around the world as Maine's international poetry journal, a publication that prizes quality, diversity and honesty in its publications and in its dealings with poets. *Off the Coast*, a quarterly print journal, publishes poetry, artwork and reviews. Arranged much like an anthology, each issue bears a title drawn from a line or phrase from one of its poems." The rights to each individual poem and print are retained by each individual artist. Publishes mss 1-2 months after acceptance. Responds in 1-2 months. Editorial decisions are not made until after the deadline for each issue. Notifications go out the first two weeks of the month following the deadline date, e.g. early April for March 15 deadline. For samples of poetry, art and reviews, visit our website: www. off-the coast.com. Contributors receive one free copy. Additional copies of the issue their work appears in available for $5, half the cover price. Sample issue for $10. Guidelines available in magazine.

HOW TO CONTACT "Send 1-3 previously unpublished poems, any subject or style, using our submission manager: www.offthecoast.sumishmash.com/submit. We accept postal submissions with SASE with sufficient postage for return. Please include contact information and brief bio with submission. We accept simultaneous submissions, but please inform us if your work is accepted elsewhere. Pays one contributor's copy. "The rights to each individual poem and print are retained by each individual artist." For reviews, send a single copy of a newly published poetry book. Please send bound books only, we do not review chapbooks."

◯ OLD RED KIMONO

Georgia Highlands College, 3175 Cedartown Highway SE, Rome GA 30161. **E-mail:** napplega@highlands.edu. **Website:** www.highlands.edu/ork/neworkweb/WELCOME.html. **Contact:** Dr. Nancy

Applegate, professor of English. *The Old Red Kimono*, published annually, prints original, high-quality poetry and fiction. Has published poetry by Walter McDonald, Peter Huggins, Ruth Moon Kempher, John Cantey Knight, Kirsten Fox, and Al Braselton. *The Old Red Kimono* is 72 pages, magazine-sized, professionally printed on heavy stock, with colored matte cover with art. Receives about 500 submissions/year, accepts about 60-70. Sample: $3. Acquires one-time rights. Responds in 3 months.

MAGAZINE'S NEEDS Submit 3-5 poems at a time. Accepts e-mail submissions. Reads submissions September 1-March 1 only. Guidelines available for SASE or on website for more submission information. Pays 2 contributor's copies.

◯◗ ON SPEC

P.O. Box 4727, Station South, Edmonton AB T6E 5G6, Canada. (780)628-7121. **E-mail:** onspec@onspec.ca. **E-mail:** onspecmag@gmail.com. **Website:** www.on-spec.ca. "We publish speculative fiction and poetry by new and established writers, with a strong preference for Canadian authored works." Buys first North American serial rights. Pays on acceptance. Publishes ms an average of 6-18 months after acceptance. Responds in 2 weeks to queries; 6 months after deadline to mss. Editorial lead time 6 months. Sample copy for $8. Guidelines for #10 SASE or on website.

◯ See website guidelines for submission announcements.

MAGAZINE'S NEEDS No rhyming or religious material. Length: 4-100 lines. Pays $50 and 1 contributor's copy.

TIPS "We want to see stories with plausible characters, a well-constructed, consistent, and vividly described setting, a strong plot and believable emotions; characters must show us (not tell us) their emotional responses to each other and to the situation and/or challenge they face. Also: don't send us stories written for television. We don't like media tie-ins, so don't watch TV for inspiration! Read, instead! Strong preference given to submissions by Canadians."

◯ OPEN MINDS QUARTERLY

The Writer's Circle, 680 Kirkwood Dr., Building 1, Sudbury ON P3E 1X3, Canada. (705)675-9193, ext. 8286. **E-mail:** openminds@nisa.on.ca. **Website:** www.nisa.on.ca. **Contact:** Dinah Laprairie, editor. *Open Minds Quarterly* provides a "venue for individuals who have experienced mental illness to express themselves via poetry, short fiction, essays, first-person accounts of living with mental illness, book/movie reviews." Wants "unique, well-written, provocative poetry." Does not want overly graphic or sexual violence. Considers poetry by children and teens. Has published poetry by Pamela MacBean, Sophie Soil, Alice Parris, and Kurt Sass. *Open Minds Quarterly* is 24 pages, magazine-sized, saddle-stapled, with 100 lb. stock cover with original artwork, includes ads. Receives about 300 poems/year, accepts about 30%. Press run is 750; 400 distributed free to potential subscribers, published writers, advertisers, and conferences and events. Single copy: $5.40 CAD, $5 USD; subscription: $35 CAD, $28.25 USD (special rates also available). Make checks payable to NISA/Northern Initiative for Social Action.

MAGAZINE'S NEEDS Submit 1-5 poems at a time. Considers previously published poems and simultaneous submissions. Accepts e-mail and disk submissions. Cover letter is required. "Info in cover letter: indication as to 'consumer/survivor' of the mental health system status." Reads submissions year round. Submit seasonal poems at least 8 months in advance. Time between acceptance and publication is 6-18 months. "Poems are first reviewed by poetry editor, then accepted/rejected by the editor. Sometimes, submissions are passed on to a third party for input or a third opinion." Seldom comments on rejected poems. Guidelines available for SASE, by fax, e-mail, or on website. Responds in up to 4 months. "Rarely" sends prepublication galleys. "All authors own their work—if another publisher seeks to reprint from our publication, we request they cite us as the source."

CONTEST/AWARD OFFERINGS "The Brainstorm Poetry Contest runs in first 2 months of each year. Contact the editor for information."

ALSO OFFERS "All material not accepted for our journal will be considered for The Writer's Circle Online, our Internet publication forum. Same guidelines apply. Same contact person."

OSIRIS

P.O. Box 297, Deerfield MA 01342. **E-mail:** amoorhead@deerfield.edu. **Contact:** Andrea Moorhead, editor. *Osiris*, published semiannually, prints contemporary poetry in English, French, and Italian without translation, and in other languages with translation, including Polish, Danish, and German. Responds in 1 month. Sometimes sends prepublication galleys. Sample: $10.

MAGAZINE'S NEEDS Wants poetry that is "lyrical, non-narrative, post-modern. Also looking for translations from non-Indo-European languages." Has published poetry by Abderrahmane Djelfaoui (Algeria); George Moore, Rob Cook, Simon Perchik, Ingrid Swanberg (USA); Flavio Ermini (Italy); Denise Desautels (Quebec); Yves Broussard (France); and Frances Presley (UK). Submit 4-6 poems at a time. "Poems should be sent by postal mail. Include short bio and SASE with submission. Translators should include a letter of permission from the poet or publisher as well as copies of the original text." Pays 3 contributor's copies.

OVER THE TRANSOM

825 Bush St., #203, San Francisco CA 94108. (415)928-3965. **E-mail:** jsh619@earthlink.net. **Contact:** Jonathan Hayes, editor. *Over The Transom*, published 2 times/year, is a free publication of poetry and prose. Open to all styles of poetry. "We look for the highest quality writing that best fits the issue." Publishes ms 2-6 months after acceptance. Responds in 2 months. Considers poetry by children and teens. Has published poetry by Garrett Caples, Richard Lopez, Glen Chesnut, Daniel J. Langton. *Over The Transom* is 32 pages, magazine-sized, saddle-stapled, with cardstock cover. Receives about 1,000 poems/year, accepts about 5%. Press run is 300 (100 subscribers); 150 distributed free to cafes, bookstores, universities, and bars. Single copy: free. Sample: $3. Make checks payable to Jonathan Hayes

MAGAZINE'S NEEDS Submit 5 poems at a time. Considers previously published poems and simultaneous submissions. Accepts e-mail submissions; no disk submissions. Must include a SASE with postal submissions. Reads submissions year round. Never comments on rejected poems. Occasionally publishes theme issues. Pays 1 contributor's copy.

OXFORD MAGAZINE

356 Bachelor Hall, Miami University, Oxford OH 45056. **E-mail:** oxmag@muohio.edu. **Website:** www.oxfordmagazine.org. *Oxford Magazine*, published annually in May online, is open in terms of form, content, and subject matter. Acquires one-time rights. Responds in 3 months.

○ Work published in *Oxford Magazine* has been included in the Pushcart Prize anthology.

MAGAZINE'S NEEDS Submit 3-5 poems at a time. Considers simultaneous submissions; no previously published poems. Submit using online submission form only.

◑ OYEZ REVIEW

Roosevelt University, Dept. of Literature & Languages, 430 S. Michigan Ave., Chicago IL 60605-1394. (312)341-3500. **E-mail:** oyezreview@roosevelt.edu. **Website:** legacy.roosevelt.edu/roosevelt.edu/oyezreview. Buys first North American serial rights. Pays 2 contributor's copies. Publishes ms an average of 2 months after acceptance. Responds in 3 months. Sample copy available by request. Guidelines available online. SASE required. Does not accept e-mail submissions unless from abroad.

○ Reading period is August 1-October 1. Responds by mid-December.

MAGAZINE'S NEEDS *Oyez Review*, published annually in January by Roosevelt University's MFA Program in Creative Writing, receives "submissions from across the nation and around the world. We're open to poetic sequences and longer poems provided they hold the reader's attention. We welcome skilled and polished work from newcomers as well as poems from established authors. The quality of the individual poem is key, not the poet's reputation." Has published poetry by Gary Fincke, Moira Egan, Gaylord Brewer, Barbara De Cesare, Prairie Markussen, Gary Held. *Oyez Review* is 90 pages, digest-sized. Accepts 5% of poems received. Press run is 800. Single copy: $5. 10 pages maximum

HOW TO CONTACT Submit up to 5 poems, no more than 10 pages of poetry at a time. No simultaneous submissions. No fax, e-mail, or disk submissions. Cover letter is required. "Be sure to include a three- to five-sentence biography and complete contact information, including phone and e-mail." Reads submissions August 1-October 1 only. Time between acceptance and publication is 2 months. Guidelines available on website. Responds in 3 months. Pays 2 contributor's copies. Acquires first North American serial rights.

◑ OYSTER BOY REVIEW

P.O. Box 1483, Pacifica CA 94044. **E-mail:** e-mail_2014@oysterboyreview.com. **Website:** www.oysterboyreview.com. **Contact:** Damon Suave, editor/publisher. Electronic and print magazine. *Oyster Boy Review*, published 4 times a year, is interested in "the underrated, the ignored, the misunderstood, and the varietal. We'll make some mistakes. 'All styles are good except the boring kind'—Voltaire." Publishes ms 6 months after acceptance. Responds in 3 months. Guidelines by e-mail or online at website.

MAGAZINE'S NEEDS Pays 2 contributor's copies.

ADDITIONAL INFORMATION Off the Cuff Books is not open to submissions or solicitations. Off the Cuff Books publishes "longer works on special projects of authors published in *Oyster Boy Review*."

TIPS "Keep writing, keep submitting, keep revising."

◑ PACKINGTOWN REVIEW

111 S. Lincoln St., Batavia IL 60510. **E-mail:** editors@packingtownreview.com. **Website:** www.packingtownreview.com. "*Packingtown Review* publishes imaginative and critical prose and poetry by emerging and established writers. We welcome submissions of poetry, scholarly articles, drama, creative nonfiction, fiction, and literary translation, as well as genre-bending pieces." Acquires first North American serial rights. Sends galleys to author. Publication is copyrighted. Pays on publication. Publishes ms a maximum of 1 year after acceptance. Responds to queries in 3 weeks. Responds to mss and poems in 3 months. Sometimes comments on/critiques rejected mss. Single copy: see website for prices. Guidelines available on website.

○ Annual. Magazine has revolving editor. Editorial term: 2 years. Next term: 2014. Literary magazine/journal. 8½x11, 250 pages. Press run: 500.

MAGAZINE'S NEEDS Submit 3-5 poems at a time. No previously published poems (considers poems posted on a public website/blog/forum previously published, but not those posted on a private, password-protected forum). No e-mail or disk submissions. Cover letter is required. "Please include a SASE. If you have simultaneously submitted these poems, please indicate in the cover letter and let us know ASAP if a poem is accepted elsewhere." Reads submissions year round. Poems are circulated to an editorial board. Sometimes comments on rejected poems. Reviews books/chapbooks of poetry and other magazines/journals. Send materials for review consideration to editor. Does not want uninspired or unrevised work. Pays 2 contributor's copies.

TIPS "We are looking for well-crafted prose. We are open to most styles and forms. We are also looking for prose that takes risks and does so successfully. We will consider articles about prose."

⬤⑂ PAINTED BRIDE QUARTERLY

Drexel University, Department of English and Philosophy, 3141 Chestnut St., Philadelphia PA 19104. **E-mail:** pbq@drexel.edu. **Website:** www.webdelsol. com/pbq. *Painted Bride Quarterly* seeks literary fiction, experimental and traditional. Buys first North American serial rights. Responds in 6 months to mss. Guidelines available online and by e-mail.

MAGAZINE'S NEEDS Submit up to 5 poems via postal mail. Does not accept e-mail submissions. "We have no specifications or restrictions. We'll look at anything."

CONTEST/AWARD OFFERINGS Sponsors an annual poetry contest and a chapbook competition. Guidelines available for SASE or on website.

TIPS "We look for freshness of idea incorporated with high-quality writing. We receive an awful lot of nicely written work with worn-out plots. We want quality in whatever—we hold experimental work to as strict standards as anything else. Many of our readers write fiction; most of them enjoy a good reading. We hope to be an outlet for quality. A good story gives, first, enjoyment to the reader. We've seen a good many of them lately, and we've published the best of them."

PALABRA

P.O. Box 86146, Los Angeles CA 90086. **E-mail:** info@ palabralitmag.com. **Website:** www.palabralitmag. com. "*PALABRA* is about exploration, risk, and ganas—the myriad intersections of thought, language, story and art—*el mas alla of letters*, symbols and spaces into meaning." Acquires first serial rights. Responds in 3-4 months to mss. Guidelines available online at website.

◯⬤ PAPERPLATES

19 Kenwood Ave., Toronto ON M6C 2R8, Canada. (416)651-2551. **E-mail:** magazine@paperplates.org. **Website:** www.paperplates.org. **Contact:** Bernard Kelly, publisher. Acquires first North American serial rights. Responds in 4-6 months. Guidelines available online at website.

⬤ No longer accepts IRCs.

MAGAZINE'S NEEDS Submit no more than 5 poems. Submit via surface mail or e-mail with short bio. Length: no more than 1,500 words.

⬤◯ THE PARIS REVIEW

62 White St., New York NY 10013. (212)343-1333. **E-mail:** queries@theparisreview.org. **Website:** www. theparisreview.org. **Contact:** Lorin Stein, editor. "Fiction and poetry of superlative quality, whatever the genre, style or mode. Our contributors include prominent, as well as less well-known and previously unpublished writers. Writers at Work interview series includes important contemporary writers discussing their own work and the craft of writing." Buys all rights, buys first English-language rights. Pays on publication. Responds in 4 months to mss. Sample copy for $12 (includes postage). Guidelines available online.

⬤ Address submissions to proper department. Do not make submissions via e-mail.

MAGAZINE'S NEEDS Submit no more than 6 poems at a time. Poetry can be sent to the poetry editor (please include a self-addressed, stamped envelope), or submitted online at http://www.theparisreview. org/poetry/. Pays $35 minimum varies according to length.

CONTEST/AWARD OFFERINGS Awards $1,000 in Bernard F. Conners Poetry Prize contest.

PARNASSUS: POETRY IN REVIEW

Poetry in Review Foundation, 205 W. 89th St., #8F, New York NY 10024. (212)362-3492. **E-mail:** parnew@aol.com. **Website:** www.parnassusreview. com. **Contact:** Herbert Leibowitz, editor and publisher. Buys one-time rights. Pays on publication. Publishes ms an average of 12-14 months after acceptance. Responds in 2 months to mss. Sample copy for $15.

MAGAZINE'S NEEDS Accepts most types of poetry.

TIPS "Be certain you have read the magazine and are aware of the editor's taste. Blind submissions are a waste of everybody's time. We'd like to see more poems that display intellectual acumen and curiosity about history, science, music, etc., and fewer trivial lyrical poems about the self, or critical prose that's academic and dull. Prose should sing."

⬤ PASSAGES NORTH

English Department, Northern Michigan University, 1401 Presque Isle Ave., Marquette MI 49855. (906)227-1203. **E-mail:** passages@nmu.edu. **Website:** www. passagesnorth.com. **Contact:** Jennifer A. Howard, editor-in-chief. *Passages North*, published annually in spring, prints poetry, short fiction, creative nonfiction, essays, and interviews. Sample: $3 (back issue). Guidelines available for SASE, by e-mail, or on website.

○ Magazine: 7×10; 200-300 pgs; 60 lb. paper. Publishes work by established and emerging writers. Has published poetry by Moira Egan, Frannie Lindsay, Ben Lerner, Bob Hicok, Gabe Gudding, John McNally, Steve Almond, Tracy Winn, and Midege Raymond. *Passages North* is 250 pages. Single copy: $13; subscription: $13/year, $23 for 2 years.

MAGAZINE'S NEEDS "We're looking for poems that give us pause, poems that surprise us, poems that keep us warm during long northern nights. We want them to sing and vibrate with energy. We're open to all forms and aesthetics." Submit up to 5 poems together in one document.

TIPS "We look for voice, energetic prose, writers who take risks. We look for an engaging story in which the author evokes an emotional response from the reader through carefully rendered scenes, complex characters, and a smart, narrative design. Revise, revise. Read what we publish."

⊜● PASSION

Crescent Moon Publishing, P.O. Box 393, Maidstone Kent ME14 5XU, United Kingdom. (44)(162)272-9593. **E-mail:** cresmopub@yahoo.co.uk. **Website:** www.crmoon.com. *Passion*, published quarterly, features poetry, fiction, reviews, and essays on feminism, art, philosophy, and the media.

○ Wants "thought-provoking, incisive, polemical, ironic, lyric, sensual, and hilarious work." Does not want "rubbish, trivia, party politics, sport, etc." Has published poetry by Jeremy Reed, Penelope Shuttle, Alan Bold, D.J. Enright, and Peter Redgrove. Single copy: £2.50 ($4 USD); subscription: £10 ($17 USD). Make checks payable to Crescent Moon Publishing.

MAGAZINE'S NEEDS Submit 5-10 poems at a time. Cover letter is required. Include brief bio and publishing credits ("and please print your address in capitals"). Pays 1 contributor's copy. *Crescent Moon* publishes about 25 books and chapbooks/year on arrangements **subsidized by the poet**. Wants "poetry that is passionate and authentic. Any form or length." Does not want "the trivial, insincere or derivative. We are also publishing two anthologies of new American poetry each year entitled *Pagan America*."

ⓘ⊕ THE PATERSON LITERARY REVIEW

Passaic County Community College, Cultural Affairs Dept., One College Blvd., Paterson NJ 07505-1179. (973)684-6555. **Fax:** (973)523-6085. **E-mail:** mGillan@pccc.edu. **Website:** www.pccc.edu/poetry. **Contact:** Maria Mazziotti Gillan, editor/executive director. *Paterson Literary Review*, published annually, is produced by the The Poetry Center at Passaic County Community College. Wants poetry of "high quality; clear, direct, powerful work." Acquires first North American serial rights. Publishes ms 6-12 months after acceptance. Reads submissions December 1-March 31 only. Responds within 1 year. Sample copy for $13, plus $1.50 postage.

○ *Paterson Literary Review* is 300-400 pages, magazine-sized, professionally printed, perfect bound, saddle-stapled, with glossy 4-color card cover. Press run is 2,500. Has published poetry and work by Diane di Prima, Ruth Stone, Marge Piercy, Laura Boss, Robert Mooney, and Abigail Stone. Work for *PLR* has been included in the *Pushcart Prize* anthology and *Best American Poetry*.

MAGAZINE'S NEEDS Submit up to 5 poems at a time. Considers simultaneous submissions. Lines/poem: 100 maximum.

ALSO OFFERS Publishes *The New Jersey Poetry Resource Book* ($5 plus $1.50 p&h) and *The New Jersey Poetry Calendar*. The Distinguished Poets Series offers readings by poets of international, national, and regional reputation. Poetryworks/USA is a series of programs produced for UA Columbia-Cablevision. See website for details about these additional resources.

TIPS Looks for "clear, moving, and specific work."

ⓘ THE PAUMANOK REVIEW

E-mail: editor@paumanokreview.com. **E-mail:** submissions@paumanokreview.com. **Website:** www.paumanokreview.com. Responds in 1 month. Guidelines available online at website.

○ J.P. Maney's *Western Exposures* was selected for inclusion in the *E2INK Best of the Web Anthology*.

MAGAZINE'S NEEDS Wants all forms of poetry. Submit up to 5 poems per submission via e-mail. Include cover letter. Length: no more than 100 lines.

TIPS "Though this is an English-language publication, it is not US-or UK-centric. Please submit accordingly. *TPR* is a publication of Wind River Press, which also publishes *Critique* magazine and select print and electronic books."

PAVEMENT SAW

Pavement Saw Press, 321 Empire St., Montpelier OH 43543. **E-mail:** info@pavementsaw.org. **Website:** http://pavementsaw.org. **Contact:** David Baratier, editor. *Pavement Saw*, published annually in August, wants "letters, short fiction, and poetry on any subject, especially work." Does not want "poems that tell; no work by a deceased writer, and no translations." Dedicates 15-20 pages of each issue to a featured writer. Acquires first rights. Responds in 4 months. Sometimes sends prepublication galleys. Seldom comments on rejected poems. Guidelines available in magazine or for SASE.

Pavement Saw is 88 pages, digest-sized, perfect-bound. Receives about 9,000 poems/year, accepts less than 1%. Press run is 550. Single copy: $8; subscription: $14. Sample: $7. Make checks payable to Pavement Saw Press. "Pavement Saw Press has been publishing steadily since the fall of 1993. Each year since 1999, we have published at least 4 full length paperback poetry collections, with some printed in library edition hard covers, 1 chapbook and a yearly literary journal anthology. We specialize in finding authors who have been widely published in literary journals but have not published a chapbook or full-length book."

MAGAZINE'S NEEDS Submit 5 poems at a time. Considers simultaneous submissions, "as long as poet has not published a book with a press run of 1,000 or more"; no previously published poems. No e-mail submissions; postal submissions only. Cover letter is required. "No fancy typefaces." Lines/poem: 1-2 pages. Pays at least 2 contributor's copies.

PEACE & FREEDOM

Peace & Freedom Press, 17 Farrow Rd., Whaplode Drove, Spalding, Lincs PE12 0TS, England. **Website:** http://pandf.booksmusicfilmstv.com/index.htm. Published semiannually; emphasizes social, humanitarian, and environmental issues. **Considers submissions from subscribers only.** "Those new to poetry are welcome. The poetry we publish is pro-animal rights/welfare, anti-war, environmental; poems reflecting love; erotic, but not obscene; humorous; spiritual, humanitarian; with or without rhyme/meter." Considers poetry by children and teens. Has

published poetry by Dorothy Bell-Hall, Freda Moffatt, Andrew Bruce, Bernard Shough, Mona Miller, and Andrew Savage. *Peace & Freedom* has a varied format. Subscription: $20 U.S., £10 UK for 6 issues. Sample: $5 U.S., £1.75 UK. "Sample copies can be purchased only from the above address. Advisable to buy a sample copy before submitting. Banks charge the equivalent of $5 to cash foreign checks in the UK, so please only send bills, preferably by registered post." Responds to submissions in less than a month usually., with SAE/IRC. Submissions from subscribers only.

MAGAZINE'S NEEDS No previously published poems or simultaneous submissions. Accepts e-mail submissions (pasted into body of message, no attachments; no more than 3 poems/e-mail); no fax submissions. Include bio. Reads submissions year round. Publishes theme issues. Upcoming themes available in magazine, for SAE with IRC, by e-mail, or on website. Responds to submissions in less than a month ("usually"), with SAE/IRC. "Work without correct postage will not be responded to or returned until proper postage is sent." Pays one contributor's copy. Reviews books of poetry. Lines/poem: 32 max.

CONTEST/AWARD OFFERINGS "*Peace & Freedom* holds regular poetry contests as does one of our other publications, *Eastern Rainbow*, which is a magazine concerning 20th-century popular culture using poetry up to 32 lines." Subscription: $20 U.S., £10 UK for 6 issues. Further details of competitions and publications available for SAE with IRC or on website.

TIPS "Too many writers have lost the personal touch that editors generally appreciate. It can make a difference when selecting work of equal merit."

PEARL

3030 E. Second St., Long Beach CA 90803. (562)434-4523. **E-mail:** pearlmag@aol.com. **Website:** www.pearlmag.com. **Contact:** Joan Jobe Smith and Marilyn Johnson, poetry editors. "*Pearl* is an eclectic publication, a place for lively, readable poetry and prose that speaks to real people about real life in direct, living language, profane or sublime." Pays with contributor's copy. Publishes ms an average of 6-12 months after acceptance. Sample copy for $10. Guidelines available online.

Submissions are accepted from Jan.-June only. Mss. received between July and Dec. will be returned unread. No e-mail submissions, except from countries outside the U.S. See guidelines.

MAGAZINE'S NEEDS "Our poetry issue contains a 12-15 page section featuring the work of a single poet. Entry fee for the Pearl Poetry Prize is $20, which includes a copy of the winning book." No sentimental, obscure, predictable, abstract or cliché-ridden poetry. 40 lines max. Send with cover letter and SASE.

TIPS "We look for vivid, *dramatized* situations and characters, stories written in an original 'voice,' that make sense and follow a clear narrative line. What makes a manuscript stand out is more elusive, though—more to do with feeling and imagination than anything else."

PEBBLE LAKE REVIEW

15318 Pebble Lake Dr., Houston TX 77095. **Website:** www.pebblelakereview.com. **Contact:** Amanda Auchter, editor. *Pebble Lake Review* accepts only original, previously unpublished poetry and prose September 1st to March 1st each year. Responds in 2-3 months. Guidelines available online.

Poems published in *Pebble Lake Review* have appeared on Verse Daily (www.versedaily.org) and were included in *Pushcart Prize XXXI: Best of the Small Presses.*

MAGAZINE'S NEEDS Submit 3-5 poems using online submission form. Include cover letter with contact information and brief bio.

THE PEDESTAL MAGAZINE

6815 Honors Court, Charlotte NC 28210. (704)643-0244. **E-mail:** pedmagazine@carolina.rr.com. **Website:** www.thepedestalmagazine.com. **Contact:** John Amen, editor-in-chief. Member: CLMP. "We are committed to promoting diversity and celebrating the voice of the individual." Buys first rights. All rights reverse back to the author/artist at publication time. "We retain the right to publish the piece in any subsequent issue or anthology without additional payment." Publishes ms 2-4 weeks after acceptance. Responds in 4-6 weeks to mss. Guidelines available online.

MAGAZINE'S NEEDS "We are open to a wide variety of poetry, ranging from the highly experimental to the traditionally formal. Submit all poems in 1 form. No need to query before submitting." No length restriction.

TIPS "If you send us your work, please wait for a response to your first submission before you submit again."

THE PEGASUS REVIEW

P.O. Box 88, Henderson MD 21640-0088. (410)482-6736. **Website:** www.sgc.edu. *The Pegasus Review*, now a quarterly, focuses on a specific theme for each issue and issued in calligraphic format. "Since themes might change it is advisable to contact editor about current themes. With us, brevity is the key. Themes may be submitted in the way of poetry, short-short fiction and essays." Has published work by Jane Stuart, Ed Galing, John Grey, and Burton R. Hoffman. Press run is 120 (100 subscribers, 2 libraries). Subscription: $12. Sample: $2.50, including shipping and handling. "We are currently accepting original poetry, prose, and artwork for consideration. Poetry and prose should be submitted electronically. Simply cut and paste it directly into an e-mail sent to: pegasus@sgc.edu." Responds within 1 month, often with a personal response.

MAGAZINE'S NEEDS Submit 3-5 poems at a time. Lines/poem: 24 maximum. Considers previously published poems, "if there is no conflict or violation of rights agreement," and simultaneous submissions, "but author must notify proper parties once specific material is accepted." "Brief cover letter with specifics as they relate to one's writing background are welcome." Include name and address on each page. "The usual SASE would be appreciated, unless told to recycle material." Pays 2 contributor's copies and an occasional book award.

TIPS "Write and circulate your work. Constantly strive to improve your writing craft through local writers' groups and/or writing conferences. Remember: writers need readers, so offer to read your work before a group (schools, senior citizen centers, libraries)."

PENNINE INK MAGAZINE

1 Neptune St., Burnley BB11 1SF, England. **E-mail:** sheridansdandl@yahoo.co.uk. **Website:** pennineink.weebly.com. **Contact:** Laura Sheridan, editor. *Pennine Ink*, published annually in January, prints poems and short prose pieces.

Pennine Ink is 48 pages, A5, with b&w illustrated cover. Receives about 400 poems/year, accepts about 40. Press run is 200. "Contributors wishing to purchase a copy of *Pennine Ink* should enclose £2 ($4 USD) per copy."

MAGAZINE'S NEEDS Submit up to 6 poems at a time. Lines/poem: 40 maximum; prose: no longer than 1,000 words. Considers previously published poems and simultaneous submissions. Accepts e-mail submissions. Seldom comments on rejected poems. Responds in 3 months. Pays 1 contributor's copy.

PENNSYLVANIA ENGLISH

(814)375-4785. **Fax:** (814)375-4785. **E-mail:** avallone@psu.edu. **Website:** www.english.iup.edu/pcea/publications.htm. **Contact:** Dr. Jess Haggerty, editor; Tony Vallone, poetry editor. *Pennsylvania English*, published annually, is "sponsored by the Pennsylvania College English Association. Our philosophy is quality. We publish literary fiction (and poetry and nonfiction). Our intended audience is literate, college-educated people." Acquires first North American serial rights. Pays upon publication. Publishes ms up tp 12 months after acceptance. Responds in up to 12 months to mss. Sometimes comments on rejected mss. Sample copy for $10. Guidelines available on website.

Magazine: 5¼×8¼; up to 200 pages; perfect bound; full-color cover featuring the artwork of a Pennsylvania artist. Reads mss during the summer. Publishes 4-6 new writers/year. Has published work by Dave Kress, Dan Leone, Paul West, Liz Rosenberg, Walt MacDonald, Amy Pence, Jennifer Richter, and Jeff Schiff.

MAGAZINE'S NEEDS Submit 3 or more poems at a time via the online submission manager at https://paenglish.submittable.com/submit. "For all submissions, please include a brief bio for the contributors' page. Be sure to include your name, address, phone number, e-mail address, institutional affiliation (if you have one), the title of your poem(s), and any other relevant information. We will edit if necessary for space." Wants poetry of "any length, any style."

TIPS "Quality of the writing is our only measure. We're not impressed by long-winded cover letters detailing awards and publications we've never heard of. Beginners and professionals have the same chance with us. We receive stacks of competently written but boring fiction. For a story to rise out of the rejection pile, it takes more than the basic competence."

PENNY DREADFUL: TALES & POEMS OF FANTASTIC TERROR

E-mail: MMPENDRAGON@aol.com. **Website:** www.mpendragon.com. *Penny Dreadful: Tales & Poems of Fanastic Terror*, published irregularly (about one/year), features goth-romantic poetry and prose. Publishes poetry, short stories, essays, letters, listings, reviews, and b&w artwork "which celebrate the darker aspects of Man, the World, and their Creator." Wants "literary horror in the tradition of Poe, M.R. James, Shelley, M.P. Shiel, and LeFanu—dark, disquieting tales and verses designed to challenge the reader's perception of human nature, morality, and man's place within the Darkness. Stories and poems should be set prior to 1910 and/or possess a timeless quality. Rhymed, metered verse preferred." Does not want "references to 20th- and 21st-century personages/events, graphic sex, strong language, excessive gore and shock elements." Has published poetry by Nancy Bennett, Michael R. Burch, Lee Clark, Louise Webster, K.S. Hardy, and Kevin N. Roberts. *Penny Dreadful* is about 170 pages, digest-sized, desktop-published, perfect-bound. Press run is 200. Subscription: $25/3 issues. Sample: $10. Make checks payable to Michael Pendragon. Acquires one-time rights. Guidelines available on website.

"Works appearing in *Penny Dreadful* have been reprinted in *The Year's Best Fantasy and Horror*." *Penny Dreadful* nominates best tales and poems for Pushcart Prizes.

MAGAZINE'S NEEDS Submit up to 12 poems at a time. Lines/poem: poems should not exceed 3 pages. Considers previously published poems and simultaneous submissions. "Due to the amount of submissions received, the editor cannot always respond. He encourages all contributors to submit work as simultaneous submissions." Accepts e-mail submissions (preferred; "include in body of message with a copy attached"). Put name and address on opening page, and name/title/page number on all following pages. SASE required with postal submissions. Reads submissions year round. Time between acceptance and publication is "indefinite." Poems are reviewed and chosen by editor. Always sends prepublication galleys. Pays 1 contributor's copy.

ADDITIONAL INFORMATION *Penny Dreadful* "includes market listings for, and reviews of, kindred magazines." Pendragon Publications also publishes *Songs of Innocence & Experience*.

THE PENWOOD REVIEW

P.O. Box 862, Los Alamitos CA 90720. **E-mail:** lcameron65@verizon.net. **E-mail:** submissions@penwoodreview.com. **Website:** www.penwoodreview.com. **Contact:** Lori Cameron, editor. *The Penwood Review* has been established to embrace high quality poetry of all kinds, and to provide a forum for poets who want to write intriguing, energetic, and disciplined poetry as an expression of their faith in God. We encourage writing that elevates the sacred while exploring its mystery and meaning in our lives. Semiannual. Wants "disciplined, high-quality, well-crafted poetry on any subject. Rhyming poetry must be written in traditional forms (sonnets, tercets, villanelles, sestinas, etc.)." Acquires one-time and electronic rights. Publishes ms 1 year after acceptance. Responds in up to 4 months. Sample copy for $6.

Has published poetry by Kathleen Spivack, Anne Babson, Hugh Fox, Anselm Brocki, Nina Tassi, and Gary Guinn. *The Penwood Review* is about 40 pages, magazine-sized, saddle-stapled, with heavy card cover. Press run is 50-100. Single copy: $8; subscription: $16. Pays with subscription discount of $10 and, with subscription, 1 additional contributor's copy.

MAGAZINE'S NEEDS Submit 3-5 poems at a time. Lines/poem: less than 2 pages preferred. No previously published poems or simultaneous submissions. Prefers e-mail submissions (pasted into body of message). Cover letter is optional. One poem to a page with the author's full name, address, and phone number in the upper right corner. "Submissions are circulated among an editorial staff for evaluations." Never comments on rejected poems. Does not want "light verse, doggerel, or greeting card-style poetry. Also, nothing racist, sexist, pornographic, or blasphemous."

PEREGRINE

Amherst Writers & Artists Press, P.O. Box 1076, Amherst MA 01004. (413)253-3307. **Fax:** (413)253-7764. **E-mail:** peregrine@amherstwriters.com. **Website:** www.amherstwriters.com. **Contact:** Jan Haag, editor. *Peregrine*, published annually, features poetry and fiction. Magazine: 6x9; 100 pages; 60 lb. white offset paper; glossy cover. "*Peregrine* has provided a forum for national and international writers since 1983, and is committed to finding excellent work by emerging as well as established writers. We welcome work reflecting diversity of voice. We like to be surprised. We look for writing that is honest, unpretentious, and memorable. We like to be surprised. All decisions are made by the editors." Annual. Member CLMP. Acquires first rights. Guidelines available online at website.

Only considers work submitted from March 15 to May 15.

MAGAZINE'S NEEDS Submit 3 single-spaced one-page poems. "We seek poems that inform and surprise us. We appreciate fresh and specific imagery and layered metaphors, but not excessive verbiage, abstractions or clichés." "We will not consider inspirational poetry, greeting-card verse, religious tirades, or nostalgia." Length: no more than 40 lines and spaces. Pays in contributor's copies.

TIPS "Check guidelines before submitting your work. Familiarize yourself with Peregrine. We look for heart and soul as well as technical expertise. Trust your own voice."

PERMAFROST: A LITERARY JOURNAL

c/o English Dept., Univ. of Alaska Fairbanks, P.O. Box 755720, Fairbanks AK 99775. **Website:** www.uaf.edu/english/permafrost. *Permafrost: A Literary Journal*, published in May/June, contains poems, short stories, creative nonfiction, b&w drawings, photographs, and prints. "We survive on both new and established writers, hoping and expecting to see the best work out there. We publish any style of poetry provided it is conceived, written, and revised with care. While we encourage submissions about Alaska and by Alaskans, we also welcome poems about anywhere, from anywhere. We have published work by E. Ethelbert Miller, W. Loran Smith, Peter Orlovsky, Jim Wayne Miller, Allen Ginsberg, and Andy Warhol." *Permafrost* is about 200 pages, digest-sized, professionally printed, flat-spined. Subscription: $9/year, $16/2 years, $22/3 years. Back-issues $5.

MAGAZINE'S NEEDS Submit up to 5 poems at a time. Considers simultaneous submissions. "Poems should be typed, with author's name, address, phone, and e-mail at the top of each page." Reads submissions September 1-March 15. Included SASE; "e-mail submissions will not be read." Sometimes comments on poems. Guidelines available on website. Responds in 2-3 months. Pays 1 contributor copy; reduced contributor rate on additional copies. Pays 1 contributor's copy. reduced contributor rate on additional copies.

PHILADELPHIA STORIES

Fiction/Art/Poetry of the Delaware Valley, 93 Old York Rd., Suite 1/#1-753, Jenkintown PA 19046. (215) 551-5889. **E-mail:** christine@philadelphiastories.org; info@philadelphiastories.org. **Website:** www.philadelphiastories.org. Carla Spataro, editorial director/co-publisher. **Contact:** Christine Weiser, executive director/co-publisher. *Philadelphia Stories*, published quarterly, publishes "fiction, poetry, essays and art written by authors living in, or originally from, Pennsylvania, Delaware, or New Jersey. *"Philadelphia Stories* also hosts 2 national writing contests: The Marguerite McGlinn Short Story Contest ($2,000 prize) and the Sandy Crimmins National Poetry Contest ($1,000 1st place prize, $250 2nd place prize). Visit our website for details. *"Philadelphia Stories* also launched a "junior" version in 2012 for Philadelphia-area writers ages 18 and younger. Visit www.philadelphiastories.org/junior for details. Acquires one-time rights. Publication is copyrighted. Pays on publication. Publishes ms 1-2 months after acceptance. Responds in 12 weeks to mss, 3 months to poems. Rarely comments on/critiques rejected mss. List of upcoming themes available for SASE, and on website. Sample copy available for $5, and on website. Guidelines available on website.

Literary magazine/journal. 8½×11; 24 pages; 70# matte text, all four-color paper; 70# Matte Text cover. Contains illustrations., photographs. Subscription: "we offer $20 memberships that include home delivery." Make checks payable to *Philadelphia Stories*. Member: CLMP.

MAGAZINE'S NEEDS Submit 3 poems at a time. Considers simultaneous submissions; no previously published poems. Accepts submissions through online submission form at www.philadelphiastories.org/submissions; no disk submissions. Cover letter is preferred. Reads submissions year round. Poems are circulated to an editorial board. "Each poem is reviewed by a preliminary board that decides on a final list; the entire board discusses this list and chooses the mutual favorites for print and Web. We send a layout proof to check for print poems." Receives about 600 poems/year, accepts about 15%. Considers poetry by teens. Has published poetry by Daniel Abdal-Hayy Moore, Scott Edward Anderson, Sandy Crimmins, Liz Dolan, Alison Hicks, and Margaret A. Robinson. Wants "polished, well crafted poems." Does not want "first drafts." Lines/poem: 36.

TIPS "All work is screened by 3 editorial board members, who rank the work. These scores are processed at the end of the quarterly submission period, and then the board meets to decide which pieces will be published in print and online. We look for exceptional, polished prose, a controlled voice, strong characters and place, and interesting subjects. Follow guidelines.

We cannot stress this enough. Read every guideline carefully and thoroughly before sending anything out. Send out only polished material. We reject many quality pieces for various reasons; try not to take rejection personally. Just because your piece isn't right for one publication doesn't mean it's bad. Selection is an extremely subjective process."

PHOEBE: A JOURNAL OF LITERATURE AND ART

MSN 2C5, George Mason University, 400 University Dr., Fairfax VA 22030. **E-mail:** phoebe@gmu.edu. **Website:** www.phoebejournal.com. "We publish mainly fiction and poetry with some visual art. *Phoebe* prides itself on supporting up-and-coming writers, whose style, form, voice, and subject matter demostrate a vigorous appeal to the senses, intellect, and emotions of our readers." Responds in 4-6 months. Guidelines available on website.

MAGAZINE'S NEEDS Submit 3-5 poems. Include SASE for mail submission. Pays in contributor's copies.

ADDITIONAL INFORMATION Check http://phoebejournal.blogspot.com for additional information and commentary about *Phoebe*.

THE PINCH

Dept. of English, The University of Memphis, Memphis TN 38152. (901)678-4591. **E-mail:** editor@thepinchjournal.com. **Website:** www.thepinchjournal.com. **Contact:** Kristen Iverson, editor-in-chief; Justin Luzader, managing editor. "Semiannual literary magazine. We publish fiction, creative nonfiction, poetry, and art of literary quality by both established and emerging artists." Give 2 copies of journal in which work appears on publication. Copyrighted. Acquires first North American serial rights. Responds in 3 months on mss. Sample copy available for $12. Guidelines available on website.

MAGAZINE'S NEEDS "We do NOT accept submissions via e-mail. Submissions sent via e-mail will not receive a response. To submit, see guidelines." Submit through mail or via online submissions manager.

CONTEST/AWARD OFFERINGS Offers an annual award in poetry. 1st Prize: $1,000 and publication; 2nd- and 3rd-Prize poems may also be published. Any previously unpublished poem of up to 2 pages is eligible. No simultaneous submissions. Poems should be typed and accompanied by a cover letter. Author's name should not appear anywhere on ms.

Manuscripts will not be returned. Guidelines available for SASE, by e-mail, or on website. **Entry fee:** $15 for up to 3 poems (includes one-year subscription). **Deadline:** January 15-March 15 (inclusive postmark dates). Winners will be notified in July; published in subsequent issue.

TIPS "We have a new look and a new edge. We're soliciting work from writers with a national or international reputation as well as strong, interesting work from emerging writers. The Pinch Literary Award (previously River City Writing Award) in Fiction offers a $1,500 prize and publication. Check our website for details."

THE PINK CHAMELEON

E-mail: dpfreda@juno.com. **Website:** www.thepinkchameleon.com. **Contact:** Dorothy Paula Freda, editor/publisher. *The Pink Chameleon*, published annually online, contains "family-oriented, upbeat poetry and stories, any genre in good taste that gives hope for the future." Acquires one-time rights for 1 year but will return rights earlier on request. Time between acceptance and publication is up to 1 year, depending on date of acceptance. Responds in 1 month to ms. Sometimes comments on rejected mss. Sample copy and writer's guidelines online.

Receives 20 unsolicited mss/month. Receives about 50 poems/year, accepts about 50%. Publishes 50% new writers/year. Has published work by Deanne F. Purcell, Martin Green, Albert J. Manachino, James W. Collins, Ron Arnold, Sally Kosmalski, Susan Marie Davniero and Glen D. Hayes.

MAGAZINE'S NEEDS Reading period is January 1-April 30 and September 1-October 31. Considers poetry by children and teens. Submit 1-4 poems at a time. Considers previously published poems; no simultaneous submissions. Accepts e-mail submissions only (pasted into body of message; no attachments. Use plain text and include a brief bio. Often comments on rejected poems. Does not want "pornography, cursing, swearing; nothing evoking despair." Line length: 6-24 lines. No payment.

TIPS "Simple, honest, evocative emotion, upbeat fiction and nonfiction submissions that give hope for the future; well-paced plots; stories, poetry, articles, essays that speak from the heart. Read guidelines carefully. Use a good, but not ostentatious, opening hook. Stories should have a beginning, middle and end that make the reader feel the story was worth his or her time. This also applies to articles and essays. In the latter 2, wrap your comments and conclusions in a neatly packaged final paragraph. Turnoffs include violence and bad language. Simple, genuine and sensitive work does not need to shock with vulgarity to be interesting and enjoyable."

PINYON

Mesa State College, Languages, Literature and Mass Communications, Mesa State College, 1100 North Ave., Grand Junction CO 81501-3122. **E-mail:** rphillis@mesa5.mesa.colorado.edu. **Website:** http://myhome.coloradomesa.edu/~rphillis/. **Contact:** Randy Phillis, editor. *Pinyon*, published annually in June, prints "the best available contemporary American poetry and fiction. No restrictions other than excellence. We appreciate a strong voice." Literary magazine/journal: 8½×5½, 120 pages, heavy paper. Contains illustrations and photographs. Press run is 300; 100 distributed free to contributors, friends, etc. Annual. Subscription: $8/year. Sample: $5. Make checks payable to Pinyon, MSC. Guidelines for SASE or online.

MAGAZINE'S NEEDS Does not want "inspirational, light verse, or sing-song poetry." Has published poetry by Mark Cox, Barry Spacks, Wendy Bishop, and Anne Ohman Youngs. *Pinyon* is about 120 pages, magazine-sized, perfect-bound. Receives about 4,000 poems/year, accepts 2%. Submit 3-5 poems at a time. No previously published poems or simultaneous submissions. Cover letter is preferred. "Name, address, e-mail, and phone number on each page. SASE required." Reads submissions August 1-December 1. "3 groups of assistant editors, led by an associate editor, make recommendations to the editor." Seldom comments on rejected poems. Pays 2 contributor's copies.

TIPS "Ask yourself if the work is something you would like to read in a publication."

PIRENE'S FOUNTAIN

E-mail: pirenesfountain@gmail.com. **Website:** pirenesfountain.com. **Contact:** Oliver Lodge, Tony Walbran, editors; Lark Vernon, senior editor; Ami Kaye, publisher and managing editor. *Pirene's Fountain* is published online 2 times per year in April and October. Poets retain copyright to their own work; rights revert to poets upon publication. Publishes ms 1-3 months after acceptance. Responds in 1-4 months. Guidelines available online.

Receives about 1,500 poems/year, accepts about 20%. A 50-100 word bio note is required with submissions. Has published work by Lisel Mueller, Linda Pastan, J.P. Dancing Bear, Alison Croggan, Dorianne Laux, Rebecca Seiferle, Joseph Millar, Kim Addonizio, Jane Hirshfield, and Jim Moore, among others.

MAGAZINE'S NEEDS Submit 3-8 poems at a time. Considers previously published poems and simultaneous submissions. Considers poetry posted on a public website/blog/forum and poetry posted on a private, password-protected forum as published. Poems are circulated to an editorial board. Never comments on rejected poems. Sometimes publishes theme issues. "Poets whose work has been selected for publication in our journal during the past calendar year (with the exception of staff /featured poets) are automatically entered for the annual award. Our editors will each choose 1 poem from all of the selections. The 5 nominated poems will be sent "blind" to an outside editor/publisher for the final decision. The winning poet will be awarded a certificate and a $100 Amazon gift card via e-mail. Pushcart and Best of the Net nominations: Editors select the best work published by PF during the year. This is open to all submitting and featured poets. Only previously unpublished poems will be considered; please indicate that in your submission. Nominated poets are notified after selections have been sent in." Does not want "blatantly religious/ political themes, anything obscene, pornographic, or discriminatory in nature."

TIPS "Please read submission guidelines carefully and send in at least 3 poems. We offer a poetry discussion group on Facebook, entitled Pirene's Fountain Poetry."

PLAINSONGS

Department of Languages and Literature, Hastings NE 68901. (402)461-7343. **Fax:** (402)461-7756. **E-mail:** plainsongs@hastings.edu. **Contact:** Laura Marvel Wunderlich, editor. *Plainsongs*, published 3 times/ year, considers poems on any subject, in any style, but free verse predominates. *Plainsongs'* title suggests not only its location on the great plains, but its preference for the living language, whether in free or formal verse. Subscription: $15 for 3 issues. Sample: $5. Acquires first rights. Responds 2 months after deadline.

MAGAZINE'S NEEDS Submit up to 6 poems at a time. No fax, e-mail, or disk submissions. Postal submissions only. Reads submissions according to the following deadlines: August 15 for winter issue; November 15 for spring issue; March 15 for fall issue. Pays 2 contributor's copies and one-year subscription.

CONTEST/AWARD OFFERINGS Three poems in each issue receive a $25 prize. "A short essay in appreciation accompanies each award poem."

PLAIN SPOKE

Blackdamp Press, 12211 State Route 43, Amsterdam OH 43903. (740) 543-3345. **E-mail:** plainspoke@ gmail.com. **Website:** www.plainspoke.net. **Contact:** Cindy Kelly, editor. "We publish work that has a sense of word economy, strong voice, Americana appeal, tightness, and shies away from the esoteric and expositional. We like to be surprised." Quarterly. Acquires first North American serial rights. Publication is copyrighted. Pays on publication. Time between acceptance and publication is 1-4 months. Responds to mss in 1-4 months. Often comments on/critiques rejected mss. Responds in 3-4 months to poetry. Sometimes comments on rejected poems. Guidelines available for SASE, via e-mail, on website.

Plain Spoke is 36-60 digest-sized,laser-printed, saddle-stitched, with a color art on cardstock cover. Receives 80 mss/month; Accepts 2-3 mss/issue, 10-12 mss/year. Receives about 2,500 poems/year, accepts about 5%. Press run is 300. Single copy: $8; subscription: $30. Make checks payable to Cindy Kelly, editor. Has published poetry by Claudia Burbank, Deborah Bogen, Doug Ramspeck, Amy Sargent.

MAGAZINE'S NEEDS Publishes "poetry heavy in sense images and with a clear, plain-spoken voice." Submit up to 6 poems at a time, preferably under 40 lines. Considers simultaneous submissions, no previously published poems (considers poetry posted on a public website/blog/forum). Accepts e-mail submissions (following guidelines). Cover letter is required. Paper submissions require an SASE. Submissions received without an SASE are recycled. No postcards. Reads submissions year round. Poems are circulated to an editorial board. Never publishes theme issues. Reviews books and chapbooks of poetry in single-book format. Send cover letter and materials for review consideration to Reviews Editor, *Plain Spoke*. Does not want "esoteric, universal, cliché." Pays 1 contributor's copy.

TIPS "Work that surprises us stands out. We don't like the predictable. We don't want to feel like we're reading a story, pull us in. Make every word count and don't rely on adverbs."

●●⑤ PLANET-THE WELSH INTERNATIONALIST

P.O. Box 44, Aberystwyth Ceredigion SY23 3ZZ, United Kingdom. **E-mail:** planet.enquiries@planetmagazine.org.uk. **Website:** www.planetmagazine.org.uk. **Contact:** Emily Trahair, associate editor. A literary/cultural/political journal centered on Welsh affairs but with a strong interest in minority cultures in Europe and elsewhere. *Planet: The Welsh Internationalist*, published quarterly, is a cultural magazine "centered on Wales, but with broader interests in arts, sociology, politics, history, and science." Wants "good poetry in a wide variety of styles. No limitations as to subject matter; length can be a problem." Has published poetry by Nigel Jenkins, Anne Stevenson, and Les Murray. *Planet* is 128 pages, A5, professionally printed, perfect-bound, with glossy color card cover. Receives about 500 submissions/year, accepts about 5%. Press run is 1,550 (1,500 subscribers, about 10% libraries, 200 shelf sales). Single copy: £6.75; subscription: £22 (£38 overseas). Sample available. Publishes ms 4-6 months after acceptance. Responds in 3 months. Sample copy for £4. Guidelines available online.

MAGAZINE'S NEEDS Please submit 4-6 poems at a time. No previously published poems or simultaneous submissions. Accepts e-mail (as attachment) and disk submissions. SASE or SAE with IRCs essential for reply. Pays £30 minimum.

TIPS "We do not look for fiction which necessarily has a 'Welsh' connection, which some writers assume from our title. We try to publish a broad range of fiction and our main criterion is quality. Try to read copies of any magazine you submit to. Don't write out of the blue to a magazine which might be completely inappropriate for your work. Recognize that you are likely to have a high rejection rate, as magazines tend to favor writers from their own countries."

●●⑤ PLEIADES

Pleiades Press, Department of English, University of Central Missouri, Martin 336, Warrensburg MO 64093. (660)543-8106. **E-mail:** pleiades@ucmo.edu. **Website:** www.ucmo.edu/englphil/pleiades. **Contact:** Kevin Prufer, editor-at-large. "We publish contemporary fiction, poetry, interviews, literary essays, special-interest personal essays, reviews for a general

and literary audience from authors from around the world." Buys first North American serial rights, buys second serial (reprint) rights. Occasionally requests rights for TV, radio reading, website. Pays on publication. Publishes ms an average of 9 months after acceptance. Responds in 2 months to queries. Responds in 1-4 months to mss. Editorial lead time 9 months. Sample copy for $5 (back issue); $6 (current issue) Guidelines available online.

○ "Also sponsors the Lena-Miles Wever Todd Poetry Series competition, a contest for the best book ms by an American poet. The winner receives $1,000, publication by Pleiades Press, and distribution by Louisiana State University Press. Deadline September 30. Send SASE for guidelines."

MAGAZINE'S NEEDS Submit 3-5 poems at a time. Cover letter preferred. "Nothing didactic, pretentious, or overly sentimental. Do not send poetry after May 31. We resume reading poetry on September 1." Pays $3/poem, and contributor copies.

TIPS "Submit only 1 genre at a time to appropriate editors. Show care for your material and your readers—submit quality work in a professional format. Include cover letter with brief bio and list of publications. Include SASE. Cover art is solicited directly from artists. We accept queries for book reviews. For summer submissions, the poetry and nonfiction editors will no longer accept mss sent between June 1 & August 31. Any sent after May 31 will be held until the end of summer. Please do not send your only copy of anything."

●●⑤ PLOUGHSHARES

Emerson College, Ploughshares, 120 Boylston St., Boston MA 02116. **Website:** www.pshares.org. **Contact:** Ladette Randolph, editor-in-chief/executive director; Andrea Martucci, managing editor. *Ploughshares*, published 3 times/year, is "a journal of new writing guest-edited by prominent poets and writers to reflect different and contrasting points of view. Translations are welcome if permission has been granted. Our mission is to present dynamic, contrasting views on what is valid and important in contemporary literature and to discover and advance significant literary talent. Each issue is guest-edited by a different writer. We no longer structure issues around preconceived themes." Editors have included Carolyn Forché, Gerald Stern, Rita Dove, Chase Twichell, and Marilyn Hacker. Has published poetry by Donald Hall, Li-Young Lee, Robert Pinsky, Brenda Hillman, and Thylias Moss. Ploughshares is 200 pages, digest-sized. Receives about 11,000 poetry, fiction, and essay submissions/year. Press run is 6,000. Subscription: $30 domestic, $30 plus shipping (see website) foreign. Sample: $14 current issue, $7 back issue, please inquire for shipping rates. Buys first North American serial rights. Pays on publication. Publishes ms an average of 6 months after acceptance. Responds in 5 months to mss. Guidelines available online.

○ A competitive and highly prestigious market. Rotating and guest editors make cracking the line-up even tougher, since it's difficult to know what is appropriate to send. Reads submissions June 1-January 15 (postmark); mss submitted January 16-May 31 will be returned unread. "We do accept electronic submissions — there is a $3 fee per submission, which is waived if you are a subscriber."

MAGAZINE'S NEEDS Submit 1-3 poems at a time.

TIPS "We no longer structure issues around preconceived themes. If you believe your work is in keeping with our general standards of literary quality and value, submit at any time during our reading period."

○ PMS POEMMEMOIRSTORY

University of Alabama at Birmingham, HB 217, 1530 3rd Ave. S, Birmingham AL 35294. (205)934-2641. **Fax:** (205)975-8125. **E-mail:** poememoirstory@gmail.com. **Website:** http://pmsj.dandoesenglish.com/. **Contact:** Kerry Madden, editor-in-chief. "*PMS poemmemoirstory* is a 140-page, perfect-bound, all-women's literary journal published annually by the University of Alabama at Birmingham. While we proudly publish the best work of the best women writers in the nation (i.e., Maxine Chernoff, Elaine Equi, Amy Gerstler, Honorée Fanonne Jeffers, Molly Peacock, Lucia Perillo, Sonia Sanchez, Ruth Stone, and Natasha Trethewey, Dr. Alison Chapman, Masha Hamilton and the Afghan Women's Writing Project, Mary Jo Bang, Heather Dundas, Donna Thomas, Jennifer Horne, Jeanie Thompson, and Nancy Rutland Glaub, among others) we also solicit a memoir for each issue written by a woman who may not be a writer, but who has experienced something of historic significance. Emily Lyons, the nurse who survived the 1998 New Woman All Women Birmingham clinic bombing by Eric Rudolph, wrote the first of these; women who

experienced the World Trade Center on September 11th, the Civil Rights Movement in Birmingham, the war in Iraq, and Hurricane Katrina have also lent us their stories." Sample copy for $10. Guidelines online.

○ Work from PMS has been reprinted in a number of award anthologies: *New Stories from the South 2005, The Best Creative Nonfiction 200* and *2008, Best American Poetry 2003* and *2004*, and *Best American Essays 2005* and *2007*.

MAGAZINE'S NEEDS "All submissions should be unpublished original work that we can recycle and be accompanied by a SASE with sufficient postage for either return of your manuscript or notification. Or use online submission form." Include cover letter and short bio. Pays 2 contributor's copies and a one-year subscription.

TIPS "We seek unpublished original work that we can recycle. Reading period runs Jan. 1-Mar. 31. Submissions received at other times of the year will be returned unread. Best way to make contact is through e-mail."

○ ③ POCKETS

The Upper Room, P.O. Box 340004, Nashville TN 37203. (615)340-7333. **Fax:** (615)340-7267. **E-mail:** pockets@upperroom.org. **Website:** pockets.upperroom.org. **Contact:** Lynn W. Gilliam, editor. Magazine published 11 times/year. "*Pockets* is a Christian devotional magazine for children ages 8-12. All submissions should address the broad theme of the magazine. Each issue is built around one theme with material which can be used by children in a variety of ways. Scripture stories, fiction, poetry, prayers, art, graphics, puzzles and activities are included. Submissions do not need to be overtly religious. They should help children experience a Christian lifestyle that is not always a neatly-wrapped moral package, but is open to the continuing revelation of God's will. Seasonal material, both secular and liturgical, is desired." Buys first North American serial rights. Pays on acceptance. Publishes ms an average of 1 year after acceptance. Responds in 8 weeks to mss. Each issue reflects a specific theme. Guidelines on website.

○ Does not accept e-mail or fax submissions.

MAGAZINE'S NEEDS Considers poetry by children. Length: 4-20 lines. Pays $25 minimum.

TIPS "Theme stories, role models, and retold scripture stories are most open to freelancers. Poetry is also open. It is very helpful if writers read our writers' guidelines and themes on our website."

POEM

Huntsville Literary Association, P.O. Box 2006, Huntsville AL 35804. **E-mail:** poem@hla-hsv.org. **Website:** www.hlahsv.org. **Contact:** Rebecca Harbor, editor; Peggy Brosious, assistant editor; Harry V. Moore, assistant editor. *Poem*, published twice/year in the spring and fall, consists entirely of poetry. "We publish both traditional forms and free verse." Wants poems "characterized by compression, rich vocabulary, significant content, and evidence of 'a tuned ear and practiced pen.' We want coherent work that moves through the particulars of the poem to make a point. We equally welcome submissions from established poets as well as from less-known and beginning poets." Does not want translations. Has published poetry by Kathryn Kirkpatrick, Peter Serchuk, and Kim Bridgford. *Poem* is 90 pages, digest-sized, flat-spined, printed on good stock paper, with a clean design and a matte cover. Prints more than 60 poems/issue, generally featured 1 to a page. Press run is 500. Single copy: $10; subscription: $20. Sample: $7 (back issue). Acquires first serial rights. Responds in 1-3 months.

MAGAZINE'S NEEDS "Submit 3-5 poems, preferably with a cover letter. Place name, address, telephone number, and e-mail address on cover letter and on each poem. Include SASE with sufficient postage. Submissions are read throughout the year. We equally welcome submissions from established poets as well as from less known and beginning poets. We publish both traditional forms and free verse. We want poems characterized by compression, rich vocabulary, significant content, and evidence of 'a tuned ear and practiced pen.' We want coherent work that moves through the particulars of the poem to make a point." "We do not want "greeting card verse" or proselytizing or didactic poems." Pays 2 contributor's copies.

POEMELEON: A JOURNAL OF POETRY

E-mail: editor@poemeleon.org. **Website:** www.poemeleon.org. **Contact:** Cati Porter, editor. "Volume VI Issue 2, The Unreal Issue, is set to launch December 2013. The Unreal Issue will feature work that could be considered magical realist, fabulist, speculative, or otherwise incorporates the strange, the surreal, and the unreal, whether or not it could possibly really exist. If you think it seems unreal, maybe we will, too. Please send only your best work, any length, any style.

Expect a response within 1-3 months after close of submissions. If you have not heard from us after 3 months, please inquire. Please submit 1 to 5 poems, 1 craft essay, or 1 book review, using the forms online. Please include a brief third-person bio in your cover letter." Acquires one-time, non-exclusive rights.

MAGAZINE'S NEEDS *Poemeleon: A Journal of Poetry*, published semiannually online, wants all forms and styles of poetry. "Does not want overly religious or sentimental, greeting card verse." Has published poetry by Sherman Alexie, David Kirby, Tony Barnstone, Catherine Daly, Ann Fisher-Wirth, Richard Garcia, Eloise Klein Healy, Bob Hicok. Poemeleon receives about 1,000 poems/year, accepts about 150-200. Number of unique visitors: 25,000/year. Submit 3-5 poems at a time. Considers previously published poems (as long as they have not appeared online) and simultaneous submissions as long as we are notified promptly if a poem is taken elsewhere). Considers poetry posted on a public website/blog/forum as published. All submissions must come through online submissions form located on the guidelines page of the website; no fax, paper, e-mail or disk submissions. Cover letter is preferred. Each issue is devoted to a particular type of poetry (past issues include poems of place, ekphrastic poems, poems in form, and the prose poem, The persona poem, humor, gender, and collaborative poetry). Please check the guidelines page for specifics before submitting. Reads submissions year round.

ADDITIONAL INFORMATION Previously published is fine, as long as it was in print, not online, and as long as you as the author retain all copyright.

CONTEST/AWARD OFFERINGS Mystery Box Contest offers a prize of the Mystery Box and publication on the website. Submit 1 poem. Guidelines available on website. **Entry fee:** none. Deadline: none.

POEMS & PLAYS

English Department, Middle Tennessee State University, Murfreesboro TN 37132. **E-mail:** gbrewer@mtsu.edu. **Website:** www.mtsu.edu/english/poemsandplays. **Contact:** Gaylord Brewer, editor. *Poems & Plays*, published annually in the spring, is an "eclectic publication for poems and short plays." No restrictions on style or content of poetry. Has published poetry by Naomi Wallace, Kate Gale, James Doyle, and Ron Koertge. *Poems & Plays* is 88 pages, digest-sized, professionally printed, perfect-bound, with coated color card cover. Receives 1,500 poems per issue, publishes 30-35 "typically." Press run is 800. Subscription: $10 for 2 issues. Acquires first rights. Pays 1 contributor's copy. Responds in 2 months. Sample copy for $6. **TIPS** Considers chapbook mss (poems or short plays) of 20-24 pages for The Tennessee Chapbook Prize. "Any combination of poems or plays, or a single play, is eligible. The winning chapbook is printed within *Poems & Plays*." Winning author receives 50 copies of the issue. SASE required. **Entry fee:** $15 (includes 1 copy of the issue). **Deadline:** Same as for the magazine (October-November). Past winners include Tammy Armstrong and Judith Sornberger. "The chapbook competition annually receives over 150 manuscripts from the US and around the world."

POESY MAGAZINE

P.O. Box 458, Santa Cruz CA 95061. (831)239-4419. E-mail: info@poesy.org; submissions@poesy.org. Website: www.poesy.org. **Contact:** Brian Morrisey, editor-in-chief. *POESY Magazine*, published biannually, is "an anthology of American poetry. *POESY*'s main concentrations are Boston, Massachusetts and Santa Cruz, California, 2 thriving homesteads for poets, beats, and artists of nature. Our goal is to unite the 2 scenes, updating poets on what's happening across the country." Wants to see "original poems that express observational impacts with clear and concise imagery. Acceptence is based on creativity, composition, and relation to the format of *POESY*." Does not want "poetry with excessive profanity. We would like to endorse creativity beyond the likes of everyday babble." Has published poetry by Lawrence Ferlinghetti, Jack Hirschman, Edward Sanders, Todd Moore, Diane Di Prima, and Julia Vinograd. *POESY* is 16 pages, magazine-sized, newsprint, glued/folded, includes ads. Receives about 1,000 poems/year, accepts about 10%. Press run is 1,000; most distributed free to local venues. Single copy: $1; subscription: $12/year. Sample: $2. Make checks payable to Brian Morrisey. Acquires first rights. Publishes ms 1 month after acceptance. Responds in 4-6 weeks. Guidelines online. **MAGAZINE'S NEEDS** Submit 3-5 poems at a time. Lines/poem: 32 maximum. Submit by e-mail or postal mail. Cover letter is preferred. Reads submissions year round. "Poems are accepted by the Santa Cruz editor/publisher based on how well the poem stimulates our format." "Please no poems about dogs, cats, angels, or the food you ate recently." Pays 3 contributor's copies.

TIPS "Our main focus is on Santa Cruz and Boston poetry, but we also accept submissions across the country. We see the poem as something to immerse the reader into a welcomed world of arresting images that jerks the eyes onto the page and leaves the reels of the mind turning long after the poem is finished. We see the poem as a work of art and save the narrative voice for the enlightenment of prose. We see the poem as a camera documenting a moment in time seen before the lens, rather than from the eyes of its beholder behind the lens. To accomplish this goal, we have to be very precise that everything we publish falls within our portrayal of the poem."

POETALK

Bay Area Poets Coalition, 1791 Solano Ave. #A11, Berkeley CA 94707-2209. **E-mail:** poetalk@aol.com. **Website:** www.bayareapoetscoalition.org. **Contact:** John Rowe (editorial board), acquisitions. *POETALK*, currently published 1-2 issues/year, is the poetry journal of the Bay Area Poets Coalition (BAPC) and publishes 60-plus poets in each issue. "*POETALK* is open to all. No particular genre. Rhyme must be well done." All rights revert to author upon publication. Usually responds in up to 6 months. Guidelines available early summer for SASE, by e-mail, or see posting on website.

  POETALK is 36 pages, digest-sized, photocopied, saddle-stapled, with heavy card cover. Press run is 400. Subscription: $5/2 issues. Sample copy: $2. Submissions are read year-round.

MAGAZINE'S NEEDS In general, poets may submit 3-5 poems at a time, no more than twice/year. Lines/poem: under 35 preferred; longer poems of "outstanding quality" considered. Considers previously published poems and simultaneous submissions, but must be noted. Cover letter is preferred. Include SASE. "Mss should be clearly typed, single-spaced, and include author's name and mailing address on every page. Please also provide an e-mail address." Pays 1 contributor's copy.

CONTEST/AWARD OFFERINGS Sponsors yearly contest.

TIPS "If you don't want suggested revisions, you need to say so clearly in your cover letter or indicate on each poem submitted." Bay Area Poets Coalition holds monthly readings (in Berkeley, CA). BAPC has 150 members; membership is $15/year (includes subscription to *POETALK* and other privileges); extra outside U.S.

POETICA MAGAZINE, REFLECTIONS OF JEWISH THOUGHT

P.O. Box 11014, Norfolk VA 23517. **E-mail:** michal-poetryeditor@poeticamagazine.com; jagodastoryeditor@poeticamagazine.com. **Website:** www.poeticamagazine.com. *Poetica Magazine, Reflections of Jewish Thought*, published 3 times/year, offers "an outlet for the many writers who draw from their Jewish backgrounds and experiences to create poetry/prose/short stories, giving both emerging and recognized writers the opportunity to share their work with the larger community." *Poetica* is 70 pages, perfect bound, full color cover, includes some ads. Receives about 500 poems/year, accepts about 60%. Press run is 350. Single copy: $10; subscription: $19.50. Poets retain all rights. Publishes ms 1 year after acceptance. Responds in 1 month.

MAGAZINE'S NEEDS Submit 1-3 poems by e-mail. Prefers PDFs. Does not want long pieces, haiku, rhyming poetry. Pays 1 contributor's copy.

TIPS "We publish original-unpublished works by Jewish and non-Jewish writers alike. We are interested in works that have the courage to acknowledge, challenge, and celebrate modern Jewish life, beyond distinctions of secular and sacred. We like accessible works that find fresh meaning in old traditions that recognize the challenges of our generation. We evaluate works on several levels, including its skillful use of craft; its ability to hold interest; and layers of meaning."

◑ POETIC MATRIX, A PERIODIC LETTER

P.O. Box 1223, Madera CA 93639. **E-mail:** poeticmatrix@yahoo.com. **Website:** www.poeticmatrix.com. **Contact:** John Peterson, editor. *Poetic Matrix, a periodic letteR*, published 2 times/year online, seeks poetry that "creates a 'place in which we can live' rather than telling us about the place; poetry that draws from the imaginal mind and is rich in the poetic experience—hence the poetic matrix. We seek writing of quality, with passion and intelligence." Acquires one-time rights. Guidelines available by e-mail or on website.

◔ Has published poetry by Lyn Lifshin, Tony White, Gail Entrekin, James Downs, Joan Michelson, and Brandon Cesmat.

MAGAZINE'S NEEDS Accepts e-mail submissions (pasted into body of message, no attachments). **Charges reading fee of $17.** Does not want poetry that talks about the experience.

TIPS "*Poetic Matrix* has a call for mss for the Slim Volume Series every 2 years. See website for when reading dates are set and for additional guidelines and awards. The Slim Volume Series is for mss of 65-75 pages."

◑ POET LORE

The Writer's Center, 4508 Walsh St., Bethesda MD 20815. **E-mail:** genevieve.deleon@writer.org. **Website:** http://poetlore.com; www.writer.org. **Contact:** Genevieve DeLeon, managing editor; Jody Bolz, editor; E. Ethelbert Miller, editor. *Poet Lore*, published semiannually, is "dedicated to the best in American and world poetry as well as timely reviews and commentary." Wants "fresh uses of traditional forms and devices, but any kind of excellence is welcome." Has published poetry by Ai, Denise Duhamel, Jefferey Harrison, Eve Jones, Carl Phillips, and Ronald Wallace. *Poet Lore* is 144 pages, digest-sized, professionally printed, perfect-bound, with glossy card cover. Receives about 4,200 poems/year, accepts 125. Press run is at least 800. Single copy: $8; subscription: $18/nonmember, $12/member. "Add $1/single copy for shipping; add $5 postage for subscriptions outside U.S." Responds in 3 months. Guidelines for SASE or online at website.

MAGAZINE'S NEEDS Considers simultaneous submissions "with notification in cover letter." No e-mail or disk submissions. "Submit typed poems (up to 5), with author's name and address on each page; SASE is required." Pays 2 contributor's copies and a one-year subscription.

◑◔ POETRY

The Poetry Foundation, 61 W. Superior St., Chicago IL 60654. (312)787-7070. **Fax:** (312)787-6650. **E-mail:** editors@poetrymagazine.org. **Website:** www.poetrymagazine.org. Christian Wiman, Editor. **Contact:** Helen Klaviter. *Poetry*'s website offers featured poems, letters, reviews, interviews, essays, and web-exclusive features. *Poetry*, published monthly by The Poetry Foundation (see separate listing in Organizations), "has no special manuscript needs and no special requirements as to form or genre: We examine in turn all work received and accept that which seems best." Has published poetry by the major voices of our time as well as new talent. *Poetry* is elegantly printed, flat-spined. Receives 90,000 submissions/year, accepts about 300-350. Press run is 16,000. Single copy: $3.75; subscription: $35 ($38 for institutions). Sample: $5.50. Buys first serial rights. Pays on publication. Publishes ms an average of 9 months after acceptance. Responds in 1-2 months to mss and queries. Sample copy for $3.75 or online at website. Guidelines available online.

MAGAZINE'S NEEDS Accepts all styles and subject matter. Submit no more than 4 poems at a time. No previously published poems or simultaneous submissions. Electronic submission preferred. When submitting by post put return address on outside of envelope; include SASE. Submissions must be typed, single-spaced, with poet's name and address on every page. Pays $10/line (with a minimum payment of $300). Reviews books of poetry in multi-book formats of varying lengths. Does not accept unsolicited reviews. Pays $10/line ($150 minimum payment).

CONTEST/AWARD OFFERINGS 7 prizes (Bess Hokin Prize, Levinson Prize, Frederick Bock Prize, J. Howard and Barbara M.J. Wood Prize, John Frederick Nims Memorial Prize, Friends of Literature Prize, Union League Civic and Arts Poetry Prize) ranging from $300 to $5,000 are awarded annually to poets whose work has appeared in the magazine that year. Only verse already published in *Poetry* is eligible for consideration; no formal application is necessary.

● POETRYBAY

P.O. Box 114, Northport NY 11768. (631)427-1950. **E-mail:** poetrybay@aol.com; info@poetrybay.com. **Website:** www.poetrybay.com. **Contact:** George Wallace, editor. *Poetrybay*, published semiannually online, seeks "to add to the body of great contemporary American poetry by presenting the work of established and emerging writers. Also, we consider essays and reviews." Has published poetry by Robert Bly, Yevgeny Yevtushenko, Marvin Bell, Diane Wakoski, Cornelius Eady, and William Heyen.

MAGAZINE'S NEEDS Submit 5 poems at a time. Considers simultaneous submissions; no previously published poems. Accepts e-mail submissions (pasted into body of message to info@poetrybay.com); no disk submissions. Time between acceptance and publication is 6-12 months. Seldom comments on rejected poems. Occasionally publishes theme issues. Guidelines available on website. Sometimes sends prepublication galleys. Acquires first-time electronic rights. Reviews books/chapbooks of poetry and other magazines/journals. Send materials for review consideration.

●○ THE POETRY CHURCH MAGAZINE

Moorside Words and Music, Eldwick Crag Farm, High Eldwick, Bingley, W. Yorkshire BD16 3BB, England. **E-mail:** reavill@globalnet.co.uk. **Contact:** Tony Reavill, editor. *The Poetry Church Magazine*, published quarterly, contains Christian poetry, prayers, and hymns. Wants "Christian or good religious poetry." Does not want "unreadable blasphemy." **Publishes subscribers' work only.** Considers poetry by children over age 10.

○ Has published poetry by Laurie Bates, Joan Sheridan Smith, Idris Caffrey, Isabella Strachan, Walter Nash, and Susan Glyn. *The Poetry Church Magazine* is 40 pages, digest-sized, photocopied, saddle-stapled, with illustrated cover. Receives about 1,000 poems/year, accepts about 500. Press run is 1,000. Single copy: free; subscription: £12 for 4 issues ($20 USD). Make checks payable in sterling to Feather Books.

MAGAZINE'S NEEDS Submit 2 poems at a time. Lines/poem: usually around 20, "but will accept longer." Considers previously published poems and simultaneous submissions. Cover letter is preferred (with information about the poet). No e-mail submissions; postal submissions only. Include SASE, or SAE and IRC. Submissions must be typed. **Publishes "only subscribers' poems as they keep us solvent."** Time between acceptance and publication is 4 months. "The editor does a preliminary reading, then seeks the advice of colleagues about uncertain poems." Responds within 1 week. Poets retain copyright.

ADDITIONAL INFORMATION Feather Books publishes the Feather Books Poetry Series, collections of around 20 Christian poems and prayers. Has recently published the Glyn family, Walter Nash, David Grieve, and Rosie Morgan Barry. "We have now published 300 poetry collections by individual Christian poets." Books are usually photocopied, saddle-stapled, with illustrated covers. "We do not insist, but **most poets pay for their work. Enquire for current costs.** If they can't afford it, but are good poets, we stand the cost. We expect poets to read *The Poetry Church Magazine* to get some idea of our standards."

POETRY INTERNATIONAL

San Diego State University, 5500 Campanile Dr., San Diego CA 92182-6020. (619)594-1522. **Fax:** (619)594-4998. **E-mail:** poetryinternational@yahoo.com. **Website:** http://poetryinternational.sdsu.edu. **Contact:** Jenny Minniti-Shippey, managing editor. *Poetry International*, published annually in November, is "an eclectic poetry magazine intended to reflect a wide range of poetry being written today." Wants "a wide range of styles and subject matter. We're particularly interested in translations." Does not want "cliché-ridden, derivative, or obscure poetry." Has published poetry by Adrienne Rich, Robert Bly, Hayden Carruth, Kim Addonizio, Maxine Kumin, and Gary Soto. *Poetry International* is 200 pages, perfect-bound, with coated cardstock cover. Press run is 1,500. Subscription: $15/1 year. "We intend to continue to publish poetry that makes a difference in people's lives, and startles us anew with the endless capacity of language to awaken our senses and expand our awareness." Responds in 6-8 months to mss.

Features the Poetry International Prize ($1,000) for best original poem. Submit up to 3 poems with a $10 entry fee.

MAGAZINE'S NEEDS Features the poetry of a different nation of the world as a special section in each issue. Does not accept e-mail submissions.

TIPS "Seeks a wide range of styles and subject matter. We read unsolicited mss. only between September 1 and December 31 of each year. Manuscripts received any other time will be returned unread."

POETRY KANTO

Kanto Poetry Center, 3-22-1 Kamariya-Minami Kanazawa-ku, Yokohama 236-8502, Japan. **E-mail:** alan@kanto-gakuin.ac.jp. **Website:** http://home.kanto-gakuin.ac.jp/~kg061001/. **Contact:** Alan Botsford, editor. *Poetry Kanto*, published annually in November by the Kanto Gakuin University, is a journal bridging east and west, featuring "outstanding poetry that navigates the divide of ocean and language from around the world. We seek exciting, well-crafted contemporary poetry in English, and also encourage and publish high-quality English translations of modern and emerging Japanese poets. All translations must be accompanied by the original poems." The magazine is unpriced. For sample, send SAE with IRCs. Guidelines available on website.

Poetry Kanto is 120 pages, 6x9, professionally printed on coated stock, perfect-bound, with glossy cover. Press run is 1,000; many are distributed free worldwide to schools, poets, and presses. See website for sample poems. Has published poetry by Jane Hirshfield, Ilya Kaminsky, Beth Ann Fennelly, Vijay Seshadri, Michael S. Collins, Mari L'Esperance, Michael Sowder, and Sarah Arvio.

MAGAZINE'S NEEDS Submit 5 poems at a time maximum. Queries welcome. No previously published poems or simultaneous submissions. Prefers e-mail submissions (as attachment in Word). Cover letter is required. Include brief bio. All postal submissions require SAE and IRCs. Reads submissions December-April. Pays 3-5 contributor's copies

POETRY NORTHWEST

Everett Community College, 2000 Tower St., Everett WA 98103. (425)388-9395. **E-mail:** editors@poetrynw.org. **Website:** www.poetrynw.org. **Contact:** Kevin Craft, editor. *Poetry Northwest* is published semiannually in April and October. "The mission of *Poetry Northwest* is to publish poetry with a vibrant sense of language at play in the world, and a strong presense of the physical world in language. We publish new, emerging, and established writers. In the words of founding editor Carolyn Kizer, we aim to 'encourage the young and the inexperienced, the neglected mature, and the rough major talents and the fragile minor ones.' All styles and aesthetics will find consideration." Acquires all rights. Returns rights to poets upon request. Pays 2 contributor's copies. Time between acceptance and publication is 3-12 months. Sometimes comments on rejected poems. Responds in 8-12 weeks. Single copy: $8. Sample: $9. Make checks payable to *Poetry Northwest*. Guidelines available on website.

Has published poetry by Theodore Roethke, Czeslaw Milosz, Anne Sexton, Harold Pinter, Thom Gunn, and Philip Larkin, Heather McHugh, Richard Kenney. *Poetry Northwest* is 40+ pages, magazine-sized, Web press-printed, saddle-stapled, with 4-color cover, includes ads. Receives about 10,000 poems/year; accepts about 1%. Press run is 2,000.

MAGAZINE'S NEEDS Submit 3-5 poems at a time once per submission period. No previously published poems; simultaneous submissions OK with notice.

Regular mail or online submission form only. No e-mail or disk submissions. Cover letter is required. Sometimes publishes theme issues. Upcoming themes available in magazine or on website. Reading period is September-March. Mss sent outside reading period will be returned unread. Always sends prepublication galleys. Reviews books of poetry in single- and multi-book format.

💥🖸 POETRY SALZBURG REVIEW

University of Salzburg, Department of English and American Studies, Erzabt-Klotz-Strasse 1, Salzburg A-5020, Austria. (43)(662)8044-4422. **Fax:** (43)(662)8044-167. **E-mail:** editor@poetrysalzburg.com. **Website:** www.poetrysalzburg.com. **Contact:** Dr. Wolfgang Goertschacher and Andreas Schachermayr, editors. *Poetry Salzburg Review*, published twice/year, contains "articles on poetry, mainly contemporary, and 60% poetry. Also includes essays on poetics, review-essays, interviews, artwork, and translations. We tend to publish selections by authors who have not been taken up by the big poetry publishers. Nothing of poor quality." Acquires first rights. Responds in 2 months.

🖸 Has published poetry by Brian W. Aldiss, Rae Armantrout, Paul Muldoon, Alice Notley, Samuel Menashe, Jerome Rothenberg, Michael Heller, Nathaniel Tarn. *Poetry Salzburg Review* is about 200 pages, A5, professionally printed, perfect-bound, with illustrated card cover. Receives about 10,000 poems/year; accepts 3%. Press run is 500. Single copy: $13; subscription: $25 (cash preferred; subscribers can also pay with PayPal). "No requirements, but it's a good idea to subscribe to *Poetry Salzburg Review*."

MAGAZINE'S NEEDS No previously published poems or simultaneous submissions. Accepts e-mail submissions (as attachment). Time between acceptance and publication is 3-6 months. Seldom comments on rejected poems. Occasionally publishes theme issues. No payment. Reviews books/chapbooks of poetry as well as books on poetics. Send materials for review consideration.

POETS AND ARTISTS (O&S)

E-mail: unitguesteditors@gmail.com. **Website:** www.poetsandartists.com. **Contact:** Didi Menendez, publisher. Reviews books of poetry, chapbooks of poetry, and other magazines/journals. Reads poetry sub-missions year round. Sometimes upcoming themes are available online at website. Rights revert to poets upon publication. Time between acceptance and publication is 1½ months. Sample copy for $25.

🖸 Prefers submissions from skilled, experienced poets; will consider work from beginning poets.

MAGAZINE'S NEEDS Paste submissions into body of e-mail message. Cover letter is unnecessary. Does not like "weird" formats.

TIPS Publisher also publishes *MiPOesias Magazine*, which has been featured in Best American Poetry, and OCHO, which has received Pushcart Prize and has been featured in *Best American Poetry*.

🖸 THE POET'S ART

171 Silverleaf Lane, Islandia NY 11749. (631)439-0427. **E-mail:** davidirafox@yahoo.com. **Contact:** David Fox, editor. *The Poet's Art*, published quarterly, is "a family-style journal, accepting work from the unpublished to the well known and all levels in between." Wants "family-friendly, positive poetry; any form considered. Topics include humor, nature, inspirational, children's poetry, or anything else that fits the family-friendly genre." Does not want "violent, vulgar, or overly depressing work. Work is read and accepted by the mentally-ill population, but they should keep in mind this is a family-friendly journal." Considers poetry by children and teens, "any age, as long as it's good quality; if under 18, get parents' permission."

🖸 *The Poet's Art* is 40 or more pages, magazine-sized, photocopied, paper-clipped or stapled, with computer cover, includes ads. Receives about 100 poems a year; accepts about 50%. Press run is 30+. Has published poetry by Sheila B. Roark, William J. Middleton, John W. (Bill) Williams, Cory Meyer, and Arthur C. Ford Sr.

MAGAZINE'S NEEDS Submit "as many poems that will fit on 1 page" at a time. Considers simultaneous submissions; "list any other small press journals (if any) poem titles". No e-mail or disk submissions; postal submissions only. Cover letter is preferred: "It's only polite. And include a SASE—a must! (I have been lax in this rule about SASEs, but I will now throw any submissions without a SASE away!)." Reads submissions year round. "I review all poems submitted and then decide what I wish to publish." Always comments on rejected poems. Reviews chapbooks of poetry and other magazines/journals, "but editors and authors must write reviews themselves. After all, who knows your magazine/journal or chapbook better than you? (Little-known/newer journals sent in by editors or contributors get first consideration for reviews)." Send to David Fox. Lines/poem: rarely accepts anything over 1 page. "I have had to institute a $2.50 charge per accepted page of poetry, which will be used for 1 or more issues to cover postage."

◐ POETS' ESPRESSO REVIEW

E-mail: PoetsEspressoReview@gmail.com. **Website:** www.poetsespresso.com. Donald R. Anderson, editor-in-chief. **Contact:** Patricia Mayorga, editor. *Poets' Espresso Review,* published quarterly online and in print, is "a small black and white publication of poetry, art, photography, recipes, and local events." Sponsored by the Writers' Guild, a club of San Joaquin Delta College. "We value variety, appropriateness for most age groups, and poetry that goes well with the season of the issue, visual and bilingual poetry (side by side with translation), and of length that will fit on our half-sheet pages." Does not want "profanity, racially prejudiced, otherwise offensive material, porn, submissions that are excessively long, illegible writing, nor your only copy of the poem." Considers poetry by all ages. "Please include contact info of parent if from a minor." Has published poetry by David Humphreys, Nikki Quismondo, Susan Richardson Harvey, Marie J. Ross, Christine Stoddard, Michael C. Ford, and Allen Field Weitzel. *Poets' Espresso Review* (print edition) is 24-28 pages, digest-sized, printed "on College's industrial printers," stapled, with color card stock cover with b&w photograph/artwork, might include ads. Accepts about 100 poems/year. Number of unique visitors (online): "small count with rapid growth." Single copy: $2; subscription: $12/year (6 issues). Sample: free in return for review or swap for a desired publication. Make checks payable to Patricia Mayorga.

ADDITIONAL INFORMATION "We occasionally publish anthologies. For info on other works we have published, please visit the websites for the books *Sun Shadow Mountain* and *Moon Mist Valley* other projects linked on the project page at www.rainflowers. org."

◑ THE POET'S HAVEN

P.O. Box 1501, Massillon OH 44648. (330)844-0177. **Website:** www.PoetsHaven.com. **Contact:** Vertigo Xavier, publisher. *The Poet's Haven* is a website "fea-

turing poetry, artwork, stories, essays, and more." Wants work that's "emotional, personal, and intimate with the author or subject. Topics can cover just about anything." Does not publish religious material. Has published poetry by Robert O. Adair, Christopher Franke, T.M. Göttl, Mary I. Huang, and Anne McMillen. Work published on *The Poet's Haven* is left on the site permanently. Receives about 1,000 poems/year, accepts about 70%.

MAGAZINE'S NEEDS Considers previously published poems and simultaneous submissions. Accepts submissions through online form only. Time between acceptance and publication is about 2 weeks. Never comments on rejected poems. Guidelines available on website. No payment for online publication. Acquires rights to publish on the website permanently and in any future print publications. Poet retains rights to have poems published elsewhere, "provided the other publishers do not require first-time or exclusive rights."

ADDITIONAL INFORMATION Publishes audio podcast as "Saturday Night With *The Poet's Haven*." Check website for submission information or to download sample episodes.

◐ THE POET'S PEN

The Society of American Poets (SOAP), 6500 Clito Rd., Statesboro GA 30461. 912-587-4400. **Website:** http://ihspub.com. **Contact:** Dr. Charles E. Cravey, editor. *The Poet's Pen*, published quarterly by The Society of American Poets, is "open to all styles of poetry and prose—both religious and secular." Does not want "gross or 'X-rated' poetry without taste or character." *The Poet's Pen* uses poetry **primarily by members and subscribers**, but outside submissions are also welcome. Subscription: included in membership, $30/year ($25 for students). Sample: $10. Has published poetry by Najwa Salam Brax, Henry Goldman, Henry W. Gurley, William Heffner, Linda Metcalf, and Charles Russ, among others Guidelines available in magazine, for SASE, or by e-mail.

Sponsors several contests each quarter, with prizes totaling $100-250. Also offers Editor's Choice Awards each quarter. The President's Award for Excellence is a prize of $50. **Deadline:** November 1. Also publishes a quarterly anthology from poetry competitions in several categories with prizes of $25-100. Guidelines available for SASE or by e-mail.

MAGAZINE'S NEEDS Submit 3 poems at a time/quarter. Considers simultaneous submissions and previously published poems, if permission from previous publisher is included. Include name and address on each page. "Submissions or inquiries will not be responded to without a #10 business-sized SASE. We do stress originality and have each new poet and/or subscriber sign a waiver form verifying originality." Publishes seasonal/theme issues. Sometimes sends prepublication galleys. Always comments on rejected poems.

✪ ○ POETS' PODIUM

2-3265 Front Rd., E. Hawkesbury ON K6A 2R2, Canada. **Website:** www.geocities.ws/poetspodium/home.html. **Contact:** Kenneth Elliot, associate editor; Catherine Heaney Barrowcliffe, associate editor; Robert Piquette, associate editor/graphic design. *Poets' Podium*, published quarterly, is a newsletter that aims "to promote the reading and writing of the poetic form, especially among those being published for the first time." Poetry specifications are open. "**Priority is given to valued subscribers.** Nevertheless, when there is room in an issue, we will publish nonsubscribers." Does not want poetry that is "gothic, erotic/sexual, gory, bloody, or that depicts violence." Subscription: $15 USD. Sample: $3 USD.

MAGAZINE'S NEEDS Submit 3 poems at a time. Lines/poem: 4 minimum, 25 maximum. Considers previously published poems and simultaneous submissions. Cover letter is required. Include SASE (or SAE and IRC), name, address, and telephone number; e-mail address if applicable. Time between acceptance and publication varies. Guidelines available for SASE (or SAE and IRC), or by fax or by e-mail. Pays 3 contributor's copies. All rights remain with the author.

TIPS "Poetry is a wonderful literary form. Try your hand at it. Send us the fruit of your labours."

◐ POINTED CIRCLE

Portland Community College—Cascade, 705 N. Killing, Portland OR 97217. **E-mail:** wendy.bourgeois@pcc.edu. **Contact:** Wendy Bourgeois, faculty advisor. Magazine: 80 pages; b&w illustrations; photos. "Anything of interest to educationally/culturally mixed audience. We will read whatever is sent, but encourage writers to remember we are a quality literary/arts magazine intended to promote the arts in the community. No pornography, nothing trite. Be mindful of deadlines and length limits." Acquires one-time rights.

○ Accepts submissions by e-mail, mail; artwork in high-resolution digital form.

MAGAZINE'S NEEDS Submit up to 6 pages of poetry. Submitted materials will not be returned; SASE for notification only. Accepts multiple submissions. No pornography, nothing trite. Pays 2 contributor's copies.

○ POLYPHONY H.S.

An International Student-Run Literary Magazine for High School Writers and Editors, Polyphony High School, 1514 Elmwood Ave., Suite 2, Evanston IL 60201. (847)910-3221. **E-mail:** info@polyphonyhs.com. **E-mail:** polyphonyhs@gmail.com. **Website:** www.polyphonyhs.com. "Our mission is to create a high-quality literary magazine written, edited, and published by high school students. We strive to build respectful, mutually beneficial, writer-editor relationships that form a community devoted to improving students' literary skills in the areas of poetry, fiction, and creative nonfiction." Acquires first rights. Pays on publication. Responds in 6-8 weeks. Sample copy available for $7.50 + $2.50 shipping/handling. Detailed guidelines online.

○ Does not accept hard copy entries.

MAGAZINE'S NEEDS "A word about centering: It's mostly the mark of a rookie writer. If you choose to center your poem, you should have a pretty compelling reason for centering it. If your reason is because you think it looks good that way, it's not a good enough reason. Avoid clichés. Please.Read your work out loud before submitting it to us. A word about profanity in poetry: one swear word goes a heckuva long way. Think carefully before using it. Ask yourself: does the poem gain anything with the word? Does it lose anything with its subtraction." Length: no more than 80 lines. Pays 2 contributor's copies.

CONTEST/AWARD OFFERINGS "We manage the Claudia Ann Seaman Awards for Young Writers; cash awards for the best poem, best story, best work of creative nonfiction. See website for details."

◐ THE PORTLAND REVIEW

Portland State University, P.O. Box 347, Portland OR 97207-0347. (503)725-4533. **E-mail:** theportlandreview@gmail.com. **Website:** portlandreview.org. **Contact:** Tim Faiella, editor. Press run is 1,000 for subscribers, libraries, and bookstores nationwide.

Single copy: $9; subscription: $27/year, $54/2 years. Sample: $8. Buys first North American serial rights. Publishes ms an average of 3-6 months after acceptance. Responds in 2-4 months to mss. Sample copy for $9. Guidelines available online. "Automatic rejection of mss not following guidelines."

MAGAZINE'S NEEDS Submit up to 5 poems at a time. No previously published poems. To submit, use submission manager on website. Include phone number, e-mail address, and other contact information. Reads submissions between September 1 and April 1. "Our website is a general introduction to our magazine, with samples of our poetry, fiction, and art. *The Portland Review* will only consider one submission per writer, per reading period. **If you would like to be considered for online publication, please specify this within your cover letter.**"

TIPS "View website for current samples and guidelines."

◐ THE POTOMAC

2020 Pennsylvania Ave., NW, Suite 443, Washington DC 20006. **E-mail:** Charles.Rammelkamp@ssa.gov. **Website:** http://thepotomacjournal.com. **Contact:** Charles Rammelkamp, editor. *The Potomac*, published semiannually online, features political commentary, cutting-edge poetry, flash fiction, and reviews. Open to all forms of poetry by new and established writers. Acquires one-time rights. Time between acceptance and publication is 3 months. Responds in 2 months. Often comments on rejected poems. Sometimes sends prepublication galleys. Sample copy free online. Guidelines available on website.

◐ Receives a "variable" number of poems/year, accepts about 30-40. Has published poetry and fiction by Robert Cooperman, Michael Salcman, Joanne Lowery, Roger Netzer, Pamela Painter, and L.D. Brodsky.

MAGAZINE'S NEEDS Submit any number of poems at a time. Considers simultaneous submissions; no previously published poems. Accepts e-mail submissions (as attachment) only; no postal or disk submissions. Cover letter is preferred. Reads submissions year round. Reviews books/chapbooks of poetry and other magazines/journals in up to 2,000 words, single- and multi-book format. Send materials for review consideration. No payment.

◐ POTOMAC REVIEW: A JOURNAL OF ARTS & HUMANITIES

Montgomery College, 51 Mannakee St., MT/212, Rockville MD 20850. (240)567-4100. **E-mail:** PotomacReviewEditor@montgomerycollege.edu. **Website:** www.montgomerycollege.edu/potomacreview. **Contact:** Professor Julie Wakeman-Linn, editor-in-chief. *Potomac Review: A Journal of Arts & Humanities*, published semiannually in November and May, "welcomes poetry, from across the spectrum, both traditional and nontraditional poetry, free verse and inform (translations accepted). Essays and creative nonfiction are also welcome." Has published work by David Wagoner, Elizabeth Spires, Ramola D, Amy Holman, and Luke Johnson. *Potomac Review* is 150 pages, digest-sized, 50 lb paper; 65 lb cover stock. Receives about 2,500 poems/year, accepts 3%. Subscription: $18/year (includes 2 issues). Sample: $10. Publishes ms 1 year after acceptance. Responds in 3 months. Guidelines available on website.

MAGAZINE'S NEEDS Submit up to 3 poems (5 pages maximum) at a time. Considers simultaneous submissions; no previously published poems. Cover letter is preferred. Include brief bio; enclose SASE. Poems are read "in house," then sent to poetry editor for comments and dialogue. Often comments on rejected poems. Does not publish theme issues. Pays 2 contributor's copies and offers 40% discount on additional copies.

CONTEST/AWARD OFFERINGS Sponsors an annual poetry contest and annual fiction contest. Guidelines available in magazine (fall/winter issue), for SASE.

TIPS "Send us interesting, well crafted stories. Have something to say in an original, provocative voice. Read recent issue to get a sense of the journal's new direction."

◐◐◐ THE PRAIRIE JOURNAL

P.O. Box 68073, 28 Crowfoot Terrace NW, Calgary AB Y3G 3N8, Canada. **E-mail:** editor@prairiejournal.org (queries only); prairiejournal@yahoo.com. **Website:** www.prairiejournal.org. **Contact:** A.E. Burke, literary editor. "The audience is literary, university, library, scholarly, and creative readers/writers." Buys first North American serial rights or buys electronic rights. In Canada, author retains copyright and owns permission to republish (with acknowledgement appreciated). Pays on publication. Publishes ms an average of 4-6 months after acceptance. Responds in 2 weeks to queries; 2-6 months to mss. Editorial lead time 2-6 months. Sample copy for $5. Guidelines available online.

○ "Use our mailing address for submissions and queries with samples or for clippings."

MAGAZINE'S NEEDS *The Prairie Journal*, published twice/year, seeks poetry "of any length; free verse, contemporary themes (feminist, nature, urban, non-political), aesthetic value, a poet's poetry." Does not want to see "most rhymed verse, sentimentality, egotistical ravings. No cowboys or sage brush." Has published poetry by Liliane Welch, Cornelia Hoogland, Sheila Hyland, Zoe Lendale, and Chad Norman. *The Prairie Journal* is 40-60 pages, digest-sized, offset-printed, saddle-stapled, with card cover, includes ads. Receives about 1,000 poems/year, accepts 10%. Press run is 600; the rest are sold on newsstands. Subscription: $10 for individuals, $18 for libraries. Sample: $8 ("use postal money order"). No U.S. stamps. No heroic couplets or greeting card verse. Length: 3-50 lines. Pays $5-50

TIPS "We publish many, many new writers and are always open to unsolicited submissions because we are 100% freelance. Do not send US stamps, always use IRCs. We have poems, interviews, stories, and reviews online (query first)."

○○ PRAIRIE SCHOONER

The University of Nebraska Press, Prairie Schooner, 123 Andrews Hall, University of Nebraska, Lincoln NE 68588. (402)472-0911. **Fax:** (402)472-1817. **E-mail:** PrairieSchooner@unl.edu. **Website:** http://prairieschooner.unl.edu. **Contact:** Marianne Kunkel, managing editor. "We look for the best fiction, poetry, and nonfiction available to publish, and our readers expect to read stories, poems, and essays of extremely high quality. We try to publish a variety of styles, topics, themes, points of view, and writers with a variety of backgrounds in all stages of their careers. We like work that is compelling—intellectually or emotionally—either in form, language, or content." Buys all rights, which are returned to the author upon request after publication. Pays on publication. Publishes ms an average of 1 year after acceptance. Responds in 1 week to queries. Responds in 3-4 months to mss. Editorial lead time 6 months. Sample copy for $6. Guidelines for #10 SASE.

○ Submissions must be received between September 1 and May 1.

MAGAZINE'S NEEDS Poetry published in Prairie Schooner has been selected for inclusion in *The Best American Poetry* and *The Pushcart Prize*. Wants "poems that fulfill the expectations they set up." No specifications as to form, length, style, subject matter, or purpose. Has published poetry by Alicia Ostriker, Marilyn Hacker, D.A. Powell, Stephen Dunn, and David Ignatow. Pays 3 copies of the issue in which the writer's work is published.

CONTEST/AWARD OFFERINGS "All manuscripts published in *Prairie Schooner* automatically will be considered for our annual prizes." These include The Strousse Award for Poetry ($500), the Bernice Slote Prize for Beginning Writers ($500), the Hugh J. Luke Award ($250), the Edward Stanley Award for Poetry ($1,000), the Virginia Faulkner Award for Excellence in Writing ($1,000), the Glenna Luschei Prize for Excellence ($1,500), and the Jane Geske Award ($250). Also, each year 10 Glenna Luschei Awards ($250 each) are given for poetry, fiction, and nonfiction. All contests are open only to those writers whose work was published in the magazine the previous year. Editors serve as judges. Also sponsors The *Prairie Schooner* Book Prize.

TIPS "Send us your best, most carefully crafted work and be persistent. Submit again and again. Constantly work on improving your writing. Read widely in literary fiction, nonfiction, and poetry. Read *Prairie Schooner* to know what we publish."

○○○○ PRISM INTERNATIONAL

Department of Creative Writing, Buch E462, 1866 Main Mall, University of British Columbia, Vancouver BC V6T 1Z1, Canada. (604)822-2514. **Fax:** (604)822-3616. **E-mail:** prismcirculation@gmail.com. **Website:** www.prismmagazine.ca. **Buys 10 poems/issue.** A quarterly international journal of contemporary writing—fiction, poetry, drama, creative nonfiction and translation. *PRISM international* is 80 pages, digest-sized, elegantly printed, flat-spined, with original color artwork on a glossy card cover. Readership: public and university libraries, individual subscriptions, bookstores—a world-wide audience concerned with the contemporary in literature. "We have no thematic or stylistic allegiances: Excellence is our main criterion for acceptance of manuscripts." Receives 1,000 submissions/year, accepts about 80. Circulation is for 1,200 subscribers. Subscription: $35/year for Canadian subscriptions, $40/year for US subscriptions, $45/year for international. Sample: $12. Buys first North American serial rights. Selected authors are paid an additional $10/page for digital rights. Pays on publication. Publishes ms an average of 4 months after acceptance. Responds in 4 months to queries. Responds in 3-6 months to mss. Sample copy for $12, more info online. Guidelines available online.

MAGAZINE'S NEEDS Wants "fresh, distinctive poetry that shows an awareness of traditions old and new. We read everything." Considers poetry by children and teens. "Excellence is the only criterion." Has published poetry by Margaret Avison, Elizabeth Bachinsky, John Pass, Warren Heiti, Don McKay, Bill Bissett, and Stephanie Bolster. Pays $40/printed page, and 1-year subscription.

HOW TO CONTACT Submit up to 6 poems at a time. No previously published poems or simultaneous submissions. No e-mail submissions. Cover letter is required. Include brief introduction and list of previous publications. Poems must be typed or computer-generated (font and point size open). Include SASE (or SAE with IRCs). "Note: American stamps are not valid postage in Canada. No SASEs with U.S. postage will be returned. Translations must be accompanied by a copy of the original." Guidelines available for SASE (or SAE with IRCs), by e-mail, or on website. Responds in up to 6 months. Editors sometimes comment on rejected poems. Acquires first North American serial rights.

ADDITIONAL INFORMATION Sponsors annual Earle Birney Prize for Poetry. Prize awarded by the outgoing poetry editor to an outstanding poetry contributor published in *PRISM international*. Enter by regular submission only: no fee required. $500 prize.

CONTEST/AWARD OFFERINGS Annual Poetry Contest. First prize: $1,000; second prize: $300; third prize: $200. Entry fee: $35 for 3 poems; $5 per additional poem. Entry fee includes one-year subscription. Deadline: see website.

TIPS "We are looking for new and exciting fiction. Excellence is still our No. 1 criterion. As well as poetry, imaginative nonfiction and fiction, we are especially open to translations of all kinds, very short fiction pieces and drama which work well on the page. Translations must come with a copy of the original language work. We pay an additional $10/printed page to selected authors whose work we place on our online version of *PRISM*."

◐ PRISM QUARTERLY

3232 S. First St., Springfield IL 62703. **E-mail:** davidpitchford@daybreakpoetry.com. **E-mail:** submissions@prismquarterly.com. **Website:** http://pitchblackbooks.netfirms.com. **Contact:** David M. Pitchford, publishing editor. *Prism Quarterly*, published by Daybreak Press, a division of Pitch-Black LLC, considers "all styles and forms of poetry." Does not want poems over 100 lines long. Considers poetry by children and teens. Has published poetry by Marge Piercy, Marcellus Leonard, Barb Robinette, and Siobhan. *Prism Quarterly* is 128 pages, digest-sized, laser-printed, perfect-bound, with cardstock cover with original artwork, includes ads. Receives about 800 poems/year, accepts about 200. Press run is 200; 25 distributed free to contributors and reviewers. Single copy: $7.95; subscription: $29.95. Make checks payable to Pitch-Black LLC. Publishes ms 2-3 months after acceptance. Responds in 1-3 months.

MAGAZINE'S NEEDS Submit no more than 3 poems at a time. Lines/poem: 100 maximum. No previously published poems or simultaneous submissions. Accepts e-mail submissions (pasted into body of message or as attachment in Rich Text Format); no disk submissions. Cover letter is required. "Please include SASE and e-mail address (if available) if response is desired for any submission." Reads submissions year-round. Submit seasonal poems 3 months in advance. Poems are circulated to an editorial board. Always comments on rejected poems. Guidelines available on website. Acquires first rights. Rights revert to poet upon publication. Pays 1 contributor's copy.

TIPS "Intermittent contests are announced at our website. Please see site for frequent updates. *Prism Quarterly* is a superlative journal of eclectic literature. The publishers welcome poets and writers in all (publishable) stages of their careers and seek a variety of themes, forms, and styles."

PROVINCETOWN ARTS

Provincetown Arts, Inc., 650 Commercial St., P.O. Box 35, Provincetown MA 02657. (508)487-3167. **E-mail:** cbusa@comcast.net. **Website:** www.provincetownarts.org. "*Provincetown Arts* focuses broadly on the artists and writers who inhabit or visit the Lower Cape, and seeks to stimulate creative activity and enhance public awareness of the cultural life of the nation's oldest continuous art colony. Drawing upon a 75-year tradition rich in visual art, literature, and theater, *Provincetown Arts* offers a unique blend of interviews, fiction, visual features, reviews, reporting, and poetry. Has published poetry by Bruce Smith, Franz Wright, Sandra McPherson, and Cyrus Cassells. 170 pages, magazine-sized, perfect-bound, with full-color glossy cover. Press run is 10,000. Buys first rights, buys one-time rights, buys second serial (reprint) rights. Pays on publication. Publishes ms an average of 4 months after acceptance. Responds in 3 weeks to queries; 2 months to mss. Editorial lead time 6 months. Sample copy for $10. Guidelines for #10 SASE.

MAGAZINE'S NEEDS Submit up to 3 poems at a time. No e-mail submissions; "all queries and submissions should be sent via postal mail." Submissions must be typed. Pays $25-100/poem plus 2 contributor's copies. Acquires first rights.

ADDITIONAL INFORMATION The Provincetown Arts Press has published 8 volumes of poetry. The Provincetown Poets Series includes *At the Gate* by Martha Rhodes, *Euphorbia* by Anne-Marie Levine (a finalist in the 1995 Paterson Poetry Prize), and *1990* by Michael Klein (co-winner of the 1993 Lambda Literary Award).

A PUBLIC SPACE

323 Dean St., Brooklyn NY 11217. (718)858-8067. **E-mail:** general@apublicspace.org. **Website:** www.apublicspace.org. **Contact:** Brigid Hughes, editor. 323 Dean St., Brooklyn, NY 11217. (718)858-8067. **E-mail:** general@apublicspace.org. **Website:** www.apublicspace.org. *A Public Space*, published quarterly, "is an independent magazine of literature and culture. In an era that has relegated literature to the margins, we plan to make fiction and poetry the stars of a new conversation. We believe that stories are how we make sense of our lives and how we learn about other lives. We believe that stories matter." Single copy: $15; subscription: $36/year or $60/2 years.

○ *A Public Space*, published quarterly, "is an independent magazine of literature and culture. In an era that has relegated literature to the margins, we plan to make fiction and poetry the stars of a new conversation. We believe that stories are how we make sense of our lives and how we learn about other lives. We believe that stories matter." Single copy: $15; subscription: $36/year or $60/2 years.

HOW TO CONTACT Submit up to 4 poems at a time. Considers simultaneous submissions; no previously published poems. Prefers submissions through online process; accepts mail. Include SASE. See website for submission dates and guidelines.

○ THE PUCKERBRUSH REVIEW

University of Maine, English Department, 413 Neville Hall, Orono ME 04469. **E-mail:** sanphip@aol.com. **Website:** http://puckerbrushreview.com. **Contact:** Sanford Phippen, Editor. *The Puckerbrush Review*, a print-only journal published twice/year, looks for "freshness and simplicity." 9×12; 80-100 pages; illustrations. Semiannual.

MAGAZINE'S NEEDS Has published poetry by Wolly Swist and Muska Nagel. Submit up to 5 poems. Click on link on website, which send an e-mail. Does not want to see "confessional, religious, sentimental, dull, feminist, incompetent, derivative" poetry.

TIPS ""Please submit your poetry, short stories, literary essays and reviews through our website link. Hard-copy submissions will no longer be accepted."

◐ PUDDING MAGAZINE: THE INTERNATIONAL JOURNAL OF APPLIED POETRY

81 Shadymere Lane, Columbus OH 43213. (614)986-1881. **E-mail:** info@puddingmagazine.com. **E-mail:** connie@puddingmagazine.com. **Website:** www.puddingmagazine.com. **Contact:** Connie Willett Everett, editor. *Pudding Magazine: The International Journal of Applied Poetry*, published "every several months," seeks "what hasn't been said before. Speak the unspeakable. Long poems okay as long as they aren't windy." *Pudding* also serves as "a forum for poems and articles by people who take poetry arts into the schools and the human services." Wants "poetry on popular culture, rich brief narratives, i.e. 'virtual journalism' (see website)." Does not want "preachments or sentimentality; obvious traditional forms without fresh approach." Has published poetry by Knute Skinner, David Chorlton, Mary Winters, and Robert Collins. *Pudding* is 70 pages, digest-sized, offset-composed on Microsoft Word PC. Press run is 1,500. Subscription: $29.95 for 4 issues. Sample: $8.95. Responds same day, unless traveling. Guidelines available on website.

MAGAZINE'S NEEDS Submit 3-10 poems at a time. Previously published submissions "respected, but include credits"; no simultaneous submissions. Cover letter is preferred ("cultivates great relationships with writers"). "Submissions without SASEs will be discarded. No postcards." Sometimes publishes theme issues. Returns rights "with *Pudding* permitted to reprint." Send anthologies and books for review consideration or listing as recommended. Pays 4 contributor's copies and $20.

TIPS "Our website is one of the greatest poetry websites in the country—calls, workshops, publication list/history, online essays, games, guest pages, calendars, poem of the month, poet of the week, much more." The website also links to the site for The Unitarian Universalist Poets Cooperative and American Poets Opposed to Executions, both national organizations.

PUERTO DEL SOL

New Mexico State University, English Department, P.O.Box 30001, MSC 3E, Las Cruces NM 88003. (505)646-3931. **E-mail:** contact@puertodelsol.org. **Website:** www.puertodelsol.org. **Contact:** Carmen Giménez Smith, editor-in-chief. "We publish innovative work from emerging and established writers and artists. Poetry, fiction, nonfiction, drama, theory, artwork, interviews, reviews, and interesting combinations thereof." Acquires one-time print and electronic rights and anthology rights. Rights revert to author after publication. Responds in 3-6 months to mss. Guidelines available online.

Magazine: 7×9; 200 pages; 60 lb. paper; 70 lb. cover stock. *Puerto del Sol* is 150 pages, digest-sized, professionally printed, flat-spined, with matte card cover with art. Press run is 1,250 (300 subscribers, 25-30 libraries). Single copies: $10. Subscriptions: $20 for 1 year, $35 for 2 years, $45 for 3 years.

MAGAZINE'S NEEDS Wants "top-quality poetry, any style, from anywhere; excellent poetry of any kind, any form." Submit 3-6 poems at a time through online submission manager. Brief cover letter is welcome. "Do not send publication vitae." One poem/page. Sometimes sends prepublication galleys. Has published poetry by Richard Blanco, Maria Ercilla, Pamela Gemin, John Repp, and Lee Ann Roripaugh. Pays 2 contributor's copies.

TIPS "We are especially pleased to publish emerging writers who work to push their art form or field of study in new directions."

PULSAR POETRY MAGAZINE

Ligden Publishers, 34 Lineacre, Grange Park, Swindon, Wiltshire SN5 6DA, England. **E-mail:** pulsar.ed@btopenworld.com. **Website:** www.pulsarpoetry.com. **Contact:** David Pike, Editor. Acquires first rights. "Originators retain copyright of their poems." Publishes ms 1 year after acceptance. Responds in 1 month. Guidelines available for SASE (or SAE and IRC) or on website.

Now is a web-zine only.

MAGAZINE'S NEEDS "We will publish poems on the Pulsar web on a quarterly basis, i.e. March, June, September and December. The selection process for poems will not alter and we will continue to publish on a merit basis only, be warned the editor is very picky! See poem submission guidelines online. We encourage the writing of poetry from all walks of life. Wants 'hard-hitting, thought-provoking work; interesting and stimulating poetry.' Does not want 'racist material. Not keen on religious poetry.' Has published poetry by A.C. Evans, Chris Hardy, Kate Edwards, Elizabeth Birchall, and Michael Newman." Pays 1 contributor's copy.

TIPS "Give explanatory notes if poems are open to interpretation. Be patient and enjoy what you are doing. Check grammar, spelling, etc. (should be obvious). Note: we are a nonprofit-making society."

PULSE ONLINE LITERARY JOURNAL

12 Center St., Rockland ME 04841. (760)243-8034. **E-mail:** mainepoet@mac.com. **Website:** www.heartsoundspressliterary.com. **Contact:** Carol Bachofner, poetry editor. *Pulse Online Literary Journal* is open to formal poetry as well as free verse. Wants "your best. Send only work revised and revised again! Translations welcome with submitted original language piece." Does not want "predictable, sentimental, greeting card verse. No gratuitous sexuality or violence. No religious verse or predictable rhyme." Has published poetry by Walt McDonald and Lyn Lifshin. Receives about 400 poems/year, accepts about 30-45%. Acquires first rights. Publishes ms 3-4 months after acceptance. Responds in 3-4 weeks. Guidelines online.

MAGAZINE'S NEEDS Submit 3-5 poems at a time. Lines/poem: up to 120. Considers previously published poems. Only accepts e-mail submissions (pasted into body of e-mail); no disk submissions. Cover letter is required. "Send bio of 50-100 words with submission." Reads submissions year round; publishes February, April, June, August, September, October, December. Sometimes comments on rejected poems. Sometimes publishes theme issues. Themes for 2009 were April-September: Urban Landscape; September-December: Movements. Reviews books/chapbooks of poetry.

CONTEST/AWARD OFFERINGS Larry Kramer Memorial Chapbook Award; William Dunbar Book-length poetry contest. Submission ofr the contest is by USPS. See website for guidelines and deadlines. Entry fee: varies with contest (multiple entries okay with additional fee for each). Deadline: April 1.

○ ⊙ PURPOSE

1251 Virginia Ave., Harrisonburg VA 22802. **E-mail:** CarolD@MennoMedia.org; purposeeditor@mpn.net. **Website:** www.mennomedia.org. **Contact:** Carol Duerksen, editor. *Purpose*, published monthly by Faith & Life Resources, an imprint of the Mennonite Publishing Network (the official publisher for the Mennonite Church in the US and Canada), is a "religious young adult/adult monthly." Focuses on "action-oriented, discipleship living." *Purpose* is digest-sized with 4-color printing throughout. Press run is 8,000. Receives about 2,000 poems/year, accepts 150. Sample (with guidelines): $2 and 9x12 SAE. Buys one-time rights. Pays on acceptance. Publishes ms an average of 18 months after acceptance. Responds in 3 months to queries. Sample copy and writer's guidelines for 6x9 SAE and $2.

MAGAZINE'S NEEDS Length: 12 lines maximum. Pays $7.50-20/poem depending on length and quality. Buys one-time rights only.

HOW TO CONTACT Considers simultaneous submissions. Prefers e-mail submissions. Postal submissions should be double-spaced, typed on one side of sheet only. Responds in 6 months. Guidelines available electronically or for SASE. Pays $7.50 to $20 per poem plus 2 contributor's copies.

TIPS "Many stories are situational, how to respond to dilemmas. Looking for first-person storylines. Write crisp, action moving, personal style, focused upon an individual, a group of people, or an organization. The story form is an excellent literary device to help readers explore discipleship issues. The first 2 paragraphs are crucial in establishing the mood/issue to

be resolved in the story. Work hard on the development of these."

○○⊙ QUANTUM LEAP

Q.Q. Press, York House, 15 Argyle Terrace, Rothesay, Isle of Bute PA20 0BD, Scotland. **Website:** www.qq-press.co.uk. *Quantum Leap*, published quarterly, uses "all kinds of poetry—free verse, rhyming, whatever—as long as it's well written and preferably well punctuated, too. We rarely use haiku." Has published poetry by Pamela Constantine, Ray Stebbing, Leigh Eduardo, Sky Higgins, Norman Bissett, and Gordon Scapens. *Quantum Leap* is 40 pages, digest-sized, desktop-published, saddle-stapled, with card cover. Receives about 2,000 poems/year, accepts about 15%. Press run is 200. Single copy: $13; subscription: $40. Sample: $10. Make checks payable to Alan Carter. "All things being equal in terms of a poem's quality, **I will sometimes favor that of a subscriber (or someone who has at least bought an issue) over a nonsubscriber,** as it is they who keep us solvent."

MAGAZINE'S NEEDS Submit 6 poems at a time. Lines/poem: 36 ("normally"). Considers previously published poems (indicate magazine and date of first publication) and simultaneous submissions. Cover letter is required. "Within the UK, send a SASE; outside it, send IRCs to the return postage value of what has been submitted." Time between acceptance and publication is usually 3 months "but can be longer now, due to magazine's increasing popularity." Sometimes comments on rejected poems. Guidelines available for SASE (or SAE and 2 IRCs). Responds in 3 weeks. Pays £2 sterling. Acquires first or second British serial rights.

CONTEST/AWARD OFFERINGS Sponsors open poetry competitions as well as competitions for subscribers only. Send SAE and IRC for details.

❶ QUARTER AFTER EIGHT

Website: www.quarteraftereight.org. **Contact:** Steve Coughlin. Acquires first North American serial rights. Rights revert to author upon publication. Publishes ms 6-12 months after acceptance. Responds in 3-5 months. Sample copy for $10. Guidelines available online at website.

○ Uses online submissions form.

MAGAZINE'S NEEDS Submit using online submissions manager.

TIPS "We look for prose and poetry that is innovative, exploratory, and—most importantly—well written. Please subscribe to our journaland read what is published to get acquainted with the QAE aesthetic."

⬤◉⑤ QUARTERLY WEST

University of Utah, 255 S. Central Campus Dr., Room 3500, Salt Lake City UT 84112. **E-mail:** quarterlywest@gmail.com. **Website:** www.quarterlywest. utah.edu. **Contact:** C.A. Schaefer & Sadie Hoagland, editors. "We publish fiction, poetry, and nonfiction in long and short formats, and will consider experimental as well as traditional works." Buys first North American serial rights, buys all rights. Pays on publication. Publishes ms an average of 6 months after acceptance. Responds in 6 months to mss. Sample copy for $7.50 or online. Guidelines available online.

   ◯   *Quarterly West* was awarded first place for Editorial Content from the American Literary Magazine Awards. Work published in the magazine has been selected for inclusion in the *Pushcart Prize* anthology and *The Best American Short Stories* anthology.

MAGAZINE'S NEEDS Submit 3-5 poems at a time using online submissions manager. Pays $15-100.

TIPS "We publish a special section of short shorts every issue, and we also sponsor a biennial novella contest. We are open to experimental work—potential contributors should read the magazine! Don't send more than 1 story/submission. Biennial novella competition guidelines available upon request with SASE. We prefer work with interesting language and detail—plot or narrative are less important. We don't do Western themes or religious work."

◉◉⑤ QUEEN'S QUARTERLY

144 Barrie St., Queen's University, Kingston ON K7L 3N6, Canada. (613)533-2667. **Fax:** (613)533-6822. **E-mail:** queens.quarterly@queensu.ca. **Website:** www. queensu.ca/quarterly. **Contact:** Joan Harcourt, editor. *Queen's Quarterly* is "a general interest intellectual review featuring articles on science, politics, humanities, arts and letters, extensive book reviews, some poetry and fiction." Requires first North American serial rights. Pays on publication. Publishes ms on average 6-12 months after acceptance. Responds in 2-3 months to queries. Free sample copy and guidelines online.

   ◯   Digest-sized, 224 pages. Press run is 3,500. Receives about 400 submissions of poetry/year, accepts 40. Has published work by Gail Anderson-Dargatz, Tim Bowling, Emma Dono-

hue, Viktor Carr, Mark Jarman, Rick Bowers, and Dennis Bock. Subscription: $20 Canadian, $25 US for U.S. and foreign subscribers. Sample: $6.50 U.S.

MAGAZINE'S NEEDS Submit up to 6 poems at a time. No simultaneous submissions. Submissions can be sent on hard copy with a SASE (no replies/returns for foreign submissions unless accompanied by an IRC) or by e-mail and will be responded to by same. Responds in 1 month. "We are especially interested in poetry by Canadian writers. Shorter poems preferred." Has published poetry by Evelyn Lau, Sue Nevill, and Raymond Souster. Each issue contains about 12 pages of poetry. Pays usually $50 (Canadian)/poem, "but it varies," plus 2 copies.

◉ QUIDDITY INTERNATIONAL LITERARY JOURNAL AND PUBLIC-RADIO PROGRAM

Benedictine University at Springfield, 1500 N. 5th St., Springfield IL 62702. **Website:** www1.ben.edu/ springfield/quiddity. **Contact:** Joanna Beth Tweedy, Founding editor. "Each work selected is considered for public-radio program feature offered by NPR-member station (WUIS (PRI affiliate). *Quiddity*, published semi-annually, is "a print journal and public-radio program featuring poetry, prose, and artwork by new, emerging, and established contributors from around the globe. Please visit the website for guidelines." Has published work by J.O.J. Nwachukwu-Agbada, Kevin Stein, Karen An-Hwei Lee, and Haider Al-Kabi. *Quiddity* is 176 pages, 7X9, perfect-bound, with 60 lb. full color cover. Receives about 3,500 poems/year, accepts about 3%. Press run is 1,000. Single copy: $9; subscription: $15/year. Make checks payable to *Quiddity*." Publishes ms 6 months to 2 years after acceptance. Responds in 6 months.

   ◯   "International submissions are encouraged."

MAGAZINE'S NEEDS Submit up to 5 poems through snail mail (hard copy) or through online submission manager. Considers simultaneous submissions; no previously published poems (previously published includes work posted on a public website/blog/forum and on private, password-protected forums). Cover letter is preferred. Address to poetry editor, SASE required (except international). See website for reading dates. Pays 1 contributor's copy.

RADIX MAGAZINE

Radix Magazine, Inc., P.O. Box 4307, Berkeley CA 94704. (510)548-5329. **E-mail:** radixmag@aol.com. **Website:** www.radixmagazine.com. **Contact:** Sharon Gallagher, editor. *"Radix Magazine*, published quarterly, is named for the Latin word for "root" and "has its roots both in the 'real world' and in the truth of Christ's teachings." Wants poems "that reflect a Christian world-view, but aren't preachy." Has published poetry by John Leax, Czeslaw Milosz, Madeleine L'Engle, and Luci Shaw. *Radix* is 32 pages, magazine-sized, offset-printed, saddle-stapled, with 60-lb. self cover. Receives about 120 poems/year, accepts about 10%. Press run varies. Subscription: $15. Sample: $5. Make checks payable to *Radix Magazine*." Interested in first North American serial rights. Publishes ms 3 months to 3 years after acceptance. Responds in 2 months to queries and to mss. Editorial lead time 6 months. Sample copy for $5. Guidelines by e-mail.

MAGAZINE'S NEEDS "Needs poetry." Submit 1-4 poems at a time. Length: 4-20 lines. Pays 2 contributor copies.

TIPS "We accept very few unsolicited manuscripts. We do not accept fiction. All articles and poems should be based on a Christian world view. Freelancers should have some sense of the magazine's tone and purpose."

THE RAG

11901 SW 34th Ave., Portland OR 97219. **E-mail:** raglitmag@gmail.com. **Website:** http://raglitmag.com. **Contact:** Seth Porter, editor; Dan Reilly, editor. "The Rag focuses on the grittier genres that tend to fall by the wayside at more traditional literary magazines. The Rag's ultimate goal is to put the literary magazine magazine back into the entertainment market while rekindling the social and cultural value short fiction once held in North American literature." Purchases first rights only. Pays on acceptance. Responds in 1 month or less for queries and in 1-2 months for mss. Editorial lead time 1-2 months.

MAGAZINE'S NEEDS "We accept all themes and styles." Submit complete ms. "5 poems or 2,000 words, whichever comes first." Pays $20-100+.

TIPS "We like gritty material; material that is psychologically believable and that has some humor in it, dark or otherwise. We like subtle themes, original characters, and sharp wit."

RAILROAD EVANGELIST

Railroad Evangelist Association, Inc., P.O. Box 5026, Vancouver WA 98668. (360)699-7208. **E-mail:** rrjoe@comcast.net. **Website:** www.railroadevangelist.com. "The *Railroad Evangelist*'s purpose and intent is to reach people everywhere with the life-changing gospel of Jesus Christ. The railroad industry is our primary target, along with model railroad and rail fans." Editorial lead time 6 weeks. Sample copy for SAE with 10x12 envelope and 3 first-class stamps. Guidelines for #10 SASE.

All content must be railroad related.

MAGAZINE'S NEEDS Length: 10-100 lines. Pays in contributor copies.

THE RAINTOWN REVIEW

Central Ave. Press, 5390 Fallriver Row Court, Columbia MD 21044. **E-mail:** theraintownreview@gmail.com. **Website:** www.theraintownreview.com. **Contact:** Anna Evans, editor-in-chief; Quincy R. Lehr, associate editor. We prefer poems that have NOT been previously published. *The Raintown Review*, published 2 times/year in Winter and Summer, contains poetry, reviews, and belletristic critical prose. Wants well-crafted poems. "We are primarily a venue for formal poetry." Has published poetry by Julie Kane, Alexandra Oliver, Rick Mullin, Annie Finch, Kevin Higgins, David Mason, A.E. Stallings, Richard Wilbur, and many others. *The Raintown Review* is 120 pages, perfect-bound. Receives about 2,500 poems/year, accepts roughly 5%. Press run is approximately 500. Subscription: $24/year, $45 for 2 years, $65 for 3 years. Sample: $12. Make checks/money orders payable to Central Ave Press. Responds in 10-12 weeks. One can also subscribe online via our website preferred method.

MAGAZINE'S NEEDS Submit 3-5 poems at a time. Lines/poem: no restrictions. Considers simultaneous submissions. Accepts e-mail submissions only (pasted into body of message); no postal submissions. Guidelines available on website.

RATTAPALLAX

Rattapallax Press, 217 Thompson St., Suite 353, New York NY 10012. (212)560-7459. **E-mail:** info@rattapallax.com. **Website:** www.rattapallax.com. **Contact:** Alan Cheuse, fiction editor. *Rattapallax*, published semiannually, is named for "Wallace Stevens's word for the sound of thunder. The magazine includes a DVD featuring poetry films and audio files. *"Rat-*

tapallax is looking for the extraordinary in modern poetry and prose that reflect the diversity of world cultures. Our goals are to create international dialogue using literature and focus on what is relevant to our society." Buys first North American serial rights, buys South American rights. Pays on publication. Publishes ms an average of 6 months after acceptance. Responds in 3 months to queries; 3 months to mss. Editorial lead time 6 months. Sample copy for $7.95. Guidelines available online.

○ *Rattapallax* is 112 pages, magazine-sized, offset-printed, perfect-bound, with 12-pt. CS1 cover; some illustrations; photos. Press run is 2,000 (100 subscribers, 50 libraries, 1,200 shelf sales); 200 distributed free to contributors, reviews, and promos. Single copy: $7.95; no subscriptions. Make checks payable to *Rattapallax*. Receives 15 unsolicited mss/month. Accepts 3 mss/issue; 6 mss/year. Agented fiction 15%. Receives about 5,000 poems/year; accepts 2%. Publishes 3 new writers/year. Has published work by Stuart Dybek, Howard Norman, Molly Giles, Rick Moody, Anthony Hecht, Sharon Olds, Lou Reed, Marilyn Hacker, Billy Collins, and Glyn Maxwell.

MAGAZINE'S NEEDS Submit via Submittable at https://rattapallax.submittable.com/submit. Often comments on rejected poems. Length: 5-200 lines. Pays 2 contributor's copies.

TIPS "The editor-in-chief, senior editor, and associate editor review all the submissions and then decide on which to accept every week. Near publication time, all accepted work is narrowed, and unused work is kept for the next issue."

○ RATTLE

12411 Ventura Blvd., Studio City CA 91604. (818)505-6777. **E-mail:** tim@rattle.com. **Website:** www.rattle.com. **Contact:** Timothy Green, editor. "Includes poems, essays, reviews, interviews with poets, and a tribute section dedicated to a specific ethnic or vocational group."

MAGAZINE'S NEEDS Wants "meaningful poetry in any form." Considers some poetry by children and teens (ages 10-18). Submit up to 5 poems at a time. Accepts e-mail submissions (pasted into body of message). Cover letter is required (with e-mail address, if possible).

CONTEST/AWARD OFFERINGS "All submissions are automatically considered for the Neil Postman Award for Metaphor, an annual $500 prize for the best use of metaphor as judged by the editors. No entry fee or special formatting is required, simply follow the regular guidelines." Also, the RATTLE Poetry Prize (see separate listing in Contests & Awards). Welcomes essays up to 2,000 words on poetry or the writing process.

○ RATTLING WALL

c/o PEN USA, 269 S. Beverly Dr. #1163, Beverly Hills CA 90212. **E-mail:** therattlingwall@gmail.com; michelle@therattlingwall.com. **Website:** http://therattlingwall.com. **Contact:** Michelle Meyering, editor. Acquires first rights. Rights revert to poet upon publication. Pays on publication. Publishes ms 2 months after acceptance. Responds in 2-4 months. Sample copy for $15. Guidelines available online.

MAGAZINE'S NEEDS Submit 3-5 poems at a time. Does not want sentimental love poetry or religious verse. Does not consider poetry by children or teens. Pays 2 contributor's copies.

○ ○ THE RAVEN CHRONICLES

A Journal of Art, Literature, & the Spoken Word, 12346 Sand Point Way N.E., Seattle WA 98125. (206)941-2955. **E-mail:** editors@ravenchronicles. org. **Website:** www.ravenchronicles.org. Responds in 3 months. Guidelines available online at website.

MAGAZINE'S NEEDS Send a maximum of 3 poems at a time via postal mail with SASE. Focus is on content that melds with form—whether traditional or experiemental.

TIPS "The Raven Chronicles publishes work which reflects the cultural diversity of the Pacific Northwest, Canada, and other areas of America. We promote art, literature and the spoken word for an audience that is hip, literate, funny, informed, and lives in a society that has a multicultural sensibility. We publish fiction, talk art/spoken word, poetry, essays, reflective articles, reviews, interviews and contemporary art. We look for work that reflects the author's experiences, perceptions and insights."

○ ○ THE READER

The Reader Organisation, The Firary Centre, Bute St., Liverpool L5 3LA, United Kingdom. **E-mail:** magazine@thereader.org.uk; info@thereader.org.uk. **Website:** www.thereader.org.uk. **Contact:** Philip Davis, editor. "*The Reader* is a quarterly literary magazine aimed at the intelligent 'common reader'—from those just beginning to explore serious literary reading to professional teachers, academics and writers. As well as publishing short fiction and poetry by new writers and established names, the magazine features articles on all aspects of literature, language, and reading; regular features, including a literary quiz and 'Our Spy in NY', a bird's-eye view of literary goings-on in New York; reviews; and readers'recommendations of books that have made a difference to them. *The Reader* is unique among literary magazines in its focus on reading as a creative, important and pleasurable activity, and in its combination of high-quality material and presentation with a genuine commitment to ordinary but dedicated readers." Also publishes literary essays, literary criticism, poetry. Pays on publication. Publishes ms 16 months after acceptance. Responds to queries and mss in 2 months. Guidelines for SASE.

TIPS "The style or polish of the writing is less important than the deep structure of the story (though of course, it matters that it's well written). The main persuasive element is whether the story moves us—and that's quite hard to quantify—it's something to do with the force of the idea and the genuine nature of enquiry within the story. When fiction is the writer's natural means of thinking things through, that'll get us. "

REALPOETIK

Athens GA **E-mail:** realpoetikblog@gmail.com. **Website:** www.realpoetik.org. "We do not want to see anything that fits neatly into categories. We subvert categories." Publishes poetry 2-4 months after acceptance. Responds in 1 month to queries. Sometimes comments on rejected mss. Sample copy online.

Publishes 20-30 new poets/year.

MAGAZINE'S NEEDS Query with or without published clips or send complete ms. Accepts submissions by e-mail.

TIPS "Be different but interesting. Complexity and consciousness are always helpful. Write short. We're a post-modern e-zine. Query us before submitting at RealPoetikblog@gmail.com."

REDACTIONS: POETRY, POETICS, & PROSE

58 S. Main St., 3rd Floor, Brockport NY 14420. **E-mail:** redactionspoetry@yahoo.com (poetry); redactionsprose@yahoo.com (prose). **Website:** www.redac-

tions.com. All rights revert back to the author. Responds in 3 months.

MAGAZINE'S NEEDS "Anything dealing with poetry."

TIPS "We only accept submissions by e-mail. We read submissions throughout the year. E-mail us and attach submission into one Word, Wordpad, Notepad, .rtf, or .txt document, or, place in the body of an e-mail. Include brief bio and your snail mail address. Query after 90 days if you haven't heard from us. See website for full guidelines for each genre, including artwork."

THE RED CLAY REVIEW

Dr. Jim Elledge, Director, M. A. in Professional Writing Program, Department of English, Kennesaw State University, 1000 Chastain Rd., #2701, Kennesaw GA 30144. **E-mail:** redclay2013@gmail.com. **Website:** http://redclayreview.com. **Contact:** Dr. Jim Elledge, director, M. A. in Professional Writing Program. Publishes ms 6 weeks after acceptance. Responds in 3-4 months. Guidelines available online.

MAGAZINE'S NEEDS Submit complete ms with cover letter. Include brief bio, list of publications, and an e-mail address must be supplied for the student, as well as the student's advisor's contact information (to verify student status). Length: no more than 300 words. Pays in contributor's copies.

TIPS "Because the editors of *RCR* are graduate student writers, we are mindful of grammatical proficiency, vocabulary, and the organizational flow of the submissions we receive. We appreciate a heightened level of writing from fellow graduate writing students; but we also hold it to a standard to which we have learned in our graduate writing experience. Have your submission(s) proofread by a fellow student or professor."

REDHEADED STEPCHILD

E-mail: redheadedstepchildmag@gmail.com. **Website:** www.redheadedmag.com/poetry. **Contact:** Malaika King Albrecht. "*The Redheaded Stepchild* only accepts poems that have been rejected by other magazines. We publish biannually, and we accept submissions in the months of August and February only. We do not accept previously published work. We do, however, accept simultaneous submissions, but please inform us immediately if your work is accepted somewhere else. We are open to a wide variety of poetry and hold no allegiance to any particular style or school. If your poem is currently displayed online on your blog or website or wherever, please do not send it to us before taking it down, at least temporarily." Acquires first rights. Rights revert to poets upon publication. Time between acceptance and publication is 3 months. Poems are circulated to an editorial board. Sometimes comments on rejected poems. Responds in 3 months. Guidelines on website.

○ Wants a wide variety of poetic styles. Does not want previously published poems. Has published poetry by Kathryn Stripling Byer, Alex Grant, Amy King, Diane Lockward, Susan Yount, and Howie Good.

MAGAZINE'S NEEDS "Submit 3-5 poems that have been rejected elsewhere with the names of the magazines that rejected the poems. We do not want multiple submissions, so please wait for a response to your first submission before you submit again. As is standard after publication, rights revert back to the author, but we request that you credit *Redheaded Stepchild* in subsequent republications. We do not accept e-mail attachments; therefore, in the body of your e-mail, please include the following: a brief bio; 3-5 poems; the publication(s) that rejected the poems."

○ REDIVIDER

Department of Writing, Literature, and Publishing, Emerson College, 120 Boylston St., Boston MA 02116. **E-mail:** editor@redividerjournal.org. **Website:** www.redividerjournal.org. Redivider, a journal of literature and art, is published twice a year by students in the graduate writing, literature and publishing department of Emerson College. Editors change each year. Prints high-quality poetry, art, fiction, and creative nonfiction. *Redivider* is 100+ pages, digest-sized, offset-printed, perfect-bound, with 4-color artwork on cover. Press run is 1,000. Single copy: $6; subscription: $10. Make checks payable to *Redivider* at Emerson College. Pays on publication. Responds in 3-6 months. Sample copy $8. Guidelines available online at website.

MAGAZINE'S NEEDS Wants "all styles of poetry. Most of all, we look for language that seems fresh and alive on the page, that tries to do something new. Read a sample copy for a good idea." Does not want "greeting card verse or inspirational verse." Submit 3-6 poems through online submissions manager. Pays 2 contributor's copies.

TIPS "Our deadlines are July 1 for the Fall issue, and December 1 for the Spring issue."

○ RED LIGHTS

2740 Andrea Drive, Allentown PA 18103-4602. (212)875-9342. **E-mail:** mhazelton@rcn.com; marilynhazelton@rcn.com. **Contact:** Marilyn Hazelton, editor. *red lights tanka journal*, published biannually in January and June, is devoted to English-language tanka and tanka sequences. Wants "print-only tanka, mainly 'free-form' but also strictly syllabic 5-7-5-7-7; will consider tanka sequences and tan-renga." Considers poetry by children and teens. Has published poetry by Sanford Goldstein, Michael McClintock, Laura Maffei, Linda Jeannette Ward, Jane Reichhold, and Michael Dylan Welch. *red lights* is 36-40 pages, offset-printed, saddle-stapled, with Japanese textured paper cover; copies are numbered. Single copy: $8; subscription: $16 U.S., $18 USD Canada, $20 USD foreign. Make checks payable to "red lights" in the U.S.

TIPS "Each issue features a '*red lights* featured tanka' on the theme of 'red lights.' Poet whose poem is selected receives 1 contributor's copy."

○ ○ THE RED MOON ANTHOLOGY OF ENGLISH LANGUAGE HAIKU

P.O. Box 2461, Winchester VA 22604-1661. **E-mail:** jim.kacian@redmoonpress.com. **Website:** www.redmoonpress.com. **Contact:** Jim Kacian, editor/publisher. *The Red Moon Anthology of English Language Haiku*, published annually in February, is "a collection of the best haiku published in English around the world." Acquires North American serial rights. Guidelines available for SASE or by e-mail.

○ *The Red Moon Anthology of English Language Haiku* is 184 pages, digest-sized, offset-printed on quality paper, with 4-color heavy-stock cover. Receives several thousand submissions/year, accepts less than 2%. Print run is 1,000 for subscribers and commercial distribution. Considers poetry by children and teens. Has published haiku and related forms by John Barlow, Cherie Hunter Day, Gary Hotham, and Billie Wilson. Subscription: $17 plus $5 p&h. Sample available for SASE or by e-mail.

MAGAZINE'S NEEDS "We do not accept direct submissions to the *Red Moon Anthology*. Rather, we employ an editorial board who are assigned journals and books from which they cull and nominate. Nominated poems are placed on a roster and judged anonymously by the entire editorial board twice a year."

ALSO OFFERS *contemporary haibun*, "an annual volume of the finest English-language haibun and haiga published anywhere in the world."

RED RIVER REVIEW

4669 Mountain Oak St., Ft. Worth TX 76244. (817)431-4691. **E-mail:** info@redriverreview.com. **Website:** www.redriverreview.com. **Contact:** Michelle Hartman, editor. "Our editorial philosophy is simple: It is the duty of the writer to accurately chronicle our times and to reflect honestly on how these events affect us. Poetry which strikes a truth, which artfully conveys the human condition is most likely to be selected. Vulgarity and coarseness are part of our daily life, and are thus valid. Life isn't always pretty. However, vulgarity and coarseness, just for the sake of the exercise, doesn't generally benefit anyone. *Red River Review* is open to all styles of writing. Abstract, beat, confessional, free verse, synthetic, formal — we will publish just about anything that has the authenticity and realism we're seeking. With this said, however, rhymed poetry of any nature is rarely accepted." Acquires first North American electronic rights and possible future anthology electronic rights. Rights revert to poets upon publication. Time between acceptance andpublication is 2 weeks. Responds in 2 weeks to poems. Sometimes comments on rejected poems. **Charges criticism fee. Handled on individual basis.** Guidelines available on website.

- Has published poetry by Naomi Shihab Nye, Larry Thomas, Rob Walker, Alan Gann, Jerry Bradley, and Ann Howells. "We are associated with the Dallas Poets Community, and therefore recommend their workshops and events to poets in the North Texas area."

MAGAZINE'S NEEDS Submit 1 poem per page, up to 5 poems at a time. Receives about 2,000 poems/year. Does not consider previously poems (poetry posted on a public website, blog. or forum. "Please be very sure you have entered your e-mail address correctly. If an acceptance comes back bad mail, we pull the poem. Please include a serious bio. If you do not respect your work, why should we?" Rarely takes rhyming or form poems, "although we live a good sonnet every now and then." Pays in contributor's copy/copies.

RED ROCK REVIEW

College of Southern Nevada, CSN Department of English, J2A, 3200 E. Cheyenne Ave., North Las Vegas NV 89030. (702)651-4094. **Fax:** (702)651-4639. **E-mail:** redrockreview@csn.edu. **Website:** sites.csn.edu/english/redrockreview/. **Contact:** Todd Moffett, senior editor. "We are dedicated to the publication of fine contemporary literature." *Red Rock Review* is about 130 pages, magazine-sized, professionally printed, perfect-bound, with 10-pt. CS1 cover. Accepts about 15% of poems received/year. Press run is 2350. Subscriptions: $9.50/year. Sample: $5.50. Buys first North American serial rights. All other rights revert to the authors and artists upon publication. No longer accepting snail mail submissions. Send all submissions as MS. Word, RTF, or PDF file attachment to redrockreview@csn.edu. Guidelines available online. Occasionally comments on rejections.

MAGAZINE'S NEEDS "We're looking for the very best literature. Poems need to be tightly crafted, characterised by expert use of language." Submit 2-3 poems at a time. Length: 80 lines. Pays in contributor's copies.

TIPS "Open to short fiction and poetry submissions from Sept. 1-May 31. Include SASE and include brief bio. No general submissions between June 1st and August 31st. See guidelines online."

REED MAGAZINE

San Jose State University, Dept. of English, One Washington Square, San Jose CA 95192. (408) 927-4458. **E-mail:** mail@reedmag.org. **Website:** www.reedmag.org/drupal. **Contact:** Cathleen Miller, faculty advisor. Pays on publication. Responds in up to 3 months. Guidelines available online at website.

- Accepts electronic submissions only.

MAGAZINE'S NEEDS Submit up to 5 poems using online submissions manager. Include contact information on first page.

TIPS "Well-writen, original, clean grammatical prose is essential. Keep submitting! The readers are students and change every year."

RENDITIONS: A CHINESE-ENGLISH TRANSLATION MAGAZINE

E-mail: renditions@cuhk.edu.hk. **Website:** www.renditions.org. *Renditions: A Chinese-English Translation Magazine*, published twice/year in May and November, uses "exclusively translations from Chinese, ancient and modern." *Poems are printed with Chinese and English texts side by side. Has published translations of the poetry of Yang Lian, Gu Cheng, Shu Ting, Mang Ke, and Bei Dao. Renditions is about 150 pages, magazine-sized, elegantly printed, perfect-bound,* with glossy card cover. Single copy: $19.90; subscription: $29.90/year, $49.90/2 years, $69.90/3 years. Responds in 2 months. Guidelines on website.

MAGAZINE'S NEEDS Submissions should be accompanied by Chinese originals. Accepts e-mail and fax submissions. "Submissions by postal mail should include two copies. Use British spelling." Sometimes comments on rejected translations. Publishes theme issues.

ADDITIONAL INFORMATION Also publishes a hardback series (Renditions Books) and a paperback series (Renditions Paperbacks) of Chinese literature in English translation. "Will consider" book mss; query with sample translations.

RHINO

The Poetry Forum, Inc., P.O. Box 591, Evanston IL 60204. **E-mail:** editors@rhinopoetry.org. **E-mail:** Online submissions form: annsbrandon@gmail.com. **Website:** www.rhinopoetry.org. **Contact:** Ralph Hamilton, editor. "This eclectic annual journal of more than 30 years accepts poetry, flash fiction (750 words or less), and poetry-in-translation from around the world that experiments, provokes, compels. More than 80 poets are showcased." Accepts general submissions April 1 - August 31. Single copy: $12. Sample: $5 (back issue). Buys first North American serial rights. Response time may exceed 6 weeks. Guidelines available online.

MAGAZINE'S NEEDS Wants "work that reflects passion, originality, engagement with contemporary culture, and a love affair with language. We welcome free verse, formal poetry, innovation, and risk-taking." Submit no more than 5 poems via online submissions manager (preferred) or by postal mail. Include cover letter.

CONTEST/AWARD OFFERINGS Founders' Prize submissions are accepted September 1 – October 31.

TIPS "Our diverse group of editors looks for the very best in contemporary writing, and we have created a dynamic process of soliciting and reading new work by local, national, and international writers. We look for idiosyncratic, rigorous, lively, passionate, and funny work."

❾❶❸ THE RIALTO

P.O. Box 309, Alysham, Norwich NR11 6LN, England. **E-mail:** info@therialto.co.uk. **Website:** www.therialto.co.uk. **Contact:** Michael Mackmin, editor. *The Rialto*, published 3 times/year, seeks "to publish the best new poems by established and beginning poets. We seek excellence and originality." Has published poetry by Alice Fulton, Jenny Joseph, Les Murray, George Szirtes, Philip Gross, and Ruth Padel. *The Rialto* is 64 pages, A4, with full-color cover. Receives about 12,000 poems/year, accepts about 1%. Press run is 1,500. Single copy: £7.50; subscription: £23 (prices listed are for U.S. and Canada). Make checks payable to *The Rialto*. "Checks in sterling only, please. Online payment also available on website." Publishes ms 5 months after acceptance. Responds in 3-4 months.

MAGAZINE'S NEEDS Submit up to 6 poems at a time. Does not accept e-mail submissions.

TIPS "*The Rialto* has recently commenced publishing first collections by poets. Please do not send book-length manuscripts. Query first." Sponsors an annual young poets competition. Details available in magazine and on website. Before submitting, "you will probably have read many poems by many poets, both living and dead. You will probably have put aside each poem you write for at least 3 weeks before considering it afresh. You will have asked yourself, 'Does it work technically?'; checked the rhythm, the rhymes (if used), and checked that each word is fresh and meaningful in its context, not jaded and tired. You will hopefully have read *The Rialto*."

❶ RIBBONS: TANKA SOCIETY OF AMERICA JOURNAL

David Bacharach, TSA Editor, 5921 Cayutaville Rd., Alpine NY 14805. **E-mail:** davidb@htva.net. **Website:** www.tankasocietyofamerica.com. **Contact:** David Bacharach, editor. Published quarterly, seeks and regularly prints "the best tanka poetry being written in English, together with reviews, critical and historical essays, commentaries, and translations." Wants "poetry that exemplifies the very best in English-language tanka, which we regard as 'the queen of short form poetry,' having a significant contribution to make to the short poem in English. All schools and approaches are welcome." Tanka should "reflect contemporary life, issues, values, and experience, in descriptive, narrative, and lyrical modes." Does not want "work that merely imitates the Japanese masters." Considers poetry by children and teens. "We have no age restrictions." Has published poetry by Cherie Hunter Day, Marianne Bluger, Sanford Goldstein, Larry Kimmel, John Stevenson, and George Swede. *Ribbons* is 60-72 pages, 6x9 perfect-bound, with color cover and art. Receives about 2,000 poems/year, accepts about 20%. Press run is 275; 15 distributed free. Single copy: $10; subscription: $30. Make checks payable to Tanka Society of America and contact Carole MacRury, Secretary/Treasurer (e-mail: macrury@whidbey.com; 1636 Edwards Dr., Point Roberts, WA 98281). Publishes ms 2 months after acceptance. Respond in 1-2 months.

MAGAZINE'S NEEDS Submit 1-8 poems at a time. Lines/poem: 5 minimum; sequences of up to 50 total lines considered. No previously published poems or simultaneous submissions. Prefers e-mail submissions (pasted into body of message); no disk submissions. "Postal submissions must include SASE." Reads submissions year-round. "See the publication or contact the editor for specific deadlines for each issue."

TIPS "Work by beginning as well as established English-language tanka poets is welcome; first-time contributors are encouraged to study the tanka form and contemporary examples before submitting. No particular school or style of tanka is preferred over another; our publications seek to showcase the full range of English-language tanka expression and subject matter through the work of new and established poets in the genre from around the world."

○ RIO GRANDE REVIEW

University of Texas at El Paso, PMB 671, 500 W. University Ave., El Paso TX 79968-0622. **E-mail:** editors@riograndereview.com. **Website:** www.utep. edu/rgr. *Rio Grande Review*, published in January and August, is a bilingual (English-Spanish) student publication from the University of Texas at El Paso. Contains poetry; flash, short, and nonfiction; short drama; photography and line art. *Rio Grande Review* is 168 pages, digest-sized, professionally printed, perfect-bound, with card cover with line art. Subscription: $8/year, $15/2 years. Guidelines available for SASE, by e-mail, or on website.

MAGAZINE'S NEEDS Poetry has a limit of 10 pages. No simultaneous submissions. Accepts e-mail submissions only (as attachment or pasted into body of message). Include short bio. Any submissions received after a reception deadline will automatically be considered for the following edition. "Permission to reprint material remains the decision of the author. However, *Rio Grande Review* does request it be given mention." Pays 2 contributor's copies.

○ ROAD NOT TAKEN: THE JOURNAL OF FORMAL POETRY, THE

E-mail: jimatshs@yahoo.com. **Website:** www.journalformalpoetry.com. **Contact:** Dr. Jim Prothero, co-editor. *The Road Not Taken: the Journal of Formal Poetry*, published quarterly online, prints formal poetry "in the tradition of Frost, Wordsworth, Tennyson, Hopkins, etc." Wants "formal poetry only. Nature and spiritual poetry always of interest but not required. Also essays/blogs on the topic of formal poetry would be of interest." Does not want free verse. Accepts poetry by children and teens; no age limitations—"it just has to be excellent." Acquires one-time rights. Rights revert to poets upon publication. Time between acceptance and publication is 2 months. Sometimes comments on rejected poems. Responds in 2 months. Guidelines available by e-mail and on website.

MAGAZINE'S NEEDS Submit 5 poems at a time. Considers previously published poems; no simultaneous submissions. (Considers poetry posted on a public website/blog/forum as published.) Accepts e-mail submissions (pasted into body of message); no fax or disk submissions. Cover letter is unnecessary. Reads submissions year round. Poems are circulated to an editorial board. "There are 2 editors: Dr. Jim Prothero and Dr. Don Williams. Poems must meet both of our approval."

◑ ROADRUNNER HAIKU JOURNAL

E-mail: scott@roadrunnerjournal.net. **Website:** www.roadrunnerjournal.net. **Contact:** Scott Metz, editor.

MAGAZINE'S NEEDS Considers haiku of any school written in English (including senryu, zappai and short poetry inspired by haiku). Please send 5 to 25 ku at a time for consideration. No single poem submissions, please (they will be ignored). Only two submissions per reading period will be considered. All poems must be unpublished and not under consideration.

◑ ⑤ ROANOKE REVIEW

Roanoke College, 221 College Lane, Salem VA 24153-3794. **E-mail:** review@roanoke.edu. **Website:** http://roanokereview.wordpress.com. **Contact:** Paul Hanstedt, editor. Magazine: 6×9; 200 pages; 60 lb. paper; 70 lb. cover. "We're looking for fresh, thoughtful material that will appeal to a broader as well as literary audience. Humor encouraged." Pays on publication for one-time rights. Publishes ms 6 months after acceptance. Responds in 1 month to queries; 6 months to mss; 3-6 months to poetry. Sometimes comments on rejected mss. Sample copy for 8×11 SAE with $2 postage. Guidelines available on website.

◑ Has published work by Siobhan Fallon, Jacob M. Appel, and JoeAnn Hart.

MAGAZINE'S NEEDS Submit original typed mss, no photocopies. Pays 2 contributor's copies "plus cash when budget allows."

TIPS "Pay attention to sentence-level writing—verbs, metaphors, concrete images. Don't forget, though, that plot and character keep us reading. We're looking for stuff that breaks the MFA story style. Be real. Know rhythm. Concentrate on strong images."

◐ THE ROCKFORD REVIEW

The Rockford Writers Guild, P.O. Box 858, Rockford IL 61105. **E-mail:** editors@rockfordwritersguild.com. **Website:** www.rockfordwritersguild.com. **Contact:** Connie Kluntz. "Published twice/year. Members only edition in summer-fall and winter-spring edition which is open to all writers. Open season to submit for the winter-spring edition of the Rock Review is August. If pubished in the winter-spring edition of the Rockford Review, payment is one copy of magazine and $5 per published piece. Credit line given. Check website for frequent updates. We are also on Facebook under Rockford Writers' Guild." Buys first North American serial rights. Pays on publication. Sample copy available for $12. Guidelines available on website.

◑ Poetry 50 lines or less, prose 1,300 words or less.

MAGAZINE'S NEEDS Wants eclectic poetry. Length: up to 50 lines. If published in the winter-spring edition of the *Rockford Review*, payment is one copy of magazine and $5 per published piece. Pays on publication.

TIPS "We're wide open to new and established writers alike—particularly short satire."

ROCKY MOUNTAIN RIDER MAGAZINE

P.O. Box 995, Hamilton MT 59840. (406)363-4085. **E-mail:** info@rockymountainrider.com. **Website:** www. rockymountainrider.com. **Contact:** Natalie Riehl, publisher. Buys first serial rights, one-time rights, as well as some reprint rights, if material has not been published in a competing publication in Montana, Idaho, Wyoming, Washington, Oregon, Colorado, or Utah. Pays on publication. Publishes ms an average of 6 months after acceptance. Responds in 2 months to queries. Responds in 3 months to mss. Sample copy for $3. Guidelines on website.

◑ *Rocky Mountain Rider Magazine* is 68+ pages, magazine-sized, Web offset-printed on SuperCal, stapled. Publishes 0-2 poems/issue; distributed free through 500+ locations in 11 states.

MAGAZINE'S NEEDS Wants "cowboy poetry; western or horse-themed poetry." Submit 1-10 poems at a time. Considers previously published poems and simultaneous submissions. No e-mail submissions; postal submissions only. Cover letter is preferred. Include SASE. Seldom comments on rejected poems. Occasionally publishes theme issues. Reviews books of poetry. Send materials for review consideration. Include SASE for returns. Pays $10/poem.

TIPS "We aren't looking for 'how-to' or training articles, and are not currently looking at any fiction. Our geographical regions of interest is the U.S. West, especially the Rocky Mountain states."

◐◑◉ ROOM

P.O. Box 46160, Station D, Vancouver BC V6J 5G5, Canada. **E-mail:** contactus@roommagazine.com. **Website:** www.roommagazine.com. "*Room* is Canada's oldest literary journal by, for, and about women. Published quarterly by a group of volunteers based in Vancouver, *Room* showcases fiction, poetry, reviews, art work, interviews and profiles about the female experience. Many of our contributors are at the beginning of their writing careers, looking for an opportunity to get published for the first time. Some later go on to great acclaim. *Room* is a space where women can speak, connect, and showcase their creativity. Each quarter we publish original, thought-provoking works that reflect women's strength, sensuality, vulnerability, and wit." *Room* is digest-sized; illustrations, photos. Press run is 1,000 (420 subscribers, 50-100 libraries, 350 shelf sales). Subscription: $22 ($32 US or foreign). Sample: $8 plus IRCs. Estab. 1975. Buys first rights. Pays on publication. Responds in 6 months. Sample copy for $13 or online at website.

MAGAZINE'S NEEDS *Room* uses "poetry by and about women, written from a feminist perspective. Nothing simplistic, clichéd. We prefer to receive 5-6 poems at a time, so we can select a pair or group." Include bio note. The mss are circulated to a collective, which "takes time." Pays honorarium plus 2 copies.

ROSEBUD

N3310 Asje Rd., Cambridge WI 53523. (608)423-9780. **E-mail:** jrodclark@smallbytes.net. **Website:** www.rsbd.net. **Contact:** Roderick Clark, publisher/managing editor; John Lehman, founder/editor-at-large. *Rosebud*, published 3 times/year in April, August, and December, has presented "many of the most prominent voices in the nation and has been listed as among the very best markets for writers." *Rosebud* is "elegantly" printed with full-color cover. Press run is 10,000. Single copy: $7.95 U.S. Subscription: $20 for 3 issues, $35 for 6 issues. Responds in 3 months. Sample copy for $6.95.

MAGAZINE'S NEEDS Wants poetry that avoids "excessive or well-worn abstractions, not to mention clichés. Present a unique and convincing world (you can do this in a few words!) by means of fresh and exact imagery, and by interesting use of syntax. Explore the deep reaches of metaphor. But don't forget to be playful and have fun with words." E-mail up to 3 poetry submissions to poetry editor John Smelcer at: jesmelcer@aol.com.

CONTEST/AWARD OFFERINGS Sponsors The William Stafford Poetry Award and the X.J. Kennedy Award for Creative Nonfiction. Guidelines for both available on website.

TIPS "Each issue will have six or seven flexible departments (selected from a total of sixteen departments that will rotate). We are seeking stories; articles; profiles; and poems of: love, alienation, travel, humor, nostalgia and unexpected revelation. Something has to 'happen' in the pieces we choose, but what happens inside characters is much more interesting to us than plot manipulation. We like good storytelling, real emotion and authentic voice."

SACRED JOURNEY

Fellowship in Prayer, Inc., 291 Witherspoon St., Princeton NJ 08542. (609)924-6863. **Fax:** (609)924-6910. **E-mail:** submissions@sacredjourney.org; lbaumann@fellowshipinprayer.org. **Website:** www.fellowshipinprayer.org. *Sacred Journey: The Journal of Fellowship in Prayer* is a quarterly multi-faith journal published winter, spring, summer, and autumn. Retains one-time rights and then the copyright is returned to the author. "Submissions may be selected for publication or on our fellowship in prayer website under 'web exclusives.' Your agreement for publication grants Fellowship in Prayer non-exclusive publication rights including the right to use and edit the work for publication in the print or electronic version of the journal *Sacred Journal* display on the Web and to retain the work indefinitely in an online archive." Responds within 4 months of receipt. Submission is considered permission for publication. "We reserve the right to edit. We will make every effort to contact the author with content revisions. Please include or be prepared to provide a bio of 50-words or less and/or a headshot phot to accompany your work, should it be selected for the print journal." Editorial lead time 3 months. Free sample copy available online. Writer guidelines are available online or by request.

"We publish articles, poems, and photographs which convey a spiritual orientation to life, promote prayer, meditation, and service to others and present topics that will foster a deeper spirit of unity among humankind. The spiritual insights, practices, and beliefs of women and men from a broad spectrum of religious traditions are welcomed."

MAGAZINE'S NEEDS "No poetry highly specific to a certain faith tradition. Nothing laden with specific faith terminology, nor a lot of Bible quotes or other quotes." Limited to 35 lines (occasionally longer).

TIPS "We are always seeking original prayers to share the richness of the world's religious traditions."

SALT HILL JOURNAL

Creative Writing Program, Syracuse University, English Deptartment, 401 Hall of Languages, Syracuse University, Syracuse NY 13244. **E-mail:** salthilljournal@gmail.com. **Website:** www.salthilljournal.com. *"Salt Hill* is published semiannually through Syracuse University's Creative Writing MFA program, which is currently ranked fifth in the nation. We strive to publish a mix of the best contemporary and emerging talent in poetry, fiction, and nonfiction. Your work, if accepted, would appear in a long tradition of exceptional contributors, including Steve Almond, Mary Caponegro, Kim Chinquee, Edwidge Danticat, Denise Duhamel, Brian Evenson, B.H. Fairchild, Mary Gaitskill, Terrance Hayes, Bob Hicok, Laura Kasischke, Etgar Keret, Phil Lamarche, Dorianne Laux, Maurice Manning, Karyna McGlynn, Ander Monson, David Ohle, Lucia Perillo, Tomaž Šalamun, Zachary Schomburg, Christine Schutt, David Shields, Charles Simic, Patricia Smith, Dara Wier, and Raúl Zurita among many others." Guidelines available online.

◐ Only accepts submissions by online submission form.

◑ THE SAME

P.O. Box 494, Mount Union PA 17066. **E-mail:** editors@thesamepress.com. **Website:** www.thesamepress.com. **Contact:** Nancy Eldredge, managing editor. *The Same*, published biannually, prints nonfiction (essays, reviews, literary criticism), poetry, and short fiction. We want eclectic poetry (formal to free verse, "mainstream" to experimental, all subject matter.) *The Same* is 50-100 pages, desktop-published and perfect bound. Single copy: $6; subscription: $12 for 2 issues, $20 for 4 issues. Publishes ms 11 months after acceptance. Responds within 2 months.

MAGAZINE'S NEEDS Submit 1-7 poems at a time. Lines/poem: 120 maximum. No previously published poems or simultaneous submissions without query. Prefers e-mail submissions (pasted into body of message). Cover letter is optional. Include SASE if you want a snail mail response. If you don't want your manuscript returned, you may omit the SASE if we can respond by e-mail. Please query before submitting fiction and nonfiction. Submissions are read year round.

ADDITIONAL INFORMATION Publishes 1-3 chapbooks/year. **Solicited mss only.** Chapbooks are 24-32 pages, desktop-published, saddle-stapled, with cardstock covers. Pays 25 author's copies (out of a press run of 100).

◯ SAMSARA: THE MAGAZINE OF SUFFERING

P.O. Box 467, Ashburn VA 20147. **E-mail:** rdfsamsara@gmail.com. **Website:** www.samsaramagazine.net. **Contact:** R. David Fulcher, editor. *Samsara, The Magazine of Suffering*, published biannually, prints poetry and fiction dealing with suffering and healing. Acquires first rights. Publishes ms 3 months after acceptance. Responds in 2 months. Sample copy for $5.50. Guidelines for SASE or on website.

◐ *Samsara* is 80 pages, magazine-sized, desktop-published, with color cardstock cover. Receives about 200 poems/year, accepts about 15%. Press run is 300 (200 subscribers). Single copy: $5.50; subscription: $10. Make checks payable to R. David Fulcher.

MAGAZINE'S NEEDS "Both metered verse and free verse poetry are welcome if dealing with the theme of suffering/healing." Has published poetry by Michael

Foster, Nicole Provencher, and Jeff Parsley. Submit up to 5 poems at a time. Lines/poem: 3 minimum, 100 maximum. Considers simultaneous submissions "if noted as such"; no previously published poems. Cover letter is preferred. Accepts e-mail submissions. Pays 1 contributor's copy.

● SANDY RIVER REVIEW

University of Maine at Farmington, 238 Main St., Farmington ME 04938. **E-mail:** srreview@gmail.com. **Website:** studentorgs.umf.maine.edu/~srreview. **Contact:** Kelsey Moore, editor. "*The Sandy River Review* seeks prose, poetry and art submissions twice a year for our Spring and Fall issues. Prose submissions may be either fiction or creative nonfiction and should be 15 pages or fewer in length; 12-point, Times Roman font; and double-spaced. Most of our art is published in b&w, and must be submitted as 300 dpi quaity, CMYK color mode, and saved as a .TIF file. We publish a wide variety of work from students as well as professional, established writers. Your submission should be polished and imaginative with strongly drawn characters and an interesting, original narrative. The review is the face of the University of Maine at Farmington's venerable BFA Creative Writing program, and we strive for the highest quality prose and poetry standard." Rights for the work return to the writer once published. Pays on publication. Publishes ms 2 months after acceptance. Guidelines available by e-mail request.

TIPS "We recommend that you take time with your piece. As with all submissions to a literary journal, submissions should be fully-completed, polished final drafts that require minimal to no revision once accepted. Double-check your prose pieces for basic grammatical errors before submitting."

◯ SANSKRIT LITERARY ARTS MAGAZINE

UNC Charlotte, 9201 University City Blvd., Student Union Room 045, Charlotte NC 28223. (704)687-7141. **E-mail:** sanskrit@uncc.edu. **Website:** http://sanskrit.uncc.edu; www.facebook.com/SanskritLitArtMagazine. **Contact:** Editor. "*Sanskrit* is UNC Charlotte's nationally recognized, award-winning literary-arts magazine. It is published once a year in April. *Sanskrit* is a collection of poems, short stories, and art from people all around the world, including students. All of the work goes through a selection process that includes our staff and university professors. Finally, each year, the magazine has a theme. This theme is completely independent from the work and is chosen by the editor as a design element to unify the magazine. The theme is kept secret until the return of the magazine in April when we have our annual gallery showing and poetry reading." Responds to mss and poems by February. Never comments on rejected mss. Guidelines available for SASE or by e-mail.

MAGAZINE'S NEEDS Submit up to 15 poems at a time. Considers simultaneous submissions. Accepts e-mail submissions. Cover letter is required. "Include 30- to 70-word third-person bio. Please do not list previous publications as a bio." Accepts submissions until the first Friday in November (deadline). Pays 1 contributor's copy.

SANTA CLARA REVIEW

Santa Clara Review, Santa Clara University, P.O. Box 3212, 500 El Camino Real, Santa Clara CA 95053-3212. (408)554-4484. **Fax:** (408)554-4454. **E-mail:** info@santaclarareview.com. **Website:** www.santaclarareview.com. "SCR is one of the oldest literary publications in the West. Entirely student-run by undergraduates at Santa Clara University the magazine draws upon submissions from SCU affiliates as well as contributors from around the globe. The magazine is published in February and May each year. In addition to publishing the magazine, the Review staff organizes a writing practicum, open mic nights, retreats for writers and artists, and hosts guest readers. Our printed magazine is also available to view free online. For contacts, queries, and general info, visit www.santaclarareview.com. SCR accepts submissions year round. Publishes ms approximately an average of 2 months after acceptance.

MAGAZINE'S NEEDS Length: Do not exceed 10 pages in length.

TIPS "Visual Art: Submit 2 works and provide us with a link to your online portfolio. Graphic Novels: 20 page max. Excerpts from larger works accepted. PDF format. Book or Album Reviews: 500-1,500 words."

◑ THE SARANAC REVIEW

CVH, Department of English, SUNY Plattsburgh, 101 Broad St., Plattsburgh NY 12901. (518)564-2414. **Fax:** (518)564-2140. **E-mail:** saranacreview@plattsburgh.edu. **Website:** http://research.plattsburgh.edu/saranacreview. **Contact:** J.L. Torres, editor. "*The Saranac Review* is committed to dissolving boundaries of all kinds, seeking to publish a diverse array of emerging and established writers from Canada and the U.S.

The Saranac Review aims to be a textual clearing in which a space is opened for cross-pollination between American and Canadian writers. In this way the magazine reflects the expansive bright spirit of the etymology of its name, Saranac, meaning 'cluster of stars.'" Published annually. *The Saranac Review* is magazine-sized, with color photo or painting on cover, includes ads. Press run is 1,000. Make checks payable to Subscriptions/*The Saranac Review*. Purchases first North American serial rights. Pays on publication. Publishes ms 8 months after acceptance. Responds in 4 months to mss. Sample copy for $6. Guidelines by e-mail or online at website.

MAGAZINE'S NEEDS *The Saranac Review*, published annually in the fall, wants poetry from both U.S. and Canadian writers. Does not want "amateurish or "greeting card" poetry." Has published poetry by Donald Revell, Ricardo Pau-Llosa, Jim Daniels, Rustin Larson, Rane Arroyo, Ross Leckie, Diane Swan, T. Alan Broughton, Brian Bartlett, Barry Dempster. Reads submissions September 1-February 15 (firm). Cover letter is appreciated. Include phone and e-mail contact information (if possible) in cover letter. Poems are circulated to an editorial board. No e-mail or disk submissions. Sometimes comments on rejected poems. Pays 2 contributor's copies.

TIPS "We publish serious, generous fiction."

◑ SCIENCE EDITOR

Council of Science Editors, 10200 W. 44th Ave., Suite 304, Wheat Ridge CO 80033. (720)881-6046. **Fax:** (303)422-8894. **E-mail:** pkbaskin@gmail.com. **Website:** www.councilscienceeditors.org. **Contact:** Patty Baskin, editor. *Science Editor*, published quarterly, is "a forum for the exchange of information and ideas among professionals concerned with publishing in the sciences." Wants "up to 90 typeset lines of poetry on the intersection of science (including but not limited to biomedicine) and communication. Geared toward adult scholars, writers, and editors in communication and the sciences." Acquires one-time rights, electronic rights. Publishes ms 3-6 months after acceptance. Responds in 3-6 weeks. Guidelines by e-mail.

◑ *Science Editor* is approximately 32 pages, magazine-sized, 4-color process, saddle-stitched, with an 80 pd Dull Cover; includes ads. "Journal is a membership benefit; dues are $164 per year; nonmember subscriptions: $55 US; $68

Int'l/year." Press run is 1,500. Single copy: $12 U.S.; $15 international. Make checks payable to Council of Science Editors (CSE). Has published poetry by Mary Knatterud, Judy Meiksin, David Goldblatt, Mary Donnelly, Nancy Overcott, Jyothirmai Gubili, Neil H. Segal, Michele Arduengo.

MAGAZINE'S NEEDS Submit up to 3 poems at a time, maximum 90 lines. Does not consider previously published poems or simultaneous submissions. Accepts e-mail submissions (pasted into the body of message), no fax or disk. "Submit both cover letter and poetry by e-mail only in the body of the same e-mail message, with no attachments." Sometimes comments on rejected poems. "*Science Editor* is posted online. Issues at least 1 year old are openly displayed accessible. Issues less than 1 year old can be accessed only by Council of Science Editors members." Rights revert to poet upon publication. Pays 3 contributor's copies.

○⑤ SCIFAIKUEST

P.O. Box 782, Cedar Rapids IA 52406. **E-mail:** gatrix65@yahoo.com. **Website:** www.samsdotpublishing.com. **Contact:** Tyree Campbell, managing editor; Teri Santitoro, editor. *Scifaikuest*, published quarterly both online and in print, features "science fiction/fantasy/horror minimalist poetry, especially scifaiku, and related forms. We also publish articles about various poetic forms and reviews of poetry collections. The online and print versions of *Scifaikuest* are different." Wants "artwork, scifaiku and speculative minimalist forms such as tanka, haibun, ghazals, senryu. No 'traditional' poetry." Has published poetry by Tom Brinck, Oino Sakai, Deborah P. Kolodji, Aurelio Rico Lopez III, Joanne Morcom, and John Dunphy. *Scifaikuest* (print edition) is 32 pages, digest-sized, offset-printed, perfect-bound, with color cardstock cover, includes ads. Receives about 500 poems/year, accepts about 160 (32%). Press run is 100/issue; 5 distributed free to reviewers. Single copy: $7; subscription: $20/year, $37 for 2 years. Make checks payable to Tyree Campbell/Sam's Dot Publishing. Member: The Speculative Literature Foundation. *Scifaikuest* was voted #1 poetry magazine in the 2004 Preditors & Editors poll.

MAGAZINE'S NEEDS Submit 5 poems at a time. Lines/poem: varies, depending on poem type. No previously published poems or simultaneous submissions. Accepts e-mail submissions (pasted into body of message). No disk submissions; artwork as e-mail attachment or inserted body of e-mail. "Submission should include snail mail address and a short (1-2 lines) bio." Reads submissions year round. Submit seasonal poems 6 months in advance. Time between acceptance and publication is 1-2 months. "Editor Teri Santitoro makes all decisions regarding acceptances." Often comments on rejected poems. Guidelines available on website. Responds in 6-8 weeks. Pays $1/poem, $4/review or article, and 1 contributor's copy. Acquires first North American serial rights.

⑨⓿ SEAM

P.O. Box 1051, Sawston, Cambridge CB22 3WT, United Kingdom. **E-mail:** seam.magazine@googlemail.com. **Website:** www.seampoetry.co.uk. **Contact:** Anne Berkeley, editor. *Seam*, published twice/year in spring and autumn, is "international in outlook and open to experimental work and authorized translations." *Seam* is 72 pages, A5, perfect-bound, with b&w cover. Receives about 2,000 poems/year, accepts about 5%. Press run is 300. Subscription: £8/year (£12 or $18 overseas). Sample: £4.50 (£5.50 or $9 overseas). Payments accepted through PayPal.

MAGAZINE'S NEEDS Submit up to 6 poems at a time. Send cover letter with e-mail address, a brief bio, a SASE or include IRCs. "We will not consider any submissions via e-mail." Wants "good contemporary poetry and "high-quality poems that engage the reader." Has published poetry by Mike Barlow, Jane Holland, Sheenagh Pugh, Julian Stannard, George Szirtes, and Tamar Yoseloff. Pays 1 contributor's copy.

THE SEATTLE REVIEW

Box 354330, University of Washington, Seattle WA 98195. (206)543-2302. **E-mail:** seaview@uw.edu. **Website:** www.seattlereview.org. **Contact:** Andrew Feld, editor-in-chief. Includes general fiction, poetry, craft essays on writing, and one interview per issue with a Northwest writer. *The Seattle Review* is 6×9; 150 pages; illustrations; photos. Semiannual. Estab. 1978. Circ. 1,000. Receives 200 unsolicited mss/month. Accepts 2-4 mss/issue; 4-8 mss/year. Publishes ms 1-2½ years after acceptance. Subscriptions: $20/three issues, $32/five issues. Back issue: $4. Buys first North American serial rights. Pays on publication. Responds in 8 months to mss. Sample copy for $6. Guidelines available online.

○   *The Seattle Review* will publish, and will only publish, long poems and novellas.

MAGAZINE'S NEEDS "We are looking for exceptional, risk-taking, intellectual and imaginative poems between ten and thirty pages in length." *The Seattle Review* will publish, and will only publish, long poems and novellas. The long poem can be: a single long poem in its entirety, a self-contained excerpt from a book-length poem, a unified sequence or series of poems. "Poetry submissions of less than ten pages in length, and prose submissions of less than forty pages, will be returned unread." Pays 4 contributor's copies and a year subscription.

HOW TO CONTACT Submit 3-5 poems via mail between October 1 and May 31, or use submission manager on website year round. Include SASE in mail. Submissions must be typed on white paper. The author's name and address should appear in the upper right hand corner. No simultaneous submissions.

TIPS "Know what we publish: no genre fiction; look at our magazine and decide if your work might be appreciated. Beginners do well in our magazine if they send clean, well-written manuscripts. We've published a lot of 'first stories' from all over the country and take pleasure in discovery."

THE SECRET PLACE

American Baptist Home Mission Societies, ABC/USA, P.O. Box 851, Valley Forge PA 19482. (610)768-2434. **E-mail:** thesecretplace@abc-usa.org. Buys first rights. Pays on acceptance. Editorial lead time 1 year. For free sample and guidelines, send 6x9 SASE.

MAGAZINE'S NEEDS Length: 4-30 lines. Pays $20.

TIPS "Prefers submissions via e-mail."

◑ SEEMS

P.O. Box 359, Lakeland College, Sheboygan WI 53082-0359. (920)565-1276 or (920)565-3871. **E-mail:** elderk@lakeland.edu. **E-mail:** seems@lakeland.edu. **Website:** www.seems.lakeland.edu. Focus on work that integrates economy of language, "the musical phrase," forms of resemblance, and the sentient. Will consider unpublished poetry, fiction, and creative nonfiction. See the editor's website at www.karlelder.com. "Links to my work and an interview may provide insight for the potential contributor." Acquires first North American serial rights and permission to publish online. Returns rights upon publication. Responds in 4 months (slower in the summer).

MAGAZINE'S NEEDS Lines/poem: open. No simultaneous submissions. No fax or e-mail submissions. Cover letter is optional. Include biographical information, SASE. Reads submissions year round. There is a 1- to 2-year backlog. "People may call or fax with virtually any question, understanding that the editor may have no answer." Guidelines available on website. Pays 1 contributor's copy.

CONTEST/AWARD OFFERINGS Subsequent issues may include themes and will alternate with chapbooks from Word of Mouth Books (query for the no-fee, any-genre, chapbook contest: elderk@lakeland.edu). See the editor's website at www.karlelder.com.

SENECA REVIEW

Hobart and William Smith Colleges, Geneva NY 14456. (315)781-3392. **E-mail:** senecareview@hws.edu. **Website:** www.hws.edu/academics/senecareview/index.aspx. "The editors have special interest in translations of contemporary poetry from around the world. Publisher of numerous laureates and award-winning poets, we also publish emerging writers and are always open to new, innovative work. Poems from *SR* are regularly honored by inclusion in *The Best American Poetry* and *Pushcart Prize* anthologies. Distributed internationally." Accepts queries by mail or online at http://senecareview.submishmash.com/submit. Responds in 3 months to mss. Guidelines available online. E-mail questions to senecareview@hws.edu.

TIPS "One submission per reading period. Mss received May 1-September 1 are returned."

THE SEWANEE REVIEW

University of the South, 735 University Ave., Sewanee TN 37383-1000. (931)598-1000. **Website:** www.sewanee.edu/sewanee_review. The *Sewanee Review* is America's oldest continuously published literary quarterly. Publishes "original fiction, poetry, essays on literary and related subjects, and book reviews for well-educated readers who appreciate good American and English literature." Only erudite work representing depth of knowledge and skill of expression is published. Buys first North American serial rights, buys second serial (reprint) rights. Pays on publication. Responds in 6-8 weeks to mss. Sample copy for $8.50 ($9.50 outside US). Guidelines available online. ◑ Does not read mss June 1-August 31.

MAGAZINE'S NEEDS Submit up to 6 poems at a time. "Please keep in mind that for each poem published in *The Sewanee Review*, approximately 250 poems are considered." Length: 40 lines maximum/poem. Pays $2.50/line, plus 2 contributor's copies (and reduced price for additional copies).

SHEARSMAN

Shearsman Books Ltd, Shearsman, 58 Velwell Rd., Exeter England EX4 4LD, U.K. **E-mail:** editor@shearsman.com. **Website:** www.shearsman.com/pages/magazine/home.html. "We are inclined toward the more exploratory end of the current spectrum. Notwithstanding this, however, quality work of a more conservative kind will always be considered seriously, provided that the work is well written. I always look for some rigour in the work, though I will be more forgiving of failure in this regard if the writer is trying to push out the boundaries." Guidelines available online.

MAGAZINE'S NEEDS No sloppy writing of any kind.

TIPS "We no longer read through the year. Our reading window for magazines is March 1-March 31 for the October issue, and September 1- September 30 for the April issue. Books may be submitted anytime. See guidelines online. Avoid sending attachments with your e-mails unless they are in PDF format. Include SASE; no IRCs."

◑ SHEMOM

2486 Montgomery Ave., Cardiff CA 92007. **E-mail:** pdfrench@cox.net. **Contact:** Peggy French, editor. *Shemom*, published 3 times/year, is a zine that "showcases writers of all ages reflecting on life's varied experiences. We often feature haiku." Includes poetry, haiku, and essays. Open to any style, but prefers free verse. "We like to hear from anyone who has a story to tell and will read anything you care to send our way." Acquires one-time rights. Publishes ms 3 months after acceptance. Responds in 1 month. Guidelines for SASE.

◑ *Shemom* is 20-30 pages. Receives about 200 poems/year, accepts 50%. Press run is 60 (30 subscribers). Single copy: $4; subscription: $12/3 issues. Make checks payable to Peggy French.

MAGAZINE'S NEEDS Submit 3-10 poems at a time. Considers previously published poems and simultaneous submissions. Accepts e-mail submissions (as attachment or pasted into body of message). "Prefer e-mail submission, but not required; if material is to be returned, please include a SASE." Pays 1 contributor's copy.

SHENANDOAH

Washington and Lee University, 17 Courthouse Square, Lexington VA 24450. (540)458-8908. **Fax:** (540)458-8461. **E-mail:** shenandoah@wlu.edu. **Website:** http://shenandoahliterary.org. **Contact:** R.T. Smith, editor. "For over half a century, *Shenandoah* has been publishing splendid poems, stories, essays, and reviews which display passionate understanding, formal accomplishment and serious mischief." Buys first North American serial rights, buys one-time rights. Pays on publication. Publishes ms an average of 10 months after acceptance. Responds in 3 months to mss. Sample copy for $12. Guidelines available online.

◑ Reads submissions September 1-May 15 only. Sponsors the annual James Boatwright III Prize for Poetry, a $1,000 prize awarded to the author of the best poem published in *Shenandoah* during a volume year.

MAGAZINE'S NEEDS Considers simultaneous submissions "only if we are immediately informed of acceptance elsewhere." No e-mail submissions. All submissions should be typed on 1 side of the paper only, with name and address clearly written on the upper right corner of the ms. Staff reviews books of poetry in 7-10 pages, multibook format. Send materials for review consideration. (Most reviews are solicited.) "No inspirational, confessional poetry." Pays $2.50/line, 1-year subscription, and 1 contributor's copy.

◑ SHIP OF FOOLS

Ship of Fools Press, University of Rio Grande, Box 1028, Rio Grande OH 45674. (740)992-3333. **Website:** http://meadhall.homestead.com/Ship.html. **Contact:** Jack Hart, editor. *Ship of Fools*, published "more or less quarterly," seeks "coherent, well-written, traditional or modern, myth, archetype, love—most types." Responds in 1 month to ms. "If longer than 6 weeks, write and ask why." Often comments on rejected poems. Sample copy: $3. Guidelines available for SASE.

◑ Has published poetry by Rhina Espaillat and Gale White. *Ship of Fools* is digest-sized, saddle-stapled, includes cover art and graphics. Press run is 237. Subscription: $10 for 4 issues.

MAGAZINE'S NEEDS No previously published poems or simultaneous submissions. Cover letter is preferred. Reviews books of poetry. Ship of Fools Press has "no plans to publish chapbooks in the next year due to time constraints." Does not want "concrete, incoherent, or greeting card poetry." Considers poetry by children and teens. Pays 1-2 contributor's copies.

SIERRA NEVADA REVIEW

999 Tahoe Blvd., Incline Village NV 89451. **E-mail:** sncreview@sierranevada.edu. **Website:** www.sierranevada.edu/800. *Sierra Nevada Review*, published annually in May, features poetry and short fiction by new writers. Wants "image-oriented poems with a distinct, genuine voice. Although we don't tend to publish 'light verse,' we do appreciate, and often publish, poems that make us laugh. No limit on length, style, etc." Does not want "sentimental, clichéd, or obscure poetry." Responds in 3 months. Guidelines available on website.

MAGAZINE'S NEEDS Submit up to 5 poems at a time. Considers simultaneous submissions; no previously published poems. Accepts e-mail submissions (pasted into body of message, no attachments). Reads submissions September 1-March 1 only. Sometimes comments on rejected poems. Pays 2 contributor's copies.

SKIDROW PENTHOUSE

68 E. Third St., Apt. 16, New York NY 10003. **E-mail:** info@skidrowpenthouse.com. **Website:** http://skidrowpenthouse.com. **Contact:** Rob Cook, editor. *Skidrow Penthouse* aims to "give emerging and idiosyncratic writers a new forum in which to publish their work. We are looking for deeply felt authentic voices, whether surreal, confessional, New York School, formal, or free verse. Work should be well crafted: attention to line-break and diction." Wants "poets who sound like themselves, not workshop professionals." Does not want "gutless posturing, technical precision with no subject matter, explicit sex and violence without craft, or abstract intellectualizing. We are not impressed by previous awards and publications."

MAGAZINE'S NEEDS Submit 3-5 poems at a time. Considers previously published poems and simultaneous submissions. "Include a legal-sized SASE; name and address on every page of your submission. No handwritten submissions will be considered." Time between acceptance and publication is one year. Seldom comments on rejected poems. Responds in 2 months. Pays one contributor's copy. Acquires one-time rights. Reviews books and chapbooks of poetry and other magazines in 1,500 words, single-book format. Send materials for review consideration." We're trying to showcase a poet in each issue by publishing up to 60-page collections within the magazine." Send query with SASE.

TIPS "We get way too many anecdotal fragments posing as poetry; too much of what we receive feels like this morning's inspiration mailed this afternoon. The majority of those who submit do not seem to have put in the sweat a good poem demands. Also, the ratio of submissions to sample copy purchases is 50:1. Just because our name is *Skidrow Penthouse* does not mean we are a repository for genre work or 'eat, shit, shower, and shave' poetry."

SKIPPING STONES: A MULTICULTURAL LITERARY MAGAZINE

P.O. Box 3939, Eugene OR 97403-0939. (541)342-4956. **E-mail:** editor@skippingstones.org. **Website:** www.skippingstones.org. **Contact:** Arun Toké, editor. "*Skipping Stones* is an award-winning multicultural, nonprofit magazine designed to promote cooperation, creativity and celebration of cultural and ecological richness. We encourage submissions by children of color, minorities and under-represented populations. We want material meant for children and young adults/teenagers with multicultural or ecological awareness themes. Think, live and write as if you were a child, tween or teen. We want material that gives insight to cultural celebrations, lifestyle, customs and traditions, glimpse of daily life in other countries and cultures. Photos, songs, artwork are most welcome if they illustrate/highlight the points. Translations are invited if your submission is in a language other than English." Themes may include cultural celebrations, living abroad, challenging, hospitality customs of various cultures, cross-cultural understanding, African, Asian and Latin American cultures, humor, international understanding, turning points and magical moments in life, caring for the earth, spirituality, and multicutural awareness. *Skipping Stones* is magazine-sized, saddle-stapled, printed on recycled paper. Published bimonthly during the school year (5 issues). Buys first North American serial rights, non-exclusive reprint, and electronic rights. Publishes ms an average of 4-8 months after acceptance. Responds only if interested. Send non-returnable samples. Editorial lead time 3-4 months. Sample: $7. Subscription: $25. Guidelines available online or for SASE.

MAGAZINE'S NEEDS Submit up to 5 poems at a time. Considers simultaneous submissions; no previously published poems. Accepts e-mail submissions. Cover letter is preferred. "Include your cultural background, experiences, and the inspiration behind your creation." Time between acceptance and publication is 6-9 months. "A piece is chosen for publication when most of the editorial staff feel good about it." Seldom comments on rejected poems. Publishes multi-theme issues. Responds in up to 4 months. Length: 30 lines maximum. Pays 2 contributor's copies, offers 40% discount for more copies and subscription, if desired. **CONTEST/AWARD OFFERINGS** Sponsors annual youth honor awards for 7- to 17-year-olds. Theme is "multicultural, social, international, and nature awareness." Guidelines available for SASE or on website. Entry fee: $3 (entitles entrant to a free issue featuring the 10 winners). Deadline: June 25.

TIPS "Be original and innovative. Use multicultural, nature, or cross-cultural themes. Multilingual submissions are welcome."

◑ SLANT: A JOURNAL OF POETRY

University of Central Arkansas, P.O. Box 5063, 201 Donaghey Ave., Conway AR 72035. (501)450-5107. **Website:** http://uca.edu/english/slant-a-journal-of-poetry. **Contact:** James Fowler, editor. *Slant: A Journal of Poetry*, published annually in May, aims "to publish a journal of fine poetry from all regions of the United States and beyond." Wants "traditional and 'modern' poetry, even experimental; moderate length, any subject on approval of Board of Readers." Doesn't want "haiku, translations." Has published poetry by Richard Broderick, Linda Casebeer, Marc Jampole, Sandra Kohler, Charles Harper Webb, and Ellen Roberts Young. *Slant* is 120 pages, professionally printed on quality stock, flat-spined, with matte card cover. Receives about 1,000 poems/year, accepts 70-75. Press run is 175 (70-100 subscribers). Sample: $10.

MAGAZINE'S NEEDS Submit up to 5 poems at a time. Lines/poem: poems should be of moderate length. No previously published poems or simultaneous submissions. Submissions should be typed; include SASE. "Put name, address (including e-mail if available), and phone number at the top of each page." Accepts submissions September 1-November 15. Comments on rejected poems "on occasion." Guidelines available in magazine, for SASE, or on website. Responds in 3-4 months from November 15 deadline. Pays 1 contributor's copy. Poet retains rights.

◒ SLATE & STYLE

2861 S. 93 Plaza APT 8, Omaha NE 68124. (402)350-1735. **E-mail:** bpollpeter@hotmail.com. **Website:** www.nfb-writers-division.net. **Contact:** Bridgit Pollpeter, editor; Robert Leslie Newman, president; Ross Pollpeter, layout and design editor. "*Slate & Style* is a quarterly publication of the Writers' division of the National Federation of the Blind (NFB Writers). It's dedicated to writing pursuits, including literary pieces along with resources and information about various writing styles. A majority of *Slate & Style*'s contributors are visually impaired, but we welcome submissions from any contributor, professional or amateur. We also accept submissions touching on any subject matter. *Slate & Style* accepts short fiction, short creative nonfiction, poetry, articles discussing and providing tips for various writing styles including literary, technical, editing, public relations and academic, literary criticism and resource information. Subject matter is not limited, though it will be up to the editor's discretion to publish." Responds in 6 weeks to submissions.

Accepts material from adults and children. Prefers e-mail submission; no hand-written or Braille submissions. Annual subscription is $15; single copy for $5. Members of the Writer's Division receive issues free of charge. An annual membership is $20. See website to pay via PayPal or e-mail newmanrl@cox.netf for other payment options.

MAGAZINE'S NEEDS Accepts submissions January 1-September 1 only. "Include a title page, along with your submission with your name, title of piece, and contact info (phone, e-mail, address. Please include a brief bio of 150 words or less. Do not send an entire history; just include key items you feel are important for readers to know. Send submissions as attachments to bpollpeter@hotmail.com. Do not paste entries into the body of the e-mail; entries simply pasted into an e-mail will not be considered. In the subject line of your e-mail, write: *Slate & Style* Submission, your name, title, and genre. Example: *Slate & Style, Bridgit Kuenning-Pollpeter, Giving Directions, poetry.* Use Microsoft Word or create an RTF document for all submissions. No other formats are accepted, and therefore will not be considered." Length: 36 lines maximum.

TIPS "Proofread and check your grammar and formatting before submitting. Submissions with too many errors will either be returned with corrections to be made if you wish to resubmit, or it will not be considered at all. *Slate & Style* will consider all submissions for publication. However, please be careful with graphic sexual and violent content, as well as language and anti-religious, anti-gender, anti-racial, and anti-homosexual orientation content. Characterization and plot often require this type of material, but it must serve a purpose. Gratuitous material with no purpose or meant only for derogatory reasons will not be considered; however, material will be published according to the discretion of the editor though. All submissions are considered for publication, but not all pieces will be published. We may keep submissions to be used for later publication. The editor may respond with comments and suggestions, giving contributors an opportunity to resubmit. Please be patient and wait the full 6 weeks before contacting us about a submission. Please direct questions and comments to Bridgit Kuenning-Pollpeter at bpollpeter@hotmail.com."

SLEEPINGFISH

Via Titta Scarpetta #28, RM Rome 00153, Italy. **E-mail:** white@sleepingfish.net. **Website:** www.sleepingfish.net. *SleepingFish*, published 1-2 times/year, is "a print or online magazine of innovative text and art." Wants "art, visual poetry, prose poems, experimental texts, graffiti, collage, multi-cultural, cross-genre work—anything that defies categorization." Does not want "conventional 'lined' or rhyming poetry (anything that looks like a 'poem'), conventional stories, genre fiction or poetry, political, religious, New Age, anything with an agenda." Acquires first rights. Returns all rights "as long as *SleepingFish* is acknowledged as first place of publication." Time between acceptance and publication is 2-6 weeks. Sometimes comments on rejected poems. Responds in 1-3 months to poems. Guidelines available on website.

Has published writings by Rick Moody, Diane Williams, Blake Butler, David Baptiste-Chirot, Miranda Mellis, Brian Evenson, Norman Lock, Peter Markus. *SleepingFish* print issues are 100-120 pages, magazine-sized, digitally printed, perfect-bound or with other binding, with 110 lb. cardstock cover in full color. Press run is 400 (10 libraries, 300 shelf sales, 100 online sales); 50 distributed free to contributors. Single copy: $15.

MAGAZINE'S NEEDS Submit 1-5 prose or visual poems at a time. Lines/poem: 1-3 pages (prose less than 1,000 words). Considers poetry by teens. Receives about 500 poems/year, accepts about 25 (5%). Considers simultaneous submissions; no previously published poems. Accepts e-mail submissions only (pasted into body of message or as small attachments (less than 2 MB) in DOC, RTF, JPG, GIF, or PDF format); no disk submissions. Cover letter is preferred. "Please send e-mail only. Reading period varies; see website for details." Sometimes publishes theme issues. "Poet should be familiar with *SleepingFish*. Online samples and work on site (www.sleepingfish.net) if you can't afford a copy." Sometimes sends prepublication galleys. Does not review books Pays 1 contributor's copy, with additional contributor copies available at half price. "Payment depends on funds."

SLIPSTREAM

Dept. W-1, Box 2071, Niagara Falls NY 14301. **E-mail:** editors@slipstream.org. **Website:** www.slipstream-press.org/index.html. **Contact:** Dan Sicoli, co-editor. "We prefer contemporary urban themes—writing from the grit that is not afraid to bark or bite. We shy away from pastoral, religious, and rhyming verse." Chapbook Contest prize is $1,000 plus 50 professionally printed copies of your chapbook. Guidelines available online.

Does not accept e-mail submissions.

MAGAZINE'S NEEDS No pastoral, religious, and rhyming verse.

SLOW TRAINS LITERARY JOURNAL

E-mail: editor@slowtrains.com. **Website:** www.slowtrains.com. **Contact:** Susannah Grace Indigo, editor. Requests one-time electronic rights with optional archiving. Responds in 2 months. Guidelines available on website.

MAGAZINE'S NEEDS "We also publish online poetry chapbooks — please query with samples of your poetry before submitting an entire chapbook. Please review our current issue before submitting." Submit via e-mail only. Length: no more than 200 lines.

TIPS "We are looking for fiction, essays, and poetry that reflect the spirit of adventure, the exploration of the soul, the energies of imagination, and the experience of Big Fun. Music, travel, sex, humor, love, loss, art, spirituality, childhood/coming of age, baseball, and dreams — these are a few of our favorite things — but most of all we want to read about the things you are passionate about."

SNOW MONKEY

E-mail: snowmonkey.editor@comcast.net. **Website:** www.ravennapress.com/snowmonkey/. Seeks writing "that's like footprints of the Langur monkeys left at 11,000 feet on Poon Hill, Nepal. Open to most themes." Responds in 2 months to mss.

MAGAZINE'S NEEDS Submit via e-mail. Does not pay.

TIPS "Send submissions as text-only in the body of your e-mail. Include your last name in the subject line. We do not currently use bios, but we love to read them."

⊙⊗ SNOWY EGRET

The Fair Press, P.O. Box 9265, Terre Haute IN 47808. **Website:** www.snowyegret.net. *Snowy Egret*, published in spring and autumn, specializes in work that is "nature-oriented: poetry that celebrates the abundance and beauty of nature or explores the interconnections between nature and the human psyche." Has published poetry by Conrad Hilberry, Lyn Lifshin, Gayle Eleanor, James Armstrong, and Patricia Hooper. *Snowy Egret* is 60 pages, magazine-sized, offset-printed, saddle-stapled. Receives about 500 poems/year, accepts about 30. Press run is 400. Sample: $8; subscription: $15/year, $25 for 2 years. Semiannual. Pays on publication. Submission guidelines online at website.

MAGAZINE'S NEEDS Guidelines available on website. Responds in 1 month. Always sends prepublication galleys. Pays $4/poem or $4/page plus 2 contributor's copies. Acquires first North American and one-time reprint rights.

TIPS Looks for "honest, freshly detailed pieces with plenty of description and/or dialogue which will allow the reader to identify with the characters and step into the setting; fiction in which nature affects character development and the outcome of the story."

⊙ SONG OF THE SAN JOAQUIN

P.O. Box 1161, Modesto CA 95353. **E-mail:** cleor36@yahoo.com. **Website:** www.ChaparralPoets.org/SSJ.html. **Contact:** Cleo Griffith, editor. *Song of the San Joaquin*, published quarterly, features "subjects about or pertinent to the San Joaquin Valley of Central California. This is defined geographically as the region from Fresno to Stockton, and from the foothills on the west to those on the east." Wants all forms and styles of poetry. "Keep subject in mind." Does not want "pornographic, demeaning, vague, or trite approaches." Considers poetry by children and teens. Acquires one-time rights.

Publishes ms 3-6 months after acceptance. Responds in up to 3 months.

MAGAZINE'S NEEDS This is a quarterly, please keep in mind the sesons of the year. Considers previously published poems. E-mail submissions are preferred; no disk submissions. Cover letter is preferred. "SASE required. All submissions must be typed on 1 side of the page only. Proofread submissions carefully. Name, address, phone number, and e-mail address should appear on all pages. Cover letter should include any awards, honors, and previous publications for each poem, and a biographical sketch of 75 words or less." Reads submissions "periodically throughout the year." Has published poetry by Robert Cooperman, Taylor Graham, Carol Louise Moon, Mimi Moriarty, Charles Rammelkamp. Open ("however, poems under 40 lines have the best chance"). Pays 1 contributor's copy.

CONTEST/AWARD OFFERINGS Poets of the San Joaquin holds an annual local young poets' contest as well as regular poetry contests. Guidelines available for SASE or by e-mail.

⊙ SO TO SPEAK

George Mason University, 4400 University Dr., MSN 2C5, Fairfax VA 22030-4444. **E-mail:** sts@gmu.edu (inquiries only). **Website:** http://sotospeakjournal.org. **Contact:** Kate Partridge, editor-in-chief. *So to Speak*, published semiannually, prints "high-quality work relating to feminism, including poetry, fiction, nonfiction (including book reviews and interviews), photography, artwork, collaborations, lyrical essays, and other genre-questioning texts." Wants "work that addresses issues of significance to women's lives and movements for women's equality and are especially interested in pieces that explore issues of race, class, and sexuality in relation to gender." Acquires first North American serial rights. Publishes ms 6-8 months after acceptance. Responds in 6 months to mss. Sample copy: $7.

⊙ *So to Speak* is 100-128 pages, digest-sized, photo-offset-printed, perfect-bound, with glossy cover; includes ads. Press run is 1,000 (75 subscribers, 100 shelf sales); 500 distributed free to students/contributors. Subscription: $12.

MAGAZINE'S NEEDS Receives about 800 poems/year; accepts 10%. Accepts submissions only via submissions manager on website. Submit 3-5 poems at a time. Considers simultaneous submissions; no previously published poems. No e-mail or paper submissions. "Please submit poems as you wish to see them in print. Be sure to include a cover letter with full contact info, publication credits, and awards received." Reads submissions August 15-October 15 and December 31-March 15. Seldom comments on rejected poems. Responds in 3 months if submissions are received during reading period. Pays 2 contributor's copies. *So to Speak* holds an annual poetry contest that awards $500. Guidelines available for SASE, by e-mail, or on website **TIPS** "We do not read between March 15 and August 15. Every writer has something they do exceptionally well; do that and it will shine through in the work. We look for quality prose with a definite appeal to a feminist audience. We are trying to move away from strict genre lines. We want high quality fiction, nonfiction, poetry, art, innovative and risk-taking work."

⬤ SOUL FOUNTAIN

90-21 Springfield Blvd., Queens Village NY 11428. (718)479-2594. **Fax:** (718)479-2594. **E-mail:** davault@ aol.com. **Website:** www.TheVault.org. **Contact:** Tone Bellizzi, editor. *Soul Fountain*, published 3 times/year, is produced by The Vault, a not-for-profit arts project of the Hope for the Children Foundation, "committed to empowering young and emerging artists of all disciplines at all levels to develop and share their talents through performance, collaboration, and networking." Prints poetry, art, photography, short fiction, and essays. Open to all. "We publish quality submitted work, and specialize in emerging voices. We favor visionary, challenging, and consciousness-expanding material." Does not want "poems about pets, nature, romantic love, or the occult. Sex and violence themes not welcome." Welcomes poetry by teens. *Soul Fountain* is 28 pages, magazine-sized, offset-printed, saddle-stapled. Subscription: $24. Sample: $7. Make checks payable to Hope for the Children Foundation. Publishes ms 1 year after acceptance. Guidelines for SASE.

MAGAZINE'S NEEDS Submit 2-3 poems at a time. Length: 1 page maximum/poem. Considers previously published poems and simultaneous submissions. Accepts e-mail submissions (pasted into body of message). Poems should be camera-ready. "When e-mailing a submission, it is necessary to include your mailing address. Cover letter not needed. SASE with postal mail submissions is not necessary, but $2 in postage is appreciated." Pays 1 contributor's copy.

⬤ SOUTH CAROLINA REVIEW

(864)656-5399. **Fax:** (864)656-1345. **E-mail:** cwayne@ clemson.edu. **Website:** www.clemson.edu/cedp/cudp/ scr/scrintro.htm. **Contact:** Wayne Chapman, editor. Magazine: 6×9; 200 pages; 60 lb. cream white vellum paper; 65 lb. color cover stock. Semiannual. Estab. 1967. Circ. 500. Literary, mainstream, poetry, essays, reviews. Does not read mss June-August or December. Receives 50-60 unsolicited mss/month. Responds in 2 months.

MAGAZINE'S NEEDS Submit 3-10 poems at a time. No previously published poems or simultaneous submissions. Cover letter is preferred. "Editor prefers a chatty, personal cover letter plus a list of publishing credits. Manuscript format should be according to new MLA Stylesheet." Submissions should be sent "in an 8x10 manila envelope so poems aren't creased." Do not submit during June, July, August, or December. Occasionally publishes theme issues.

⬤ SOUTH DAKOTA REVIEW

University of South Dakota, 414 E. Clark St., Vermillion SD 57069. (605)677-5184. **E-mail:** sdreview@ usd.edu. **Website:** www.usd.edu/sdreview. **Contact:** Brian Bedard and Lee Ann Roripaugh, editors. *South Dakota Review*, published quarterly, prints "poetry, fiction, criticism, and scholarly and personal essays. When material warrants, emphasis is on the American West; writers from the West; Western places or subjects. There are frequent issues with no geographical emphasis; periodic special issues on one theme, one place, or one writer." Wants "originality, sophistication, significance, craft—i.e., professional work." Press run is 500-600 (450 subscribers, half libraries). Single copy: $10; subscription: $30/year, $45/2 years. Sample: $8. Acquires first, second serial (reprint) rights. Publishes ms 1-6 months after acceptance. Responds in 10-12 weeks.

◗ *Pushcart* and *Best American Essays* nominees.

MAGAZINE'S NEEDS Has published poetry by Allan Safarik, Joanna Gardner, Nathaniel Hansen, and Jeanine Stevens. Submit up to 5 poems at a time. Postal submission or online submission using submission manager found on website. Cover letter is required. Must include SASE. Reads submissions year round.

TIPS "We like very well written, thematically ambitious, character-centered short fiction. Contemporary western American setting appeals, but is not necessary. No formula stories, horror, science fiction, or adolescent 'I' narrators. SDR rejects manuscripts because of careless writing, often careless typing, stories too personal ('I' confessional), aimlessness, unclear or unresolved conflicts, or subject matter that the editor finds clichéd, sensationalized, pretentious, or trivial."

⬤ SOUTHERN CALIFORNIA REVIEW

3501 Trousdale Pkwy., Mark Taper Hall, THH 355J, University of Southern California, Los Angeles CA 90089. **E-mail:** scr@college.usc.edu. **Website:** http://dornsife.usc.edu/mpw/literary-journal. Responds in 3-6 months. Sample copy for $10. Guidelines online at website.

MAGAZINE'S NEEDS Submit up to 3 poems in any form at a time. Submit via postal mail or online submissions manager. Include cover letter. Pays in contributor's copies.

CONTEST/AWARD OFFERINGS The Ann Stanford Poetry Prize.

SOUTHERN HUMANITIES REVIEW

Auburn University, 9088 Haley Center, Auburn University AL 36849. (334)844-9088. **Fax:** (334)844-9027. **E-mail:** shrengl@auburn.edu. **E-mail:** shrsubmissions@auburn.edu. **Website:** www.cla.auburn.edu/shr. **Contact:** Karen Beckwith, managing editor. *Southern Humanities Review* publishes fiction, poetry, and critical essays on the arts, literature, philosophy, religion, and history for a well-read, scholarly audience. "We contract for all rights until publication. Then copyright reverts to author." Responds in 1-2 weeks to queries. Sample copy for $5 in U.S.; $7 everywhere else. Guidelines online.

MAGAZINE'S NEEDS Send 3-5 poems at a time. "We seldom print a poem longer than 2 pages."

CONTEST/AWARD OFFERINGS Sponsors the Theodore Christian Hoepfner Award, a $50 prize for the best poem published in a given volume of *Southern Humanities Review.*

TIPS "Send us the ms with SASE. If we like it, we'll take it or we'll recommend changes. If we don't like it, we'll send it back as promptly as possible. Read the journal. Send typewritten, clean copy, carefully proofread. We also award the annual Hoepfner Prize of $100 for the best published essay or short story of the year. Let someone whose opinion you respect read your story and give you an honest appraisal. Rewrite, if necessary, to get the most from your story."

◑ SOUTHERN POETRY REVIEW

Armstrong Atlantic State University, 11935 Abercorn St., Savannah GA 31419. (912)344-3196. **E-mail:** tony.morris@armstrong.edu; james.smith@armstrong.edu. **Website:** www.southernpoetryreview.org. **Contact:**

Tony Morris, managing editor; James Smith, co-editor; Robert Parham, co-editor. Member: CLMP. *Southern Poetry Review*, published twice a year, is one of the oldest poetry journals in America. Southern Poetry Review is 80-88 pages, digest-sized, perfect-bound, with 80 lb. matte cardstock cover with b&w photography, includes ads. Single copy: $7.00. Acquires one-time rights. Publishes ms 6 months after acceptance. Responds in 2 months. Guidelines available in magazine, for SASE, by e-mail, or on website.

◒   Work appearing in *Southern Poetry Review* received a 2005 Pushcart Prize and often has poems selected for VerseDaily.org.

MAGAZINE'S NEEDS Wants "poetry eclectically representative of the genre; no restrictions on form, style, or content." Has published poetry by Cathy Smith Bowers, Carl Dennis, Robert Morgan, Linda Pastan, Margaret Gibson, and R. T. Smith. Considers simultaneous submissions (with notification in cover letter); no previously published poems ("previously published" includes poems published or posted online). No e-mail or disk submissions. Cover letter is preferred. "Include SASE for reply; ms returned only if sufficient postage is included." Reads submissions year round. Poems are circulated to an editorial board ("multiple readers, lively discussion and decision-making"). Sometimes comments on rejected poems. Always sends pre-publication galleys. Does not want fiction, essays, or reviews. Pays 2 contributor's copies.

CONTEST/AWARD OFFERINGS Sponsors annual Guy Owen Contest. See website for guidelines.

THE SOUTHERN REVIEW

(225)578-5108. **Fax:** (225)578-5098. **E-mail:** southern-review@lsu.edu. **Website:** www.lsu.edu/tsr. **Contact:** Jeanne Leiby, Editor. Reading period: September1-June 1. All mss. submitted during summer months will be recycled. Buys first North American serial rights. Pays on publication. Publishes ms an average of 6 months after acceptance. Responds in 2 months. Sample copy for $8. Guidelines available online.

MAGAZINE'S NEEDS *The Southern Review*, published quarterly, "has been committed to finding the next new voices in literature. In our pages were published the early works of Eudora Welty, John Berryman, Delmore Schwartz, Peter Taylor, Randall Jarrell, Mary McCarthy, and Nelson Algren, to name only a few. More recently, we can claim Robert Pinsky, Michael S. Harper, and David Kirby as being among those whom we helped "discover." Has published poetry by Aimee Baker, Wendy Barker, David Bottoms, Nick Courtright, Robert Dana, Oliver de la Paz, Ed Falco, Piotr Florczyk, Rigoberto Gonzalez, Ava Leavell Haymon, and Philip Schultz. *The Southern Review* is 200 pages, digest-sized, flat-spined, with full color cover. Receives about 10,000 poetry submissions/year. Press run is 3,200 (2,100 subscribers, 70% libraries). Subscription: $40. Sample: $12. 1-4 pages Pays $30/page

HOW TO CONTACT Submit up to 1-5 pages of poetry at a time. No previously published poems. No fax or e-mail submissions. "We do not require a cover letter, but we prefer one giving information about the author and previous publications." Reads submissions September-May. Guidelines available for SASE or on website. Responds in 1-2 months. Pays $25/printed page plus 2 contributor's copies. Acquires first North American serial rights. Staff reviews books of poetry in 3,000 words, multi-book format. Send materials for review consideration.

TIPS "Careful attention to craftsmanship and technique combined with a developed sense of the creation of story will always make us pay attention."

🌀📀 SOUTH POETRY MAGAZINE

PO BOX 3744, Cookham Maidenhead SL6 9UY, England. **E-mail:** south@southpoetry.org. **Website:** www. southpoetry.org. *SOUTH Poetry Magazine*, published biannually in Spring and Autumn, is based in "the southern counties of England. Poets from or poems about the South region are particularly welcome, but poets from all over the world are encouraged to submit work on all subjects." Has published poetry by Ian Caws, Stella Davis, Lyn Moir, Elsa Corbluth, Paul Hyland, and Sean Street. *SOUTH* is 68 pages, digest-sized, litho-printed, saddle-stapled, with gloss-laminated duotone cover. Receives about 1,500 poems/year, accepts about 120. Press run is 350 (250 subscribers). Single copy: £5.80; subscription: £10/year, £18/2 years. Make cheques (in sterling) payable to *SOUTH Poetry Magazine*. Publishes ms 2 months after acceptance. Guidelines online.

MAGAZINE'S NEEDS Submit up to 3 poems at a time in duplicate. Print and use submission form on website. Selection does not begin prior to the deadline and may take up to eight weeks or more from that date."

TIPS "Buy the magazine and read it. That way you will see the sort of work we publish, and whether your work is likely to fit in. You'll also be contributing to its continued success."

● THE SOUTHEAST REVIEW

Florida State University, Tallahassee FL 32306-1036. **Website:** southeastreview.org. **Contact:** Katie Cortese, editor-in-chief. "The mission of *The Southeast Review* is to present emerging writers on the same stage as well-established ones. In each semi-annual issue, we publish literary fiction, creative nonfiction, poetry, interviews, book reviews and art. With nearly 60 members on our editorial staff who come from throughout the country and the world, we strive to publish work that is representative of our diverse interests and aesthetics, and we celebrate the eclectic mix this produces. We receive approximately 400 submissions per month and we accept less than 1-2% of them. We will comment briefly on rejected mss when time permits." Acquires first North America serial rights, which then revert to the author. Publishes ms 2-6 months after acceptance. Responds in 2-6 months.

○ Magazine: 6×9; 160 pages; 70 lb. paper; 10 pt. Krome Kote cover; photos. Publishes 4-6 new writers/year. Has published work by Elizabeth Hegwood, Anthony Varallo, B.J. Hollars, Tina Karelson, and John Dufresne.

MAGAZINE'S NEEDS Submit 3-5 poems at a time through online manager. "All submissions must be typed (poetry single-spaced) and properly formatted then uploaded to our online Submission Manager as a .doc or .rtf file only. Submission Manager restricts you from sending us your work more than twice per year. Please wait until you receive a reply regarding a submission before you upload the next." Does not accept e-mail, paper, or previously published submissions. Accepts submissions year-round, "though please be advised that the response time is slower during the summer months." Reviews books and chapbooks of poetry. "Book reviews may be submitted at any time through our online submission manager." Pays 2 contributor's copies.

CONTEST/AWARD OFFERINGS Sponsors an annual poetry contest. Winner receives $500 and publication; 9 finalists will also be published. **Entry fee:** $15 for 3 poems. **Deadline:** March. Guidelines available on website.

TIPS "*The Southeast Review* accepts regular submissions for publication consideration year-round exclusively through the online Submission Manager. Any breaks, hiatuses, or interruptions to the reading period will be announced online, and are more likely to occur during the summer months. *SER* does not, under any circumstances, accept work via e-mail. **Except during contest season, paper submissions sent through regular postal mail will not be read or returned**. Please note that, during contest season, entries to our World's Best Short Short Story, Poetry, and Creative Nonfiction competitions must still be sent through regular postal mail. Avoid trendy experimentation for its own sake (present-tense narration, observation that isn't also revelation). Fresh stories, moving, interesting characters and a sensitivity to language are still fiction mainstays. We also publish the winner and runners-up of the World's Best Short Story Contest, Poetry Contest, and Creative Nonfiction Contest."

SOUTHWESTERN AMERICAN LITERATURE

Center for the Study of the Southwest, Texas State University-San Marcos, Brazos Hall, 601 University Dr., San Marcos TX 78666. (512)245-2224. **Fax:** (512)245-7462. **E-mail:** delateja@txstate.edu; swpublications@txstate.edu. **Website:** www.txstate.edu/cssw/publications/sal.html. **Contact:** Jesús F. de la Teja, editor-in-chief. Responds in 2-4 months. "Please feel free to e-mail the editors (swpublications@txstate.edu) after 6 months to check on the status of your work." Sample copy for $11. Guidelines online.

MAGAZINE'S NEEDS "Generally speaking, we seek material covering the Greater Southwest or material written by southwestern writers." Length: no more than 100 lines. Pays 2 contributor's copies.

TIPS "We look for crisp language, an interesting approach to material; a regional approach is desired but not required. Read widely, write often, revise carefully. We are looking for stories that probe the relationship between the tradition of Southwestern American literature and the writer's own imagination in creative ways. We seek stories that move beyond stereotype and approach the larger defining elements and also ones that, as William Faulkner noted in his Nobel Prize acceptance speech, treat subjects central to good literature—the old verities of the human heart, such as honor and courage and pity and suffering, fear and humor, love and sorrow."

SOUTHWEST REVIEW

P.O. Box 750374, Dallas TX 75275-0374. (214)768-1037. **Fax:** (214)768-1408. **E-mail:** swr@smu.edu. **Web-site:** www.smu.edu/southwestreview. **Contact:** Willard Spiegelman, editor-in-chief. "The majority of our readers are well-read adults who wish to stay abreast of the latest and best in contemporary fiction, poetry, and essays in all but the most specialized disciplines." Quarterly. Acquires first North American serial rights. Sends galleys to author. Publishes ms 6-12 months after acceptance. Responds in 1-4 months to mss. Occasionally comments on rejected mss. Sample copy for $6. Guidelines available for SASE or online.

Magazine: 6×9; 150 pages. Receives 200 unsolicited mss/month. Has published work by Alice Hoffman, Sabina Murray, Alix Ohlin. Publishes fiction, literary essays, poetry.

MAGAZINE'S NEEDS Submissions accepted online for a $2 fee. No fee for submissions sent by mail. No simultaneous or previously published work accepted. Submit up to 6 poems at a time. Reading period: September 1-May 31. No arbitrary limits on length. Accepted pieces receive nominal payment upon publication and copies of the issue.

CONTEST/AWARD OFFERINGS The Elizabeth Matchett Stover Memorial Award presents $250 to the author of the best poem or groups of poems (chosen by editors) published in the preceding year. Also offers The Morton Marr Poetry Prize.

TIPS "Despite the title, we are not a regional magazine. Before you submit your work, it's a good idea to take a look at recent issues to familiarize yourself with the magazine. We strongly advise all writers to include a cover letter. Keep your cover letter professional and concise and don't include extraneous personal information, a story synopsis, or a resume. When authors ask what we look for in a strong story submission the answer is simple regardless of graduate degrees in creative writing, workshops, or whom you know. We look for good writing, period."

SOU'WESTER

Department of English, Box 1438, Southern Illinois University, Edwardsville IL 62026. **Website:** http://sou-wester.org. *Sou'wester* appears biannually in spring and fall. "We lean toward poetry with strong imagery, successful association of images, and skillful use of figurative language." Has published poetry by Robert Wrigley, Beckian Fritz Goldberg, Eric Pankey, Betsy Sholl, and Angie Estes. *Sou'wester* has 30-40 pages of poetry in each digest-sized, 100-page issue. *Sou'wester* is professionally printed, flat-spined, with textured matte card cover, press run is 300 for 500 subscribers of which 50 are libraries. Receives 3,000 poems (from 600 poets) each year, accepts 36-40, has a 6-month backlog. Subscription: $18/2 issues. Returns rights. Responds in 3 months. Sample: $8.

○ Uses online submission form.

MAGAZINE'S NEEDS Submit up to 5 poems via online journal manager. Accepts simultaneous submissions. No previously published poems. No e-mail submissions. Reads submissions from September 1 through May 1. Editor comments on rejected poems "usually, in the case of those that we almost accept." Pays 2 contributor's copies and a 1-year subscription.

THE SOW'S EAR POETRY REVIEW

217 Brookneill Dr., Winchester VA 22602. **E-mail:** sowsearpoetry@yahoo.com. **Website:** www.sows-ear.kitenet.net. **Contact:** Kristin Camitta Zimet. "*The Sow's Ear* prints fine poetry of all styles and lengths, complemented by b&w art. We also welcome reviews, interviews, and essays related to poetry. We are open to group submissions. Our 'Crossover' section features poetry married to any other art form, including prose, music, and visual media." Acquires first publication rights. Publishes ms an average of 1-6 months after acceptance. Responds in 2 weeks to queries. Responds in 3 months to mss. Editorial lead time 1-6 months. Sample copy for $8. Guidelines available for SASE, by e-mail, or on website.

MAGAZINE'S NEEDS Submit up to 5 poems at a time. Considers simultaneous submissions "if you tell us promptly when work is accepted elsewhere"; no previously published poems, although will consider poems from chapbooks if they were never published in a magazine. Previously published poems may be included in 'Crossover' if rights are cleared. No e-mail submissions, except for poets outside the US; postal submissions only. Include brief bio and SASE. Pays 2 contributor's copies. Inquire about reviews, interviews, and essays. Contest/Award offerings: *The Sow's Ear* Poetry Competition and *The Sow's Ear* Chapbook Contest. Open to any style or length. No limits on line length.

TIPS "We like work that is carefully crafted, keenly felt, and freshly perceived. We respond to poems with voice, a sense of place, delight in language, and a meaning that unfolds. We look for prose that opens new dimensions to appreciating poetry."

○⑤ SPACE AND TIME

458 Elizabeth Ave., Somerset NJ 08873. **E-mail:** ww.spaceandtimemagazine.com. **Website:** www.spaceandtimemagazine.com. **Contact:** Hildy Silverman, editor-in-chief. Magazine. 48 pages, matte paper, glossy cover. Contains illustrations. "We love stories that blend elements—horror and science fiction, fantasy with SF elements, etc. We challenge writers to try something new and send us their unclassifiable works—what other publications reject because the work doesn't fit in their 'pigeonholes.'" Acquires first North American serial rights and one-time rights. Pays on publication. Publishes ms 3-6 months after acceptance. Sample copy available for $6.50. Additional copies $5. Guidelines available only on website.

MAGAZINE'S NEEDS "Multiple submissions okay within reason (don't send an envelope stuffed with 10 poems). Submit embedded in an e-mail or as a Word doc or .rtf attacment." Pays $5 per poem.

○⑤ SPACEPORTS & SPIDERSILK

Sam's Dot Publishing, P.O. Box 782, Cedar Rapids IA 52406-0782. **Website:** www.samsdotpublishing.com. *Spaceports & Spidersilk*, published quarterly online, prints "fantasy, science fiction, sword and sorcery, alternate history, myths/folktales, spooky short stories, poems, illustrations, puzzles, nonfiction articles, and movie and book reviews, all for a reading audience of 9-18 years old." Wants "fantasy, science fiction, spooky horror, and speculative poetry" appropriate to age group. Does not want "horror with excessive blood and gore." Considers poetry by children and teens. Has published poetry by Bruce Boston, Karen A. Romanko, Guy Belleranti, Aurelio Rico Lopez III, and Kristine Ong Muslim. Receives about 180 poems/year, accepts about 30 (16%). Acquires first, exclusive worldwide electronic rights for 90 days. Publishes ms 1-3 months after acceptance. Responds in 4-6 weeks. Guidelines available online at website.

MAGAZINE'S NEEDS Submit up to 5 poems at a time. Lines/poem: 25 maximum. Considers previously published poems; no simultaneous submissions. Accepts e-mail submissions only (pasted into body of message). "Submission should include snail mail address and a short (1-2 lines) bio." Reads submissions year round. Often comments on rejected poems. Reviews books/chapbooks of poetry. Send materials for review consideration to Tyree Campbell. Pays $2/original poem, $1/reprint.

◐○ SPEEDPOETS ZINE

86 Hawkwood St., Brisbane QL 4122, Australia. (61)
(7)3420-6092. **E-mail:** speedpoets@yahoo.com.au.
Website: http://speedpoets.com. **Contact:** Graham
Nunn, editor. *SpeedPoets Zine*, published monthly,
showcases "the community of poets that perform at the
monthly SpeedPoets readings in Brisbane, as well as
showcasing poets from all around the world." Publishes ms 2 weeks after acceptance. Responds in 2 weeks.
Guidelines available by e-mail.

○ *SpeedPoets Zine* is 28 pages, digest-sized, photocopied, folded and stapled, with color cover.
Press run is 100. Single copy: $5 for overseas/in-
terstate contributors. Payable to Graham Nunn
via PayPal (in AUD only, or send well-concealed
cash). Has published poetry by Robert Smith,
Steve Kilbey, Brentley Frazer, Jayne Fenton Ke-
ane, and Marie Kazalia.

MAGAZINE'S NEEDS Submit 2 poems at a time.
Considers previously published poems. Accepts e-mail
submissions (pasted into body of message—no attachments); no disk submissions. Cover letter is preferred.
Reads submissions year round. Does not want long submissions. Lines/poem: 25 maximum.

○◉ SPIDER

Cricket Magazine Group, 70 E. Lake St., Suite 300, Chicago IL 60601. **Website:** www.cricketmag.com; www.
spidermagkids.com. **Contact:** Marianne Carus, editor-
in-chief; Suzanne Beck, managing art director. *SPIDER*,
published monthly, is a reading and activity magazine
for children ages 6-9. "It's specially written and edited
for children who have reached that amazing age when
they first get excited about reading on their own." *SPI-
DER* is 38 pages, 8x10, staple-bound. Receives more
than 1,200 submissions/month, accepts 25-30. Subscription: $35.97/year (12 issues). Sample: $5; sample
pages available on website.

MAGAZINE'S NEEDS Wants "serious and humorous poetry, nonsense rhymes." Submit no more than 5
poems at a time. Length: no more than 20 lines. Pays
up to $3/line.

◑ SPILLWAY

P.O. Box 7887, Huntington Beach CA 92615. (714)968-
0905. **E-mail:** mifanwy.kaiser@gmail.com; spillway2@
tebotbach.org. **Website:** http://tebotbach.org/spillway.
html. **Contact:** Mifanwy Kaiser, publisher; Susan Ter-
ris, editor. Published semi-annually in June and December, *Spillway* celebrates "writing's diversity and

power to affect our lives." Open to all voices, schools,
and tendencies. Acquires one-time rights. Responds
in up to 6 months.

○ *Spillway* is about 125 pages, digest-sized, attractively printed, perfect-bound, with 2-color
or 4-color card cover. Press run is 2,000. "We
recommend ordering a sample copy before you
submit, though acceptance does not depend
upon purchasing a sample copy." Single copy is
$13.50, includes shipping and handling; 1 year
subscription is $23, includes shipping and han-
dling; 2 year subscription is $40, includes ship-
ping and handling. To order, visit the website
and use PayPal, or make checks payable to Tebot
Bach with "Spillway" in the notation line.

MAGAZINE'S NEEDS Submit 3-5 poems at a time
(6 pages maximum total). No fiction. Theme for June
2013: "The Road Taken/Not Taken." Theme for December 2013: "The Long & Short of It." For more complete
information about upcoming themes and submission
periods, check our website. E-mail submissions only
to spillway2@tebotbach.org (MS Word attachment);
no disk or fax submissions. Cover letter is required. Include brief bio. Responds in up to 6 months. Pays 1 contributor's copy. Reviews books of poetry in 500-1,500
words. Accepts queries by e-mail. Send materials for
review consideration.

◑ SPINNING JENNY

c/o Black Dress Press, P.O. Box 1067, New York NY
10014. **E-mail:** editor@spinning-jenny.com. **Website:**
www.spinning-jenny.com. **Contact:** C.E. Harrison,
editor. *Spinning Jenny*, published once/year in the fall
(usually September), has published poetry by Abra-
ham Smith, Cynthia Cruz, Michael Morse, and Joyelle
McSweeney. Authors retain rights. Responds within 4
months. Single copy: $10; subscription: $20 for 2 issues.
Guidelines available on website.

○ *Spinning Jenny* is 96 pages, digest-sized, perfect-
bound, with heavy card cover. "We accept less
than 5% of unsolicited submissions." Press run
is 1,000.

MAGAZINE'S NEEDS "*Spinning Jenny* is an open forum for poetry. We are pleased to consider experimental writing and work by unpublished authors. However,
writers are strongly encouraged to review a recent issue
of the magazine before submitting their work." Submit
up to 6 poems using online submission form. Pays in
contributor's copies.

SPITBALL: THE LITERARY BASEBALL MAGAZINE

5560 Fox Rd., Cincinnati OH 45239. **Website:** www. spitballmag.com. **Contact:** Mike Shannon, editor-in-chief. *Spitball: The Literary Baseball Magazine*, published semiannually, is "a unique magazine devoted to poetry, fiction, and book reviews exclusively about baseball. Newcomers are very welcome, but remember that you have to know the subject; we do, and our readers do. Perhaps a good place to start for beginners is one's personal reactions to the game, a game, a player, etc., and take it from there." Writers submitting to *Spitball* for the first time must buy a sample copy (waived for subscribers). "This is a one-time-only fee, which we regret, but economic reality dictates that we insist those who wish to be published in *Spitball* help support it, at least at this minimum level." *Spitball* is 96 pages, digest-sized, computer-typeset, perfect-bound. Receives about 1,000 submissions/year, accepts about 40. Press run is 1,000. Subscription: $12. Sample: $6.

MAGAZINE'S NEEDS Submit a "batch" of poems at a time ("we prefer to use several of same poet in an issue rather than a single poem"). Lines/poem: open. No previously published poems or simultaneous submissions. Cover letter is required. Include brif bio and SASE. "Many times we are able to publish accepted work almost immediately." Pays 2 contributor's copies."All material published in *Spitball* will be automatically considered for inclusion in the next *Best of Spitball* anthology."1) Poems submitted to *Spitball* will be considered automatically for Poem of the Month, to appear on the website. 2) "We sponsor the Casey Award (for best baseball book of the year) and hold the Casey Awards Banquet in late February or early March. Any chapbook of baseball poetry should be sent to us for consideration for the 'Casey' plaque that we award to the winner each year."

TIPS "Take the subject seriously. We do. In other words, get a clue (if you don't already have one) about the subject and about the poetry that has already been done and published about baseball. Learn from it— think about what you can add to the canon that is original and fresh—and don't assume that just anybody with the feeblest of efforts can write a baseball poem worthy of publication. And most importantly, stick with it. Genius seldom happens on the first try."

SPLIZZ

4 St. Marys Rise, Burry Port, Carms SA16 0SH, Wales. **E-mail:** splizzmag@yahoo.co.uk. **Contact:** Amanda Morgan, editor. *Splizz*, published quarterly, features poetry, prose, reviews of contemporary music, and background to poets. Responds in 2 months. Sometimes sends prepublication galleys. Guidelines available in magazine, for SASE (or SAE and IRC), or by e-mail.

Wants "any kind of poetry. We have no restrictions regarding style, length, subjects." Does not want "anything racist or homophobic." Has published Colin Cross (UK), Anders Carson (Canada), Paul Truttman (US), Jan Hansen (Portugal), and Gregory Arena (Italy). *Splizz* is 60-64 pages, A5, saddle-stapled; includes ads. Receives about 200-300 poems/year; accepts about 90%. Press run is 150 (35 subscribers). Single copy: £2.20 (UK); subscription: £8.80 (UK). E-mail for current rates. Payments accepted in cash or PayPal to splizz@tiscali.co.uk. "No checks please."

MAGAZINE'S NEEDS Submit 5 poems at a time. No previously published poems or simultaneous submissions. Accepts e-mail submissions (as attachment). Cover letter is required. Include short bio. Typed submissions preferred. Name and address must be included on each page of submitted work. Include SAE with IRCs. Time between acceptance and publication is 4 months. Often comments on rejected poems. Charges criticism fee. "Just enclose SAE/IRC for response,and allow 1-2 months for delivery. For those sending IRCs, please ensure that they have been correctly stamped by your post office." Reviews books/chapbooks of poetry or other magazines in 50-300 words. Send materials for review consideration. E-mail for further enquiries.

SPOUT MAGAZINE

P.O. Box 581067, Minneapolis MN 55458. **E-mail:** editors@spoutpress.org. **Website:** www.spoutpress.org. **Contact:** Michelle Filkins. As the counterpart to Spout Press, Spout magazine features poetry, art, fiction, and thought pieces with diverse voices and styles. Publishes ms 2-3 months after acceptance. Responds in 4 months. Guidelines online at website.

MAGAZINE'S NEEDS Submit up to 5 poems at a time. Considers previously published poems and simultaneous submissions. Cover letter is preferred. "Poems are reviewed by 2 of 3 editors; those selected for final review are read again by all three."

ⓞ SPRING: THE JOURNAL OF THE E.E. CUMMINGS SOCIETY

129 Lake Huron Hall, Grand Valley State University, Allendale MI 49401. **E-mail:** websterm@gvsu.edu. **Website:** www.gvsu.edu/english/cummings/Index. html. **Contact:** Michael Webster, editor. *Spring: The Journal of the E.E. Cummings Society*, published annually (usually in the fall), is designed "to broaden the audience for E.E. Cummings, and to explore various facets of his life and art." **Contributors are required to subscribe.** Reads May-August. Responds in 6 months. Guidelines for SASE.

MAGAZINE'S NEEDS Wants poems in the spirit of Cummings, primarily poems of 1 page or less. Submit as e-mail attachment. Include cover letter. Does not want "amateurish" work.

ⓞ SRPR (SPOON RIVER POETRY REVIEW)

4241 Department of English, Illinois State University, Normal IL 61790. **E-mail:** krhotel@ilstu.edu. **Website:** http://srpr.org. *SRPR (Spoon River Poetry Review)*, published biannually, is "one of the nation's oldest continuously published poetry journals. We seek to publish the best of all poetic genres, experimental as well as mainstream, and are proud of our commitment to regional as well as international poets and readers. *SRPR* includes, alongside poems from emerging and established poets, a chapbook-length selection of poetry by our featured *SRPR* poet, a substantial interview with the featured poet, and a long review-essay on books of recently published poetry written by established poet-critics. The Summer/Fall issue also spotlights the winner and runners-up of our highly competitive editor's prize contest." Acquires first North American serial rights. Responds in 2-6 months. Guidelines available in magazine or on website.

ⓞ   Accepts submissions from September 15 to February 15 (postmarked).

MAGAZINE'S NEEDS "We publish the best of all poetic genres, including translations, and are proud of our commitment to regional as well as international poets. At SRPR, both innovative and mainstream poems are welcome, though all poetry we publish must be as intellectually and emotionally ambitious as it is formally attentive." Submit 3-5 poems at a time. Submit using online submission form or by postal mail with SASE. Pays 2 contributor's copies and a one-year subscription.

ⓞ STAND MAGAZINE

School of English, University of Leeds, Leeds LS2 9JT, United Kingdom. (44)(113)343-4794. **E-mail:** stand@leeds.ac.uk. **Website:** www.standmagazine.org. **Contact:** Jon Glover, managing editor. Quarterly literary magazine. "U.S. submissions can be made through the Virginia office (see separate listing)." Pays on publication. Guidelines available online at website.

ⓞ   Does not accept e-mail submissions.

MAGAZINE'S NEEDS Submit through postal mail only. Include SASE.

ST. ANTHONY MESSENGER

Franciscan Media, 28 W. Liberty St., Cincinnati OH 45202-6498. (513)241-5615. **Fax:** (513)241-0399. **E-mail:** mageditors@franciscanmedia.org. **Website:** www.stanthonymessenger.org. **Contact:** John Feister, editor. "*St. Anthony Messenger* is a Catholic family magazine which aims to help its readers lead more fully human and Christian lives. We publish articles which report on a changing church and world, opinion pieces written from the perspective of Christian faith and values, personality profiles, and fiction which entertains and informs." Buys first North American serial rights, buys electronic rights. first worldwide serial rights. Pays on acceptance. Publishes ms an average of 1 year after acceptance. Responds in 3 weeks to queries. Responds in 2 months to mss. Sample copy for 9x12 SAE with 4 first-class stamps. Guidelines available online.

MAGAZINE'S NEEDS Submit "a few" poems at a time. "Please include your phone number and a SASE with your submission. Do not send us your entire collection of poetry. Poems must be original." Submit seasonal poems several months in advance. "Our poetry needs are very limited." Length: up to 20-25 lines; "the shorter, the better." Pays $2/line; $20 minimum.

TIPS "The freelancer should consider why his or her proposed article would be appropriate for us, rather than for *Redbook* or *Saturday Review*. We treat human problems of all kinds, but from a religious perspective. Articles should reflect Catholic theology, spirituality, and employ a Catholic terminology and vocabulary. We need more articles on prayer, scripture, Catholic worship. Get authoritative information (not merely library research); we want interviews with experts. Write in popular style; use lots of examples, stories, and personal quotes. Word length is an important consideration."

⑤ STAR*LINE

Science Fiction Poetry Association, 1412 NE 35th St., Ocala FL 34479. **E-mail:** starline@sfpoetry.com. **Website:** www.sfpoetry.com. **Contact:** Marge Simon, editor. *Star*Line*, published quarterly by the Science Fiction Poetry Association (see separate listing in Organizations), is a newsletter and poetry magazine. "Open to all forms—free verse, traditional forms, light verse—as long as your poetry shows skilled use of the language and makes a good use of science fiction, science, fantasy, horror, or speculative motifs." Buys first North American serial rights. Responds in 1 month. Guidelines online.

MAGAZINE'S NEEDS Submit 3-5 poems at a time. Lines/poem: preferably under 50. No simultaneous submissions. Accepts e-mail submissions (preferred; pasted into body of message, no attachments). Cover letter is preferred (brief). Submissions must be typed. Pays $3 for 10 lines or less; $5 for 11-50 lines; 10¢ per line rounded to the next dollar for 51+ lines.

ALSO OFFERS The Association also publishes *The Rhysling Anthology*, a yearly collection of nominations from the membership "for the best science fiction/fantasy long and short poetry of the preceding year and *Dwarf Stars*, an annual collection of poetry ten lines or fewer."

◐ STEPPING STONES MAGAZINE: ALIMIA

First Step Press, P.O. Box 902, Norristown PA 19404-0902. **E-mail:** info@ssmalmia.com. **Website:** http://ssmalmia.com. **Contact:** Trinae A. Ross, publisher. *Stepping Stones Magazine: ALIMIA*, a web publication with a rolling publication date, seeks "poetry as diverse as are the authors themselves. Poems should have something to say other than, 'Hi, I'm a poem please publish me.'" Does not want "poems that promote intolerance for race, religion, gender, or sexual preference." Responds in 2 months.

◐ Has published poetry by Richard Fenwick, Karlanna Lewis, and Stephanie Kaylor. Receives about 600 poems/year, accepts about 10-15%.

MAGAZINE'S NEEDS Submit no more than 5 poems at a time. Considers previously published poems and simultaneous submissions. Prefers e-mail submissions; should include cover letter and formatted with a simple font and saved as .doc, .rtf, or .odf. Attach submissions and cover letter to e-mail and send to poetry@ssmalmia.com. Reads submissions year round. Guidelines available for SASE, by sending an e-mail to info@ssmalmia.com, or on the website. Pays one contributor's copy and free advertising space, though will implement a pay schedule when funding permits.

ALSO OFFERS "The continuing goal of SSM: ALMIA is to provide sanctuary for new and established writers, to hone their skills and commune with one another within the comfort of our electronic pages."

◐ STILL CRAZY

P.O. Box 777, Worthington OH 43085. (614)746-0859. **E-mail:** editor@crazylitmag.com. **Website:** www.crazylitmag.com. **Contact:** Barbara Kussow, editor. "*Still Crazy* publishes writing by people over age 50 and writing by people of any age if the topic is about people over 50 years old." Acquires one-time rights. Rights revert to author upon publication. Time between acceptance and publication is up to 1 year. Simultaneous submissions OK, but notify editor as soon as possible if work is accepted elsewhere. Responds in 6 months to mss. Sometimes sends prepublication galleys. Sometimes comments on/critiques rejected mss. Sometimes publishes theme issues. Guidelines on website.

◐ Accepts 3-4 mss/issue; 6-8/year. Occasionally considers previously published poems. "Do not submit material that has been published elsewhere online." Publication is not copyrighted. Reads submissions year round.

MAGAZINE'S NEEDS Wants poems that tell a story; writing by people over age 50 and writing by people of any age if the topic is about people over 50. The editor is particularly interested in material that challenges the stereotypes of older people and that portrays older people's inner lives as rich and rewarding. Does not want "rhyming poetry, or poetry that is too sentimental." Lines/poem: 30 (maximum). Pays 1 contributor's copy.

TIPS Looking for "interesting characters and interesting situations that might interest readers of all ages. Humor and lightness welcomed."

◐ STIRRING: A LITERARY COLLECTION

Stirring: A Literary Collection, c/o Erin Elizabeth Smith, Department of English, 301 McClung Tower, University of Tennessee, Knoxville TN 37996. **E-mail:** eesmith81@gmail.com. **Website:** www.sundresspublications.com/stirring/. **Contact:** Erin Elizabeth Smith, managing and poetry editor. Acquires first North American serial rights. Publishes ms 1-2 weeks after acceptance. Responds in 2-5 months. E-mail for guidelines.

○ *"Stirring* is one of the oldest continually-published literary journals on the web. *Stirring* is a monthly literary magazine that publishes poetry, short fiction, creative nonfiction, and photography by established and emerging writers."

MAGAZINE'S NEEDS Wants free verse, formal poetry, etc. Doesn't want religious verse or children's verse. Has published poetry by Dorianne Laux, Sharon Olds, Patricia Smith, Chad Davidson. Receives about 1,500 poems/year, accepts 60.

○ ⑤ STONE SOUP

Children's Art Foundation, P.O. Box 83, Santa Cruz CA 95063-0083. (831)426-5557. **E-mail:** editor@stonesoup.com. **Website:** http://stonesoup.com. **Contact:** Ms. Gerry Mandel, editor. *Stone Soup* is 48 pages, 7x10, professionally printed in color on heavy stock, saddle-stapled, with coated cover with full-color illustration. Receives 5,000 poetry submissions/year, accepts about 12. Press run is 15,000. Subscription: $37/year (U.S.). "We have a preference for writing and art based on real-life experiences; no formula stories or poems. We only publish writing by children ages 8 to 13. We do not publish writing by adults." Buys all rights. Pays on publication. Publishes ms an average of 4 months after acceptance. Sample copy by phone only. Guidelines available online.

○ "Stories and poems from past issues are available online."

MAGAZINE'S NEEDS Wants free verse poetry. Does not want rhyming poetry, haiku, or cinquain. Pays $40/poem, a certificate, and 2 contributor's copies, plus discounts.

TIPS "All writing we publish is by young people ages 13 and under. We do not publish any writing by adults. We can't emphasize enough how important it is to read a couple of issues of the magazine. You can read stories and poems from past issues online. We have a strong preference for writing on subjects that mean a lot to the author. If you feel strongly about something that happened to you or something you observed, use that feeling as the basis for your story or poem. Stories should have good descriptions, realistic dialogue, and a point to make. In a poem, each word must be chosen carefully. Your poem should present a view of your subject, and a way of using words that are special and all your own."

① STORYSOUTH

5603B W. Friendly Ave., Suite 282, Greensboro NC 27410. **E-mail:** terry@storysouth.com. **Website:** www.storysouth.com. **Contact:** Terry Kennedy, editor. "*storySouth* accepts unsolicited submissions of fiction, poetry, and creative nonfiction during two submission periods annually: March 15-June 15 and September 15-December 15. Long pieces are encouraged. Please make only one submission in a single genre per reading period." Acquires one-time rights. Publishes ms 1 month after acceptance. Responds in 2-6 months to mss. Writers' guidelines online.

MAGAZINE'S NEEDS Experimental, literary, regional (South), translations. Submit 3-5 poems via online submissions manager. No word/line limit.

TIPS "What really makes a story stand out is a strong voice and a sense of urgency—a need for the reader to keep reading the story and not put it down until it is finished."

THE STORYTELLER

2441 Washington Rd., Maynard AR 72444. (870)647-2137. **E-mail:** storytellermag1@@yahoo.com. **Website:** www.thestorytellermagazine.com. Buys first rights. Publishes ms an average of 1-12 months after acceptance. Responds in 1 week to queries. Responds in 2 weeks to mss. Editorial lead time 6 months. Sample copy for 4 first-class stamps. Guidelines for #10 SASE.

MAGAZINE'S NEEDS Submit with SASE. Does not want long rambling. Length: 40 lines.

CONTEST/AWARD OFFERINGS Sponsors a quarterly contest. "Readers vote on their favorite poems. Winners receive a copy of the magazine and a certificate. We also nominate for the Pushcart Prize." See website for yearly contest announcements and winners.

TIPS "*The Storyteller* is one of the best places you will find to submit your work, especially new writers. Our best advice, be professional. You have one chance to make a good impression. Don't blow it by being unprofessional."

① THE STRAY BRANCH

E-mail: thestraybranchlitmag@yahoo.com. **Website:** www.thestraybranch.org. **Contact:** Debbie Berk, editor/publisher. *The Stray Branch* is "open to form and style; however free verse is preferred. Shorter poems have a better chance of being published. Looking for edgy, darker material written from the gut, reflecting the heart and human condition known as 'existence.' Topics include depression, mental illness, loss, sorrow, addiction, recovery, abuse, survival, daily existence, self struggles, and discovery through words. Personal, confessional poems are welcomed and embraced here. Rhyming poems are OK. Does not want over-schooled, arrogant, self-rigteous, religious, political, sentimental, or happy and light pretty poetry. No erotic or sexually explicit poetry." Acquires one-time rights ("includes material published on the web"). Rights revert to poets upon publication. Responds in 3-4 weeks to submissions. Guidelines available on website.

○ *The Stray Branch* does not accept work from children or teens, or work written for children or teens. E-mail submisssions only. Has published work by Andy Robertson, Keith Estes, Kate Sjostrand, Lena Vanelslander, Michael Grover, and Justin Blackburn. Issue price: $10; $7 for contributors with the use of a contributor discount code.

MAGAZINE'S NEEDS Submit up to 6 poems within the body of the e-mail or as attatchments. No simultaneous submissions. Previously published works are OK.

○ STRAYLIGHT

UW-Parkside, English Department, 900 Wood Rd., P.O. Box 2000, Kenosha WI 53141. (262)595-2139. **Fax:** (262)595-2271. **E-mail:** submissions@straylightmag. com. **Website:** www.straylightmag.com. **Contact:** Fiction editor. (Magazine has revolving editor. Editorial term: 1 year. *Straylight*, published biannually, seeks fiction and "poetry of almost any style as long as it's inventive." *Straylight* is digest-sized. Single copy: $10; subscription: $19. Make checks payable to *Straylight*. Acquires first North American serial rights. Publication is copyrighted. Pays on publication. Publishes ms 6 months after acceptance. Responds to queries in 2 weeks. Responds to mss in 2 months. Rarely comments on/critiques rejected mss. Sample copy available for $10. Guidelines available for SASE and on website.

○ Literary magazine/journal: 6x9 115 pages, quality paper, uncoated index stock cover. Contains illustrations. Includes photographs.

MAGAZINE'S NEEDS Submit 3-6 poems at a time. No previously published poems or simultaneous submissions. Accepts e-mail submissions (preferred, as .rtf or .doc attachment); no fax or disk submissions. Cover letter is required. Include contact information on all pages of submission. Reads submissions August 15-April 15. Submit seasonal poems 3 months in advance. Time between acceptance and publication is 6

months. Never comments on rejected poems. Sometimes publishes theme issues. Upcoming themes available on website. Responds in 2 months. Rights revert to poet upon publication. Pays 2 contributor's copies. Additional payment when funding permits.

TIPS "We tend to publish character-based and inventive fiction with cutting-edge prose. We are unimpressed with works based on strict plot twists or novelties. Read a sample copy to get a feel for what we publish."

○○ STRIDE MAGAZINE

E-mail: editor@stridemagazine.co.uk. **E-mail:** submissions@stridemagazine.co.uk. **Website:** www. stridemagazine.co.uk. **Contact:** Rupert Loydell, editor. *Stride Magazine*, published online, is "a gathering of new poetry, short prose, articles, news, reviews, and whatever takes our fancy. *Stride* is regularly updated with new contributions."

MAGAZINE'S NEEDS Submit 4-5 poems at a time. Accepts e-mail submissions (pasted into body of message; no attachments). "Attachments or snail mail without SAEs will not be considered or replied to."

○ STRUGGLE: A MAGAZINE OF PROLETARIAN REVOLUTIONARY LITERATURE

P.O. Box 28536, Detroit MI 48228. (313)273-9039. **E-mail:** timhall11@yahoo.com. **Website:** www.strugglemagazine.net. **Contact:** Tim Hall, editor. "A quarterly magazine featuring African American, Latino and other writers of color, prisoners, disgruntled workers, activists in the anti-war, anti-racist and other mass movements and many writers discontented with the Bush imperialist juggernaut and the Democratic and labor-leader capitulation to it. While we urge literature in the direction of revolutionary working-class politics and a vision of socialism as embodying a genuine workers' power, in distinction to the state-capitalist regimes of the former Soviet Union, present-day China, North Korea, Cuba, etc., we accept a broader range of rebellious viewpoints in order to encourage creativity and dialogue." No rights acquired. Responds in 3-4 months to queries generally. Sample copies for $3; $5 for double-size issues; subscriptions $10 for 4 issues; make checks payable to Tim Hall, Special Account, not to *Struggle*.

MAGAZINE'S NEEDS Submit up to 8 poems at a time or one story or plan up to 20 pages. Accepts e-mail submissions (pasted into body of message, no attachments), but prefers postal mail. "Writers must include SASE. Name and address must appear on the opening page of each poem."

STUDIO, A JOURNAL OF CHRISTIANS WRITING

727 Peel St., Albury NS 2640, Australia. (61)(2)6021-1135. **Fax:** (61)(2)6021-1135. **E-mail:** studio00@bigpond.net.au. **Contact:** Paul Grover, publisher. *Studio, A Journal of Christians Writing,* published quarterly, prints "poetry and prose of literary merit, offering a venue for previously published, new, and aspiring writers, and seeking to create a sense of community among Christians writing." Also publishes occasional articles as well as news and reviews of writing, writers, and events of interest to members. Wants "shorter pieces (of poetry) but with no specification as to form or length (necessarily less than 200 lines), subject matter, style, or purpose. People who send material should be comfortable being published under this banner: *Studio, A Journal of Christians Writing.*" Acquires first Australian rights. Pays 1 contributor's copy. Time between acceptance and publication is 6-9 months. Response time is 2 months to poems. Responds in 1 week to queries and to mss. Editorial lead time 3 months. Sample copy for $10 (AUD; airmail to U.S.). Guidelines by e-mail.

Has published poetry by John Foulcher, Les Murray, and other Australian poets. *Studio* is 36 pages, digest-sized, professionally printed on high-quality recycled paper, saddle-stapled, with matte card cover. Press run is 300 (all subscriptions). Subscription: $60 AUD for overseas members. Conducts a biannual poetry and short story contest.

MAGAZINE'S NEEDS Lines/poem: less than 200. Considers simultaneous submissions. Cover letter is required. Include brief details of previous publishing history, if any. SAE with IRC required. "Submissions must be typed and double-spaced on 1 side of A4 white paper. Name and address must appear on the reverse side of each page submitted." Reviews books of poetry in 250 words, single-book format. Send materials for review consideration.

CONTEST/AWARD OFFERINGS Conducts a biannual poetry and short story contest.

STUDIO ONE

Mary Commons, College of St. Benedict, 37 S. College Ave., St. Joseph MN 56374. **E-mail:** studio1@csbsju.edu. **Website:** http://clubs.csbsju.edu/studio1. *Studio*

One, published annually in May, is a "literary and visual arts magazine designed as a forum for local, regional, and national poets/writers. No specifications regarding form, subject matter, or style of poetry submitted." Considers poetry by children and teens. Has published poetry by Bill Meissner, Eva Hooker, and Larry Schug. *Studio One* is 50-80 pages, typeset, with soft cover. Receives 600-800 submissions/year. No subscriptions. Make checks payable to *Studio One.* Submissions are accepted August-December. The deadline is January 1 for spring publication. The reading/judging period between late November and February. Results will be sent by May. Submissions sent after the judging period concludes will be retained for consideration in the following year's publication. "Sample copy can be obtained by sending a self-addressed, stamped manila envelope and $6."

MAGAZINE'S NEEDS Submit no more than 5 poems at a time. Lines/poem: "poetry no more than 2 pages stands a better chance of publication." Considers simultaneous submissions; no previously published poems. Accepts e-mail submissions (pasted into body of message); "clearly show page breaks and indentations." Seldom comments on rejected poems.

SUBLIMINAL INTERIORS, A LITERARY ARTS MAGAZINE

E-mail: subliminalinteriors@gmail.com; submit@subliminalinteriors.net. **Website:** www.subliminalinteriors.net. **Contact:** Lisa Minner, Managing Editor. Monthly online literary magazine. "Seeking a variety of voices and styles in poetry and nonfiction, as well as sharp and thought-provoking photography. The abstract and the concrete are both welcomed. Send us interesting and passionate work." Buys first rights, electronic rights. Responds in 1 week on queries; 1 month on manuscripts. Editorial lead time is 1 month. Sample copy online at website. Writer's guidelines available by e-mail and online at website.

SUBTROPICS

University of Florida, P.O. Box 112075, 4008 Turlington Hall, Gainesville FL 32611-2075. **E-mail:** subtropics@english.ufl.edu. **Website:** www.english.ufl.edu/subtropics. **Contact:** David Leavitt. "Magazine published twice year through the University of Florida's English department. *Subtropics* seeks to publish the best literary fiction, essays, and poetry being written today, both by established and emerging authors. We will consider works of fiction of any length, from short shorts to novellas and self-contained novel excerpts. We give the same latitude to essays. We appreciate work in translation and, from time to time, republish important and compelling stories, essays, and poems that have lapsed out of print by writers no longer living." Member CLMP. Buys first North American serial rights, buys one-time rights. Pays on acceptance. Publishes ms an average of 6 months after acceptance. Responds in 1 month to queries and mss. Rarely comments on/critiques rejected mss Sample copy available for $12.95. Guidelines available on website.

○ Literary magazine/journal: 9x6, 160 pages. Includes photographs.

MAGAZINE'S NEEDS Submit in hard copy by mail. Include cover letter with contact information on both letter and on submission. Responds by e-mail. Submission period September 1-May 1. Does not return ms. "We do not accept simultaneous submissions in poetry." Pays $100 per poem.

TIPS "We publish longer works of fiction, including novellas and excerpts from forthcoming novels. Each issue will include a short-short story of about 250 words on the back cover. We are also interested in publishing works in translation for the magazine's English-speaking audience."

THE SUN

107 N. Roberson St., Chapel Hill NC 27516. (919)942-5282. **Fax:** (919)932-3101. **Website:** www.thesunmagazine.org. Sy Safransky, editor. **Contact:** Luc Sanders, assistant editor. "We are open to all kinds of writing, though we favor work of a personal nature." Buys first rights, buys one-time rights. Pays on publication. Publishes ms an average of 6-12 months after acceptance. Responds in 3-6 months to queries. Responds in 3-6 months to mss. Sample copy for $5. Guidelines available online.

○ Magazine: 812×11; 48 pages; offset paper; glossy cover stock; photos.

MAGAZINE'S NEEDS Submit up to 6 poems at a time. Considers previously published poems but strongly prefers unpublished work; no simultaneous submissions. "Poems should be typed and accompanied by a cover letter and SASE." Guidelines available with SASE or on website. Responds within 3-6 months. Acquires first serial or one-time rights. Rarely publishes poems that rhyme. Pays $100-500 on publication plus contributor's copies and subscription.

TIPS "Do not send queries except for interviews. We're looking for artful and sensitive photographs that aren't overly sentimental. We're open to unusual work. Read the magazine to get a sense of what we're about. Send the best possible prints of your work. Our submission rate is extremely high. Please be patient after sending us your work. Send return postage and secure return packaging."

◑ SUNSPINNER

E-mail: sunspinnermagazine@yahoo.com. **Website:** www.sunspinner.org. **Contact:** Ellen Lewis and Lisa Swanstrom, editors. *Sunspinner*, published biannually online, is based in southern California and features "fiction and poetry from writers everywhere. There are no restrictions on style or subject matter, and submissions are always welcome." Has published poetry by Ryan G. Van Cleave, Lyn Lifshin, Linda Mastrangelo, and Gary Lehman. Publishes ms 6 months after acceptance. Responds in 4-6 months. Guidelines on website.

MAGAZINE'S NEEDS Submit 3-5 poems at a time. Considers previously published poems ("provided the author retains all rights") and simultaneous submissions. Accepts e-mail (pasted into body of message or as attachment in Microsoft Word) and disk submissions. Cover letter is preferred. "Please include a brief bio with each submission." Reads submissions year round. "Works accepted by *Sunspinner* will be archived for an indefinite period of time and removed at the author's request. Authors retain all rights to work featured in *Sunspinner*."

◑ SUNSTONE

Website: www.sunstonemagazine.com. *Sunstone*, published 6 times/year, prints "scholarly articles of interest to an open, Mormon audience; personal essays; fiction and poetry." Wants "both lyric and narrative poetry that engages the reader with fresh, strong images, skillful use of language, and a strong sense of voice and/or place." Does not want "didactic poetry, sing-song rhymes, or in-process work." Has published poetry by Susan Howe, Anita Tanner, Robert Parham, Ryan G. Van Cleave, Robert Rees, and Virgil Suaárez. *Sunstone* is 64 pages, magazine-sized, professionally printed, saddle-stapled, with semi-glossy paper cover. Receives more than 500 poems/year, accepts 40-50. Press run is 3,000. Subscription: $45 for 6 issues. Sample: $10 postpaid. Acquires first North American serial rights. Publishes ms 2 years after acceptance. Responds in 3 months. Guidelines for SASE.

MAGAZINE'S NEEDS Submit up to 5 poems at a time. Lines/poem: 40 maximum. No previously published poems or simultaneous submissions. Include name and address on each poem. Seldom comments on rejected poems. Pays 5 contributor's copies.

SYCAMORE REVIEW

Purdue University Dept. of English, 500 Oval Dr., West Lafayette IN 47907. (765) 494-3783. **Fax:** (765) 494-3780. **E-mail:** sycamore@purdue.edu. **Website:** www.sycamorereview.com. **Contact:** Alisha Karabinus, managing editor; Jessica Jacobs, editor-in-chief. "Strives to publish the best writing by new and established writers. Looks for well crafted and engaging work, works that illuminate our lives in the collective human search for meaning. We would like to publish more work that takes a reflective look at our national identity and how we are perceived by the world. We look for diversity of voice, pluralistic worldviews, and political and social context." Buys first North American serial rights.

○ *Sycamore Review* is Purdue University's internationally acclaimed literary journal, affiliated with Purdue's College of Liberal Arts and the Dept. of English. Art should present politics in a language that can be felt.

MAGAZINE'S NEEDS Submissions should be typed, double-spaced, with numbered pages and the author's name and the title easily visible on each page. Does not publish creative work by any student currently attending Purdue University. Former students should wait one year before submitting.

TIPS "We look for originality, brevity, significance, strong dialogue, and vivid detail. We sponsor the Wabash Prize for Poetry (deadline: mid-October) and Fiction (deadline: March 1). $1,000 award for each. All contest submissions will be considered for regular inclusion in the *Sycamore Review*. No e-mail submissions—no exception. Include SASE."

● ● TAKAHE

P.O. Box 13-335, Christchurch 8001, New Zealand. (03)359-8133. **E-mail:** admin@takahe.org.nz. **Website:** www.takahe.org.nz/index.php. The Takahe Collective Trust is a non-profit organisation that aims to support emerging and published writers, poets, artists and cultural commentators. The Takahē magazine appears three times a year and publishes short stories, poetry and art by established and emerging writers and artists as well as essays and interviews (by invitation), and book reviews in these related areas. Ac-

quires first rights. Responds in 4 months. Guidelines available online.

MAGAZINE'S NEEDS No simultaneous submissions. No e-mail submissions. "**Please note:** U.S. stamps should not be used on SAEs. They do not work in New Zealand. Please enclose IRCs or supply e-mail address." Cover letter is required. " Submit up to 6 poems at a time. Pays 1 contributor's copy.

TIPS "We pay a flat rate to each writer/poet appearing in a particular issue regardless of the number/length of items. Editorials and literary commentaries are by invitation only."

● ○ TALENT DRIPS EROTIC LITERARY EZINE

Cleveland OH 44102. (216)799-9775. **E-mail:** talentdripseroticpublishing@yahoo.com. **Website:** http://eroticatalentdrips.wordpress.com. **Contact:** Kimberly Steele, founder. *Talent Drips*, published monthly online, focuses solely on showcasing new erotic fiction. Acquires electronic rights only. Rights revert to authors and poets upon publication. Work archived on the site for 1 year. Time between acceptance and publication is 2 months. Responds in 3 weeks. Guidelines on website.

MAGAZINE'S NEEDS Submit 2-3 poems at a time, maximum 30 lines each by e-mail to talentdripseroticpublishing@yahoo.com. Considers previously published and simultaneous submissions. Accepts e-mail pasted into body of message. Reads submissions during publication months only. Pays $10 for each accepted poem.

CONTEST/AWARD OFFERINGS Talent Drips Erotic Literary EZine Poet of the Year Contest is held annually. Prizes: $75, $50, and certificate. Deadline: December 15. Guidelines on website.

TIPS "Please read our take on the difference between *erotica* and *pornography;* it's on the website. *Talent Drips* does not accept pornography. And please keep poetry 30 lines or less."

TALES OF THE TALISMAN

Hadrosaur Productions, P.O. Box 2194, Mesilla Park NM 88047-2194. **E-mail:** hadrosaur@zianet.com. **Website:** www.talesofthetalisman.com. **Contact:** David Lee Summers, editor. "*Tales of the Talisman* is a literary science fiction and fantasy magazine. We publish short stories, poetry, and articles with themes related to science fiction and fantasy. Above all, we are looking for thought-provoking ideas and good writing. Speculative fiction set in the past, present, and future is welcome. Likewise, contemporary or historical fiction is welcome as long as it has a mythic or science fictional element. Our target audience includes adult fans of the science fiction and fantasy genres along with anyone else who enjoys thought-provoking and entertaining writing." Buys one-time rights. Pays on acceptance. Publishes ms an average of 9 months after acceptance. Responds in 1 week to queries. Responds in 1 month to mss. Editorial lead time 9-12 months. Sample copy for $8. Guidelines available online.

○ Fiction and poetry submissions are limited to reading periods of January 1-February 15 and July 1-August 15.

MAGAZINE'S NEEDS "Do not send 'mainstream' poetry with no science fictional or fantastic elements. Do not send poems featuring copyrighted characters, unless you're the copyright holder." Length: 3-50 lines.

TIPS "Let your imagination soar to its greatest heights and write down the results. Above all, we are looking for thought-provoking ideas and good writing. Our emphasis is on character-oriented science fiction and fantasy. If we don't believe in the people living the story, we generally won't believe in the story itself."

◐ TALKING RIVER

Division of Literature and Languages, 500 8th Ave., Lewiston ID 83501. (208)792-2189. **Fax:** (208)792-2324. **E-mail:** talkingriver@lcmail.lcsc.edu. **Website:** www.lcsc.edu/talkingriverreview. **Contact:** Kevin Goodan, editorial advisor. Acquires one-time rights. Publishes ms 1-2 years after acceptance. Responds in 3 months to mss. Sample copy for $6. Writer's guidelines for #10 SASE.

MAGAZINE'S NEEDS Pays contributor's copies; additional copies $4.

TIPS "We look for the strong, the unique; we reject clichéd images and predictable climaxes."

◐ TARPAULIN SKY

P.O. Box 189, Grafton VT 05146. **E-mail:** editors@tarpaulinsky.com. **E-mail:** submissions@tarpaulinsky.com. **Website:** www.tarpaulinsky.com. *Tarpaulin Sky*, published biannually in print and online, features "highest-quality poetry, prose, cross-genre work, art, photography, interviews, and reviews. We are open to all styles and forms, providing the forms appear inevitable and/or inextricable from the poems. We are especially fond of inventive/experimental and cross-/trans-genre work. The best indication of our aesthetic is found in the journal we produce: Please read it be-

fore submitting your work. Also, hardcopy submissions may be received by different editors at different times; check guidelines before submitting." Has published poetry by Jenny Boully, Matthea Harvey, Bin Ramke, Eleni Sikelianos, Juliana Spahr, and Joshua Marie Wilkinson. Receives about 3,000 poems/year. Acquires first rights. Publishes ms 2-6 months after acceptance. Responds in 1-4 months.

MAGAZINE'S NEEDS Submit 4-6 poems at a time. Considers simultaneous submissions; no previously published poems. Accepts e-mail submissions ("best received as attachments in .rtf or .pdf formats"); no disk submissions. Cover letter is preferred. Reads submissions year round. "Poems are read by all editors. We aim for consensus." Rarely comments on rejected poems. Guidelines available for SASE, by e-mail, or on website. Pays in contributor's copies and "by waiving readings fees for Tarpaulin Sky Press Open Reading Periods."

◑ TAR RIVER POETRY

Mail Stop 159, Erwin Hall, East Fifth St., East Carolina University, Greenville NC 27858. **E-mail:** TarRiverPoetry@gmail.com. **Website:** www.tarriverpoetry.com. **Contact:** Luke Whisnant, editor. *Tar River Poetry*, published twice/year, is an "'all-poetry' magazine that publishes 40-50 poems per issue, providing the talented beginner and experienced writer with a forum that features all styles and forms of verse." Wants "skillful use of figurative language; poems that appeal to the senses." Does not want "sentimental, flat-statement poetry." *Tar River Poetry* is 64 pages, 9x5, professionally printed with color cover. Receives 6,000-8,000 submissions/year, accepts 60-80. Press run is 900 (500 subscribers, 125 libraries). Subscription: $12 for 1 year; $20 for 2 years. Sample: $7 postpaid. Has published poetry by William Stafford, Sharon Olds, Carolyn Kizer, A.R. Ammons, and Claudia Emerson. Has also published "many other well-known poets, as well as numerous new and emerging poets." Acquires first rights and reassigns reprint rights after publication. Responds in 6 weeks. Rarely comments on rejections "due to volume of submissions." Guidelines available for SASE or on website.

○ "We only consider submissions during *2* six-week reading periods: 1 in the fall (usually September 15-November 1) and 1 in the spring (February 1-March 15); check our website for reading periods before submitting. Work submitted at other times will not be considered."

MAGAZINE'S NEEDS Submit no more than 5 poems at a time. Simultaneous submissions okay. No previously published poems. Accepts e-mail submissions only; no print submissions; print submissions will be returned unread. "Detailed submission instructions appear on the website, along with writer's guidelines." Check website for reading periods: "we do not read mss from May through August—submissions will be returned unread." Reviews books of poetry in 4,000 words maximum, single- or multi-book format. Query for reviews. Pays 2 contributor's copies.

TIPS Familiarize yourself with the type of poetry we publish before submitting. Sample copies are available, or visit our website to read sample poems. "Writers of poetry should first be readers of poetry. Read and study traditional and contemporary poetry."

TATTOO HIGHWAY

E-mail: submissions@tattoohighway.org. **Website:** www.tattoohighway.org. **Contact:** Sara McAulay, editor and graphics; Rochelle Nameroff, poetry editor. Guidelines available online at website.

MAGAZINE'S NEEDS Welcomes any and all forms. "E-mail submissions to submissions@tattoohighway. org as a Rich Text Format (RTF) attachment or as plain text in the body of your message, and with TH and the issue number in the subject line."

TIPS "Interpret our themes literally or loosely, as you wish. Our tastes are eclectic. We like fresh, vivid language, and we like stories and poems that are actually about something — that acknowledge a world beyond the writer's own psyche. If they have an edge, if they provoke us to think or make us laugh, so much the better. We strongly suggest reading a previous issue or two before submitting."

THE TEACHER'S VOICE

P.O. Box 150384, Kew Gardens NY 11415. **E-mail:** editor@the-teachers-voice.org. **Website:** www.the-teachers-voice.org. **Contact:** Andres Castro, founding/managing editor. *The Teacher's Voice*, was founded as an experimental hardcopy literary magazine and is now free and online. "We publish poetry, short stories, creative nonfiction, and essays that reflect the many different American teacher experiences." Wants "all styles and forms. We ask to see critical creative writing that takes risks without being overly self-indulgent or inaccessible. We welcome work that ranges from 'art for art's

sake' to radically social/political. Writing that illuminates the most pressing/urgent issues in American education and the lives of teachers gets special attention." Has published poetry by Edward Francisco, Sapphire, Hal Sirowitz, and Antler. Receives about 1,000 poems/ year, accepts about 10%. Acquires first electronic rights. Guidelines on website.

MAGAZINE'S NEEDS Submit 3-5 poems at a time. Cover letter is preferred. "Are you a teacher, administrator, parent, student, librarian, custodian, coach, security officer, etc? We do not accept responsibility for submissions or queries not accompanied by a SASE with adequate postage." Poems are circulated to an editorial board.

ADDITIONAL INFORMATION "Since we publish open as well as theme issues (that require enough thematic pieces to be compiled) and do rely on readership financial support, our publishing schedule and format may vary from year to year. We publish hardcopy limited press collections when funds allow. Our production goal is to showcase strong cohesive collections that support our mission and satisfy the needs of particular issues. For the moment, our new focus on electronic publishing is a matter of survival that offers many new possibilities and opportunities in keeping with the changing times."

CONTEST/AWARD OFFERINGS Sponsors *The Teacher's Voice* Annual Chapbook Contest and *The Teacher's Voice* Annual Poetry Contest for Unpublished Poets. Final contest judges have included, Sapphire, Jack Hirschman, and Taylor Mali. Guidelines for both contests available for SASE, by e-mail, or on website.

TEARS IN THE FENCE

Portman Lodge, Durweston, Blandford Forum, Dorset DT11 0QA, England. **E-mail:** tearsinthefence@gmail. com. **Website:** http://tearsinthefence.com. *Tears in the Fence*, published twice a year, is a "small press magazine of poetry, fiction, interviews, essays, and reviews. We are open to a wide variety of poetic styles. Work that shows social and poetic awareness whilst prompting close and divergent readings. However, we like to publish a variety of work." Sample: $13.

Has published Aidan Semmens, Hannah Silva, Paul Kareem Tayyar, Edward Field, Carrie Etter, Nathaniel Tarn, Anthony Barnett, Geraldine Clarkson, Sheila E. Murphy. *Tears in the Fence* is 176 pages, A5, docutech-printed on 110-gms. paper, perfect-bound, with matte card cover.

Press run is 800 (522 subscribers). Subscription: $35/3 issues.

MAGAZINE'S NEEDS Submit 6 poems at a time. Accepts e-mail (pasted into body of message) and disk submissions. Cover letter with brief bio is required. Poems must be typed; include SASE. Time between acceptance and publication is 3 months. Pays 1 contributor's copy. Books for review to Ian Brinton, Brescia House, 2 Capel Road, Faversham, Kent, ME13 8RL, England.

ALSO OFFERS The magazine runs a regular series of readings in London, and an annual international literary festival.

TEXAS POETRY CALENDAR

Dos Gatos Press, 1310 Crestwood Rd., Austin TX 78722. (512)467-0678. **E-mail:** editors@dosgatospress.org; managingeditor@dosgatospress.org. **E-mail:** https://dosgatospress.submittable.com/submit. **Website:** www.dosgatospress.org. **Contact:** Scott Wiggerman and David Meischen, publishers; Cindy Huyser and Laurie Ann Guerrero, editors. *Texas Poetry Calendar*, published annually in July, features a "week-by-week calendar side-by-side with poems with a Texas connection." Wants "a wide variety of styles, voices, and forms, including rhyme—though a Texas connection is preferred. Humor is welcome! Poetry only!" Does not want "children's poetry, erotic poetry, profanity, obscure poems, previously published work, or poems over 35 lines." Publishes me 3-4 months after acceptance.

Texas Poetry Calendar is about 144 pages, digest-sized, offset-printed, spiral-bound, with full-color cardstock cover. Receives about 600 poems/year, accepts about 80-85. Press run is 1,000; 80-85 distributed free to contributors. Single copy: $13.95 plus $3 shipping. Make checks payable to Dos Gatos Press.

MAGAZINE'S NEEDS Submit 3 poems through Submittable: https://dosgatospress.submittable.com/submit. No simultaneous submissions; no previously published poems. No fax, e-mail, or snail mail submissions; only electronic submissions via Submittable. Cover letter is required. "Include a short bio (100-200 words) and poem titles in cover letter. Also include e-mail address and phone number. Do not include poet's name on the poems themselves!" Reads submissions February-May. Poems are circulated to an editorial board. Never comments on rejected poems,

but nominates poems for Pushcart Prizes each year. Deadline: February 21 (postmark). Lines/poem: 35 maximum, "including spaces and title."

TEXAS REVIEW

Texas Review Press, Department of English, Sam Houston State University, Box 2146, Huntsville TX 77341-2146. (936)294-1992. **Fax:** (936)294-3070. **E-mail:** eng_pdr@shsu.edu; cww006@shsu.edu. **Website:** www.shsu.edu/~www_trp. **Contact:** Dr. Paul Ruffin, editor/director. "We publish top quality poetry, fiction, articles, interviews and reviews for a general audience." Semiannual. Pays on publication for first North American serial, one-time rights. Sends galleys to author. Publishes ms 6-12 months after acceptance. Responds in 2 weeks to queries; 3-6 months to mss. Sometimes comments on rejected mss. Sample copy for $5. Writer's guidelines for SASE and on website.

Magazine: 6×9; 148-190 pages; best quality paper; 70 lb. cover stock; illustrations; photos. Receives 40-60 unsolicited mss/month. Accepts 4 mss/issue; 6 mss/year. **Publishes some new writers/year.** Does not read mss May-September. A member of the Texas A&M University Press consortium.

MAGAZINE'S NEEDS No previously published poems or simultaneous submissions. Include SASE. Reads submissions September 1-April 30 only. Time between acceptance and publication is 6 months. Poems are circulated to an editorial board. Seldom comments on rejected poems. Pays one-year subscription and one contributor's copy (may request more).

CONTEST/AWARD OFFERINGS Sponsors the X.J. Kennedy Poetry Prize (for best full-length book of poetry) and the Robert Phillips Poetry Chapbook Prize (for best poetry chapbook). Both competitions award $200 and publication for the winning mss. **Entry fee:** $20. Guidelines available for SASE (specifying "for poetry/fiction contest guidelines") or on website.

THEMA

Thema Literary Society, P.O. Box 8747, Metairie LA 70011-8747. **E-mail:** thema@cox.net. **Website:** http://themaliterarysociety.com. **Contact:** Gail Howard, poetry editor. "*THEMA* is designed to stimulate creative thinking by challenging writers with unusual themes, such as 'The Box Under the Bed' and 'Put It In Your Pocket, Lillian.' Appeals to writers, teachers of creative writing, and general reading audience." Acquires one-time rights. Pays on acceptance. Publishes ms, on average, within 6 months after acceptance. Responds in 1 week to queries. Responds in 5 months to mss. Sample $10 U.S./$15 foreign. Upcoming themes and guidelines available in magazine, for SASE, by e-mail, or on website.

○ *THEMA* is 100 pages, digest-sized professionally printed, with glossy card cover. Receives about 400 poems/year, accepts about 8%. Press run is 400 (230 subscribers, 30 libraries). Subscription: $20 U.S./$30 foreign. Has published poetry by Beverly Boyd, Elizabeth Creith, James Penha and Matthew J. Spireng.

MAGAZINE'S NEEDS Submit up to 3 poems at a time. Include SASE. "All submissions should be typewritten on standard 812x11 paper. Submissions are accepted all year, but evaluated after specified deadlines." Specify target theme. Editor comments on submissions. "Each issue is based on an unusual premise. Please send SASE for guidelines before submitting poetry to find out the upcoming themes." Does not want "scatologic language, alternate lifestyle, explicit love poetry." Pays $10/poem and 1 contributor's copy.

○ THICK WITH CONVICTION

E-mail: twczine@yahoo.com. **Website:** www.angelfire.com/poetry/thickwithconviction. **Contact:** Arielle Lancaster-LaBrea, Kayla Middlebrook, Kristina Marie Blanton, Taylor Copeland. *Thick With Conviction*, published biannually online, is "run by four twentysomething women who are looking for fresh and exciting voices in poetry. We don't want to take a nap while we're reading, so grab our attention, make us sit up and catch our breath." Wants all genres of poetry, "poems that make us exhale a deep sigh after reading them. Basically, if we can't feel the words in front of us, we're not going to be happy. We'd like to see new and cutting edge poets who think outside the box, but still know how to keep things from getting too strange and inaccessible." Does not want "teen angst poems, religious poems, or greeting card tripe." Has published poetry by Kendall A. Bell, April Michelle Bratten, KristinaMarie Darling, James H. Duncan, Paul Hostovsky and Kelsey Upward. Receives about 300 poems/year, accepts about 15%. Never comments on rejected poems. Acquires one-time rights. Rights revert to poet upon publication. Publishes ms 3 months after acceptance. Responds in "roughly 2-3 months." Guidelines available on website.

MAGAZINE'S NEEDS Submit 3-5 poems at a time. Lines/poem: no limit. Considers previously published poems; no simultaneous submissions. Accepts e-mail submissions (pasted into body of message; "any attachments will be deleted"); no disk submissions. Cover letter and bio is required. Reads submissions year-round.

THINK JOURNAL

Reason Publishing LLC, P.O. Box 454, Downingtown PA 19335. **E-mail:** thinkjournal@yahoo.com. **Website:** www.thinkjournalreview.com. **Contact:** Christine Yurick, editor. "*Think Journal*, published quarterly, "focuses on words that have meaning, that are presented in a clear way, and that exhibit the skills demanded by craft. The journal prints work that achieves a balance between form and content. The most important traits that will be considered are form, structure, clarity, content, imagination, and style." Buys one-time rights. Publishes ms an average of 6-9 months after acceptance. Responds in 2-4 weeks to queries. Responds in 6-9 months to mss. Editorial lead time 6 months.

○ *Think Journal* is 55 pages, digest-sized, desktop-printed, perfect-bound with a cardstock cover containing original artwork. Single copy: $7; subscription: $20/year. Sample $6. Make checks payable to Christine Yurick.

MAGAZINE'S NEEDS Accepts submissions by e-mail, mail. "Always include a SASE with submissions. Cover letter and brief biography preferred. Please include your e-mail address on the cover page for further communications. Include your name and address on each page of your submission." Reads submissions year round. Does not accept previously published or simultaneous submissions. Publication is payment, along with 1 free contributor's copy.

TIPS "Please visit the website to view samples of previously published work, or purchase a sample issue. Also looking for graphic design artwork for the cover."

○○ THIRD WEDNESDAY: A LITERARY ARTS MAGAZINE

174 Greenside Up, Ypsilanti MI 48197. (734) 434-2409. **E-mail:** submissions@thirdwednesday.org; LaurenceWT@aol.com. **Website:** http://thirdwednesday.org. **Contact:** Laurence Thomas, editor. "*Third Wednesday* publishes quality (a subjective term at best) poetry, short fiction, and artwork by experienced writers and artists. We welcome work by established writers/artists, as well as those who are not yet well known, but headed for prominence." Acquires first rights. Pays on

acceptance. Publishes ms 3 months after acceptance. Responds to mss in 6-8 weeks. Sometimes comments on/critiques rejected mss. Sample copy available for $8. Guidelines available for SASE, or via e-mail.

◐ Quarterly literary magazine/journal: 60-65 pages. Contains illustrations. Includes photographs. Receives 5-10 mss/month. Accepts 3-5 mss/issue. Receives 800 poems/year. Has published poetry by Wanda Coleman, Philip Dacey, Richard Luftig, Simon Perchik, Marge Piercy, Charles Harper Webb. Press run is 125. Single copy: $8; subscription: $30. Make checks payable to *Third Wednesday*.

MAGAZINE'S NEEDS Submit 1-5 poems at a time. Wants "all styles and forms of poetry, from formal to experimental. Emphasis is placed on the ideas conveyed, craft and language, beauty of expression, and the picture that extends beyond the frame of the poem." Does not want "hate-filled diatribes, pornography (though eroticism is acceptable), prose masquerading as poetry, first drafts of anything." Acquires first North American serial rights, electronic rights. "*TW* retains the right to reproduce accepted work as samples on our website." Rights revert to poet upon publication. Pays $3 and 1 contributor's copy.

TIPS "Of course, originality is important, along with skill in writing, deft handling of language, and meaning, which goes hand in hand with beauty—whatever that is. Short fiction is specialized and difficult, so the writer should read extensively in the field."

◐ 34TH PARALLEL

P.O. Box 4823, Irvine CA 92623. **E-mail:** 34thParallel@gmail.com. **Website:** www.34thparallel.net. **Contact:** Tracey Boone Swan, Martin Chipperfield, editors. *34th Parallel*, published quarterly in print and online, seeks "to promote and publish the exceptional writing of new and emerging writers overlooked by large commercial publishing houses and mainstream presses. Wants work that experiments with and tests boundaries. Anything that communicates a sense of wonder, reality, tragedy, fantasy, and/or brilliance. Does not want historical romance, science fiction, erotica, Gothic horror, book reviews, or nonfiction." Sample copy $11. Guidelines on website.

MAGAZINE'S NEEDS "In the subject heading of your e-mail, type in 'story submissions' or 'poetry submission' or 'image submission.' Will discard as spam those submissions that do not contain one of these subject headings. Submit 1 poem only. Considers simultaneous submissions; no previously published poems. Accepts electronic submissions. Cover letter is required, containing a short bio about your life, your writing, and where we can see some of your other work online. Reads submissions year round. Often comments on rejected poems." Pays 1 contributor's copy in PDF format.

◐ TIGER'S EYE

Tiger's Eye Press, P.O. Box 9723, Denver CO 80209. (541)285-8355. **E-mail:** tigerseyepoet@yahoo.com. **Website:** www.tigerseyejournal.com. **Contact:** Colette Jonopulos and JoAn Osborne, editors. *Tiger's Eye: A Journal of Poetry*, published annually, features both established and undiscovered poets. Acquires one-time rights. Publishes ms 3 months after acceptance. Responds in 6 months. Guidelines available in magazine or on website.

MAGAZINE'S NEEDS "Besides publishing the work of several exceptional poets in each issue, we feature two poets in interviews, giving the reader insight into their lives and writing habits." Wants "both free verse and traditional forms; no restrictions on subject or length. We welcome sonnets, haibun, haiku, ghazals, villenelles, etc. We pay special attention to unusual forms and longer poems that may have difficulty being placed elsewhere. Poems with distinct imagery and viewpoint are read and re-read by the editors and considered for publication." Submit 3-5 poems. Length: no more than 5 pages. Pays one contributor's copy to each poet, 2 to featured poets.

ADDITIONAL INFORMATION *Tiger's Eye* nominates for *The Pushcart Prize*.

CONTEST/AWARD OFFERINGS Tiger's Eye Chapbook Contest (see separate listing in Contests & Awards). "Our annual poetry contest awards $500, $100, $50. Send 20-25 poems, cover letter with poet's name and contact information (no identifying information on mss pages) SASE, and $15 entry fee. **Deadline: August 31.**

TIMBER JOURNAL

E-mail: timberjournal@gmail.com. **Website:** www.timberjournal.com. **Contact:** Oren Silverman, managing editor; Caroline Davidson, poetry editor; Gabrielle Fuentes, fiction editor. Timber is a literary journal, run by students in the MFA program at the University of Colorado-Boulder, dedicated to the promotion of innovative literature. "We publish work that explores the boundaries of poetry, fiction, creative nonfiction, and digital literatures. We produce both an online journal in which we explore the potentials of the digital medium, and a semi-annual 'book object,' which is a venue for more traditional print-based work." Reading period September 1-February 15. Include 30-50 word bio with submission. Guidelines available online.

MAGAZINE'S NEEDS Looking for innovative poetry. Submit 3-5 poems (less than 3 poems will not be reviewed). Pays one contributor copy.

TIPS "We are looking for innovative poetry, fiction, creative nonfiction, and digital lit (screenwriting, digital poetry, multimedia lit, etc.)."

◑◎ TIME OF SINGING: A MAGAZINE OF CHRISTIAN POETRY

P.O. Box 149, Conneaut Lake PA 16316. **E-mail:** timesing@zoominternet.net. **Website:** www.timeofsinging.com. **Contact:** Lora Zill, editor. "*Time of Singing* publishes Christian poetry in the widest sense, but prefers literary'type. Welcome forms, fresh rhyme, well-crafted free verse. Like writers who take chances, who don't feel the need to tie everything up neatly." Buys first North American serial rights, buys first rights, buys one-time rights, buys second serial (reprint) rights. Publishes ms within 1 year of acceptance. Responds in 3 months to mss. Editorial lead time 6 months. Sample copy for $4/each or 2 for $7. Guidelines for SASE or on website.

○ Magazine: 44 pages, digest-sized, offset from typescript. Receives more than 800 submissions/year, accepts about 175. Press run is 250 (150 subscribers). Subscription: $17 USD, $21 USD Canada, $30 USD overseas. Sample: $4, or 2 for $7 (postage paid). Has published poetry by John Grey, Luci Shaw, Bob Hostetler, Tony Cosier, Barbara Crooker, and Charles Waugaman.

MAGAZINE'S NEEDS Wants free verse and well-crafted rhyme; would like to see more forms. Accepts e-mail submissions (pasted into body of message or as attachment). Poems should be single-spaced. Comments "with suggestions for improvement if close to publication. *TOS* has published poets from England, South Africa, Mexico, New Zealand, Scotland, Russia, Australia, and Ireland." Does not want "collections of uneven lines, sermons that rhyme, greeting card type poetry, unstructured 'prayers,' and trite sing-song rhymes." Length: 3-60 lines. All contributors receive 1 copy of the issue in which their work appears and the opportunity to purchase more at the contributor's rate

ADDITIONAL INFORMATION "*Time of Singing* also welcomes general inspirational and nature poems. I prefer poems that don't preach, and "show" rather than "tell." Sermons and greeting card poetry have valid purposes, but aren't appropriate for this magazine. I suggest you obtain a sample back issue to help you ascertain TOS's style. I welcome fresh rhyme, beg for more forms, appreciate well-crafted free verse, and consider poems up to 60 lines in length. I try to respond within 3 months, and make every effort to publish poems within one year of acceptance."

CONTEST/AWARD OFFERINGS Sponsors theme contests for specific issues. Guidelines available for SASE, by e-mail, or on website.

TIPS "Read widely and study the craft. You need more than feelings and religious jargon to make it into *TOS*. It's helpful to get honest critiques of your work. Cover letter not necessary. Your poems speak for themselves."

TIN HOUSE

McCormack Communications, P.O. Box 10500, Portland OR 97210. (503)219-0622. **Fax:** (503)222-1154. **E-mail:** info@tinhouse.com. **Website:** www.tinhouse.com. **Contact:** Cheston Knapp, managing editor; Holly Macarthur, founding editor. "We are a general interest literary quarterly. Our watchword is quality. Our audience includes people interested in literature in all its aspects, from the mundane to the exalted." Buys first North American serial rights, buys anthology rights. Pays on publication. Publishes ms an average of 6 months after acceptance. Responds in 6 weeks to queries. Responds in 3 months to mss. Editorial lead time 6 months. Sample copy for $15. Guidelines available online.

MAGAZINE'S NEEDS "No prose masquerading as poetry." Send complete ms September 1-May 31 via regular mail or online submission form. No fax or e-mail submissions. Pays $50-150.

TIPS "Remember to send an SASE with your submission."

TOAD SUCK REVIEW

E-mail: toadsuckreview@gmail.com. **Website:** http://toadsuckreview.org. **Contact:** Mark Spitzer, editor. Prefers submissions from skilled, experienced poets; will consider work from beginning poets. "Born from the legendary *Exquisite Corpse Annual*, the innovative *Toad Suck Review* is a cutting edge mixture of poetry, fiction, creative nonfiction, translations, reviews, and artwork with a provocative sense of humor and an interest in diverse cultures and politics. No previously published work. 'Previously published' work includes: poetry posted on a public website/blog/forum, and poetry posted on a private, password-protected forum. Reads mss in the summer. " Acquires one-time rights. Pays contributor's copies upon publication. Publishes ms 4 months after acceptance. Responds to mss in 1 week to 9 months. Sample copy for $15. Guidelines available free for SASE or on website.

○ The journal received a Library Journal award for being one of the 10 best lit mags published in 2012. *Toad Suck Review* is a 6 x 11 magazine, 200 pages, perfect bound flat spine. Lifetime subscription: $75. Has published work by Charles Bukowski, Lawrence Ferlinghetti, Edward Abbey, Gary Snyder, Anne Waldman, Ed Sanders, Tyrone Jaeger, Jean Genet, Louis-Ferdinand Céline, Antler, David Gessner, C.D. Wright, Amiri Baraka.

MAGAZINE'S NEEDS "All forms and styles are welcome, especially those that take risks and shoot for something new." Submit in e-mail as attachment. Receives about 777 poems/year; accepts 17. Sometimes comments on rejected poems. Does not want rhyming, repetitive, pastoral, or religious poetry. Length: 1-111 lines. Pays contributor's copies.

TIPS "Our guidelines are very open and ambiguous. Don't send us too much and don't make it too long. If you submit in an e-mail, use rtf. We're easy. If it works, we'll be in touch. It's a brutal world—wear your helmet."

○ TOASTED CHEESE

E-mail: editors@toasted-cheese.com. **E-mail:** submit@toasted-cheese.com. **Website:** www.toasted-cheese.com. "*Toasted Cheese* accepts submissions of previously unpublished fiction, flash fiction, creative nonfiction, and poetry. Our focus is on quality of work, not quantity. Some issues will therefore contain fewer/more pieces than previous issues. We don't restrict publication based on subject matter. We encourage submissions from innovative writers in all genres." Acquires electronic rights. Responds in 4 months to mss. Sample copy online. Follow online submission guidelines.

MAGAZINE'S NEEDS Receives 150 unsolicited mss/month. Accepts 1-10 mss/issue; 5-30 mss/year. Publishes 15 new writers/year. Send complete ms in body of e-mail; no attachments. Accepts submissions by e-mail. Sponsors awards/contests "No first drafts."

TIPS "We are looking for clean, professional writing from writers of any level. Accepted stories will be concise and compelling. We are looking for writers who are serious about the craft: tomorrow's literary stars before they're famous. Take your submission seriously, yet remember that levity is appreciated. You are submitting not to traditional 'editors' but to fellow writers who appreciate the efforts of those in the trenches. Follow online submission guidelines."

◑ TORCH: POETRY, PROSE AND SHORT STORIES BY AFRICAN AMERICAN WOMEN

3720 Gattis School Rd., Suite 800, Round Rock TX 78664. **E-mail:** info@torchpoetry.org (inquiries), poetry@torchpoetry.org (submissions). **Website:** www.torchpoetry.org. **Contact:** Amanda Johnston, editor. *TORCH: Poetry, Prose, and Short Stories by African American Women*, published semiannually online, provides "a place to publish contemporary poetry, prose, and short stories by experienced and emerging writers alike. We prefer our contributors to take risks, and offer a diverse body of work that examines and challenges preconceived notions regarding race, ethnicity, gender roles, and identity." Has published poetry by Sharon Bridgforth, Patricia Smith, Crystal Wilkinson, Tayari Jones, and Natasha Trethewey. Reads submissions April 15-August 31 only. Sometimes comments on rejected poems. Always sends prepublication galleys. No payment. "Within *TORCH*, we offer a special section called Flame that features an interview, biography, and work sample by an established writer as well as an introduction to their Spark—an emerging writer who inspires them and adds to the boundless voice of creative writing by Black women." A free online newsletter is available; see website. Acquires rights to publish accepted work in online issue and in archives. Rights revert to authors upon publication. Publishes ms 2-7 months after acceptance. Guidelines available on website.

MAGAZINE'S NEEDS Submit via e-mail only, as one MS word attachment.

TRAVEL NATURALLY

Internaturally, Inc., P.O. Box 317, Newfoundland NJ 07435-0317. (973)697-3552. **Fax:** (973)697-8313. **E-mail:** naturally@internaturally.com. **Website:** www.internaturally.com. "*Travel Naturally* looks at why millions of people believe that removing clothes in public is a good idea, and at places specifically created for that purpose—with good humor, but also in earnest.

Travel Naturally takes you to places where your personal freedom is the only agenda, and to places where textile-free living is a serious commitment." Buys first rights, buys one-time rights. Pays on publication. Editorial lead time 4 months. Sample copy for $9. Guidelines available.

○ *Travel Naturally* is 72 pages, magazine-sized, printed on glossy paper, saddle-stapled.

MAGAZINE'S NEEDS Wants poetry about the naturalness of the human body and nature; any length. Consideers previously published poems and simultaneous submissions. Accepts e-mail and fax submissions. "Name and address must be submitted with e-mail."

TIPS "*Travel Naturally* invokes the philosophies of naturism and nudism, but also activities and beliefs in the mainstream that express themselves, barely: spiritual awareness, New Age customs, pagan and religious rites, alternative and fringe lifestyle beliefs, artistic expressions, and many individual nude interests. Our higher purpose is simply to help restore our sense of self. Although the term 'nude recreation' may, for some, conjure up visions of sexual frivolities inappropriate for youngsters—because that can also be technically true—these topics are outside the scope of *Travel Naturally*. Here the emphasis is on the many varieties of human beings, of all ages and backgrounds, recreating in their most natural state, at extraordinary places, their reasons for doing so, and the benefits they derive. We incorporate a travel department to advise and book vacations in locations reviewed in travel articles."

◑ TRIBECA POETRY REVIEW

P.O. Box 2061, New York NY 10013. **E-mail:** editor@tribecareview.org. **Website:** www.tribecareview.org. **Contact:** Kenlynne Rini Mulroy, editor. *Tribeca Poetry Review*, published biennially in even-numbered years, is "a publication emerging out of the thick poetic history that is downtown New York. It seeks to expose its readers to the best smattering of poetry we can get our hands on. *TPR* will showcase new pieces by seasoned poets as well as illuminate the work of fresh voices." Acquires first North American serial rights. Reads submissions year round. Time between acceptance and publication is up to 2 years. Sometimes comments on rejected poems. Responds as soon as possible; can be up to 6 months. Guidelines on website. Now accepting electronic submissions to editor@tribecareview.org.

○ *Tribeca Poetry Review* is approximately 100 pages, digest-sized, professionally printed, flat-spine bound, with artwork cover. Press run is 1,000.

MAGAZINE'S NEEDS Submit no more than 5 poems at a time, up to 10 pages in total, to editor@tribecareview.org. No previously published poems or simultaneous submissions. Cover letter is required. "Please do not use your cover letter as a place to explain your poems. The letter is a place to introduce yourself and your work but not sell or explain either. Your name, address, contact phone, and e-mail should be on each page submitted." Wants "the kind of poetry that squirms in your head for days, hopefully longer, after reading it. Send us your best work. Will publish all forms (including traditional poesy, spoken word, or your experimental pieces) providing they translate well on the page, are intelligent, and well-crafted. New York City poets are always encouraged to submit their work, but this is *not* strictly a regional publication. Does not want "overly self-absorbed poems; pieces so abstract that all meaning and pleasure is lost on anyone but the poet; first drafts, goofy word play, trite nostalgia." Considers poetry by teens. "It's the poem itself that needs to resonate with readers, so the age of the poet means little. Occasionally, poetry by a 14 year old is more profound than the drivel generated by those adults who hang out unnecessarily in coffee shops and believe themselves 'poets.'" Pays 2 contributor's copies.

◑ TULANE REVIEW

122 Norman Mayer, New Orleans LA 70118. **E-mail:** tulane.review@gmail.com. **E-mail:** litsoc@tulane.edu. **Website:** www.tulane.edu/~litsoc/treview.html. *Tulane Review*, published biannually, is a national literary journal seeking quality submissions of prose, poetry, and art. "We consider all types of poetry." Wants "imaginative poems with bold, inventive images." Has published poetry by Tom Chandler, Ace Boggess, Carol Hamilton, and Brady Rhoades. *Tulane Review* is 70 pages, 7×9, perfect-bound, with 100# cover with full-color artwork. Receives about 1,200 poems/year, accepts about 50 per issue. Single copy: $8; subscription: $15. Make checks payable to *Tulane Review*.

○ *Tulane Review* is the recipient of an AWP Literary Magazine Design Award.

MAGAZINE'S NEEDS Submit up to 5 poems at a time. Considers simultaneous submissions; previously published pieces will be considered. Accepts e-mail submissions; no fax or disk submissions. Cover letter is required. Include 1-3 sentence biography. Reads submissions year-round. Poems are reviewed anonymously by a review board under a poetry editor's supervision. Length: 1-2 pages. Pays 2 contributor's copies.

THE TULE REVIEW

P.O. Box 160406, Sacramento CA 95816. (916)451-5569. **E-mail:** tulereview@sacramentopoetrycenter.org. **Website:** www.sacramentopoetrycenter.org. **Contact:** Theresa McCourt or Linda Collins. *The Tule Review*, published 1-2 times/year, uses "poetry, book reviews, and essays concerning contemporary poetry" Acquires first North American serial rights. Publishes ms 1-6 months after acceptance. Responds in 3-4 monts. Guidelines and upcoming themes available by e-mail, or on website.

Only accepts submissions using online submissions manager.

MAGAZINE'S NEEDS Submit up to 6 poems at a time using online submission form. Provide short, 5 line bio. Reads submissions year round. Wants "all styles and forms of poetry." Primarily publishes poets living in the greater Sacramento area, but accepts work from anywhere. Length: no more than 96 lines. Pays 1 contributor's copy.

TUNDRA: THE JOURNAL OF THE SHORT POEM

22230 NE 28th Place, Sammamish WA 98074-6408. **E-mail:** welchm@aol.com. **Website:** http://sites.google.com/site/tundrashortpoem/. **Contact:** Michael Dylan Welch, editor. *Tundra: The Journal of the Short Poem* showcases all short poetry, including haiku, tanka, and other genres. Wants "short poems of 13 or fewer lines rooted in immediate and objective imagery, including haiku and tanka." Does not want religious, topical, or confessional poetry. Has published poetry by Dana Gioia, X.J. Kennedy, Jane Hirshfield, Peter Pereira, Robert Bly, and Madeleine DeFrees. *Tundra* is 128 pages, digest-sized, offset-printed, perfect-bound, with glossy cover. Receives about 14,000 poems/year, accepts less than 1%. Press run is 1,200 (700 subscribers, 10 libraries, 50 shelf sales); 10 distributed free to such places as poetry centers. Single copy: $9; subscription: $21 for 3 issues. Make checks payable to Michael Dylan Welch. Acquires first rights. Publishes ms 1 year after acceptance. Responds in 3-4 months. Guidelines available for SASE, by e-mail, or on website.

MAGAZINE'S NEEDS Submit 3-5 poems at a time ("up to 10 is okay if as short as haiku"). Accepts e-mail submissions (pasted into body of message; no attach-

ments); no disk submissions. "Always include your full postal address with each e-mail submission." Cover letter is optional; "okay the first time you submit, but unnecessary thereafter unless you write something you are sure the editor needs to know. *Tundra* does not publish bios, so there's no need to include them except for the editor's information. Please include a #10 SASE with sufficient postage for return of the manuscript or for a response." Pays 1 contributor's copy.

TIPS "If your work centers on immediate and objective imagery, *Tundra* is interested. All poems must be 13 or fewer lines, with only very rare exceptions (where each line is very short). If you think that a haiku is merely 5-7-5 syllables, then I do not want to see your work (see 'Becoming a Haiku Poet' online at http://sites.google.com/site/graceguts/essays/becoming-a-haiku-poet for reasons why). Due to the excessive volume of inappropriate submissions for *Tundra* in the past, I now encourage only well-established poets to submit."

TURTLE MAGAZINE FOR PRESCHOOL KIDS

U.S. Kids, 1100 Waterway Blvd., Indianapolis IN 46202. **Website:** www.turtlemag.org. "Colorful and entertaining..perfect for reading aloud." *Turtle Magazine for Preschool Kids* uses read-aloud stories, especially suitable for bedtime or naptime reading, for children ages 2-5. Also uses poems, simple science experiments, easy recipes and health-related articles. Wants light-hearted poetry appropriate for the age group. Buys all rights. Pays on publication. Responds in 3 months to queries. Sample copy for $3.99. Guidelines free with SASE and on website.

MAGAZINE'S NEEDS "We're especially looking for short poems (4-8 lines) and slightly longer action rhymes to foster creative movement in preschoolers. We also use short verse on our inside front cover and back cover." Pays $25 minimum.

TIPS "Writers should present their material in a way that is appropriate for kids, but which does not talk down to them. Reading our editorial guidelines is not enough. Careful study of current issues will acquaint writers with each title's personality, various departments, and regular features. We are looking for more short rebus stories, easy science experiments, and simple, nonfiction health articles. We are trying to include more material for our youngest readers. Material must be entertaining and written from a healthy lifestyle perspective. Our need for health-related material, especially features that encourage fitness, is ongoing. Health subjects must be age-appropriate. When writing about them, think creatively and lighten up! Always keep in mind that in order for a story or article to educate preschoolers, it first must be entertaining—warm and engaging, exciting, or genuinely funny. Here the trend is toward leaner, lighter writing. There will be a growing need for interactive activities. Writers might want to consider developing an activity to accompany their concise manuscripts."

○ UP AND UNDER: THE QND REVIEW

P.O. Box 115, Hainesport NJ 08036. **E-mail:** qndpoets@ yahoo.com. **Website:** www.quickanddirtypoets.com. **Contact:** Kendall Bell, editor. *Up and Under: The QND Review,* published annually in March, is "a journal with an eclectic mix of poetry: sex, death, politics, IKEA, Mars, food, and jug handles alongside a smorgasbord of other topics covered in such diverse forms as the sonnet, villanelle, haiku, and free verse. We are interested in excellent poetry with no bias between free verse or traditional forms." Does not want "greeting card verse, graphic pornography." Has published poetry by Dan Maguire, Gina Larkin, Leonard Gontarek, Autumn Konopka, John Grey and Taylor Graham. *Up and Under* is 50-60 pages, digest-sized, laser-printed, saddle-stapled, with card cover with photograph, includes ads. Receives about 300 poems/year, accepts about 30 (or 10%). Press run is 100. Single copy: $7. Chapbooks are available online or through U.S. Mail. Make checks payable to Kendall Bell. Acquires one-time rights. Publishes ms 3-6 months after acceptance. Responds in 2-3 months. Guidelines available in magazine, for SASE, or on website.

MAGAZINE'S NEEDS Submit up to 5 poems. Length: no limit. Pays 1 contributor's copy.

◐○ URTHONA MAGAZINE

71 The Broadway, Granchester, Cambridge CB3 9NQ, UK. **E-mail:** urthonamag@gmail.com. **Website:** www. urthona.com. *Urthona,* published biannually, explores the arts and Western culture from a Buddhist perspective. Wants "poetry rousing the imagination." Does not want "undigested autobiography, political, or New Agey poems." Acquires one-time rights. Publishes ms 8 months after acceptance. Responds in 6 months.

○ *Urthona* is 60 pages, A4, offset-printed, saddle-stapled, with 4-color glossy cover; includes ads. Receives about 300 poems/year, accepts about 40. Press run is 1,200 (200 subscribers, plus shelf

sales in Australia and America). "See website for current subscription rates." Sample (including guidelines): $7.99 USD, $8.99 CAD. Has published poetry by Peter Abbs, Robert Bly, and Peter Redgrove.

MAGAZINE'S NEEDS Submit 6 poems at a time. No previously published poems or simultaneous submissions. Accepts e-mail submissions (as attachment). Cover letter is preferred. Poems are circulated to an editorial board and are read and selected by poetry editor. Other editors have right of veto. Reviews books/chapbooks of poetry and other magazines in 600 words. Send materials for review consideration. Pays 1 contributor's copy.

U.S. 1 WORKSHEETS

U.S. 1 Poets' Cooperative, U.S. 1 Worksheets, P.O. Box 127, Kingston NJ 08528. **E-mail:** info@US1Poets.com. **Website:** www.us1poets.com. "*U.S. 1 Worksheets,* published annually, uses high-quality poetry and, on occasion, short fiction. We prefer complex, well-written work. Responds in 3-6 months to mss. Guidelines available online.

MAGAZINE'S NEEDS Submit up to 5 poems at a time. Considers simultaneous submissions if indicated; no previously published poems. "We are looking for well-crafted poetry with a focused point of view." Submit no more than 7 pages.

ADDITIONAL INFORMATION The U.S. 1 Poets' Cooperative co-sponsors (with the Princeton Public Library) a series of monthly poetry readings (U.S. 1 Poets Invite) at the Princeton Public Library. "There is no formal membership, only the willingness of participants to share their work."

TIPS "Mss are accepted from April 15-June 30 and are read by rotating editors from the cooperative. Send us something unusual, something we haven't seen before, but make sure it's poetry. Proofread carefully."

U.S. CATHOLIC

Claretian Publications, 205 W. Monroe St., Chicago IL 60606. (312)236-7782. **Fax:** (312)236-8207. **E-mail:** editors@uscatholic.org. **E-mail:** submissions@uscatholic.org. **Website:** www.uscatholic.org. "*U.S. Catholic* is dedicated to the belief that it makes a difference whether you're Catholic. We invite and help our readers explore the wisdom of their faith tradition and apply their faith to the challenges of the 21st century." Buys all rights. Pays on acceptance. Publishes ms an average of 2-3 months after acceptance. Responds in 1 month to queries. Responds in 2 months to mss. Editorial lead time 8 months. Sample copy for large SASE. Guidelines by e-mail or on website.

○ Please include SASE with written ms.

MAGAZINE'S NEEDS Submit 3-5 poems at a time. Lines/poem: 50 maximum. Considers simultaneous submissions; no previously published poems. Accepts e-mail submissions (pasted into body of message; no attachments). Cover letter is preferred. No light verse. Length: 50 lines. Pays $75.

○○❸ VALLUM: CONTEMPORARY POETRY

P.O. Box 598, Victoria Station, Montreal QC H3Z 2Y6, Canada. (514)937-8946. **Fax:** (514)937-8946. **E-mail:** info@vallummag.com. **Website:** www.vallummag. com. **Contact:** Joshua Auerbach and Eleni Zisimatos, editors. "Poetry/fine arts magazine published twice/ year. Publishes exciting interplay of poets and artists. Content for magazine is selected according to themes listed on website. Material is not filed but is returned by SASE. E-mail response is preferred. Seeking exciting, unpublished, traditional or avant-garde poetry that reflects contemporary experience." Buys first North American serial rights. Copyright remains with the author. Pays on publication. Sample copies available for $10. Guidelines available on website.

○ *Vallum* is 100 pages, digest sized (7x8½), digitally printed, perfect-bound, with color images on coated stock cover. Includes ads. Press run is 1,800. Single copy: $10 CDN; subscription: $17/ year CDN; $21 U.S. (shipping included). Make checks payable to *Vallum*.

MAGAZINE'S NEEDS Does not want "hate" poetry. Pays $30 honorarium for accepted poems.

ADDITIONAL INFORMATION "The Vallum Chapbook Series publishes 2-3 chapbooks by both well-known and emerging poets. Past editions include *Gospel of X* by George Elliott Clarke, *The Art of Fugue* by Jan Zwicky and *Address* by Franz Wright. *Vallum* does not currently accept unsolicited mss for this project."

CONTEST/AWARD OFFERINGS "Sponsors annual contest. First Prize: $500, Second Prize: $250 and publication in an issue of *Vallum*. Honourable mentions may be selected but are not eligible for cash prizes. Submit 4-5 poems. Entry fee: $20 USD / CAD (includes subscription to *Vallum*). Deadline: June 30. Guidelines available in magazine, by e-mail, and on website. Poems may be submitted in any style or on any subject;

max. 4-5 poems, up to 25-40 lines per poem. Entries should be labelled 'Vallum Contest' and submitted by regular mail. Submissions are not returned. In addition to cash prizes, winners will be announced on our website and published in the forthcoming issue."

① VALPARAISO POETRY REVIEW

Department of English, Valparaiso University, Valparaiso IN 46383-6493. (219)464-5278. **Fax:** (219)464-5511. **E-mail:** vpr@valpo.edu. **Website:** www.valpo. edu/vpr/. **Contact:** Edward Byrne, editor. *Valparaiso Poetry Review: Contemporary Poetry and Poetics*, published semiannually online, accepts "submissions of unpublished poetry, book reviews, author interviews, and essays on poetry or poetics that have not yet appeared online and for which the rights belong to the author. Query for anything else." Wants poetry of any length or style, free verse or traditional forms. Has published poetry by Charles Wright, Cornelius Eady, Dorianne Laux, Dave Smith, Claudia Emerson, Billy Collins, Brian Turner, Daisy Fried, Stanley Plumly, and Annie Finch. Receives about 9,000 poems/year, accepts about 1%. Acquires one-time rights. "All rights remain with author." Publishes ms 6-12 months after acceptance. Responds in 6 weeks. Guidelines online.

MAGAZINE'S NEEDS Submit 3-5 poems at a time (no more than 5). Considers previously published poems ("original publication must be identified to ensure proper credit") and simultaneous submissions. Accepts e-mail submissions (pasted into body of message, no attachments); no fax or disk submissions. **Postal submissions preferred.** Cover letter is preferred. Include SASE. Reads submissions year round. Seldom comments on rejected poems. Reviews books of poetry in single- and multi-book format. Send materials for review consideration.

❸① VAN GOGH'S EAR: BEST WORLD POETRY & PROSE

French Connection Press, 12 rue Lamartine, Paris 75009, France. (33)(1)4016-0535. **Fax:** (33)(1)4016-0701. **E-mail:** info@frenchcx.com. **Website:** www.frenchcx. com. *Van Gogh's Ear*, published annually in April, is an anthology series "devoted to publishing powerful poetry and prose in English and English translations by major voices and innovative new talents from around the globe." Poetry published in *Van Gogh's Ear* has appeared in *The Best American Poetry*. Acquires one-time rights. Time between acceptance and publication is 1 year. Responds in 9 months. Seldom comments on rejections. Always sends prepublication galleys. "Every submission is closely read by all members of the editorial board and voted upon. Our continued existence, and continued ability to read your work, depends mainly on subscriptions/donations. Therefore, we must ask that you at least purchase a sample copy before submitting work." Guidelines available in anthology or on website.

○ *Van Gogh's Ear* is 280 pages, digest-sized, offset-printed, perfect-bound, with 4-color matte cover with commissioned artwork. Receives about 1,000 poems/year, accepts about 30%. Press run is 2,000 (105 subscribers, 25 libraries, 1,750 shelf/online sales); 120 distributed free to contributors and reviewers. Single copy: $19; subscription: $36 for 2 years. Has published poetry by Tony Curtis, Yoko Ono, James Dean, Xaviera Hollander, and Charles Manson.

MAGAZINE'S NEEDS Submit 6 poems at a time. No previously published poems or simultaneous submissions. No fax, e-mail, or disk submissions. Cover letter is preferred. "**Send to the French Connection Press address only!** Please include SASE (or SAE with IRCs) or e-mail address along with a brief bio of up to 120 words." Reads submissions May 1-October 31. **Charges $10 (USD) reading fee for non-subscribers.** Lines/poem: 165 maximum. Pays 1 contributor's copy.

TIPS "As a 501(c)(3) nonprofit enterprise, *Van Gogh's Ear* needs the support of individual poets, writers, and readers to survive. Any donation, large or small, will help *Van Gogh's Ear* continue to publish the best cross-section of contemporary poetry and prose. Because of being an anglophone publication based in France, *Van Gogh's Ear* is unable to get any grants or funding. Your contribution will be tax-deductible. Make donation checks payable to Committee on Poetry-*VGE*, and mail them (donations **only**) to the Allen Ginsberg Trust, P.O. Box 582, Stuyvesant Station, New York NY 10009. All U.S. checks/money orders for reading fees, subscriptions, and purchases must be made out to French Connection Press and sent to Michael Hathaway, 522 E. South Ave., St. John KS 67576-2212."

VEGETARIAN JOURNAL

P.O. Box 1463, Baltimore MD 21203-1463. (410)366-8343. **E-mail:** vrg@vrg.org. **Website:** www.vrg.org. **Contact:** Debra Wasserman, editor. Estab. 1982. *Vegetarian Journal* is 36 pages, magazine-sized, professionally printed, saddle-stapled, with glossy card cover. Press run is 20,000. Sample: $3. The Vegetarian Re-

source Group offers an annual contest for ages 18 and under: $50 prize in 3 age categories for the best contribution on any aspect of vegetarianism. "Most entries are essay, but we would accept poetry with enthusiasm." **Deadline:** May 1 (postmark). Details available at website: http://www.vrg.org/essay/

MAGAZINE'S NEEDS "Please, no submissions of poetry from adults; 18 and under only."

TIPS Areas most open to freelancers are recipe section and feature articles. "Review magazine first to learn our style. Send query letter with photocopy sample of line drawings of food."

◐○ VERANDAH LITERARY & ART JOURNAL

Faculty of Arts, Deakin University, 221 Burwood Hwy., Burwood, Victoria 3125, Australia. (61)(3)9251-7134. **E-mail:** verandah@deakin.edu.au. **Website:** www.deakin.edu.au/verandah. *Verandah*, published annually in September, is "a high-quality literary journal edited by professional writing students. It aims to give voice to new and innovative writers and artists." Acquires first Australian publishing rights. Some prizes awarded. Pays 1 contributor's copy, "with prizes awarded accordingly." Sample: $20 AUD. Guidelines available on website.

○ "The first edition of *Verandah* was launched in 1985, beneath the shade of the 'wide verandahs' of Victoria College. Established as a student-run publication, from its inception *Verandah* has attracted high quality work by both established and emerging writers and artists for annual publication." Has published work by Christos Tsiolka, Dorothy Porter, Seamus Heaney, Les Murray, Ed Burger, and John Muk Muk Burke. *Verandah* is 120 pages, professionally printed on glossy stock, flat-spined, with full-color glossy card cover.

MAGAZINE'S NEEDS Submit by mail or e-mail. However, electronic version of work must be available if accepted by *Verandah*. **Do not submit work without the required submission form (available for download on website).** Reads submissions by June 1 deadline (postmark). Length: 100 lines maximum.

⊘ VERSE

English Department, University of Richmond, Richmond VA 23173. **Website:** http://versemag.blogspot.com; http://english.richmond.edu/resources/verse.html. **Contact:** Brian Henry, co-editor; Andrew Zawacki, co-editor. *Verse*, published 3 times/year, is "an international poetry journal which also publishes interviews with poets, essays on poetry, and book reviews." Wants "no specific kind; we look for high-quality, innovative poetry. Our focus is not only on American poetry, but on all poetry written in English, as well as translations." Has published poetry by James Tate, John Ashbery, Barbara Guest, Gustaf Sobin, and Rae Armantrout. *Verse* is 128-416 pages, digest-sized, professionally printed, perfect-bound, with card cover. Receives about 5,000 poems/year, accepts 1%. Press run is 1,000. Single copy: $10; subscription: $18 for individuals, $39 for institutions. Sample: $6. Everyone submitting work to the print magazine will receive a free copy of Verse (cover price $12-15). All contributors to the print magazine will receive at least $200 (possibly more) plus two copies and a one-year subscription. There is no reading fee for submissions to the *Verse* site and no payment for contributors to the *Verse* site. All submissions to the print magazine will also be considered for the *Verse* site, so if a portfolio isn't selected for the print magazine, individual pieces still might be accepted for the *Verse* site.

TIPS "Read widely and deeply. Avoid inundating a magazine with submissions; constant exposure will not increase your chances of getting accepted."

THE VIEW FROM HERE MAGAZINE

E-mail: editor@viewfromheremagazine.com; rear.view.poetry@gmail.com. **Website:** www.viewfromheremagazine.com. **Contact:** Mike French, senior editor; Claire King, managing fiction editor. "We are a print and online literary magazine designed and edited by an international team. We bring an entertaining mix of wit and insight all packaged in beautifully designed pages." Buys first rights.

MAGAZINE'S NEEDS "The Rear View Poetry realm showcases new, emerging talent as well as the seasoned voice. Our poets are word wizards, prophets, mystics and lyricists who are afraid to demand attention by painting the world with their vision." May submit 3 poems at a time.

TIPS "Due to the amount of submissions, work sent without a brief cover letter or introduction will be dismissed."

THE VIRGINIA QUARTERLY REVIEW

P.O. Box 400223, Charlottesville VA 22904. **E-mail:** vqr@vqronline.org. **Website:** www.vqronline.org. *The Virginia Quarterly Review* uses about 45-50 pages of poetry in each issue. No length or subject restrictions. Issues have largely included lyric and narrative free verse, most of which features a strong message or powerful voice. *The Virginia Quarterly Review* is 256 pages, digest-sized, flat-spined. Press run is 7,000. Responds in 1-3 months. Guidelines on website.

MAGAZINE'S NEEDS Submit up to 5 poems at a time. No simultaneous submissions. Accepts online submissions only at http://vqronline.org/submission/. Pays $5/line.

CONTEST/AWARD OFFERINGS Sponsors the Emily Clark Balch Prize for Poetry, an annual award of $1,000 given to the best poem or group of poems published in the *Review* during the year.

THE WALLACE STEVENS JOURNAL

University of Antwerp, Prinsstraat 13, B-200 Antwerp, Belgium. **E-mail:** bart.eeckhout@ua.ac.be. **Website:** www.press.jhu.edu/journals/wallace_stevens_journal. **Contact:** James Finnegan, poetry editor: jforjames@aol.com. *The Wallace Stevens Journal*, published semi-annually by the Wallace Stevens Society, uses "poems about or in the spirit of Wallace Stevens or having some relation to his work. No bad parodies of Stevens's anthology pieces."

The Wallace Stevens Journal is 100-160 pages, digest-sized, typeset, flat-spined, with glossy cover with art. Receives 200 poems/year, accepts 15-20. Press run is 400 + institutional subscriptions through Project Muse (Johns Hopkins University Press). Subscription: $30 (includes membership in the Wallace Stevens Society). Has published poetry by David Athey, Jacqueline Marcus, Charles Wright, X.J. Kennedy, A.M. Juster, and Robert Creeley.

WATERWAYS: POETRY IN THE MAINSTREAM

Ten Penny Players, Inc., 393 Saint Pauls Ave., Staten Island NY 10304-2127. (718)442-7429. **Website:** www.tenpennyplayers.org. **Contact:** Barbara Fisher and Richard Spiegel, poetry editors. *Waterways: Poetry in the Mainstream*, published 11 times/year, prints work by adult poets. "We publish theme issues and are trying to increase an audience for poetry and the printed and performed word. While we do 'themes,' sometimes an idea for a future magazine is inspired by a submission, so we try to remain open to poets' inspirations. Poets should be guided, however, by the fact that we are children's and animal rights advocates and are a NYC press. We are open to reading material from people we have never published, writing in traditional and experimental poetry forms." Does not want "haiku or rhyming poetry; never use material of an explicit sexual nature." Acquires one-time publication rights. Responds in less than 1 month. Sometimes comments on rejected poems. Sample: $5. Guidelines available for SASE or on website.

Ⓠ *Waterways* is 40 pages, 4¼x7, photocopied from various type styles, saddle-stapled, with matte card cover. Back issues of *Waterways* are published online at www.tenpennyplayers.org and at scribd.com in addition to being available in the limited printing paper edition. Accepts 60% of poems submitted. Press run is 150. Subscription: $45. Has published poetry by Ida Fasel, Will Inman, and Richard Kostelanetz.

MAGAZINE'S NEEDS Submit less than 10 poems at a time (for first submission). Considers simultaneous submissions. Accepts e-mail submissions (pasted into body of message). Pays 1 contributor's copy.

ADDITIONAL INFORMATION Ten Penny Players publishes chapbooks "by children and young adults only—not by submission—they come through our workshops in the library and schools. Adult poets are published through our Bard Press imprint, **by invitation only**. Books evolve from the relationship we develop with writers we publish in *Waterways* and to whom we would like to give more exposure."

TIPS "Since we've taken the time to be very specific in our response, writers should take seriously our comments and not waste their emotional energy and our time sending material that isn't within our area of interest. Sending for our theme sheet and a sample issue and then objectively thinking about the writer's own work is practical and wise. Mss that arrive without a return envelope are not sent back."

⬤🌎 WEBER: THE CONTEMPORARY WEST

Weber State University, 1405 University Circle, Ogden UT 84408-1405. **Website:** www.weber.edu/weberjournal. *Weber: The Contemporary West*, published 3 times/year, is "an interdisciplinary journal interested in relevant works covering a wide range of topics." Wants "three or four poems; we publish multiple poems from a poet." Does not want "poems that are flippant, prurient, sing-song, or preachy." Has published poetry by Naomi Shihab Nye, Carolyn Forche, Stephen Dunn, Billy Col-

lins, William Kloefkorn, David Lee, Gary Gildner, and Robert Dana. *Weber* is 150 pages, offset-printed on acid-free paper, perfect-bound, with color cover. Receives about 250-300 poems/year, accepts 30-40. Press run is 1,000; 90% libraries. Subscription: $20 ($30 for institutions); $40 for outside the US. Sample: $10 (back issue). Acquires all rights. Copyright reverts to author after first printing. Publishes ms 15 months after acceptance. Responds in 6 months. Themes and guidelines available in magazine, for SASE, by e-mail, or on website.

Ⓠ Poetry published in *Weber* has appeared in *The Best American Poetry*.

MAGAZINE'S NEEDS Submit 3-4 poems at a time, 2 copies of each (one without name). Considers simultaneous submissions; no previously published poems. Cover letter is preferred. Poems are selected by an anonymous (blind) evaluation. Always sends prepublication galleys. Pays 2 contributor's copies, a year's subscription, and a small honorarium ($100-300) depending on fluctuating grant monies.

CONTEST/AWARD OFFERINGS The Dr. Sherwin W. Howard Poetry Award, a $500 cash prize, is awarded annually to the author of the best set of poems published in *Weber* during the previous year. The competition is announced each year in the Spring/Summer issue.

WEST BRANCH

Stadler Center for Poetry, Bucknell University, Lewisburg PA 17837-2029. (570)577-1853. **Fax:** (570)577-1885. **E-mail:** westbranch@bucknell.edu. **Website:** www.bucknell.edu/westbranch. *West Branch* publishes poetry, fiction, and nonfiction in both traditional and innovative styles. Buys first North American serial rights. Pays on publication. Sample copy for $3. Guidelines available online.

MAGAZINE'S NEEDS Pays $20-100 ($10/page).

TIPS "All submissions must be sent via our online submission manager. Please see website for guidelines. We recommend that you acquaint yourself with the magazine before submitting."

🌎⬤🌎 WESTERLY

Westerly Centre (M202), The University of Western Australia, 35 Stirling Hwy., Crawley WA 6009, Australia. **E-mail:** westerly@uwa.edu.au. **Website:** http://westerly.uwa.edu.au. *Westerly*, published annually in July and November, prints quality short fiction, poetry, literary critical, socio-historical articles, and book reviews with special attention given to Australia, Asia, and the Indian Ocean region. "We don't dictate to writers on rhyme, style, experimentation, or anything else. We are willing to publish short or long poems. We do assume a reasonably well-read, intelligent audience. Past issues of *Westerly* provide the best guides. Not consciously an academic magazine."

🞰 *Westerly* is about 200 pages, digest-sized, "electronically printed." Press run is 1,200. Subscription information available on website.

MAGAZINE'S NEEDS Submit up to 3 poems or 1 short story (2 if quite short-suggested maximum length 5,000 words) at a time. No simultaneous submissions. Submit via post or e-mail. Cover letters should be brief and non-confessional. All mss must show the name and address of the sender and should be single spaced in size 12 Times New Roman font. Deadline for July edition is March 31; deadline for November edition is July 31. Time between acceptance and publication may be up to 1 year, depending on when work is submitted. "Please wait for a response before forwarding any additional submissions for consideration." Contributors receive payment, plus 1 complimentary copy. Acquires first publication rights; requests acknowledgment on reprints. Reviews books of poetry in multi-book format in an annual review essay. Send materials for review consideration. For further information on contributing, see website.

CONTEST/AWARD OFFERINGS The Patricia Hackett Prize (value approximately $750 AUD) is awarded annually for the best contribution published in the previous year's issue of *Westerly*.

WESTERN HUMANITIES REVIEW

University of Utah, English Department, 255 S. Central Campus Dr., Room 3500, Salt Lake City UT 84112-0494. (801)581-6070. **Fax:** (801)585-5167. **E-mail:** whr@mail.hum.utah.edu. **Website:** www.hum.utah.edu/whr. **Contact:** Barry Weller, editor; Nate Liederbach, managing editor. Buys one-time rights. Pays in contributor copies. Publishes ms an average of 1 year after acceptance. Responds in 6 months. Sample copy for $10. Guidelines available online.

MAGAZINE'S NEEDS Considers simultaneous submissions but no more than 5 poems or 25 pages per reading period. No fax or e-mail submissions. Reads submissions October 1-April 1 only. Wants "quality poetry of any form, including translations." Has published poetry by Charles Simic, Olena Kalytiak Davis, Ravi Shankar, Karen Volkman, Dan Beachy-Quick,

Lucie Brock-Broido, Christine Hume, and Dan Chiasson. Innovative prose poems may be submitted as fiction or nonfiction to the appropriate editor. Pays 2 contributor's copies.

CONTEST/AWARD OFFERINGS Sponsors an annual contest for Utah writers.

TIPS "Because of changes in our editorial staff, we urge familiarity with recent issues of the magazine. We do not publish writer's guidelines because we think that the magazine itself conveys an accurate picture of our requirements. Please, no e-mail submissions."

WESTVIEW: A JOURNAL OF WESTERN OKLAHOMA

Southwestern Oklahoma State University, 100 Campus Dr., Weatherford OK 73096. **E-mail:** james.silver@swosu.edu; westview@swosu.edu. *Westview: A Journal of Western Oklahoma*, published semiannually, is "particularly interested in writers from the Southwest; however, we are open to quality work by poets from elsewhere. We publish free verse, prose poems, and formal poetry."

🞰 Has published poetry by Carolynne Wright, Miller Williams, Walter McDonald, Robert Cooperman, Alicia Ostriker, and James Whitehead. *Westview* is 64 pages, magazine-sized, perfect-bound, with full-color glossy card cover. Receives about 500 poems/year; accepts 7%. Press run is 700 (300 subscribers, about 25 libraries). Subscription: $15/2 years. Sample: $6.

MAGAZINE'S NEEDS Submit 5 poems at a time. Cover letter is required, including biographical data for contributor's note. Comments on submissions "when close." Mss are circulated to an editorial board. Responds within 4-6 months. Pays 1 contributor's copy.

WESTWARD QUARTERLY: THE MAGAZINE OF FAMILY READING

Laudemont Press, P.O. Box 369, Hamilton IL 62341. (800)440-4043. **E-mail:** editor@wwquarterly.com. **Website:** www.wwquarterly.com. **Contact:** Shirley Anne Leonard, editor. *WestWard Quarterly: The Magazine of Family Reading* prints poetry. Wants "all forms, including rhyme—we welcome inspirational, positive, reflective, humorous material promoting nobility, compassion, and courage." Does not want "experimental or avant-garde forms, offensive language, depressing or negative poetry." Considers poetry by children and teens. Has published poetry by Wynne Alexander, Leland Jamieson, Joyce I. Johnson, Michael

Keshigian, Richard Luftig, Arlene Mandell, Dennis Ross, J. Alvin Speers, Jane Stuart, Charles Waugaman. *WestWard Quarterly* is 32 pages, digest-sized, laser-printed, saddle-stapled, with inkjet color cover with scenic photos, includes ads. Receives about 1,500 poems/year, accepts about 12%. Press run is 150 (60 subscribers). Single copy: $4 ($6 foreign); subscription: $15/year ($18 foreign). Contributors to an issue may order extra copies at a discounted price. Make checks payable to Laudemont Press. Acquires one-time rights. Time between acceptance and publication is "months." Responds in "weeks." Often comments on rejected poems. Guidelines available for SASE, by e-mail, or on website.

Every issue includes a "Featured Writer" and a piece on improving writing skills and a piece on improving writing skills or writing different forms of poetry.

MAGAZINE'S NEEDS Submit up to 5 poems at a time. Considers previously published poems and simultaneous submissions. Prefers e-mail submissions (pasted into body of message); no disk submissions. Reads submissions year round. Lines/poem: 40 maximum. Pays 1 contributor's copy.

WHISKEY ISLAND MAGAZINE

Rhodes Tower 1636, Cleveland OH 44115. (216)687-2000. **E-mail:** whiskeyisland@csuohio.edu. **Website:** www.csuohio.edu/class/english/whiskeyisland. "This is a nonprofit literary magazine that has been published (in one form or another) by students of Cleveland State University for over 30 years. Also features the Annual Student Creative Writing Contest." Responds in 3 months to mss.

"We accept original poetry, prose, and art submissions from August 15 through May 1 of each year. We accept simultaneous submissions and ask that you identify them as such in your cover letter. No multiple submissions, please, and no previously published work either. Reporting time is about 3 months."

MAGAZINE'S NEEDS "Submit 3-5 poems at one time. Please combine all the poems you wish to submit into one document."

TIPS "See submissions page. Wait at least a year before submitting again."

WICKED ALICE

dancing girl press, 410 S. Michigan #921, Chicago IL 60605. **E-mail:** wickedalicepoetry@yahoo.com. **Website:** www.sundresspublications.com/wickedalice.

Contact: Kristy Bowen, editor. "*Wicked Alice* is a women-centered poetry journal dedicated to publishing quality work by both sexes, depicting and exploring the female experience." Wants "work that has a strong sense of image and music. Work that is interesting and surprising, with innovative, sometimes unusual, use of language. We love humor when done well, strangenes, wackiness. Hybridity, collage, intertexuality." Does not want greeting card verse. Has published poetry by Daniela Olszewska, Rebecca Loudon, Robyn Art, Simone Muench, Brandi Homan, Karyna McGlynn. Receives about 500 poems/year, accepts about 8%. Acquires one-time rights. Responds in 1-6 months. Guidelines on website.

MAGAZINE'S NEEDS Wants "work that has a strong sense of image and music. Work that is interesting and surprising, with innovative, sometimes unusual, use of language. We love humor when done well, strangenes, wackiness. Hybridity, collage, intertexuality." Does not want greeting card verse.

WILD GOOSE POETRY REVIEW

Hickory NC 28235-5009. **E-mail:** asowens1@yahoo.com. **Website:** www.wildgoosepoetryreview.com. *Wild Goose Poetry Review*, published quarterly online, is "looking for good contemporary poetry. No particular biases. Enjoy humor, strong imagery, strong lines, narrative, lyric, etc. Not a fan of abstraction, cliche, form for the sake of form, shock for the sake of shock. As in any good poem, everything should be purposeful." Rights revert to poet upon publication. Time between acceptance and publication is up to 3 months. Usually responds to mss within 1 month.

Receives more than 1,000 poems/year, accepts less than 10%. No previously published poems or simultaneous submissions. Reviews books/chapbooks of poetry. Send materials for review consideration to Scott Owens. Has published poetry by Anthony Abbott, Karen Douglass, Lisa Zaran.

MAGAZINE'S NEEDS Accepts e-mail submissions only, pasted into body of e-mail; no attachments; no disk submissions. Cover letter is preferred; include bio. Reads submissions year round.

WILD VIOLET

P.O. Box 39706, Philadelphia PA 19106. **E-mail:** wildvioletmagazine@yahoo.com. **Website:** www.wildviolet.net. **Contact:** Alyce Wilson, editor. Guidelines online at website.

MAGAZINE'S NEEDS *Wild Violet*, published quarterly online, aims "to make the arts more accessible, to make a place for the arts in modern life." Wants "poetry that is well crafted, that engages thought, that challenges or uplifts the reader. We have published free verse, haiku, blank verse, and other forms. If the form suits the poem, we will consider any form." Does not want "abstract, self-involved poetry; poorly managed form; excessive rhyming; self-referential poems that do not show why the speaker is sad, happy, or in love." Has published poetry by Lyn Lifshin, Andrew H. Oerke, Erik Kestler, Anselm Brocki, Carol Frith, Richard Fammereeé, Joanna Weston and Graham Burchell. Accepts about 15% of work submitted.

HOW TO CONTACT Submit 3-5 poems at a time. Considers simultaneous submissions (with notification); no previously published poems. Accepts e-mail submissions (pasted into body of message, or as text or Word attachment); no disk submissions. Cover letter is preferred. Reads submissions year round. Submit seasonal poems 3 months in advance. Time between acceptance and publication is 3 months. "Decisions on acceptance or rejection are made by the editor." Seldom comments on rejected poems, unless requested. Occasionally publishes theme issues. Guidelines available by e-mail or on website. Responds in up to 3 months. Pays by providing a bio and link on contributor's page. Requests electronic rights to publish and archive accepted works. Reviews books/chapbooks of poetry in 250 words, single-book format. Query for review consideration.

CONTEST/AWARD OFFERINGS Sponsors an annual poetry contest, offering 1st Prize: $100 and publication in *Wild Violet*; 2 Honorable Mentions will also be published. Guidelines available by e-mail or on website. **Entry fee:** $5/poem. Judged by independent judges.

TIPS "We look for stories that are well-paced and show character and plot development. Even short shorts should do more than simply paint a picture. Manuscripts stand out when the author's voice is fresh and engaging. Avoid muddying your story with too many characters and don't attempt to shock the reader with an ending you have not earned. Experiment with styles and structures, but don't resort to experimentation for its own sake."

◑ WILLARD & MAPLE

163 S. Willard St., Freeman 302, Box 34, Burlington VT 05401. (802)860-2700 ext.2462. **E-mail:** willardand-maple@champlain.edu. *Willard & Maple*, published annually in spring, is a student-run literary magazine from Champlain College's Professional Writing Program that considers short fiction, essays, reviews, fine art, and poetry by adults, children and teens." Wants "creative work of the highest quality." Does not want any submissions over 10 typed pages in length; all submissions must be in English. Pays on publication for one-time rights. Time between acceptance and publication is less than 1 year. Responds in 6 months to queries; 6 months to mss. Writer's guidelines for SASE or send e-mail.

○ *Willard & Maple* is 200 pages, digest-sized, digitally printed, perfect-bound. Receives about 500 poems/year, accepts about 20%. Press run is 600 (80 subscribers, 4 libraries); 200 are distributed free to the Champlain College writing community. Single copy: $12. Contact Lulu Press for contributor's copy.

MAGAZINE'S NEEDS Submit up to 5 poems at a time. No previously published poems. Accepts e-mail and disk submissions. Cover letter is required. "Please provide current contact information including an e-mail address. Single-space submissions, 1 poem/page." Reads submissions September 1-March 31. "All editors receive a blind copy to review. They meet weekly throughout the academic year. These meetings consist of the submissions being read aloud, discussed, and voted upon." Seldom comments on rejected poems. Occasionally publishes theme issues. Upcoming themes available by e-mail. Reviews books/chapbooks of poetry and other magazines/journals in 1,200 words. Send materials for review consideration to the poetry editor. Lines/poem: 100 maximum. Pays 2 contributor's copies.

TIPS "The power of imagination makes us infinite."

WILLOW REVIEW

College of Lake County Publications, College of Lake County, 19351 W. Washington St., Grayslake IL 60030-1198. (847)543-2956. **E-mail:** com426@clcillinois.edu. **Website:** www.clcillinois.edu/community/willowreview.asp. **Contact:** Michael Latza, editor. *Willow Review*, published annually, is interested in poetry, creative nonfiction, and fiction of high quality. "We have no preferences as to form, style, or subject, as long as each poem stands on its own as art and communicates ideas." All rights revert to author upon publication. Pays on publication. Responds to mss in 3-4 months. Guidelines available on website.

The editors award prizes for best poetry and prose in the issue. Prize awards vary contingent on the current year's budget but normally ranges from $100-400. There is no reading fee or separate application for these prizes. All accepted mss. are eligible. *Willow Review* is 88-96 pages, digest-sized, professionally printed, flat-spined, with a 4-color cover featuring work by an Illinois artist. Press run is 1,000. Subscription: $18 for 3 issues, $30 for 6 issues. Sample: $5 (back issue). International: add $5 per issue. Has published poetry by Lisel Mueller, Lucien Stryk, David Ray, Louis Rodriguez, John Dickson, and Patricia Smith.

MAGAZINE'S NEEDS Submit up to 5 poems at a time. Considers simultaneous submissions "if indicated in the cover letter"; no previously published poems. No e-mail submissions; postal submissions only. Include SASE; **"mss will not be returned unless requested."** Reads submissions September-May. Pays 2 contributor's copies.

CONTEST/AWARD OFFERINGS Prizes totaling $400 are awarded to the best poetry and short fiction/creative nonfiction in each issue.

ALSO OFFERS The College of Lake County Reading Series (4-7 readings/academic year) has included Thomas Lux, Isabel Allende, Donald Justice, Galway Kinnell, Lisel Mueller, Amiri Baraka, and others. One reading is for contributors to *Willow Review*. Readings, usually held on Thursday evenings and widely publicized in Chicago and suburban newspapers, are presented to audiences of about 150 students and faculty of the College of Lake County and other area colleges, as well as residents of local communities.

TIPS "Include SASE. No e-mail submissions, please. *Willow Review* can be found on EBSCOhost databases, assuring a broader targeted audience for our authors' work. *Willow Review* is a nonprofit journal partially supported by a grant from the Illinois Arts Council (a state agency), College of Lake County Publications, private contributions, and sales."

WINDFALL: A JOURNAL OF POETRY OF PLACE

Windfall Press, P.O. Box 19007, Portland OR 97280-0007. **E-mail:** bsiverly@comcast.net. **Website:** www.windfalljournal.com. **Contact:** Bill Siverly and Michael McDowell, co-editors. *Windfall: A Journal of Poetry of Place*, published semiannually in March and September, is "looking for poems of place, specifically places in the Pacific Northwest (the broad bioregion extending from the North Slope of Alaska to the San Francisco Bay Area, and from the Rocky Mountains to the Pacific Coast). 'Place' can be named or unnamed; but if unnamed, then location should be clearly implied or suggested by observed detail. The poet does not have to be living in the Pacific Northwest, but the poem does. We favor poetry based on imagery derived from sensory observation. *Windfall* also favors poetry that occurs in lines and stanzas." Does not want "language poetry, metapoetry, surrealism, 'Internet poetry' (constructed from search engine information rather than experience), abstract, or self-centered poetry of any kind." Acquires first North American serial rights. "Poem may appear in sample pages on *Windfall* website." Rights revert to poet upon publication. Publishes ms 2 months after acceptance. Responds within 6 months ("depends on when poems are submitted in the biannual cycle"). Guidelines available in magazine or on website.

Has published poetry by Judith Barrington, Gloria Bird, Barbara Drake, Clem Starck, Tom Wayman, and Robert Wrigley. *Windfall* is 52 pages, digest-sized, stapled, with art on covers ("all are drawings or prints by Portland artist Sharon Bronzan"). Receives about 160 poems/year, accepts about 60. Press run is 250. Single copy: $7; subscription: $14/year. Make checks payable to Windfall Press.

MAGAZINE'S NEEDS Submit 5 poems at a time. Lines/poem: up to 50. Considers simultaneous submissions; no previously published poems. Accepts e-mail submissions (as attachment). Cover letter is preferred. "SASE required for submissions by US mail." Reads submissions "after the deadlines for each issue: February 1 for Spring, and August 1 for Fall."

WINDHOVER

A Journal of Christian Literature, P.O. Box 8008, 900 College St., Belton TX 76513. (254)295-4561. **E-mail:** windhover@umhb.edu. **Website:** http://undergrad.umhb.edu/english/windhover-journal. **Contact:** Dr. Nathaniel Hansen, editor. "*Windhover* is devoted to promoting writers and literature with a Christian perspective and with a broad definition of that perspective. We accept poetry, short fiction, nonfiction, creative nonfiction." Publishes ms 1 year after acceptance. Sample copy for $10. Writer's guidelines available at http://undergrad.umhb.edu/english/windhover-journal.

Magazine: 6×9; white bond paper.

MAGAZINE'S NEEDS Accepts electronic submissions only through online submission manager; no e-mailed submissions. Include estimated word count, brief bio, and list of publications. Reading period is February 1-September 1. Deadlines for submissions is June 1 for next issue. Pays 2 contributor's copies.

TIPS "We particularly look for convincing plot and character development."

WINDSOR REVIEW

Department of English, University of Windsor, Windsor ON N9B 3P4, Canada. (519)253-3000; (519) 253-4232, ext. 2290. **Fax:** (519)971-3676. **E-mail:** uwrevu@uwindsor.ca. **Website:** www.uwindsor.ca. **Contact:** Marty Gervais, art editor. "We try to offer a balance of fiction and poetry distinguished by excellence." Buys one-time rights. Pays on publication. Publishes ms an average of 6 months after acceptance. Responds in 1 month to queries; 6 weeks to mss. Sample copy for $7 (U.S.). Guidelines available online.

TIPS "Good writing, strong characters, and experimental fiction is appreciated."

WISCONSIN REVIEW

University of Wisconsin Oshkosh, 800 Algoma Blvd., Oshkosh WI 54901. (920)424-2267. **E-mail:** wisconsinreview@uwosh.edu. **Website:** www.uwosh.edu/wisconsinreview. *Wisconsin Review*, published semiannually, is a "contemporary poetry, prose, and art magazine run by students at the University of Wisconsin Oshkosh." Wants all forms and styles of poetry. Does not want "poetry that is racist, sexist, or unnecessarily vulgar." Considers poetry by children and teens. "Minors may submit material by including a written letter of permission from a parent or guardian." Acquires first rights. Time between acceptance and publication is 4+6 months. Responds in 6-9 months. Sometimes comments on rejected poems. Guidelines available in magazine, for SASE, by e-mail, and on website.

Wisconsin Review is around 100 pages, digest-sized, perfect-bound, with 4-color glossy cover-stock. Receives about 400 poetry submissions/year, accepts about 50; Press run is 1,000. Single copy: $7.50; subscription: $10 plus $3 extra per issue for shipments outside the U.S.

MAGAZINE'S NEEDS Submit up to 5 poems at a time. Does not consider previously published poems or simultaneous submissions. Does not accept e-mail submissions. "Online submissions are accepted only through http://wisconsinreview.submittable.com/submit." Type 1 poem/page, single-spaced, with name and address of writer on each page. Cover letter is required. Include 3-5 sentence bio and SASE if submitting by mail. Reads submissions September through May. Submit seasonal poems 6 months in advance. Does not review books and chapbooks of poetry, other magazines and journals. Pays 2 contributor's copies.

TIPS "We are open to any poetic form and style, and look for outstanding imagery, new themes, and fresh voices - poetry that induces emotions."

WOLF, THE

E-mail: editor@wolfmagazine.co.uk. **E-mail:** thewolfpoetry@hotmail.com. **Website:** www.wolfmagazine.co.uk. *The Wolf*, published 3 times per year, publishes "international translations, critical prose, and interviews with leading contemporary poets, which are frequently mentioned as distinguishing characteristics of the magazine. The poetry, however, comes purely through work submitted. There is no special treatment with regard to the consideration of any poet or poem. Since January 2008, *The Wolf* has benefited from Arts Council funding. Since receiving its grant the magazine has increased its content by a third and is perfect bound." $12 single issue, including postage and packing; $35 subscription. Accepts PayPal. Responds in 6 months. Sample copy on website. Guidelines available online.

MAGAZINE'S NEEDS "Please submit no more than 5 poems. We accept any poetry of various styles or theme. But it's advisable to read a few issues of the magazine to see what gets in. The editor prefers poems to hold a modernist aesthetic over the postmodern. Experimental over mainstream. Serious over light verse. It's worth seeing how this fits in with recent publications of *The Wolf*." Pays 1 contributor's copy.

ADDITIONAL INFORMATION Also accepts critical essays on any poetry subject between 2,000-3,000 words. Welcomes artwork or photographs.

THE WORCESTER REVIEW

1 Ekman St., Worcester MA 01607. (508)797-4770. **E-mail:** twr.diane@gmail.com. **Website:** www.theworcesterreview.org. **Contact:** Diane Mulligan, managing editor. *The Worcester Review*, published annually by the Worcester County Poetry Association, encourages "critical work with a New England connection; no geographic limitation on poetry and fiction." Wants "work that is crafted, intuitively honest and

empathetic. We like high quality, creative poetry, art-work, and fiction. Critical articles should be connected to New England." Acquires one-time rights. Publishes ms within 1 year of acceptance. Accepts about 10% un-solicited mss. Agented fiction less than 10%. Responds in 4-8 months to mss. Sometimes comments on reject-ed mss. Sample copy: $8. Guidelines available for SASE or on website.

Magazine: 6×9; 60 lb. white offset paper; 10 pt. CS1 cover stock; illustrations; photos. Has pub-lished poetry by Kurt Brown, Cleopatra Mathis, and Theodore Deppe. *The Worcester Review* is 160 pages, digest-sized, professionally printed in dark type on quality stock, perfect-bound, with matte card cover. Press run is 600. Subscription: $30 (includes membership in WCPA).

MAGAZINE'S NEEDS Submit up to 5 poems at a time. Cover letter is optional. Print submissions should be typed on 8 1/2 x 11 paper, with poet's name and e-mail address in upper left corner of each page. Include SASE or e-mail for reply. Pays 2 contributor's copies plus small honorarium.

TIPS "We generally look for creative work with a blend of craftsmanship, insight and empathy. This does not exclude humor. We won't print work that is shoddy in any of these areas."

WRITE ON!! POETRY MAGAZETTE

P.O. Box 901, Richfield UT 84701-0901. **E-mail:** jim-nipoetry@yahoo.com. **Contact:** Jim Garman, editor. *Write On!! Poetry Magazette*, published monthly, fea-tures "poetry from poets around the world." Wants po-etry of "any style; all submissions must be suitable for all ages to read." Does not want "adult themes or vulgar material." Considers poetry by children and teens. Ac-quires one-time rights "which return to author upon publication." Time between acceptance and publica-tion is 1 month. Responds in approximately 4 weeks or less. Never comments on rejected poems. Guidelines available by e-mail.

Write On!! is 24 pages, digest-sized, photostat-copied, saddle-stapled. Receives about 500 po-ems/year, accepts about 50%. Press run is 50. Single copy: $4. Sample: $3. Make checks pay-able to Jim Garman. Has published poetry by Robert Kernell, B.Z. Niditch, Ron Koppelberger, Joey Graham, and Marilyn O. Bailey.

MAGAZINE'S NEEDS Submit 1-6 poems at a time. Considers previously published poems and simultane-ous submissions. Accepts e-mail submissions (pasted into body of message, no attachments). Reads submis-sions year round. Occasionally publishes theme issues. Lines/poem: 6 minimum, 28 maximum. No payment or free copies provided. "*Write On!!* contains no ads, no sponsors; all costs are covered out of pocket or by those desiring a copy."

THE WRITE PLACE AT THE WRITE TIME

E-mail: submissions@thewriteplaceatthewritetime. org. **Website:** www.thewriteplaceatthewritetime.org. **Contact:** Nicole M. Bouchard, editor-in-chief. Ac-quires electronic rights, archive rights, and one-time reprint rights. Responds to queries in 2-6 weeks. Fre-quently comments on rejected mss. Guidelines avail-able on website or by e-mail: questions@thewriteplace-atthewritetime.org.

"We encourage new and seasoned writers to send in submissions for the next issue, benefit from resources we provide, read the current issue and enjoy themselves. It is our personal touch, on everything from the feedback we give to our aesthetic to the lasting relationships we cultivate with our contributors, that distin-guishes us as having a community-like atmo-sphere dedicated to a humanitarian approach to the arts. We publish 3 issues a year, and our writers range from previously unpublished to having written for *The New York Times*, *Time* magazine, *The Wall Street Journal*, *Glimmer Train*, *Newsweek*, and *Business Week*, and they come from all over the world."

TIPS "Visit the website for details before submitting. Our publication is copyrighted. We send pre-publica-tion galleys to authors depending on whether the story underwent significant edits. We like to work closely with our writers. If the material is only slightly edited, then we don't."

WRITER'S BLOC

Texas A&M University-Kingsville, Dept. of Language and Literature, MSC 162, Fore Hall 201B, Kingsville TX 78363. (361)593-2640. **E-mail:** octavio.quintanil-la@tamuk.edu. **Website:** www.tamuk.edu/artsci/lan-glit/writers_bloc.html. **Contact:** Octavio Quintanilla. *Writer's Bloc*, published annually, prints poetry, fiction, creative nonfiction, and graphic art. "About half of our pages are devoted to the works of Texas A&M Univer-sity-Kingsville students and half to the works of writ-ers and artists from all over the world." Wants quality poetry; no restrictions on content or form. *Writer's Bloc* is 96 pages, digest-sized. Press run is 300. Subscription: $7. Sample: $7. Guidelines online or in magazine.

MAGAZINE'S NEEDS Submit no more than 3 pages of poetry at a time ("prose poems okay"). No e-mail submissions; postal submissions only. "Submissions should be typed, double-spaced; SASE required for reply." Reads submissions September-February only. "Manuscripts are published upon recommendation by a staff of students and faculty." Seldom comments on rejected poems. "Acceptance letters are sent out in October." Length: no more than 50 lines. Pays 1 contributor's copy.

THE WRITER'S CHRONICLE

Association of Writers & Writing Programs (AWP), Carty House MS 1E3, George Mason University, Fairfax VA 22030-4444. (703)993-4301. **Fax:** (703)993-4302. **E-mail:** chronicle@awpwriter.org. **Website:** www.awpwriter.org. "*Writer's Chronicle* strives to: present the best essays on the craft and art of writing poetry, fiction and nonfiction; help overcome the over-specialization of the literary arts by presenting a public forum for the appreciation, debate and analysis of contemporary literature; present the diversity of accomplishments and points of view within contemporary literature; provide serious and committed writers and students of writing the best advice on how to manage their professional lives; provide writers who teach with new pedagogical approaches for their classrooms; provide the members and subscribers with a literary community as a compensation for a devotion to a difficult and lonely art; provide information on publishing opportunities, grants and awards; and promote the good works of AWP, its programs and its individual members." Buys first North American serial rights for print and Web. Pays on publication. Responds in 2 weeks to queries. Editorial lead time 3 months. Sample copy free. Guidelines free and online.

TIPS "In general, the editors look for articles that demonstrate an excellent working knowledge of literary issues and a generosity of spirit that esteems the arguments of other writers on similar topics. When writing essays on craft, do not use your own work as an example. Keep in mind that 18,000 of our readers are students or just-emerging writers. They must become good readers before they can become good writers, so we expect essays on craft to show exemmplary close readings of a variety of contemporary and older

works. Essays must embody erudition, generosity, curiosity and discernment rather than self-involvement. Writers may refer to their own travails and successes if they do so modestly, in small proportion to the other examples. We look for a generosity of spirit—a general love and command of literature as well as an expert, writerly viewpoint."

WRITER'S DIGEST

F+W Media, Inc., 10151 Carver Rd., Suite #200, Blue Ash OH 45242. (513)531-2690. **E-mail:** wdsubmissions@fwmedia.com. **Website:** www.writersdigest.com. "Our readers look to us for specific ideas and tips that will help them succeed, whether success means getting into print, finding personal fulfillment through writing or building and maintaining a thriving writing career and network." Buys first North American print and perpetual world digital rights. Pays 25% print reprint fee. Pays on acceptance. Publishes ms an average of 6-9 months after acceptance. Responds in 2-4 months to queries and mss. Guidelines and editorial calendar available online (writersdigest.com/submissionguidelines).

○   The magazine does not accept or read e-queries with attachments.

TIPS "*InkWell* is the best place for new writers to break in. We recommend you consult our editorial calendar before pitching feature-length articles. Check our writer's guidelines for more details."

◐ THE WRITING DISORDER

P.O. Box 93613, Los Angeles CA 90093. (323)336-5822. **E-mail:** submit@thewritingdisorder.com. **Website:** www.thewritingdisorder.com. **Contact:** C.E. Lukather, editor; Paul Garson, managing editor; Julianna Woodhead, poetry editor. Quarterly literary magazine featuring new and established writers. "*The Writing Disorder* is an online literary magazine devoted to literature, art, and culture. The mission of the magazine is to showcase new and emerging writers—particularly those in writing programs—as well as established ones. The magazine also features original artwork, photography, and comic art. Although it strives to publish original and experimental work, *The Writing Disorder* remains rooted in the classic art of storytelling." Acquires first North American serial rights. Pays on publication Publishes ms an average of 3-6 months after acceptance. Responds in 6-12 weeks to queries; 3-6 months to ms. Editorial lead time 3 months. Sample copy online. Guidelines available online.

MAGAZINE'S NEEDS Query. Annual print anthology of best work published online. Pays contributor's a copy of anthology to writer's whose work has been selected for inclusion.

TIPS "We are looking for work from new writers, writers in writing programs, and students and faculty of all ages."

◐ XAVIER REVIEW

Website: www.xula.edu/review. **Contact:** Ralph Adamo, editor. "*Xavier Review* accepts poetry, fiction, translations, creative nonfiction, and critical essays. Content focuses on African American, Caribbean, and Southern literature, as well as works that touch on issues of religion and spirituality. We do, however, accept quality work on all themes. (Please note: This is not a religious publication.)"

MAGAZINE'S NEEDS Submit 3-5 poems at a time. Include 2-3 sentence bio and SASE. E-mail submissions are generally not accepted; links to sites are ignored. "Overseas authors only may submit by e-mail attachment." Pays 2 contributor's copies; offers 40% discount on additional copies.

◐◑ YEMASSEE

University of South Carolina, Department of English, Columbia SC 29208. (803)777-2085. **Fax:** (803)777-9064. **E-mail:** editor@yemasseejournalonline.org. **Website:** http://yemasseejournalonline.org. **Contact:** Lauren Eyler, editor-in-chief. "*Yemassee* is the University of South Carolina's literary journal. Our readers are interested in high quality fiction, poetry, drama, and creative nonfiction. We have no editorial slant; quality of work is our only concern. We publish in the fall and spring, printing three to five stories and 12-15 poems per issue. We tend to solicit reviews, essays, and interviews but welcome unsolicited queries. We do not favor any particular aesthetic or school of writing." Buys first North American serial rights, buys electronic rights. Publishes ms an average of 4-6 months after acceptance. Responds in 1-4 months to queries and mss. Editorial lead time 3 months. Sample copy for $5. Guidelines available online.

◐ Stories from *Yemassee* have been published in *New Stories From the South*. As of 2012, only accepts submissions through online submissions manager.

MAGAZINE'S NEEDS Submit 3-5 poems combined into a single document. "Submissions for all genres should include a cover letter that lists the titles of the pieces included, along with your contact information (including author's name, address, e-mail address, and phone number)." Does not want workshop poems, unpolished drafts, generic/unoriginal themes, bad Hemingway. Does not want "poems of such a highly personal nature that their primary relevance is to the author; bad Ginsberg." Length: 1-120 lines. Pays in contributor's copies.

CONTEST/AWARD OFFERINGS Pocataligo Poetry Contest: $500 award; submission deadline: March 15, annual.

◐ ZYLOPHONE POETRY JOURNAL

E-mail: rogerbarrow52@yahoo.com. **Website:** www.poetezines.4mg.com. **Contact:** J. Rogers Barrow. *Zylophone* is published semiannually in print and online. Wants all common formats. Has published poetry by Edward W. Cousins, Daisy Whitmore, David Barger. *Zylophone* is 16 pages, tabloid-sized, staple-bound with line drawing artwork. Receives about 60 poems/year; accepts about 12. Press run is 20. Sample copy is $6. Publishes ms 6 weeks after acceptance. Guidelines by e-mail.

MAGAZINE'S NEEDS Submit 3 poems at a time by e-mail. Lines/poem: 4-16 lines. Considers simultaneous submissions; no previously published work. Cover letter is preferred. Reads submissions year round. Pays 1 contributor's copy.

ZYZZYVA

466 Geary Street, Suite 401, San Francisco CA 94102. (415)440-1510. **E-mail:** editor@zyzzyva.org. **Website:** www.zyzzyva.org. **Contact:** Laura Cogan, editor; Oscar Villalon, managing editor. "We feature work by writers currently living on the West Coast or in Alaska and Hawaii only. We are essentially a literary magazine, but of wide-ranging interests and a strong commitment to nonfiction." Buys first North American serial and one time anthology rights. Pays on acceptance. Publishes ms an average of 3 months after acceptance. Responds in 1 week to queries. Responds in 1 month to mss. Sample copy for $7 or online. Guidelines available online.

◐ Accepts submissions year-round. Does not accept online submissions.

MAGAZINE'S NEEDS Submit by mail. Length: no maximum page count. Pays $50

TIPS "We are not currently seeking work about any particular theme or topic; that said, reading recent issues is perhaps the best way to develop a sense for the length and quality we are looking for in submissions."

BOOK/CHAPBOOK PUBLISHERS

//

Every poet dreams of publishing a collection of his or her work. However, it's surprising how many poets still envision putting out a thick, hardbound volume containing hundreds of poems. In reality, poetry books are usually slim, often paperback, with varying levels of production quality, depending on the publisher.

More common than full-length poetry books (i.e., 50-150 pages by modern standards) are poetry *chapbooks*, small editions of approximately 24-32 pages. They may be printed on quality paper with beautiful cover art on heavy stock; or they may be photocopied sheets of plain printer paper, folded and stapled or hand-sewn along the spine.

In this section you'll find a variety of presses and publishers of poetry books and chapbooks. However, it's a reflection of how poetry publishing works in the early 21st century that many book/chapbook publishing opportunities appear in the Contest & Awards section instead.

GETTING STARTED, FINDING A PUBLISHER

If you don't have a publisher in mind, read randomly through the listings, making notes as you go. (Don't hesitate to write in the margins, underline, use highlighters; it also helps to flag markets that interest you with Post-It Notes). Browsing the listings is an effective way to familiarize yourself with the kind of information presented and the publishing opportunities that are available at various skill levels. If you're thinking of a specific publisher by name, however, begin with the General Index. Here all *Poet's Market* listings are alphabetized.

AHSAHTA PRESS

MFA Program in Creative Writing, Boise State University, 1910 University Dr., MS 1525, Boise ID 83725. (208)426-4210. **E-mail:** ahsahta@boisestate.edu. **E-mail:** jholmes@boisestate.edu. **Website:** ahsahtapress.boisestate.edu. **Contact:** Janet Holmes, director. Publishes trade paperback originals. Pays 8% royalty on retail price. Publishes ms 2 years after acceptance. Responds in 3 months to mss. Book catalog available online.

NEEDS "We are booked years in advance and are not currently reading manuscripts, with the exception of the Sawtooth Poetry Prize competition, from which we publish 2-3 mss per year."

HOW TO CONTACT Open readings during May beginning in 2013. Submit complete ms. Considers multiple and simultaneous submissions. Reading period is temporarily suspended due to backlog, but the press publishes runners-up as well as winners of the Sawtooth Poetry Prize. Forthcoming, new, and backlist titles available on website. Most backlist titles: $9.95; most current titles: $18.

TIPS "Ahsahta's motto is that poetry is art, so our readers tend to come to us for the unexpected—poetry that makes them think, reflect, and even do something they haven't done before."

AMERICAN CARRIAGE HOUSE PUBLISHING

P.O. Box 1130, Nevada City CA 95959. (530)432-8860. **Fax:** (530)432-7379. **Website:** www.americancarriagehousepublishing.com. **Contact:** Lynn Taylor, editor (parenting, reference, child, women). Publishes trade paperback and electronic originals. Pays outright purchase of $300-3,000. Publishes ms 1 year after acceptance. Responds in 3 months. Catalog free on request.

NEEDS Wholesome poetry.

TIPS "We are looking for proposals, both fiction and nonfiction, preferably wholesome topics."

ANAPHORA LITERARY PRESS

104 Banff Dr., Apt. 101, Edinboro PA 16412. (814)273-0004. **E-mail:** pennsylvaniajournal@gmail.com. **Website:** www.anaphoraliterary.com. **Contact:** Anna Faktorovich, editor-in-chief (general interest). "We are actively seeking submissions at this time. The genre is not as important as the quality of work. You should have a completed full-length ms ready to be emailed or mailed upon request." "In the Winter of 2010, Anaphora began accepting book-length single-author submissions. We are actively seeking single and multiple-author books in fiction (poetry, novels, and short story collections) and nonfiction (academic, legal, business, journals, edited and un-edited dissertations, biographies, and memoirs). E-mail submissions. Profits are split 50/50 with single-author writers. There are no costs to have a book produced by Anaphora. We do not offer any free contributor copies." Format publishes in trade paperback originals and reprints; mass market paperback originals and reprints. Pays 10-30% royalty on retail price. "We currently publish journals, which are authored by several people. If we publish a novel or a critical book by a single author, we will share our profits with the author." Publishes 2 months after acceptance. Responds in 1 month on queries, proposals, and mss. Catalog and guidelines available online at website.

NEEDS Confession, contemporary, experimental, occult, picture books, plays, poetry, poetry in translation.

HOW TO CONTACT Contact by mail or e-mail. Looking for single and multiple-author books in poetry. Query with 10 sample poems.

TIPS "Our audience is academics, college students and graduates, as well as anybody who loves literature. Regardless of profits, we love publishing great books and we enjoy reading submissions. So, if you are reading this book because you love writing and hope to publish as soon as possible, send a query letter or a submission to us. But, remember—proofread your work (most of our editors are English instructors)."

ANHINGA PRESS

P.O. Box 3665, Tallahassee FL 32315. (850)422-1408. **Fax:** (850)442-6323. **E-mail:** info@anhinga.org. **Website:** www.anhinga.org. **Contact:** Rick Campbell, editor. Publishes only full-length collections of poetry (60-80 pages). No individual poems or chapbooks. Publishes hardcover and trade paperback originals. Pays 10% royalty on retail price. Offers Anhinga Prize of $2,000. Responds in 3 months to queries, proposals, and mss. Book catalog and contest for #10 SASE or online. Guidelines available online.

NEEDS Query with SASE and 10-page sample (not full ms) by mail. No e-mail queries.

ANVIL PRESS

P.O. Box 3008 MPO, Vancouver BC V6B 3X5, Canada. (604)876-8710. **Fax:** (604)879-2667. **E-mail:** info@anvilpress.com. **Website:** www.anvilpress.com. **Con-**

tact: Brian Kaufman. "Anvil Press publishes contemporary adult fiction, poetry, and drama, giving voice to up-and-coming Canadian writers, exploring all literary genres, discovering, nurturing, and promoting new Canadian literary talent. Currently emphasizing urban/suburban themed fiction and poetry; de-emphasizing historical novels." Publishes trade paperback originals. Pays advance. 8 months Responds in 6 months. Book catalog for 9×12 SAE with 2 first-class stamps. Guidelines available online.

○ Canadian authors only. No e-mail submissions.

NEEDS "Get our catalog, look at our poetry. We do very little poetry-maybe 1-2 titles per year."

HOW TO CONTACT Query and submit 8-12 poems with SASE.

TIPS "Audience is young, informed, educated, aware, with an opinion, culturally active (films, books, the performing arts). No U.S. authors. Research the appropriate publisher for your work."

ARC PUBLICATIONS

Nanholme Mill, Shaw Wood Rd., Todmorden, Lancashire OL14 6DA, England. **E-mail:** editorarcuk@btinternet.com. **Website:** www.arcpublications.co.uk. **Contact:** John W. Clarke. Responds in 6 weeks.

NEEDS Publishes "contemporary poetry from new and established writers from the UK and abroad, specializing in the work of world poets writing in English, and the work of overseas poets in translation."

HOW TO CONTACT Send 16-24 pages of poetry and short cover letter.

ASHLAND POETRY PRESS

401 College Avenue, Ashland OH 44805. (419)289-5957. **Fax:** (419)289-5255. **E-mail:** app@ashland.edu. **Website:** www.ashland.edu/aupoetry. **Contact:** Sarah M. Wells, managing editor. Publishes trade paperback originals. Makes outright purchase of $500-1,000. Publishes book 10 months after acceptance. Responds in 1 month to queries; 6 months to mss. Book catalog available online. Guidelines available online.

NEEDS "We accept unsolicited manuscripts through the Snyder Prize competition each spring-the deadline is April 30. Judges are mindful of dedication to craftsmanship and thematic integrity."

TIPS "We rarely publish a title submitted off the transom outside of our Snyder Prize competition."

AUTUMN HOUSE PRESS

87½ Westwood St., Pittsburgh PA 15211. (412)381-4261. **E-mail:** info@autumnhouse.org. **Website:** www.autumnhouse.org. Sharon Dilworth, fiction editor. **Contact:** Michael Simms, editor-in-chief (fiction). "We are a non-profit literary press specializing in high-quality poetry and fiction. Our editions are beautifully designed and printed, and they are distributed nationally. Approximately one-third of our sales are to college literature and creative writing classes." Member CLMP, AWP, Academy of American Poets. "We distribute our own titles. We do extensive national promotion through ads, web-marketing, reading tours, bookfairs and conferences." "We are open to all genres. The quality of writing concerns us, not the genre." You can also learn about our annual Fiction Prize, Poetry Prize and Chapbook Award competitions, as well as our online journal, *Coal Hill Review*. (Please note that Autumn House accepts unsolicited manuscripts *only* through these competitions.) Hardcover, trade paperback, and electronic originals. Format: acid-free paper; offset printing; perfect and casebound (cloth) bound; sometimes contains illustrations. Average print order: 1,500. Debut novel print order: 1,500. Pays 7% royalty on wholesale price. Pays $0-2,500 advance. Publishes 9 months after acceptance. Responds in 1-3 days on queries and proposals; 3 months on mss Catalog free on request. Guidelines online at website; free on request; or for #10 SASE.

NEEDS Since 2003, the annual Autumn House Poetry Contest has awarded publication of a full-length manuscript and $2,500 to the winner. *We ask that all submissions from authors new to Autumn House come through one of our annual contests.* All finalists will be considered for publication.

HOW TO CONTACT Submit only through our annual contest. See guidelines online.

TIPS "The competition to publish with Autumn House is very tough. Submit only your best work."

THE BACKWATERS PRESS

3502 N. 52nd St., Omaha NE 68104. (402)451-4052. **Website:** www.thebackwaterspress.org. **Contact:** Greg Kosmicki, editor.

NEEDS Only considers submissions to Backwaters Prize. More details on website.

BEAR STAR PRESS

185 Hollow Oak Dr., Cohasset CA 95973. (530)891-0360. **Website:** www.bearstarpress.com. **Contact:** Beth Spencer, publisher/editor. "Bear Star is committed to publishing the best poetry it can attract. Each

year it sponsors the Dorothy Brunsman contest, open to poets from Western and Pacific states. From time to time we add to our list other poets from our target area whose work we admire." Publishes trade paperback originals. Pays $1,000, and 25 copies to winner of annual Dorothy Brunsman contest. Publishes book 9 months after acceptance. Responds in 2 weeks to queries. Guidelines available online.

NEEDS Wants well-crafted poems. No restrictions as to form, subject matter, style, or purpose. "Poets should enter our annual book competition. Other books are occasionally solicited by publisher, sometimes from among contestants who didn't win."

HOW TO CONTACT Query and submit complete ms. Online form.

CONTEST/AWARD OFFERINGS The Dorothy Brunsman Poetry Prize awards $1,000 and publication by Bear Star Press to the best book-length ms by a poet who resides in the Western states (within Mountain or Pacific time zones, plus Alaska and Hawaii) and serves as their primary pool for finding new manuscripts. "You need not enter the contest to submit to us, but our first allegiance is to mss that come with a reading fee since they help to keep the press going."

TIPS "Send your best work, consider its arrangement. A 'wow' poem early keeps me reading."

◑Ⓢ BIRCH BOOK PRESS

P.O. Box 81, Delhi NY 13753. **Fax:** (607)746-7453. **E-mail:** birchbrook@copper.net. **Website:** www.birchbrookpress.info. **Contact:** Tom Tolnay, editor/publisher; Barbara dela Cuesta, associate editor. Birch Brook Press "is a letterpress book printer/typesetter/designer that uses monies from these activities to publish several titles of its own each year with cultural and literary interest." Specializes in literary work, flyfishing, baseball, outdoors, theme anthologies, occasional translations of classics, and books about books. Specializes "mostly in anthologies with specific themes." Books are "handset letterpress editions printed in our own shop." Member, Small Press Center, Publishers Marketing Association, Academy of American Poets. Distributes titles through Barnes&Noble.com, Amazon.com, Gazelle Book Services in Europe, Multicultural Books in Canada. Abe Books, and Alibris Books online. Promotes titles through website, catalogs, direct mail and group ads, book fairs. Occasionally publishes trade paperback originals. Pays modest royalty on acceptance. Publishes ms 10-18 months after ac-

ceptance. Responds in 3 to 6 months to mss. Book catalog available online.

HOW TO CONTACT Query first with a few sample poems or chapters, or send entire ms. No e-mail submissions; submissions by postal mail only. Must include SASE with submissions. Occasionally comments on rejected poems. Royalty on co-op contracts.

TIPS "Write well on subjects of interest to BBP, such as outdoors, flyfishing, baseball, music, literary stories, fine poetry, and occasional novellas, books about books."

BKMK PRESS

(816)235-2558. **Fax:** (816)235-2611. **E-mail:** bkmk@umkc.edu. **Website:** www.umkc.edu/bkmk. **Contact:** Ben Furnish, managing editor. "BkMk Press publishes fine literature. Reading period January-June." Publishes trade paperback originals Responds in 4-6 months to queries Guidelines available online

HOW TO CONTACT Submit 10 sample poems and SASE.

TIPS "We skew toward readers of literature, particularly contemporary writing. Because of our limited number of titles published per year, we discourage apprentice writers or 'scattershot' submissions."

◑Ⓢ BLACK LAWRENCE PRESS

326 Bingham St., Pittsburgh PA 15211. **E-mail:** editors@blacklawrencepress.com. **Website:** www.blacklawrencepress.com. **Contact:** Diane Goettel, executive editor. Black Lawrence press seeks to publish intriguing books of literature—novels, short story collections, poetry collections, chapbooks, anthologies, and creative nonfiction. Will also publish the occasional translation from German. Has published books by Mary Biddinger, Marc McKee, Patrick Michael Finn, David Rigsbee, Laura McCullough, Adam Prince, Charlotte Pence, and T.J. Beitelman. Publishes 15-20 books/year, mostly poetry and fiction. Manuscripts are selected through open submission and competition. Books are 20-400 pages, offset-printed or high-quality POD, perfect-bound, with 4-color cover. Pays royalties. Responds in 6 months to mss.

CONTEST/AWARD OFFERINGS The St. Lawrence Book Award, The Hudson Prize, and The Black River Chapbook Competition.

Ⓢ BLACK MOUNTAIN PRESS

P.O. Box 9907, Asheville NC 28815. (828)273-3332. **E-mail:** jackmoe@theBlackMountainPress.com. **Website:** www.theBlackMountainPress.com. **Contact:**

Jack Moe, editor (how-to, poetry); James Robining-ski (short story collections, novels). Publishes hard-cover, trade paperback, and electronic originals. Pays 5-10% royalty on retail price. Pays $100-500 advance. Publishes ms 5 months after acceptance. Responds in 4-6 months to mss. Book catalog and ms guidelines available online at website.

HOW TO CONTACT Submit complete ms.

TIPS "Don't be afraid of sending your anti-government, anti-religion, anti-art, anti-literature, experimental, avant-garde efforts here. But don't send your work before it's fully cooked, we do, however, enjoy fresh, natural, and sometimes even raw material, just don't send in anything that is "glowing" unless it was savaged from a FoxNews book-burning event."

BLACK OCEAN

Fax: (617)849-5678. **E-mail:** carrie@blackocean.org. **Website:** www.blackocean.org. **Contact:** Carrie Olivia Adams, poetry editor. Responds in 6 months to mss.

NEEDS Wants poetry that is well-considered, risks itself, and by its beauty and/or bravery disturbs a tiny corner of the universe. Manuscripts are selected through open submission. Books are 60+ pages.

HOW TO CONTACT Book/chapbook mss may include previously published poems. We have an open submission period in May of each year; specific guidelines are updated and posted on our website in the months preceding.

BLAZEVOX [BOOKS]

76 Inwood Place, Buffalo NY 14209. **E-mail:** editor@blazevox.org. **Website:** www.blazevox.org. **Contact:** Geoffrey Gatza, editor/publisher. "We are a major publishing presence specializing in innovative fictions and wide-ranging fields of innovative forms of poetry and prose. Our goal is to publish works that are challenging, creative, attractive, and yet affordable to individual readers. Articles of submission depend on many criteria, but overall items submitted must conform to one ethereal trait, your work must not suck. This put plainly, bad art should be punished; we will not promote it. However, all submissions will be reviewed and the author will receive feedback. We are human too." Pays 10% royalties on fiction and poetry books, based on net receipts. This amount may be split across multiple contributors. "We do not pay advances." Guidelines online.

HOW TO CONTACT Submit complete ms via e-mail.

TIPS "We actively contract and support authors who tour, read and perform their work, play an active part of the contemporary literary scene, and seek a readership."

BLUE LIGHT PRESS

1563 45th Ave., San Francisco CA 94122. **E-mail:** bluelightpress@aol.com. **Website:** www.bluelight-press.com. **Contact:** Diane Frank, chief editor. "We like poems that are imagistic, emotionally honest, and push the edge—where the writer pushes through the imagery to a deeper level of insight and understanding. No rhymed poetry." Has published poetry by Alice Rogoff, Tom Centolella, Rustin Larson, Tony Krunk, Lisha Adela Garcia, Becky Sakellariou, and Christopher Buckley. "Books are elegantly designed and artistic." Chapbooks are 30 pages, digest-sized, professionally printed, with original cover art.

NEEDS "We have an online poetry workshop with a wonderful group of American and international poets—open to new members 3 times per year. Send an e-mail for info. We work in person with local poets, and will edit/critique poems by mail; $40 for four poems."

HOW TO CONTACT Does not accept e-mail submissions. **Deadlines:** January 30 full-sized ms. and June 15 for chapbooks. "Read our guidelines before sending your ms."

BLUE MOUNTAIN PRESS

Blue Mountain Arts, Inc., P.O. Box 4219, Boulder CO 80306. (800)525-0642. **E-mail:** BMPbooks@sps.com. **Website:** www.sps.com. **Contact:** Patti Wayant, editorial director. Publishes hardcover originals, trade paperback originals, electronic originals. Pays royalty on wholesale price. Publishes ms 6-8 months after acceptance. Responds in 2-4 months to queries, mss, and proposals. Guidelines available by e-mail.

> *"Please note: We are not accepting works of fiction, rhyming poetry, children's books, chapbooks, or memoirs."*

NEEDS "We publish poetry appropriate for gift books, self-help books, and personal growth books. We do not publish chapbooks or literary poetry."

HOW TO CONTACT Query. Submit 10+ sample poems.

BOA EDITIONS, LTD.

250 N. Goodman St., Suite 306, Rochester NY 14607. (585)546-3410. **Fax:** (585)546-3913. **E-mail:** conners@

boaeditions.org; hall@boaeditions.org. **Website:** www.boaeditions.org. Melissa Hall, development director/office manager. **Contact:** Peter Conners, editor. "BOA Editions publishes distinguished collections of poetry, fiction and poetry in translation. Our goal is to publish the finest American contemporary poetry, fiction and poetry in translation." Publishes hardcover and trade paperback originals. Negotiates royalties. Pays variable advance. Publishes ms 18 months after acceptance. Responds in 1 week to queries; 5 months to mss. Book catalog available online. Guidelines available online.

NEEDS "Readers who, like Whitman, expect of the poet to `indicate more than the beauty and dignity which always attach to dumb real objects . . . They expect him to indicate the path between reality and their souls,' are the audience of BOA's books." BOA Editions, a Pulitzer Prize-winning, not-for-profit publishing house acclaimed for its work, reads poetry mss for the American Poets Continuum Series (new poetry by distinguished poets in mid- and late career), the Lannan Translations Selection Series (publication of 2 new collections of contemporary international poetry annually, supported by The Lannan Foundation of Santa Fe, NM), The A. Poulin, Jr. Poetry Prize (to honor a poet's first book; mss considered through competition), and The America Reader Series (short fiction and prose on poetics). Has published poetry by Naomi Shihab Nye, W.D. Snodgrass, Lucille Clifton, Brigit Pegeen Kelly, and Li-Young Lee.

HOW TO CONTACT Check website for reading periods for the American Poets Continuum Series and The Lannan Translation Selection Series. "Please adhere to the general submission guidelines for each series." Guidelines available for SASE or on website.

⊘ BOTTOM DOG PRESS, INC.

P.O. Box 425, Huron OH 44839. **E-mail:** LsmithDog@smithdocs.net. **Website:** http://smithdocs.net. **Contact:** Larry Smith, director; Allen Frost, Laura Smith, Susanna Sharp-Schwacke, associate editors. Bottom Dog Press, Inc., "is a nonprofit literary and educational organization dedicated to publishing the best writing and art from the Midwest and Appalachia."

💬 "Query via e-mail first."

① BRICK ROAD POETRY PRESS, INC.

P.O. Box 751, Columbus GA 31902. (706)649-3080. **Fax:** (706)649-3094. **E-mail:** editor@brickroadpoetrypress.com. **Website:** www.brickroadpoetrypress.

com. **Contact:** Ron Self and Keith Badowski, co-editors/founders.

NEEDS Publishes poetry only: books (single author collections), e-zine, and annual anthology. "We prefer poetry that offers a coherent human voice, a sense of humor, attentiveness to words and language, narratives with surprise twists, persona poems, and/or philosophical or spiritual themes explored through the concrete scenes and images." Does not want over-emphasis on rhyme, intentional obscurity or riddling, highfalutin vocabulary, greeting card verse, overt religious statements of faith and/or praise, and/or abstractions. Publishes 10-12 poetry books/year and 1 anthology/year. Accepted poems meeting our theme requirements are published on our website. Mss accepted through open submission and competition. Books are 110 pages, print-on-demand, perfectbound, paperback with full color art or photograph covers.

HOW TO CONTACT "We accept .doc, .rtf, or .pdf file formats. We prefer electronic submissions but will reluctantly consider hard copy submissions by mail if USPS Flat Rate Mailing Envelope is used and with the stipulation that, should the author's work be chosen for publication, an electronic version (.doc or .rtf) must be prepared in a timely manner and at the poet's expense." Please include cover letter with poetry publication/recognition highlights and something intriguing about your life story or ongoing pursuits. "We would like to develop a connection with the poet as well as the poetry." Please include the collection title in the cover letter. "We want to publish poets who are engaged in the literary community, including regular submission of work to various publications and participation in poetry readings, workshops, and writers' groups. That said, we would never rule out an emerging poet who demonstrates ability and motivation to move in that direction." Pays royalties and 15 author copies. Initial print run of 150, print-on-demand thereafter.

CONTEST/AWARD OFFERINGS Brick Road Poetry Contest is an annual contest with a $1,000 prize. Entry fee: $25. Learn more online.

TIPS "The best way to discover all that poetry can be and to expand the limits of your own poetry is to read expansively. We recommend the following poets: Kim Addonizio, Ken Babstock, Coleman Barks, Billy Collins, Morri Creech, Alice Friman, Beth A. Gylys, Jane Hirshfield, Jane Kenyon, Ted Kooser, Stanley Kunitz,

Thomas Lux, Barry Marks, Michael Meyerhofer, Linda Pastan, Mark Strand, and Natasha D. Trethewey."

☁ BROKEN JAW PRESS

Box 596, STN A, Fredericton NB E3B 5A6, Canada. (506)454-5127. **E-mail:** editors@brokenjaw.com. **Website:** www.brokenjaw.com. "We publish poetry, fiction, drama and literary nonfiction, including translations and multilingual books." "Publishes almost exclusively Canadian-authored literary trade paperback originals and reprints." Pays 10% royalty on retail price. Pays $0-500 advance. Publishes ms 18 months after acceptance. Responds in 1 year to mss. Book catalog for 6×9 SAE with 2 first-class Canadian stamps in Canada or download PDF from website. Guidelines available online.

○ *Currently not accepting unsolicited mss and queries.*

TIPS "Unsolicited queries and manuscripts are not welcome at this time."

BROOKS BOOKS

3720 N. Woodridge Dr., Decatur IL 62526. **E-mail:** brooksbooks@sbcglobal.net. **Website:** www.brooksbookshaiku.com. **Contact:** Randy Brooks, editor (haiku poetry, tanka poetry). "Brooks Books, formerly High/Coo Press, publishes English-language haiku books, chapbooks, magazines, and bibliographies." Publishes hardcover, trade paperback, and electronic originals. Outright purchase based on wholesale value of 10% of a press run. Publishes ms 1 year after acceptance. Responds in 2 months to queries; 3 months to proposals and mss. Book catalog free on request or online at website. Guidelines free on request, for #10 SASE.

NEEDS "We celebrate English language haiku by promoting & publishing in a variety of media. Our goal is to share our joy of the art of reading & writing haiku through our little chapbook-size magazine, *Mayfly*. Also, we celebrate the art of haiga, lifetime contributions of haiku writers, the integration of visual arts (photography or painting) and contemporary English language haiku by leading poets.

HOW TO CONTACT Query.

TIPS "The best haiku capture human perception—moments of being alive conveyed through sensory images. They do not explain nor describe nor provide philosophical or political commentary. Haiku are gifts of the here and now, deliberately incomplete so that the reader can enter into the haiku moment to

open the gift and experience the feelings and insights of that moment for his or her self. Our readership includes the haiku community, readers of contemporary poetry, teachers and students of Japanese literature and contemporary Japanese poetics."

⊕ C&R PRESS

812 Westwood Ave., Chattanooga TN 37405. (423)645-5375. **Website:** www.crpress.org. **Contact:** Chad Prevost, editorial director and publisher; Ryan G. Van Cleave, executive director and publisher. Publishes hardcover, trade paperback, mass market paperback, and electronic originals. Publishes ms 1 year after acceptance. Responds in up to 1 month on queries and proposals, 1-2 months on mss. Catalog and guidelines available online at website.

NEEDS "We remain committed to our annual first book of poetry contest, the De Novo Award. However, we also feature 1-2 montly paid reading periods when we consider any and all poetry projects. Please check the website for updated guidelines."

HOW TO CONTACT Submit complete ms.

⊘ CALAMARI PRESS

Via Titta Scarpetta #28, Rome 00153, Italy. **E-mail:** derek@calamaripress.net. **Website:** www.calamaripress.com. Calamari Press publishes books of literary text and art. Publishes 1-2 books/year. Manuscripts are selected by invitation. Occasionally has open submission period— check website. Helps to be published in *SleepingFish* first." See separate listing in magazines/journals. Order books through the website, Powell's, or SPD. Publishes paperback originals. Pays in author's copies. Manuscript published 2-6 months after acceptance. Responds to mss in 2 weeks. Writer's guidelines on website.

NEEDS Calamari Press publishes books of literary text and art. Publishes 1-2 books/year. Manuscripts are selected by invitation. Occasionally has open submission period— check website.

HOW TO CONTACT Helps to be published in *SleepingFish* first." See separate listing in magazines/journals. Order books through the website, Powell's, or SPD.

CAROLINA WREN PRESS

120 Morris St., Durham NC 27701. (919)560-2738. **E-mail:** carolinawrenpress@earthlink.net. **Website:** www.carolinawrenpress.org. **Contact:** Andrea Selch, president. "We publish poetry, fiction, and memoirs by, and/or about people of color, women, gay/lesbian

issues, health and mental health topics in children's literature." Publishes ms 2 year after acceptance. Responds in 3 months to queries; 6 months to mss. Guidelines are available on our website in December, with information about electronic submissions.

Accepts simultaneous submissions, but "let us know if work has been accepted elsewhere."

NEEDS Publishes 2 poetry books/year, "usually through the Carolina Wren Press Poetry Series Contest. Otherwise we primarily publish women, minorities, and North Carolina authors." Has published "a half-red sea" by Evie Shockley, as well as poetry by Lee Ann Brown, Minnie Bruce Pratt, William Pitt Root and Erica Hunt. Guidelines on website. We are not accepting unsolicited submissions except through our Poetry Series Contest.

HOW TO CONTACT Accepts e-mail queries, but send only letter and description of work, no large files. Carolina Wren Press Poetry Contest for a First of Second Book takes submissions, electronically, from January to March of odd-numbered years.

CONTEST/AWARD OFFERINGS The Carolina Wren Press Poetry Series—full-length poetry manuscripts by authors who have not had more than one full-length book published. Submissions are accepted from January to March in odd-numbered years. There is a $20 reading fee for this contest. Full guidelines should be followed - check the website December to see the current guidelines.

TIPS "Best way to get read is to submit to a contest."

● CHRISTIAN BOOKS TODAY LTD

136 Main St., Buckshaw Village Chorley, Lancashire PR7 7BZ, United Kingdom. **E-mail:** md@christianbookstoday.com. **E-mail:** submissions@christianbookstoday.com. **Website:** www.christianbookstoday.com. **Contact:** Jason Richardson, MD (nonfiction); Lynda McIntosh, editor (fiction). Publishes trade paperback originals/reprints and electronic originals/reprints. Pays 10% royalty on retail price or 50% of title profit. Publishes ms 6 months after acceptance. Responds in 1 month to queries; 2 months to proposals and mss. Catalog and guidelines available online.

TIPS "We appeal to a general Christian readership. We are not interested in Hallmark stories, nor fantasy, or mysticism. We want work by Christians rather than Christian writing. If you want to take a risk in subject, you are particularly encouraged to submit. We actively seek out writers who want to build a ca-

reer with us and who understand we do what we do because we love it."

● CLEVELAND STATE UNIVERSITY POETRY CENTER

2121 Euclid Ave., RT 1841, Cleveland OH 44115. (216)687-3986. **Fax:** (216)687-6943. **E-mail:** poetrycenter@csuohio.edu. **Website:** www.csuohio.edu/poetrycenter. **Contact:** Frank Giampietro, manager.

NEEDS The Cleveland State University Poetry Center publishes "full-length collections by established and emerging poets, through competition and solicitation, as well as occasional poetry anthologies, texts on poetics, and novellas. Eclectic in its taste and inclusive in its aesthetic, with particular interest in lyric poetry and innovative approaches to craft. Not interested in light verse, devotional verse, doggerel, or poems by poets who have not read much contemporary poetry." Recent CSU Poetry Center publications include *The Hartford Book*, by Samuel Amadon; *Mother Was a Tragic Girl*, by Sandra Simonds; *I Live in a Hut*, by S.E. Smith; *Uncanny Valley*, by Jon Woodward.

HOW TO CONTACT "Most manuscripts we publish are accepted through the competitions. All manuscripts sent for competitions are considered for publication. Outside of competitions, manuscripts are accepted by solicitation only."

● COACH HOUSE BOOKS

(416)979-2217. **Fax:** (416)977-1158. **E-mail:** editor@chbooks.com. **Website:** www.chbooks.com. **Contact:** Alana Wilcox, editor. Publishes trade paperback originals by Canadian authors. Pays 10% royalty on retail price. Publishes ms 1 year after acceptance. Responds in 6 months to queries. Guidelines available online.

TIPS "We are not a general publisher, and publish only Canadian poetry, fiction, artist books and drama. We are interested primarily in innovative or experimental writing."

● ● COFFEE HOUSE PRESS

79 13th NE, Suite 110, Minneapolis MN 55413. (612)338-0125. **Fax:** (612)338-4004. **E-mail:** info@coffeehousepress.org. **Website:** www.coffeehousepress.org. **Contact:** Chris Fischbach, associate publisher. This successful nonprofit small press has received numerous grants from various organizations including the NEA, the McKnight Foundation and Target. Books published by Coffee House Press have won numerous honors and awards. Example: The Book of Medicines by Linda Hogan won the Colo-

rado Book Award for Poetry and the Lannan Foundation Literary Fellowship. Publishes hardcover and trade paperback originals. Responds in 4-6 weeks to queries; up to 6 months to mss. Book catalog and ms guidelines online.

HOW TO CONTACT As of September 1, 2010, Coffee House Press will only accept submissions during two annual reading periods: September 1-October 31 and March 1-April 30. Submissions postmarked outside of these two reading periods will not be considered or returned. In addition, until further notice, Coffee House Press will not accept unsolicited poetry submissions. Please check our web page periodically for future updates to this policy.

TIPS Look for our books at stores and libraries to get a feel for what we like to publish. No phone calls, e-mails, or faxes."

COTEAU BOOKS

(306)777-0170. **Fax:** (306)522-5152. **E-mail:** coteau@coteaubooks.com. **Website:** www.coteaubooks.com. **Contact:** Geoffrey Ursell, publisher. "Our mission is to publish the finest in Canadian fiction, nonfiction, poetry, drama, and children's literature, with an emphasis on Saskatchewan and prairie writers. De-emphasizing science fiction, picture books." Publishes trade paperback originals and reprints. Pays 10% royalty on retail price. 12 months. Responds in 3 months to queries and manuscripts. Book catalog available free. Guidelines available online.

NEEDS Coteau Books is a "small literary press that publishes poetry, fiction, drama, anthologies, criticism, young adult novels—**by Canadian writers only**." Has published *The Crooked Good* by Louise Bernice Halfe, *Wolf Tree* by Alison Calder, and *Love of Mirrors* by Gary Hyland.

HOW TO CONTACT Submit mss (80-100 poems only) typed with at least 12-point font. No simultaneous or non-Canadian submissions. No e-mail or fax submissions. Cover letter is required. Include publishing credits and bio, and SASE for return of ms. Accepts poetry mss from September 1-December 31 only. Responds to queries and mss in 4 months. Always sends prepublication galleys. Author receives 10% royalties and 10 author's copies. Order samples by sending 9x12 SASE for catalog. Submit 20-25 sample poems and complete ms.

ADDITIONAL INFORMATION Website includes title and ordering information, author interviews, awards, news and events, submission guidelines, and links.

TIPS "Look at past publications to get an idea of our editorial program. We do not publish romance, horror, or picture books but are interested in juvenile and teen fiction from Canadian authors. Submissions, even queries, must be made in hard copy only. We do not accept simultaneous/multiple submissions. Check our website for new submission timing guidelines."

CRESCENT MOON PUBLISHING

P.O. Box 393, Maidstone Kent ME14 5XU, UK. (44)(162)272-9593. **E-mail:** cresmopub@yahoo.co.uk. **Website:** www.crescentmoon.org.uk. **Contact:** Jeremy Robinson, director (arts, media, cinema, literature); Cassidy Hushes (visual arts). "Our mission is to publish the best in contemporary work, in poetry, fiction, and critical studies, and selections from the great writers. Currently emphasizing nonfiction (media, film, music, painting). De-emphasizing children's books." Publishes hardcover and trade paperback originals. Pays royalty. Pays negotiable advance. Publishes ms 18 months after acceptance. Responds in 2 months to queries; 4 months to proposals and mss. Book catalog and ms guidelines free.

NEEDS "We prefer a small selection of the poet's very best work at first. We prefer free verse or non-rhyming poetry. Do not send too much material."

HOW TO CONTACT Query and submit 6 sample poems.

TIPS "Our audience is interested in new contemporary writing."

CROSS-CULTURAL COMMUNICATIONS

Cross-Cultural Literary Editions, Ltd.; Express Editions; Ostrich Editions, 239 Wynsum Ave., Merrick NY 11566. (516)869-5635. **Fax:** (516)379-1901. **E-mail:** cccpoetry@aol.com. **Website:** www.cross-cultural-communications.com. **Contact:** Stanley H. Barkan, publisher/editor-in-chief (bilingual poetry); Bebe Barkan, Mia Barkan Clarke, art editors (complementary art to poetry editions). Publishes hardcover and trade paperback originals. Publishes book 1 year after acceptance. Responds in 1 month to proposals; 2 months to mss. Book catalog (sample flyers) for #10 SASE.

HOW TO CONTACT For bilingual poetry submit 3-6 short poems in original language with English translation, a brief (3-5 lines) bio of the author and translator(s).

TIPS "Best chance: poetry from a translation."

CRYSTAL SPIRIT PUBLISHING, INC.

P.O. Box 12506, Durham NC 27709. **E-mail:** crystalspiritinc@gmail.com. **Website:** www.crystalspiritinc.com. **Contact:** Vanessa S. O'Neal, senior editor; Elise L. Lattier, editor. "Our readers are lovers of high-quality books that are sold in book and gift stores and placed in libraries and schools. They support independent authors and they expect works that will provide them with entertainment, inspiration, romance, and education. Our audience loves to read and will embrace niche authors that love to write." Publishes hardcover, trade paperback, mass market paperback, and electronic originals. Pays 20-45% royalty on retail price. Publishes ms 3-6 months after acceptance. Responds in 3-6 months to mss. Book catalog and ms guidelines available online at website.

NEEDS "All poetry must have titles. Include a description of the collective works and type of poetry."

HOW TO CONTACT Submit 10 sample poems.

TIPS "Submissions are accepted for publication throughout the year, but the decisions for publishing considerations are made in March, June, September, and December. Works should be positive and non-threatening. Typed pages only. Non-typed entries will not be reviewed or returned. Ensure that all contact information is correct, abide by the submission guidelines and do not send follow-up e-mails or calls."

⊘ DAVID R. GODINE, PUBLISHER

15 Court Square, Suite 320, Boston MA 02108. (617)451-9600. **Fax:** (617)350-0250. **E-mail:** info@godine.com. **Website:** www.godine.com. "We publish books that matter for people who care."

This publisher is no longer considering unsolicited mss of any type. Only interested in agented material.

DIAL BOOKS FOR YOUNG READERS

Imprint of Penguin Group USA, 375 Hudson St., New York NY 10014. (212)366-2000. **Website:** www.penguin.com/youngreaders. **Contact:** Lauri Hornik, president/publisher; Kathy Dawson, associate publisher; Kate Harrison, senior editor; Liz Waniewski, editor; Alisha Niehaus, editor; Jessica Garrison, editor; Lily Malcom, art director. "Dial Books for Young Readers publishes quality picture books for ages 18 months-6 years; lively, believable novels for middle readers and young adults; and occasional nonfiction for middle readers and young adults." Publishes hard-

cover originals. Pays royalty. Pays varies advance. Responds in 4-6 months to queries. Book catalog for 9 X12 envelope and 4 first-class stamps.

TIPS "Our readers are anywhere from preschool age to teenage. Picture books must have strong plots, lots of action, unusual premises, or universal themes treated with freshness and originality. Humor works well in these books. A very well-thought-out and intelligently presented book has the best chance of being taken on. Genre isn't as much of a factor as presentation."

DIVERSION PRESS

E-mail: diversionpress@yahoo.com. **Website:** www.diversionpress.com. Publishes hardcover, trade and mass market paperback originals. Pays 10% royalty on wholesale price. Publishes ms 1-2 years after acceptance. Responds in 2 weeks to queries. Responds in 1 month to proposals. Guidelines available online.

NEEDS "Poetry will be considered for anthology series and for our poetry award."

HOW TO CONTACT Submit 5 sample poems.

TIPS "Read our website and blog prior to submitting. We like short, concise queries. Tell us why your book is different, not like other books. Give us a realistic idea of what you will do to market your book—that you will actually do. We will ask for more information if we are interested."

DREAMLAND BOOKS INC.

P.O.Box 1714, Minnetonka MN 55345. (612)281-4704. **E-mail:** dreamlandbooks@inbox.com. **Website:** www.dreamlandbooksinc.com.

NEEDS "We ARE accpeting poetry and flash story submissions for our poetry journal Cellar Door Poetry. We accept all forms of poetry, but will not publish any work that promotes violence or pornography."

DUFOUR EDITIONS

(610)458-5005 or (800)869-5677. **Fax:** (610)458-7103. **Website:** www.dufoureditions.com. We publish literary fiction by good writers which is well received and achieves modest sales. De-emphsazing poetry and nonfiction. Publishes hardcover originals, trade paperback originals and reprints. Pays $100-500 advance. 18 months Responds in 3 months to queries. Responds in 3 months to proposals. Responds in 6 months to manuscripts. Book catalog available free.

HOW TO CONTACT Query.

TIPS Audience is sophisticated, literate readers especially interested in foreign literature and translations, and a strong Irish-Celtic focus, as well as work from U.S. writers. Check to see if the publisher is really a good match for your subject matter.

ÉCRITS DES FORGES

992-A, rue Royale, Trois-Rivières QC G9A 4H9, Canada. (819)840-8492. **Website:** www.ecritsdesforges. com. **Contact:** Stéphane Despatie, director. Pays royalties of 10-20%. Responds to queries in 6 months.

NEEDS Écrits des Forges publishes poetry only that is "authentic and original as a signature. We have published poetry from more than 1,000 poets coming from most of the francophone countries: Andreé Romus (Belgium), Amadou Lamine Sall (Seéneégal), Nicole Brossard, Claude Beausoleil, Jean-Marc Desgent, and Jean-Paul Daoust (Québec)." Publishes 45-50 paperback books of poetry/year. Books are usually 80-88 pages, digest-sized, perfect-bound, with 2-color covers with art.

HOW TO CONTACT Query first with a few sample poems and a cover letter with brief bio and publication credits. Order sample books by writing or faxing.

FABER & FABER INC.

Farrar, Straus & Giroux, 18 W. 18th St., New York NY 10011. (212)741-6900. **E-mail:** fsg.editorial@fsgbooks. com. **Website:** us.macmillan.com/faberandfaber.aspx. Responds in 6-8 weeks.

HOW TO CONTACT "All submissions must be submitted through the mail—we do not accept electronic submissions, or submissions delivered in person. Please include a cover letter describing your submission, along with the first 50 pages of the manuscript. If you are submitting poems, please include 3-4 poems."

FABER & FABER LTD

Bloomsbury House, 74-77 Great Russell St., London WC1B 3DA, United Kingdom. 020 7465 0045. **Fax:** 020 7465 0034. **Website:** www.faber.co.uk. **Contact:** Lee Brackstone, Hannah Griffiths, Angus Cargill, (fiction); Walter Donohue, (film); Dinah Wood, (plays); Julian Loose, Neil Belton, (nonfiction); Paul Keegan, (poetry); Belinda Matthews, (music); Suzy Jenvy, Julia Wells, (children's). Faber & Faber have rejuvenated their nonfiction, music and children's titles in recent years and the film and drama lists remain market leaders. Publishes hardcover and paperback originals and reprints. Pays royalty. Pays varying advances with each project. Responds in 3 months to mss. Book catalog available online.

Faber & Faber will consider unsolicited proposals for poetry only.

NEEDS Address poetry to 'Poetry Submissions Department' and include an SAE for return. For more information, ring 020 7465 0045.

HOW TO CONTACT Submit 6 sample poems.

TIPS Explore the website and downloadable book catalogues thoroughly to get a feel for the lists in all categories and genres.

FANTASTIC BOOKS PUBLISHING

Lilac Tree Farm, Honeypots Ln., Elstronwick East Yorkshire HU12 9BP, United Kingdom. +44 (07415)388882. **E-mail:** fantasticbookspublishing@ gmail.com. **Website:** www.fantasticbookspublishing. com. **Contact:** Daniel Grubb, CEO/COO. Publishes trade paperback and electronic originals. Pays 40-100% on wholesale price. No advance. Publishes ms 3-4 months after acceptance. Responds in 1 week to queries; 1 month to proposals; 3 months to mss. Catalog and guidelines available online at website.

50% author-subsidy published.

HOW TO CONTACT Submit 3 sample poems.

TIPS "Be yourself. Don't try to come across as anything different. We work very closely with our clients and it is our intention to get to know you and to welcome you into our publishing family. This helps us market and promote your book to your target audience. It also helps the reputation of the publishing industry which, in these times of constant change, is what we intend to do by being honest, transparent and, above all, sincere with our clients."

FARRAR, STRAUS & GIROUX

18 W. 18th St., New York NY 10011. (646)307-5151. **E-mail:** fsg.editorial@fsgbooks.com. **Website:** us.macmillan.com. **Contact:** Children's Editorial Department. (Specialized: children) "We publish original and well-written material for all ages." Publishes hardcover originals and trade paperback reprints Pays 2-6% royalty on retail price for paperbacks, 3-10% for hardcovers. Pays $3,000-25,000 advance. 18 months Responds in 2 months to queries. Responds in 3 months to manuscripts For catalog fax request or email to: childrens.publicity@fsgbooks.com Guidelines available online

NEEDS Publishes one book of children's poetry "every once in a while," in trade hardcover only. Open to book-length submissions of children's poetry only. Has published Valerie Worth's *Peacock and Other Po-*

ems, Tony Johnston's *An Old Shell*, and Helen Frost's *Keesha's House* (a novel in poems).

HOW TO CONTACT Query first with sample poems and cover letter with brief bio and publication credits. Considers simultaneous submissions. Seldom comments on rejected poems. Send SASE for reply. Responds to queries in up to 2 months, to mss in up to 4 months. "We pay an advance against royalties; the amount depends on whether or not the poems are illustrated, etc." Also pays 10 author's copies.

TIPS Audience is full age range, preschool to young adult. Specializes in literary fiction.

FENCE BOOKS

(518)591-8162. **E-mail:** fence.fencebooks@gmail.com; robfence@gmail.com. **Website:** www.fenceportal.org. **Contact:** Rob Arnold, Submissions Manager. "*Fence is closed to submissions right now.* We'll have another reading period in the Spring. Fence Books offers 2 book contests (in addition to the National Poetry Series) with 2 sets of guidelines and entry forms on our website." Hardcover originals. Guidelines available online.

NEEDS Enter National Poetry Series Contest. See Open Competition Guidelines online. Also the annual Fence Books Motherwell Prize 2011 ($5,000) for a first or second book of poetry by a woman. Submit 48-60 pages during the month of November; and Fence Modern Poets Series 2011, for a poet writing in English at any stage in his or her career. $25 entry fee.

HOW TO CONTACT Submissions may be sent through regular USPS mail, UPS, Fedex-type couriers, or certified mail.

TIPS "At present Fence Books is a self-selecting publisher; mss come to our attention through our contests and through editors' investigations. We hope to become open to submissions of poetry and fiction mss in the near future."

✚ FIRST EDITION DESIGN PUBLISHING

5202 Old Ashwood Dr., Sarasota FL 34233. (941)921-2607. **Fax:** (617)249-1694. **E-mail:** support@firsteditiondesign.com. **E-mail:** submission@firsteditiondesign.com. **Website:** www.firsteditiondesignpublishing.com. **Contact:** Deborah E. Gordon, executive editor; Tom Gahan, marketing director. Pays royalty 30-70% on retail price. Accept to publish time is 1 week to 2 months. Send SAE for catalog. Guidelines available free on request or online at website.

HOW TO CONTACT Submit complete ms electronically.

TIPS "Follow our FAQs listed on our website."

◐◑⑤ FLARESTACK POETS

69 Beaks Hill Road, Birmingham B38 8BL, United Kingdom. **E-mail:** meria@btinternet.com; jacquierowe@hotmail.co.uk. **Website:** www.flarestackpoets.co.uk. **Contact:** Meredith Andrea and Jacqui Rowe. Pays 25% royalty and 6 contributor's copies. Responds in 6 weeks.

NEEDS Flarestack Poets wants "poems that dare outside current trends, even against the grain." Does not want "poems that fail to engage with either language or feeling." First chapbooks appearing in Autumn 2009. Publishes 8 chapbooks/year and 1 anthology. Manuscripts are selected through open submission and competition. "Our first chapbooks are winners of the 2009 Flarestack Poets Pamphlet competition. Thereafter we will consider open submissions." Chapbooks are 20-30 pages, professional photocopy, saddle-stitched, card cover.

HOW TO CONTACT Query first with a few sample poems and a cover letter with brief bio and publication credits. Ms may include previously published poems.

● FLOATING BRIDGE PRESS

909 NE 43rd St., #205, Seattle WA 98105. **E-mail:** floatingbridgepress@yahoo.com. **Website:** www.floatingbridgepress.org.

NEEDS Floating Bridge Press publishes chapbooks and anthologies by Washington State poets, selected through an annual competition (see below). Has published *After* by Nancy Pagh, *In the Convent We Become Clouds* by Annette Spaulding-Convy, *Toccata & Fugue* by Timothy Kelly, and *The Former St. Christopher* by Michael Bonacci, among others. The press also publishes *Floating Bridge Review*, an annual anthology featuring the work of Washington State poets. *Floating Bridge Review* is 86-144 pages, digest-sized, offset-printed, perfect-bound, with glossy cardstock cover. For a sample chapbook or anthology, send $13 postpaid.

CONTEST/AWARD OFFERINGS For consideration, **Washington State poets only** should submit a chapbook ms of 20-24 pages of poetry. In addition to publication, the winner receives $500, 15 author's copies, and a reading in the Seattle area. All entrants receive a copy of the winning chapbook and will be considered for inclusion in *Floating Bridge Review*. Poet's name must not appear on the ms. Include a separate page with ms title, poet's name, address, phone number, and acknowledgments of any previous publications. Include SASE for results only; mss will not be returned. **Entry fee:** $12. **Deadline:** usual reading period is November 1-February 15 (postmark). Considers previously published individual poems and simultaneous submissions. Mss are judged anonymously.

⊕ FOLDED WORD

5209 Del Vista Way, Rocklin CA 95765. Phone/**Fax:** (916)624-5088. **E-mail:** editors@foldedword.com. **Website:** www.foldedword.com. Editor-in-Chief: J.S. Graustein. Poetry Editor: Rose Auslander. Fiction Editor: Casey Murphy. "Folded Word is an independent literary press. Our focus? Connecting new voices to readers. Our goal? To make poetry and fiction accessible for the widest audience possible both on and off the page."

TIPS "E-mail is the best way to reach us."

◐ FOUR WAY BOOKS

Box 535, Village Station, New York NY 10014. **E-mail:** editors@fourwaybooks.com. **Website:** www.fourwaybooks.com. **Contact:** Martha Rhodes, director. "Four Way Books is a not-for-profit literary press dedicated to publishing poetry and short fiction by emerging and established writers. Each year, Four Way Books publishes the winners of its national poetry competitions, as well as collections accepted through general submission, panel selection, and solicitation by the editors."

NEEDS Four Way Books publishes poetry and short fiction. Considers full-length poetry mss only. Has published poetry by D. Nurkse, Noelle Kocot, Susan Wheeler, Nancy Mitchell, Henry Israeli, and Paul Jenkins. Publishes 8-11 books a year. Books are about 70 pages, offset-printed digitally, perfect-bound, with paperback binding, art/graphics on covers. Does not want individual poems or poetry intended for children/young readers.

HOW TO CONTACT See website for complete submission guidelines and open reading period in June. Book mss may include previously published poems. Responds to submissions in 4 months. Payment varies. Order sample books from Four Way Books online or through bookstores.

FRONT STREET

Boyds Mills Press, 815 Church St., Honesdale PA 18431. **Website:** www.frontstreetbooks.com. **Contact:** Acquisitions Editor. "We are an independent publisher of books for children and young adults." Publishes hardcover originals and trade paperback reprints. Pays royalty on retail price. Pays advance. 1 year Responds in 3 months. Book catalog available online. Guidelines available online.

HOW TO CONTACT Submit book-length collection of poems. "Keep in mind that the strongest collections demonstrate a facility with multiple poetic forms."

TIPS "Read through our recently published titles and review our website. Check to see what's on the market and in our catalog before submitting your story. Feel free to query us if you're not sure."

● FUTURECYCLE PRESS

Website: www.futurecycle.org. **Contact:** Diane Kistner, director/editor-in-chief. Pays 10% royalty and 25 author's copies. Responds to mss in 3 months. Guidelines available online at website.

NEEDS Wants "poetry from highly skilled poets, whether well known or emerging. With a few exceptions, we are eclectic in our editorial tastes." Does not want concrete or visual poetry. Has published David Chorlton, John Laue, Temple Cone, Neil Carpathios, Tania Runyan, Timothy Martin, Joanne Lowery. Publishes 4 poetry books/year and 2 chapbooks/year. Ms. selected through open submission and competition. "We read unsolicited mss. but also conduct a yearly poetry book competition." Books are 60-90 pages; offset print, perfect-bound, with glossy, full color cover stock, b&w inside. Chapbooks are 20-40 pages, offset print, saddle-stitched.

HOW TO CONTACT Submit complete ms, no need to query.

⊘ GHOST PONY PRESS

P.O. Box 260113, Madison WI 53726. **E-mail:** ghostponypress@hotmail.com. **Website:** ghostponypress.com. **Contact:** Ingrid Swanberg, editor/publisher. Ghost Pony Press has published 3 books of poetry by próspero saíz, including *the bird of nothing & other poems* (168 pages, 7x10, with sewn and wrapped binding; paperback available for $20, signed and numbered edition for $35). Also published *zen concrete & etc.* by d.a. levy (268 pages, magazine-sized, perfect-bound, illustrated; paperback available for $27.50).

HOW TO CONTACT Query first, with a few sample poems (5-10) and cover letter with brief bio and publication credits. Include SASE. Considers previously published material for book publication. Accepts submissions by postal mail only; no e-mail submissions. Editor sometimes comments briefly on rejected poems. No promised response time. "We currently have a considerable backlog."

GINNINDERRA PRESS

P.O. Box 3461, Port Adelaide 5015, Australia. (61)(2)6258-9060. **Fax:** (61)(2)6258-9069. **E-mail:** stephen@ginninderrapress.com.au. **Website:** www.ginninderrapress.com.au. **Contact:** Stephen Matthews, publisher. Ginninderra Press works "to give publishing opportunities to new writers." Has published poetry by Alan Gould and Geoff Page. Books are usually up to 72 pages, A5, laser-printed, saddle-stapled or thermal-bound, with board covers. Responds to queries within 1 week; mss in 2 months.

Publishes books by Australian authors only.

HOW TO CONTACT Query first, with a few sample poems and a cover letter with brief bio and publication credits. Considers previously published poems.

GIVAL PRESS

Gival Press, LLC, P.O. Box 3812, Arlington VA 22203. (703)351-0079. **E-mail:** givalpress@yahoo.com. **Website:** www.givalpress.com. **Contact:** Robert L. Giron, editor-in-chief (area of interest: literary). Publishes trade paperback, electronic originals, and reprints. Royalties (% varies). 12 months Responds in 1 month to queries, 3 months to proposals & mss. Book catalog available online, free on request/for #10 SASE Guidelines available online, by email, free on request/for #10 SASE

HOW TO CONTACT Query via email; provide description, bio, etc.; submit 5-6 sample poems via email.

TIPS "Our audience is those who read literary works with depth to the work. Visit our website—there is much to be read/learned from the numerous pages."

GOOSE LANE EDITIONS

(506)450-4251. **Fax:** (506)459-4991. **Website:** www.gooselane.com/submissions.php. **Contact:** Angela Williams, publishing assistant. "Goose Lane publishes literary fiction and nonfiction from well-read and highly skilled Canadian authors." Publishes hardcover and paperback originals and occasional reprints. Pays 8-10% royalty on retail price. Pays $500-3,000, negotiable advance. Responds in 6 months to queries.

NEEDS Goose Lane is a small literary press publishing Canadian fiction, poetry, and nonfiction. **Considers mss by Canadian poets only.** Receives about 400 mss/year, publishes 15-20 books/year, 4 of which are poetry collections. Has published *Beatitudes* by Herménégilde Chiasson and *I & I* by George Elliott Clarke.

HOW TO CONTACT "Call to inquire whether we are reading submissions." Accepts submissions by postal mail only. Guidelines available on website. Always sends prepublication galleys. Authors may receive royalties of up to 10% of retail price on all copies sold. Copies available to author at 40% discount.

TIPS "Writers should send us outlines and samples of books that show a very well-read author with highly developed literary skills. Our books are almost all by Canadians living in Canada; we seldom consider submissions from outside Canada. If I were a writer trying to market a book today, I would contact the targeted publisher with a query letter and synopsis, and request manuscript guidelines. Purchase a recent book from the publisher in a relevant area, if possible. Always send an SASE with IRCs or suffient return postage in Canadian stamps for reply to your query and for any material you'd like returned should it not suit our needs. Specializes in high quality Canadian literary fiction, poetry, and nonfiction. We consider submissions from outside Canada only when the author is Canadian and the book is of extraordinary interest to Canadian readers. We do not publish books for children or for the young adult market."

GRAYWOLF PRESS

250 Third Ave. N., Suite 600, Minneapolis MN 55401. **E-mail:** wolves@graywolfpress.org. **Website:** www.graywolfpress.org. **Contact:** Katie Dublinski, editorial manager (nonfiction, fiction). "Graywolf Press is an independent, nonprofit publisher dedicated to the creation and promotion of thoughtful and imaginative contemporary literature essential to a vital and diverse culture." Publishes trade cloth and paperback originals. Pays royalty on retail price. Pays $1,000-25,000 advance. Publishes 18 months after acceptance. Responds in 3 months to queries. Book catalog available free. Guidelines available online.

NEEDS Graywolf Press is considered one of the nation's leading nonprofit literary publishers. "Graywolf introduces and promotes some of the most exciting and creative writers of our times." Considers only mss by poets widely published in magazines and journals of merit; **does not generally consider unsolicited mss but considers queries**. Has published poetry by Elizabeth Alexander, Vijay Seshadri, Tess Gallagher, Tony Hoagland, Matthea Harvey, D.A. Powell, and many more. Publishes around 9 collections of poetry, 1-2 collections of poetry in translation, and 1-2 collections of essays on poetry/year. "We are interested in linguistically challenging work." Query with SASE.

HOW TO CONTACT *No unsolicited mss.* Query first, with 10 pages of poetry (as a sample from the ms) and cover letter with brief bio and publication credits through online submission form. See website for guidelines. SASE required for reply. No e-mail queries. Reads queries in January, May, and September. Responds to queries in 3-6 months. Order sample books through website, or request catalog through online submission form.

⊘ GROVE/ATLANTIC, INC.

841 Broadway, 4th Floor, New York NY 10003. (212)614-7850. **Fax:** (212)614-7886. **E-mail:** info@groveatlantic.com. **Website:** www.groveatlantic.com. "Due to limited resources of time and staffing, Grove/Atlantic cannot accept manuscripts that do not come through a literary agent. In today's publishing world, agents are more important than ever, helping writers shape their work and navigate the main publishing houses to find the most appropriate outlet for a project." Publishes hardcover and trade paperback originals, and reprints. Pays 7 ½-12 ½% royalty. Makes outright purchase of $5-500,000. Book published 9 months after acceptance of ms. Responds in 1 month to queries; 2 months to proposals; 4 months to mss. Book catalog available online.

HOW TO CONTACT Agented submissions only.

⊘♲ GUERNICA EDITIONS

Box 117, Station P, Toronto ON M5S 2S6, Canada. (416)576-9403. **Fax:** (416)981-7606. **E-mail:** michaelmirolla@guernicaeditions.com. **Website:** www.guernicaeditions.com. **Contact:** Antonio D'Alfonso, editor/publisher (poetry, nonfiction, novels). Guernica Editions is a literary press that produces works of poetry, fiction and nonfiction often by writers who are ignored by the mainstream. Publishes trade paperback originals and reprints. Pays 8-10% royalty on retail price, or makes outright purchase of $200-5,000. Pays $200-2,000 advance. Publishes 15 months after acceptance. Responds in 1 month to queries. Re-

sponds in 6 months to proposals. Responds in 1 year to manuscripts Book catalog available online.

NEEDS Feminist, gay/lesbian, literary, multicultural, poetry in translation. We wish to have writers in translation. Any writer who has translated Italian poetry is welcomed. Full books only. No single poems by different authors, unless modern, and used as an anthology. First books will have no place in the next couple of years.

HOW TO CONTACT Query.

HIGH PLAINS PRESS

P.O. Box 123, 403 Cassa Rd., Glendo WY 82213. (307)735-4370. **Fax:** (307)735-4590. **E-mail:** editor@highplainspress.com. **Website:** www.highplainspress.com. **Contact:** Nancy Curtis, publisher. High Plains Press is a regional book publishing company specializing in books about the American West, with special interest in things relating to Wyoming. Publishes hardcover and trade paperback originals. Pays 10% royalty on wholesale price. Pays $200-1,200 advance. Publishes book 2 years after acceptance of ms. Responds in 3 months to queries and proposals; 12 months on mss. Book catalog available online. Guidelines available online.

NEEDS "We publish 1 poetry volume a year. Require connection to West. Consider poetry in August."

HOW TO CONTACT Submit 5 sample poems.

TIPS "Our audience comprises general readers interested in history and culture of the Rockies."

⬎ HIPPOPOTAMUS PRESS

22 Whitewell Rd., Frome Somerset BA11 4EL, UK. (44)(173)466-6653. **E-mail:** rjhippopress@aol.com. **Contact:** R. John, editor; M. Pargitter (poetry); Anna Martin (translation). "Hippopotamus Press publishes first, full collections of verse by those well represented in the mainstream poetry magazines of the English-speaking world." Publishes hardcover and trade paperback originals. Pays 7½-10% royalty on retail price. Pays advance. Publishes book 10 months after acceptance. Responds in 1 month to queries. Book catalog available free.

NEEDS "Read one of our authors—poets often make the mistake of submitting poetry without knowing the type of verse we publish."

HOW TO CONTACT Query and submit complete ms.

TIPS "We publish books for a literate audience. We have a strong link to the Modernist tradition. Read what we publish."

HIS WORK CHRISTIAN PUBLISHING

P.O. Box 563, Ward Cove AK 99928. (206)274-8474. **Fax:** (614)388-0664. **E-mail:** hiswork@hisworkpub. com. **Website:** www.hisworkpub.com. **Contact:** Angela J. Perez, acquisitions editor. Publishes trade paperback and electronic originals and reprints; also, hardcover originals. Pays 10-20% royalty on wholesale price. Publishes book 1-2 years after acceptance. Responds in 1-3 months to queries; 1-2 months to *requested* manuscripts. Book catalog available online. "Guidelines available online and updated regularly. Please check these before submitting to see what we are looking for."

NEEDS "We only plan to publish 1-2 titles per year in poetry. Send us only your best work."

HOW TO CONTACT Submit 15 sample poems.

TIPS "Audience is children and adults who are looking for the entertainment and relaxation you can only get from jumping into a good book. Submit only your best work to us. Submit only in the genres we are interested in publishing. Do not submit work that is not suitable for a Christian audience."

HOLIDAY HOUSE, INC.

(212)688-0085. **Fax:** (212)421-6134. **E-mail:** info@ holidayhouse.com. **Website:** holidayhouse.com. **Contact:** Mary Cash, editor-in-chief. "Holiday House publishes children's and young adult books for the school and library markets. We have a commitment to publishing first-time authors and illustrators. We specialize in quality hardcovers from picture books to young adult, both fiction and nonfiction, primarily for the school and library market." Publishes hardcover originals and paperback reprints. Pays royalty on list price, range varies. Agent's royalty. Publishes 1-2 years after acceptance. Responds in 4 months. Guidelines for #10 SASE.

NEEDS A trade children's book house. Has published hardcover books for children by John Updike and Walter Dean Myers. Publishes one poetry book/ year, averaging 32 pages.

HOW TO CONTACT "The acceptance of complete book mss of high-quality children's poetry is limited." Please send the entire manuscript, whether submitting a picture book or novel by mail. Does not accept submissions by e-mail or fax.

TIPS "We need manuscripts with strong stories and writing."

⊘ ⊘ ⊛ HOUSE OF ANANSI PRESS

110 Spadina Ave., Suite 801, Toronto ON M5V 2K4, Canada. (416)363-4343. **Fax:** (416)363-1017. **Website:** www.anansi.ca. Pays 8-10% royalties. Pays $750 advance and 10 author's copies. Responds to queries within 1 year, to mss (if invited) within 4 months.

NEEDS House of Anansi publishes literary fiction and poetry by Canadian and international writers. "We seek to balance the list between well-known and emerging writers, with an interest in writing by Canadians of all backgrounds. We publish Canadian poetry only, and poets must have a substantial publication record—if not in books, then definitely in journals and magazines of repute." Does not want "children's poetry or poetry by previously unpublished poets." Has published *Power Politics* by Margaret Atwood and *Ruin & Beauty* by Patricia Young. Books are generally 96-144 pages, trade paperbacks with French sleeves, with matte covers.

HOW TO CONTACT Canadian poets should query first with 10 sample poems (typed double-spaced) and a cover letter with brief bio and publication credits. Considers simultaneous submissions. Poems are circulated to an editorial board. Often comments on rejected poems.

ILIUM PRESS

2407 S. Sonora Dr., Spokane WA 99037. (509)928-7950. **E-mail:** contact@iliumpress.com; submissions@iliumpress.com. **Website:** www.iliumpress. com. **Contact:** John Lemon, owner/editor (literature, epic poetry, how-to). Publishes trade paperback originals and reprints, electronic originals and reprints. Pays 20%-50% royalties on receipts. Publishes ms up to 1 year after acceptance. Responds in 6 months to queries/proposals/mss. Guidelines available on website www.iliumpress.com.

NEEDS "Submit only book-length narrative epic poems in metered blank or sprung verse. All others will be rejected. See submission guidelines on website."

HOW TO CONTACT Query with first 20 pages and SASE.

TIPS "Read submission guidelines and literary preferences on the website: www.iliumpress.com."

○ INSOMNIAC PRESS

520 Princess Ave., London ON N6B 2B8, Canada. (416)504-6270. **E-mail:** mike@insomniacpress.com. **Website:** www.insomniacpress.com. **Contact:** Mike O'Connor, publisher. Publishes trade paperback origi-

nals and reprints, mass market paperback originals, and electronic originals and reprints. Pays 10-15% royalty on retail price. Pays $500-1,000 advance. 6 months Guidelines available online

NEEDS "Our poetry publishing is limited to 2-4 books per year and we are often booked up a year or two in advance."

HOW TO CONTACT Submit complete ms.

TIPS "We envision a mixed readership that appreciates up-and-coming literary fiction and poetry as well as solidly researched and provocative nonfiction. Peruse our website and familiarize yourself with what we've published in the past."

ITALICA PRESS

595 Main St., Suite 605, New York NY 10044-0047. (917)371-0563. **E-mail:** inquiries@italicapress.com. **Website:** www.italicapress.com. **Contact:** Ronald G. Musto and Eileen Gardiner, publishers. "Italica Press publishes English translations of modern Italian fiction and medieval and Renaissance nonfiction." Publishes trade paperback originals Pays 7-15% royalty on wholesale price; author's copies. 1 year Responds in 1 month to queries. Responds in 4 months to manuscripts. Book catalog and guidelines available online.

NEEDS Italica is a small press publisher of English translations of Italian works in paperbacks, averaging 175 pages. Has published *Contemporary Italian Women Poets*, a dual-language (English/Italian) anthology edited and translated by Anzia Sartini Blum and Lara Trubowitz, and *Women Poets of the Italian Renaissance*, a dual-language anthology, edited by Laura Anna Stortoni, translated by Laura Anna Stortoni and Mary Prentice Lillie. Poetry titles are always translations and generally dual language.

HOW TO CONTACT Query with 10 sample translations of medieval and Renaissance Italian poets. Include cover letter, bio, and list of publications. Accepts simultaneous submissions, but translation should not be "totally" previously published. Accepts e-mail submissions; no fax submissions. Responds to queries in 3 weeks, to mss in 3 months. Always sends prepublication galleys. Pays 7-15% royalties plus 10 author's copies. Acquires English language rights.

TIPS "We are interested in considering a wide variety of medieval and Renaissance topics (not historical fiction), and for modern works we are only interested in translations from Italian fiction by well-known Italian authors." *Only* fiction that has been previously published in Italian. A *brief* call saves a lot of postage. 90% of proposals we receive are completely off base—but we are very interested in things that are right on target. Please send return postage if you want your ms returned.

ALICE JAMES BOOKS

238 Main St., Farmington ME 04938. (207)778-7071. **Fax:** (207)778-7766. **E-mail:** interns@alicejames-books.org; frank@alicejamesbooks.org. **Website:** www.alicejamesbooks.org. **Contact:** Meg Willing, managing editor; Carey Salerno, executive director; Ellen Marlow, editorial assistant. "Alice James Books is a nonprofit cooperative poetry press. The founders' objectives were to give women access to publishing and to involve authors in the publishing process. The cooperative selects mss for publication through both regional and national competitions." Publishes trade paperback originals. Pays through competition awards. Publishes ms 1 year after acceptance. Responds promptly to queries; 4 months to mss. Book catalog for free or on website. Guidelines for #10 SASE or on website.

NEEDS "Alice James Books is a nonprofit cooperative poetry press. The founders' objectives were to give women access to publishing and to involve authors in the publishing process. The cooperative selects mss for publication through both regional and national competitions." Seeks to publish the best contemporary poetry by both established and beginning poets, with particular emphasis on involving poets in the publishing process. Has published poetry by Jane Kenyon, Jean Valentine, B.H. Fairchild, and Matthea Harvey. Publishes flat-spined paperbacks of high quality, both in production and contents. Does not want children's poetry or light verse. Publishes 6 paperback books/year, 80 pages each, in editions of approximately 1,500.

HOW TO CONTACT Query.

TIPS "Send SASE for contest guidelines or check website. Do not send work without consulting current guidelines."

THE JOHNS HOPKINS UNIVERSITY PRESS

2715 N. Charles St., Baltimore MD 21218. (410)516-6900. **Fax:** (410)516-6968. **E-mail:** jmm@press.jhu.edu. **Website:** www.press.jhu.edu. **Contact:** Jacqueline C. Wehmueller, executive editor (consumer health, psychology and psychiatry, and history of medicine; jcw@press.jhu.edu); Matthew McAdam, editor (mxm@jhu@press.edu); Robert J. Brugger, senior acquisitions editor (American history; rjb@ press.jhu.edu); Vincent J. Burke, exec. editor (biology; vjb@press.jhu.edu); Juliana McCarthy, acquisitions editor (humanities, classics, and ancient studies; jmm@press.jhu.edu); Ashleigh McKown, assistant editor (higher education, history of technology, history of science; aem@press.jhu.edu); Suzanne Flinchbaugh, Associate Editor (Political Science, Health Policy, and Co-Publishing Liaison; skf@ press.jhu.edu; Greg Nicholl, Assistant Editor (Regional Books, Poetry and Fiction, and Anabaptist and Pietist Studies; gan@press.jhu.edu). Publishes hardcover originals and reprints, and trade paperback reprints. Pays royalty. Publishes ms 1 year after acceptance.

NEEDS "One of the largest American university presses, Johns Hopkins publishes primarily scholarly books and journals. We do, however, publish short fiction and poetry in the series Johns Hopkins: Poetry and Fiction, edited by John Irwin."

● ALFRED A. KNOPF

1745 Broadway, 21st Floor, New York NY 10019. **Website:** knopf.knopfdoubleday.com. Publishes hardcover and paperback originals. Royalties vary. Offers advance. Publishes ms 1 year after acceptance. Responds in 2-6 months to queries.

WENDY LAMB BOOKS

Imprint of Random House Children's Books/Random House, Inc., 1745 Broadway, New York NY 10019. (212)782-9000. **Fax:** (212)782-9452. **E-mail:** wlamb@randomhouse.com; cmeckler@randomhouse.com. **Website:** www.randomhouse.com. "Query letter with SASE for reply. A query letter should briefly describe the book you have written, the intended age group, and your brief biography and publishing credits, if any. Please send the first 10 pages (or to the end of the chapter) of your manuscript. Our turn around time is approximately 4-8 weeks." Publishes hardcover originals. Pays royalty. Guidelines for #10 SASE.

◐ Literary fiction and nonfiction for readers 8-15.

HOW TO CONTACT Submit 4 sample poems.

TIPS "Please note that we do not publish picture books. Please send the first 10 pages of your ms (or until the end of the first chapter) along with a cover letter, synopsis, and SASE. Before you submit, please take a look at some of our recent titles to get an idea of what we publish."

●◐ LAPWING PUBLICATIONS

1 Ballysillan Dr., Belfast BT14 8HQ, Northern Ireland. +44 2890 500 796. **Fax:** +44 2890 295 800. **E-mail:** lapwing.poetry@ntlworld.com. **Website:** www. lapwingpoetry.com. **Contact:** Dennis Greig, editor. Pays 20 author's copies, no royalties. Responds to queries in 1 month; mss in 2 months.

◐ Lapwing will produce work only if and when resources to do so are available.

NEEDS Lapwing publishes "emerging Irish poets and poets domiciled in Ireland, plus the new work of a suitable size by established Irish writers. Non-Irish poets are also published. Poets based in continental Europe have become a major feature. Emphasis on first collections preferrably not larger than 80 pages. Logistically, publishing beyond the British Isles is always difficult for 'hard copy' editions. PDF copies via e-mail are £3 or 3€ per copy. No fixed upperl limit to number of titles per year. Hard copy prices are £8 to £10 per copy. No e-reader required." Wants poetry of all kinds, but, "no crass political, racist, sexist propaganda, even of a positive or 'pc' tenor." Has published Alastair Thomson, Clifford Ireson, Colette Wittorski, Gilberte de Leger, Aubrey Malone, and Jane Shaw Holiday. Pamphlets up to 32 pages, chapbooks up to 44 pages, books 48-112 pages; New Belfast binding, simulated perfect binding for books, otherwise saddle stitching.

HOW TO CONTACT "Submit 6 poems in the first instance; depending on these, an invitation to submit more may follow." Considers simultaneous submissions. Accepts e-mail submissions in body of message or in DOC format. Cover letter is required. "All submissions receive a first reading. If these poems have minor errors or faults, the writer is advised. If poor quality, the poems are returned. Those 'passing' first reading are retained, and a letter of conditional offer is sent." Often comments on rejected poems. "After initial publication, irrespective of the quantity, the work will be permanently available using 'print-on-demand' production; such publications will not always be printed exactly as the original, although the content will remain the same."

TIPS "At present we are unable to accept new work from beyond mainland Europe and the British Isles due to increased delivery costs."

LEDGE HILL PUBLISHING

P.O. Box 337, Alton NH 03809. **E-mail:** info@ledge-hillpublishing.com. **Website:** www.ledgehillpublishing.com. **Contact:** Amanda Eason. Publishes hardcover, trade paperback, and mass market paperback originals. Pays 2-15% royalty. Publishes ms 3 months after acceptance. Responds in 1 month to queries and proposals; 2 months to mss. Book catalog available online at website. Guidelines free on request by e-mail or online at website.

HOW TO CONTACT Submit complete ms.

LEE & LOW BOOKS

95 Madison Ave., #1205, New York NY 10016. (212)779-4400. **E-mail:** general@leeandlow.com. **Website:** www.leeandlow.com. Jennifer Fox, senior editor; Emily Hazel, assistant editor. **Contact:** Louise May, editor-in-chief (multicultural children's fiction/nonfiction). "Our goals are to meet a growing need for books that address children of color, and to present literature that all children can identify with. We only consider multicultural children's books. Currently emphasizing material for 5-12 year olds. Sponsors a yearly New Voices Award for first-time picture book authors of color. Contest rules online at website or for SASE." Publishes hardcover originals and trade paperback reprints. Pays net royalty. Pays authors advances against royalty. Pays illustrators advance against royalty. Photographers paid advance against royalty. Publishes book 2 years after acceptance. Responds in 6 months to mss if interested. Book catalog available online. Guidelines available online or by written request with SASE.

HOW TO CONTACT Submit complete ms.

TIPS "Check our website to see the kinds of books we publish. Do not send mss that don't fit our mission."

LES FIGUES PRESS

P.O. Box 7736, Los Angeles CA 90007. **E-mail:** info@lesfigues.com. **Website:** www.lesfigues.com. **Contact:** Teresa Carmody and Vanessa Place, co-directors. Les Figues Press is an independent, nonprofit publisher of poetry, prose, visual art, conceptual writing, and translation. With amission is to create aesthetic conversations between readers, writers, and artists, Les-Figues Press favors projects which push the boundaries of genre, form, and general acceptability. Submissions are only reviewed through its annual NOS Book Contest.

LETHE PRESS

118 Heritage Ave., Maple Shade NJ 08052. (609)410-7391. **E-mail:** editor@lethepressbooks.com. **Website:** www.lethepressbooks.com. **Contact:** Steve Berman, publisher. "Lethe Press is a small press seeking gay and lesbian themed poetry collections." Lethe Books are distributed by Ingram Publications and Bookazine, and are available at all major bookstores, as well as the major online retailers.

NEEDS "Lethe Press is an independent publishing house specializing in speculative fiction, books of gay interest, poetry, spirituality, as well as classic works of the occult & supernatural. Named after the Greek river of memory and forgetfulness (and pronounced Lee-Thee), Lethe Press is devoted to ideas that are often neglected or forgotten by mainstream publishers."

HOW TO CONTACT Send query letter. Accepts queries by e-mail. Rarely accepts unsolicited mss.

LOUISIANA STATE UNIVERSITY PRESS

3990 W. Lakeshore Dr., Baton Rouge LA 70808. (225)578-6294. **Fax:** (225)578-6461. **E-mail:** mkc@lsu.edu. **Website:** www.lsupress.org. John Easterly, executive editor (poetry, fiction, literary studies); Rand Dotson, senior editor (U.S. History & Southern Studies). **Contact:** MK Callaway, director. Publishes in the fall and spring. Publishes hardcover and paperback originals, and reprints. Publishes 8 poetry titles per year and 2 works of original fiction as part of the Yellow Shoe Fiction series. Pays royalty. Publishes ms 1 year after acceptance. Responds in 1 month to queries. Book catalog and ms guidelines free and online.

NEEDS A highly respected publisher of collections by poets such as Claudia Emerson, David Kirby, Brendan Galvin, Fred Chappell, Marilyn Nelson, and Henry Taylor. Publisher of the Southern Messenger Poets series edited by Dave Smith." "No unsolicited poetry mss. for the foreseeable future. We have filled our slots until 2014."

LUNA BISONTE PRODS

E-mail: bennett.23@osu.edu. **Website:** www.johnmbennett.net. **Contact:** John M. Bennett, editor/publisher.

NEEDS "Interested in avant-garde and highly experimental work only." Has published poetry by Jim Leftwich, Sheila E. Murphy, Al Ackerman, Richard

Kostelanetz, Carla Bertola, Olchar Lindsann, and many others.

HOW TO CONTACT Query first, with a few sample poems and cover letter with brief bio and publication credits. "Keep it brief. Chapbook publishing usually depends on grants or other subsidies, and is usually by solicitation. **Will also consider subsidy arrangements on negotiable terms.**" A sampling of various Luna Bisonte Prods products is available for $20.

⊘ MAVERICK DUCK PRESS

E-mail: maverickduckpress@yahoo.com. **Website:** www.maverickduckpress.com. **Contact:** Kendall A. Bell, editor. Maverick Duck Press is a "publisher of chapbooks from undiscovered talent. We are looking for fresh and powerful work that shows a sense of innovation or a new take on passion or emotion. Previous publication in print or online journals could increase your chances of us accepting your manuscript." Does not want "unedited work." Pays 20 author's copies (out of a press run of 50).

HOW TO CONTACT Send ms in Microsoft Word format with a cover letter with brief bio and publication credits. Chapbook mss may include previously published poems. "Previous publication is always a plus, as we may be more familiar with your work. Chapbook mss should have 16-24 poems, but no more than 24 poems."

⊘🌐 MARGARET K. MCELDERRY BOOKS

Imprint of Simon & Schuster Children's Publishing Division, Simon & Schuster, 1230 Sixth Ave., New York NY 10020. (212)698-7200. **Website:** www.simonsayskids.com. **Contact:** Justin Chanda, vice president; Karen Wojtyla, editorial director; Gretchen Hirsch, associate editor; Emily Fabre, assistant editor. Ann Bobco, executive art director. "Margaret K. McElderry Books publishes hardcover and paperback trade books for children from pre-school age through young adult. This list includes picture books, middle grade and teen fiction, poetry, and fantasy. The style and subject matter of the books we publish is almost unlimited. We do not publish textbooks, coloring and activity books, greeting cards, magazines, pamphlets, or religious publications." Pays authors royalty based on retail price. Pays illustrator royalty of by the project. Pays photographers by the project. Original artwork returned at job's completion. Offers $5,000-8,000 advance for new authors. Guidelines for #10 SASE.

NEEDS *No unsolicited mss.*
HOW TO CONTACT Query and submit 3 sample poems.
TIPS "Read! The children's book field is competitive. See what's been done and what's out there before submitting. We look for high quality: an originality of ideas, clarity and felicity of expression, a well organized plot, and strong character-driven stories. We're looking for strong, original fiction, especially mysteries and middle grade humor. We are always interested in picture books for the youngest age reader. Study our titles."

MERRIAM PRESS

133 Elm St., Suite 3R, Bennington VT 05201. (802)447-0313. **E-mail:** ray@merriam-press.com. **Website:** www.merriam-press.com. "Merriam Press specializes in military history - particularly World War II history. We are also branching out into other genres." Publishes hardcover and softcover trade paperback originals and reprints Pays 10% royalty on actual selling price. Publishes ms 6 months or less after acceptance. Responds quickly (e-mail preferred) to queries. Book catalog available for $5 or visit website to view all available titles and access writer's guidelines and info.

TIPS "Our military history books are geared for military historians, collectors, model kit builders, wargamers, veterans, general enthusiasts. We now publish some historical fiction and poetry and will consider well-written books on a variety of non-military topics."

⊘ MIAMI UNIVERSITY PRESS

356 Bachelor Hall, Miami University, Oxford OH 45056. **E-mail:** tumakw@muohio.edu. **Website:** www.muohio.edu/mupress. **Contact:** Keith Tuma, editor; Dana Leonard, managing editor. Publishes 1-2 books of poetry/year and one novella, in paperback editions.
HOW TO CONTACT Miami University Press is unable to respond to unsolicited mss and queries.

🕐 MILKWEED EDITIONS

1011 Washington Ave. S., Suite 300, Minneapolis MN 55415. (612)332-3192. **Fax:** (612)215-2550. **E-mail:** submissions@milkweed.org. **Website:** www.milkweed.org. "Milkweed Editions publishes with the intention of making a humane impact on society, in the belief that literature is a transformative art uniquely able to convey the essential experiences of the human heart and spirit. To that end, Milkweed

Editions publishes distinctive voices of literary merit in handsomely designed, visually dynamic books, exploring the ethical, cultural, and esthetic issues that free societies need continually to address." Publishes hardcover, trade paperback, and electronic originals; trade paperback and electronic reprints. Pays authors variable royalty based on retail price. Offers advance against royalties. Pays varied advance from $500-10,000. Publishes book in 18 months. Responds in 6 months to queries, proposals, and mss. Book catalog available online. Guidelines available online.

NEEDS Milkweed Editions is "looking for poetry manuscripts of high quality that embody humane values and contribute to cultural understanding." Not limited in subject matter. Open to writers with previously published books of poetry or a minimum of 6 poems published in nationally distributed commercial or literary journals. Considers translations and bilingual mss. Has published *Fancy Beasts*, by Alex Lemon, *Reading Novalis in Montana*, by Melissa Kwasny, and *The Book of Props*, by Wayne Miller.

HOW TO CONTACT Submit through website. No fax or e-mail submissions. Do not send originals. Accepts and reads unsolicited mss all year. Guidelines available on website. Responds in up to 6 months. Order sample books through website. Query with SASE; submit completed ms

TIPS "We are looking for excellent writing with the intent of making a humane impact on society. Please read submission guidelines before submitting and acquaint yourself with our books in terms of style and quality before submitting. Many factors influence our selection process, so don't get discouraged. Nonfiction is focused on literary writing about the natural world, including living well in urban environments."

MOON TIDE PRESS

P.O. Box 50184, Irvine CA 92619. **E-mail:** publisher@moontidepress.com. **Website:** www.moontidepress.com. **Contact:** Michael Miller, publisher.

HOW TO CONTACT Query first.

TIPS "Keep in mind that when we open and read your ms, it will probably be in the middle of a large stack of other submissions, and many of those will be well-meaning but undistinguished collections about the same few themes. So don't be afraid to take risks. Surprise and entertain us. Give us something that the next ten poets in the stack won't."

MOVING PARTS PRESS

10699 Empire Grade, Santa Cruz CA 95060. (831)427-2271. **E-mail:** frice@movingpartspress.com. **Website:** www.movingpartspress.com. **Contact:** Felicia Rice, poetry editor. Moving Part Press publishes handsome, innovative books, broadsides, and prints that "explore the relationship of word and image, typography and the visual arts, the fine arts and popular culture." Published *Codex Espangliensis: from Columbus to the Border Patrol* (1998) with performance texts by Guillermo Goómez-Penña and collage imagery by Enrique Chagoya; *Cosmogonie Intime/An Intimate Cosmogony* (2005), a limited edition artists' book with poems by Yves Peyreé, translated by Elizabeth R. Jackson, and drawings by Ray Rice.

HOW TO CONTACT Does not accept unsolicited mss.

MY GREEN PUBLISHER LLC

P.O. Box 702, Richland MT 49083. **E-mail:** mygreenpublisher@gmail.com. **Website:** www.mygreenpublisher.com. **Contact:** Fiona Thomas, editor-in-chief. Publishes trade paperback and electronic originals. Pays 15% royalty on wholesale price (paperback); 20% royalty on wholesale price (ebook). Publishes ms 6-12 months after acceptance. Responds in 3 days to queries; 1 month to proposals and mss. Book catalog available online. Guidelines availble online or by e-mail.

HOW TO CONTACT Submit complete ms.

NEW ISSUES POETRY & PROSE

Western Michigan University, 1903 W. Michigan Ave., Kalamazoo MI 49008-5463. (269)387-8185. **Fax:** (269)387-2562. **E-mail:** new-issues@wmich.edu. **Website:** wmich.edu/newissues. **Contact:** Managing Editor. Established 1996. Contests: The Green Rose Prize in Poetry offers $2,000 and publication of a book of poems by an established poet who has published one or more full-length collections of poetry. New Issues may publish as many as 3 additional mss from this competition. Considers simultaneous submissions, but New Issues must be notified of acceptance elsewhere. Submit a ms of at least 48 pages, typed, single-spaced preferred. Clean photocopies acceptable. Do not bind; use manila folder or metal clasp. Include cover page with poet's name, address, phone number, and title of the ms. Also include brief bio, table of contents, and acknowledgments page. No e-mail or fax submissions. Include SASP for notification of receipt of ms and SASE for results only; mss will be recycled. Guidelines available for SASE, by fax, e-mail, or on website. Please visit the AWP website for guidelines to submit to the AWP Award Series in the Novel contest. Publishes 18 months after acceptance. Guidelines available online, by e-mail, or by SASE.

NEEDS New Issues Poetry & Prose offers two contests annually. The Green Rose Prize is awarded to an author who has previously published at least one full-length book of poems. The New Issues Poetry Prize, an award for a first book of poems, is chosen by a guest judge. Past judges have included Philip Levine, C.K. Williams, C.D. Wright, and Campbell McGrath. New Issues does not read manuscripts outside our contests. Graduate students in the Ph.D. and M.F.A. programs of Western Michigan Univ. often volunteer their time reading manuscripts. Finalists are chosen by the editors. New Issues often publishes up to two additional manuscripts selected from the finalists.

HOW TO CONTACT Query first. All unsolicited mss returned unopened. "The press considers for publication only manuscripts submitted during its competition reading periods and often accepts two or more manuscripts for publication in addition to the winner."

NEW RIVERS PRESS

MSU Moorhead, 1104 Seventh Ave. S., Moorhead MN 56563. **E-mail:** kelleysu@mnstate.edu. **Website:** www.newriverspress.com. Suzzanne Kelley, managing editor. **Contact:** Alan Davis. New Rivers Press publishes collections of poetry, novels, nonfiction, translations of contemporary literature, and collections of short fiction and nonfiction. "We continue to publish books regularly by new and emerging writers, but we also welcome the opportunity to read work of every character and to publish the best literature available nationwide. Each fall through the Many Voices Project competition, we choose 2 books: 1 poetry and 1 prose."

NEEDS The Many Voices Project awards $1,000, a standard book contract, publication of a book-length ms by New Rivers Press, and national distribution. All previously published poems must be acknowledged. "We will consider simultaneous submissions if noted as such. If your manuscript is accepted elsewhere during the judging, you must notify New Rivers Press immediately. If you do not give such notification and your manuscript is selected, your entry gives New Rivers Press permission to go ahead with publication." Submit 50-80 pages of poetry. Entry form

(required) and guidelines available on website. **Entry fee:** $25. **Deadline:** submit September 15-November 1 (postmark).

HOW TO CONTACT Guidelines available on website.

NINETY-SIX PRESS

Furman University, 3300 Poinsett Hwy., Greenville SC 29613. (864)294-3152. **Fax:** (864)294-2224. **E-mail:** gil.allen@furman.edu. **Website:** http://library.furman.edu/specialcollections/96Press/index.htm. **Contact:** Gilbert Allen, editor. For a sample, send $10.

TIPS "South Carolina poets only. Check our website for guidelines."

NORTH ATLANTIC BOOKS

2526 MLK Jr. Way, Berkeley CA 94704. **Website:** www.northatlanticbooks.com. **Contact:** Douglas Reil, associate publisher; Erin Wiegand, senior acquisitions editor. Publishes hardcover, trade paperback, and electronic originals; trade paperback and electronic reprints. Pays royalty percentage on wholesale price. Publishes ms 14 months after acceptance. Responds in 3-6 months to queries, proposals, mss. Book catalog free on request (if available). Guidelines online.

HOW TO CONTACT Submit 15-20 sample poems.

W.W. NORTON & COMPANY, INC.

500 Fifth Ave., New York NY 10110. (212)354-5500. **Fax:** (212)869-0856. **Website:** www.wwnorton.com. **Contact:** Trish Marks. "W. W. Norton & Company, the oldest and largest publishing house owned wholly by its employees, strives to carry out the imperative of its founder to "publish books not for a single season, but for the years" in fiction, nonfiction, poetry, college textbooks, cookbooks, art books and professional books."

"Due to the workload of our editorial staff and the large volume of materials we receive, *Norton is no longer able to accept unsolicited submissions.* If you are seeking publication, we suggest working with a literary agent who will represent you to the house."

OBERLIN COLLEGE PRESS

50 N. Professor St., Oberlin College, Oberlin OH 44074. (440)775-8408. **Fax:** (440)775-8124. **E-mail:** oc.press@oberlin.edu. **Website:** www.oberlin.edu/ocpress. **Contact:** Linda Slocum, managing editor. Publishes hardcover and trade paperback originals. Pays 7½-10% royalty. Responds promptly to queries; 2 months to mss.

NEEDS "*FIELD Magazine*—submit 2-6 poems through website "submissions" tab; FIELD Translation Series—query with SASE and sample poems; FIELD Poetry Series—*no unsolicited mss.* Enter mss in FIELD Poetry Prize ($1,000 and a standard royalty contract) held annually in May. Submit electronically through field poetry prize link on website at www.oberlin.edu/ocpress."

HOW TO CONTACT Submit 2-6 sample poems.

TIPS "Queries for the FIELD Translation Series: send sample poems and letter describing project. Winner of the annual FIELD poetry prize determines publication. Do not send unsolicited manuscripts."

OOLIGAN PRESS

369 Neuberger Hall, 724 SW Harrison St., Portland OR 97201. (503)725-9410. **E-mail:** ooligan@ooliganpress.pdx.edu. **Website:** www.ooliganpress.pdx.edu. Publishes trade paperback, and electronic originals and reprints. Pays negotiable royalty on retail price. Book catalog available online. Guidelines available online.

NEEDS Ooligan is a general trade press that "specializes in publishing authors from the Pacific Northwest and/or works that have specific value to that community. We are limited in the number of poetry titles that we publish as poetry represents only a small percentage of our overall acquisitions. We are open to all forms of style and verse; however, we give special preference to translated poetry, prose poetry, and traditional verse. Although spoken word, slam, and rap poetry are of interest to the press, we will not consider such work if it does not translate well to the written page. Ooligan does not publish chapbooks." Has published *Deer Drink the Moon*, edited by Liz Nakazawa and *American Scream* and *Palindrome Apocalypse* by the Croatian poet Durbravaka Oraic-Tolid, translated by Julienne Eden Busic.

HOW TO CONTACT Query, submit 20 sample poems, submit complete ms.

TIPS "For children's books, our audience will be middle grades and young adult, with marketing to general trade, libraries, and schools. Good marketing ideas increase the chances of a manuscript succeeding."

ORCHARD BOOKS

557 Broadway, New York NY 10012. **E-mail:** mcroland@scholastic.com. **Website:** www.scholastic.com. **Contact:** Ken Geist, vice president/editorial director;

David Saylor, vice president/creative director. Most commonly offers an advance against list royalties.

⊘ *Orchard is not accepting unsolicited manuscripts.*

TIPS "Read some of our books to determine first whether your manuscript is suited to our list."

⊘ ORCHISES PRESS

P.O. Box 320533, Alexandria VA 22320. (703)683-1243. **E-mail:** lathbury@gmu.edu. **Website:** mason.gmu.edu/~lathbury. **Contact:** Roger Lathbury, editor-in-chief. Orchises Press is a general literary publisher specializing in poetry with selected reprints and textbooks. No new fiction or children's books. Publishes hardcover and trade paperback originals and reprints. Pays 36% of receipts after Orchises has recouped its costs. Publishes book 1 year after acceptance. Responds in 3 months to queries. Guidelines available online.

NEEDS Poetry must have been published in respected literary journals. *Orchises Press no longer reads unsolicited mss.* Publishes free verse, but has strong formalist preferences.

HOW TO CONTACT Query and submit 5 sample poems.

PALETTES & QUILLS

330 Knickerbocker Ave., Rochester NY 14615. (585)456-0217. **E-mail:** palettesnquills@gmail.com. **Website:** www.palettesnquills.com. **Contact:** Donna M. Marbach, publisher/owner.

NEEDS Palettes & Quills "is at this point, a poetry press only, and produces only a handful of publications each year, specializing in anthologies, individual chapbooks, and broadsides." Wants "work that should appeal to a wide audience." Does not want "poems that are sold blocks of text, long-lined and without stanza breaks. Wildly elaborate free-verse would be difficult and in all likelihood fight with art background, amateurish rhyming poem, overly sentimental poems, poems that use excessive profanity, or which denigrate other people, or political and religious diatribes."

HOW TO CONTACT Query first with 3-5 poems and a cover letter with brief bio and publication credits for individual unsolicited chapbooks. May include previously published poems. Chapbook poets would get 20 copies of a run; broadside poets and artists get 5-10 copies and occasionally paid $10 for reproduction rights. Anthology poets get 1 copy of the anthology. All poets and artists get a discount on purchases that include their work.

CONTEST/AWARD OFFERINGS Palettes & Quills Biennial Chapbook Contest, held biennially. Prize: $200 plus 50 copies of chapbook and discount on purchase of others. Guidelines available for SASE or on website. Entry fee: $20. Past judges: Ellen Bass, Dorianne Laux, and J.P. Dancing Bear.

PELICAN PUBLISHING COMPANY

1000 Burmaster St., Gretna LA 70053. (504)368-1175. **Fax:** (504)368-1195. **E-mail:** editorial@pelicanpub.com. **Website:** www.pelicanpub.com. **Contact:** Nina Kooij, editor-in-chief. "We believe ideas have consequences. One of the consequences is that they lead to a best-selling book. We publish books to improve and uplift the reader. Currently emphasizing business and history titles." Publishes 20 young readers/year; 1 middle reader/year. "Our children's books (illustrated and otherwise) include history, biography, holiday, and regional. Pelican's mission is to publish books of quality and permanence that enrich the lives of those who read them." Publishes hardcover, trade paperback and mass market paperback originals and reprints. Pays authors in royalties; buys ms outright "rarely." Illustrators paid by "various arrangements." Advance considered. Publishes a book 9-18 months after acceptance. Responds in 1 month to queries; 3 months to mss. Book catalog and ms guidelines online.

NEEDS Pelican Publishing Company is a medium-sized publisher of popular histories, cookbooks, regional books, children's books, and inspirational/motivational books. Considers poetry for "hardcover children's books only (1,100 words maximum), preferably with a regional focus. However, our needs for this are very limited; we publish 20 juvenile titles per year, and most of these are prose, not poetry." Two of Pelican's popular series are prose books about Gaston the Green-Nosed Alligator by James Rice, and Clovis Crawfish by Mary Alice Fontenot. Books are 32 pages, magazine-sized, include illustrations.

TIPS "We do extremely well with cookbooks, popular histories, and business. We will continue to build in these areas. The writer must have a clear sense of the market and knowledge of the competition. A query letter should describe the project briefly, give the author's writing and professional credentials, and promotional ideas."

PEMMICAN PUBLICATIONS, INC.

90 Sutherland Ave., Winnipeg MB R2W 3C7, Canada. (204)589-6346. **Fax:** (204)589-2063. **E-mail:** pemmican@pemmican.mb.ca. **Website:** www.pemmican-publications.ca. **Contact:** Randal McIlroy, managing editor (Metis culture & heritage). "Pemmican Publications is a Metis publishing house, with a mandate to publish books by Metis authors and illustrators and with an emphasis on culturally relevant stories. We encourage writers to learn a little about Pemmican before sending samples. Pemmican publishes titles in the following genres: Adult Fiction, which includes novels, story collections and anthologies; Non-Fiction, with an emphasis on social history and biography reflecting Metis experience; Children's and Young Adult titles; Aboriginal languages, including Michif and Cree." Publishes trade paperback originals and reprints. Pays 10% royalty on retail price. Publishes book 1-2 years after acceptance. Responds to queries, proposals, and mss in 3 months. Book catalog available free with SASE. Guidelines available online.

HOW TO CONTACT Submit 10 sample poems and complete ms.

TIPS "Our mandate is to promote Metis authors, illustrators and stories. No agent is necessary."

PERENNIAL

HarperCollins Publishers, 10 E. 53rd St., New York NY 10022. (212)207-7000. **Website:** www.harpercollins.com. **Contact:** Acquisitions Editor. Perennial publishes a broad range of adult literary fiction and nonfiction paperbacks that create a record of our culture. Publishes trade paperback originals and reprints. Book catalog available free.

"With the exception of Avon romance, HarperCollins does not accept unsolicited submissions or query letters. Please refer to your local bookstore, the library, or a book entitled *Literary Marketplace* on how to find the appropriate agent for you."

NEEDS Don't send poetry unless you have been published in several established literary magazines already. *Agented submissions only.*

TIPS See our website for a list of titles or write to us for a free catalog.

PERSEA BOOKS

277 Broadway, Suite 708, New York NY 10007. (212)260-9256. **Fax:** (212)267-3165. **E-mail:** info@perseabooks.com. **Website:** www.perseabooks.com.

"We are pleased to receive query letters from authors and literary agents for fiction and nonfiction manuscripts." Responds in 8 weeks to proposals; 10 weeks to mss. Guidelines online.

NEEDS "We have a longstanding commitment to publishing extraordinary contemporary poetry and maintain an active poetry program. At this time, due to our commitment to the poets we already publish, we are limited in our ability to add new collections."

HOW TO CONTACT Send an e-mail to poetry@perseabooks.com describing current project and publication history, attaching a pdf or Word document with up to 12 sample pages of poetry. "If the timing is right and we are interested in seeing more work, we will contact you."

⊘ PERUGIA PRESS

P.O. Box 60364, Florence MA 01062. **E-mail:** info@perugiapress.com. **Website:** www.perugiapress.com. **Contact:** Susan Kan, director.

⊘ PLAN B PRESS

P.O. Box 4067, Alexandria VA 22303. (215)732-2663. **E-mail:** planbpress@gmail.com. **Website:** www.planbpress.com. **Contact:** Steven Allen May, president. Plan B Press is a "small publishing company with an international feel. Our intention is to have Plan B Press be part of the conversation about the direction and depth of literary movements and genres. Plan B Press's new direction is to seek out authors rarely-to-never published, sharing new voices that might not otherwise be heard. Plan B Press is determined to merge text with image, writing with art." Publishes poetry and short fiction. Wants "experimental poetry, concrete/visual work." Has published poetry by Lamont B. Steptoe, Michele Belluomini, Jim Mancinelli, Lyn Lifshin, Robert Miltner, and Steven Allen May. Publishes 1 poetry book/year and 5-10 chapbooks/year. Manuscripts are selected through open submission and through competition (see below). Books/chapbooks are 24-48 pages, with covers with art/graphics. Pays author's copies. Responds to queries in 1 month; mss in 3 months.

NEEDS Wants to see: experimental, concrete, visual poetry. Does not want "sonnets, political or religious poems, work in the style of Ogden Nash."

HOW TO CONTACT Query first, with a few sample poems and a cover letter with brief bio and publication credits. Book/chapbook mss may include previously published poems.

● PRESA :S: PRESS

P.O. Box 792, 8590 Belding Rd. NE, Rockford MI 49341. **E-mail:** presapress@aol.com. **Website:** www.presapress.com. **Contact:** Roseanne Ritzema, editor. Presa :S: Press publishes "perfect-bound paperbacks and saddle-stitched chapbooks of poetry. Wants "imagistic poetry where form is an extension of content, surreal, experimental, and personal poetry." Does not want "overtly political or didactic material." Pays 10-25 author\quotes copies. Time between acceptance and publication is 8-12 weeks. Responds to queries in 2-4 weeks; to mss in 8-12 weeks Guidelines available in magazine, for SASE, and by e-mail.

NEEDS Needs poems, reviews, essays, photos, criticism, and prose. Dedicates 6-8 pages of each issue to a featured poet. Considers previously published poems. (Considers poetry posted on a public website/blog/forum and poetry posted on a private, password-protected forum as published.) Acquires first North American serial rights and the right to reprint in anthologies. Rights revert to poets upon publication. Accepts postal submissions only. Cover letter is preferred. Reads submissions year round. Poems are circulated to an editorial board. Never comments on rejected poems. Never publishes theme issues. Reviews books and chapbooks of poetry. Send materials for review consideration to Roseanne Ritzema.

HOW TO CONTACT Query first, with a few sample poems and a cover letter with brief bio and publication credits. Book/chapbook mss may include previously published poems.

⊕ PRESS 53

P.O. Box 30314, Winston-Salem NC 27101. **E-mail:** kevin@press53.com. **Website:** www.press53.com. **Contact:** Kevin Morgan Watson, publisher. "Press 53 was founded in October 2005 and quickly began earning a reputation as a quality publishing house of short story and poetry collections." Open submission period in November each year. Responds in 6 months to mss. Guidelines online.

NEEDS "We love working with poets who have been widely published and are active in the poetry community. We publish only full-length poetry collections of roughly 70 pages or more." Prefers that at least 30-40% of the poems in the collection be previously published.

HOW TO CONTACT In November, submit via Submittable on site: letter of introduction with info about yourself and poetry collection, the number of poems in collection, where the poems have been published, and a few ideas for marketing book, along with complete ms.

TIPS "We are looking for writers who are actively involved in the writing community, writers who are submitting their work to journals, magazines and contests, and who are getting published and earning a reputation for their work."

PRINCETON UNIVERSITY PRESS

41 William St., Princeton NJ 08540. (609)258-4900. **Fax:** (609)258-6305. **Website:** www.pupress.princeton.edu. **Contact:** Hanne Winarsky, editor. "The Lockert Library of Poetry in Translation embraces a wide geographic and temporal range, from Scandinavia to Latin America to the subcontinent of India, from the Tang Dynasty to Europe of the modern day. It especially emphasizes poets who are established in their native lands and who are being introduced to an English-speaking audience. The series, many of whose titles are bilingual editions, calls attention to some of the most widely-praised poetry available today. In the Lockert Library series, each book is given individual design treatment rather than stamped into a series mold. We have published a wide range of poets from other cultures, including well-known writers such as Hoölderlin and Cavafy, and those who have not yet had their due in English translation, such as Goöran Sonnevi. Manuscripts are judged with several criteria in mind: the ability of the translation to stand on its own as poetry in English; fidelity to the tone and spirit of the original, rather than literal accuracy; and the importance of the translated poet to the literature of his or her time and country."

NEEDS Submit hard copy of proposal with sample poems or full ms. Cover letter is required. Reads submissions year round. Mss will not be returned. Comments on finalists only. Responds in 3-4 months.

✪ RAGGED SKY PRESS

P.O. Box 312, Annandale NJ 08801. **E-mail:** info@raggedsky.com. **Website:** www.raggedsky.com. **Contact:** Ellen Foos, publisher; Vasiliki Katsarou, managing editor; Arlene Weiner, editor. Produces books of poetry and inspired prose. Ragged Sky is a small, highly selective cooperative press. "We work with our authors closely." Learn more online.

⊘ RED HEN PRESS

P.O. Box 3537, Granada Hills CA 91394. (818)831-0649. **Fax:** (818)831-6659. **E-mail:** redhenpressbooks.com. **Website:** www.redhen.org. **Contact:** Mark E. Cull, publisher/editor (fiction). "*Red Hen Press is not currently accepting unsolicited material.* At this time, the best opportunity to be published by Red Hen is by entering one of our contests. Please find more information in our award submission guidelines." Publishes trade paperback originals. Publishes ms 1 year after acceptance. Responds in 1 month to queries; 2 months to proposals; months to mss. Book catalog available free. Guidelines available online.

HOW TO CONTACT Submit to Benjamin Saltman Poetry Award.

CONTEST/AWARD OFFERINGS The Benjamin Saltman Award is awarded annually for the best poetry book collection. Submit 48 to 96 pages of poetry. Postmark deadline is August 31. $25 entry fee. SASE for notification only. Please include name, address, title, email address, and telephone number on cover sheet only. Award: $3,000 and publication of collection.

TIPS "Audience reads poetry, literary fiction, intelligent nonfiction. If you have an agent, we may be too small since we don't pay advances. Write well. Send queries first. Be willing to help promote your own book."

⊘ RED MOON PRESS

P.O. Box 2461, Winchester VA 22604. (540)722-2156. **E-mail:** jim.kacian@redmoonpress.com. **Website:** www.redmoonpress.com. **Contact:** Jim Kacian, editor/publisher. Red Moon Press "is the largest and most prestigious publisher of English-language haiku and related work in the world." Publishes 6-8 volumes/year, usually 3-5 anthologies and individual collections of English-language haiku, as well as 1-3 books of essays, translations, or criticism of haiku. Under other imprints, the press also publishes chapbooks of various sizes and formats.

HOW TO CONTACT Query with book theme and information, and 30-40 poems or draft of first chapter. Responds to queries in 2 weeks, to mss (if invited) in 3 months. "Each contract separately negotiated."

◐ RONSDALE PRESS

3350 W. 21st Ave., Vancouver BC V6S 1G7, Canada. (604)738-4688. **Fax:** (604)731-4548. **E-mail:** ronsdale@shaw.ca. **Website:** http://ronsdalepress.com.

Contact: Ronald B. Hatch (fiction, poetry, nonfiction, social commentary); Veronica Hatch (YA novels and short stories). "Ronsdale Press is a Canadian literary publishing house that publishes 12 books each year, four of which are young adult titles. Of particular interest are books involving children exploring and discovering new aspects of Canadian history." Publishes trade paperback originals. Pays 10% royalty on retail price. Publishes book 1 year after acceptance. Responds to queries in 2 weeks; mss in 2 months. Book catalog for #10 SASE. Guidelines available online.

NEEDS Poets should have published some poems in magazines/journals and should be well-read in contemporary masters.

HOW TO CONTACT Submit complete ms.

TIPS "Ronsdale Press is a literary publishing house, based in Vancouver, and dedicated to publishing books from across Canada, books that give Canadians new insights into themselves and their country. We aim to publish the best Canadian writers."

ROSE ALLEY PRESS

4203 Brooklyn Ave. NE, #103A, Seattle WA 98105. (206)633-2725. **E-mail:** rosealleypress@juno.com. **Website:** www.rosealleypress.com. **Contact:** David D. Horowitz. "Rose Alley Press primarily publishes books featuring rhymed metrical poetry and an annually updated booklet about writing and publication. We do not read or consider unsolicited manuscripts."

SAKURA PUBLISHING & TECHNOLOGIES

P.O. Box 1681, Hermitage PA 16148. (330)360-5131. **E-mail:** skpublishing124@gmail.com. **Website:** www.sakura-publishing.com. **Contact:** Derek Vasconi, talent finder and CEO. Publishes hardcover, trade paperback, mass market paperback and electronic originals and reprints. Pays royalty of 20-60% on wholesale price or retail price. Publishes ms 6 months after acceptance. Responds in 1 month to queries, mss, proposals. Book catalog available for #10 SASE. Guidelines available online at website or by e-mail.

SALMON POETRY

Knockeven, Cliffs of Moher, County Clare , Ireland. 353(0)65 708 1941. **Fax:** 353(0)65 708 1941. **E-mail:** info@salmonpoetry.com. **E-mail:** jessie@salmonpoetry.com. **Website:** www.salmonpoetry.com. **Contact:** Jessie Lendennie, editor. Publishes mass market paperback originals.

NEEDS "Salmon Press has become one of the most important publications in the Irish literary world, specialising in the promotion of new poets, particularly women poets. Established as an alternative voice. Walks tightrope between innovation and convention. Was a flagship for writers in the west of Ireland. Salmon has developed a cross-cultural, internatonal literary dialog, broadening Irish Literature and urging new perspectives on established traditions."

TIPS "If we are broad minded and willing to nurture the individual voice inherent in the work, the artist will emerge."

SATURNALIA BOOKS

105 Woodside Rd., Ardmore PA 19003. (267) 278-9541. **E-mail:** info@saturnaliabooks.com. **Website:** www.saturnaliabooks.org. **Contact:** Henry Israeli, publisher. "We do not accept unsolicited submissions. We hold a contest, the Saturnalia Books Poetry Prize, annually in which 1 anonymously submitted title is chosen by a poet with a national reputation for publication. Submissions are accepted during the month of March. The submission fee is $30, and the prize is $2,000 and 20 copies of the book. See website for details." Publishes trade paperback originals and digital versions for e-readers. Pays authors 4-6% royalty on retail price. Pays $400-2,000 advance. Responds in 4 months on mss. Catalog on website. Guidelines available on website.

HOW TO CONTACT "Saturnalia Books has no bias against any school of poetry, but we do tend to publish writers who take chances and push against convention in some way, whether it's in form, language, content, or musicality." Submit complete ms to contest only.

TIPS "Our audience tend to be young avid readers of contemporary poetry. Read a few sample books first."

SECOND AEON PUBLICATIONS

19 Southminster Rd., Roath, Cardiff CF23 5AT, Wales. +44(29)2049-3093. **Fax:** +44(29)2049-3093. **E-mail:** peter@peterfinch.co.uk. **Website:** www.peterfinch.co.uk. **Contact:** Peter Finch, poetry editor.

Does not accept unsolicited mss.

HOW TO CONTACT *Does not accept unsolicited mss.*

SHEARSMAN BOOKS, LTD

50 Westons Hills Dr., Emersons Green Bristol BS16 7DF, UK. **E-mail:** editor@shearsman.com. **Website:** www.shearsman.com. **Contact:** Tony Frazer, editor.

Publishes trade paperback originals. Pays 10% royalty on retail price after 150 copies have sold; authors also receive 10 free copies of their books. Responds in 2-3 months to mss. Book catalog available online. Guidelines available online.

NEEDS "Shearsman only publishes poetry, poetry collections, and poetry in translation (from any language but with an emphasis on work in Spanish & in German). Some critical work on poetry and also memoirs and essays by poets. Mainly poetry by British, Irish, North American, & Australian poets." No children's books.

TIPS "Book ms submission: most of the ms must have already appeared in the UK or USA magazines of some repute, & it has to fill 70-72 pages of half letter or A5 pages. You must have sufficient return postage. Submissions can also be made by email. It is unlikely that a poet with no track record will be accepted for publication as there is no obvious audience for the work. Try to develop some exposure to UK & US magazines & try to assemble a ms only later."

◑ STEEL TOE BOOKS

Department of English, Western Kentucky University, 1906 College Heights Blvd. #11086, Bowling Green KY 42101. (270)745-5769. **E-mail:** tom.hunley@wku.edu. **Website:** www.steeltoebooks.com. **Contact:** Dr. Tom C. Hunley, director. Steel Toe Books publishes "full-length, single-author poetry collections. Our books are professionally designed and printed. We look for workmanship (economical use of language, high-energy verbs, precise literal descriptions, original figurative language, poems carefully arranged as a book); a unique style and/or a distinctive voice; clarity; emotional impact; humor (word plays, hyperbole, comic timing); performability (a Steel Toe poet is at home on the stage as well as on the page)." Does not want "dry verse, purposely obscure language, poetry by people who are so wary of being called 'sentimental' they steer away from any recognizable human emotions, poetry that takes itself so seriously that it's unintentionally funny." Has published poetry by Allison Joseph, Susan Browne, James Doyle, Martha Silano, Mary Biddinger, John Guzlowski, Jeannine Hall Gailey, and others. Publishes 1-3 poetry books/year. Manuscripts are normally selected through open submission.

HOW TO CONTACT "Check the website for news about our next open reading period." Book mss may include previously published poems. Responds to mss in 3 months. Pays $500 advance on 10% royalties and 10 author's copies. Order sample books by sending $12 to Steel Toe Books. *Must purchase a manuscript in order to submit*. See website for submission guidelines.

➕ SUBITO PRESS

University of Colorado at Boulder, Dept. of English, 226 UCB, Boulder CO 80309-0226. **E-mail:** subitopressucb@gmail.com. **Website:** www.subitopress.org. Subito Press is a non-profit publisher of literary works. Each year Subito publishes one work of fiction and one work of poetry through its contest. Submissions are open annually during the month of July. Trade paperback originals. Guidelines online.

HOW TO CONTACT Submit complete ms to contest.

TIPS "We publish two books of innovative writing a year through our poetry and fiction contests. All entries are also considered for publication with the press."

SWAN ISLE PRESS

P.O. Box 408790, Chicago IL 60640. (773)728-3780. **E-mail:** info@swanislepress.com. **Website:** www.swanislepress.com. Publishes hardcover and trade paperback originals. Pays 7 1/2-10% royalty on wholesale price. Publishes book 18 months after acceptance. Responds in 6 months to queries. Responds in 12 months to manuscripts. Book catalog available online. Guidelines available online.

💬 *"We do not accept unsolicited mss."*

HOW TO CONTACT Query and submit complete ms.

SWAN SCYTHE PRESS

1468 Mallard Way, Sunnyvale CA 94087. **E-mail:** robert.pesich@gmail.com. **Website:** www.swanscythe.com. **Contact:** Robert Pesich, editor.

NEEDS "After publishing 25 chapbooks, a few full-sized poetry collections,and 1 anthology, then taking a short break from publishing, Swan Scythe Press is now re-launching its efforts with some new books, under a new editorship, in 2010. We have also begun a new series of books, called Poetas/Puentes, from emerging poets writing in Spanish, translated into English. We will also consider manuscripts in indigenous languages from North, Central and South America, translated into English. Has published poetry by Emmy Perez, Maria Melendez, John Olivares Espinoza, Karen An-hwei Lee, Pos Moua, and Walter Pavlich. Order books/chapbooks by using paypal at the Swan Scythe Press or order through website.

HOW TO CONTACT Query first before submitting a ms via email or through website.

SYNERGEBOOKS

948 New Highway 7, Columbia TN 38401. (863)956-3015. **Fax:** (863)588-2198. **E-mail:** synergebooks@aol.com. **Website:** www.synergebooks.com. **Contact:** Debra Staples, publisher/acquisitions editor. "SynergEbooks is first and foremost a digital publisher, so most of our marketing budget goes to those formats. Authors are required to direct-sell a minimum of 100 digital copies of a title before it's accepted for print." Publishes trade paperback and electronic originals. Pays 15-40% royalty; makes outright purchase. Book catalog and guidelines available online.

NEEDS Anthologies must be a unique topic or theme.

HOW TO CONTACT Query and submit 1-5 sample poems.

TIPS "At SynergEbooks, we work with the author to promote their work."

◐ TARPAULIN SKY PRESS

P.O. Box 189, Grafton VT 05146. **E-mail:** editors@tarpaulinsky.com. **Website:** www.tarpaulinsky.com. **Contact:** Colie Collen, editor-in-chief. Tarpaulin Sky Press publishes cross- and trans-genre works as well as innovative poetry and prose. Produces full-length books and chapbooks, hand-bound books and trade paperbacks, and offers both hand-bound and perfect-bound paperback editions of full-length books. "We're a small, author-centered press endeavoring to create books that, as objects, please our authors as much their texts please us." Has published books and chapbooks by Jenny Boully, Danielle Dutton, Joyelle McSweeney, Chad Sweeney, Andrew Michael Roberts, and Max Winter, as well as a collaborative book by Noah Eli Gordon as Joshua Marie Wilkinson.

HOW TO CONTACT Writers whose work has appeared in or been accepted for publication in *Tarpaulin Sky* (see separate listing in Magazines/Journals) may submit chapbook or full-length manuscripts at any time, with no reading fee. Tarpaulin Sky Press also considers chapbook and full-length manuscripts from writers whose work has not appeared in the journal, but **asks for a $20 reading fee**. Make checks/money orders to Tarpaulin Sky Press. Cover letter is preferred. Reads periods may be found on the website.

⊘ TEBOT BACH

P.O. Box 7887, Huntington Beach CA 92615. (714)968-0905. **E-mail:** info@tebotbach.org. **Website:** www.te-botbach.org. **Contact:** Mifanwy Kaiser, editor/publisher. 2 years Responds to queries and mss, if invited, in 3 months.

NEEDS Offers two contests per year. The Patricia Bibby First Book Contest and The Clockwise Chapbook contest. Go to www.tebotbach.org and www.spillway.org for further information on programs and guidelines for submission.

HOW TO CONTACT Query first via e-mail, with a few sample poems and cover letter with brief bio.

ADDITIONAL INFORMATION Also publishes *Spillway: A Literary Journal*.

TEXAS TECH UNIVERSITY PRESS

P.O. Box 41037, 3003 15th St., Suite 201, Lubbock TX 79409. (806)742-2982. **Fax:** (806)742-2979. **E-mail:** judith.keeling@ttu.edu. **Website:** www.ttupress.org. **Contact:** Judith Keeling, editor-in-chief; Robert Mandel, director. Texas Tech University Press, the book publishing office of the university since 1971 and an AAUP member since 1986, publishes nonfiction titles in the areas of natural history and the natural sciences; eighteenth-century and Joseph Conrad studies; studies of modern Southeast Asia, particularly the Vietnam War; costume and textile history; Latin American literature and culture; and all aspects of the Great Plains and the American West, especially history, biography, memoir, sports history, and travel. In addition, the Press publishes several scholarly journals, acclaimed series for young readers, an annual invited poetry collection, and literary fiction of Texas and the West. Guidelines online.

NEEDS "TTUP publishes an annual invited first-book poetry manuscript (please note that we cannot entertain unsolicited poetry submissions)."

TIA CHUCHA PRESS

c/o Tia Chucha's Centro Cultural, 13197-A Gladstone Blvd., Sylmar CA 91342. **E-mail:** info@tiachucha.com. **Website:** www.tiachucha.com. **Contact:** Luis Rodriguez, director. Tia Chucha's Centro Cultural is a non-profit learning and cultural arts center. We support andpromote the continued growth, development and holistic learning of our community through the many powerful means of the arts. Tia Centra provides a positive space for people to activate what we all share as humans: the capacity to create, to imagine and to express ourselves in an effort to improve the quality of life for our community. Publishes hardcover and trade paperback originals. Pays 10% royalty on wholesale price. Publishes ms 1 year after acceptance. Responds in 9 months to mss. Guidelines available free.

NEEDS No restrictions as to style or content. We do cross-cultural and performance-oriented poetry. It has to work on the page, however.

HOW TO CONTACT Query and submit complete ms.

TIPS We will cultivate the practice. Audience is those interested.

⦿⦸ TIGHTROPE BOOKS

602 Markham St., Toronto ON M6G 2L8, Canada. (647)348-4460. **E-mail:** info@tightropebooks.com. **Website:** www.tightropebooks.com. **Contact:** Shirarose Wilensky, editor. Publishes hardcover and trade paperback originals. Pays 5-15% royalty on retail price. Pays advance of $200-300. Publishes book 1 year after acceptance. Responds if interested. Catalog and guidelines free on request and online.

⦿   Temporarily suspending all submissions.

TIPS "Audience is young, urban, literary, educated, unconventional."

⦿⑂ TIMBERLINE PRESS

5710 S. Kimbark #3, Chicago IL 60637. **E-mail:** timberline@vacpoetry.org. **Website:** http://vacpoetry. org/timberline. "Since January 2011, Timberline Press (founded by Clarence Wolfshohl in 1975) has been the fine press imprint of Virtual Artists Collective. We print chapbooks—usually poetry—usually 20-30 pages, hand bound, limited editions of 50-100. We generally print no more than 2 or 3 books a year."

⦿   *"Please note that we are not currently accepting new submissions."*

TOKYO ROSE RECORDS/CHAPULTEPEC PRESS

4222 Chambers, Cincinnati OH 45223. **E-mail:** ChapultepecPress@hotmail.com. **Website:** www. tokyoroserecords.com. **Contact:** David Garza. Publishes trade paperback originals. Pays 50% of profits and author's copies. Publishes book 6 months after acceptance. Book catalog available online.

NEEDS Chapultepec Press publishes books of poetry/ literature, essays, social/political issues, art, music, film, history, popular science; library/archive issues, and bilingual works. Wants "poetry that works as a unit, that is caustic, fun, open-ended, worldly, mature, relevant, stirring, evocative. Bilingual. Looking for authors who have a publishing history. No poetry collections without a purpose, that are mere collections. Also looking for broadsides/posters/illumina-

tions." Publishes 1-2 books/year. Books are usually 1-100 pages.

HOW TO CONTACT Query first. Submit 5-15 sample poems.

TIPS Tokyo Rose Records/Chapultepec Press specializes in shorter-length publications (100 pages or less). Order sample books by sending $5 payable to David Garza.

TUPELO PRESS

P.O. Box 1767, North Adams MA 01247. (413)664-9611. **E-mail:** publisher@tupelopress.org. **E-mail:** www.tupelopress.org/submissions. **Website:** www. tupelopress.org. **Contact:** Jeffrey Levine, publish/editor-in-chief; Elyse Newhouse, associate publisher; Jim Schley, managing editor. "We're an independent nonprofit literary press. Also sponsor these upcoming competitions: Dorset Prize: $10,000. Entries must be postmarked between September 1 and December 31, 2011. Guidelines are online; Snowbound Series chapbook Award: $1,000 and 50 copies of chapbook. See website for submission period and guidelines. Every July we have Open Submissions. We accept book-length poetry, poetry collections (48 + pages), short story collections, novellas, literary nonfiction/memoirs and up to 80 pages of a novel." Guidelines available online.

NEEDS "Our mission is to publish thrilling, visually and emotionally and intellectually stimulating books of the highest quality, inside and out. We want contemporary poetry, etc. by the most diverse list of emerging and established writers in the U.S."

HOW TO CONTACT Submit complete ms.

⦿⦿⑂ TURNSTONE PRESS

206-100 Arthur St., Winnipeg MB R3B 1H3, Canada. (204)947-1555. **Fax:** (204)942-1555. **E-mail:** info@ turnstonepress.com. **E-mail:** editor@turnstonepress. com. **Website:** www.turnstonepress.com. "Turnstone Press is a literary publisher, not a general publisher, and therefore we are only interested in literary fiction, literary non-fiction—including literary criticism—and poetry. We do publish literary mysteries, thrillers, and noir under our Ravenstone imprint. We publish only Canadian authors or landed immigrants, we strive to publish a significant number of new writers, to publish in a variety of genres, and to have 50% of each year's list be Manitoba writers and/or books with Manitoba content." Publishes ms 2 years after acceptance. Responds in 4-7 months. Guidelines available online at website.

HOW TO CONTACT Poetry manuscripts should be a minimum 70 pages. Submit complete ms. Include cover letter.

TIPS "As a Canadian literary press, we have a mandate to publish Canadian writers only. Do some homework before submitting works to make sure your subject matter/genre/writing style falls within the publishers area of interest."

THE UNIVERSITY OF AKRON PRESS

120 E. Mill St., Suite 415, Akron OH 44325. (330)972-5342. **Fax:** (330)972-8364. **E-mail:** uapress@uakron.edu. **Website:** www.uakron.edu/uapress. **Contact:** Thomas Bacher, director and acquisitions. "The University of Akron Press is the publishing arm of The University of Akron and is dedicated to the dissemination of scholarly, professional, and regional books and other content." Publishes hardcover and paperback originals and reissues. Pays 7-15% royalty. Publishes book 9-12 months after acceptance. Responds in 2 weeks to queries/proposals; 3-4 months to solicited mss. Query prior to submitting Guidelines available online.

NEEDS Follow the guidelines and submit mss only for the contest: www.uakron.edu/uapress/poetry.html. "We publish two books of poetry annually, one of which is the winner of The Akron Poetry prize. We also are interested in literary collections based around one theme, especially collections of translated works."

HOW TO CONTACT If you are interested in publishing with The University of Akron Press, please fill out form online.

THE UNIVERSITY OF ARKANSAS PRESS

McIlroy House, 105 N. McIlroy Ave., Fayetteville AR 72701. (479)575-3246. **Fax:** (479)575-6044. **E-mail:** lmalley@uark.edu; jewatki@uark.edu. **Website:** uapress.com. **Contact:** Lawrence J. Malley, director and editor-in-chief and Julie Watkins, editor. "The University of Arkansas Press publishes series on Ozark studies, the Civil War in the West, poetry and poetics, and sport and society." Publishes hardcover and trade paperback originals and reprints. Publishes book 1 year after acceptance. Responds in 3 months to proposals. Book catalog and ms guidelines on website or on request.

HOW TO CONTACT University of Arkansas Press publishes four poetry books per year through the Miller Williams Poetry Prize. See Contests section of this book for more information.

⊘ THE UNIVERSITY OF CHICAGO PRESS

1427 E. 60th St., Chicago IL 60637. Voicemail: (773)702-7700. **Fax:** (773)702-2705 or (773)702-9756. **Website:** www.press.uchicago.edu. **Contact:** Randolph Petilos, poetry and medieval studies editor. "The University of Chicago Press has been publishing scholarly books and journals since 1891. Annually, we publish an average of four books in our Phoenix Poets series and two books of poetry in translation. Occasionally, we may publish a book of poetry outside Phoenix Poets, or as a paperback reprint from another publisher." Has recently published work by Andrea Zanzotto, Janet Foxman, David Ferry, Francesca Abbate, Andrew Feld, John Peck, Jennifer Clarvoe, Bruce Smith, Gail Mazur, Eleanor Wilner, Peter Balakian, Atsuro Riley, Tom Yuill, Robert Pack, Amelia Rosselli, Tommaso Campanella, Milo De Angelis, Mark Halliday, and Joshua Weiner.

UNIVERSITY OF IOWA PRESS

100 Kuhl House, 119 W. Park Rd., Iowa City IA 52242. (319)335-2000. **Fax:** (319)335-2055. **E-mail:** uipress@uiowa.edu. **Website:** www.uiowapress.org. **Contact:** Holly Carver, director; Joseph Parsons, acquisitions editor. "We publish authoritative, original nonfiction that we market mostly by direct mail to groups with special interests in our titles, and by advertising in trade and scholarly publications." Publishes hardcover and paperback originals. Pays 7-10% royalty on net receipts. Publishes book 1 year after acceptance. Book catalog available free. Guidelines available online.

NEEDS Currently publishes winners of the Iowa Poetry Prize Competition, Kuhl House Poets, poetry anthologies. Competition guidelines available on website.

UNIVERSITY OF NEBRASKA PRESS

1111 Lincoln Mall, Lincoln NE 68588. (800)755-1105. **Fax:** (402)472-6214. **E-mail:** pressmail@unl.edu. **E-mail:** arold1@unl.edu. **Website:** nebraskapress.unl.edu. **Contact:** Heather Lundine, editor-in-chief; Alison Rold, production manager. "We primarily publish nonfiction books and scholarly journals, along with a few titles per season in contemporary and regional prose and poetry. On occasion, we reprint previously published fiction of established reputation, and we have several programs to publish literary works in translation." Publishes hardcover and trade paper-

back originals and trade paperback reprints. Book catalog available free. Guidelines available online.
NEEDS Contemporary, regional.

⑤ UNIVERSITY OF NEW MEXICO PRESS

1717 Roma Ave., Albuquerque NM 87106. (505)277-3324 or (800)249-7737. **Fax:** (505)277-3343. **E-mail:** clark@unm.edu. **E-mail:** wcwhiteh@unm.edu. **Website:** www.unmpress.com. **Contact:** W. Clark Whitehorn, editor-in-chief. "The Press is well known as a publisher in the fields of anthropology, archeology, Latin American studies, art and photography, architecture and the history and culture of the American West, fiction, some poetry, Chicano/a studies and works by and about American Indians. We focus on American West, Southwest and Latin American regions." Publishes hardcover originals and trade paperback originals and reprints. Pays variable royalty. Pays advance. Book catalog available for free. Please read and follow the submission query guidelines on the Author Information page online. Do not send your entire ms or additional materials until requested. If your book is accepted for publication, you will be notified.

① UNIVERSITY OF WISCONSIN PRESS

1930 Monroe St., 3rd Floor, Madison WI 53711. (608)263-1110. **Fax:** (608)263-1132. **E-mail:** uwiscpress@uwpress.wisc.edu. **E-mail:** kadushin@wisc.edu. **Website:** www.wisc.edu/wisconsinpress. Gwen Walker, acquisitions editor. **Contact:** Raphael Kadushin, senior acquisitions editor; Gwen Walker, acquisitions editor. Publishes hardcover originals, paperback originals, and paperback reprints. Pays royalty. Publishes ms 9-18 months after acceptance. Responds in 2 weeks to queries; 8 weeks to mss. Rarely comments on rejected mss. Guidelines online.

○ Check online guidelines for latest submission guidelines.

NEEDS The University of Wisconsin Press Awards the Brittingham Prize in Poetry and Felix Pollack Prize in Poetry. Each winning poet receives $2,500 ($1,000 cash prize and $1,500 honorarium to cover expenses of reading in Madison). Prizes awarded annually for the two best book-length manuscripts of original poetry submitted in the open competition. Submission period September 1-30. More details online.
TIPS "Make sure the query letter and sample text are well-written, and read guidelines carefully to make sure we accept the genre you are submitting."

UNTREED READS PUBLISHING

506 Kansas St., San Francisco CA 94107. (415)621-0465. **Fax:** (415)621-0465. **E-mail:** general@untreedreads.com. **E-mail:** submissions@untreedreads.com. **Website:** www.untreedreads.com. K.D. Sullivan, CEO/publisher (nonfiction-all genres, especially business). **Contact:** Jay A. Hartman, editor-in-chief (fiction-all genres). Publishes electronic originals and reprints. Pays 50-60% royalty on retail price. Responds in 1/2 month on queries, 1 month on proposals, and 1 1/2 months on mss. Catalog and guidelines available online at website.
NEEDS "We are not accepting individual poems currently, but will accept proposals for poetry collections."
TIPS "For our fiction titles we lean toward a literary audience. For nonfiction titles, we want to be a platform for business people, entrepreneurs, and speakers to become well known in their fields of expertise. However, for both fiction and nonfiction we want to appeal to many audiences."

○ VÉHICULE PRESS

3861 Boulevard st-Laurent, P.O.B. 42094 BP Roy, Montreal QC H2W 2T3, Canada. (514)844-6073. **Fax:** (514)844-7543. **E-mail:** vp@vehiculepress.com. **Website:** www.vehiculepress.com. **Contact:** Simon Dardick, president/publisher. "Montreal's Véhicule Press has published the best of Canadian and Quebec literature-fiction, poetry, essays, translations, and social history." Publishes trade paperback originals by Canadian authors mostly. Pays 10-15% royalty on retail price. Pays $200-500 advance. Publishes ms 1 year after acceptance. Responds in 4 months to queries. Book catalog for 9 x 12 SAE with IRCs.
NEEDS Contact Carmine Starnino with SASE. Vehicule Press is a "literary press with a poetry series, Signal Editions, publishing the work of Canadian poets only." Publishes flat-spined paperbacks. Has published *The Empire's Missing Links* by Walid Bitar, *36 Cornelian Avenue* by Christopher Wiseman, and *Morning Gothic* by George Ellenbogen. Publishes Canadian poetry that is "first-rate, original, content-conscious."
TIPS "Quality in almost any style is acceptable. We believe in the editing process."

○⑤ WAKE FOREST UNIVERSITY PRESS

P.O. Box 7333, Winston-Salem NC 27109. (336)758-5448. **Fax:** (336)758-5636. **E-mail:** wfupress@wfu.edu. **Website:** www.wfu.edu/wfupress. **Contact:** Jefferson Holdridge, director/poetry editor; Dillon Johnston, advisory editor. "We publish only poetry from Ireland. I am able to consider only poetry written by native Irish poets. I must return, unread, poetry from American poets." Query with 4-5 samples and cover letter. Sometimes sends prepublication galleys. Buys North American or U.S. rights. Pays on 10% royalty contract, plus 6-8 author's copies. Negotiable advance. Responds to queries in 1-2 weeks; to submissions (*if invited*) in 2-3 months.

NEEDS Has published *Collected Poems* by John Montague; *Ghost Orchid* by Michael Longley; *Selected Poems* by Medbh McGuckian; and *The Wake Forest Book of Irish Women's Poetry*.

⦿⑤ WASHINGTON WRITERS' PUBLISHING HOUSE

P.O. Box 15271, Washington DC 20003. **E-mail:** wwphpress@gmail.com. **Website:** www.washingtonwriters.org. **Contact:** Patrick Pepper, president. Guidelines for SASE or on website.

NEEDS Washington Writers' Publishing House considers book-length mss for publication by poets living within 75 driving miles of the U.S. Capitol (Baltimore area included) through competition only. Publishes 1-2 poetry books/year.

HOW TO CONTACT "No specific criteria, except literary excellence."

CONTEST/AWARD OFFERINGS Offers $1,000 and 50 copies of published book plus additional copies for publicity use. Manuscripts may include previously published poems. Submit an electronic copy by e-mail to wwphpress@gmail.com (use PDF, .doc, or rich text format) or 2 hard copies by snail mail of a poetry ms of 50-70 pages, single-spaced (poet's name should not appear on ms pages). Include separate page of publication acknowledgments plus 2 cover sheets: one with ms title, poet's name, address, telephone number, and e-mail address, the other with ms title only. Include SASE for results only; mss will not be returned (will be recycled). Guidelines available for SASE or on website. "Author should indicate where they heard about WWPH." **Entry fee:** $25. **Deadline:** July 1-November 1 (postmark). Order sample books on website or by sending $12 plus $3 s&h to Washington Writers' Publishing House, P.O. Box 15271, Washington DC 20003.

WAVE BOOKS

1938 Fairview Ave. E., Suite 201, Seattle WA 98102. (206)676-5337. **E-mail:** info@wavepoetry.com. **Website:** www.wavepoetry.com. **Contact:** Charlie Wright, publisher; Joshua Beckman and Matthew Zapruder, editors; Heidi Broadhead, managing editor. "Wave Books is an independent poetry press based in Seattle, Washington, dedicated to publishing the best in contemporary American poetry, poetry in translation, and writing by poets. The Press was founded in 2005, merging with established publisher Verse Press. By publishing strong innovative work in finely crafted trade editions and handmade ephemera, we hope to continue to challenge the values and practices of readers and add to the collective sense of what's possible in contemporary poetry." Publishes hardcover and trade paperback originals. Catalog online.

⦿ "No children's fiction or nonfiction for Wave library. Please no unsolicited mss or queries. We will post calls for submissions on our website."

⦸⑤ WESLEYAN UNIVERSITY PRESS

215 Long Lane, Middletown CT 06459. (860)685-7711. **Fax:** (860)685-7712. **E-mail:** stamminen@wesleyan.edu. **Website:** www.wesleyan.edu/wespress. **Contact:** Suzanna Tamminen, director and editor-in-chief. "Wesleyan University Press is a scholarly press with a focus on poetry, music, dance and cultural studies." Wesleyan University Press is one of the major publishers of poetry in the nation. Publishes 4-6 titles/year. Has published poetry by James Dickey, Joy Harjo, James Tate, and Yusef Komunyakaa. Guidelines available for SASE or on website. Responds to queries in 2 months; to mss in 4 months. Pays royalties plus 10 author's copies. Poetry publications from Wesleyan tend to get widely (and respectfully) reviewed. **"We are accepting manuscripts by invitation only until further notice."** Publishes hardcover originals and paperbacks. Book catalog available free. Ms guidelines online or with #10 SASE.

NEEDS We do not accept unsolicited manuscripts.

HOW TO CONTACT Query first with SASE. Considers simultaneous submissions.

⦸ WHITE EAGLE COFFEE STORE PRESS

P.O. Box 383, Fox River Grove IL 60021. **E-mail:** WECSPress@aol.com. **Website:** whiteeaglecoffeestorepress.com. **Contact:** Frank Edmund Smith, publisher. White Eagle is a small press publishing 2-3 chapbooks/year. "Alternate chapbooks are published by invitation and by competition. Author published by invitation becomes judge for next competition." Wants "any kind of poetry. No censorship at this press. Literary values are the only standard." Does not want "sentimental or didactic writing." Has published poetry by Timothy Russell, Connie Donovan, Scott Lumbard, Linda Lee Harper, Scott Beal, Katie Kingston, and Brian Brodeur. Sample: $6.95. *Regular submissions by invitation only.*

NEEDS Winner receives $500 and 25 author's copies. All entrants will receive a copy of the winning chapbook. Considers previously published poems and simultaneous submissions, with notice. Submit complete chapbook ms (20-24 pages), paginated, with table of contents. Poet's name should not appear on ms pages. Include 2 cover sheets: 1 with ms title, poet's name, address, phone number, and brief biography; second with ms title and 125-word statement about poet's work to be included in chapbook (poet's name should not appear on second cover sheet). Include list of credits for previously published poems. **Entry fee:** $15. **Deadline:** October 31 (postmark). "Each competition is judged by either the author of the most recent chapbook published by invitation or by previous competition winners." Responds 3 months after deadline.

HOW TO CONTACT No e-mail submissions. Include SASE for results only; mss will not be returned. Guidelines available for SASE or on website.

TIPS "Poetry is about a passion for language. That's what we're about. We'd like to provide an opportunity for poets of any age who are fairly early in their careers to publish something substantial. We're excited by the enthusiasm shown for this press and by the extraordinary quality of the writing we've received."

WISDOM PUBLICATIONS

199 Elm St., Somerville MA 02144. (617)776-7416, ext. 28. **Fax:** (617)776-7841. **E-mail:** editors@wisdompubs. org. **Website:** www.wisdompubs.org. **Contact:** David Kittlestrom, senior editor. "Wisdom Publications is dedicated to making available authentic Buddhist works for the benefit of all. We publish translations, commentaries, and teachings of past and contemporary Buddhist masters and original works by leading Buddhist scholars. Currently emphasizing popular applied Buddhism, scholarly titles." Publishes hardcover originals and trade paperback originals and reprints. Pays 4-8% royalty on wholesale price. Pays advance. Publishes ms within 2 years of acceptance. Book catalog and ms guidelines online.

TIPS "We are basically a publisher of Buddhist books-all schools and traditions of Buddhism. Please see our catalog or our website before you send anything to us to get a sense of what we publish."

WORDSONG

815 Church St., Honesdale PA 18431. **Fax:** (570)253-0179. **E-mail:** submissions@boydsmillspress.com; eagarrow@boydsmillspress.com. **Website:** www.wordsongpoetry.com. "We publish fresh voices in contemporary poetry." Pays authors royalty or work purchased outright. Responds to mss in 3 months.

NEEDS Submit complete ms or submit through agent. Label package "Manuscript Submission" and include SASE. "Please send a book-length collection of your own poems. Do not send an initial query."

TIPS "Collections of original poetry, not anthologies, are our biggest need at this time. Keep in mind that the strongest collections demonstrate a facility with multiple poetic forms and offer fresh images and insights. Check to see what's already on the market and on our website before submitting."

YALE UNIVERSITY PRESS

(203)432-0960. **Fax:** (203)432-0948. **E-mail:** niamh. cunningham@yale.edu. **Website:** www.yale.edu/yup. **Contact:** Niamh Cunningham, (203)432-0975. Christopher Rogers, editorial director (history and current events); Jean E. Thomson Black, executive editor (science, medicine); Vadim Staklo, Associate Editor (reference books, Annals of Communism, Slavic Studies); William Frucht, Executive Editor (politics, law, and economics); Michelle Komie, Senior Editor (art, architecture); Patricia Fidler, Publisher (art, architecture); Tim Shea, Editor (languages, ESL); Alison Mackeen, Editor (literature, literary studies, media studies); Sarah Miller, Associate Editor, General Interest; Ileene Smith, Exec. Editor-at-large, General Interest; Laura Davulis, Editor (digital development); Jennifer Banks, Senior Editor (Religion, Religious History, Classics). Estab. 1908. "Yale University Press publishes scholarly and general interest books." Publishes hardcover and trade paperback originals Book catalog and ms guidelines online

NEEDS Publishes 1 book each year. Submit to Yale Series of Younger Poets Competition. Open to poets under 40 who have not had a book previously published. Submit ms of 48-64 pages by November 15. Rules and guidelines available online or with SASE.

HOW TO CONTACT Submit complete ms.

TIPS "Audience is scholars, students and general readers."

CONTESTS
AND AWARDS

//

This section contains a wide array of poetry competitions and literary awards. These range from state poetry society contests (with a number of modest monetary prizes) to prestigious honors bestowed by private foundations, elite publishers and renowned university programs. Because these listings reflect such a variety of skill levels and degrees of competitiveness, it's important to read each carefully and note its unique requirements. *Never* enter a contest without consulting the guidelines and following directions to the letter (including manuscript formatting, number of lines or pages of poetry accepted, amount of entry fee, entry forms needed and other details).

Important note: As we gathered information for this edition of *Poet's Market*, we found that some competitions hadn't yet established their 2014 fees and deadlines. In such cases, we list the most recent information available as a general guide. Always consult current guidelines for updates before entering any competition.

WHERE TO ENTER?

While it's perfectly okay to "think big," being realistic may improve your chances of winning a prize for your poetry. Entering smaller and less established contests may improve your odds of winning. That said, all contests are incredibly competitive, especially when any form of monetary compensation or publication opportunity is the prize.

If you are new to poetry, try finding contests that offer entry prizes, such as a complimentary subscription to a journal or a copy of the winning book. That way you'll still get something you can enjoy and study, even if you don't win:

✪ 10 MINUTE PLAY CONTEST & FESTIVAL

Weathervane Playhouse, 1301 Weathervane Lane, Akron OH 44313. (330)836-2626. **E-mail:** info@weathervaneplayhouse.com. **Website:** www.weathervaneplayhouse.com. Annual 8x10 TheatreFest. Must be US citizen 18 years or older. All rights remain with writers. "The mission of the Weathervane Playhouse 8x10 TheatreFest is to promote the art of play writing, present new works, and introduce area audiences to the short play form. The competition will provide Weathervane with recognition for quality and innovative theatre." Deadline: mid-May. Prizes: 1st Place: $350; 2nd Place: $250; Audience Favorite: $150; 5 runners-up: $50. Eight finalists receive full productions of their plays during TheatreFest, held in mid-July. First round judges include individuals with experience in every area of stagecraft, including tech designers, actors, directors, stage managers, and playwrights.
TIPS "Please see visit www.weathervaneplayhouse.com/special-events for this year's specific dates, guidelines, etc."

◑ THE 49TH PARALLEL POETRY AWARD

Western Washington University, Mail Stop 9053, Bellingham WA 98225. **E-mail:** bhreview@wwu.edu. **Website:** www.bhreview.org. The annual 49th Parallel Poetry Award offers 1st Prize of $1,000, plus publication in and a year's subscription to *Bellingham Review*. Runners-up and finalists may be considered for publication. Submissions must be unpublished and not accepted for publication elsewhere. Considers simultaneous submissions, but work must be withdrawn from the competition if accepted for publication elsewhere. Submit up to 3 poems. "Poems within a series will each be treated as a separate entry." For each entry, include a 3x5 index card stating the title of the work, the category (poetry), the poet's name, phone number, address, and e-mail. "Make sure writing is legible on this card. Author's name must not appear anywhere on the manuscript." Include SASE for results only; mss will not be returned. Guidelines available for SASE or on website. **Entry fee:** $18 for first entry (up to 3 poems); $10 each additional poem. Make checks payable to *Bellingham Review*. "Everyone entering the competition will receive a complimentary two-issue subscription to *Bellingham Review*." **Deadline:** April 1. Given for a poem or group of poems of any style or length. Prize: $1,000.

◔ ACORN-PLANTOS AWARD FOR PEOPLES POETRY

Acorn-Plantos Award Committee, 36 Sunset Ave., Hamilton ON L8R 1V6, Canada. **E-mail:** jeffseff@allstream.net. **Contact:** Jeff Seffinga. "Annual contest for work that appeared in print in the previous calender year. This award is given to the Canadian poet who best (through the publication of a book of poems) exemplifies populist or peoples poetry in the tradition of Milton Acorn, Ted Plantos, et al. Work may be entered by the poet or the publisher; the award goes to the poet. Entrants must submit 5 copies of each title. Poet must be a citizen of Canada or a landed immigrant. Publisher need not be Canadian." Deadline: June 30 $500 (CDN) and a medal. Judged by a panel of poets in the tradition who are not entered in the current year.

◐ AGHA SHAHID ALI PRIZE IN POETRY

University of Utah Press, J. Willard Marriott Lib., Ste 5400, 295 S. 1500 East, Salt Lake City UT 84112. (801)581-6771. **Fax:** (801)581-3365. **Website:** www.uofupress.com/ali-poetry-prize.php. The University of Utah Press and the University of Utah Department of English offer an annual award of $1,000, publication of a book-length poetry ms, and a reading in the Guest Writers Series. Poems must be unpublished as a collection, but individual poems may have been previously published elsewhere. Considers simultaneous submissions; "however, entrants must notify the Press immediately if the collection submitted is accepted for publication elsewhere during the competition." Submit 48-64 typed pages of poetry, with no names or other identifying information appearing on title page or within ms. Include cover sheet with complete contact information (name, address, telephone, e-mail address). Submissions must be in English. Mss will not be returned. Guidelines available on website. **Entry fee:** $25/book submission. Competition receives over 300 mss/year. Winner announced on press website in November; series editor contacts winning poet. Copies of winning books are available for $14.95 from University of Utah Press ((800)621-2736 for order fulfillment) or through website. Honoring the memory of a celebrated poet and a beloved teacher, the Agha Shahid Ali Prize in Poetry is awarded annually and is sponsored by The University of Utah Press and The University of Utah Department of English. Deadline: March 31. Prize: $1,000.

THE AMERICAN POETRY JOURNAL BOOK PRIZE

P.O. Box 2080, Aptos CA 95001-2080. **E-mail:** editor@americanpoetryjournal.com. **Website:** www.americanpoetryjournal.com. The American Poetry Journal Book Prize awards $500 and book publication. Submit 50-65 paginated pages of poetry, table of contents, acknowledgments, bio, and e-mail address (for results). No SASE required; mss will be recycled. Guidelines available on website. **Entry fee:** $25. Make checks payable to Dream Horse Press. **Deadline:** February 28 (check website for updates). Winners of previous contests were Lisa Lewis, and Mark Conway, and Quinn Latimer. The American Poetry Journal Book Prize awards $500 and book publication. Deadline: February 28. Prize: $1,000 and 20 published copies. All entries will be considered for publication.

THE AMY AWARD FOR POETRY

Poets & Writers, Poets & Writers, 90 Broad St., Suite 2100, New York NY 10004. **E-mail:** admin@pw.org. **E-mail:** amyaward@pw.org. **Website:** www.pw.org/about-us/amy_award. **Contact:** Elliot Figman, executive director. The Amy Award, sponsored by Poets & Writers, Inc., offers honorarium, books, plus a reading in NYC. **Entrants must be women 30 years of age or under who reside on Long Island or in the New York metropolitan region.** Submit 3 lyric poems of no more than 50 lines each, online or with SASE, and application. Guidelines available on website. **Entry fee:** none. **Deadline:** June, 2014. Past winners include Genevieve Burger-Weiser, Lisabeth Burton, K.D. Henley, and Alexandra Wilder. "The Amy Award was established by Edward Butscher and Paula Trachtman of East Hampton in memory of Mrs. Trachtman's daughter, Amy Rothholz, an actor and poet who died at age 25." The Amy Award celebrates promising young women poets from the New York City Area. Deadline: June 1. Prize: An invitation to read at the awards presentation and reception in New York City in autumn 2013, an honorarium, and a one-year subscription to Poets & Writers Magazine and a selection of poetry books. Up to three winners will be selected.

ANABIOSIS PRESS CHAPBOOK CONTEST

2 South New St., Bradford MA 01835. (978)469-7085. **E-mail:** rsmyth@anabiosispress.org. **Website:** www.anabiosispress.org. **Contact:** Richard Smyth, editor.

Deadline: June 30 (postmark). $100, plus publication of the winning chapbook, and 75 copies of the first run.

ANDERBO POETRY PRIZE

Anderbo Poetry Prize, 270 Lafayette St., Suite 705, New York NY 10012. **E-mail:** rrofihe@yahoo.com. **E-mail:** editors@anderbo.com. **Website:** www.anderbo.com. **Contact:** Rick Rofihe. Poet must not have have been previously published on anderbo.com. Limit six poems per poet. Poems should be typed on 8½ x 11 paper with the poet's name and contact info on the upper right corner of each poem. See guidelines online. Deadline: December 15. Prize: $500, publication on anderbo.com.

ANNUAL VENTURA COUNTY WRITERS CLUB POETRY CONTEST WITH TWO DIVISIONS FOR YOUNG POETS

Ventura County Writers Club Poetry Contest, P.O. Box 3373, Thousand Oaks CA 91362. (805)524-6970. **E-mail:** info@venturacountywriters.com. **Website:** www.venturacountywriters.com. **Contact:** Kate Sexton, president. The Ventura County Writers Club announced its twelfth annual Poetry Contest, which includes an exciting Audio/Visual category to address more forms of poetry. The contest will continue its two youth categories for poets under 18: Division A is open to entrants ages 13 to 18; and, Division B is open to poets ages 12 and under. Poets 18 and older are invited to enter in the Adult category. The contest is open to poets worldwide as long as the poem is in English. Deadline: February 15. Prize: The adult and A/V categories will award $100 for first place, $75 for second and $50 for third place. The two youth categories will award $50 for first place, $35 for second and $25 for third place.

ANNUAL WORLD HAIKU COMPETITION & ANNUAL WORLD TANKA CONTEST

P.O. Box 17331, Arlington VA 22216. **E-mail:** lpezinesubmissions@gmail.com. **Website:** http://lyricalpassionpoetry.yolasite.com. **Contact:** Raquel D. Bailey. Contest is open to all writers. "Promotes Japanese short form poetry." Deadline: November 30, 2012. (Dates are subject to change each year. See website for details) Monetary compensation and publication. Judged by experienced editors and award-winning writers from the contemporary writing community. **TIPS** "E-mail and snail mail entries accepted."

ARIZONA LITERARY CONTEST & BOOK AWARDS

6145 W. Echo Lane, Glendale AZ 85302. (623)847-9343. **E-mail:** info@azauthors.com. **Website:** www.azauthors.com. Arizona Authors Association sponsors annual literary contest in poetry, short story, essay, unpublished novels, and published books (fiction, nonfiction, and children's literature). Awards publication in *Arizona Literary Magazine*, and prizes by Five Star Publications, Inc. Competition receives 1,000 entries/year. Deadline: Reads submissions January 1-July 1 $100 1st Prize, $50 2nd Prize, and $25 3rd Prize in each category. Judges: Arizona authors, editors, and reviewers. Winners announced at an award banquet by November 8.

○ ARIZONA STATE POETRY SOCIETY ANNUAL CONTEST

7111 E. Buena Terra Way, Scottsdale AZ 85253. (480)575-1222. **Website:** azpoetry.webs.com. Offers a variety of cash prizes in several categories ranging from $10-125; 1st, 2nd, and 3rd Prize winners are published in Sandcutters , ASPS's quarterly publication, which also lists names of Honorable Mention winners. See guidelines for detailed submission information (available for SASE or on website). **Entry fee:** varies according to category; see guidelines. **Deadline:** approximately September 15 (postmark). Competition receives over 1,000 entries/year. "ASPS sponsors a variety of monthly contests for members. Membership is available to anyone anywhere." Deadline: Approximately September 15. Offers a variety of cash prizes in several categories ranging from $10-125; 1st, 2nd, and 3rd Prize winners are published in Sandcutters , ASPS's quarterly publication, which also lists names of Honorable Mention winners.

ART AFFAIR ANNUAL WRITING CONTEST

Art Affair, P.O. Box 54302, Oklahoma City OK 73154. **E-mail:** artaffair@aol.com. **Website:** www.shadetreecreations.com. **Contact:** Barbara Shepherd. Purpose of contest is to encourage new and established writers and to publicly recognize them for their efforts. Open to any writer or poet. Deadline: October 1 (every year). To encourage new and established writers and to publicly recognize them for their efforts. Open to any writer or poet. Deadline: October 1. Prizes: Short Story: 1st Prize: $50; 2nd Prize: $25; 3rd Prize: $15. Western Short Story: 1st Prize: $50; 2nd Prize: $25; 3rd Prize: $15. Poetry: 1st Prize: $40; 2nd Prize: $25; 3rd Prize: $15. (all winners also receive certificates. Additional certificates for Honorable Mentions will be awarded at discretion of the judges). **TIPS** "Guidelines and entry forms available for SASE and on website."

THE ART OF MUSIC BIENNIAL WRITING CONTEST

P.O. Box 85, Del Mar CA 92014. (619)884-1401. **Fax:** (858)755-1104. **E-mail:** info@theartofmusicinc.org. **E-mail:** eaxford@aol.com. **Website:** www.theartofmusicinc.org; www.pianopress.com. **Contact:** Elizabeth C. Axford. Offered biannually. Categories are: Essay, short story, poetry, song lyrics, and illustrations for cover art. Acquires one-time rights. All entries must be accompanied by an entry form indicating category and age; parent signature is required of all writers under age 18. Poems may be of any length and in any style; essays and short stories should not exceed 5 double-spaced, typewritten pages. All entries shall be previously unpublished (except poems and song lyrics) and the original work of the author. Inquiries accepted by e-mail, phone. Short stories should be no longer than 5 pages typed and double spaced. Open to any writer. "Make sure all work is fresh and original. Music-related topics only." Results announced October 31. Winners notified by mail. For contest results, send SASE or visit website. "The purpose of the contest is to promote the art of music through writing." Deadline: June 30. Prize: Trophy, certificate, publication online and in the eBook, *The Art of Music: A Collection of Writings*. Judged by a panel of published poets, authors and songwriters.

○ ATLANTIC WRITING COMPETITION FOR UNPUBLISHED MANUSCRIPTS

Writers' Federation of Nova Scotia, 1113 Marginal Rd., Halifax NS B3H 4P7. (902)423-8116. **Fax:** (902)422-0881. **E-mail:** programs@writers.ns.ca. **Website:** www.writers.ns.ca. **Contact:** Hillary Titley. "Annual contest for beginners to try their hand in a number of categories: adult novel, writing for children, poetry, short story, juvenile/young adult novel, creative non-fiction, and play. Because our aim is to help Atlantic Canadian writers grow, judges return written comments when the competition is concluded." "We encourage writers in Atlantic Canada to explore and expand their talents by sending in their new, untried work." Deadline: November 9. Prizes vary based on categories. See website for details.

AUTUMN HOUSE POETRY, FICTION, AND NONFICTION PRIZES

P.O. Box 60100, Pittsburgh PA 15211. (412)381-4261. **E-mail:** msimms@autumnhouse.org. **Website:** http://autumnhouse.org. **Contact:** Michael Simms, editor. Offers annual prize of $2,500 and publication of book-length ms with national promotion. Submission must be unpublished as a collection, but individual poems, stories, and essays may have been previously published elsewhere. Considers simultaneous submissions. Submit 50-80 pages of poetry or 200-300 pages of prose ("blind judging—2 cover sheets requested"). Guidelines available for SASE, by e-mail, or on website. Competition receives 1,500 entries/year. Winners announced through mailings, website, and ads in *Poets & Writers*, *American Poetry Review,* and *Writer's Chronicle* (extensive publicity for winner). Copies of winning books available from Amazon.com, Barnes & Noble, and other retailers. "Autumn House is a nonprofit corporation with the mission of publishing and promoting poetry and other fine literature. We have published books by Gerald Stern, Ruth L. Schwartz, Ed Ochester, Andrea Hollander Budy, George Bilgere, Jo McDougall, and others." Deadline: June 30, annually 2012 judges were Stephen Dunn, Stewart O'Nan, and Phillip Lopate.

TIPS "Include only your best work."

BARROW STREET PRESS BOOK CONTEST

P.O. Box 1558, Kingston RI 02881. **E-mail:** submissions@barrowstreet.org. **Website:** www.barrowstreet.org. Barrow Street Press publishes one poetry book/year through the annual Barrow Street Press Book Contest. Winner receives $1,000 and publication. Submit a 50- to 70-page ms of original, previously unpublished poetry in English. Manuscript should be typed, single-spaced on white 8½x11 paper. Clear photocopies acceptable. Include 2 title pages and an acknowledgments page listing any poems previously published in journals or anthologies. Author's name, address, and daytime phone number should appear on first title page only, and nowhere else in ms. Include SASE for results only; no mss will be returned. Guidelines available on website. **Entry fee:** $25; include mailer with $2.13 postage for copy of winning book. Make checks payable to Barrow Street. **Deadline:** June 30. 2012 Judge is Lynn Emanuel. The Barrow Street Press Book Contest award will be given

for the best previously unpublished manuscript of poetry in English. Deadline: June 30. Judged by Afaa Michael Weaver.

ELINOR BENEDICT POETRY PRIZE

E-mail: passages@nmu.edu. **Website:** passagesnorth.com/contests/. **Contact:** Jennifer A. Howard, Editor-in-Chief. Contest sponsored by Passages North, Dept. of English, Northern Michigan University, 1401 Presque Isle Ave., Marquette MI 49855. (906)227-1203. **Fax:** (906)227-1096. **E-mail:** passages@nmu.edu. **Website:** myweb.nmu.edu/~passages. Acquisitions: Kate Myers Hanson. Contest. $1,000 first prize and publication. $10 for up to three poems entry fee ($3 for each additional poem after that). T. Johnston, Managing Editor, PN. Given biennially for a poem or a group of poems. Deadline: March 22. Prize: $1,000. Judged by Aimee Nezhukumatathil.

THE PATRICIA BIBBY FIRST BOOK AWARD

Patricia Bibby Award, Tebot Bach, P.O. Box 7887, Huntington Beach CA 92615-7887. **E-mail:** mifanwy@tebotbach.org. **Website:** www.tebotbach.org. **Contact:** Mifanwy Kaiser. Deadline: October 31 (postmark). Prize: $1,000 and book will be published. Judged by Ralph Angel in 2013.

BINGHAMTON UNIVERSITY MILT KESSLER POETRY BOOK AWARD

Binghamton University Creative Writing Program, Department of English, General Literature, and Rhetoric, Library North Room 1149, Vestal Parkway East, P.O. Box 6000, Binghamton NY 13902-6000. (607)777-2713. **Fax:** (607)777-2408. **E-mail:** cwpro@binghamton.edu. **Website:** www2.binghamton.edu/english/creative-writing/binghamton-center-for-writers. **Contact:** Maria Mazziotti Gillan, creative writing program director. Offers annual award for a book of poetry judged best of those published during the previous year. Deadline: March 1. Prize: $1,000.

BLUE MOUNTAIN ARTS/SPS STUDIOS POETRY CARD CONTEST

P.O. Box 1007, Boulder CO 80306. (303)449-0536. **Fax:** (303)447-0939. **E-mail:** poetrycontest@sps.com. **Website:** www.sps.com. "We're looking for original poetry that is rhyming or non-rhyming, although we find that non-rhyming poetry reads better. Poems may also be considered for possible publication on greeting cards or in book anthologies. Contest is offered biannually. Guidelines available online." Deadline: December 31 and June 30. Prizes: 1st Place: $300; 2nd Place: $150; 3rd Place: $50. Blue Mountain Arts editorial staff.

THE FREDERICK BOCK PRIZE

(312)787-7070. **Fax:** (312)787-6650. **E-mail:** editors@ poetrymagazine.org. **Website:** www.poetryfoundation.org. Several prizes are awarded annually for the best work printed in *Poetry* during the preceding year. Only poems already published in the magazine are eligible for consideration, and no formal application is necessary. The winners are announced in the November issue. Upon acceptance, *Poetry* licenses exclusive worldwide first serial rights, including electronic rights, for publication, as well as non-exclusive rights to reprint, reuse, and archive the work, in any format, in perpetuity. Copyright reverts to author upon first publication. Any writer may submit poems to *Poetry*. Prize: $500.

BOULEVARD EMERGING POETS CONTEST

PMB 325, 6614 Clayton Rd., Richmond Heights MO 63117. **E-mail:** kellyleavitt@boulevardmagazine.org. **Website:** www.boulevardmagazine.org. **Contact:** Kelly Leavitt, managing editor. Annual Emerging Poets Contest offers $1,000 and publication in *Boulevard* (see separate listing in Magazines/Journals) for the best group of 3 poems by a poet who has not yet published a book of poetry with a nationally distributed press. "All entries will be considered for publication and payment at our regular rates." Submissions must be unpublished. Considers simultaneous submissions. Submit 3 poems, typed; may be a sequence or unrelated. On page one of first poem type poet's name, address, phone number, and titles of the 3 poems. Include ASP for notification of receipt of ms; mss will not be returned. Guidelines available on website. **Entry fee:** $15/group of 3 poems, $15 for each additional group of 3 poems; includes one-year subscription to *Boulevard*. Make checks payable to Boulevard. **Deadline:** June 1 (postmark). Judge: editors of *Boulevard* magazine. "No one editorially or financially affiliated with *Boulevard* may enter the contest." Annual Emerging Poets Contest offers $1,000 and publication in *Boulevard* (see separate listing in Magazines/Journals) for the best group of 3 poems by a poet who has not yet published a book of poetry with a nationally distributed press. "All entries will be considered for

publication and payment at our regular rates." Deadline: June 1. Prize: $1,000 and publication.

BRICK ROAD POETRY BOOK CONTEST

Brick Road Poetry Press, Inc., P.O. Box 751, Columbus GA 31902. (706)649-3080. **Fax:** (706)649-3094. **E-mail:** editor@brickroadpoetrypress.com. **Website:** www.brickroadpoetrypress.com. **Contact:** Ron Self and Keith Badowski, co-editors/founders. Offers annual award. The 1st Prize winner will receive a publication contract with Brick Road Poetry Press, $1,000, and 25 copies of the printed book. The winning book will be published in both print and e-book formats. "We may also offer publication contracts to the top finalists." Submissions must be unpublished as a collection, but individual poems may have been previously published elsewhere. Submit 70-100 pages of poetry. Guidelines available by e-mail or online. Competition receives 150 entries/year. Judged by Ron Self and Keith Badowski. Winners notified February 15. Copies of winning books available for $15.95. "The mission of Brick Road Poetry Press is to publish and promote poetry that entertains, amuses, edifies and surprises a wide audience of appreciative readers. We are not qualified to judge who deserves to be published, so we concentrate on publishing what we enjoy. Our preference is for poetry geared toward dramatizing the human experience in a language rich with sensory image and metaphor, recognizing that poetry can be, at one and the same time, both familiar as the perspiration of daily labor and outrageous as a carnival sideshow." Deadline: November 1

TIPS "The best way to discover all that poetry can be and to expand the limits of your own poetry is to read expansively."

BRIGHT HILL PRESS POETRY CHAPBOOK COMPETITION

Bright Press Hill & Literary Center, P.O. Box 193, 94 Church St., Treadwell NY 13846. (607)829-5055. **E-mail:** brighthillpress@stny.rr.com. **Website:** www. brighthillpress.org. The annual Bright Hill Press Chapbook Award offers $300, publication of a chapbook-length ms, and 25 author's copies. Guidelines available for SASE, by e-mail, or on website. Deadline: December 15. Prize: a publication contract with Bright Hill Press and $1,000, publication in print format, and 30 copies of the printed book.

TIPS "Publish your poems in literary magazines before trying to get a whole ms published. Publishing individual poems is the best way to hone your complete ms."

BRITTINGHAM PRIZE IN POETRY

University of Wisconsin Press, 1930 Monroe Street, 3rd Floor, Madison WI 5311-2059. (608)263-1110. **Fax:** (608)263-1132. **E-mail:** rwallace@wisc.edu. **E-mail:** uwiscpress@uwpress.wisc.edu. **Website:** uwpress.wisc.edu. **Contact:** Ronald Wallace, poetry editor. The annual Brittingham Prize in Poetry is 1 of 2 prizes awarded by The University of Wisconsin Press (see separate listing for the Felix Pollak Prize in Poetry in this section). Submissions must be unpublished as a collection, but individual poems may have been published elsewhere (publication must be acknowledged). Considers simultaneous submissions if notified of selection elsewhere. Submit 50-80 unbound ms pages, typed single-spaced (with double spaces between stanzas). Clean photocopies are acceptable. Include 1 title page with poet's name, address, and telephone number and 1 with title only. No translations. SASE required. Will return results only; mss will not be returned. Guidelines available for SASE or on website. **Entry fee:** $25. **NOTE:** $25 fee applies to consideration of same entry for the Felix Pollak Prize in Poetry—1 fee for 2 contest entries. Make checks/money orders payable to University of Wisconsin Press. 2012 Brittingham Prize winner was Jazzy Danziger, *Darkroom*. Qualified readers will screen all mss. Judge by "a distinguished poet who will remain anonymous until the winners are announced in mid-February." The annual Brittingham Prize in Poetry is 1 of 2 prizes awarded by The University of Wisconsin Press (see separate listing for the Felix Pollak Prize in Poetry in this section). The Brittingham Prize in Poetry is awarded annually to the best book-length manuscript of original poetry submitted in an open competition. The award is administered by the University of Wisconsin–Madison English Department, and the winner is chosen by a nationally recognized poet. The resulting book is published by the University of Wisconsin Press. Deadline: Submit September 1-27 (postmark). Prize: Offers $1,000, plus publication, with an additional $1,500 honorarium to cover expenses of a reading in Madison.

BURNSIDE REVIEW CHAPBOOK COMPETITION

P.O. Box 1782, Portland OR 97207. **E-mail:** sid@burnsidereview.org. **Website:** www.burnsidereview.org. **Contact:** Sid Miller, editor. Deadline: June 30. Competition begins March 15. Prize: $200 and 10 copies of the chapbook printed by Burnside Review Press. Judged by Ed Skoog.

GERALD CABLE BOOK AWARD

Silverfish Review Press, P.O. Box 3541, Eugene OR 97403. (541)344-5060. **E-mail:** sfrpress@earthlink.net. **Website:** www.silverfishreviewpress.com. **Contact:** Rodger Moody, editor. Offers annual award of $1,000, publication by Silverfish Review Press, and 25 author copies to a book-length ms of original poetry by an author who has not yet published a full-length collection. No restrictions on the kind of poetry or subject matter; no translations. Individual poems may have been previously published elsewhere, but must be acknowledged. Considers simultaneous submissions (notify immediately of acceptance elsewhere). Submit at least 48 pages of poetry, no names or identification on ms pages. Include separate title sheet with poet's name, address, and phone number. Include SASP for notification of receipt and SASE for results; no mss will be returned. Accepts e-mail submissions in Word, plain text, or rich text; send entry fee and SASE by regular mail. Guidelines available for SASE, by e-mail, or on website. **Entry fee:** $25. Make checks payable to Silverfish Review Press. **Deadline:** October 15 (postmark). Winner announced in March. Copies of winning books available through website. "All entrants who enclose a booksize envelope and $2.23 in postage will receive a free copy of a recent winner of the book award."

TIPS "Now accepting e-mail submissions (save money on postage and photocopying); use Paypal for reading fee payment, see website for instructions."

CAROLINA WREN PRESS POETRY CONTEST FOR A FIRST OR SECOND BOOK

120 Morris St., Durham NC 27701. (919)560-2738. **Fax:** (919)560-2759. **E-mail:** carolinawrenpress@earthlink.net. **Website:** www.carolinawrenpress.org. **Contact:** Ravi Shankar, founding editor. The biennial Carolina Wren Press Poetry Contest for a First or Second Book offers $1,000 and publication by Carolina Wren Press (see separate listing in Book/Chapbook Publishers). Open only to poets who have

published no more than 1 full-length collection (48 pages or more). Submissions must be unpublished as a collection, but individual poems may have been previously published elsewhere. Manuscripts that have been previously self-published or that are available online in their entirety are not eligible. Considers simultaneous submissions (notify immediately of acceptance elsewhere). Submit 2 copies of a poetry ms of 48-72 pages. Page count should include title page, table of contents, and optional dedication page. See guidelines for complete formatting and submission details. Include SASE for results only; mss will not be returned. Guidelines available for SASE, by e-mail, or on website (in September). **Entry fee:** $20. 2011 judge: Lee Ann Brown. Past judges: William Pitt Root, Evie Shockley, Minnie Bruce Pratt. Copies of winning books available through website, Amazon, or local bookstore. Carolina Wren Press is a nonprofit organization whose mission is to publish quality writing, especially by writers historically neglected by mainstream publishing, and to develop diverse and vital audiences through publishing, outreach, and educational programs. Deadline: March 31. Prize: $1,000 and publication in 2015.

JAMIE CAT CALLAN HUMOR PRIZE

Category in the Soul Making Keats Literary Competition, The Webhallow House, 1544 Sweetwood Dr., Broadmoor Village CA 94015-2029. **E-mail:** Eileen-Malone@comcast.net. **Website:** www.soulmaking-contest.us. **Contact:** Eileen Malone. Deadline: November 30. Prize: First Place: $100; Second Place: $50; Third Place: $25. Judged by Jamie Cat Callan.

❶❷ THE CENTER FOR BOOK ARTS POETRY CHAPBOOK COMPETITION

The Center for Book Arts, 28 W. 27th St., 3rd Floor, New York NY 10001. (212)481-0295. **Fax:** (866)708-8994. **E-mail:** info@centerforbookarts.org. **Website:** www.centerforbookarts.org. Contest needs poetry chapbooks. Offered annually for unpublished collections of poetry. Individual poems may have been previously published. Collection must not exceed 500 lines or 24 pages (does not include cover page, title pages, table of contents, or acknowledgements pages). Copies of winning chapbooks available through website. "Center for Book Arts is a nonprofit organization dedicated to the traditional crafts of bookmaking and contemporary interpretations of the book as an art object. Through the Center's Education, Exhibition,

and Workspace Programs, we ensure that the ancient craft of the book remains a viable and vital part of our civilization." Deadline: December 15 (postmarked). Prize: $500 award, $500 honorarium for a reading, publication, and 10 copies of chapbook. Judged by Harryette Mullen and Sharon Dolin in 2013.

❶ CIDER PRESS REVIEW BOOK AWARD

P.O. Box 33384, San Diego CA 92163. **E-mail:** editor@ciderpressreview.com. **Website:** http://ciderpressreview.com/bookaward. Annual award from *Cider Press Review*. Deadline: submit September 1 - November 30 (postmark). Prize: $1,500, publication, and 25 author's copies of a book length collection of poetry. Author receives a standard publishing contract. Initial print run is not less than 1,000 copies. CPR acquires first publication rights. The 2012 judge was Gray Jacobik.

❶ CLEVELAND STATE UNIVERSITY POETRY CENTER FIRST BOOK

Dept. of English, 2121 Euclid Ave., Cleveland OH 44115-2214. (216)687-2000. **E-mail:** poetrycenter@csuohio.edu. **Website:** www.csuohio.edu/poetrycenter/. **Contact:** Frank Giampietro, Interim Director. Offers $1,000, publication in the CSU Poetry Series, and a paid reading at Cleveland State for the best full-length volume of original poetry by a poet who has not published or committed to publish a collection of poetry in a book of 48 or more pages with a press run of at least 500 copies. "The CSU Poetry Center reserves the right to consider all finalists for publication." Considers simultaneous submissions; "please inform us if the manuscript is accepted elsewhere." "Eclectic in taste and inclusive in its aesthetic, with particular interest in lyric poetry and innovative approaches to craft. Not interested in light verse, devotional verse, doggerel, or poems by poets who have not read my contemporary poetry." Submit a minimum of 48 pages of poetry, numbered. Include table of contents and acknowledgements page. Include 2 cover pages: one with ms title, poet's name, address, phone number, and e-mail; one with ms title only. No identifying information on ms pages; no cover letter or biographical information. Clearly mark outside of mailing envelope and each cover page "First Book." Accepts multiple submissions with separate entry fee for each; send in the same envelope marked " Multiple." Include SASP for notification of receipt of ms (optional) and SASE for notification of results;

mss are not returned. Guidelines available on website. **Entry fee:** $25. Make checks payable to Cleveland State University. Entrants notified by mail in summer. 2012 judge: Nick Flynn (intimate friends, relatives, current and former students of the First Book judge, students in an academic degree-conferring program or its equivalent are not eligible to enter)." The Poetry Center has retained its focus on publishing collections of contemporary poetry by established and emerging authors, while preserving its original legacy of providing educational outreach to the literary community of Northeast Ohio and maintaining a regular poetry reading series which now brings an average of fifteen poets a year from across the country to give public readings at Cleveland State University. The Poetry Center is committed to acquiring, through first-book and open-book competitions, stylistically distinctive and skillfully crafted collections from an aesthetically diverse range of authors. Offered for the best full-length volumes of original poetry in English. Deadline: March 13. Contest opens November 1 of the previous year. Prize: $1,000 and publication in the CSU Poetry Series. The 2013 competition is judged by Tracy K. Smith.

◑ CLEVELAND STATE UNIVERSITY POETRY CENTER OPEN COMPETITION

Dept. of English, 2121 Euclid Ave., Cleveland OH 44115-2214. (216)687-2000. **E-mail:** poetrycenter@csuohio.edu. **Website:** www.csuohio.edu/poetrycenter/contest1.html. **Contact:** Frank Giampietro, Interim Director. For the best full-length volume of original poetry by a poet who has published at least one full-length collection of poetry in a book of 48 pages or more with a press run of 500. Deadline: March 13. Submission period begins November 1. Prize: $1,000 and publication in the CSU Poetry Series.

CLOCKWISE CHAPBOOK COMPETITION

Tebot Bach, Tebot Bach, Clockwise, P.O. Box 7887, Huntington Beach CA 92615. (714)968-0905. **Fax:** (714)968-4677. **E-mail:** mifanwy@tebotbach.org. **Website:** www.tebotbach.org/clockwise.html. **Contact:** Gail Wronsky. Purpose of award is to honor the winning entry. Deadline: April 15. Prize: Book Publication in Perfect Bound Editions. Judged by Gail Wronsky.

CLOUDBANK CONTEST

P.O. Box 610, Corvallis OR 97339. **E-mail:** michael@cloudbankbooks.com. **Website:** www.cloudbank-books.com. **Contact:** Michael Malan, poetry and short fiction. Prize: $200 and publication, plus an extra copy of the issue in which the winning poem appears Judged by Michael Malan (final) and Reading Board (initial).

◑ THE COLORADO PRIZE FOR POETRY

Colorado Review/Center for Literary Publishing, Department of English, Colorado State University, 9105 Campus Delivery, Ft. Collins CO 80523. (970)491-5449. **E-mail:** creview@colostate.edu. **Website:** http://coloradoprize.colostate.edu. **Contact:** Stephanie G'Schwind, editor. Submission must be unpublished as a collection, but individual poems may have been published elsewhere. Submit mss of 48-100 pages of poetry (no set minimum or maximum) on any subject, in any form, double- or single-spaced. Include 2 titles pages: 1 with ms title only, the other with ms title and poet's name, address, and phone number. Enclosed SASP for notification of receipt and SASE for results; mss will not be returned. Guidelines available for SASE or by e-mail. "Guidelines available for SASE or online at website. Poets can also submit online via our online submission manager through our website." To connect writers and readers by publishing exceptional writing. Annual deadline is early January. Check website for exact deadline $2,000 and publication of a book-length ms.

○ CONCRETE WOLF POETRY CHAPBOOK CONTEST

P.O. Box 1808, Kingston WA 98346. **E-mail:** concretewolf@yahoo.com. **Website:** http://concretewolf.com. The Concrete Wolf Poetry Chapbook award offers publication and 100 author copies of a perfectly bound chapbook. Considers simultaneous submissions if notified of acceptance elsewhere. "We prefer chapbooks that have a theme, either obvious (i.e., chapbook about a divorce) or understated (i.e., all the poems mention the color blue). We like a collection that feels more like a whole than a sampling of work. We have no preference as to formal or free verse. We probably slightly favor lyric and narrative poetry to language and concrete, but excellent examples of any style get our attention." Deadline: November 30. Prize: 100 copies of a perfect-bound chapbook.

THE CONNECTICUT RIVER REVIEW POETRY CONTEST

P.O. Box 792, Manchester CT 06045. **E-mail:** conpoetry@comcast.net. **Website:** ct-poetry-society.org.

Deadline: September 30. Submissions period begins on August 1. Prize: 1st Place: $400; 2nd Place: $100; 3rd Place: $50.

CPR EDITOR'S PRIZE BOOK AWARD

P.O. Box 33384, San Diego CA 92163. **E-mail:** editor@ciderpressreview.com. **Website:** http://ciderpressreview.com/bookaward. Annual award from *Cider Press Review*. Deadline: submit April 1 - June 30 (postmark). Prize: $1,000, publication, and 25 author's copies of a book length collection of poetry. Author receives a standard publishing contract. Initial print run is not less than 1,000 copies. CPR acquires first publication rights. Judged by *Cider Press Review* editors.

CRAB ORCHARD SERIES IN POETRY FIRST BOOK AWARD

First Book Award, Dept. of English, Mail Code 4503, Southern Illinois University Carbondale, 1000 Faner Drive, Carbondale IL 62901. (618)453-6833. **E-mail:** jtribble@siu.edu. **Website:** www.craborchardreview.siu.edu. **Contact:** Jon Tribble, series editor. "A first book of poems will be selected for publication from an open competition of manuscripts, in English, by a U.S. citizen or permanent resident who has neither published, nor committed to publish, a volume of poetry 48 pages or more in length in an edition of over 500 copies* (individual poems may have been previously published; for the purposes of the Crab Orchard Series in Poetry, a manuscript which was in whole or in part submitted as a thesis or dissertation as a requirement for the completion of a degree is considered unpublished and is eligible)." Deadline: July 6. Prize: Offers $3,500 ($2,000 prize plus $1,500 honorarium for a reading at Southern Illinois University Carbondale) and publication.

LOIS CRANSTON MEMORIAL POETRY PRIZE

CALYX, Inc., P.O. Box B, Corvallis OR 97339. **E-mail:** calyx@proaxis.com. **Website:** www.calyxpress.org/LoisPrize.html. This poetry prize in Lois Cranston's name honors the memory of her commitment to the creative work of women from all walks of life. Deadline: May 31 (submission period begins on March 1). Prize: $300, publication, and one-volume subscription.

CWW ANNUAL WISCONSIN WRITERS AWARDS COMPETITION

Council for Wisconsin Writers, **Website:** www.wisconsinwriters.org. **Contact:** Geoff Gilpin; Jerriane Hayslett and Karla Huston, awards co-chairs; and Carolyn Washburne, Christopher Latham Sholes Award and Major Achievement Award co-chair. Offered annually for work published by Wisconsin writers the previous calendar year. Nine awards: Major/life achievement alternate years; short fiction; short nonfiction; nonfiction book; poetry book; fiction book; children's literature; Lorine Niedecker Poetry Award; Sholes Award for Outstanding Service to Wisconsin Writers Alternate Years; Essay Award for Young Writers. Open to Wisconsin residents. Guidelines, rules, and entry form on website. Deadline: January 31 (postmark). Prizes: $500 and a week-long residency at Shake Rag Alley or Maplewood Lodge in Mineral Point. Essay Contest: $150. "This year only the Essay Award for Young Writers prize will be $250."

THE ROBERT DANA ANHINGA PRIZE FOR POETRY

Anhinga Press, P.O. Box 3665, Tallahassee FL 32315. (850)577-0745. **Fax:** (850)577-0745. **E-mail:** info@anhinga.org. **Website:** www.anhinga.org. **Contact:** Rick Campbell, poetry editor. Offered annually for a book-length collection of poetry by an author who has not published more than 1 book of poetry. Guidelines for SASE or on website. Open to any writer writing in English. Submissions will be accepted from February 15-May 15. Prize: $2,000, a reading tour of selected Florida colleges and uninversities, and the winning manuscript will be published. Past judges include Donald Hall, Joy Harjo, Robert Dana, Mark Jarman, and Tony Hoagland. Past winners include Frank X. Gaspar, Earl S. Braggs, Julia Levine, Keith Ratzlaff, and Lynn Aarti Chandhok, and Rhett Iseman Trull.

DANA AWARDS IN THE NOVEL, SHORT FICTION, ESSAY AND POETRY

(336)644-8028. **E-mail:** danaawards@pipeline.com. **E-mail:** danaawards@gmail.com. **Website:** www.danaawards.com. **Contact:** Mary Elizabeth Parker, chair. Four awards offered annually for unpublished work written in English. Purpose is monetary award for work that has not been previously published or received monetary award, but will accept work published simply for friends and family. Works previously published online are not eligible. No work accepted by or for persons under 16 for any of the 4 awards: **Novel**—For the first 40 pages of a novel completed or in progress; **Fiction**—short fiction (no memoirs) up to 10,000 words; **Essay**—personal essay, memoir, or creative nonfiction up to 10,000 words; **Poetry**—for best group of 5 poems based on excellence of all 5 (no light verse, no single poem over 100 lines). Deadline: October 31 (postmarked). Prizes: $1,000 for each of the 4 awards.

◐ DANCING POETRY CONTEST

AEI Contest Chair, Judy Cheung, 704 Brigham Ave., Santa Rosa CA 95404-5245. (707)528-0912. **E-mail:** jhcheung@comcast.net. **Website:** www.dancingpoetry.com. **Contact:** Judy Cheung, contest chair. "We always look for something new and different including new twists to old themes, different looks at common situations, inovative concepts for dynamic, thought provoking entertainment." Deadline: May 15. Prizes: Three Grand Prizes wil receive $100 each plus the poems will be danced and videotaped; six First Prizes will receive $50 each; twelve Second Prizes will receive $25 each; and thirty Third Prizes will receive $10 each.

DER-HOVANESSIAN PRIZE

New England Poetry Club, 654 Green St., No. 2, Cambridge MA 02139. **E-mail:** contests@nepoetryclub.org. **Website:** www.nepoetryclub.org. **Contact:** NEPC contest coordinator. For a translation from any language into English. Send a copy of the original. Funded by John Mahtesian. Deadline: May 31. Prize: $200. Judges are well-known poets and sometimes winners of previous NEPC contests.

◑ DIAGRAM/NEW MICHIGAN PRESS CHAPBOOK CONTEST

Department of English, P.O. Box 210067, University of Arizona, Tucson AZ 85721-0067. **E-mail:** nmp@thediagram.com. **Website:** thediagram.com/contest.html. **Contact:** Ander Monson, editor. The annual *DIAGRAM*/New Michigan Press Chapbook Contest offers $1,000, plus publication and author's copies, with discount on additional copies. Also publishes 2-4 finalist chapbooks each year. Deadline: April 1. Prize: $1,000 plus publication.

DOBIE PAISANO PROJECT

The Graduate School, The University of Texas at Austin, Attn: Dobie Paisano Program, 110 Inner Campus Drive Stop G0400, Austin TX 78712-0531. (512)232-3609. **Fax:** (512)471-7620. **E-mail:** gbarton@austin.utexas.edu. **Website:** www.utexas.edu/ogs/Paisano. **Contact:** Gwen Barton. "Sponsored by the Graduate School at The University of Texas at Austin and the Texas Institute of Letters, the Dobie Paisano Fellowship Program provides solitude, time, and a comfortable place for Texas writers or writers who have written significantly about Texas." Deadline: January 15. "The Ralph A. Johnston memorial Fellowship is for a period of 4 months with a stipend of $5,000 per month. It is aimed at writers who have already demonstrated some publishing and critical success. The Jesse H. Jones Writing Fellowship is for a period of approximately 6 months with a stipend of $3,000 per month. It is aimed at, but not limited to, writers who are early in their careers."

TIPS "Guidelines and application forms are on the website or may be requested by sending a SASE (2-ounce postage) to the above address and attention of 'Dobie Paisano Fellowship Project.'"

●◑ T.S. ELIOT PRIZE

Dutch Houses, 307-308 High Holborn, London WCIV 7LL, United Kingdom. **E-mail:** editor@poetrybooks.co.uk. **Website:** www.poetrybooks.co.uk. Offers annual award for the best poetry collection published in the UK/Republic of Ireland each year. Deadline: early August. Prize: £15,000 will be awarded to the best collection of new verse in English. The ten shortlisted poets will also receive a cheque for £1,000.

T.S. ELIOT PRIZE FOR POETRY

Truman State University Press, 100 E. Normal Ave., Kirksville MO 63501. (660)785-7336. **Fax:** (660)785-4480. **E-mail:** tsup@truman.edu. **Website:** tsup.truman.edu. **Contact:** Nancy Rediger. "The manuscript may include individual poems previously published in journals or anthologies, but may not include a significant number of poems from a published chapbook or self-published book." Submit 60-100 pages. Include 2 title pages: 1 with poet's name, address, phone number, and ms title; the other with ms title only. Include SASE for acknowledgment of ms receipt only; mss will not be returned. Guidelines available for SASE or on website. Competition receives about 500 entries/year. Deadline: October 31. Prize: $2,000 and publication. Judge announced after close of competition.

◑ EMERGING VOICES

P.O. Box 6037, Beverly Hills CA 90212. (323)424-4939. **Fax:** (323)424-4944. **E-mail:** pen@penusa.org.

Website: www.penusa.org. Annual program offering $1,000 stipend and 8-month fellowship to writers in the early stages of their literary careers. Program includes one-on-one sessions with mentors, seminars on topics such as editing or working with agents, courses in the Writers' Program at UCLA Extension, and literary readings. Participants selected according to potential and lack of access to traditional publishing and/or educational opportunities. Must be over the age of 18. Graduates of Creative Writing B.A., M.F.A., and Ph.D. programs or students currently enrolled in B.A., M.A., or M.F.A. programs are not eligible. Participants need not be published, but "the program is directed toward poets and writers of fiction and creative nonfiction with clear ideas of what they hope to accomplish through their writing. Mentors are chosen from PEN's comprehensive membership of professional writers and beyond. Participants are paired with established writers sharing similar writing interests and often with those of the same ethnic and cultural backgrounds." Program gets underway in January. See website for brochure and complete guidelines. Application Fee: $10. Deadline: September 5. "Materials must arrive in the PEN offices by the submission deadline—no exceptions." Emerging Voices is a literary fellowship program that aims to provide new writers, who lack access, with the tools they will need to launch a professional writing career. During the eight month fellowship, each Emerging Voices fellow participates in a professional mentorship, hosted Q & A evenings with prominent local authors, a series of master classes focused on genre, a voice class, a volunteer project, and several public readings. Deadline: September 5. Accepting applications starting May 6. Offers a $1,000 stipend.

◑ ERSKINE J. POETRY PRIZE

P.O. Box 22161, Baltimore MD 21203. **E-mail:** sreichert@smartishpace.com. **Website:** www.smartishpace.com. **Contact:** Stephen Reichert, editor. Deadline: September 1. Prize: Winning poet receives $200. Top three poets and all finalists (usually about 10) are published in Smartish Place.

◐◑ FAR HORIZONS AWARD FOR POETRY

The Malahat Review, University of Victoria, P.O. Box 1700, Stn CSC, Victoria BC V8W 2Y2, Canada. (250)721-8524. **Fax:** (250)472-5051. **E-mail:** malahat@uvic.ca. **Website:** www.malahatreview.ca. **Contact:**

John Barton, editor. The biennial Far Horizons Award for Poetry offers $1,000 CAD and publication in The Malahat Review (see separate listing in Magazines/Journals). Open to "emerging poets from Canada, the United States, and elsewhere" who have not yet published a full-length book (48 pages or more). Submissions must be unpublished. No simultaneous submissions. Submit up to 3 poems per entry, each poem not to exceed 60 lines; no restrictions on subject matter or aesthetic approach. Include separate page with poet's name, address, e-mail, and poem title(s); no identifying information on mss pages. No e-mail submissions. Do not include SASE for results; mss will not be returned. Full guidelines available on website. Winner and finalists contacted by e-mail. Winner published in fall in *The Malahat Review* and announced on website, Facebook page, and in quarterly e-newsletter, *Malahat lite*. Deadline: May 1 of even-numbered years. Prize: $1,000.

JANICE FARRELL POETRY PRIZE

Category in the Soul-Making Keats Literary Competition, under the auspice of the National League of American Pen Women, The Webhallow House, 1544 Sweetwood Dr., Broadmoor Village CA 94015. **E-mail:** SoulKeats@aol.com. **Website:** www.soul-makingcontest.us. **Contact:** Eileen Malone. "Poetry may be double- or single-spaced. One-page poems only, and only 1 poem/page. All poems must be titled. Three poems/entry. Indicate category on each poem. Identify with 3x5 card only. Open to all writers." Judged by a local San Francisco successfully published poet. Deadline: November 30. Prize: Cash prizes.

FIELD POETRY PRIZE

Oberlin College Press/FIELD, 50 N. Professor St., Oberlin OH 44074-1095. (440)775-8408. **Fax:** (440)775-8124. **E-mail:** oc.press@oberlin.edu. **Website:** www.oberlin.edu/ocpress/prize.htm. **Contact:** Marco Wilkinson, managing editor. The annual FIELD Poetry Prize for a book-length collection of poems offers $1,000 and publication in the FIELD Poetry Series. Mss of 50-80 pages must be submitted during May through our online submissions manager. See our website for details. Entry Fee: $28; includes one-year subscription to FIELD: Contemporary Poetry and Poetics (see separate listing in Magazines/Journals). 2012 winner was Mary Ann Samyn (My Life in Heaven). "Offered annually for unpublished work. Contest seeks to encourage the finest in contemporary poetry writing. Open to any writer." Deadline: Submit in May only. Prize: $1,000 and the book is published in Oberlin College Press's FIELD Poetry Series.

● THE FINCH PRIZE FOR POETRY

The National Poetry Review, P.O. Box 2080, Aptos CA 95001-2080. **E-mail:** editor@nationalpoetry review. com. **Website:** www.nationalpoetryreview.com. **Contact:** C.J. Sage, editor. The Finch Prize for Poetry offers $500 plus publication in *The National Poetry Review*. All entries will be considered by the editor for publication. Deadline: June 30 (postmark). Prize: $500 plus possible publication.

○ FLORIDA FIRST COAST WRITERS' FESTIVAL NOVEL, SHORT FICTION, PLAYWRITING & POETRY AWARDS

Florida Community College at Jacksonville, 4501 Capper Road, Jacksonville FL 32218-4499. (904)766-6601. **Fax:** (904)766-6654. **Website:** opencampus.fccj. org/WF/. Conference and contest "to create a healthy writing environment, honor writers of merit and find a novel manuscript to recommend to New York publishers for 'serious consideration." Deadline: December 1.

FOUR WAY BOOKS POETRY PRIZES

Four Way Books, P.O. Box 535, Village Station, New York NY 10014. **E-mail:** editors@fourwaybooks.com. **Website:** www.fourwaybooks.com. Four Way Books runs different prizes annually. The Intro Prize in Poetry, The Four Way Books Levis Poetry Prize. Open to all poets, regardless of publication history. Submissions guidelines will be posted on site at the end of December. For guidelines send a SASE or download from website. Deadline: March 31. Prize: $1,000 and book publication. Judged by James Longenbach (2013).

◐ FREEFALL SHORT PROSE AND POETRY CONTEST

Freefall Literary Society of Calgary, 922 9th Ave. SE, Calgary AB T2G 0S4, Canada. **E-mail:** freefallmagazine@yahoo.ca. **Website:** www.freefallmagazine.ca. **Contact:** Lynn C. Fraser, managing editor. Offered annually for unpublished work in the categories of poetry (5 poems/entry) and prose (3,000 words or less). The purpose of the award in both categories is to recognize writers and offer publication credits in a literary magazine format. Contest rules and entry form online. Acquires first Canadian serial rights; ownership reverts to author after one-time publica-

tion. Deadline: December 31. Prize: 1st Place: $300 (CAD); 2nd Place: $150 (CAD); 3rd Place: $75; Honourable Mention: $25. All prizes include publication in the spring edition of *FreeFall Magazine*. Winners will also be invited to read at the launch of that issue if such a launch takes place. Honorable mentions in each category will be published and may be asked to read. Travel expenses not included. Judged by current guest editor for issue (who are also published authors in Canada).

● GEORGETOWN REVIEW

Georgetown Review, 400 East College St., Box 227, Georgetown KY 40324. (502) 863-8308. **Fax:** (502) 863-8888. **E-mail:** gtownreview@georgetowncollege. edu. **Website:** georgetowncolleged.edu/georgetown-review. **Contact:** Steve Carter, editor. Our magazine is a collaboration between English faculty at Georgetown College and undergrads who learn the editing business as they go and who always amaze their elders with their dedication and first-rate work. Deadline: October 15 Prize: $1,000 and publication; runners-up receive publication.

ALLEN GINSBERG POETRY AWARDS

The Poetry Center at Passaic County Community College, One College Blvd., Paterson NJ 07505. (973)684-6555. **Fax:** (973)523-6085. **E-mail:** mgillan@pccc. edu. **Website:** www.pccc.edu/poetry. **Contact:** Maria Mazziotti Gillan, executive director. All winning poems, honorable mentions, and editor's choice poems will be published in *Paterson Literary Review*. Winners will be asked to participate in a reading that will be held in the Paterson Historic District. Submissions must be unpublished. Deadline: April 1 (postmark). Prize: 1st Prize: $1,000; 2nd Prize: $200; 3rd Prize: $100.

GIVAL PRESS POETRY AWARD

Gival Press, LLC, P.O. Box 3812, Arlington VA 22203. (703)351-0079. **E-mail:** givalpress@yahoo.com. **Website:** www.givalpress.com. **Contact:** Robert L. Giron, editor. "Offered annually for a previously unpublished poetry collection as a complete ms, which may include previously published poems; previously published poems must be acknowledged, and poet must hold rights. Guidelines for SASE, by e-mail, or online." The competition seeks to award well-written, original poetry in English on any topic, in any style. Deadline: December 15 (postmarked). Prize: $1,000, publication, and 20 copies of the publication. The editor narrows entries to the top 10; previous winner selects top 5 and chooses the winner—all done anonymously.

TIPS "Open to any writer, as long as the work is original, not a translation, and is written in English. The copyright remains in the author's name; certain rights fall to the publisher per the contract."

◑ GOVERNOR GENERAL'S LITERARY AWARD FOR POETRY

Canada Council for the Arts, 350 Albert St., P.O. Box 1047, Ottawa ON K1P 5V8, Canada. (613)566-4414, ext. 5573. **Fax:** (613)566-4410. **Website:** www.canadacouncil.ca/prizes/ggla. Offered for the best English-language and the best French-language work of poetry by a Canadian. Publishers submit titles for consideration. Deadline depends on the book's publication date. Books in English: March 15, June 1, or August 7. Books in French: March 15 or July 15. Prize: Each laureate receives $25,000; non-winning finalists receive $1,000.

● GUGGENHEIM FELLOWSHIPS

John Simon Guggenheim Memorial Foundation, 90 Park Ave., New York NY 10016. (212)687-4470. **E-mail:** fellowships@gf.org. **Website:** www.gf.org. Guggenheim Fellowships are awarded each year to poets, as well as fiction and creative nonfiction writers, "on the basis of unusually distinguished achievement in the past and exceptional promise for future accomplishment." Previously, fellowships were awarded to 34 writers; amounts averaged $36,672 each. Submit career summary, statement of intent, and no more than 3 published books. Guidelines, application form (required), and additional information available for SASE, by e-mail, or on website. **Entry fee:** none. Often characterized as "midcareer" awards, Guggenheim Fellowships are intended for men and women who have already demonstrated exceptional capacity for productive scholarship or exceptional creative ability in the arts. Fellowships are awarded through two annual competitions: one open to citizens and permanent residents of the United States and Canada, and the other open to citizens and permanent residents of Latin America and the Caribbean. Candidates must apply to the Guggenheim Foundation in order to be considered in either of these competitions. The Foundation receives between 3,500 and 4,000 applications each year. Although no one who applies is guaranteed success in the competition, there is no prescreen-ing: all applications are reviewed. Approximately 200 Fellowships are awarded each year. Deadline: September 15.

HACKNEY LITERARY AWARDS

1305 2nd Ave. N, #103, Birmingham AL 35203. (205)226-4921. **E-mail:** info@hackneyliterary-awards.org. **Website:** www.hackneyliteraryawards. org. **Contact:** Myra Crawford, PhD, executive director. Offered annually for unpublished novels, short stories (maximum 5,000 words) and poetry (50 line limit). Guidelines on website. Deadline: September 30 (novels), November 30 (short stories and poetry) Prize: $5,000 in annual prizes for poetry and short fiction ($2,500 national and $2,500 state level). 1st Place: $600; 2nd Place: $400; 3rd Place: $250); plus $5,000 for an unpublished novel. Competition winners will be announced on the website each March.

KATHRYN HANDLEY PROSE POEM PRIZE

Category in the Soul-Making Keats Literary Competition, under the auspice of the National League of American Pen Women, The Webhallow House, 1544 Sweetwood Dr., Broadmoor Village CA 94015-2029. **E-mail:** SoulKeats@aol.com. **Website:** www.soul-makingcontest.us. **Contact:** Eileen Malone. Open annually to all writers. Poetry may be double- or single-spaced. 1-page prose poems only, and only 1 prose poem/page. Three poems/entry. Indicate category on each poem. Identify only with 3x5 card. Deadline: November 30. Prizes: 1st Place: $100; 2nd Place: $50; 3rd Place: $25.

◐ THE HODDER FELLOWSHIP

Lewis Center for the Arts, 185 Nassau Street, Princeton NJ 08544. (609)258-1500. **E-mail:** anikolop@princeton.edu. **Website:** www.princeton.edu/arts/lewis_center/society_of_fellows. **Contact:** Angelo Nikolopoulos, program assistant, Creative Writing. The Hodder Fellowship will be given to writers of exceptional promise to pursue independent projects at Princeton University during the current academic year. Typically the fellows are poets, playwrights, novelists, creative nonfiction writers and translators who have published one highly acclaimed work and are undertaking a significant new project that might not be possible without the "studious leisure" afforded by the fellowship. Deadline: November 1 (postmarked). Prize: $68,000 stipend.

ERIC HOFFER AWARD

Hopewell Publications, LLC, P.O. Box 11, Titusville NJ 08560-0011. **Fax:** (609)964-1718. **E-mail:** info@hopepubs.com. **Website:** www.hofferaward.com. **Contact:** Christopher Klim, chair. "Annual contest for previously published books. Recognizes excellence in independent publishing in many unique categories: Art (titles capture the experience, execution, or demonstration of the arts); Poetry (all styles); General Fiction (nongenre-specific fiction); Commercial Fiction (genre-specific fiction); Children (titles for young children); Young Adult (titles aimed at the juvenile and teen markets); Culture (titles demonstrating the human or world experience); Memoir (titles relating to personal experience); Business (titles with application to today's business environment and emerging trends); Reference (titles from traditional and emerging reference areas); Home (titles with practical applications to home or home-related issues, including family); Health (titles promoting physical, mental, and emotional well-being); Self-help (titles involving new and emerging topics in self-help); Spiritual (titles involving the mind and spirit, including relgion); Legacy (titles over 2 years of age that hold particular relevance to any subject matter or form). Open to any writer of published work within the last 2 years, including categores for older books. Also awards the Montaigne Medal for most though-provoking book, the Da Vinci Eye for best cover, and the First Horizon Award for best new authors. Results published in the US Review of Books."

THE BESS HOKIN PRIZE

Poetry, 61 W. Superior St., Chicago IL 60654. (312)787-7070. **Fax:** (312)787-6650. **E-mail:** editors@poetrymagazine.org. **Website:** www.poetrymagazine.org. Offered annually for poems published in *Poetry* during the preceding year (October-September). Upon acceptance, *Poetry* licenses exclusive worldwide first serial rights, including electronic rights, for publication, as well as non-exclusive rights to reprint, reuse, and archive the work, in any format, in perpetuity. Copyright reverts to author upon first publication. "Established in 1947 through the generosity of our late friend and guarantor, Mrs. David Hokin, and is given annually in her memory." Prize: $1,000.

FIRMAN HOUGHTON PRIZE

New England Poetry Club, 654 Green St., Apt. 2, Cambridge MA 02139 . **E-mail:** contests@nepoetry-clug.org. **Website:** www.nepoetryclub.org. **Contact:** NEPC contest coordinator. For a lyric poem in honor of the former president of NEPC. Deadline: May 31 Prize: $250. Judges are well-known poets and sometimes winners of previous NEPC contests.

◑ TOM HOWARD/JOHN H. REID POETRY CONTEST

Tom Howard Books, Tom Howard Books, c/o Winning Writers, 351 Pleasant St., PMB 222, Northampton MA 01060-3961. (866)946-9748. **Fax:** (413)280-0539. **E-mail:** johnreid@mail.qango.com. **Website:** www.winningwriters.com. **Contact:** John Reid, award director. Any type of original short story, essay or other work of prose is eligible. Competition receives about 1,000 entries/year. Winners announced in February at WinningWriters.com. Entrants who provide valid e-mail addresses will also receive notification. Deadline: April 30. Prizes: First prize: $3,000. Second prize: $1,000. Third prize: $400. Fourth prize: $250. There will also be six Most Highly Commended Awards of $150 each. The top 10 entries will be published on the Winning Writers website (over one million page views per year) and announced in Tom Howard Contest News and the Winning Writers Newsletter.

THE JULIA WARD HOWE/BOSTON AUTHORS AWARD

The Boston Authors Club, 45 Pine Crest Rd., Newton MA 02459. (617)244-0646. **E-mail:** bostonauthors@aol.com; SarahM45@aol.com. **Website:** www.bostonauthorsclub.org. **Contact:** Sarah Lamstein. This annual award honors Julia Ward Howe and her literary friends who founded the Boston Authors Club in 1900. It also honors the membership over 110 years, consisting of novelists, biographers, historians, governors, senators, philosophers, poets, playwrights, and other luminaries. There are 2 categories: trade books and books for young readers (beginning with chapter books through young adult books). Works of fiction, nonfiction, memoir, poetry, and biography published in 2010 are eligible. Authors must live or have lived (college counts) within a 100-mile radius of Boston within the last 5 years. Subsidized books, cook books and picture books are not eligible. Fee is $25 per title.

◑ THE LYNDA HULL MEMORIAL POETRY PRIZE

Crazyhorse, Department of English, College of Charleston, 66 George St., Charleston SC 29424.

(843)953-4470. **E-mail:** crazyhorse@cofc.edu. **Website:** http://crazyhorse.cofc.edu. **Contact:** Prize Director. The annual Lynda Hull Memorial Poetry Prize offers $2,000 and publication in *Crazyhorse*. All entries will be considered for publication. Submissions must be unpublished. Submit online or by mail up to 3 original poems (no more than 10 pages). Include cover page (placed on top of ms) with poet's name, address, e-mail, and telephone number; no identifying information on mss (blind judging). Accepts multiple submissions with separate fee for each. Include SASP for notification of receipt of ms and SASE for results only; mss will not be returned. Guidelines available for SASE or on website. Deadline: January 31.

INDIANA REVIEW ½ K (SHORT-SHORT/PROSE-POEM) CONTEST

Indiana Review, Ballantine Hall 465, 1020 E. Kirkwood Ave., Indiana University, Bloomington IN 47405-7103. (812)855-3439. **Fax:** (812)855-9535. **E-mail:** inreview@indiana.edu. **Website:** http://indianareview.org. **Contact:** Jennifer Luebers, editor. Offered annually for unpublished work. Maximum story/poem length is 500 words. Guidelines available in March for SASE, by phone, e-mail, on website, or in publication. Deadline: May 31. Prize: $1,000, plus publication, contributor's copies, and a year's subscription to *Indiana Review*.

INDIANA REVIEW POETRY PRIZE

Indiana Review, Poetry Prize, Indiana Review, Ballantine Hall 465, 1020 E. Kirkwood Ave., Bloomington IN 47405-7103. (812)855-3439. **Fax:** (812)855-9535. **E-mail:** inreview@indiana.edu. **Website:** www.indianareview.org. **Contact:** Michael Mlekoday, Poetry Editor. Offered annually for unpublished work. Open to any writer. Send no more than 3 poems per entry. Guidelines on website and with SASE request. Deadline: April 1. Prize: $1,000 Honorarium and Publication. Judged by Nikky Finney in 2013.

○ INKWELL ANNUAL POETRY CONTEST

Manhattanville College, 2900 Purchase St., Purchase NY 10577. (914)323-5239. **Fax:** (914)323-3122. **E-mail:** inkwell@mville.edu. **Website:** www.inkwelljournal.org. **Contact:** Competition Poetry Editor. *Inkwell* is dedicated to discovering new talent and bringing the work of up and coming writers and artists to a wider audience. We encourage diverse voices and have an open submission policy for poetry, prose

and artwork. It is published twice a year and staffed by faculty and graduate students of Manhattanville's MFA Program in Writing. Deadline: August 1-October 30. Prize: $1,000 and publication in *Inkwell*.

○ THE INTRO PRIZE IN POETRY

Four Way Books, P.O. Box 535, Village Station, New York NY 10014. (212)334-5430. **E-mail:** editors@fourwaybooks.com. **Website:** www.fourwaybooks.com. The Intro Prize in Poetry, offered biennially in even-numbered years, awards publication by Four Way Books, honorarium ($1,000), and a reading at one or more participating series. Open to U.S. poets who have not yet published a book-length collection. "Submit one manuscript, 48-100 pages suggested. You may submit via e-mail or regular mail by the deadline. For complete information, you must refer to our guidelines on our website." **Entry fee:** $28. **Deadline:** March 31 (postmark). Winner announced by mail and on website. Copies of winning books available through Four Way Books online and at bookstores (to the trade through University Press of New England). Given biennially (on even years) for a first poetry colletion. Prize: $1,000 and publication by Four Way Books. The winner is invited to participate in a reading in New York City.

IOWA POETRY PRIZES

University of Iowa Press, 119 West Park Rd., 100 Kuhl House, Iowa City IA 52242. (319)335-2000. **Fax:** (319)335-2055. **E-mail:** uipress@uiowa.edu. **Website:** www.uiowapress.org. Offered annually to encourage poets and their work. Submissions must be postmarked during the month of April; put name on title page only. This page will be removed before ms is judged. Open to writers of English (US citizens or not). Mss will not be returned. Previous winners are not eligible. Deadline: April 30. Prize: Publication under standard royalty agreement.

○ THE IOWA REVIEW AWARD IN POETRY, FICTION, AND NONFICTION

308 EPB, University of Iowa, Iowa City IA 52242. **E-mail:** iowa-review@uiowa.edu. **Website:** www.iowareview.org. *The Iowa Review* Award in Poetry, Fiction, and Nonfiction presents $1,500 to each winner in each genre, $750 to runners-up. Winners and runners-up published in *The Iowa Review*. Deadline: Submit January 1-31 (postmark) 2013 Judges: Mary Jo Bang, Z.Z. Packer, Susan Orlean.

JOSEPH HENRY JACKSON AWARD

225 Bush Street, Suite 500, San Francisco CA 94104-4224. (415)733.8500. **Fax:** (415)477.2783. **E-mail:** info@sff.org. **Website:** www.sff.org. Awards an author of an unpublished work-in-progress of fiction (novel or short stories), nonfictional prose, or poetry. Deadline: March 31. Prize: $2,000.

● HAROLD MORTON LANDON TRANSLATION AWARD

The Academy of American Poets, The Academy of American Poets, 75 Maiden Lane, Suite 901, New York NY 10038. (212)274-0343 ext. 13. **E-mail:** awards@poets.org. **Website:** www.poets.org. **Contact:** Patricia Guzman, Programs Assistant. Recognizes a published translation of poetry from any language into English. Deadline: February 15. Prize: $1,000. Judged by a noted translator.

LEAGUE OF UTAH WRITERS CONTEST

The League of Utah Writers, P.O. Box 88, Logan UT 84323. (435)755-7609. **E-mail:** luwcontest@gmail.com. **Website:** www.luwriters.org. **Contact:** Tim Keller, Contest Chair. Open to any writer, the LUW Contest provides authors an opportunity to get their work read and critiqued. Multiple categories are offered; see webpage for details. Entries must be the original and unpublished work of the author. Winners are announced at the Annual Writers Round-Up in September. Those not present will be notified by e-mail. Submission Period: March 15 to June 15. Entries are judged by professional authors and editors from outside the League.

THE LEDGE ANNUAL POETRY CHAPBOOK CONTEST

E-mail: info@theledgemagazine.com. **Website:** www.theledgemagazine.com. **Contact:** Timothy Monaghan, Editor-in-Chief. The Ledge Press, 40 Maple Ave., Bellport NY 11713. **Website:** www.theledgemagazine.com. The Ledge Poetry Chapbook Contest offers an annual prize of $1,000, publication by The Ledge Press, and 25 chapbook copies. Considers simultaneous submissions. Accepts multiple submissions with separate entry fee for each. " No restrictions on form or content. Excellence is the only criterion." Submit 16-28 pages of poetry with bio and acknowledgements, if any. Include title page with poet's name, address, phone number, and e-mail address (if applicable). Include SASE for results or return of ms. Guidelines available on web-

site. **Entry fee:** $18; all entrants will receive a copy of the winning chapbook upon publication. **Deadline:** October 31. Sample chapbooks available for $8 postpaid. Winner announced in March. Offered annually to publish an outstanding collection of poems. Prize: $1,000 and publication and 25 copies of the chapbook.

⊕ LES FIGUES PRESS NOS BOOK CONTEST

P.O. Box 7736, Los Angeles CA 90007. **E-mail:** info@lesfigues.com. **Website:** www.lesfigues.com. Les Figues Press creates aesthetic conversations between writers/artists and readers, especially those interested in innovative/experimental/avant-garde work. The Press intends in the the most premeditated fashion to champion the trinity of Beauty, Belief, and Bawdry. Annual NOS (not otherwise specific) book prize given for best ms of poetry, prosem or writing in between. Electronic submissions only. See website for contest guidelines. Deadline: September 30. Prize: $1,000, plus publication by Les Figues Press. Each entry receives LFP book.

LET'S WRITE LITERARY CONTEST

The Gulf Coast Writers Association, P.O. Box 10294, Gulfport MS 39505. **E-mail:** writerpllevin@gmail.com. **Website:** www.gcwriters.org. **Contact:** Philip Levin. "The Gulf Coast Writers Association sponsors this nationally recognized contest, which accepts unpublished poems and short stories from authors all around the US. This is an annual event which has been held for over 20 years." Deadline: April 15. 1st Prize: $100; 2nd Prize: $60; 3rd Prize: $25. **TIPS** "See guidelines online."

LEVIS READING PRIZE

(804)828-1329. **Fax:** (804)828-8684. **E-mail:** kileyk@vcu.edu. **E-mail:** englishgrad@vcu.edu. **Website:** www.has.vcu.edu/eng/resources/levis_prize/levis_prize.htm. **Contact:** Katelyn Kiley, Levis Fellow. "Offered annually for books of poetry published in the previous year to encourage poets early in their careers. The entry must be the writer's first or second published book of poetry. Previously published books in other genres, or previously published chapbooks or self-published material, do not count as books for this purpose." Deadline: January 15 Prize: $2,000 and an expense-paid trip to Richmond to present a public reading.

THE RUTH LILLY POETRY PRIZE

(312)787-7070. **Fax:** (312)787-6650. **E-mail:** editors@poetrymagazine.org. **Website:** www.poetrymagazine.org. Awarded annually, the $100,000 Ruth Lilly Poetry Prize honors a living U.S. poet whose lifetime accomplishments warrant extraordinary recognition. Established in 1986 by Ruth Lilly, the Prize is one of the most prestigious awards given to American poets and is one of the largest literary honors for work in the English language. Deadline: Varies. Prize: $100,000.

◑ LITERAL LATTÉ FOOD VERSE AWARDS

200 East 10th St., Suite 240, New York NY 10003. **Website:** www.literal-latte.com. **Contact:** Lisa Erdman. The annual Literary *Latté Food* for Verse Awards offers 1st Prize: $500 for best poem with food as an ingredient. All styles and subjects welcome. All entries considered for publication in *Literal Latté*. Submissions must be unpublished. Include cover page with poet's name, address, phone number, e-mail, and poem titles/first lines; no identifying information on mss pages. Guidelines available by e-mail, or on website. **Entry fee:** $10 for up to 6 poems, $15 for 12 poems. Make checks/money orders payable to *Literal Latté*. **Deadline:** January 15 (postmark).

THE MACGUFFIN NATIONAL POET HUNT CONTEST

The MacGuffin, The MacGuffin, Schoolcraft College, 18600 Haggerty Rd., Livonia MI 48152. (734)462-4400, ext. 5327. **Fax:** (734)462-4679. **E-mail:** macguffin@schoolcraft.edu. **Website:** www.macguffin.org. **Contact:** Gordon Krupsky, managing editor. The MacGuffin, established in 1984, is a national literary magazine from Schoolcraft College in Livonia, Michigan. The mission of The MacGuffin is to encourage, support, and enhance the literary arts in the Schoolcraft College community, the region, the state, and the nation. Deadline: must be postmarked between April 1 and June 3. Prize: $500.

NAOMI LONG MADGETT POETRY AWARD

Lotus Press, Inc., P.O. Box 21607, Detroit MI 48221. **E-mail:** lotuspress@comcast.net. **Website:** www.lotuspress.org. **Contact:** Constance Withers. Offered annually to recognize an unpublished book-length poetry ms by an African American. Guidelines for SASE, by e-mail, or online. Deadline: January 2-March 1 $500 and publication by Lotus Press.

◐ "Interested poets should not submit a manuscript without consulting the guidelines that are available on our website."

◑ MAIN STREET RAG'S ANNUAL POETRY BOOK AWARD

P.O. Box 690100, Charlotte NC 28227. (704)573-2516. **E-mail:** editor@mainstreetrag.com. **Website:** www.MainStreetRag.com. **Contact:** M. Scott Douglass, editor/publisher. Main Street Rag's Annual Poetry Book Award offers a 1st Prize of $1,000 and 50 copies of book; runners-up may also be offered publication. Submit 48-84 pages of poetry, no more than 1 poem/page (individual poems may be longer than 1 page). Guidelines available on website. January 31

◑◐ THE MALAHAT REVIEW LONG POEM PRIZE

The Malahat Review, Box 1700 STN CSC, Victoria BC V8W 2Y2, Canada. **E-mail:** malahat@uvic.ca (queries only). **Website:** www.malahatreview.ca. **Contact:** John Barton, editor. "Long Poem Prize offered in alternate years with the Novella Contest." Offers 2 awards of $1,000 CAD each for a long poem or cycle (10-20 printed pages). Includes publication in *The Malahat Review* and a 1-year subscription. Open to "entries from Canadian, American, and overseas authors." Submissions must be unpublished. No simultaneous submissions. Submit a single poem or cycle of poems, 10-20 published pages (a published page equals 32 lines or less, including breaks between stanzas); no restrictions on subject matter or aesthetic approach. Include separate page with poet's name, address, e-mail, and title; no identifying information on mss pages. No e-mail submissions. Do not include SASE for results; mss will not be returned. Guidelines available on website. "Preliminary reading by editorial board; final judging by 3 recognized poets. Obtains first world rights. After—publication rights revert to the author. Open to any writer." Winners published in the summer issue of *The Malahat Review*, announced in summer on website, Facebook page, and in quarterly e-newsletter *Malahat lite*. Deadline: February 1 of odd-numbered years. Prizes: Two $1,000 prizes.

● THE MORTON MARR POETRY PRIZE

Southwest Review, Southern Methodist University, P.O. Box 750374, Dallas TX 75275. (214)768-1037. **Fax:** (214)768-1408. **E-mail:** swr@mail.smu.edu. **Website:** www.smu.edu/southwestreview. **Contact:** Prize coordinator. Annual award for poem(s) by a writer who has not yet published a book of poetry. Submit no more than 6 poems in a "traditional" form (e.g., sonnet, sestine, villanelle, rhymed stanzas, blank verse, et al.). Submissions will not be returned. All entrants will receive a copy of the issue in which the winning poems appear. Postmarked deadline for entry is September 30. Prizes: $1,000 for 1st place; $500 for 2nd place; plus publication in the Southwest Review.

●○ MELBOURNE POETS UNION NATIONAL POETRY COMPETITION

Melbourne Poets Union, P.O. Box 266, 246 Flinders Lane, 8009, VI 8009, Australia. **Website:** http://home.vicnet.net.au/~mpuinc. **Contact:** Dr. Kevin Brophy. Offers annual prizes of $1,500 AUD, plus book vouchers and book prizes. Submissions must be unpublished. Submit unlimited number of poems on any subject, in any form, up to 50 lines. "Open to Australian residents living in Australia or overseas." Entry form and guidelines available for SASE (or SAE and IRC). Deadline: October 31. Prize: $1,000 for first place; $300 for second place; and $200 for third place.

MIDLAND AUTHORS AWARD

Society of Midland Authors, Society of Midland Authors, P.O. Box 10419, Chicago IL 60610-0419. **E-mail:** loerzel@comcast.net. **Website:** www.midlandauthors.com. **Contact:** Robert Loerzel, President. Since 1957, the Society has presented annual awards for the best books written by Midwestern authors. "Established in 1915, the Society of Midland Authors Award (SMA) is presented to one title in each of six categories 'to stimulate creative effort,' one of SMA's goals, to be honored at the group's annual awards banquet in May." Deadline: February 1. Prize: cash prize of at least $300 and a plaque that is awarded at the SMA banquet.

○ MILFORD FINE ARTS COUNCIL NATIONAL POETRY CONTEST

40 Railroad Ave., South, Milford CT 06460. (203)878-6647. **E-mail:** milfordfac@optonline.net. **Website:** www.milfordarts.org. **Contact:** Tom Bouton, Writer's Group Chairperson. Offers annual award of 1st Prize: $100; 2nd Prize: $50; 3rd Prize: $25; plus winners will be published in Milford Fine Arts Council's annual publication, *High Tide*. Submissions must be unpublished. No simultaneous submissions. Poems entered may not have won any other prizes or honorable mentions. Poets must be 18 years and older. "Poems must be typed single-spaced on white standard paper, 10-30 lines (including title), no more than 48 characters/line, on any subject, in any style, rhymed or unrhymed. Use standard font, clear and legible, 1 poem/page, no script or fax. NO foul language. No bio or date, only the words 'Unpublished Original' typed above the poem." Include poet's name, address, ZIP code, and phone number or e-mail address in the middle back of the submitted poem, no identifying information on the front of the page. Poems will be judged on form, clarity, originality, and universal appeal. "Entries may be considered for publication in *High Tide*. If you do not want your poems considered for publication, then you must print on the back of the poem (below your name, address, and ZIP code) 'For National Poetry Contest Only.'" Include SASE for results only, with NOTIFICATION printed on bottom left corner of envelope; no poems will be returned. Guidelines available for SASE or on website. **Entry fee:** $3 for one poem, $6 for 3 poems, $2 for each additional poem after 3. Contestants may enter an unlimited number of poems (will be judged individually, not as a group). Check or money order accepted, no cash. **Deadline:** March 31.

VASSAR MILLER PRIZE IN POETRY

University of North Texas Press, 1155 Union Circle, #311336, Denton TX 76203. (940)565-2142. **Fax:** (940)565-4590. **Website:** http://untpress.unt.edu. **Contact:** John Poch. Annual prize awarded to a collection of poetry. Deadline: November 15. Winner will receive $,1000 and publication by University of North Texas Press. Judged by a "different eminent writer selected each year. Some prefer to remain anonymous until the end of the contest."

TIPS "No limitations to entrants. In years when the judge is announced, we ask that students of the judge not enter to avoid a perceived conflict. All entries should contain identifying material only on the one cover sheet. Entries are read anonymously."

◐ MISSISSIPPI REVIEW PRIZE

Mississippi Review, 118 College Dr., #5144, Hattiesburg MS 39406-0001. (601)266-4321. **Fax:** (601)266-5757. **E-mail:** msreview@usm.edu; rief@mississippireview.com. **Website:** www.mississippireview.com. "Our annual contest awards prizes of $1,000 in fiction and in poetry. Winners and finalists will make up next winter's print issue of the national literary magazine *Mississippi Review*. Contest is open to all writers in English except current or former students or employees of The University of Southern Mississippi. Fiction entries should be 1,000-5,000 words, poetry entries should be three poems totaling 10 pages or less. There is no limit on the number of entries you may submit. Entry fee is $15 per entry, payable to the *Mississippi Review*. Each entrant will receive a copy of the prize issue. No manuscripts will be returned. Previously published work is ineligible. Contest opens April 2. Deadline is October 1. Winners will be announced in late January and publication is scheduled for May next year. Entries should have 'MR Prize,' author name, address, phone, e-mail and title of work on page 1."

TIPS "No mss returned."

JENNY MCKEAN MOORE VISITING WRITER

English Deptartment, George Washington University, Rome Hall, 801 22nd St. NW, Suite 760, Washington DC 20052. (202)994-6180. **Fax:** (202)994-7915. **E-mail:** tvmallon@gwu.edu. **Website:** http://columbian. gwu.edu/departmentsprograms/english/creativewriting/activitiesevents. **Contact:** Thomas Mallon, director of Creative Writing. "The position is filled annually, bringing a visiting writer to The George Washington University. During each semester the Writer teaches 1 creative-writing course at the university as well as a community workshop. Each year we seek someone specializing in a different genre—fiction, poetry, creative nonfiction. For the 2012-13 academic year we will be looking for a poet. Guidelines for application will be announced in *The Writer's Chronicle*. Annual stipend between $50,000 and $60,000, plus reduced-rent townhouse on campus (not guaranteed)." Application Deadline: November 1. Prize: Annual stipend varies, depending on endowment performance; most recently, stipend was $58,000, plus reduced-rent townhouse (not guaranteed).

THE KATHRYN A. MORTON PRIZE IN POETRY

Sarabande Books, Inc., P.O. Box 4456, Louisville KY 40204. (502)458-4028. **E-mail:** info@sarabandebooks. org. **Website:** www.SarabandeBooks.org. **Contact:** Sarah Gorham, editor-in-chief. Member: CLMP. The Kathryn A. Morton Prize in Poetry is awarded annually to a book-length ms (at least 48 pages). All finalists are considered for publication. Competition receives approximately 1,400 entries. 2012 judge was Cole Swensen. "To avoid conflict of interest, students in a degree-granting program or close friends of a judge are ineligible to enter the contest in the genre for which their friend or teacher is serving as judge. Sarabande, as a member of CLMP, complies with its Contest Code of Ethics." Deadline: Submit January 1-February 15 (postmark) only. Prize: $2,000, publication, and a standard royalty contract.

SHEILA MARGARET MOTTON PRIZE

New England Poetry Club, 2 Farrar St., Cambridge MA 02138. (617)744-6034. **E-mail:** info@nepoetryclub.org. **Website:** www.nepoetryclub.org. **Contact:** NEPC contest coordinator. Checks for all contests should be made to New England Poetry Club. All entries should be sent in duplicate with name, address, phone, and email of writer on only one copy. (Judges receive copies without names). Deadline: May 31. Prize: $500. Judges are well-known poets and sometimes winners of previous NEPC contests.

ERIKA MUMFORD PRIZE

New England Poetry Club, 654 Green St., Apt. 2, Cambridge MA 02139. **E-mail:** contests@nepoetryclub.org. **Website:** www.nepoetryclub.org/contests. htm. **Contact:** NEPC contest coordinator. Offered annually for a poem in any form about foreign culture or travel. Funded by Erika Mumford's family and friends. Deadline: May 31 $250. Judges are well-known poets and sometimes winners of previous NEPC contests.

● NATIONAL BOOK AWARDS

The National Book Foundation, 90 Broad St., Suite 604, New York NY 10004. (212)685-0261. **E-mail:** nationalbook@nationalbook.org. **Website:** www. nationalbook.org. Prize: Presents $10,000 in each of 4 categories (fiction, nonfiction, poetry, and young people's literature), plus 16 short-list prizes of $1,000 each to finalists. Submissions must be previously published and **must be entered by the publisher**. General guidelines available on website; interested publishers should phone or e-mail the Foundation. **Entry fee:** $125/title. **Deadline:** See website for current year's deadline.

● THE NATIONAL POETRY REVIEW BOOK PRIZE

The National Poetry Review, P.O. Box 2080, Aptos CA 95001-2080. **E-mail:** editor@nationalpoetryreview. com. **Website:** www.nationalpoetryreview.com. **Contact:** C.J. Sage, editor. Deadline: June 30 (postmark).

Prize: $1,000 plus publication and 15 copies of the book.

NATIONAL WRITERS ASSOCIATION POETRY CONTEST

The National Writers Association, 10940 S. Parker Rd. #508, Parker CO 80134. (303)841-0246. **E-mail:** natlwritersassn@hotmail.com. **Website:** www.nationalwriters.com. **Contact:** Sandy Whelchel, director. "Annual contest to encourage the writing of poetry, an important form of individual expression but with a limited commercial market." Deadline: October 1. 1st Place: $100; 2nd Place: $50; 3rd Place: $25.

HOWARD NEMEROV SONNET AWARD

320 Hunter Dr., Evansville IN 47711. **E-mail:** mona.3773@yahoo.com. **Website:** www.theformalist.evansville.edu/home.htm. **Contact:** Mona Baer, contest coordinator. *The Formalist* sponsors the annual Howard Nemerov Sonnet Award. 2011 winner was Robert W. Crawford. 2011 judge was A. M. Juster. Deadline: November 15 postmark. Prize: Offers $1,000 prize for a single sonnet. Winner and 11 finalists will be published in *Measure: A Review of Formal Poetry*.

● THE PABLO NERUDA PRIZE FOR POETRY

Nimrod International Journal, 800 S. Tucker Dr., Tulsa OK 74104. (918)631-3080. **Fax:** (918)631-3033. **E-mail:** nimrod@utulsa.edu. **Website:** www.utulsa.edu/nimrod. **Contact:** Eilis O'Neal. Annual award to discover new writers of vigor and talent. Open to US residents only. Submissions must be unpublished. Work must be in English or translated by original author. Submit 3-10 pages of poetry (1 long poem or several short poems). Poet's name must not appear on ms. Include cover sheet with poem title(s), poet's name, address, phone and fax numbers, and e-mail address (poet must have a US address by October of contest year to enter). Mark "Contest Entry" on submission envelope and cover sheet. Include SASE for results only; mss will not be returned. Guidelines available for #10 SASE or on website. **Entry fee:** $20; includes 1-year subscription (2 issues) to *Nimrod*. Make checks payable to *Nimrod*. Winners will be announced on *Nimrod*'s website. Deadline: April 30. Prizes: 1st Place: $2,000 and publication; 2nd Place: $1,000 and publication. Judged by the *Nimrod* editors (finalists). A recognized author selects the winners.

◑ THE NEW CRITERION POETRY PRIZE

Website: www.newcriterion.com. Deadline: September 30. Prize: $3,000.

◑ NEW LETTERS PRIZE FOR POETRY

New Letters Awards for Writers, UMKC, University House, 5101 Rockhill Rd., Kansas City MO 64110. **Website:** www.newletters.org. The annual New Letters Poetry Prize awards $1,500 and publication in *New Letters* (see separate listing in Magazines/Journals) to the best group of 3-6 poems. All entries will be considered for publication in *New Letters*. **Deadline:** May 18 (postmark) $1,500.

NEW MILLENNIUM AWARDS FOR FICTION, POETRY, AND NONFICTION

New Millennium Writings, NMW, Room M2, P.O. Box 2463, Knoxville TN 37901. (423)428-0389. **Website:** www.newmillenniumwritings.com/awards. "No restrictions as to style, content or number of submissions. Previously published pieces OK if online or under 5,000 print circulation. Send any time between now and midnight, June 17, for the Summer Awards program, January 31 for the Winter Awards. Simultaneous and multiple submissions welcome. Each fiction or nonfiction piece is a separate entry and should total no more than 6,000 words, except for the Short-Short Fiction Award, which should total no more than 1,000 words. (Nonfiction includes essays, profiles, memoirs, interviews, creative nonfiction, travel, humor, etc.) Each poetry entry may include up to 3 poems, not to exceed 5 pages total. All 20 poetry finalists will be published. Include name, phone, address, e-mail, and category on cover page only." Deadline: postmarked on or before January 31. Prize: $1,000 for Best Poem; $1,000 for Best Fiction; $1,000 for Best Nonfiction; $1,000 for Best Short-Short Fiction.

NEW SOUTH WRITING CONTEST

E-mail: newsouth@gsu.edu. **Website:** newsouthjournal.com/contest. **Contact:** Matt Sailor, editor-in-chief. Offered annually to publish the most promising work of up-and-coming writers of poetry (up to 3 poems) and fiction (9,000 word limit). Rights revert to writer upon publication. Guidelines online. Deadline: March 15. Prize: 1st Place: $1,000 in each category; 2nd Place: $250; and publication to winners. Judged by Marily Kallet in poetry and Amber Sparks in prose. **TIPS** "We look for engagement with language and characters we care about."

◑ NEW WOMEN'S VOICES CHAPBOOK COMPETITION

Finishing Line Press, P.O. Box 1626, Georgetown KY 40324. (859)514-8966. **E-mail:** FinishingBooks@aol. com. **Website:** www.finishinglinepress.com. **Contact:** Leah Maines, poetry editor. The New Women's Voices Chapbook Competition offers publication by Finishing Line Press for a chapbook-length ms by a woman poet who has not yet published a full-length collection (previous chapbook publication is okay). Deadline: February 15. Prize: $1,000 and print and Kindle publication.

◑ JESSIE BRYCE NILES MEMORIAL CHAPBOOK AWARD

The Comstock Review, 4956 St. John Dr., Syracuse NY 13215. (315)488-8077. **E-mail:** poetry@comstockreview.org. **Website:** www.comstockreview.org. The Jesse Bryce Niles Memorial Chapbook Award runs every other year, next in 2013, and offers $1,000 plus publication and 50 author's copies; each entrant also receives a copy. Submissions must be unpublished as a collection, but individual poems may have been previously published in journals. Considers simultaneous submissions "as long as the poet notifies us immediately upon acceptance elsewhere." Submit 25-34 pages of poetry, single-spaced (1 page=38 lines maximum, including spacing between lines; poems may run longer than 1 page). **Manuscripts either too short or too long will be disqualified.** "Do not count title page, acknowledgments, dedication, or bio in the page length. Do not send illustrations, photos, or any other graphics attached to the poems. You may submit a table of contents, which may list the manuscript name only, not the poet's name (not counted in page total for manuscript)." Manuscripts should be paginated and secured with a binder clip; no staples or plastic covers. Include 2 cover pages: 1 with ms title, poet's name, address, phone number, and e-mail address; second with ms title only. List acknowledgments on a separate, removable page with same identifying information. Poet's name should not appear on poems. Include SASE for results only; mss will not be returned. Guidelines available for SASE or on website. **Entry fee:** $25/chapbook. **Deadline:** submit August 1-September 30 (postmark). **Offered every other year.** Deadline: September 30. Contest begins August 1. Prize: $1,000 and 50 copies of chapbook.

Judged by Kathleen Bryce Niles. All chapbooks are screened by the editors.

THE JOHN FREDERICK NIMS MEMORIAL PRIZE

Poetry, 61 W. Superior St., Chicago IL 60654. (312)787-7070. **Fax:** (312)787-6650. **E-mail:** poetry@poetry-magazine.org. **E-mail:** mail@poetryfoundation.org. **Website:** www.poetrymagazine.org. Offered annually for poems published in *Poetry* during the preceding year (October-September). Upon acceptance, *Poetry* licenses exclusive worldwide first serial rights, including electronic rights, for publication, as well as non-exclusive rights to reprint, reuse, and archive the work, in any format, in perpetuity. Copyright reverts to author upon first publication. Copyrights are returned to the authors on request. The John Frederick Nims Memorial Prize for translation work is permanently endowed through a fund established by Bonnie Larkin Nims, Trustees of The Poetry Foundation, and friends of the late poet, translator, and Editor of *Poetry*. Prize: $500.

NORTH CAROLINA WRITERS' FELLOWSHIPS

North Carolina Arts Council, North Carolina Arts Council, Writers' Fellowships, Department of Cultural Resources, Raleigh NC 27699-4632. (919)807-6512. **Fax:** (919)807-6532. **E-mail:** debbie.mcgill@ncmail.net. **Website:** www.ncarts.org. **Contact:** Debbie McGill, literature director. The North Carolina Arts Council offers grants in two categories to writers, spoken-word artists, playwrights, and screenwriters: fellowships (every other year) and residency grants (every year). Offered every even year to support writers of fiction, poetry, literary nonfiction, literary translation, and spoken word. See website for guidelines and other eligibility requirements. Deadline: November 1. Prize: $10,000 grant. Reviewed by a panel of literature professionals (writers and editors).

◐ NSW PREMIER'S LITERARY AWARD THE KENNETH SLESSOR PRIZE

Website: www.sl.nsw.gov.au. (Specialized: Australian citizens only) Offers annual award of $30,000 for a book of poetry (collection or long poem) published in the previous year. **Open to Australian citizens only.** Books may be nominated by poets or by their agents or publishers. Write for entry form and guidelines or check website. **Deadline:** November (check guidelines). Winners will be announced in May. "Obtain copy of guidelines before entering." The NSW Premier's Literary Awards have a proud history, both in celebrating achievement by Australian writers and in helping to establish values and standards in Australian literature. The Kenneth Slessor Prize is offered to a poet for a book of collected poems or for a single poem of substantial length published in book form. A collection of poems may consist partly of work previously published in book form, but this work must be clearly identified by the nominator. In such cases the judges will assess only the new work and determine whether it is sufficient, in quantity and quality, to merit an award. The NSW Government is committed to increasing public engagement with the arts. Administered by the State Library of NSW, the NSW Premier's Literary Awards provide an opportunity to highlight the importance of literacy and to encourage everyone to enjoy and learn from the work of our writers. These annual awards honour distinguished achievement by Australian writers, contribute to Australia's artistic reputation, and draw international attention to some of our best writers and to the cultural environment that nurtures them. Deadline: November 23. Prize: $30,000. Judged by an independent committee of writers, academics, critics and other sector professionals who have been appointed by the NSW Premier.

OHIOANA POETRY AWARD

Ohioana Library Association, 274 E. First Ave., Suite 300, Columbus OH 43201. (614)466-3831. **Fax:** (614)728-6974. **E-mail:** ohioana@ohioana.org. **Website:** www.ohioana.org. "Offers annual Ohioana Book Awards. Up to 6 awards may be given for books (including books of poetry) by authors born in Ohio or who have lived in Ohio for at least 5 years." The Ohioana Poetry Award of $1,000 (with the same residence requirements), made possible by a bequest of Helen Krout, is given yearly "to an individual whose body of published work has made, and continues to make, a significant contribution to poetry, and through whose work as a writer, teacher, administrator, or in community service, interest in poetry has been developed." Competition receives several hundred entries. 2009 Ohioana Poetry Award winner was William Greenway (*Everywhere at Once*). Ohioana Quarterly regularly reviews books by Ohio authors and is available through membership in Ohioana Library Association ($25/year). The Ohioana Library is dedicated to collecting, preserving, and promoting the written work of Ohio's writers, artists, and musicians. Given periodically to an Ohio poet for a body of published work that had made, and continues to make, a significant contribution to poetry, and through whose work as a writer, teacher, administrator, or in community service, interest in poetry has been developed. Deadline: December 31. Prize: $1,000.

OPEN SEASON AWARDS

The Malahat Review, University of Victoria, P.O. Box 1700, Stn CSC, Victoria BC V8V 2Y2, Canada. **Fax:** (250)472-5051. **E-mail:** malahat@uvic.ca. **Website:** www.malahatreview.ca. **Contact:** John Barton, editor. The annual Open Season Awards offers $1,000 CAD and publication in *The Malahat Review*. The Open Season Awards accepts entries of poetry, fiction, and creative nonfiction. Submissions must be unpublished. No simultaneous submissions. Submit up to 3 poems per entry, each poem not to exceed 100 lines; one piece of fiction (2500 words max.), or one piece of creative nonfiction (2500 words max.), no restrictions on subject matter or aesthetic approach. Include separate page with writer's name, address, e-mail, and title(s); no identifying information on mss pages. No e-mail submissions. Do not include SASE for results; mss will not be returned. Guidelines available on website. Winner and finalists contacted by e-mail. Winners published in spring issue of *Malahat Review* announced in winter on website, facebook page, and in quarterly e-newsletter, *Malahat lite*. Deadline: November 1 of each year. Prize: Offers $1,000 CAD and publication in *The Malahat Review* in each category.

THE PATERSON POETRY PRIZE

(973)684-6555. **Fax:** (973)523-6085. **E-mail:** mgillan@pccc.edu. **Website:** www.pccc.edu/poetry. **Contact:** Maria Mazziotti Gillan, executive director. The Paterson Poetry Prize offers an annual award of $1,000 for the strongest book of poems (48 or more pages) published in the previous year. The winner will be asked to participate in an awards ceremony and to give a reading at The Poetry Center. Minimum press run: 500 copies. Publishers may submit more than 1 title for prize consideration; 3 copies of each book must be submitted. Include SASE for results; books will not be returned (all entries will be donated to The Poetry Center Library). Guidelines and application form (required) available for SASE or on website. Deadline: February 1 (postmark). Prize: $1,000.

⊕ THE KATHERINE PATERSON PRIZE FOR YOUNG ADULT AND CHILDREN'S WRITING

Hunger Mountain, Vermont College of Fine Arts, 36 College St., Montpelier VT 05602. (802)828-8517. **E-mail:** hungermtn@vcfa.edu. **Website:** www.hungermtn.org. **Contact:** Miciah Bay Gault, editor. The annual Katherine Paterson Prize for Young Adult and Children's Writing offers $1,000 and publication in *Hunger Mountain*; 3 runners-up receive $100 and are also published. Submit young adult or middle grade mss, and writing for younger children, short stories, picture books, or novel excerpts, under 10,000 words. Guidelines available on website. "An annual prize for Young Adult and Children's Literature. A chance for your YA and Children's Lit to be read by Hunger Mountain editors and guest judges." Deadline: June 30. Prize: $1,000 and publication for the first place winner; $100 each and publication for the three category winners.

⊙ PAVEMENT SAW PRESS CHAPBOOK AWARD

321 Empire St., Montpelier OH 43543-1301. **E-mail:** info@pavementsaw.org. **E-mail:** editor@pavement-saw.org. **Website:** www.pavementsaw.org. **Contact:** David Baratier, editor. "Pavement Saw Press has been publishing steadily since the fall of 1993. Each year since 1999, we have published at least 4 full-length paperback poetry collections, with some printed in library edition hard covers, 1 chapbook and a yearly literary journal anthology. We specialize in finding authors who have been widely published in literary journals but have not published a chapbook or full-length book." Deadline: December 31 (postmark). Prize: Chapbook Award offers $500, publication, and 50 author copies.

⊙ PEARL POETRY PRIZE

Pearl Editions, 3030 E. Second St., Long Beach CA 90803. (562)434-4523. **Fax:** (562)434-4523. **E-mail:** pearlmag@aol.com. **Website:** www.pearlmag.com. **Contact:** Marilyn Johnson, editor/publisher. The annual Pearl Poetry Prize awards $1,000, publication, and 25 author's copies for a book-length ms. Guidelines available for SASE or on website. "Offered annually to provide poets with further opportunity to publish their poetry in book-form and find a larger audience for their work. Mss must be original works written in English. Guidelines for SASE or online.

Open to all writers." Deadline: Submit May 1-June 30 only. Prize: $1,000 and publication by Pearl Editions.

○ JUDITH SIEGEL PEARSON AWARD

Judith Siegel Pearson Award, c/o Department of English, Wayne State University, Attn: Rhonda Agnew, 5057 Woodward Ave, Ste. 9408, Detroit MI 48202. (313)577-2450. **Fax:** (313)577-8618. **E-mail:** ad2073@wayne.edu. **Contact:** Rhonda Agnew. Offers an annual award of up to $500 for the best creative or scholarly work on a subject concerning women. The type of work accepted rotates each year: Drama in 2012; poetry in 2013 (poetry, 20 pages maximum); essays in 2014; fiction in 2015. Open to all interested writers and scholars. Submissions must be unpublished. Guidelines available by e-mail. No late or electronic submissions accepted. The award is an annual prize for the best creative or scholarly work on a subject concerning women. Deadline: February 25.

● JEAN PEDRICK PRIZE

New England Poetry Club, 654 Green St., Apt. 2, Cambridge MA 02139. **E-mail:** contests@nepoetryclub.org. **Website:** www.nepoetryclub.org. **Contact:** NEPC contest coordinator. Prize for a chapbook published in the last two years. Deadline: May 31. Prize: $100. Judges are well-known poets and sometimes winners of previous NEPC contests.

PEN CENTER USA LITERARY AWARDS

PEN Center USA, P.O. Box 6037, Beverly Hills CA 90212. (323)424-4939. **E-mail:** awards@penusa.org. **E-mail:** pen@penusa.org. **Website:** www.penusa.org. Offered for work published or produced in the previous calendar year. Open to writers living west of the Mississippi River. Award categories: fiction, poetry, research nonfiction, creative nonfiction, translation, children's/young adult, drama, screenplay, teleplay, journalism. Deadline for book categories: 4 copies must be received by December 31. Deadline for non-book categories: 4 copies must be received by January 31. Prize: $1,000.

PEN/JOYCE OSTERWEIL AWARD FOR POETRY

PEN American Center, 588 Broadway, Suite 303, New York NY 10012. (212)334-1660, ext. 126. **E-mail:** awards@pen.org. **Website:** www.pen.org. **Contact:** Jasmine Davey, literary awards coordinator. *Candidates may only be nominated by members of PEN.* This award recognizes the high literary character of the published work to date of a new and emerging American poet of any age, and the promise of further literary achievement. Nominated writer may not have published more than 1 book of poetry. Offered in odd-numbered years and alternates with the PEN/Voelcker Award for Poetry. Deadline: February 1. Prize: $5,000. Judged by a panel of 3 judges selected by the PEN Awards Committee.

PEN/VOELCKER AWARD FOR POETRY

PEN American Center, 588 Broadway, Suite 303, New York NY 10012. (212)334-1600, ext. 108. **E-mail:** awards@pen.org. **Website:** www.pen.org. **Contact:** Jasmine Davey, literary awards coordinator. Deadline: See website. Prize: $5,000 stipend. Judged by a panel of 3 poets or other writers.

Biannual award. No award in 2013.

PERUGIA PRESS PRIZE

Perugia Press, P.O. Box 60364, Florence MA 01062. **E-mail:** info@perugiapress.com. **Website:** www.perugiapress.com. **Contact:** Susan Kan. The Perugia Press Prize is for a first or second poetry book by a woman. Poet must have no more than 1 previously published book of poems (chapbooks don't count). Submissions must be unpublished as a collection, but individual poems may have been previously published in journals, chapbooks, and anthologies. Considers simultaneous submissions if notified of acceptance elsewhere. "Follow online guidelines carefully. Electronic submissions available through our website." No translations or self-published books. Multiple submissions accepted if accompanied by separate entry fee for each. Entry fee: $25. Make checks payable to Perugia Press. "Use USPS or electronic submission, not FedEx or UPS." Winner announced by April 1 by e-mail or SASE (if included with entry). Deadline: Submit August 1-November 15 (postmark) Prize: $1,000 and publication. Judges: Panel of Perugia authors, booksellers, scholars, etc.

THE RICHARD PETERSON POETRY PRIZE

Crab Orchard Review, Dept. of English, Mail Code 4503, Faner Hall 2380, Southern Illinois University at Carbondale, 1000 Faner Drive, Carbondale IL 62901. (618)453-6833. **Fax:** (618)453-8224. **E-mail:** jtribble@siu.edu. **Website:** www.craborchardreview.siu.edu. **Contact:** Jon Tribble, managing editor. Deadline: May 4. Prize: $2,000 plus publication.

THE PINCH LITERARY AWARD IN FICTION AND POETRY

(901)678-4591. **E-mail:** editor@thepinchjournal.com. **Website:** www.thepinchjournal.com. Offered annually for unpublished short stories of 5,000 words maximum or up to three poems. Guidelines on website. Cost: $20, which is put toward one issue of *The Pinch*. Deadline: March 15. Prize: 1st place Fiction: $1,500 and publication; 1st place Poetry: $1,000 and publication.

PLAN B PRESS POETRY CHAPBOOK CONTEST

P.O. Box 4067, Alexandria VA 22303. (215)732-2663. **E-mail:** planbpress@gmail.com. **Website:** www.planbpress.com. **Contact:** Contest Coordinator. A small independent publishing company that primarily produces high-quality, limited-run poetry chapbooks. "Our primary focus for the past five years has been to publish collections by authors at the beginning of their careers, i.e. their 1st-3rd works. Lately we have also decided to play up our natural strength of creating books that are visually appealing, combining imagery and words, and packaging the collections as a completed thought- a collectable, covetable object." Deadline: March 1. Prize: $235, publication by Plan B Press, and 50 author's copies

PNWA LITERARY CONTEST

Pacific Northwest Writers Association, PMB 2717-1420 NW Gilman Blvd., Suite 2, Issaquah WA 98027. (425)673-2665. **Fax:** (425)961-0768. **E-mail:** pnwa@pnwa.org. **Website:** www.pnwa.org. **Contact:** Kelli Liddane. **Open to students.** Annual contest. Purpose of contest: "Valuable tool for writers as contest submissions are critiqued (2 critiques)." Unpublished submissions only. Submissions made by author. Deadline: February 18. Prizes: 1st: $700; 2nd: $300.

POETRY 2013 INTERNATIONAL POETRY COMPETITION

Atlanta Review, P.O. Box 8248, Atlanta GA 31106. **E-mail:** atlanta.review@yahoo.com. **Website:** www.atlantareview.com. **Contact:** Dan Veach, Editor/Publisher. *Atlanta Review* (see separate listing in Magazines/Journals) sponsors an annual international poetry competition, offering $1,000 Grand Prize, 20 International Publication Awards (winners will be published in *Atlanta Review*), and 30 International Merit Awards (includes certificate, Honorable Mention in *Atlanta Review*, and free issue). Poems must not have been published in a nationally distributed print publication. Online entry available at journal website. For mail entry: put your name and address on each page (e-mail and phone optional). Include SASE for results only; no entries will be returned. Guidelines available on website. **Entry fee:** $5 for the first poem, $3 for each additional poem. Make checks payable to *Atlanta Review*. International entrants must use online entry. **Deadline:** March 1, 2013. Winners will be announced in the summer; Contest Issue published in October. Contest Issue available for $4, or free with $10 subscription to *Atlanta Review*. "Atlanta Review is an international poetry journal devoted to bringing surprise, wonder and delight to readers around the world. Its unique blend of quality and human appeal have made it one of the world's best-selling poetry journals. Here you'll find Nobel and Pulitzer Prize winners galore, but also poems that touch the deepest feelings of the writer and the reader. Atlanta Review is a haven for our common humanity, the things that unite us across the boundaries of nation, race, and religion. It is a voice we need more urgently than ever in today's world." Deadline: March 1. Winners announced in the summer. Prize: $1,000 grand prize; 20 entrants will be published in the Contest Issue of Atlanta Review; and 30 Merit Awards, where poet's name will appear in Atlanta Review, with a certificate and a free contest issue. Judged by the Editor of Atlanta Review.

○ THE POETRY SOCIETY OF VIRGINIA ADULT AND STUDENT CONTESTS

P.O. Box 6706, Virginia Beach VA 23456-0706. **E-mail:** ggterr@infionline.net. **E-mail:** nancy1734@aol.com. **Website:** www.ooetrysocietyofvirginia.org. **Contact:** Guy Terrell, Adult Contest Co-Chair. Adult contest offers many categories for original, unpublished poems—both specified and unspecified forms and topics. Student contest is school grade-specific. Offers numerous cash prizes (varies by year). One poem per category may be submitted. Submit 2 copies of each poem. Both copies must have the category name and number on top left of page. One copy must contain poet's name, address, e-mail, and phone number on top right of page, as well as membership status. Guidelines available for SASE or on website (guidelines must be followed). **Entry fee:** $4/poem for adults; no fee for students and PSV members. ("Membership fee of $25 covers entries in all categories and can be sent with entry and membership form, available on website or for SASE.") Designate entries as "adult" or "student" and send to Contest Chair at the above address. **Deadline:** January 19 (postmark) annually (Edgar Allan Poe's birthday). Winning entries may be published in a booklet or on the PSV website unless author indicates otherwise on each poem entered. "Follow guidelines to ensure inclusion of poem in contest. Always include SASE for any return information." Prize: Multiple prizes with different prize amounts are offered. See website for details.

⊘ POETS & PATRONS ANNUAL CHICAGOLAND POETRY CONTEST

Sponsored by Poets & Patrons of Chicago, 416 Gierz St., Downers Grove IL 60515. **E-mail:** eatonb1016@aol.com. **Website:** www.poetsandpatrons.org. **Contact:** Barbara Eaton, director. Annual contest for unpublished poetry. Guidelines available for self-addressed, stamped envelope. The purpose of the contest is to encourage the crafting of poetry. Deadline: September 1 Prize is $45, $20, $10 cash. Poet retains rights. Judged by out-of-state professionals.

◑ FELIX POLLAK PRIZE IN POETRY

University of Wisconsin Press, 1930 Monroe Street, 3rd Floor, Madison WI 53711-2059. (608)263-1110. **Fax:** (608)263-1120. **E-mail:** uwiscpress@uwpress.wisc.edu. **Website:** uwpress.wisc.edu. The Felix Pollak Prize in Poetry is awarded annually to the best book-length manuscript of original poetry submitted in an open competition. The award is administered by the University of Wisconsin–Madison English department, and the winner is chosen by a nationally recognized poet. The resulting book is published by the University of Wisconsin Press.

● A. POULIN, JR. POETRY PRIZE

BOA Editions, Ltd., BOA Editions, Ltd., P.O. Box 30971, Rochester NY 14604. **E-mail:** conners@boaeditions.org. **Website:** www.boaeditions.org. BOA Editions, Ltd. sponsors the annual A. Poulin, Jr. Poetry Prize for a poet's first book. The A. Poulin, Jr. Poetry Prize is awarded to honor a poet's first book, while also honoring the late founder of BOA Editions, Ltd., a not-for-profit publishing house of poetry and poetry in translation. Deadline: Submit between August 1-Nov. 30. Prize: Awards $1,500 honorarium and book publication in the A. Poulin, Jr. New Poets of America Series. Judged by Dorianne Laux.

PRAIRIE SCHOONER BOOK PRIZE

Prairie Schooner and the University of Nebraska Press, Prairie Schooner Prize Series, Attn: Fiction, 123 Andrews Hall, Lincoln NE 68588-0334. (402)472-0911. **E-mail:** PSBookPrize@unl.edu. **Website:** prairieschooner.unl.edu. **Contact:** Kwame Dawes, editor. Annual competition/award for story collections. Deadline: March 15. Prize: $3,000 and publication through the University of Nebraska Press.

⊕ PRESS 53 OPEN AWARDS

Press 53, 411 W. Fourth St., Suite 101A, Winston-Salem NC 27101. **E-mail:** kevin@press53.com. **Website:** www.press53.com. **Contact:** Kevin Morgan Watson, publisher. The Press 53 Open Awards Writing Contest is open to writers anywhere in the world who write in English (excluding Press 53 employees and family members). Previously published pieces are accepted so long as any previous publishing agreements do not prohibit Press 53 from publishing the work in the winning anthology. Deadline: March 31. Prize: 1st Place: Press 53 Open Award, publication, 2 complimentary copies of anthology; 2nd Place: Personalized certificate, complimentary copy of anthology; Honorable Mention: Personalized certificate, complimentary copy of anthology.

◑ THE PSA NEW YORK CHAPBOOK FELLOWSHIPS

Poetry Society of America, 15 Gramercy Park, New York NY 10003. (212)254-9628. **Fax:** (212)673-2352. **Website:** www.poetrysociety.org. **Contact:** Contest Coordinator. Open to any New York City resident (in the 5 boroughs) who is 30 or under and has not published a full-length poetry collection. Poets who apply to the New York Chapbook Fellowships cannot apply to the National Chapbook Fellowships. Does not accept entries by fax or e-mail. Guidelines available for SASE or on website. Deadline: entries accepted between October 1 and December 22. Prize: Offers 2 prizes of $1,000 and publication of each of winning chapbook mss, with distribution by the Poetry Society of America. 2013 judges include Mary Ruefle and John Yau.

PUSHCART PRIZE

Pushcart Press, P.O. Box 380, Wainscott NY 11975. (631)324-9300. **Website:** www.pushcartprize.com. **Contact:** Bill Henderson. Published every year since 1976, The Pushcart Prize - Best of the Small Presses series "is the most honored literary project in America.

Hundreds of presses and thousands of writers of short stories, poetry and essays have been represented in the pages of our annual collections." Little magazine and small book press editors (print or online) may make up to six nominations from their year's publicatoins by the deadline. The nominations may be any combination of poetry, short fiction, essays or literary whatnot. Editors may nominate self-contained portions of books — for instance, a chapter from a novel. Deadline: December 1.

◐ RATTLE POETRY PRIZE

RATTLE, 12411 Ventura Blvd., Studio City CA 91604. (818) 505-6777. **E-mail:** tim@rattle.com. **E-mail:** prize@rattle.com. **Website:** www.rattle.com. **Contact:** Timothy Green, editor. *Rattle*'s mission is to promote the practice of poetry. "More than anything, our goal is to promote a community of active poets." Deadline: July 15. Prize: One $5,000 winner and ten $100 finalists will be selected in a blind review by the editors of *Rattle* and printed in the Winter issue; one $1,000 Readers' Choice Award will then be chosen from among the Finalists by subscriber and entrant vote. Judged by the editors of *Rattle*.

◌ THE RBC BRONWEN WALLACE AWARD FOR EMERGING WRITERS

The Writers' Trust of Canada, 90 Richmond St. East, Suite 200, Toronto, Ontario M5C 1P1, Canada. (416)504-8222. **Fax:** (416)504-9090. **E-mail:** info@writerstrust.com. **Website:** www.writerstrust.com. **Contact:** Amanda Hopkins. Presented annually to "a Canadian writer under the age of 35 who is not yet published in book form. The award, which alternates each year between poetry and short fiction, was established in memory of poet Bronwen Wallace." Deadline: January 31. Prize: $5,000 and $1,000 to 2 finalists.

◌ REGINA BOOK AWARD

Saskatchewan Book Awards, Inc., P.O. Box 20025, Regina SK S4P 4J7, Canada. (306)569-1585. **E-mail:** director@bookawards.sk.ca. **Website:** www.bookawards.sk.ca. Offered annually. "In recognition of the vitality of the literary community in Regina, this award is presented to a Regina author for the best book, judged on the quality of writing." Books from the following categories will be considered: Children's; drama; fiction (short fiction by a single author, novellas, novels); nonfiction (all categories of nonfiction writing except cookbooks, directories, how-to books, or bibliographies of minimal critical content); poetry. Deadline: November 1. $2,000 (CAD).

BEULLAH ROSE POETRY PRIZE

P.O. Box 22161, Baltimore MD 21203. **E-mail:** cbanks@smartishpace.com. **Website:** www.smartishpace.com. **Contact:** Clare Banks, associate editor. To recognize exceptional poetry by women. Deadline: Octobr 1. Prize: $200. Judged by Clare Banks and Traci O'Dea.

LORI RUDNITSKY FIRST BOOK PRIZE

Persea Books, P.O. Box 1388, Columbia MO 65205. **Website:** www.perseabooks.com. "This annual competition sponsors the publication of a poetry collection by an American woman poet who has yet to publish a full-length book of poems." Deadline: October 31. Prize: $1,000, plus publication of book. In addition, the winner receives the option of an all-expenses-paid residency at the Civitella Ranieri Center, a renowned artists retreat housed in a 15th-century castle in Umbertide, Italy.

THE SACRAMENTIO POETRY CENTER BOOK PRIZE

The Sacramento Poetry Center, P.O. Box 160406, Sacramento CA 95816. (916)240-1897. **E-mail:** buchanan@csus.edu. **Website:** www.sacramentopoetrycenter.org. **Contact:** Brad Buchanan. The Sacramento Poetry Center is a non-profit organization dedicated to furthering the cause of poetry in the Sacramento area and nationwide. We welcome work from anyone, anywhere. Deadline: May 10. Contest begins January 1. Prize: Winning book manuscript will be published by The Sacramento Poetry Center Press.

ERNEST SANDEEN PRIZE IN POETRY

University of Notre Dame, Dept. of English, 356 O'Shaughnessy Hall, Notre Dame IN 46556-5639. (574)631-7526. **Fax:** (574)631-4795. **E-mail:** creative-writing@nd.edu. **Website:** http://english.nd.edu/creative-writing/publications/sandeen-sullivan-prizes. **Contact:** Director of Creative Writing. The Sandeen Prize in Poetry is awarded to the author who have published at least one volume of short fiction or one volume of poetry. Awarded biannually, but judged quadrennially. Submissions Period: May 1 - Septhember 1. Prize: A $1,000 prize, a $500 award and a $500 advance against royalties from the Notre Dame Press.

MAY SARTON AWARD

New England Poetry Club, 654 Green St., No. 2, Cambridge MA 02139. **Website:** www.nepoetryclub.org. **Contact:** NEPC contest coordinator. "Given intermittently to a poet whose work is an inspiration to other poets. Recipients are chosen by the board." To recognize emerging poets of exceptional promise and distinguished achievement. Established to honor the memory of longtime Academy Fellow May Sarton, a poet, novelist, and teacher who during her career encouraged the work of young poets. Deadline: May 31. Prize: $250. Judges are well-known poets and sometimes winners of previous NEPC contests.

SASKATCHEWAN FIRST BOOK AWARD

Saskatchewan Book Awards, Inc., P.O. Box 20025, Regina SK S4P 4J7, Canada. (306)569-1585. **E-mail:** director@bookawards.sk.ca. **Website:** www.bookawards.sk.ca. Offered annually. "This award is presented to a Saskatchewan author for the best first book, judged on the quality of writing." Books from the following categories will be considered: Children's; drama; fiction (short fiction by a single author, novellas, novels); nonfiction (all categories of nonfiction writing except cookbooks, directories, how-to books, or bibliographies of minimal critical content); and poetry. Deadline: November 1 Prize: $2,000 (CAD).

SASKATCHEWAN POETRY AWARD

Saskatchewan Book Awards, Inc., P.O. Box 20025, Regina SK S4P 4J7, Canada. (306)569-1585. **E-mail:** director@bookawards.sk.ca. **Website:** www.bookawards.sk.ca. Offered annually. "This award is presented to a Saskatchewan author for the best book of poetry, judged on the quality of writing." Deadline: November 1. Prize: $2,000 (CAD).

THE SCARS EDITOR'S CHOICE AWARDS

829 Brian Court, Gurnee IL 60031-3155. **E-mail:** editor@scars.tv. **Website:** http://scars.tv. **Contact:** Janet Kuypers, editor/publisher (whom all reading fee checks need to be made out to). Award "to showcase good writing in an annual book." Categories: short stories, poetry. Entry fee: $19/short story, and $15/poem. Deadline: Revolves for appearing in different upcoming books as winners. Prize: Publication of story/essay and 1 copy of the book. Entries may be unpublished or previously published, "as long as you retain the rights to your work." Open to any writer.

For guidelines, visit website. Accepts inquiries by e-mail. "E-mail is always preferred for inquiries and submissions. (If you have access to e-mail, we will request that you e-mail your contest submission, and we will hold it until we receive the reading fee payment for the submission.)" Length: "We appreciate shorter works. Shorter stories, more vivid and more real storylines in writing have a good chance." Results announced at book publication, online. Winners notified by mail when book is printed. For contest results, send SASE or e-mail or look at the contest page at website. Award to showcase good writing in an annual book.

THE MONA SCHREIBER PRIZE FOR HUMOROUS FICTION & NONFICTION

E-mail: brad.schreiber@att.net. **Website:** www.bradschreiber.com. **Contact:** Brad Schreiber. "The purpose of the contest is to award the most creative humor writing, in any form less than 750 words, in either fiction or nonfiction, including but not limited to stories, articles, essays, speeches, shopping lists, diary entries, and anything else writers dream up." Deadline: December 1. Prizes: 1st Place: $500; 2nd Place: $250; 3rd Place: $100. Judge: Brad Schreiber, author, journalist, consultant, and instructor. Complete rules and previous winning entries on website. **TIPS** "No SASE's, please. Non-US entries should enclose US currency or checks written in US dollars. Include email address. No previously published work."

⊙ SKIPPING STONES HONOR (BOOK) AWARDS

P.O. Box 3939, Eugene OR 97403. Phone/fax: (541)342-4956. **E-mail:** editor@skippingstones.org. **Website:** www.skippingstones.org. **Contact:** Arun N. Toké. Annual awards since 1994 to "promote multicultural and/or nature awareness through creative writings for children and teens and their educators. We seek authentic, exceptional, child/youth friendly books that promote intercultural, international, intergenerational harmony, and understanding through creative ways. Writings that come out of your own experiences and cultural understanding seem to have an edge." Deadline: February 1. Prizes: Honor certificates; gold seals; reviews; press release/publicity. Judged by "a multicultural committee of teachers, librarians, parents, students and editors."

SLAPERING HOL PRESS CHAPBOOK COMPETITION

(914)332-5953. **Fax:** (914)332-4825. **E-mail:** info@writerscenter.org. **Website:** www.writerscenter.org. **Contact:** Margo Stever, editor. 300 Riverside Dr., Sleepy Hollow NY 10591-1414. (914)332-5953. **Fax:** (914)332-4825. **E-mail:** info@writerscenter.org. **Website:** www.slaperingholpress.org. Established 1990. **Contact:** Margo Stever. The Slapering Hol Press Chapbook Competition offers an annual award of $1,000, publication, 10 author's copies, and a reading at The Hudson Valley Writers' Center (see separate listing in Organizations). Open only to poets who have not previously published a book or chapbook. Submit 16-20 pages of poetry (collection or one long poem), any form or style. Manuscript should be anonymous with separate cover sheet containing name, address, phone number, e-mail address, a bio, and acknowledgments. Include SASE for results only; manuscripts will not be returned. Guidelines available for SASE, by fax, e-mail, or on website. **Entry fee:** $15. Make checks payable to The Hudson Valley Writers' Center. Winner will be announced in September. Competition receives more than 300 entries. 2006 winner was Mary Kaiser (Falling Into Velázquez). Winning chapbooks available through website and www.amazon.com. The annual competition is open to poets who have not published a book or chapbook, though individual poems may have already appeared. To provide publishing opportunities for emerging poets. Deadline: May 15. Prize: $1,000, publication of chapbook, 20 copies of chapbook, and a reading at The Hudson Valley Writers' Center. Uses a blind judging system.

SLIPSTREAM ANNUAL POETRY CHAPBOOK CONTEST

E-mail: editors@slipstreampress.org. **Website:** www.slipstreampress.org. **Contact:** Dan Sicoli, co-editor. Slipstream Magazine is a yearly anthology of some of the best poetry you'll find today in the American small press. Offered annually to help promote a poet whose work is often overlooked or ignored. Open to any writer. Deadline: December 1. Prize: $1,000 plus 50 professionally-printed copies of your book.

◑ SLOPE EDITIONS BOOK PRIZE

4 Lynde St., Nashua NH 03064. **E-mail:** ethan@slope.org. **Website:** www.slopeeditions.org. **Contact:** Christopher Janke, senior editor and Ethan Paquin, edi-

tor-in-chief. Deadline: March 15. Prize: $1,000 plus publication.

THE BERNICE SLOTE AWARD

Prairie Schooner, 123 Andrews Hall, PO Box 880334, Lincoln NE 68588-0334. (402)472-0911. **Fax:** (402)472-1817. **E-mail:** PrairieSchooner@unl.edu. **Website:** www.prairieschooner.unl.edu. **Contact:** Kwame Dawes. Offered annually for the best work by a beginning writer published in Prairie Schooner in the previous year. Celebrates the best and finest writing that they have published for the year. Prize: $500.

HELEN C. SMITH MEMORIAL AWARD FOR POETRY

E-mail: tilsecretary@yahoo.com. **Website:** http://texasinstituteofletters.org/. Offered annually for the best book of poems published January 1-December 31 of previous year. Poet must have been born in Texas, have lived in the state at some time for at least 2 consecutive years, or the subject matter must be associated with the state. See website for guidelines. Deadline: early January. Prize: $1,200.

◐ KAY SNOW WRITING CONTEST

Willamette Writers, Willamette Writers, 2108 Buck St., West Linn OR 97068. (503)305-6729. **Fax:** (503)344-6174. **E-mail:** wilwrite@willamettewriters. com. **Website:** www.willamettewriters.com. **Contact:** Lizzy Shannon, contest director. "Willamette Writers is the largest writers' organization in Oregon and one of the largest writers' organizations in the United States. It is a non-profit, tax-exempt Oregon corporation led by volunteers. Elected officials and directors administer an active program of monthly meetings, special seminars, workshops and annual writing conference. Continuing with established programs and starting new ones is only made possible by strong volunteer support." "The purpose of this annual writing contest, named in honor of Willamette Writer's founder, Kay Snow, is to help writers reach professional goals in writing in a broad array of categories and to encourage student writers." Deadline: April 23. Prize: One first prize of $300, one second place prize of $150, and a third place prize of $50 per winning entry in each of the six categories.

◐ THE RICHARD SNYDER MEMORIAL PUBLICATION PRIZE

Ashland Poetry Press, 401 College Ave., Ashland University, Ashland OH 44805. **E-mail:** app@ash-land.edu. **Website:** www.ashlandpoetrypress.com. **Contact:** Sarah Wells, managing editor. Offers annual award of $1,000 plus book publication in a paper-only edition of 1,000 copies. Submissions must be unpublished in book form. Considers simultaneous submissions. Submit 50-80 pages of poetry. Competition receives 375 entries/year. Winners will be announced in *Writer's Chronicle* and *Poets & Writers*. Copies of winning books available from Small Press Distribution and directly from the Ashland University Bookstore online. The Ashland Poetry Press publishes 2-4 books of poetry/year. Deadline: April 30 (annually). 2013 judge: Alicia Ostriker.

◐ SOUL MAKING KEATS LITERARY COMPETITION

The Webhallow House, 1544 Sweetwood Dr., Broad-moor Vlg CA 94015-2029. **E-mail:** SoulKeats@mail. com. **Website:** www.soulmakingcontest.us. **Contact:** Eileen Malone, Award Director. Annual open contest offers cash prizes in each of 13 literary categories, including poetry and prose poem. Competition receives 600 entries/year. Names of winners and judges are posted on website. Winners announced in January by SASE and on website. Winners are invited to read at the Koret Auditorium, San Francisco. Event is televised. Deadline: November 30. Prizes: 1st Prize: $100; 2nd Prize: $50; 3rd Prize: $25.

◐ THE SOW'S EAR CHAPBOOK COMPETITION

The Sow's Ear Review, P.O. Box 127, Millwood VA 22646. (540)955-3955. **E-mail:** rglesman@gmail. com. **Website:** www.sows-ear.kitenet.net. **Contact:** Robert G. Lesman, managing editor. *The Sow's Ear Poetry Review* sponsors an annual chapbook competition. Open to adults. Deadline: May 1 (postmark). Prize: Offers $1,000, publication as the spring issue of the magazine, 25 author's copies, and distribution to subscribers.

◐ THE SOW'S EAR POETRY COMPETITION

The Sow's Ear Review, P.O. Box 127, Millwood VA 22646. **E-mail:** rglesman@gmail.com. **Website:** www.sows-ear.kitenet.net. **Contact:** Robert G. Lesman, managing editor. Deadline: November 1. Prize: $1,000, publication, and the option of publication for approximately twenty finalists.

● SPARK QUARTERLY WRITING CONTEST

Spark: A Creative Anthology (Empire & Great Jones Creative Arts Foundation), 13024 S. 3100 W, Riverton UT 84065. **E-mail:** editor@sparkanthology.org. **Website:** www.SparkAnthology.org/contests. **Contact:** Brian Lewis, contest director. "This contest is open to any writer without restriction on age, location, genre, or previous publication credits. We encourage both established and emerging writers to participate. Prizes are awarded for excellent poetry and excellent prose, with no regard to the entrant's previous publication experience. Prose includes both fiction and nonfiction, and poetry includes all forms and meters." "Grand Prize (one each for Poetry and Prose) always includes cash and publication." Judged by "staff of *Spark: A Creative Anthology* plus two previously-published professional writers as 'Guest Judges' who are not on Spark staff. Guest Judges change with each contest."

○ STEVENS POETRY MANUSCRIPT CONTEST

NFSPS Stevens Poetry Manuscript Competition, 3520 State Road 56, Mechanicsburg OH 43044. **E-mail:** downejm@auburn.edu. **Website:** www.nfsps.org. **Contact:** Amy Jo Zook, Chair. National Federation of State Poetry Societies (NFSPS) offers annual award of $1,000, publication of ms, and 50 author's copies for the winning poetry manuscript by a single author. Submission Period: August 1-October 15. Prize: $1,000, publication and 50 copies of the book.

THE ELIZABETH MATCHETT STOVER MEMORIAL AWARD

Southwest Review, Southern Methodist University, P.O. Box 750374, Dallas TX 75275-0374. (214)768-1037. **Fax:** (214)768-1408. **E-mail:** swr@mail.smu.edu. **Website:** www.smu.edu/southwestreview. **Contact:** Jennifer Cranfill, senior editor, and Willard Spiegelman, editor-in-chief. "Offered annually to the best works of poetry that have appeared in the magazine in the previous year. Please note that mss are submitted for publication, not for the prizes themselves. Guidelines for SASE and online." $300 Judged by Jennifer Cranfill and Willard Spiegelman.
TIPS "Not an open contest. Annual prize in which winners are chosen from published pieces during the preceding year."

● STROKESTOWN INTERNATIONAL POETRY COMPETITION

Strokestown International Poetry Festival, Strokestown Poetry Festival Office, Strokestown, County Roscommon , Ireland. (+353) 71 9633759. **E-mail:** director@strokestownpoetry.org. **Website:** www.strokestownpoetry.org. **Contact:** Martin Dyar, Director. This annual competition was established to promote excellence in poetry and participation in the reading and writing of it. Acquires first publication rights. Deadline: January .Prize: €3,000 Judged by Iggy McGovern and Michael Schmidt

● MAY SWENSON POETRY AWARD

Utah State University Press, Swenson Poetry Award, 3078 Old Main Hill, Logan UT 84322-3078. (435)797-1362. **Fax:** (435)797-0313. **E-mail:** michael.spooner@usu.edu. **Website:** www.usupress.org. **Contact:** Michael Spooner, director. "This annual competition, named for May Swenson, honors her as one of America's most provocative and vital writers." Deadline: September 30. Prize: $1,000 and publication. Previous judges include Harold Bloom, Grace Schulman, Billy Collins, and Edward Field. See website for guidelines and the full series of Swenson volumes.

TEXAS INSTITUTE OF LETTERS BOB BUSH MEMORIAL AWARD FOR FIRST BOOK OF POETRY

Website: http://texasinstituteofletters.org. Offered annually for best first book of poetry published in previous year. Writer must have been born in Texas, have lived in the state at least 2 consecutive years at some time, or the subject matter should be associated with the state. See website for exact date $1,000.

THE TEXAS INSTITUTE OF LETTERS LITERARY AWARDS

E-mail: Betwx@aol.com. **Website:** www.texasinstituteofletters.org. The Texas Institute of Letters gives annual awards for books by Texas authors, including the Helen C. Smith Memorial Award for Best Book of Poetry. Books must have been first published in the year in question, and entries may be made by authors or by their publishers. Complete guidelines and award information available on website.

● TIGER'S EYE POETRY CHAPBOOK CONTEST

Tiger's Eye Press, P.O. Box 9723, Denver CO 80209. (541)285-8355. **E-mail:** tigerseyepoet@yahoo.com.

Website: www.tigerseyejournal.com. **Deadline:** August 31 (postmark). Submissions accepted starting April 1. Prize: $100 and 25 copies.

◑ LENA-MILES WEVER TODD POETRY SERIES BOOK COMPETITION

Pleiades Press, Lena-Miles Wever Todd Poetry Prize, Dept of English, Martin 336, University of Central Missouri, Warrensburg MO 64093. (660)543-8106. **E-mail:** pleiades@ucmo.edu. **Website:** www.ucmo.edu/pleiades/. **Contact:** Wayne Miller, editor. The annual Lena-Miles Wever Todd Poetry Series Book Competition is open to all American writers, regardless of previous publication. Submission must be unpublished as a collection, but individual poems may have been previously published elsewhere. Submit at least 48 pages of poetry (one copy). Include 2 cover sheets: one with ms title, poet's name, address, and phone number; the second with ms title only. Also include acknowledgments page for previously published poems. Include SASE for results; for an additional large SASE with $1.28 postage affixed, entrant will receive a copy of the winning book. Guidelines available for SASE or on website. **Deadline:** November 15. **Prize:** $2,000 and the winning collection will be published in paperback and nationally distributed.

◑ TUFTS POETRY AWARDS

Claremont Graduate University, Claremont Graduate University, School of Arts & Humanities, 831 N. Dartmouth Ave., Claremont CA 91711-6165. (909)621-8612. **Website:** www.cgu.edu/tufts. **Contact:** Wendy Martin, program director. "Unlike many literary awards, which are coronations for a successful career or body of work, the Kingsley Tufts Poetry Award was created to both honor the poet and provide the resources that allow artists to continue working towards the pinnacle of their craft." "Any poet will tell you that the only thing more rare than meaningful recognition is a meaningful payday. For two outstanding poets each year, the Kingsley and Kate Tufts awards represent both." **Deadline:** must be submitted between September 1 and August 31. **Prize:** $100,000 for the Kingsley Tufts Poetry Award and $10,000 for the Kate Tufts Discovery Award.

◑ UTMOST CHRISTIAN POETRY CONTEST

Utmost Christian Writers Foundation, 121 Morin Maze, Edmonton Alberta T6K 1V1, Canada. (780)265-4650. **E-mail:** nnharms@telusplanet.net.

Website: www.utmostchristianwriters.com. **Contact:** Nathan Harms, executive director. Utmost is founded on — and supported by — the dreams, interests and aspirates of individual people. **Deadline:** February 28. **Prizes:** 1st Place: $1,000; 2nd Place: $500; 10 prizes of $100 are offered for honorable mention; $300 for best rhyming poem and $200 for an honorable mention rhyming poem. Judged by a committee of the Directors of Utmost Christian Writers Foundation (who work under the direction of Barbara Mitchell, chief judge).

TIPS "Besides providing numerous resources for Christian writers and poets, Utmost also provides a marketplace where Christian writers and poets can sell their work. Please follow our guidelines. We receive numerous unsuitable submissions from writers. We encourage writers to submit suitable material. The best way to do this is to read the guidelines specific to your project—poetry, book reviews, articles—and then take time to look at the material we have already published in that area. The final step is to evaluate your proposed submission in comparison to the material we have used previously. If you complete these steps and strongly feel that your material is appropriate for us, we encourage you to submit it. Please use the submission link on the appropriate Web page. For example, if you are submitting a poem, please click the 'Poetry Gallery' link and use the submission link 'Poetry Guidelines'. If you fail to follow these instructions, it's possible your submission will be lost."

◎ DANIEL VARUJAN AWARD

New England Poetry Club, 654 Green St., Apt. 2, Cambridge MA 02139. **E-mail:** contests@nepoetryclub.org. **Website:** www.nepoetryclub.org. **Contact:** NEPC contest coordinator. "For a poem on any subject, worthy of poet Daniel Varujan who was executed by the Ottoman Turks in the 1915 genocide of the Armenian population. Jailed while awaiting execution he finished a manuscript of sweet pastoral poems." **Deadline:** May 31 **Prize:** $1,000. Judges are well-known poets and sometimes winners of previous NEPC contests.

○ MARICA AND JAN VILCEK PRIZE FOR POETRY

Bellevue Literary Review, New York University School of Medicine, OBV-A612, 550 First Ave., New York NY 10016. (212)263-3973. **E-mail:** info@BLReview.org. **Website:** www.BLReview.org. **Contact:** Stacy Bodziak. The annual Marica and Jan Vilcek Prize for Poetry recognizes outstanding writing related to themes of health, healing, illness, the mind, and the body. All entries will be considered for publication. No previously published poems (including Internet publication). Submit up to 3 poems (5 pages maximum). Electronic (online) submissions only; combine all poems into 1 document and use first poem as document title. See guidelines for additional submission details. Guidelines available for SASE or on website. July 1 Offers $1,000 for best poem and publication in *Bellevue Literary Review*. Previous judges include Mark Doty, Cornelius Eady, Naomi Shihab Nye, and Tony Hoagland.

WERGLE FLOMP HUMOR POETRY CONTEST

Winning Writers, 351 Pleasant St., PMB 222, Northampton MA 01060. (866)946-9748. **Fax:** (413)280-0539. **E-mail:** adam@winningwriters.com. **Website:** www.winningwriters.com. **Contact:** Adam Cohen. "This annual contest seeks today's best humor poems. One poem of any length should be submitted. The poem should be in English. Inspired gibberish is also accepted. See website for guidelines, examples, and to submit your poem. Nonexclusive right to publish submissions on WinningWriters.com, in e-mail newsletter, and in press releases." April 1 $2,500 in prizes, with a top prize of $1,000. Jendi Reiter.

TIPS "Submissions may be previously published and may be entered in other contests. Competition receives about 2,000 entries/year. Winners are announced on August 15 at WinningWriters.com. Entrants who provide a valid e-mail address will also receive notification."

⊙ WESTERN AUSTRALIAN PREMIER'S BOOK AWARDS

State Library of Western Australia, Alexander Library Bldg., Perth Cultural Centre, Perth WA 6000, Australia. **Website:** www.slwa.wa.gov.au/pba.html. Competition receives about 30-40 entries in poetry category per year. Winners announced in September each year at a presentation given by the Premier of Western Australia. "The contest is organized by the State Library of Western Australia, with money provided by the Western Australian State Government to support literature." January 31 each year $10,000 AUD for a published book of poetry. Winner also eligible for Premier's Prize of $25,000 AUD.

WILLA LITERARY AWARD

E-mail: pamtartaglio@yahoo.com. **Website:** www.womenwritingthewest.org. **Contact:** Pam Tartaglio. The WILLA Literary Award honors the best in literature featuring women's or girls' stories set in the West published each year. Women Writing the West (WWW), a nonprofit association of writers and other professionals writing and promoting the Women's West, underwrites and presents the nationally recognized award annually (for work published between January 1 and December 31). The award is named in honor of Pulitzer Prize winner Willa Cather, one of the country's foremost novelists. The award is given in 7 categories: Historical fiction, contemporary fiction, original softcover fiction, creative nonfiction, scholarly nonfiction, poetry, and children's/young adult fiction/nonfiction. Deadline: February 1. Winner receives $100 and a trophy. Finalist receives a plaque. Award announcement is in early August, and awards are presented to the winners and finalists at the annual WWW Fall Conference. Judged by professional librarians not affiliated with WWW.

THE J. HOWARD AND BARBARA M.J. WOOD PRIZE

Poetry, 61 W. Superior St., Chicago IL 60654. (312)787-7070. **Fax:** (312)787-6650. **E-mail:** editors@poetry-magazine.org. **Website:** www.poetrymagazine.org. Offered annually for poems published in *Poetry* during the preceding year (October-September). Upon acceptance, *Poetry* licenses exclusive worldwide first serial rights, including electronic rights, for publication, as well as non-exclusive rights to reprint, reuse, and archive the work, in any format, in perpetuity. Copyright reverts to author upon first publication. Prize: $5,000.

⊙ WORKING PEOPLE'S POETRY COMPETITION

Blue Collar Review, P.O. Box 11417, Norfolk VA 23517. **E-mail:** red-ink@earthlink.net. **Website:** www.partisanpress.org. The Working People's Poetry Competition offers $100 and a 1-year subscription to *Blue Collar Review* (see separate listing in Magazines/Journals) and "1 year posting of winning poem on our website. Poetry should be typed as you would like to see it published, with your name and address on each page. Include cover letter with entry." Guidelines available on website. Deadline: May 15

WRITER'S DIGEST ANNUAL WRITING COMPETITION

10151 Carver Road, Suite #200, Blue Ash OH 45242. (715)445-4612, ext. 13430. **E-mail:** WritersDigest-WritingCompetition@fwmedia.com. **Website:** www.writersdigest.com. Annual competition with several categories, including rhyming poetry and non-rhyming poetry. Deadline: June 3. Prizes: Thousands of dollars in prizes.

WRITER'S DIGEST INTERNATIONAL SELF-PUBLISHED BOOK AWARDS

10151 Carver Road, Suite #200, Blue Ash OH 45242. (715)445-4612, ext. 13430. **E-mail:** WritersDigest-WritingCompetition@fwmedia.com. **Website:** www.writersdigest.com. **Contact:** Nicole Florence. Contest open to all English-language self-published books for which the authors have paid the full cost of publication, or the cost of printing has been paid for by a grant or as part of a prize. Categories include: Mainstream/Literary Fiction, Genre Fiction, Nonfiction, Inspirational (spiritual/new age), Life Stories (biographies/autobiographies/family histories/memoirs), Children's Books, Reference Books (directories/encyclopedias/guide books), Poetry, Middle-Grade/Young Adult Books. Deadline: May 1; Early bird deadline: April 1. Grand Prize: $3,000, promotion in *Writer's Digest* and *Publisher's Weekly*, and 10 copies of the book will be sent to major review houses with a guaranteed review in *Midwest Book Review*; 1st Place (9 winners): $1,000, promotion in *Writer's Digest*; Honorable Mentions: promotion in *Writer's Digest*, $50 of Writer's Digest Books, and a certificate.

GRANTS:

State & Provincial

//

Arts councils in the United States and Canada provide assistance to artists (including poets) in the form of fellowships or grants. These grants can be substantial and confer prestige upon recipients; however, only state or province residents are eligible. Because deadlines and available support vary annually, query first (with a SASE) or check websites for guidelines.

UNITED STATES ARTS AGENCIES

ALABAMA STATE COUNCIL ON THE ARTS, 201 Monroe St., Montgomery AL 36130-1800. (334)242-4076. E-mail: staff@arts.alabama.gov. Website: www.arts.state.al.us.

ALASKA STATE COUNCIL ON THE ARTS, 411 W. Fourth Ave., Suite 1-E, Anchorage AK 99501-2343. (907)269-6610 or (888)278-7424. E-mail: aksca_info@eed.state.ak.us. Website: www.eed.state.ak.us/aksca.

ARIZONA COMMISSION ON THE ARTS, 417 W. Roosevelt St., Phoenix AZ 85003-1326. (602)771-6501. E-mail: info@azarts.gov. Website: www.azarts.gov.

ARKANSAS ARTS COUNCIL, 1500 Tower Bldg., 323 Center St., Little Rock AR 72201. (501)324-9766. E-mail: info@arkansasarts.com. Website: www.arkansasarts.com.

CALIFORNIA ARTS COUNCIL, 1300 I St., Suite 930, Sacramento CA 95814. (916)322-6555. E-mail: info@caartscouncil.com. Website: www.cac.ca.gov.

COLORADO COUNCIL ON THE ARTS, 1625 Broadway, Suite 2700, Denver CO 80202. (303)892-3802. E-mail: online form. Website: www.coloarts.state.co.us.

COMMONWEALTH COUNCIL FOR ARTS AND CULTURE (Northern Mariana Islands), P.O. Box 5553, CHRB, Saipan MP 96950. (670)322-9982 or (670)322-9983. E-mail: galaidi@vzpacifica.net. Website: www.geocities.com/ccacarts/ccacwebsite.html.

CONNECTICUT COMMISSION ON CULTURE & TOURISM, Arts Division, One Financial Plaza, 755 Main St., Hartford CT 06103. (860)256-2800. Website: www.cultureandtourism.org.

DELAWARE DIVISION OF THE ARTS, Carvel State Office Bldg., 4th Floor, 820 N. French St., Wilmington DE 19801. (302)577-8278 (New Castle Co.) or (302)739-5304 (Kent or Sussex Counties). E-mail: delarts@state.de.us. Website: www.artsdel.org.

DISTRICT OF COLUMBIA COMMISSION ON THE ARTS & HUMANITIES, 410 Eighth St. NW, 5th Floor, Washington DC 20004. (202)724-5613. E-mail: cah@dc.gov. Website: http://dcarts.dc.gov.

FLORIDA ARTS COUNCIL, Division of Cultural Affairs, R.A. Gray Building, Third Floor, 500 S. Bronough St., Tallahassee FL 32399-0250. (850)245-6470. E-mail: info@florida-arts.org. Website: http://dcarts.dc.gov.

GEORGIA COUNCIL FOR THE ARTS, 260 14th St., Suite 401, Atlanta GA 30318. (404)685-2787. E-mail: gaarts@gaarts.org. Website: www.gaarts.org.

GUAM COUNCIL ON THE ARTS & HUMANITIES AGENCY, P.O. Box 2950, Hagatna GU 96932. (671)646-2781. Website: www.guam.net.

HAWAII STATE FOUNDATION ON CULTURE & THE ARTS, 2500 S. Hotel St., 2nd Floor, Honolulu HI 96813. (808)586-0300. E-mail: ken.hamilton@hawaii.gov. Website: http.state.hi.us/sfca.

IDAHO COMMISSION ON THE ARTS, 2410 N. Old Penitentiary Rd., Boise ID 83712. (208)334-2119 or (800)278-3863. E-mail: info@arts.idaho.gov. Website: www.arts.idaho.gov.

ILLINOIS ARTS COUNCIL, James R. Thompson Center, 100 W. Randolph, Suite 10-500, Chicago IL 60601. (312)814-6750. E-mail: iac.info@illinois.gov. Website: www.state.il.us/agency/iac.

INDIANA ARTS COMMISSION, 150 W. Market St., Suite 618, Indianapolis IN 46204. (317)232-1268. E-mail: IndianaArtsCommission@iac.in.gov. Website: www.in.gov/arts.

INSTITUTE OF PUERTO RICAN CULTURE, P.O. Box 9024184, San Juan PR 00902-4184. (787)724-0700. E-mail: www@icp.gobierno.pr. Website: www.icp.gobierno.pr.

IOWA ARTS COUNCIL, 600 E. Locust, Des Moines IA 50319-0290. (515)281-6412. Website: www.iowaartscouncil.org.

KANSAS ARTS COMMISSION, 700 SW Jackson, Suite 1004, Topeka KS 66603-3761. (785)296-3335. E-mail: KAC@arts.state.ks.us. Website: http://arts.state.ks.us.

KENTUCKY ARTS COUNCIL, 21st Floor, Capital Plaza Tower, 500 Mero St., Frankfort KY 40601-1987. (502)564-3757 or (888)833-2787. E-mail: kyarts@ky.gov. Website: http://artscouncil.ky.gov.

LOUISIANA DIVISION OF THE ARTS, Capitol Annex Bldg., 1051 N. 3rd St., 4th Floor, Room #420, Baton Rouge LA 70804. (225)342-8180. Website: www.crt.state.la.us/arts.

MAINE ARTS COMMISSION, 193 State St., 25 State House Station, Augusta ME 04333-0025. (207)287-2724. E-mail: MaineArts.info@maine.gov. Website: www.mainearts.com.

MARYLAND STATE ARTS COUNCIL, 175 W. Ostend St., Suite E, Baltimore MD 21230. (410)767-6555. E-mail: msac@msac.org. Website: www.msac.org.

MASSACHUSETTS CULTURAL COUNCIL, 10 St. James Ave., 3rd Floor, Boston MA 02116-3803. (617)727-3668. E-mail: mcc@art.state.ma.us. Website: www.massculturalcouncil.org.

MICHIGAN COUNCIL OF HISTORY, ARTS, AND LIBRARIES, 702 W. Kalamazoo St., P.O. Box 30705, Lansing MI 48909-8205. (517)241-4011. E-mail: artsinfo@michigan.gov. Website: www.michigan.gov/hal/0,1607,7-160-17445_19272---,00.html.

MINNESOTA STATE ARTS BOARD, Park Square Court, 400 Sibley St., Suite 200, St. Paul MN 55101-1928. (651)215-1600 or (800)866-2787. E-mail: msab@arts.state.mn.us. Website: www.arts.state.mn.us.

MISSISSIPPI ARTS COMMISSION, 501 N. West St., Suite 701B, Woolfolk Bldg., Jackson MS 39201. (601)359-6030. Website: www.arts.state.ms.us.

MISSOURI ARTS COUNCIL, 815 Olive St., Suite 16, St. Louis MO 63101-1503. (314)340-6845 or (866)407-4752. E-mail: moarts@ded.mo.gov. Website: www.missouriartscouncil.org.

MONTANA ARTS COUNCIL, 316 N. Park Ave., Suite 252, Helena MT 59620-2201. (406)444-6430. E-mail: mac@mt.gov. Website: www.art.state.mt.us.

NATIONAL ASSEMBLY OF STATE ARTS AGENCIES, 1029 Vermont Ave. NW, 2nd Floor, Washington DC 20005. (202)347-6352. E-mail: nasaa@nasaa-arts.org. Website: www.nasaa-arts.org.

NEBRASKA ARTS COUNCIL, 1004 Farnam St., Plaza Level, Omaha NE 68102. (402)595-2122 or (800)341-4067. Website: www.nebraskaartscouncil.org.

NEVADA ARTS COUNCIL, 716 N. Carson St., Suite A, Carson City NV 89701. (775)687-6680. E-mail: online form. Website: http://dmla.clan.lib.nv.us/docs/arts.

NEW HAMPSHIRE STATE COUNCIL ON THE ARTS, 21/2 Beacon St., 2nd Floor, Concord NH 03301-4974. (603)271-2789. Website: www.nh.gov/nharts.

NEW JERSEY STATE COUNCIL ON THE ARTS, 225 W. State St., P.O. Box 306, Trenton NJ 08625. (609)292-6130. Website: www.njartscouncil.org.

NEW MEXICO ARTS, DEPT. OF CULTURAL AFFAIRS, P.O. Box 1450, Santa Fe NM 87504-1450. (505)827-6490 or (800)879-4278. Website: www.nmarts.org.

NEW YORK STATE COUNCIL ON THE ARTS, 175 Varick St., New York NY 10014. (212)627-4455. Website: www.nysca.org.

NORTH CAROLINA ARTS COUNCIL, 109 East Jones St., Cultural Resources Building, Raleigh NC 27601. (919)807-6500. E-mail: ncarts@ncmail.net. Website: www.ncarts.org.

NORTH DAKOTA COUNCIL ON THE ARTS, 1600 E. Century Ave., Suite 6, Bismarck ND 58503. (701)328-7590. E-mail: comserv@state.nd.us. Website: www.state.nd.us/arts.

OHIO ARTS COUNCIL, 727 E. Main St., Columbus OH 43205-1796. (614)466-2613. Website: www.oac.state.oh.us.

OKLAHOMA ARTS COUNCIL, Jim Thorpe Building, 2101 N. Lincoln Blvd., Suite 640, Oklahoma City OK 73105. (405)521-2931. E-mail: okarts@arts.ok.gov. Website: www.arts.state.ok.us.

OREGON ARTS COMMISSION, 775 Summer St. NE, Suite 200, Salem OR 97301-1280. (503)986-0082. E-mail: oregon.artscomm@state.or.us. Website: www.oregonartscommission.org.

PENNSYLVANIA COUNCIL ON THE ARTS, 216 Finance Bldg., Harrisburg PA 17120. (717)787-6883. Website: www.pacouncilonthearts.org.

RHODE ISLAND STATE COUNCIL ON THE ARTS, One Capitol Hill, Third Floor, Providence RI 02908. (401)222-3880. E-mail: info@arts.ri.gov. Website: www.arts.ri.gov.

SOUTH CAROLINA ARTS COMMISSION, 1800 Gervais St., Columbia SC 29201. (803)734-8696. E-mail: info@arts.state.sc.us. Website: www.southcarolinaarts.com.

SOUTH DAKOTA ARTS COUNCIL, 711 E. Wells Ave., Pierre SD 57501-3369. (605)773-3301. E-mail: sdac@state.sd.us. Website: www.artscouncil.sd.gov.

TENNESSEE ARTS COMMISSION, 401 Charlotte Ave., Nashville TN 37243-0780. (615)741-1701. Website: www.arts.state.tn.us.

TEXAS COMMISSION ON THE ARTS, E.O. Thompson Office Building, 920 Colorado, Suite 501, Austin TX 78701. (512)463-5535. E-mail: front.desk@arts.state.tx.us. Website: www.arts.state.tx.us.

UTAH ARTS COUNCIL, 617 E. South Temple, Salt Lake City UT 84102-1177. (801)236-7555. Website: http://arts.utah.gov.

VERMONT ARTS COUNCIL, 136 State St., Drawer 33, Montpelier VT 05633-6001. (802)828-3291. E-mail: online form. Website: www.vermontartscouncil.org.

VIRGIN ISLANDS COUNCIL ON THE ARTS, 5070 Norre Gade, St. Thomas VI 00802-6872. (340)774-5984. Website: http://vicouncilonarts.org.

VIRGINIA COMMISSION FOR THE ARTS, Lewis House, 223 Governor St., 2nd Floor, Richmond VA 23219. (804)225-3132. E-mail: arts@arts.virginia.gov. Website: www.arts.state.va.us.

WASHINGTON STATE ARTS COMMISSION, 711 Capitol Way S., Suite 600, P.O. Box 42675, Olympia WA 98504-2675. (360)753-3860. E-mail: info@arts.wa.gov. Website: www.arts.wa.gov.

WEST VIRGINIA COMMISSION ON THE ARTS, The Cultural Center, Capitol Complex, 1900 Kanawha Blvd. E., Charleston WV 25305-0300. (304)558-0220. Website: www.wvculture.org/arts.

WISCONSIN ARTS BOARD, 101 E. Wilson St., 1st Floor, Madison WI 53702. (608)266-0190. E-mail: artsboard@arts.state.wi.us. Website: www.arts.state.wi.us.

WYOMING ARTS COUNCIL, 2320 Capitol Ave., Cheyenne WY 82002. (307)777-7742. E-mail: ebratt@state.wy.us. Website: http://wyoarts.state.wy.us.

CANADIAN PROVINCES ARTS AGENCIES

ALBERTA FOUNDATION FOR THE ARTS, 10708-105 Ave., Edmonton AB T5H 0A1. (780)427-9968. Website: www.affta.ab.ca/index.shtml.

BRITISH COLUMBIA ARTS COUNCIL, P.O. Box 9819, Stn. Prov. Govt., Victoria BC V8W 9W3. (250)356-1718. E-mail: BCArtsCouncil@gov.bc.ca. Website: www.bcartscouncil.ca.

THE CANADA COUNCIL FOR THE ARTS, 350 Albert St., P.O. Box 1047, Ottawa ON K1P 5V8. (613)566-4414 or (800)263-5588 (within Canada). Website: www.canadacouncil.ca.

MANITOBA ARTS COUNCIL, 525-93 Lombard Ave., Winnipeg MB R3B 3B1. (204)945-2237 or (866)994-2787 (in Manitoba). E-mail: info@artscouncil.mb.ca. Website: www.artscouncil.mb.ca.

NEW BRUNSWICK ARTS BOARD (NBAB), 634 Queen St., Suite 300, Fredericton NB E3B 1C2. (506)444-4444 or (866)460-2787. Website: www.artsnb.ca.

NEWFOUNDLAND & LABRADOR ARTS COUNCIL, P.O. Box 98, St. John's NL A1C 5H5. (709)726-2212 or (866)726-2212. E-mail: nlacmail@nfld.net. Website: www.nlac.nf.ca.

NOVA SCOTIA DEPARTMENT OF TOURISM, CULTURE, AND HERITAGE, Culture Division, 1800 Argyle St., Suite 601, P.O. Box 456, Halifax NS B3J 2R5. (902)424-4510. E-mail: cultaffs@gov.ns.ca. Website: www.gov.ns.ca/dtc/culture.

ONTARIO ARTS COUNCIL, 151 Bloor St. W., 5th Floor, Toronto ON M5S 1T6. (416)961-1660 or (800)387-0058 (in Ontario). E-mail: info@arts.on.ca. Website: www.arts.on.ca.

PRINCE EDWARD ISLAND COUNCIL OF THE ARTS, 115 Richmond St., Charlottetown PE C1A 1H7. (902)368-4410 or (888)734-2784. E-mail: info@peiartscouncil.com. Website: www.peiartscouncil.com.

QUÉBEC COUNCIL FOR ARTS & LITERATURE, 79 boul. René-Lévesque Est, 3e étage, Quebec QC G1R 5N5. (418)643-1707 or (800)897-1707. E-mail: info@calq.gouv.qc.ca. Website: www.calq.gouv.qc.ca.

THE SASKATCHEWAN ARTS BOARD, 2135 Broad St., Regina SK S4P 1Y6. (306)787-4056 or (800)667-7526 (Saskatchewan only). E-mail: sab@artsboard.sk.ca. Website: www.artsboard.sk.ca.

YUKON ARTS FUNDING PROGRAM, Cultural Services Branch, Dept. of Tourism & Culture, Government of Yukon, Box 2703 (L-3), Whitehorse YT Y1A 2C6. (867)667-8589 or (800)661-0408 (in Yukon). E-mail: arts@gov.yk.ca. Website: www.tc.gov.yk.ca/216.html.

CONFERENCES,
WORKSHOPS &
FESTIVALS

There are times when we want to immerse ourselves in learning. Or perhaps we crave a change of scenery, the creative stimulation of being around other artists, or the uninterrupted productivity of time alone to work.

That's what this section of *Poet's Market* is all about, providing a selection of writing conferences and workshops, artist colonies and retreats, poetry festivals, and even a few opportunities to go traveling with your muse. These listings give the basics: contact information, a brief description of the event, lists of past presenters, and offerings of special interest to poets. Contact an event that interests you for additional information, including up-to-date costs and housing details.

(Please note that most directors had not finalized their 2014 plans when we contacted them for this edition of *Poet's Market*. However, where possible, they provided us with their 2013 dates, costs, faculty names or themes to give you a better idea of what each event has to offer.)

Before you seriously consider a conference, workshop or other event, determine what you hope to get out of the experience. Would a general conference with one or two poetry workshops among many other types of sessions be acceptable? Or are you looking for something exclusively focused on poetry? Do you want to hear poets speak about poetry writing, or are you looking for a more participatory experience, such as a one-on-one critiquing session or a group workshop? Do you mind being one of hundreds of attendees, or do you prefer a more intimate setting? Are you willing to invest in the expense of traveling to a conference, or would something local better suit your budget? Keep these questions and others in mind as you read these listings, view Web sites and study conference brochures.

ABROAD WRITERS CONFERENCES

17363 Sutter Creek Rd., Sutter Creek CA 95685. (209)296-4050. **E-mail:** abroadwriters@yahoo. com. **Website:** www.abroad-crwf.com/index.html. "Abroad Writers Conferences are devoted to introducing our participants to world views here in the United States and Abroad. Throughout the world we invite several authors to come join us to give readings and to participate on a panel. Our discussion groups touch upon a wide range of topics from important issues of our times to publishing abroad and in the United States. Our objective is to broaden our cultural and scientific perspectives of the world through discourse and writing." Conferences are held throughout the year in various places worldwide. See website for scheduling details. Conference duration: 7-10 days. "Instead of being lost in a crowd at a large conference, Abroad Writers' Conference prides itself on holding small group meetings where participants have personal contact with everyone. Stimulating talks, interviews, readings, Q&A's, writing workshops, film screenings, private consultations and social gatherings all take place within a week to ten days. Abroad Writers' Conference promises you true networking opportunities and full detailed feedback on your writing."

COSTS/ACCOMMODATIONS Prices start at $2,750. Discounts and upgrades may apply. Participants must apply to program no later than 3 months before departure. To secure a place you must send in a deposit of $1,000. Balance must be paid in full twelve weeks before departure. See website for pricing details.

ADDITIONAL INFORMATION Agents participate in conference. Application is online at website.

AMERICAN CHRISTIAN WRITERS CONFERENCES

P.O. Box 110390, Nashville TN 37222-0390. (800)219-7483. **Fax:** (615)834-7736. **E-mail:** acwriters@aol.com. **Website:** www.acwriters.com. **Contact:** Reg Forder, director. ACW hosts dozens of annual two-day writers conferences and mentoring retreat across America taught by editors and professional freelance writers. These events provide excellent instruction, networking opportunities, and valuable one-on-one time with editors. Annual conferences promoting all forms of Christian writing (fiction, nonfiction, scriptwriting). Conferences are held between March and November during each year.

COSTS/ACCOMMODATIONS Special rates are available at the host hotel (usually a major chain like Holiday Inn). Costs vary based on conference. Prices also depend on whether it is a conference or a mentoring retreat.

ADDITIONAL INFORMATION Send a SASE for conference brochures/guidelines.

ART WORKSHOPS IN GUATEMALA

4758 Lyndale Ave. S., Minneapolis MN 55419-5304. (612)825-0747. **E-mail:** info@artguat.org. **Website:** www.artguat.org. **Contact:** Liza Fourre, director. Annual. Workshops held year-round. Maximim class size: 10 students per class.

COSTS/ACCOMMODATIONS All transportation and accommodations included in price of conference. See website. Includes tuition, lodging, breakfast, ground transportation.

ADDITIONAL INFORMATION Conference information available now. For brochure/guidelines visit website, e-mail or call. Accepts inquiries by e-mail, phone.

ASPEN SUMMER WORDS LITERARY FESTIVAL & WRITING RETREAT

Aspen Writers' Foundation, 110 E. Hallam St., #116, Aspen CO 81611. (970)925-3122. **Fax:** (970)925-5700. **E-mail:** info@aspenwriters.org. **Website:** www.aspenwriters.org. **Contact:** Natalie Lacy, programs coordinator. ASW is one part laboratory and one part theater. It is comprised of two tracks— the Writing Retreat and the Literary Festival — which approach the written word from different, yet complementary angles. The Retreat features introductory and intensive workshops with some of the nation's most notable writing instructors and includes literature appreciation symposia and professional consultations with literary agents and editors. The Writing Retreat supports writers in developing their craft by providing a winning combination of inspiration, skills, community, and opportunity. The Literary Festival is a booklover's bliss, where the written word takes center stage. Since 2005, each edition of the Festival has celebrated a particular literary heritage and culture by honoring the stories and storytellers of a specific region. Annual conference held the fourth week of June. Conference duration: 5 days. Average attendance: 150 at writing retreat; 300+ at literary festival.

COSTS/ACCOMMODATIONS Discount lodging at the conference site will be available. 2013 rates to be announced. Free shuttle around town. Check website each year for updates.

ADDITIONAL INFORMATION Check website for details on when to buy tickets and passes. Aspen Summer Words runs between June 16-21, 2013.

ATLANTIC CENTER FOR THE ARTS

1414 Art Center Ave., New Smyrna Beach FL 32168. (386)427-6975. **Fax:** (386)427-5669. **E-mail:** program@atlanticcenterforthearts.org. **Website:** www.atlanticcenterforthearts.org. Internship and residency programs. A Florida artist-in-residence program in which artists of all disciplines work with current prominent artists in a supportive and creative environment.

COSTS/ACCOMMODATIONS $850; $25 non-refundable application fee. Financial aid is availableParticipants responsible for all meals.Accommodations available on site. See website for application schedule and materials.

AUSTIN INTERNATIONAL POETRY FESTIVAL

(512)777-1888. **E-mail:** lynn@aipf.org. **E-mail:** james@aipf.org. **Website:** www.aipf.org. **Contact:** Ashley S. Kim, festival director. Annual Austin Internatinal Poetry Festival (AIPF) April 11-14, is open to the public. This four-day citywide, all-inclusive celebration of poetry and poets has grown to become "the largest non-juried poetry festival in the U.S." The festival will include up to 20 live local readings, youth anthology read, 20 poetry workshops, 5 open mics, 5 music and poetry presentations, two anthology competions and complete readings, two poetry slams, an all-night open mic and a poetry panel symposium. API projects over 250 registered poets from the international, national, state, and local areas

COSTS/ACCOMMODATIONS Includes anthology submission fee, program bio, scheduled reading at one of AIPF's 15 venues, participation in all events, 1 catered meal, workshop participation, and more.

ADDITIONAL INFORMATION Offers multiple poetry contests as part of festival. Guidelines available on website. Registration form available on website. "Largest non-juried poetry festival in the U.S.!"

BREAD LOAF WRITERS' CONFERENCE

(802)443-5286. **Fax:** (802)443-2087. **E-mail:** ncargill@middlebury.edu. **E-mail:** blwc@middlebury.edu. **Website:** www.middlebury.edu/blwc. **Contact:** Michael Collier, Director. Annual conference held in late August. Conference duration: 11 days. Offers workshops for fiction, nonfiction, and poetry. Agents, editors, publicists, and grant specialists will be in attendance.

COSTS/ACCOMMODATIONS Bread Loaf Campus in Ripton, Vermont. $2,714 (includes tuition, housing).

ADDITIONAL INFORMATION Conference Date: August 14-24. Location: mountain campus of Middlebury College. Average attendance: 230.

CAPE COD WRITERS CENTER ANNUAL CONFERENCE

P.O. Box 408, Osterville MA 02655. **E-mail:** writers@capecodwriterscenter.org. **Website:** www.capecodwriterscenter.org. **Contact:** Nancy Rubin Stuart, executive director. Duration: 5 days; first week in August. Offers workshops in fiction, commercial fiction, nonfiction, poetry, writing for children, humor, memoir, pitching your book, screenwriting, digital communications, getting published, ms evaluation, mentoring sessions with faculty. Held at Resort and Conference Center of Hyannis, Hyannis, MA.

COSTS/ACCOMMODATIONS Vary, depending on the number of courses selected.

CELEBRATION OF SOUTHERN LITERATURE

Southern Lit Alliance, 3069 S. Broad St., Suite 2, Chattanooga TN 37408-3056. (423)267-1218 or (800)267-4232. **Fax:** (423)267-1018. **E-mail:** srobinson@southernlitalliance.org. **Website:** www.southernlitalliance.org. **Contact:** Susan Robinson. "The Celebration of Southern Literature stands out because of its unique collaboration with the Fellowship of Southern Writers, an organization founded by towering literary figures like Eudora Welty, Cleanth Brooks, Walker Percy, and Robert Penn Warren to recognize and encourage literature in the South. The 2013 celebration marked 24 years since the Fellowship selected Chattanooga for its headquarters and chose to collaborate with the Celebration of Southern Literature. Up to 50 members of the Fellowship will participate in this year's event, discussing hot topics and reading from their latest works. The Fellowship will also award 11 literary prizes and induct 2 new members, making this event the place to discover up-and-coming voices in Southern literature. The Southern Lit Alliance's Celebration of Southern Literature attracts more than 1,000 readers and writers from all over the U.S. It strives to maintain an informal atmosphere where conversations will thrive, inspired by a common passion for the written word. The Southern Lit Alliance (formerly The Arts & Education Council) started as 1 of 12 pilot agencies founded by a Ford Foundation grant in 1952. The Alliance is the only organization of the 12 still in existence. The Southern Lit Alliance celebrates southern writers and readers through community education and innovative literary arts experiences."

FINE ARTS WORK CENTER

24 Pearl St., Provincetown MA 02657. (508)487-9960 ext. 103. **Fax:** (508)487-8873. **E-mail:** workshops@ fawc.org. **Website:** www.fawc.org. Weeklong workshops in creative writing and the visual arts. Location: The Fine Arts Work Center in Provincetown.

COSTS/ACCOMMODATIONS Summer Workshop Program fees range $600-725. Limited accommodations available at the Work Center for $675 for 6 nights. Additional accommodations available locally. Cost: $600-725/week, $675/week (housing).

ADDITIONAL INFORMATION See website for details and an application form.

⊕ HAIKU NORTH AMERICA CONFERENCE

1275 Fourth St. PMB #365, Santa Rosa CA 95404. **E-mail:** welchm@aol.com. **Website:** www.haikunorthamerica.com. **Contact:** Michael Dylan Welch. Biannual conference held August 14-18 on board the historic Queen Mary ocean liner, permanently docked in Long Beach, California. Haiku North America (HNA) is the largest and oldest gathering of haiku poets in the United States and Canada. There are no membership fees and HNA provides breaking news and interaction at the HNA blog. All haiku poets and interested parties are welcome. It is a long weekend of papers, panels, workshops, readings, performances, book sales, and much socialization with fellow poets, translators, scholars, editors, and publishers. Both established and aspiring haiku poets are welcome.

COSTS/ACCOMMODATIONS Typically around $200, including a banquet and some additional meals. Accommodations at discounted hotels nearby are an additional cost. Information available on website as details are finalized closer to the conference date.

HIGHLAND SUMMER CONFERENCE

Box 7014, Radford University, Radford VA 24142-7014. (540)831-5366. **Fax:** (540)831-5951. **E-mail:** tburriss@

radford.edu; rbderrick@radford.edu. **Website:** www. radford.edu/content/cehd/home/departments/appalachian-studies.html. **Contact:** Dr. Theresa Burriss, Ruth Derrick. The Highland Summer Writers' Conference is a one-week lecture-seminar workshop combination conducted by well-known guest writers. It offers the opportunity to study and practice creative and expository writing within the context of regional culture. The course is graded on Pass/Fail basis for undergraduates and letter grades for graduate students. It may be taken twice for credit. The class runs Monday through Friday 9 a.m.-noon and 1:30-4:30 p.m., with extended hours on Wednesday, and readings and receptions by resident teachers on Tuesday and Thursday evening in McConnell Library 7:30-9:30 p.m. The evening readings are free and open to the public.

COSTS/ACCOMMODATIONS "We do not have special rate arrangements with local hotels. We do offer accommodations on the Radford University campus in a recently refurbished residence hall."

ADDITIONAL INFORMATION Conference leaders typically critique work done during the one-week conference, and because of the one-week format, students will be asked to bring preliminary work when they arrive at the conference, as well as submit a portfolio following the conference. Brochures/guidelines are available in March by request.

HOFSTRA UNIVERSITY SUMMER WRITING WORKSHOPS

University College for Continuing Education, 250 Hofstra University, Hempstead NY 11549-2500. (516)463-7200. **Fax:** (516)463-4833. **E-mail:** ce@hofstra.edu. **Website:** hofstra.edu/academics/ce. **Contact:** Colleen Slattery, Senior Associate Dean. Hofstra University's 2-week Summer Writers Program, a cooperative endeavor of the Creative Writing Program, the English Department, and Hofstra University Continuing Education (Hofstra CE), offers 8 classes which may be taken on a noncredit or credit basis, for both graduate and undergraduate students. Led by master writers, the Summer Writing Program operates on the principle that true writing talent can be developed, nurtured and encouraged by writer-in-residence mentors. Through instruction, discussion, criticism and free exchange among the program members, writers begin to find their voice and their style. The program provides group and individual sessions for each writer. The Summer Writing Program includes a banquet, guest speakers, and exposure to authors such as Oscar Hijuelos, Robert Olen Butler (both Pulitzer Prize winners), Maurice Sendak, Cynthia Ozick, Nora Sayre, and Denise Levertov. Often agents, editors, and publishers make presentations during the conference, and authors and students read from published work and works in progress. These presentations and the conference banquet offer additional opportunities to meet informally with participants, master writers and guest speakers. Average attendance: 65. Conference offers workshops in short fiction, nonfiction, poetry, and occasionally other genres such as screenplay writing or writing for children. Site is the university campus on Long Island, 25 miles from New York City.

COSTS/ACCOMMODATIONS Free bus operates between Hempstead Train Station and campus for those commuting from New York City on the Long Island Rail Road. Dormitory rooms are available. Check website for current fees. Credit is available for undergraduate and graduate students. Choose one of 9 writing genres and spend two intensive weeks studying and writing in that genre.

ADDITIONAL INFORMATION Students entering grades 9-12 can now be part of the Summer Writers Program with a special section for high school students. Through exercises and readings, students will learn how to use their creative impulses to improve their fiction, poetry and plays and learn how to create cleaner and clearer essays. During this intensive 2-week course, students will experiment with memoir, poetry, oral history, dramatic form and the short story, and study how to use character, plot, point of view and language.

INDIANA UNIVERSITY WRITERS' CONFERENCE

464 Ballantine Hall, 1020 E. Kirkwood Ave., Bloomington IN 47405-7103. (812)855-1877. **Fax:** (812)855-9535. **E-mail:** writecon@indiana.edu. **Website:** www.indiana.edu/~writecon. **Contact:** Bob Bledsoe, director. Annual. Conference/workshops held in May. Average attendance: 115. "The Indiana University Writers' Conference believes in a craft-based teaching of fiction writing. We emphasize an exploration of creativity through a variety of approaches, offering workshop-based craft discussions, classes focusing on technique, and talks about the careers and concerns of a writing life." 2013 faculty: Alix Lambert, Scott Hutchins, Nathaniel Perry, Lloyd Suh.

COSTS/ACCOMMODATIONS Information on accommodations available on website. 2013: Workshop, $550/week; classes only, $300/week.

ADDITIONAL INFORMATION Fiction workshop applicants must submit up to 25 pages of prose. Registration information available for SASE, by e-mail, or on website. Spaces still available in all workshops and classes for 2013.

INTERNATIONAL CREATIVE WRITING CAMP

111-11th Ave.SW, Minot ND 58701-6081. (701)838-8472. **Fax:** (701)838-1351. **E-mail:** info@internationalmusiccamp.com. **Website:** www.internationalmusiccamp.com. **Contact:** Joseph Alme, interim director. Writer and illustrator workshops geared toward beginner, intermediate and advanced levels. **Open to students.** Sessions offered include those covering poems, plays, mystery stories, essays. Workshop held June 23-29, 2013. Registration limited to 40. The summer camp location at the International Peace Garden on the Border between Manitoba and North Dakota is an ideal site for creative thinking. Excellent food, housing, and recreation facilities are available.

COSTS/ACCOMMODATIONS Before May 1, $375; after May 1—$390. Write for more information.

IOWA SUMMER WRITING FESTIVAL

The University of Iowa, C215 Seashore Hall, University of Iowa, Iowa City IA 52242. (319)335-4160. **Fax:** (319)335-4743. **E-mail:** iswfestival@uiowa.edu. **Website:** uiowa.edu/~iswfest. Annual festival held in June and July. Conference duration: Workshops are 1 week or a weekend. Average attendance: Limited to 12 people/class, with over 1,500 participants throughout the summer. "We offer courses across the genres: novel, short story, poetry, essay, memoir, humor, travel, playwriting, screenwriting, writing for children, and women's writing. Held at the University of Iowa campus." Speakers have included Marvin Bell, Lan Samantha Chang, John Dalton, Hope Edelman, Katie Ford, Patricia Foster, Bret Anthony Johnston, Barbara Robinette Moss, among others.

COSTS/ACCOMMODATIONS Accommodations available at area hotels. Information on overnight accommodations available by phone or on website. $590 for full week; $305 for weekend workshop. Housing and meals are separate.

ADDITIONAL INFORMATION Brochures are available in February. Inquire via e-mail or on website.

JACKSON HOLE WRITERS CONFERENCE

PO Box 1974, Jackson WY 83001. (307)413-3332. **E-mail:** nicole@jacksonholewritersconference.com. **Website:** jacksonholewritersconference.com. Annual conference held June 27-29. Conference duration: 4 days. Average attendance: 110. Covers fiction, creative nonfiction, and young adult and offers ms critiques from authors, agents, and editors. Agents in attendance will take pitches from writers. Paid manuscript critique programs are available.

COSTS/ACCOMMODATIONS $365 if registered by May 12. Accompanying teen writer: $175. Pre-Conference Writing Workshop: $150.

ADDITIONAL INFORMATION Held at the Center for the Arts in Jackson, Wyoming and online.

KENYON REVIEW WRITERS WORKSHOP

Kenyon College, Gambier OH 43022. (740)427-5207. **Fax:** (740)427-5417. **E-mail:** kenyonreview@kenyon.edu; writers@kenyonreview.org. **Website:** www.kenyonreview.org. **Contact:** Anna Duke Reach, director. Annual 8-day workshop held in June. Participants apply in poetry, fiction, or creative nonfiction, and then participate in intensive daily workshops which focus on the generation and revision of significant new work. Held on the campus of Kenyon College in the rural village of Gambier, Ohio. Workshop leaders have included David Baker, Ron Carlson, Rebecca McClanahan, Meghan O'Rourke, Linda Gregorson, Dinty Moore, Tara Ison, Jane Hamilton, Lee K. Abbott, and Nancy Zafris.

COSTS/ACCOMMODATIONS The workshop operates a shuttle to and from Gambier and the airport in Columbus, Ohio. Offers overnight accommodations. Participants are housed in Kenyon College student housing. The cost is covered in the tuition. $1,995; includes tuition, room and board.

ADDITIONAL INFORMATION Application includes a writing sample. Admission decisions are made on a rolling basis. Workshop information is available online at www.kenyonreview.org/workshops in November. For brochure send e-mail, visit website, call, fax. Accepts inquiries by SASE, e-mail, phone, fax.

KUNDIMAN POETRY RETREAT

P.O. Box 4248, Sunnyside NY 11104. **E-mail:** info@kundiman.org. **Website:** www.kundiman.org. **Contact:** June W. Choi, executive director. Held annualy June 19-23 at Fordham University's Rose Hill campus.

"Opento Asian American poets. Renowned faculty will conduct workshops and provide one-on-one mentorship sessions with fellows. Readings and informal social gatherings will also be scheduled. Fellows selected based on sample of 6-8 poems and short essay answer. Applications should be received between December 15-February 1."

COSTS/ACCOMMODATIONS Room and board is free to accepted Fellows. $350

ADDITIONAL INFORMATION Additional information, guidelines, and online application available on website.

MENDOCINO COAST WRITERS CONFERENCE

1211 Del Mar Dr., Fort Bragg CA 95437. (707)937-9983. **E-mail:** info@mcwc.org. **Website:** www.mcwc.org. Annual conference held in July. Average attendance: 80. Provides workshops for fiction, nonfiction, and poetry. Held at a small community college campus on the northern Pacific Coast. Workshop leaders have included Kim Addonizio, Lynne Barrett, John Dufresne, John Lescroart, Ben Percy, Luis Rodriguez, and Ellen Sussman. Agents and publishers will be speaking and available for meetings with attendees.

COSTS/ACCOMMODATIONS Information on overnight accommodations is made available. $525+ (includes panels, meals, 2 socials with guest readers, 4 public events, 3 morning intensive workshops in 1 of 6 subjects, and a variety of afternoon panels and lectures).

ADDITIONAL INFORMATION Emphasis is on writers who are also good teachers. Registration opens March 15. Send inquiries via e-mail.

MONTEVALLO LITERARY FESTIVAL

Sta. 6420, University of Montevallo, Montevallo AL 35115. (205)665-6420. **Fax:** (205)665-6422. **E-mail:** murphyj@montevallo.edu. **Website:** www.montevallo.edu/english. **Contact:** Dr. Jim Murphy, director. Takes place annually, April 12.

COSTS/ACCOMMODATIONS Offers overnight accommodations at Ramsay Conference Center on campus. Call (205)665-6280 for reservations. Free on-campus parking. Additional information available at www.montevallo.edu/cont_ed/ramsay.shtm. Readings are free. Readings, plus lunch, reception, and dinner is $20. Master Class only is $30. Master Class with everything else is $50.

ADDITIONAL INFORMATION To enroll in a fiction workshop, contact Bryn Chancellor (bchancellor@montevallo.edu). Information for upcoming festival available in February For brochure, visit website. Accepts inquiries by mail (with SASE), e-mail, phone, and fax. Editors participate in conference. "This is a friendly, relaxed festival dedicated to bringing literary writers and readers together on a personal scale." Poetry workshop participants submit up to 5 pages of poetry; e-mail as Word doc to Jim Murphy (murphyj@montevallo.edu) at least 2 weeks prior to festival.

JENNY MCKEAN MOORE COMMUNITY WORKSHOPS

English Department, George Washington University, 801 22nd St. NW, Rome Hall, Suite 760, Washington DC 20052. (202) 994-6180. **Fax:** (202) 994-7915. **E-mail:** tvmallon@gwu.edu. **Website:** www.gwu.edu/~english/creative_jennymckeanmoore.html. **Contact:** Thomas Mallon, director of creative writing. Workshop held each semester at the university. Average attendance: 15. Concentration varies depending on professor—usually fiction or poetry. The Creative Writing department brings an established poet or novelist to campus each year to teach a writing workshop for GW students and a free community workshop for adults in the larger Washington community. Details posted on website in June, with an application deadline at the end of August or in early September.

ADDITIONAL INFORMATION Admission is competitive and by ms.

MOUNT HERMON CHRISTIAN WRITERS CONFERENCE

P.O. Box 413, Mount Hermon CA 95041. **E-mail:** info@mounthermon.org. **Website:** mounthermon.org. Annual professional conference (always held over the Palm Sunday weekend, Friday noon through Tuesday noon). Average attendance: 450. Sponsored by and held at the 440-acre Mount Hermon Christian Conference Center near San Jose, California in the heart of the coastal redwoods, we are a broad-ranging conference for all areas of Christian writing, including fiction, nonfiction, fantasy, children's, teen, young adult, poetry, magazines, inspirational and devotional writing. This is a working, how-to conference, with Major Morning tracks in all genres (including a track especially for teen writers), and as many as 20 optional workshops each afternoon. Faculty-to-student ratio is about 1 to 6. The bulk of our more than

70 faculty members are editors and publisher representatives from major Christian publishing houses nationwide. Speakers have included T. Davis Bunn, Debbie Macomber, Jerry Jenkins, Bill Butterworth, Dick Foth and others.

COSTS/ACCOMMODATIONS Registrants stay in hotel-style accommodations. Meals are buffet style, with faculty joining registrants. See website for cost updates. Registration fees include tuition, all major morning sessions, keynote sessions, and refreshment breaks. Room and board varies depending on choice of housing options. Costs vary from $617 to $1565 based on housing rates.

ADDITIONAL INFORMATION "The residential nature of our conference makes this a unique setting for one-on-one interaction with faculty/staff. There is also a decided inspirational flavor to the conference, and general sessions with well-known speakers are a highlight. Registrants may submit 2 works for critique in advance of the conference, then have personal interviews with critiquers during the conference. All conference information is online by December 1 of each year. Send inquiries via e-mail. Tapes of past conferences are also available online."

NAPA VALLEY WRITERS' CONFERENCE

Napa Valley College, 1088 College Ave., St. Helena CA 94574. (707)967-2900. **Website:** www.napawritersconference.org. **Contact:** John Leggett and Anne Evans, program directors. Established 1981. Annual weeklong event, July 28-August 2. Location: Upper Valley Campus in the historic town of St. Helena, 25 miles north of Napa in the heart of the valley's wine growing community. Excellent cuisine provided by Napa Valley Cooking School. Average attendance: 48 in poetry and 48 in fiction. "Serious writers of all backgrounds and experience are welcome to apply." Offers poets workshops, lectures, faculty readings, ms critiques, and meetings with editors. "Poetry session provides the opportunity to work both on generating new poems and on revising previously written ones."

COSTS/ACCOMMODATIONS Total participation fee is $900.

ADDITIONAL INFORMATION The conference is held at the Upper Valley Campus of Napa Valley College, located in the heart of California's Wine Country. During the conference week, attendees' meals are provided by the Napa Valley Cooking School, which offers high quality, intensive training for aspiring chefs.

The goal of the program is to provide each student with hands-on, quality, culinary and pastry skills required for a career in a fine-dining establishment. The disciplined and professional learning environment, availability of global externships, low student teacher ratio and focus on sustainability make the Napa Valley Cooking School unique.

THE NEW LETTERS WEEKEND WRITERS CONFERENCE

University of Missouri-Kansas City, 5101 Rockhill Rd., Kansas City MO 64110-2499. (816)235-1168. **Fax:** (816)235-2611. **E-mail:** newletters@umkc.edu. **Website:** http://cas.umkc.edu/ce/. **Contact:** Robert Stewart, director. Annual conference held in late June. Conference duration: 3 days. Average attendance: 75. The conference brings together talented writers in many genres for seminars, readings, workshops, and individual conferences. The emphasis is on craft and the creative process in poetry, fiction, screenwriting, playwriting, and journalism, but the program also deals with matters of psychology, publications, and marketing. The conference is appropriate for both advanced and beginning writers. The conference meets at the university's beautiful Diastole Conference Center. Two- and 3-credit hour options are available by special permission from the director, Robert Stewart. **COSTS/ACCOMMODATIONS** Registrants are responsible for their own transportation, but information on area accommodations is available. Participants may choose to attend as a noncredit student or they may attend for 1 hour of college credit from the University of Missouri-Kansas City. Conference registration includes Friday evening reception and keynote speaker, Saturday and Sunday continental breakfast and lunch. **ADDITIONAL INFORMATION** Those registering for college credit are required to submit a ms in advance. Ms reading and critique are included in the credit fee. Those attending the conference for noncredit also have the option of having their ms critiqued for an additional fee. Brochures are available for a SASE after March. Accepts inquiries by e-mail and fax.

PHILADELPHIA WRITERS' CONFERENCE

(215) 619-7422. **E-mail:** dresente@mc3.edu. **E-mail:** info@pwcwriters.org. **Website:** www.pwcwriters. org. **Contact:** Dana Resente. Annual. Conference held June 7-9. Average attendance: 160-200. Conference covers many forms of writing: novel, short story, genre fiction, nonfiction book, magazine writing, blogging, juvenile, poetry. **COSTS/ACCOMMODATIONS** Holiday Inn, Independence Mall, Fourth and Arch Streets, Philadelphia, PA 19106-2170. "Hotel offers discount for early registration." Advance registration is $205; walk-in registration is $225. The banquet and buffet are $40 each. Master classes are $50. **ADDITIONAL INFORMATION** Sponsors contest. "Length is generally 2,500 words for fiction or nonfiction. 1st Prize, in addition to cash and certificate, gets free tuition for following year." Also offers ms critique. Accepts inquiries by e-mail and SASE. Agents and editors attend conference. Visit us on the web for further agent and speaker details."

PIMA WRITERS' WORKSHOP

Pima College, 2202 W. Anklam Rd., Tucson AZ 85709. (520)206-6084. **Fax:** (520)206-6020. **E-mail:** mfiles@ pima.edu. **Contact:** Meg Files, director. Writer conference geared toward beginner, intermediate and advanced levels. **Open to students.** The conference features presentations and writing exercises on writing and publishing stories for children and young adults, among other genres. Annual conference. Workshop held in May. Cost: $100 (can include ms critique). Participants may attend for college credit. Meals and accommodations not included. Features a dozen authors, editors, and agents talking about writing and publishing fiction, nonfiction, poetry, and stories for children. Write for more information.

POETRY WEEKEND INTENSIVES

40 Post Ave., Hawthorne NJ 07506. (973)423-2921. **Fax:** (973)523-6085. **E-mail:** mariagillan@verizon. net. **Website:** www.mariagillan.com; www.mariagillan.blogspot.com. **Contact:** Maria Mazziotti Gillan, executive director. Usually held 2 times/year in June and December. Average attendance: 26. **COSTS/ACCOMMODATIONS** Location: generally at St. Marguerite's Retreat House, Mendham, NJ; also several other convents and monasteries. $425, including meals. Offers a $25 early bird discount. Housing in on-site facilities included in the $425 price. **ADDITIONAL INFORMATION** Individual poetry critiques available. Poets should bring poems to weekend. Registration form available for SASE or by fax or e-mail. Maria Mazziotti Gillan is the director of the Creative Writing Program of Binghamton University-State University of New York, exec. director of the

Poetry Center at Passaic County Community College, and edits Paterson Literary Review. Laura Boss is the editor of *Lips* magazine. Fifteen professional development credits are available for each weekend.

SAN DIEGO STATE UNIVERSITY WRITERS' CONFERENCE

(619)594-2517. **Fax:** (619)594-8566. **E-mail:** sdsuwritersconference@mail.sdsu.edu. **Website:** ces.sdsu.edu/writers. Annual conference held in January/February. Conference duration: 2 days. Average attendance: 375. Covers fiction, nonfiction, scriptwriting and e-books. Held at the Doubletree Hotel in Mission Valley. Each year the conference offers a variety of workshops for the beginner and advanced writers. This conference allows the individual writer to choose which workshop best suits his/her needs. In addition to the workshops, editor reading appointments and agent/editor consultation appointments are provided so attendees may meet with editors and agents one-on-one to discuss specific questions. A reception is offered Saturday immediately following the workshops, offering attendees the opportunity to socialize with the faculty in a relaxed atmosphere. Last year, approximately 60 faculty members attended.

COSTS/ACCOMMODATIONS Attendees must make their own travel arrangements. Approximately $365-485

SANTA BARBARA WRITERS CONFERENCE

27 W. Anapamu St., Suite 305, Santa Barbara CA 93101. (805)568-1516. **E-mail:** info@sbwriters.com. **Website:** www.sbwriters.com. Annual conference held June 8-13. Average attendance: 200. Covers fiction, nonfiction, journalism, memoir, poetry, playwriting, screenwriting, travel writing, young adult, children's literature, humor, and marketing. Speakers have included Ray Bradbury, William Styron, Eudora Welty, James Michener, Sue Grafton, Charles M. Schulz, Clive Cussler, Fannie Flagg, Elmore Leonard, and T.C. Boyle. Agents will appear on a panel; in addition, there will be an agents and editors day that allows writers to pitch their projects in one-on-one meetings.

COSTS/ACCOMMODATIONS Hyatt Santa Barbara. Conference registration is $550 on or before March 16 and $625 after March 16.

ADDITIONAL INFORMATION Register online or contact for brochure and registration forms.

○ SASKATCHEWAN FESTIVAL OF WORDS

217 Main St. N., Moose Jaw SK S6J 0W1, Canada. **Website:** www.festivalofwords.com. Annual 4-day event, third week of July (2013 dates: July 18-21). Location: Moose Jaw Library/Art Museum complex in Crescent Park. Average attendance: about 4,000 admissions. "Canadian authors up close and personal for readers and writers of all ages inmystery, poetry, memoir, fantasy, graphic novels, history, and novel. Each summer festival includes 60 events within 2 blocks of historic Main Street. Audience favorite activities include workshops for writers, audience readings, drama,performance poetry, concerts, panels, and music."

COSTS/ACCOMMODATIONS Information available at www.templegardens.sk.ca, campgrounds, and bed and breakfast establishments. Complete information about festival presenters, events, costs, and schedule also available on website.

SCHOOL OF THE ARTS AT RHINELANDER UW-MADISON CONTINUING STUDIES

21 N Park St., 7th Floor, Madison WI 53715-1218. (608)262-7389. **E-mail:** lkaufman@dcs.wisc.edu. **Website:** continuingstudies.wisc.edu/lsa/soa/. "Each summer for nearly 50 years, more than 250 people have gathered in northern Wisconsin for a week of study, performance, exhibits, and other creative activities. More than 50 workshops in writing, body/mind/spirit; food and fitness; art and folk art; music; and digital media are offered. Participants can choose from any and all 1-, 2-, and 5-day classes to craft their own mix for creative exploration and renewal." Dates: July 20-24. Location: James Williams Middle School and Rhineland High School, Rhinelander, WI. Average attendance: 250.

COSTS/ACCOMMODATIONS Informational available from Rhinelander Chamber of Commerce. Ranges from $20-300 based on workshops.

SEWANEE WRITERS' CONFERENCE

735 University Ave., 119 Gailor Hall, Stamler Center, Sewanee TN 37383-1000. (931) 598-1654. **E-mail:** allatham@sewanee.edu. **Website:** www.sewaneewriters.org. **Contact:** Adam Latham. Annual conference held July 23 - August 4. Average attendance: 144. "We offer genre-based workshops in fiction, poetry, and playwriting. The conference uses the facilities of Sewanee: The University of the South. The university is a collec-

tion of ivy-covered Gothic-style buildings located on the Cumberland Plateau in mid-Tennessee. Editors, publishers, and agents structure their own presentations, but there is always opportunity for questions from the audience." A score of writing professionals will visit. The Conference will offer its customary Walter E. Dakin Fellowships and Tennessee Williams Scholarships as well as awards in memory of Stanley Elkin, Donald Justice, Howard Nemerov, Father William Ralston, Peter Taylor, Mona Van Duyn, and John N. Wall. Additional scholarships have been made possible by Georges and Anne Borchardt and Gail Hochman. Each participant—whether contributor, scholar, or fellow—receives financial support.

COSTS/ACCOMMODATIONS Participants are housed in single rooms in university dormitories. Bathrooms are shared by small groups. Motel or B&B housing is available, but not abundantly so. $1,000 for tuition and $700 for room, board, and activity costs

SOUTH COAST WRITERS CONFERENCE

Southwestern Oregon Community College, P.O. Box 590, 29392 Ellensburg Ave., Gold Beach OR 97444. (541)247-2741. **Fax:** (541)247-6247. **E-mail:** scwc@socc.edu. **Website:** www.socc.edu/scwriters. Annual conference held Presidents Day weekend in February. Conference duration: 2 days. Covers fiction, poetry, children's, nature, songwriting, and marketing. William Sullivan is the next scheduled keynote speaker, and presenters include Linda Barnes, Merritt "Biff" Barnes, Judy Cox, Bruce Holbert, Elizabeth Lyon, Carolyn J. Rose, Johnny Shaw, Lauren Sheehan, William Sullivan, and Bob Welch.

ADDITIONAL INFORMATION See website for cost and additional details.

STEAMBOAT SPRINGS WRITERS CONFERENCE

Steamboat Springs Arts Council, Eleanor Bliss Center for the Arts at the Depot, 1001 13th St., Steamboat Springs CO 80487. (970)879-9008. **Fax:** (970)879-8138. **E-mail:** info@steamboatwriters.com. **Website:** www.steamboatwriters.com. **Contact:** Susan de Wardt. Annual conference held in mid-July. Conference duration: 1 day. Average attendance: approximately 35. Attendance is limited. Featured areas of instruction change each year. Held at the restored train Depot. Speakers have included Carl Brandt, Jim Fergus, Avi, Robert Greer, Renate Wood, Connie Willis, Margaret Coel, and Kent Nelson.

COSTS/ACCOMMODATIONS Tuition: $50 early registration, $65 after May 4

ADDITIONAL INFORMATION Brochures are available in April for a SASE. Send inquiries via e-mail.

SUMMER WRITING PROGRAM

Naropa University, 2130 Arapahoe Ave., Boulder CO 80302. (303)245-4600. **Fax:** (303)546-5287. **E-mail:** swpr@naropa.edu. **Website:** www.naropa.edu/swp. **Contact:** Kyle Pivarnik, administrative coordinator. Annual. Workshops held July 1-27. Workshop duration: 4 weeks. Average attendance: 250. Offers college credit. Accepts inquiries by e-mail, phone."With 13 workshops to choose from each of the 4 weeks of the program, students may study poetry, prose, hybrid/cross-genre writing, small press printing, or book arts." Site: "All workshops, panels, lectures and readings are hosted on the Naropa University main campus. Located in downtown Boulder, the campus is within easy walking distance of restaurants, shopping, and the scenic Pearl Street Mall."

COSTS/ACCOMMODATIONS Housing is available at Snow Lion Apartments. Additional info is available on the housing website: www.naropa.edu/student-life/housing/index.php. In 2013: $500/week, $2,000 for all 4 weeks (non-credit students).

ADDITIONAL INFORMATION Writers can elect to take the Summer Writing Program for noncredit, graduate, or undergraduate credit. The registration procedure varies, so consider whether or not you'll be taking the SWP for academic credit. All participants can elect to take any combination of the first, second, third, and/or fourth weeks. To request a catalog of upcoming program or to find additional information, visit www.naropa.edu/swp. Naropa University alsowelcomes participants with disabilities. Contact Andrea Rexilius at (303)546-5296 or arexilius@naropa.edu before May 15 to inquire about accessibility and disability accommodations needed to participate fully in this event.

TAOS SUMMER WRITERS' CONFERENCE

Department of English Language and Literature, MSC 03 2170, 1 University of New Mexico, Albuquerque NM 87131-0001. (505)277-5572. **Fax:** (505)277-2950. **E-mail:** taosconf@unm.edu. **Website:** www.unm.edu/~taosconf. **Contact:** Sharon Oard Warner. Annual conference held July 14-21. Offers workshops in novel writing, short story writing, screenwriting, poetry, creative nonfiction, travel writing, historical fiction, memoir, and revision. Participants may also schedule a consultation with a visiting agent/editor.

COSTS/ACCOMMODATIONS Held at the Sagebrush Inn and Conference Center. Weeklong workshop registrations are $650

☾ THE SCHOOL FOR WRITERS SUMMER WORKSHOP

The Humber School for Writers, Humber Institute of Technology & Advanced Learning, 3199 Lake Shore Blvd. W., Toronto ON M8V 1K8, Canada. (416)675-6622. **E-mail:** antanas.sileika@humber.ca; hilary.higgins@humber.ca. **Website:** www.creativeandperformingarts.humber.ca/content/writers.html. The School for Writers Summer Workshop has moved to the fall with the International Festival of Authors. Workshop the last week in October through first week in November. Conference duration: 1 week. Average attendance: 100. New writers from around the world gather to study with faculty members to work on their novels, short stories, poetry, or creative nonfiction. Agents and editors participate in conference. Include a work-in-progress with your registration. Faculty has included Martin Amis, David Mitchell, Rachel Kuschner, Peter Carey, Roddy Doyle, Tim O'Brien, Andrea Levy, Barry Unsworth, Edward Albee, Ha Jin, Julia Glass, Mavis Gallant, Bruce Jay Friedman, Isabel Huggan, Alistair MacLeod, Lisa Moore, Kim Moritsugu, Francine Prose, Paul Quarrington, Olive Senior, and D.M. Thomas, Annabel Lyon, Mary Gaitskill, M. G. Vassanji.

COSTS/ACCOMMODATIONS Nearby hotels are available. around $800 (in 2013). Some limited scholarships are available.

ADDITIONAL INFORMATION Accepts inquiries by e-mail, phone, and fax.

UNIVERSITY OF NORTH DAKOTA WRITERS CONFERENCE

(701)777-3321. **E-mail:** writersconference@und.nodak.edu. **Website:** www.undwritersconference.org. Established 1970. Annual 4- to 5-day event. 2011 dates: March 29-April 2. Location: the University of North Dakota Memorial Union. Average attendance: 3,000-5,000. "Some individual events have as few as 20, some over 1,000." Annual conference held March 19-23. Offers panels, readings, and films focused around a specific theme. Almost all events take place in the UND Memorial Union, which has a variety of small rooms and a 1,000-seat main hall. Past speakers include Art Spiegelman, Truman Capote, Sir Salman Rushdie, Allen Ginsberg, Alice Walker, and Louise Erdrich.

COSTS/ACCOMMODATIONS All events are free and open to the public. Accommodations available at area hotels. Information on overnight accommodations available on website. All events are free and open to the public. Donations accepted.

ADDITIONAL INFORMATION Schedule and other information available on website.

VERMONT STUDIO CENTER

P.O. Box 613, 80 Pearl Street, Johnson VT 05656. (802)635-2727. **Fax:** (802)635-2730. **E-mail:** info@vermontstudiocenter.org. **Website:** www.vermontstudiocenter.org. **Contact:** Gary Clark, Writing Program Director. From 2-12 weeks, year-round; most residents stay for 4 weeks. Community size: 50+ writers and visual artists/month. Founded by artists in 1984, the Vermont Studio Center is the largest international artists' and writers' Residency Program in the United States, hosting 50 visual artists and writers each month from across the country and around the world. The Studio Center provides 4-12 week studio residencies on an historic 30-building campus along the Gihon River in Johnson, Vermont, a village in the heart of the northern Green Mountains.

COSTS/ACCOMMODATIONS "The cost of a 4-week residency is $3,750. Generous fellowship and grant assistance available. "Accommodations available on site. "Residents live in single rooms in ten modest, comfortable houses adjacent to the Red Mill Building. Rooms are simply furnished and have shared baths. Complete linen service is provided. The Studio Center is unable to accommodate guests at meals, overnight guests, spouses, children or pets."

ADDITIONAL INFORMATION Fellowships application deadlines are February 15, June 15 and October 1. Writers encouraged to visit website for more information. May also e-mail, call, fax.

WESLEYAN WRITERS CONFERENCE

Wesleyan University, 294 High St., Room 207, Middletown CT 06459. (860)685-3604. **Fax:** (860)685-2441. **E-mail:** agreene@wesleyan.edu. **Website:** www.wesleyan.edu/writing/conference. Annual conference held June 12-16. Average attendance: 100. Focuses on the novel, fiction techniques, short stories, poetry, screenwriting, nonfiction, literary journalism, memoir, mixed media work and publishing. The conference is held on the campus of Wesleyan University, in the hills overlooking the Connecticut River. Features a faculty of award-winning writers, seminars and readings of new fiction, poetry, nonfiction and mixed media forms - as well as guest lectures on a range of topics including publishing. Both new and experienced writers are welcome. Participants may attend seminars in all genres. Speakers have included Esmond Harmsworth (Zachary Schuster Agency), Daniel Mandel (Sanford J. Greenburger Associates), Dorian Karchmar, Amy Williams (ICM and Collins McCormick), Mary Sue Rucci (Simon & Schuster), Denise Roy (Simon & Schuster), John Kulka (Harvard University Press), Julie Barer (Barer Literary) and many others. Agents will be speaking and available for meetings with attendees. Participants are often successful in finding agents and publishers for their mss. Wesleyan participants are also frequently featured in the anthology *Best New American Voices*.

COSTS/ACCOMMODATIONS Meals are provided on campus. Lodging is available on campus or in town.

ADDITIONAL INFORMATION Ms critiques are available, but not required. Scholarships and teaching fellowships are available, including the Joan Jakobson Awards for fiction writers and poets; and the Jon Davidoff Scholarships for nonfiction writers and journalists. Inquire via e-mail, fax, or phone.

WESTERN RESERVE WRITERS & FREELANCE CONFERENCE

7700 Clocktower Dr., Kirtland OH 44094. (440) 525-7812. **E-mail:** deencr@aol.com. **Website:** www.deannaadams.com. **Contact:** Deanna Adams, director/conference coordinator. Biannual. Last conference held September 28, 2013. Conference duration: 1 day or half-day. Average attendance: 120. "The Western Reserve Writers Conferences are designed for all writers, aspiring and professional, and offer presentations in all genres—nonfiction, fiction, poetry, essays, creative nonfiction, and the business of writing, including Web writing and successful freelance writing." Site: "Located in the main building of Lakeland Community College, the conference is easy to find and just off the I-90 freeway. The Fall 2013 conference featured top-notch presenters from newspapers and magazines, along with published authors, freelance writers, and professional editors. Presentations included developing issues in today's publishing and publishing options, turning writing into a lifelong vocation, as well as workshops on plotting, creating credible characters,

writing mysteries, romance writing, and tips on submissions, getting books into stores, and storytelling for both fiction and nonfiction writers. Included throughout the day are one-on-one editing consults, Q&A panel, and book sale/author signings."

COSTS/ACCOMMODATIONS Fall all-day conference includes lunch: $95. Spring half-day conference, no lunch: $69.

ADDITIONAL INFORMATION Brochures for the conferences are available by January (for spring conference) and July (for fall). Also accepts inquiries by e-mail and phone. Check Deanna Adams' website for all updates. Editors and agents often attend the conferences.

WINTER POETRY & PROSE GETAWAY

18 N. Richards Ave., Ventnor NJ 08406. (888)887-2105. **E-mail:** info@wintergetaway.com. **Website:** www.wintergetaway.com. **Contact:** Peter Murphy. Annual January conference at the Jersey Shore. "This is not your typical writers' conference. Advance your craft and energize your writing at the Winter Getaway. Enjoy challenging and supportive workshops, insightful feedback, and encouraging community. Choose from small, intensive workshops in memoir, novel, YA, nonfiction, and poetry."

COSTS/ACCOMMODATIONS See website or call for current fee information.

ADDITIONAL INFORMATION Previous faculty has included Julianna Baggott, Christian Bauman, Laure-Anne Bosselaar, Kurt Brown, Mark Doty (National Book Award winner), Stephen Dunn (Pulitzer Prize winner), Dorianne Laux, Carol Plum-Ucci, James Richardson, Mimi Schwartz, Terese Svoboda, and more.

WRITER'S DIGEST CONFERENCE

F+W Media, Inc., 10151 Carver Road, Suite 200, Blue Ash OH 45242. **E-mail:** jill.ruesch@fwmedia.com. **Website:** www.writersdigestconference.com. The Writer's Digest Conference features an amazing line up of speakers to help writers with the craft and business of writing. The most popular feature of this conference is the agent pitch slam, in which potential authors are given the ability to pitch their books directly to agents. For the 2013 conference, there will be more than 50 agents in attendance. The 2013 conference will be held in New York City on April 5-7. For more details, see the website.

WRITERS OMI AT LEDIG HOUSE

55 Fifth Ave., 15th Floor, New York NY 10003. (212)206-6114. **E-mail:** writers@artomi.org. **Website:** www.artomi.org. Residency duration: 2 weeks to 2 months. Average attendance and site: "Up to 20 writers per session—10 at a given time—live and write on the stunning 300 acre grounds and sculpture park that overlooks the Catskill Mountains." Deadline: October 20.

COSTS/ACCOMMODATIONS Residents provide their own transportation. Offers overnight accommodations.

ADDITIONAL INFORMATION "Agents and editors from the New York publishing community are invited for dinner and discussion. Bicycles, a swimming pool, and nearby tennis court are available for use."

WRITING WORKSHOP AT CASTLE HILL

1 Depot Rd., P.O. Box 756, Truro MA 02666-0756. **E-mail:** cherie@castlehill.org. **Website:** www.castlehill.org. Poetry, Fiction, Memoir workshops geared toward intermediate and advanced levels. **Open to students.** Workshops by Keith Althaus: Poetry; Anne Bernays: Elements of Fiction; Elizabeth Bradfield: Poetry in Plein Air & Broadsides and Beyond: Poetry as Public Art; Melanie Braverman: In Pursuit of Exactitude: Poetry; Josephine Del Deo: Preoccupation in Poetry; Martin Espada: Barbaric Yamp: A Poetry Workshop; Judy Huge: Finding the Me in Memoir; Justin Kaplan: Autobiography. See website under Summer 2011 Writers for dates and more information.

THE HELENE WURLITZER FOUNDATION

P.O. Box 1891, Taos NM 87571. (575)758-2413. **Fax:** (575)758-2559. **E-mail:** hwf@taosnet.com. **Website:** www.wurlitzerfoundation.org. **Contact:** Michael A. Knight, executive director. The Foundation's purpose is to provide a quiet haven where artists may pursue their creative endeavors without pressure to produce while they are in residence.

COSTS/ACCOMMODATIONS "Provides individual housing in fully furnished studio/houses (casitas), rent and utility free. Artists are responsible for transportation to and from Taos, their meals, and the materials for their work. Bicycles are provided upon request."

ORGANIZATIONS

There are many organizations of value to poets. These groups may sponsor workshops and contests, stage readings, publish anthologies and chapbooks or spread the word about publishing opportunities. A few provide economic assistance or legal advice. The best thing organizations offer, though, is a support system to which poets can turn for a pep talk, a hard-nosed (but sympathetic) critique of a manuscript or simply the comfort of talking and sharing with others who understand the challenges, and joys, of writing poetry.

Whether national, regional or as local as your library or community center, each organization has something special to offer. The listings in this section reflect the membership opportunities available to poets with a variety of organizations. Some groups provide certain services to both members and nonmembers.

To find out more about groups in your area (including those that may not be listed in *Poet's Market*), contact your YMCA, community center, local colleges and universities, public library and bookstores (and don't forget newspapers and the Internet). If you can't find a group that suits your needs, consider starting one yourself. You might be surprised to discover there are others in your locality who would welcome the encouragement, feedback and moral support of a writer's group.

THE ACADEMY OF AMERICAN POETS

75 Maiden Lane, Suite 901, New York NY 10038. (212)274-0343. **Fax:** (212)274-9427. **E-mail:** academy@poets.org. **Website:** www.poets.org. Executive Director: Tree Swenson. Established 1934. The Academy of American Poets was founded to support the nation's poets at all stages of their careers and to foster the appreciation of contemporary poetry. Levels of membership/dues: begin at $35/year (contributing member). Administers The Walt Whitman Award; The James Laughlin Award; The Harold Morton Landon Translation Award; The Lenore Marshall Poetry Prize; The Raiziss/de Palchi Translation Award; and The Wallace Stevens Award. Also awards The Fellowship of the Academy of American Poets ($25,000 to honor distinguished poetic achievement, no applications accepted) and The University & College Poetry Prizes. Publishes American Poet , an informative semiannual journal sent to all Academy members. The Academy's other programs include National Poetry Month (April), the largest literary celebration in the world; the Poetry Audio Archive, a 700-volume audio library capturing the voices of contemporary American poets for generations to come; an annual series of poetry readings and special events; and Poets. org, which includes thousands of poems, hundreds of essays and interviews, lesson plans for teachers, a National Poetry Almanac, a national Calendar of Events, and the National Poetry Map.

AMERICAN BOOKSELLERS FOUNDATION FOR FREE EXPRESSION

19 Fulton St., Suite 1504, New York NY 10038. (212)587-4025 ext. 15. **Fax:** (212)587-2436. **E-mail:** chris@abffe.com. **Website:** www.abffe.com. "The American Booksellers Foundation for Free Expression is the bookseller's voice in the fight against censorship. Founded by the American Booksellers Association, ABFFE's mission is to promote and protect the free exchange of ideas, particularly those contained in books, by opposing restrictions on the freedom of speech; issuing statements on significant free expression controversies; participating in legal cases involving First Amendment rights; collaborating with other groups with an interest in free speech; providing education about the importance of free expression to booksellers, other members of the book industry, politicians, the press and the public." Levels of membership/dues: $50. ABFFE is the bookseller's voice in all free speech controversies involving books and other written material. We alerted booksellers to the dangers posed by the USA Patriot Act and helped them communicate their concerns to Congress. We are also active on the local level. ABFFE opposes efforts to ban books in public schools and libraries and files amicus briefs in cases challenging school censorship. ABFFE is a sponsor of Banned Books Week. Additional information available on the website.

⊕ AMERICAN HAIKU ARCHIVES

California State Library, Library & Courts II Bldg, 900 N St., Sacramento CA 95814. **E-mail:** WelchM@aol.com. **Website:** www.americanhaikuarchives.org. **Contact:** Michael Dylan Welch. California State Library, Library & Courts II Bldg, Sacramento CA 95814. **E-mail:** WelchM@aol.com. **Website:** www.americanhaikuarchives.org. The American Haiku Archives, founded in 1996, is "the world's largest public collection of haiku and related poetry books and papers outside Japan." This repository is housed at the California State Library in Sacramento, California, and is dedicated to preserving the history of North American haiku. Materials are publicly available for research purposes through the library's California History Room. The American Haiku Archives actively seeks donations of books, journals, recordings, letters, ephemera, and personal papers relating to haiku poetry in all languages, but especially North American languages. The American Haiku Archives also appoints an honorary curator every July for a one-year term. The intent of this appointment is to honor leading haiku poets, translators, or scholars for their accomplishments or service in support of haiku poetry as a literary art. Past honorary curators have been Gary Snyder, Stephen Addiss, George Swede, H. F. Noyes, Hiroaki Sato, Francine Porad, Makoto Ueda, William J. Higginson, Leroy Kanterman, Lorraine Ellis Harr, Robert Spiess, Cor van den Heuvel, Jerry Kilbride, and Elizabeth Searle Lamb. Additional information about the archives is available on the website. The American Haiku Archives, founded in 1996, is "the world's largest public collection of haiku and related poetry books and papers outside Japan." This repository is housed at the California State Library in Sacramento, California, and is dedicated to preserving the history of North American haiku. Materials are publicly available for research purposes through the library's California History Room. The American Haiku Archives actively seeks donations of books, journals, recordings, letters, ephemera, and personal papers relating to haiku poetry in all languages, but especially North American languages. The American Haiku Archives also appoints an honorary curator every July for a one-year term. The intent of this appointment is to honor leading haiku poets, translators, or scholars for their accomplishments or service in support of haiku poetry as a literary art. Past honorary curators have been Gary Snyder, Stephen Addiss, George Swede, H. F. Noyes, Hiroaki Sato, Francine Porad, Makoto Ueda, William J. Higginson, Leroy Kanterman, Lorraine Ellis Harr, Robert Spiess, Cor van den Heuvel, Jerry Kilbride, and Elizabeth Searle Lamb. Additional information about the archives is available on the website.

ARIZONA AUTHORS ASSOCIATION

6145 West Echo Lane, Glendale AZ 85302. (623)847-9343. **E-mail:** info@azauthors.com. **Website:** www.azauthors.com. **Contact:** Toby Heathcotte, president. Purpose of organization: to offer professional, educational and social opportunities to writers and authors, and serve as a network. Members must be authors, writers working toward publication, agents, publishers, publicists, printers, illustrators, etc. Membership cost: $45/year writers; $30/year students; $60/year other professionals in publishing industry. Holds regular workshops and meetings. Publishes bimonthly newsletter and *Arizona Literary Magazine*. Sponsors Annual Literary Contest in poetry, essays, short stories, novels, and published books with cash prizes and awards bestowed at a public banquet. Winning entries are also published or advertised in the *Arizona Literary Magazine*. First and second place winners in poetry, essay and short story categories are entered in the Pushcart Prize. Winners in published categories receive free listings by www.fivestarpublications.com. Send SASE or view website for guidelines.

THE AUTHORS GUILD, INC.

31 E. 32nd St., 7th Floor, New York NY 10016. (212)564-5904. **Fax:** (212)564-5363. **E-mail:** staff@authorsguild.org. **Website:** www.authorsguild.org. **Contact:** Paul Aiken, executive director. Purpose of organization: to offer services and materials intended to help authors with the business and legal aspects of their work, including contract problems, copyright matters, freedom of expression and taxation. Guild has 8,000 members. Qualifications for membership:

Must be book author published by an established American publisher within 7 years or any author who has had 3 works (fiction or nonfiction) published by a magazine or magazines of general circulation in the last 18 months. Associate membership also available. Annual dues: $90. Different levels of membership include: associate membership with all rights except voting available to an author who has a firm contract offer or is currently negotiating a royalty contract from an established American publisher. "The Guild offers free contract reviews to its members. The Guild conducts several symposia each year at which experts provide information, offer advice and answer questions on subjects of interest and concern to authors. Typical subjects have been the rights of privacy and publicity, libel, wills and estates, taxation, copyright, editors and editing, the art of interviewing, standards of criticism and book reviewing. Transcripts of these symposia are published and circulated to members. The *Authors Guild Bulletin*, a quarterly journal, contains articles on matters of interest to writers, reports of Guild activities, contract surveys, advice on problem clauses in contracts, transcripts of Guild and League symposia and information on a variety of professional topics. Subscription included in the cost of the annual dues."

CALIFORNIA STATE POETRY SOCIETY

CSPS/CQ, P.O. Box 7126, Orange CA 92863. **E-mail:** pearlk@covad.net. **Website:** www.californiaquarterly.blogspot.com. **Contact:** The Membership Chair. The California State Poetry Society "is dedicated to the adventure of poetry and its dissemination. Although located in California, its members are from all over the U.S. and abroad." Levels of membership/dues: $30/year. Benefits include membership in the National Federation of State Poetry Societies (NFSPS); 4 issues of California Quarterly, *Newsbriefs*, and *The Poetry Letter*. Sponsors monthly and annual contests. Additional information available for SASE.

FURIOUS FLOWER POETRY CENTER

Website: www.jmu.edu/furiousflower. **Contact:** Joanne Gabbin, PhD, Founder/Exec. Director. (Specialized: African American poetry) MSC 3802, James Madison University, Harrisonburg VA 22807. (540)568-8883. **Fax:** (540)568-8888. **E-mail:** gabbinjv@jmu.edu. **Website:** www.jmu.edu/furiousflower. Established 1999. **Contact:** Joanne Gabbin, PhD, Executive Director. A non-membership-based organization. "The mission of the Furious Flower Poetry Center is to advance the genre of African American poetry by providing opportunities for education, research, and publication." Sponsors workshops and conferences related to African American poetry, including an annual poetry camp for children of the community. Sponsored national conferences in 1994 and 2004. Nationally known writers give readings that are open to the public. Sponsors open mic readings for the public; also sponsors the Central Shenandoah Valley Slam Team. Additional information available by e-mail or on website. The mission of the Furious Flower Poetry Center is to advance the genre of African American Poetry by providing opportunities for education, research, and publication. Furious Flower Poetry Center serves as a resource for the campus and local Harrisonburg community. The Center hosts visiting poets, sponsors poetry workshops for emerging poets, holds an annual poetry camp for children in the community, and produces scholarly texts, videos and DVDs on African American poetry. Furious Flower has sponsored two decade-defining conferences celebrating the African American poetic tradition.

GEORGIA POETRY SOCIETY

P.O. Box 2184, Columbia GA 31902. **E-mail:** gps@georgiapoetrysociety.org. **Website:** www.georgiapoetrysociety.org. Statewide organization open to any person who is in accord with the objectives to secure fuller public recognition of the art of poetry, stimulate an appreciation of poetry, and enhance the writing and reading of poetry. Currently has 200 members. Levels of membership/dues: Active, $30 ($40 family), fully eligible for all aspects of membership; Student, $15, does not vote or hold office, and must be full-time enrolled student through college level; Lifetime, same as Active but pays a one-time membership fee of $500, receives free anthologies each year, and pays no contest entry fees. Membership includes affiliation with NFSPS. Holds at least one workshop annually. Contests are sponsored throughout the year, some for members only. "Our contests have specific general rules, which should be followed to avoid the disappointment of disqualification. See the website for details." Publishes Georgia Poetry Society Newsletter, a quarterly, and The Reach of Song, an annual anthology devoted to contest-winning poems and member works. Each quarterly meeting (open to the public) features at least one poet of regional promi-

nence. Also sponsors a monthly open mic at the Columbus Library (Macon Rd) in Columbus, GA (open to the public). Sponsors Poetry in the Schools project. Additional information available on website. Statewide organization open to any person who is in accord with the objectives to secure fuller public recognition of the art of poetry, stimulate an appreciation of poetry, and enhance the writing and reading of poetry. Currently has 200 members. Levels of membership/dues: Active, $30 ($40 family), fully eligible for all aspects of membership; Student, $15, does not vote or hold office, and must be full-time enrolled student through college level; Lifetime, same as Active but pays a one-time membership fee of $500, receives free anthologies each year, and pays no contest entry fees. Membership includes affiliation with NFSPS. Holds at least one workshop annually.

HAIKU SOCIETY OF AMERICA

P.O. Box 31, Nassau NY 12123. **E-mail:** hsa-9AT@comcast.net. **Website:** www.hsa-haiku.org. The Haiku Society of America is composed of haiku poets, editors, critics, publishers, and enthusiasts dedicated to "promoting the creation and appreciation of haiku and related forms (haibun, haiga, renku, senryu, sequences, and tanka) among its members and the public." Currently has over 800 members. Levels of membership/dues: $33 U.S.; $30 seniors or full-time students (in North America); $35 USD in Canada and Mexico; $45 USD for all other areas. Membership benefits include a year's subscription (3 issues in 2011) to the Society's journal, Frogpond (see separate listing in Magazines/Journals), and to the quarterly HSA Newsletter Ripples; the annual information sheet; an annual address/e-mail list of HSA members; and eligibility to submit work to the members' anthology. Administers the following annual awards: The Harold G. Henderson Awards for haiku, The Gerald Brady Awards for senryu, The Bernard Lionel Einbond Awards for renku, The Merit Book Awards, and The Nicholas Virgilio Haiku Awards for youth. A haibun contest is being offered as well. Guidelines available in the newsletter or on website. Meets quarterly at various locations throughout the U.S. Additional information available for SASE or on website.

INTERNATIONAL WOMEN'S WRITING GUILD

International Women's Writing Guild, P.O. Box 810, Gracie Station, New York NY 10028. (212)737-

7536. **Fax:** (212)737-9469. **E-mail:** iwwg@iwwg.org; dirhahn@iwwg.org. **Website:** www.iwwg.org. **Contact:** Hannelore Hahn, founder/executive editor. IWWG is "a network for the personal and professional empowerment of women through writing." Qualifications: Open to any woman connected to the written word regardless of professional portfolio. Membership cost: $55/65 annually. "IWWG sponsors several annual conferences a year in all areas of the U.S. The major conference is held in June of each year at Yale University in New Haven, Connecticut. It is a weeklong conference attracting 350 women internationally." Also publishes a 32-page newsletter, *Network*, 4 times/year; offers dental and vision insurance at group rates, referrals to literary agents.

IOWA POETRY ASSOCIATION

2325 61st St., Des Moines IA 50322. (515)279-1106. **Website:** www.iowapoetry.com. Established 1945. **Contact:** Lucille Morgan Wilson, editor. Statewide organization open to "anyone interested in poetry, with a residence or valid address in the state of Iowa." Currently has about 425 members. Levels of membership/dues: Regular ($8/year) and Patron ($15 or more/year; "same services, but patron members contribute to cost of running the association"). Offerings include "semiannual workshops to which a poem may be sent in advance for critique; annual contest—also open to nonmembers—with no entry fee; IPA Newsletter , published 5 or 6 times/year, including a quarterly national publication listing of contest opportunities; and an annual poetry anthology, Lyrical Iowa , containing prize-winning and high-ranking poems from contest entries, available for $10 postpaid. No requirement for purchase to ensure publication." Semiannual workshops "are the only 'meetings' of the association." Additional information available for SASE or on website.

THE LIT

2026 Murray Hill, Suite 103, Cleveland OH 44106. **E-mail:** info@the-lit.org. **Website:** www.the-lit.org. **Contact:** Judith Mansour, Exec. Director. 2570 Superior Ave., Suite 203, Cleveland, OH 44114. **E-mail:** info@the-lit.org. **Website:** www.the-lit.org. Established 1974. **Contact:** Judith Mansour-Thomas, executive director. Founded "to foster a supportive community for poets and writers throughout Northern Ohio and to expand the audience for creative writing among the general public." Currently has 300 mem-

bers. Levels of membership/dues are regular: $35/year; students and seniors $25. Membership benefits include subscription to Muse Magazine and discounts on services and facilities at the Literary Center. The Literary Center offers classes and an event space for writers and readers. The Lit conducts a monthly workshop where poets can bring their work for discussion. Publishes a monthly calendar of literary events in NE Ohio; a quarterly magazine, Muse , which includes articles on the writing life, news, markets, and an annual writing contest in all genres; and 2 chapbooks/year featuring an anthology of work by area poets. "The Lit also sponsors a dramatic reading series, 'Poetry: Mirror of the Arts,' which unites poetry and other art forms performed in cultural settings; and 'Writers & Their Friends,' a biennial literary showcase of new writing (all genres), performed dramatically by area actors, media personalities, and performance poets." Additional information available for SASE, by e-mail, or on website.

LLENYDDIAETH CYMRU / LITERATURE WALES

(44)(29)2047-2266. **Fax:** (44)(29)2049-2930. **E-mail:** post@academi.org. **Website:** www.academi.org. Academi is the Welsh National Literature Promotion Agency and Society of Writers and is open to "the population of Wales and those outside Wales with an interest in Welsh writing." Currently has 2,000 members.Levels of membership/dues: associate, full, and fellow; £15/year (waged) or £7.50/year (unwaged). Offerings include promotion of readings, events, conferences, exchanges, tours; employment of literature-development workers; publication of a quarterly events magazine; publication of a literary magazine in Welsh (Taliesin). Sponsors conferences/workshops and contests/awards. Publishes A470: What's On In Literary Wales , a magazine appearing quarterly containing information on literary events in Wales. Academi is also a resident company of the Wales Millenium Centre, where it runs the Glyn Jones Centre, a resource centre for writers and the public. Additional information available for SASE (or SAE and IRC), by fax, e-mail, or on website.

THE LOFT LITERARY CENTER

Suite 200, Open Book, 1011 Washington Ave. S, Minneapolis MN 55414. (612)215-2575. **E-mail:** loft@loft.org. **Website:** www.loft.org. "The Loft is the largest and most comprehensive literary center in the country, serving both writers and readers with a variety of readings, Spoken Word performances, educational programs, contests and grants, and writing facilities." Supporting members (starting at $60/year - $25 for students/low income) receive benefits including discounted tuition, admission charges, and contest fees; check-out privileges at The Loft's Rachel Anne Gaschott Resource Library; rental access to the Book Club Meeting Room and writers' studios and more. Information on additional benefit levels, classes/workshops, contests and grants, and readings by local and national writers available at the website.

NATIONAL WRITERS ASSOCIATION

10904 S. Parker Rd., #508, Parker CO 80138. (303)841-0246. **Fax:** (303)841-2607. **E-mail:** natlwritersassn@hotmail.com. **Website:** www.nationalwriters.com. Purpose of organization: association for freelance writers. Qualifications for membership: associate membership—must be serious about writing; professional membership—must be published and paid writer (cite credentials). Membership cost: $65 associate; $85 professional; $35 student. Sponsors workshops/conferences: TV/screenwriting workshops, NWAF Annual Conferences, Literary Clearinghouse, editing and critiquing services, local chapters, National Writer's School. Open to non-members. Publishes industry news of interest to freelance writers; how-to articles; market information; member news and networking opportunities. Nonmember subscription: $20. Sponsors poetry contest; short story contest; article contest; novel contest. Awards cash for top 3 winners; books and/or certificates for other winners; honorable mention certificate places 5-10. Contests open to nonmembers.

NATIONAL WRITERS UNION

256 W. 38th St., Suite 703, New York NY 10018. (212)254-0279. **Fax:** (212)-254-0673. **E-mail:** nwu@nwu.org. **Website:** www.nwu.org. Purpose of organization: Advocacy for freelance writers. Qualifications for membership: "Membership in the NWU is open to all qualified writers, and no one shall be barred or in any manner prejudiced within the Union on account of race, age, sex, sexual orientation, disability, national origin, religion or ideology. You are eligible for membership if you have published a book, a play, three articles, five poems, one short story or an equivalent amount of newsletter, publicity, technical, commercial, government or institutional copy. You are also eligible for membership if you have written an equal amount of unpublished material and you are actively writing and attempting to publish your work" Membership cost: annual writing income less than $5,000-$120/year; $5,001-15,000-$195; $15,001-30,000-$265/year; $30,001-$45,000-$315 a year; $45,001- and up -$340/year. Holds workshops throughout the country. Members only section on website offers rich resources for freelance writers. Skilled contract advice and grievance help for members.

NEW HAMPSHIRE WRITERS' PROJECT

2500 North River Rd., Manchester NH 03106. (603)314-7980. **Fax:** (603)314-7981. **E-mail:** info@nhwritersproject.org. **Website:** www.nhwritersproject.org. **Contact:** Kathy Wurtz, Exec. Director. Statewide organization open to writers at all levels in all genres. Currently has 600+ members. Levels of membership/dues: $55/year; $25/year for seniors and students. Offerings include workshops, seminars, an annual conference, and a literary calendar. Sponsors daylong workshops and 4- to 6-week intensive courses. Also sponsors the biennial New Hampshire Literary Awards for outstanding literary achievement (including The Jane Kenyon Award for Outstanding Book of Poetry). Publishes *NH Writer*, a quarterly newsletter for and about New Hampshire writers. Members and nationally known writers give readings that are open to the public. Additional information available by fax, e-mail, or on website.

THE NORTH CAROLINA POETRY SOCIETY

NCPS, 3814 Hulon Dr., Durham NC 27705. **E-mail:** caren@windstream.net. **Website:** www.ncpoetrysociety.org. The North Carolina Poetry Society holds poetry-related contests and gives away several awards each year, for both Adults and Students (which includes 3rd Graders all the way to University Undergraduates). Contact through website: www.ncpoetrysociety.org or mail to: NCPS, 3814 Hulon Drive, Durham, NC 27705. Include SASE for reply. Established 1932. Statewide organization open to non-NC residents. Purpose: to encourage the reading, writing, study, and publication of poetry. NCPS brings poets together in meetings that feature workshops, presentations by noted poets and publishers, book and contest awards, and an annual anthology of award-winning poems. Currently has 350 members from NC and beyond. Levels of membership: Adult ($25/year) and Student ($10/year). NCPS conducts 6 general meetings and numerous statewide workshops/events each year. Sponsors annual Poetry Contest with categories for adults and students. Contests are open to anyone, with small fee for nonmembers. **Deadline** in January (verify date via Website or mail.) Winning poems are published in *Pinesong*, NCPS's annual anthology. A free copy is given to all winners, who are also invited to read at Awards Day. NCPS also sponsors the annual Brockman-Campbell Book Award for a book of poetry over 20 pages by a North Carolina poet (native-born or current resident for 3 years. Prize: $200 and a reading. Entry fee: none for members, $10 for non-members. Deadline: May 1.) NCPS also cosponsors the Gilbert-Chappell Distinguished Poet Series with The North Carolina Center for the Book, for the purpose of mentoring young poets across the state. Please visit NCPS's Website for more information or to see additional benefits offered to members.

NORTH CAROLINA WRITERS' NETWORK

P.O. Box 21591, Winston-Salem NC 27120. (336)293-8844. **E-mail:** mail@ncwriters.org. **Website:** www.ncwriters.org. Supports the work of writers, writers' organizations, independent bookstores, little magazines and small presses, and literary programming statewide. Currently has 1,000 members. Levels of membership/dues: $75/year; seniors/students, $55/year. Membership benefits include The Writers' Network News, a 24-page quarterly newsletter containing organizational news, trend in writing and publishing, and other literary material of interest to writers; and access to the NCWN online resources, other writers, workshops, writer's residencies, conferences, readings and competitions, and NCWN's critiquing and editing service. Annual fall conference features nationally known writers, publishers, and editors, held in a different North Carolina location each November. Sponsors competitions in short fiction, nonfiction, and poetry for North Carolina residents and NCWN members. Guidelines available for SASE or on website.

OHIO POETRY ASSOCIATION

5580 Beverly Hills Dr., Apt B, Columbus OH 43213. (740)694-5013. **E-mail:** david@ohiopoetryassn.org. **Website:** www.ohiopoetryassn.com. Established in 1929 as Verse Writers' Guild of Ohio. **Contact:** Bob Casey, president. Promotes the art of poetry, and furthers the support of poets and others who support poetry. Statewide membership with additional members in several other states, Japan, and England. Af-

filiated with the National Federation of State Poetry Societies (NFSPS). Open to poets and writers of all ages and ability, as well as to non-writing lovers of poetry. Currently has about 215 members. Levels of membership/dues: Regular ($18); Student (including college undergrads, $8); Associate ($8); Senior ($15); Life; and Honorary. Member benefits include regular contests; meeting/workshop participation; assistance with writing projects; networking; twice-yearly magazine, Common Threads (see separate listing in Magazines/Journals), publishing only poems by members; quarterly Ohio Poetry Association Newsletter; quarterly NFSPS newsletters (Strophes); automatic NFSPS membership; and contest information and lower entry fees for NFSPS contests. Members are automatically on the mailing list for Ohio Poetry Day contest guidelines (OPA financially supports Ohio Poetry Day; see separate listing in Contests & Awards). Individual chapters regularly host workshops and seminars. Members and nationally known writers give readings that are open to the public (at quarterly meetings; public is invited). Sponsors open mic readings for members and the public. Past readers have included Lisa Martinovic, David Shevin, Michael Bugeja, David Citino, and Danika Dinsmore. Members meet quarterly (September, December, March, May). Additional information available by e-mail or on website. "In short, OPA provides poets with opportunities to share info, critique, publish, sponsor contests, and just socialize."

PEN AMERICAN CENTER

588 Broadway, Suite 303, New York NY 10012. (212)334-1660. **Fax:** (212)334-2181. **E-mail:** pen@pen.org. **Website:** www.pen.org. Purpose of organization: "An association of writers working to advance literature, to defend free expression, and to foster international literary fellowship." Qualifications for membership: "The standard qualification for a writer to become a member of PEN is publication of two or more books of a literary character, or one book generally acclaimed to be of exceptional distinction. Also eligible for membership: editors who have demonstrated commitment to excellence in their profession (usually construed as five years' service in book editing); translators who have published at least two book-length literary translations; playwrights whose works have been produced professionally; and literary essayists whose publications are extensive even if they have not

yet been issued as a book. Candidates for membership may be nominated by a PEN member or they may nominate themselves with the support of two references from the literary community or from a current PEN member. Membership dues are $100 per year and many PEN members contribute their time by serving on committees, conducting campaigns and writing letters in connection with freedom-of-expression cases, contributing to the PEN journal, participating in PEN public events, helping to bring literature into underserved communities, and judging PEN literary awards. PEN members receive a subscription to the PEN journal, the PEN Annual Report, and have access to medical insurance at group rates. Members living in the New York metropolitan and tri-state area, or near the Branches, are invited to PEN events throughout the year. Membership in PEN American Center includes reciprocal privileges in PEN American Center branches and in foreign PEN Centers for those traveling abroad. Application forms are available on the Web at www.pen.org. Associate Membership is open to everyone who supports PEN's mission, and your annual dues ($40; $20 for students) provides crucial support to PEN's programs. When you join as an Associate Member, not only will you receive a subscription to the *PEN Journal* http://pen.org/page.php/prmID/150 and notices of all PEN events but you are also invited to participate in the work of PEN. PEN American Center is the largest of the 141 centers of PEN International, the world's oldest human rights organization and the oldest international literary organization. PEN International was founded in 1921 to dispel national, ethnic, and racial hatreds and to promote understanding among all countries. PEN American Center, founded a year later, works to advance literature, to defend free expression, and to foster international literary fellowship. The Center has a membership of 3,400 distinguished writers, editors, and translators. In addition to defending writers in prison or in danger of imprisonment for their work, PEN American Center sponsors public literary programs and forums on current issues, sends prominent authors to inner-city schools to encourage reading and writing, administers literary prizes, promotes international literature that might otherwise go unread in the United States, and offers grants and loans to writers facing financial or medical emergencies. In carrying out this work, PEN American Center builds upon the achievements of such dedicated past members as W.H. Auden, James Baldwin, Willa Cather, Robert Frost, Langston Hughes, Thomas Mann, Arthur Miller, Marianne Moore, Susan Sontag, and John Steinbeck. The Children's Book Authors' Committee sponsors annual public events focusing on the art of writing for children and young adults and on the diversity of literature for juvenile readers. The PEN/Phyllis Naylor Working Writer Fellowship was established in 2001 to assist a North American author of fiction for children or young adults (**E-mail:** awards@pen.org). Visit www.pen.org for complete information. Sponsors several competitions per year. Monetary awards range from $2,000-35,000.

POETRY SOCIETY OF NEW HAMPSHIRE

31 Reservoir, Farmington NH 03835. (603)332-0732. **E-mail:** poetrysocietyofnh@gmail.com. **Website:** www.poetrysocietyofnewhampshire.org. A statewide organization for anyone interested in poetry. Currently has 200 members. Levels of membership/dues: Junior ($10); Regular ($20). Offerings include annual subscription to quarterly magazine, The Poet's Touchstone ; critiques, contests, and workshops; public readings; and quarterly meetings with featured poets. The Poet's Touchstone is available to nonmembers for $6 (single issue). Members and nationally known writers give readings that are open to the public. Sponsors open mic readings for members and the public. Additional information available for SASE or by e-mail. "We do sponsor a national contest four times a year with $100, $50, and $25 prizes paid out in each one. People from all over the country enter and win."

THE POETRY SOCIETY OF SOUTH CAROLINA

P.O. Box 1090, Charleston SC 29402. **E-mail:** flatbluesky@hotmail.com. **Website:** www.poetrysocietysc.org. The Poetry Society of South Carolina supports "the reading, writing, study, and enjoyment of poetry." Statewide organization open to anyone interested in poetry. Offers programs in Charleston that are free and open to the public September-May (except for members-only holiday party in December). Currently has 150 members. Levels of membership/dues: $15 student, $25 individual, $35 family, $50 patron, and $100 business or sponsor. Membership year runs July 1-June 30. Membership benefits include discounts to PSSC-sponsored seminars and workshops held in various SC locations; a copy of the annual

Yearbook of contest-winning poems; eligibility to read at the open mic and to enter contests without a fee; and an invitation to the annual holiday party. Sponsors a monthly Writers' Group, a January open mic reading featuring PSSC members, a Charleston Poetry Walk during Piccolo Spoleto in June, and a May Forum leading to an audience-selected poetry prize. Sponsors two yearly contests, totaling 20-25 contest categories, some with themes; some are open to all poets, others open only to SC residents or PSSC members. Guidelines available on website. **Deadline:** November 15 (Fall round) and February 15 (Spring round). Also offers the Skylark Prize, a competition for SC high school students. Sometimes offers a chapbook competition. Members and nationally known writers give readings that are open to the public. Poets have included Billy Collins, Henry Taylor, Cathy Smith Bowers, and Richard Garcia, as well as emerging poets from the region. Additional information available by e-mail or on website.

UNIVERSITY OF ARIZONA POETRY CENTER

1508 E. Helen St., P.O. Box 210129, Tucson AZ 85721. (520)626-3765. **E-mail:** poetry@email.arizona.edu. **Website:** www.poetrycenter.arizona.edu. **Contact:** Gail Browne, Exec. Director. 1508 E. Helen St., P.O. Box 210150, Tucson AZ 85721. (520)626-3765. **Fax:** (520)621-5566. **E-mail:** poetry@u.arizona.edu. **Website:** www.poetrycenter.arizona.edu. **Contact:** Gail Browne, executive director. Established 1960. "Open to the public, the University of Arizona Poetry Center is a contemporary poetry archive and a nationally acclaimed poetry collection that includes over 70,000 items. Programs and services include a library with a noncirculating poetry collection and space for small classes; online lesson plan library; High School Bilingual Corrido Contest; K-16 field trip program; summer camps; poetry-related meetings and activities; facilities, research support, and referral information about poetry and poets for local and national communities; Reading Series; community creative writing classes and workshops; a summer residency offered each year to two writers (one prose, one poetry) selected by jury; and poetry awards, readings, and special events for high school, undergraduate, and graduate students. Additional information available by phone, e-mail, or website. Become a 'Friend of the Poetry Center' by making an annual contribution."

WORDS WITHOUT BORDERS

P.O. Box 1658, New York NY 10276. **E-mail:** info@ wordswithoutborders.org. **Website:** www.wordswith- outborders.org. P.O. Box 1658, New York NY 10276.**E- mail:** info@wordswithoutborders.org. **Website:** www. wordswithoutborders.org. "Words Without Borders opens doors to international exchange through translation, publications, and promotion of the world's best writing. Our ultimate aim is to introduce exciting international writing to the general public—travelers, teachers, students, publishers, and a new generation of eclectic readers— by presenting international literature not as a static, elite phenomenon, but a portal through which to explore the world. The heart of WWB's work is its online magazine. Monthly issues feature new selections of contemporary world literature, most of which would never have been accessible to English-speaking readers without WWB." Members and international writers give readings that are open to the public. See website for additional information. "Words Without Borders opens doors to international exchange through translation, publications, and promotion of the world's best writing. Our ultimate aim is to introduce exciting international writing to the general public—travelers, teachers, students, publishers, and a new generation of eclectic readers— by presenting international literature not as a static, elite phenomenon, but a portal through which to explore the world. The heart of WWB's work is its online magazine. Monthly issues feature new selections of contemporary world literature, most of which would never have been accessible to English-speaking readers without WWB. Members and international writers give readings that are open to the public. Finally, Words without Borders is building an education program in order to expose students at both the high school and college levels to a broader spectrum of contemporary international literature. Our goal is to provide content and resources fostering the use of contemporary literature in the classroom. We hope that in reaching out to students we can create a passion for international literature, a curiosity about other cultures, and help cultivate true world citizens. See website for additional information."

WRITERS' FEDERATION OF NOVA SCOTIA

1113 Marginal Rd., Halifax NS B3H 4P7, Canada. (902)423-8116. **Fax:** (902)422-0881. **E-mail:** talk@

writers.ns.ca. **Website:** www.writers.ns.ca. Purpose of organization: "to foster creative writing and the profession of writing in Nova Scotia; to provide advice and assistance to writers at all stages of their careers; and to encourage greater public recognition of Nova Scotian writers and their achievements." Regional organization open to anybody who writes. Currently has 800+ members. Levels of membership/dues: $45 CAD annually ($20 CAD students). Offerings include resource library with over 2,500 titles, promotional services, workshop series, annual festivals, mentorship program. Publishes *Eastword*, a bimonthly newsletter containing "a plethora of information on who's doing what; markets and contests; and current writing events and issues." Members and nationally known writers give readings that are open to the public. Additional information available on website.

☼ WRITERS GUILD OF ALBERTA

11759 Groat Rd., Edmonton AB T5M 3K6, Canada. (780)422-8174. **Fax:** (780)422-2663. **E-mail:** mail@writersguild.ab.ca. **Website:** www.writersguild.ab.ca. Purpose of organization: to support, encourage and promote writers and writing, to safeguard the freedom to write and to read, and to advocate for the well-being of writers in Alberta. Currently has over 1,000 members. Offerings include retreats/conferences; monthly events; bimonthly magazine that includes articles on writing and a market section; weekly electronic bulletin with markets and event listings; and the Stephan G. Stephansson Award for Poetry (Alberta residents only). Membership cost: $60/year; $30 for seniors/students. Holds workshops/conferences. Publishes a newsletter focusing on markets, competitions, contemporary issues related to the literary arts (writing, publishing, censorship, royalties etc.). Sponsors annual Literary Awards in five categories (novel, nonfiction, children's literature, poetry, drama). Awards include $1,500, leather-bound book, promotion and publicity. Open to nonmembers.

THE WRITERS ROOM

Website: www.writersroom.org. 740 Broadway, 12th Floor, New York NY 10003. (212)254-6995. **Fax:** (212)533-6059. **E-mail:** writersroom@writersroom. org. **Website:** www.writersroom.org. Established 1978. Provides a "home away from home" for any writer who needs space to work. Open 24 hours a day, 7 days a week, **for members only**. Currently has about 350 members. Emerging and established writers may apply. Levels of membership/dues: vary from $$525 to $750/half year, plus one-time initiation fee of $75. Large loft provides desk space, Internet access, storage, and more. Call for application or download from website.

POETS IN EDUCATION

Whether known as PITS (Poets in the Schools), WITS (Writers in the Schools), or similar names, programs exist nationwide that coordinate residencies, classroom visits and other opportunities for experienced poets to share their craft with students. Many state arts agencies include such "arts in education" programs in their activities (see Grants on page 424 for contact information). Another good source is the National Assembly of State Arts Agencies (see below), which offers an online directory of contact names and addresses for arts education programs state-by-state. The following list is a mere sampling of programs and organizations that link poets with schools. Contact them for information about their requirements (some may insist poets have a strong publication history, others may prefer classroom experience) or check their websites where available.

THE ACADEMY OF AMERICAN POETS, 584 Broadway, Suite 604, New York NY 10012-5243. (212)274-0343. E-mail: academy@poets.org. website: www.poets.org (includes links to state arts in education programs).

ARKANSAS WRITERS IN THE SCHOOLS, WITS Director, 333 Kimpel Hall, University of Arkansas, Fayetteville AR 72701. (479)575-5991. E-mail: wits@cavern.uark.edu. website: www.uark.edu/~wits.

CALIFORNIA POETS IN THE SCHOOLS, 1333 Balboa St. #3, San Francisco CA 94118. (415)221-4201. E-mail: info@cpits.org. website: www.cpits.org.

E-POETS.NETWORK, a collective online cultural center that promotes education through videoconferencing (i.e., "distance learning"); also includes the *Voces y Lugares* project. website: http://learning.e-poets.net (includes online contact form).

IDAHO WRITERS IN THE SCHOOLS, Log Cabin Literary Center, 801 S. Capitol Blvd., Boise ID 83702. (208)331-8000. E-mail: info@thecabinidaho.org. website: www.thecabin idaho.org.

INDIANA WRITERS IN THE SCHOOLS, University of Evansville, Dept. of English, 1800 Lincoln Ave., Evansville IN 47722. (812)488-2962. E-mail: rg37@evansville.edu. website: http://english.evansville.edu/WritersintheSchools.htm.

MICHIGAN CREATIVE WRITERS IN THE SCHOOLS, ArtServe Michigan, 17515 W. Nine Mile Rd., Suite 1025, Southfield MI 48075. (248)557-8288 **OR** 1310 Turner St., Suite B, Lansing MI 48906. (517)371-1720 (toll free at (800)203-9633). E-mail: online form. website: www.artservemichigan.org.

NATIONAL ASSEMBLY OF STATE ARTS AGENCIES, 1029 Vermont Ave. NW, 2nd Floor, Washington DC 20005. (202)347-6352. E-mail: nasaa@nasaa-arts.org. website: www.nasaa-arts.org.

NATIONAL ASSOCIATION OF WRITERS IN EDUCATION (NAWE), P.O. Box 1, Sheriff Hutton, York YO60 7YU England. (44)(1653)618429. website: www.nawe.co.uk.

OREGON WRITERS IN THE SCHOOLS, Literary Arts, 224 NW 13th Ave., Suite 306, Portland OR 97209. (503)227-2583. E-mail: john@literary-arts.org. website: www.literary-arts.org/wits.

PEN IN THE CLASSROOM (PITC), Pen Center USA, Þco Antioch University, 400 Corporate Pointe, Culver City CA 90230. (310)862-1555. E-mail: pitc@penusa.org. website: www.penusa.org/go/classroom.

"PICK-A-POET," The Humanities Project, Arlington Public Schools, 1439 N. Quincy St., Arlington VA 22207. (703)228-6299. E-mail: online form. website: www.humanitiesproject.org.

POTATO HILL POETRY, 6 Pleasant St., Suite 2, South Natick MA 01760. (888)5-POETRY. E-mail: info@potatohill.com. website: www.potatohill.com (includes online contact form).

SEATTLE WRITERS IN THE SCHOOLS (WITS), Seattle Arts & Lectures, 105 S. Main St., Suite 201, Seattle WA 98104. (206)621-2230. website: www.lectures.org/wits.html.

TEACHERS & WRITERS COLLABORATIVE, 520 Eighth Ave., Suite 2020, New York NY 10018. (212)691-6590 or (888)BOOKS-TW (book orders). E-mail: info@twc.org. website: www.twc.org. "A catalog of T&W books is available online, or call toll-free to request a print copy.

TEXAS WRITERS IN THE SCHOOLS, 1523 W. Main, Houston TX 77006. (713)523-3877. E-mail: mail@witshouston.org. website: www.writersintheschools.org.

WRITERS & ARTISTS IN THE SCHOOLS (WAITS), COMPAS, Landmark Center, Suite 304, 75 Fifth St. West, St. Paul MN 55102-1496. (651)292-3254. E-mail: daniel@compas.org. website: www.compas.org.

YOUTH VOICES IN INK, Badgerdog Literary Publishing, Inc., P.O. Box 301209, Austin TX 78703-0021. (512)538-1305. E-mail: info@badgerdog.org. website: www.badgerdog.org.

GLOSSARY OF LISTING TERMS

A3, A4, A5. Metric equivalents of 11¾×16½, 8¼×11¾, and 5⅞×8¼ respectively.

ACKNOWLEDGMENTS PAGE. A page in a poetry book or chapbook that lists the publications where the poems in the collection were originally published; may be presented as part of the copyright page or as a separate page on its own.

ANTHOLOGY. A collection of selected writings by various authors.

ATTACHMENT. A computer file electronically "attached" to an e-mail message.

AUD. Abbreviation for Australian Dollar.

B&W. Black & white (photo or illustration).

BIO. A short biographical statement often requested with a submission.

CAD. Abbreviation for Canadian Dollar.

CAMERA-READY. Poems ready for copy camera platemaking; camera-ready poems usually appear in print exactly as submitted.

CHAPBOOK. A small book of about 24-50 pages.Circulation. The number of subscribers to a magazine/journal.

CLMP. Council of Literary Magazines and Presses; service organization for independent publishers of fiction, poetry, and prose.

CONTRIBUTOR'S COPY. Copy of book or magazine containing a poet's work, sometimes given as payment.

COVER LETTER. Brief introductory letter accompanying a poetry submission.

COVERSTOCK. Heavier paper used as the cover for a publication.

DIGEST-SIZED. About 5½×8½, the size of a folded sheet of conventional printer paper.

DOWNLOAD. To "copy" a file, such as a registration form, from a website.

ELECTRONIC MAGAZINE. See *online magazine*.

EURO. Currency unit for the 27 member countries of the European Union; designated by EUR or the INSERT EURO symbol.

FAQ. Frequently Asked Questions.

FONT. The style/design of type used in a publication; typeface.

GALLEYS. First typeset version of a poem, magazine, or book/chapbook.

GLBT. Gay/lesbian/bisexual/transgender (as in "GLBT themes").

HONORARIUM. A token payment for published work.

IRC. International Reply Coupon; a publisher can exchange IRCs for postage to return a manuscript to another country.

JPEG. Short for *Joint Photographic Experts Group*; an image compression format that allows digital images to be stored in relatively small files for electronic mailing and viewing on the Internet.

MAGAZINE-SIZED. About 8½×11, the size of an unfolded sheet of conventional printer paper.

MS. Manuscript.

MSS. Manuscripts.

MULTI-BOOK REVIEW. Several books by the same author or by several authors reviewed in one piece.

OFFSET-PRINTED. Printing method in which ink is transferred from an image-bearing plate to a "blanket" and then from blanket to paper.

ONLINE MAGAZINE. Publication circulated through the Internet or e-mail.

P&H. Postage & handling.

P&P. Postage & packing.

"PAYS IN COPIES." See *contributor's copy.*

PDF. Short for *Portable Document Format*, developed by Adobe Systems, that captures all elements of a printed document as an electronic image, allowing it to be sent by e-mail, viewed online, and printed in its original format.

PERFECT-BOUND. Publication with glued, flat spine; also called "flat-spined."

POD. See *print-on-demand.*

PRESS RUN. The total number of copies of a publication printed at one time.

PREVIOUSLY PUBLISHED. Work that has appeared before in print, in any form, for public consumption.

PRINT-ON-DEMAND. Publishing method that allows copies of books to be published as they're requested, rather than all at once in a single press run.

PUBLISHING CREDITS. A poet's magazine publications and book/chapbook titles.

QUERY LETTER. Letter written to an editor to raise interest in a proposed project.

READING FEE. A monetary amount charged by an editor or publisher to consider a poetry submission without any obligation to accept the work.

RICH TEXT FORMAT. Carries the .rtf filename extension. A file format that allows an exchange of text files between different word processor operating systems with most of the formatting preserved.

RIGHTS. A poet's legal property interest in his/her literary work; an editor or publisher may acquire certain rights from the poet to reproduce that work.

ROW. "Rest of world."

ROYALTIES. A percentage of the retail price paid to the author for each copy of a book sold.

SADDLE-STAPLED. A publication folded, then stapled along that fold; also called "saddle-stitched."

SAE. Self-addressed envelope.

SASE. Self-addressed, stamped envelope.

SASP. Self-addressed, stamped postcard.

SIMULTANEOUS SUBMISSION. Submission of the same manuscript to more than one publisher at the same time.

SUBSIDY PRESS. Publisher who requires the poet to pay all costs, including typesetting, production, and printing; sometimes called a "vanity publisher."

TABLOID-SIZED. 11×15 or larger, the size of an ordinary newspaper folded and turned sideways.

TEXT FILE. A file containing only textual characters (i.e., no graphics or special formats).

UNSOLICITED MANUSCRIPT. A manuscript an editor did not ask specifically to receive.

URL. Stands for "Uniform Resource Locator," the address of an Internet resource (i.e., file).

USD. Abbreviation for United States Dollar.

GLOSSARY OF POETRY TERMS

This glossary is provided as a quick-reference only, briefly covering poetic styles and terms that may turn up in articles and listings in *Poet's Market*. For a full understanding of the terms, forms, and styles listed here, as well as common literary terms not included, consult a solid textbook or handbook, such as John Drury's *The Poetry Dictionary* (Writer's Digest Books).

ABSTRACT POEM: conveys emotion through sound, textures, and rhythm and rhyme rather than through the meanings of words.

ACROSTIC: initial letters of each line, read downward, form a word, phrase, or sentence.

ALLITERATION: close repetition of consonant sounds, especially initial consonant sounds. (Also known as *consonance*.)

ALPHABET POEM: arranges lines alphabetically according to initial letter.

AMERICAN CINQUAIN: derived from Japanese haiku and tanka by Adelaide Crapsey; counted syllabic poem of 5 lines of 2-4-6-8-2 syllables, frequently in iambic feet.

ANAPEST: foot consisting of 2 unstressed syllables followed by a stress (- - ').

ASSONANCE: close repetition of vowel sounds. Avant-garde: work at the forefront--cutting edge, unconventional, risk-taking.

BALLAD: narrative poem often in ballad stanza (4-line stanza with 4 stresses in lines 1 and 3, 3 stresses in lines 2 and 4, which also rhyme).

BALLADE: 3 stanzas rhymed *ababbcbC* (*C* indicates a refrain) with envoi rhymed *bcbC*.

BEAT POETRY: anti-academic school of poetry born in '50s San Francisco; fast-paced free verse resembling jazz.

BLANK VERSE: unrhymed iambic pentameter.

CAESURA: a deliberate rhetorical, grammatical, or rhythmic pause, break, cut, turn, division, or pivot in poetry.

CHANT: poem in which one or more lines are repeated over and over.

CINQUAIN: any 5-line poem or stanza; also called "quintain" or "quintet." (See also *American cinquain*.)

CONCRETE POETRY: see *emblematic poem*.

CONFESSIONAL POETRY: work that uses personal and private details from the poet's own life.

CONSONANCE: see *alliteration*.

COUPLET: stanza of 2 lines; pair of rhymed lines.

DACTYL: foot consisting of a stress followed by 2 unstressed syllables (' - -).

DIDACTIC POETRY: poetry written with the intention to instruct.

ECLECTIC: open to a variety of poetic styles (as in "eclectic taste").

EKPHRASTIC POEM: verbally presents something originally represented in visual art, though more than mere description.

ELEGY: lament in verse for someone who has died, or a reflection on the tragic nature of life.

EMBLEMATIC POEM: words or letters arranged to imitate a shape, often the subject of the poem.

ENJAMBMENT: continuation of sense and rhythmic movement from one line to the next; also called a "run-on" line.

ENVOI: a brief ending (usually to a ballade or sestina) no more than 4 lines long; summary.

EPIC POETRY: long narrative poem telling a story central to a society, culture, or nation.

EPIGRAM: short, witty, satirical poem or saying written to be remembered easily, like a punchline.

EPIGRAPH: a short verse, note, or quotation that appears at the beginning of a poem or section; usually presents an idea or theme on which the poem elaborates, or contributes background information not reflected in the poem itself.

EPITAPH: brief verse commemorating a person/group of people who died.

EXPERIMENTAL POETRY: work that challenges conventional ideas of poetry by exploring new techniques, form, language, and visual presentation.

FIBS: short form based on the mathematical progression known as the Fibonacci sequence; syllable counts for each line are 1/1/2/3/5/8/13 (count for each line is derived by adding the counts for the previous two lines).

FLARF: a malleable term that may refer to 1) poetic and creative text pieces by the Flarflist Collective; any poetry created from search engine (such as Google) results; any intentionally bad, zany, or trivial poetry.

FOOT: unit of measure in a metrical line of poetry. Found poem: text lifted from a non-poetic source such as an ad and presented as a poem.

FREE VERSE: unmetrical verse (lines not counted for accents, syllables, etc.).

GHAZAL: Persian poetic form of 5-15 unconnected, independent couplets; associative jumps may be made from couplet to couplet.

GREETING CARD POETRY: resembles verses in greeting cards; sing-song meter and rhyme.

HAIBUN: originally, a Japanese form in which elliptical, often autobiographical prose is interspersed with haiku.

HAIKAI NO RENGA: see *renku.*

HAY(NA)KY: a 3-line form, with 1 word in line 1, 2 words in line 2, and 3 words in line 3.

HAIKU: originally, a Japanese form of a single vertical line with 17 sound symbols in a 5-7-5 pattern. In English, typically a 3-line poem with fewer than 17 syllables in no set pattern, but exhibiting a 2-part juxtapositional structure, seasonal reference, imagistic immediacy, and a moment of keen perception of nature or human nature. The term is both singular and plural.

HOKKU: the starting verse of a renga or renku, in 5, 7, and then 5 sound symbols in Japanese; or in three lines, usually totaling fewer than 17 syllables, in English; the precursor for what is now called haiku. (See also *haiku.*)

IAMB: foot consisting of an unstressed syllable followed by a stress (- ').

IAMBIC PENTAMETER: consists of 5 iambic feet per line.

IMAGIST POETRY: short, free verse lines that present images without comment or explanation; strongly influenced by haiku and other Oriental forms.

KYRIELLE: French form; 4-line stanza with 8-syllable lines, the final line a refrain.

LANGUAGE POETRY: attempts to detach words from traditional meanings to produce something new and unprecedented.

LIMERICK: 5-line stanza rhyming *aabba*; pattern of stresses/line is traditionally 3-3-2-2-3; often bawdy or scatalogical.

LINE: basic compositional unit of a poem; measured in feet if metrical.

LINKED POETRY: written through the collaboration of 2 or more poets creating a single poetic work.

LONG POEM: exceeds length and scope of short lyric or narrative poem; defined arbitrarily, often as more than 2 pages or 100 lines.

LYRIC POETRY: expresses personal emotion; music predominates over narrative or drama.

METAPHOR: 2 different things are likened by identifying one as the other (A=B).

METER: the rhythmic measure of a line.

MINUTE: a 12-line poem consisting of 60 syllables, with a syllabic line count of 8,4,4,4,8,4,4,4, 8,4,4,4; often consists of rhyming couplets.

MODERNIST POETRY: work of the early 20th century literary movement that sought to break with the past, rejecting outmoded literary traditions, diction, and form while encouraging innovation and reinvention.

NARRATIVE POETRY: poem that tells a story.

NEW FORMALISM: contemporary literary movement to revive formal verse.

NONSENSE VERSE: playful, with language and/or logic that defies ordinary understanding.

OCTAVE: stanza of 8 lines.

ODE: a songlike, or lyric, poem; can be passionate, rhapsodic, and mystical, or a formal address to a person on a public or state occasion.

PANTOUM: Malayan poetic form of any length; consists of 4-line stanzas, with lines 2 and 4 of one quatrain repeated as lines 1 and 3 of the next; final stanza reverses lines 1 and 3 of the previous quatrain and uses them as lines 2 and 4; traditionally each stanza rhymes *abab*.

PETRARCHAN SONNET: octave rhymes *abbaabba*; sestet may rhyme *cdcdcd, cdedce, ccdccd, cddcdd, edecde,* or *cddcee.*

PROSE POEM: brief prose work with intensity, condensed language, poetic devices, and other poetic elements.

QUATRAIN: stanza of 4 lines.

REFRAIN: a repeated line within a poem, similar to the chorus of a song.

REGIONAL POETRY: work set in a particular locale, imbued with the look, feel, and culture of that place.

RENGA: originally, a Japanese collaborative form in which 2 or more poets alternate writing 3 lines, then 2 lines for a set number of verses (such as 12, 18, 36, 100, and 1,000). There are specific rules for seasonal progression, placement of moon and flower verses, and other requirements. (See also *linked poetry.*)

RENGAY: an American collaborative 6-verse, thematic linked poetry form, with 3-line and 2-line verses in the following set pattern for 2 or 3 writers (letters represent poets, numbers indicate the lines in each verse): A3-B2-A3-B3-A2-B3 or A3-B2-C3-A2-B3-C2. All verses, unlike renga or renku, must develop at least one common theme.

RENKU: the modern term for renga, and a more popular version of the traditionally more aristocratic renga. (See also *linked poetry.*)

RHYME: words that sound alike, especially words that end in the same sound.

RHYTHM: the beat and movement of language (rise and fall, repetition and variation, change of pitch, mix of syllables, melody of words).

RONDEAU: French form of usually 15 lines in 3 parts, rhyming *aabba aabR aabbaR* (*R* indicates a refrain repeating the first word or phrase of the opening line).

SENRYU: originally, a Japanese form, like haiku in form, but chiefly humorous, satirical, or ironic, and typically aimed at human foibles. (See also *haiku* and *zappai.*)

SEQUENCE: a group or progression of poems, often numbered as a series.

SESTET: stanza of 6 lines.

SESTINA: fixed form of 39 lines (6 unrhymed stanzas of 6 lines each, then an ending 3-line stanza), each stanza repeating the same 6 non-rhyming end-words in a different order; all 6 end-words appear in the final 3-line stanza.

SHAKESPEAREAN SONNET: rhymes *abab cdcd efef gg.*Sijo: originally a Korean narrative or thematic lyric form. The first line introduces a situation or problem that is countered or developed in line 2, and concluded with a twist in line 3. Lines average 14-16 syllables in length.

SIMILE: comparison that uses a linking word (*like, as, such as, how*) to clarify the similarities.

SONNET: 14-line poem (traditionally an octave and sestet) rhymed in iambic pentameter; often presents an argument but may also present a description, story, or meditation.

SPONDEE: foot consisting of 2 stressed syllables (' ').

STANZA: group of lines making up a single unit; like a paragraph in prose.

STROPHE: often used to mean "stanza"; also a stanza of irregular line lengths.

SURREALISTIC POETRY: of the artistic movement stressing the importance of dreams and the subconscious, nonrational thought, free associations, and startling imagery/juxtapositions.

TANKA: originally, a Japanese form in one or 2 vertical lines with 31 sound symbols in a 5-7-5-7-7 pattern. In English, typically a 5-line lyrical poem with fewer than 31 syllables in no set syllable pattern, but exhibiting a caesura, turn, or pivot, and often more emotional and conversational than haiku.

TERCET: stanza or poem of 3 lines.

TERZA RIMA: series of 3-line stanzas with interwoven rhyme scheme (*aba, bcb, cdc . . .*).

TROCHEE: foot consisting of a stress followed by an unstressed syllable (' -).

VILLANELLE: French form of 19 lines (5 tercets and a quatrain); line 1 serves as one refrain (repeated in lines 6, 12, 18), line 3 as a second refrain (repeated in lines 9, 15, 19); traditionally, refrains rhyme with each other and with the opening line of each stanza.

VISUAL POEM: see *emblematic poem.*

WAKA: literally, "Japanese poem," the precursor for what is now called tanka. (See also *tanka.*)

WAR POETRY: poems written about warfare and military life; often written by past and current soldiers; may glorify war, recount exploits, or demonstrate the horrors of war.

ZAPPAI: originally Japanese; an unliterary, often superficial witticism masquerading as haiku or senryu; formal term for joke haiku or other pseudo-haiko.

ZEUGMA: a figure of speech in which a single word (or, occasionally, a phrase) is related in one way to words that precede it, and in another way to words that follow it.

SUBJECT INDEX

AFRICAN AMERICAN
Furious Flower Poetry Center 466
hArtworks 249
Torch 361

ANIMALS/PETS
Advocate, PKA's Publication 180
Peace & Freedom 299
Rocky Mountain Rider Magazine 330

ANTHOLOGY/ANIMAL/BEST OF
AMAZE 184
Birch Book Press 380
Blue Light Press 381
Brick Road Poetry Press, Inc. 382
Caribbean Writer, The 208
Chantarelle's Notebook 211
Confrontation 219
contemporary haibun 220
Diagram 228
Down in the Dirt 230
Floating Bridge Press 388
Four Way Books 389
FreeXpresSion 242
Georgia Poetry Society 467
Great American Poetry Show, The 246
Haiku Society of America 467
iota 257
Iowa Poetry Association 468
Literal Latté 267
LIT, The 468
North Carolina Poetry Society, The 469
nthposition 292
Painted Bride Quarterly 297
Passion 298
Peace & Freedom 299

Poetry Church Magazine, The 311
Poet's Haven, The 314
Poet's Pen, The 314
Red Moon Press 402
Scifaikuest 334
Song of the San Joaquin 340
Southern California Review 342
Star*Line 349
Teacher's Voice, The 356
Tebot Bach 405
VAN GOGH'S EAR 365
Words Without Borders 472

BILINGUAL/FOREIGN LANGUAGE
American Dissident 184
Babel 194
Borderlands 204
Écrits des Forges 387
Italica Press 393
Llenyddiaeth Cymru / Literature Wales 468
Milkweed Editions 396
M.I.P. Company 279
Osiris 295
Rio Grande Review 329
Skipping Stones 337
Tokyo Rose Records/Chapultepec Press 406
Wake Forest University Press 408

BUDDHISM
Bottom Dog Press, Inc. 382

CHRISTIAN
Alive Now 183
Ancient Paths 186
devozine 228
Evangel 235
Image 256

Lutheran Digest, The 271
Mature Years 276
Mennonite, The 276
Pockets 307
Poetry Church Magazine, The 311
Purpose 321
Radix Magazine 323
Studio, A Journal of Christians Writing 352
Time of Singing 360

COWBOY POETRY/AMERICAN WEST

High Plains Press 391
Rocky Mountain Rider Magazine 330
South Dakota Review 341

CULTURES/COMMUNITIES VARIOUS

African Voices 181
Babel 194
Caribbean Writer, The 208
FACES Magazine 236
Italian Americana 258
Lapwing Publications 394
Plain Spoke 305
Rattapallax 323
Toad Suck Review 360
Wake Forest University Press 408
Westerly 368

EROTICA

M.I.P. Company 279
Peace & Freedom 299

FANTASY

Anaphora Literary Press 378
Aoife's Kiss 187
Beyond Centauri 199
Fickle Muses 236
Fifth Di..., The 237
Illumen 255
Leading Edge 265
Mythic Delirium 282
Scifaikuest 334
Space and Time 345
Spaceports & Spidersilk 345
Star*Line 349
Tales of the Talisman 354

FORM/STYLE

Able Muse 178
ABRAXAS 178
Alimentum, The Literature of Food 183
AMAZE 184
Amy Award for Poetry, The 413
bear creek haiku 197
Blood Lotus 201
Capilano Review, The 208
Clark Street Review 215
Cold Mountain Review 217
Deronda Review, The 227
Eclectic Muse, The 232
Ekphrasis 232
Ghost Pony Press 389

Indefinite Space 256
Iodine Poetry Journal 257
Luna Bisonte Prods 395
Lutheran Digest, The 271
Lyric, The 272
Malahat Review Long Poem Prize, The 428
Marr Poetry Prize, The Morton 428
Measure 276
Naugatuck River Review 284
Ooligan Press 399
Plan B Press 401
Poetry Society of Virginia Adult and Student Contests,
    The 436
Raintown Review, The 323
Road Not Taken 329
SleepingFish 339
SpeedPoets Zine 346
Spring 348
Stevens Journal, The Wallace 367
Tarpaulin Sky 355
Tarpaulin Sky Press 405
Tundra 363
VAN GOGH'S EAR 365
Windfall 372

FORM/STYLE ASIAN

American Tanka 186
bear creek haiku 197
contemporary haibun 220
Frogpond 243
Haiku Society of America 467
Modern Haiku 281
Poetry Kanto 312
Poetry Society of Virginia Adult and Student Contests,
    The 436
red lights 326
Red Moon Anthology of English Language Haiku,
    The 326
Red Moon Press 402
Ribbons 328
Roadrunner Haiku Journal 329
Scifaikuest 334
Shemom 336
Tundra 363

GAY/LESBIAN/BISEXUAL/TRANSGEN-
    DERED

Babel 194
Carolina Wren Press 383
Lethe Press 395

GOTHIC/HORROR/DARK POETRY

Anaphora Literary Press 378
Beyond Centauri 199
Darkling Magazine 226
Hungur Magazine 254
Mythic Delirium 282
Penny Dreadful 301
Scifaikuest 334
Space and Time 345
Spaceports & Spidersilk 345

Star*Line 349
Tales of the Talisman 354

HISPANIC/LATINO
Moving Parts Press 397

HUMOR/SATIRE
Anaphora Literary Press 378
asinine poetry 192
babysue* 195
Brick Road Poetry Book Contest 416
Brick Road Poetry Press, Inc. 382
Cider Press Review 214
Deronda Review, The 227
Jewish Women's Literary Annual 259
Nuthouse 293
Peace & Freedom 299
Poet's Art, The 313
Talking River 355
Timberline Press 406
Wergle Flomp Humor Poetry Contest 443

JEWISH
Poetica Magazine, Reflections of Jewish Thought 310

LOVE/ROMANCE
Anaphora Literary Press 378
Deronda Review, The 227
Peace & Freedom 299

MEDICAL/HEALTH ISSUES
Bellevue Literary Review 197
CHEST 213
Hospital Drive 252
Jack and Jill 259
Journal of the American Medical Association (JAMA) 260
Kaleidoscope 261
Samsara 332
Slate & Style 338
Turtle Magazine for Preschool Kids 363
Vilcek Prize for Poetry, Marica and Jan 442

MEMBERSHIP/SUBSCRIPTION
Bell's Letters Poet 198
Common Threads 218
Lone Stars Magazine 269
Magnolia Quarterly, The 274
Moccasin, The 280
Peace & Freedom 299
Poetry Church Magazine, The 311
Poet's Pen, The 314
Poets' Podium 315
Quantum Leap 321
Spring 348

MINORITIES
Carolina Wren Press 383
Haight Ashbury Literary Journal 248

MYSTERY/SUSPENSE
Anaphora Literary Press 378
Ellery Queen's Mystery Magazine 233

NATURE ECOLOGY, SEASONS, OUTDOORS
Albatross 182
Avocet, A Journal of Nature Poems 194
Earthshine 231
Kerf, The 263
Mature Years 276
Modern Haiku 281
Peace & Freedom 299
Poet's Art, The 313
Poet's Pen, The 314
Road Not Taken 329
Skipping Stones 337
Snowy Egret 340
Sunstone 353
Timberline Press 406

ONLINE MARKETS
Able Muse 178
Agnieszka's Dowry (AgD) 182
AMAZE 184
Aoife's Kiss 187
Apple Valley Review 188
asinine poetry 192
Babel 194
Chantarelle's Notebook 211
C/Oasis 216
Convergence 221
Diagram 228
Dirty Napkin, The 229
DMQ Review 229
Down in the Dirt 230
Drown In My Own Fears 230
Earthshine 231
Fickle Muses 236
Fifth Di..., The 237
ForPoetry.Com 241
Green Hills Literary Lantern 246
Hospital Drive 252
Jerry Jazz Musician 259
KotaPress Loss Journal 263
Languageandculture.net 264
La Petite Zine 264
Literal Latté 267
Literal Latté Food Verse Awards 428
Literary Mama 267
Living Poets Magazine 268
Long Story Short, An E-zine for Writers 269
miller's pond 279
Mudlark 282
New Verse News, The 288
nthposition 292
Oxford Magazine 295
Painted Bride Quarterly 297
Pedestal Magazine, The 300
Poemeleon 308
Poetic Matrix, a periodic letteR 310
Poetrybay 311
Poets' Espresso Review 314

Poet's Haven, The 314
Potomac, The 316
Pulse Online Literary Journal 320
Red River Review 327
Road Not Taken 329
Roadrunner Haiku Journal 329
Scifaikuest 334
Spaceports & Spidersilk 345
Stepping Stones Magazine 349
Stirring 349
storySouth 350
Stride Magazine 351
Sunspinner 353
Tarpaulin Sky 355
Thick With Conviction 358
Torch 361
Valparaiso Poetry Review 365
Wild Goose Poetry Review 370
Wild Violet 370

POETRY BY CHILDREN

Advocate, PKA's Publication 180
African Voices 181
American Tanka 186
Aoife's Kiss 187
Apple Valley Review 188
Beyond Centauri 199
Ceremony, a journal of poetry and other arts 210
Chantarelle's Notebook 211
Confrontation 219
contemporary haibun 220
Current Accounts 224
Deronda Review, The 227
Earthshine 231
Fifth Di..., The 237
Frogpond 243
Georgetown Review 244
Home Planet News 251
Homestead Review 251
Hungur Magazine 254
Idiom 23 255
Illumen 255
Jerry Jazz Musician 259
Jewish Currents 259
Kerf, The 263
Leading Edge 265
Lone Stars Magazine 269
Long Story Short, An E-zine for Writers 269
Louisville Review, The 271
Lutheran Digest, The 271
Moccasin, The 280
Modern Haiku 281
North Carolina Poetry Society, The 469
Off the Coast 293
Open Minds Quarterly 294
Over The Transom 295
Oyster Boy Review 296
Peace & Freedom 299
Pockets 307
Poetica Magazine, Reflections of Jewish Thought 310

Poetry Church Magazine, The 311
Poetry Society of Virginia Adult and Student Contests, The 436
Poet's Art, The 313
Poets' Espresso Review 314
Poet's Pen, The 314
Potomac Review 316
Prism International 317
Prism Quarterly 318
RATTLE 324
red lights 326
Red Moon Anthology of English Language Haiku, The 326
Ribbons 328
Road Not Taken 329
Roadrunner Haiku Journal 329
Same, The 332
Scifaikuest 334
Ship of Fools 336
Skipping Stones 337
Slate & Style 338
Song of the San Joaquin 340
Spaceports & Spidersilk 345
Star*Line 349
Storyteller, The 350
Studio One 352
Tears in the Fence 356
Vallum 365
Vegetarian Journal 366
WestWard Quarterly 369
Write On!! Poetry Magazette 374

POETRY BY TEENS

Advocate, PKA's Publication 180
AMAZE 184
American Tanka 186
Aoife's Kiss 187
Apple Valley Review 188
Beyond Centauri 199
Ceremony, a journal of poetry and other arts 210
Challenger international 211
Chantarelle's Notebook 211
Cloudbank 215
Common Threads 218
Confrontation 219
contemporary haibun 220
Current Accounts 224
Deronda Review, The 227
devozine 228
Drown In My Own Fears 230
Earthshine 231
Fifth Di..., The 237
Frogpond 243
Georgetown Review 244
Hanging Loose 248
hArtworks 249
Home Planet News 251
Homestead Review 251
Hungur Magazine 254
Idiom 23 255

Illumen 255
Jerry Jazz Musician 259
Jewish Currents 259
Kerf, The 263
Languageandculture.net 264
Leading Edge 265
Lone Stars Magazine 269
Long Story Short, An E-zine for Writers 269
Louisville Review, The 271
Lutheran Digest, The 271
Mobius 280
Moccasin, The 280
Modern Haiku 281
North Carolina Poetry Society, The 469
North Central Review 290
Off the Coast 293
Open Minds Quarterly 294
Over The Transom 295
Peace & Freedom 299
Pegasus Review, The 300
Philadelphia Stories 302
Pirene's Fountain 304
Poetica Magazine, Reflections of Jewish Thought 310
Poetry Church Magazine, The 311
Poetry Society of Virginia Adult and Student Contests, The 436
Poet's Art, The 313
Poets' Espresso Review 314
Poet's Pen, The 314
Potomac Review 316
Prism International 317
Prism Quarterly 318
Quiddity International Literary Journal and Public-Radio Program 322
RATTLE 324
red lights 326
Red Moon Anthology of English Language Haiku, The 326
Ribbons 328
Road Not Taken 329
Roadrunner Haiku Journal 329
Same, The 332
Scifaikuest 334
Ship of Fools 336
Skipping Stones 337
Slate & Style 338
SleepingFish 339
Song of the San Joaquin 340
Soul Fountain 341
Spaceports & Spidersilk 345
St. Anthony Messenger 348
Star*Line 349
Storyteller, The 350
Studio One 352
Tears in the Fence 356
Thick With Conviction 358
Think Journal 358
Tribeca Poetry Review 362
Vallum 365

Vegetarian Journal 366
WestWard Quarterly 369
Write On!! Poetry Magazette 374

POETRY FOR CHILDREN

Advocate, PKA's Publication 180
Anaphora Literary Press 378
Beyond Centauri 199
Cobblestone 216
Dial Books for Young Readers 386
Dig Magazine 228
FACES Magazine 236
Farrar, Straus & Giroux 387
Holiday House, Inc. 392
Jack and Jill 259
Ladybug 263
Louisville Review, The 271
Pockets 307
Poet's Art, The 313
Skipping Stones 337
Spaceports & Spidersilk 345
Spider 346
Storyteller, The 350
Turtle Magazine for Preschool Kids 363

POETRY FOR TEENS

Advocate, PKA's Publication 180
Anaphora Literary Press 378
Beyond Centauri 199
Challenger international 211
Cobblestone 216
devozine 228
Dial Books for Young Readers 386
Dig Magazine 228
FACES Magazine 236
Farrar, Straus & Giroux 387
hArtworks 249
Holiday House, Inc. 392
Louisville Review, The 271
Purpose 321
Skipping Stones 337
Spaceports & Spidersilk 345
Storyteller, The 350

POLITICAL

American Dissident 184
Blue Collar Review 202
Cold Mountain Review 217
Haight Ashbury Literary Journal 248
Left Curve 265
Minnesota Review, The 279
Mobius 280
New Verse News, The 288
nthposition 292
Pudding Magazine 319
Struggle 351
Teacher's Voice, The 356
Toad Suck Review 360
Tokyo Rose Records/Chapultepec Press 406
Working People's Poetry Competition 443

REGIONAL

Amy Award for Poetry, The 413
Anaphora Literary Press 378
Arc Publications 379
Borderlands 204
Bottom Dog Press, Inc. 382
Briar Cliff Review, The 205
Caribbean Writer, The 208
Cleveland State University Poetry Center 384
Coteau Books 385
Cottonwood 222
Dead Mule School of Southern Literature, The 226
Eliot Prize, T.S. (UK, Ireland) 421
Floating Bridge Press 388
Goose Lane Editions 390
House of Anansi Press 392
Idiom 23 255
Iowa Poetry Association 468
Jackson Award, Joseph Henry 427
Journal of New Jersey Poets 260
Kaimana 261
Kelsey Review 262
Lapwing Publications 394
Llenyddiaeth Cymru / Literature Wales 468
Louisiana Literature 270
Louisiana Review, The 270
Manoa 275
Melbourne Poets Union National Poetry Competition 429
New Rivers Press 398
Ninety-Six Press 398
North Carolina Literary Review 290
North Carolina Poetry Society, The 469
NSW Premier's Literary Award The Kenneth Slessor Prize 432
Ohioana Poetry Award 433
Ooligan Press 399
Permafrost 302
Philadelphia Stories 302
Plainsongs 305
POESY Magazine 309
Prairie Journal, The 316
PSA New York Chapbook Fellowships, The 437
Rocky Mountain Rider Magazine 330
Ronsdale Press 402
Song of the San Joaquin 340
South Dakota Review 341
SOUTH Poetry Magazine 343
Southwestern American Literature 344
Talking River 355
Tebot Bach 405
Texas Institute of Letters Literary Awards, The 441
Texas Poetry Calendar 357
Toad Suck Review 360
Tribeca Poetry Review 362
Tule Review, The 363
Vehicule Press 408
Washington Writers' Publishing House 409
Westerly 368
Western Australian Premier's Book Awards 443

Westview 369
Windfall 372
Writers Guild of Alberta 473

RELIGIOUS POETRY
Poet's Pen, The 314

RELIGIOUS VARIOUS
Soul Making Keats Literary Competition 440

SCIENCE FICTION
Aoife's Kiss 187
Beyond Centauri 199
Fifth Di..., The 237
Illumen 255
Leading Edge 265
Mythic Delirium 282
Scifaikuest 334
Spaceports & Spidersilk 345
Star*Line 349
Tales of the Talisman 354

SENIOR CITIZEN/AGING
Mature Years 276

SOCIAL ISSUES
Blue Collar Review 202
Bottom Dog Press, Inc. 382
Carolina Wren Press 383
Haight Ashbury Literary Journal 248
Left Curve 265
Minnesota Review, The 279
Mobius 280
New Verse News, The 288
Open Minds Quarterly 294
Peace & Freedom 299
Pudding Magazine 319
Radix Magazine 323
Rattapallax 323
Skipping Stones 337
Struggle 351
Sunstone 353
Teacher's Voice, The 356
Tokyo Rose Records/Chapultepec Press 406
Westerly 368
Working People's Poetry Competition 443

SPECIALIZED VARIOUS
Alimentum, The Literature of Food 183
American Dissident 184
Anaphora Literary Press 378
Binghamton University Milt Kessler Poetry Book Award 415
Cobblestone 216
Dig Magazine 228
Ekphrasis 232
Exit 13 Magazine 235
Fickle Muses 236
Illumen 255
Jerry Jazz Musician 259
Kerf, The 263
KotaPress Loss Journal 263
Literal Latté Food Verse Awards 428

Literary Mama 267
LUNGFULL!magazine 271
Mythic Delirium 282
New Verse News, The 288
Poet's Art, The 313
Pudding Magazine 319
Samsara 332
Shemom 336
Slate & Style 338
SleepingFish 339
Soul Making Keats Literary Competition 440
Spring 348
Stevens Journal, The Wallace 367
Teacher's Voice, The 356
Tufts Poetry Awards 442
Vegetarian Journal 366
Wergle Flomp Humor Poetry Contest 443
Windfall 372

SPIRITUALITY/INSPIRATIONAL
Alive Now 183
Avocet, A Journal of Nature Poems 194
Bottom Dog Press, Inc. 382
devozine 228
Lutheran Digest, The 271
Modern Haiku 281
Peace & Freedom 299
Penwood Review, The 301
Poet's Art, The 313
Poet's Pen, The 314
St. Anthony Messenger 348
Studio, A Journal of Christians Writing 352
Sunstone 353

SPORTS/RECREATION
Jack and Jill 259
Journal of Asian Martial Arts 260
Spitball 347
Turtle Magazine for Preschool Kids 363

STUDENTS
Anaphora Literary Press 378
Lyric, The 272
North Carolina Poetry Society, The 469
North Central Review 290
Poetry Society of Virginia Adult and Student Contests,
    The 436

THEMES
Alive Now 183
Arc Poetry Magazine 189
Asheville Poetry Review 192
Awakenings Review, The 194
Barrow Street 196
Bellevue Literary Review 197
Ceremony, a journal of poetry and other arts 210
Cobblestone 216
Concrete Wolf Poetry Chapbook Contest 419
Confrontation 219
Country Dog Review, The 222
Crab Orchard Review 222
Cream City Review 223

Curriculum Vitae 225
Dalhousie Review 226
Darkling Magazine 226
devozine 228
Diagram 228
Dig Magazine 228
Dirty Napkin, The 229
Drown In My Own Fears 230
Drunken Boat 230
FACES Magazine 236
Folio, A Literary Journal at American University 240
Fourth River, The 241
FreeFall Magazine 242
FreeXpresSion 242
Green Mountains Review 246
Gulf Stream Magazine 247
Haight Ashbury Literary Journal 248
Home Planet News 251
Hospital Drive 252
Illuminations 255
Journal of the American Medical Association (JAMA)
    260
Kaleidoscope 261
La Petite Zine 264
Left Curve 265
Literary Review 267
Living Poets Magazine 268
Louisiana Literature 270
Lullwater Review 271
Mennonite, The 276
Michigan Quarterly Review 277
Midwest Quarterly, The 278
Minnesota Review, The 279
Nimrod 289
Notre Dame Review 292
nthposition 292
Over The Transom 295
Packingtown Review 296
Painted Bride Quarterly 297
Peace & Freedom 299
Pedestal Magazine, The 300
Pegasus Review, The 300
Pirene's Fountain 304
Pockets 307
Poemeleon 308
Poetica Magazine, Reflections of Jewish Thought 310
Poetrybay 311
Poetry Salzburg Review 313
Poets' Espresso Review 314
Poet's Pen, The 314
Pudding Magazine 319
Pulse Online Literary Journal 320
Quiddity International Literary Journal and Public-
    Radio Program 322
Radix Magazine 323
Renditions 327
Ribbons 328
Rocky Mountain Rider Magazine 330
Skipping Stones 337

Song of the San Joaquin 340
South Carolina Review 341
South Dakota Review 341
Stand Magazine 348
Straylight 351
THEMA 357
Torch 361
Tule Review, The 363
Vallum 365
Waterways 367
Weber 368
Wild Violet 370
Words Without Borders 472
Write On!! Poetry Magazette 374

TRANSLATIONS

ABRAXAS 178
Anaphora Literary Press 378
Apple Valley Review 188
Arc Publications 379
Aries 189
Arts & Letters Journal of Contemporary Culture 191
Asheville Poetry Review 192
Black Lawrence Press 380
Carolina Quarterly, The 209
Cider Press Review 214
Cold Mountain Review 217
Connecticut River Review, The 220
Crab Creek Review 222
Crab Orchard Review 222
Curriculum Vitae 225
Dancing Poetry Contest 421
Epicenter 233
Faultline 236
FIELD 237
Frogpond 243
Ghost Pony Press 389
Green Mountains Review 246
Guernica Editions 391
Illuminations 255
Indiana Review 256
Italica Press 393
Jewish Currents 259
Journal, The 261
Kenyon Review, The 262
Lake Effect 264
Landon Translation Award, Harold Morton 427
Languageandculture.net 264
Literary Review 267
Lullwater Review 271
MacGuffin, The 273
Manhattan Review, The 275
Milkweed Editions 396
Modern Haiku 281
Moving Parts Press 397
New England Review 285
New Laurel Review, The 286
New Rivers Press 398
New Yorker, The 288
Nimrod 289

Ooligan Press 399
Osiris 295
Poet Lore 310
Poetry International 312
Poetry Kanto 312
Poetry Salzburg Review 313
Princeton University Press 402
Prism International 317
Puerto del Sol 320
Pulse Online Literary Journal 320
Quarterly West 322
Red Moon Press 402
Renditions 327
Rhino 328
Ribbons 328
Seneca Review 335
Southern Humanities Review 342
Spillway 346
SRPR (Spoon River Poetry Review) 348
Stand Magazine 348
storySouth 350
Sycamore Review 354
Toad Suck Review 360
University of Chicago Press, The 407
Vallum 365
VAN GOGH'S EAR 365
Verse 366
Western Humanities Review 369
Wolf, The 373
Words Without Borders 472

WOMEN VARIOUS

Amy Award for Poetry, The 413
Carolina Wren Press 383
Chapman 212
Haight Ashbury Literary Journal 248
International Women's Writing Guild 467
Jewish Women's Literary Annual 259
Lilith Magazine 266
Literary Mama 267
Long Story Short, An E-zine for Writers 269
New Women's Voices Chapbook Competition 432
Pearson Award, Judith Siegel 434
Perugia Press Prize 435
Room 330
Rose Poetry Prize, Beullah 438
So to Speak 340
Struggle 351
Torch 361

WORKING CLASS ISSUES

Blue Collar Review 202
Bottom Dog Press, Inc. 382
Struggle 351
Working People's Poetry Competition 443

GENERAL INDEX

2River View 178
10 Minute Play Contest & Festival 412
49th Parallel Poetry Award, The 412
Aasra Punjabi English Magazine 178
Able Muse 178
ABRAXAS 178
Abroad Writers Conferences 452
ABZ 179
Academy of American Poets, The 465
ACM 179
Acorn 179
Acorn-Plantos Award for Peoples Poetry 412
Acumen Magazine 180
Adirondack Review, The 180
Advocate, PKA's Publication 180
African Voices 181
Agni 181
Agnieszka's Dowry (AgD) 182
Aguilar Expression, The 182
Ahsahta Press 378
Albatross 182
Alimentum, The Literature of Food 183
Ali Prize in Poetry, Agha Shahid 412
Alive Now 183
All Genres Literary Magazine 183
AMAZE 184
Ambit 184
American Booksellers Foundation for Free Expression 465
American Carriage House Publishing 378
American Christian Writers Conferences 452
American Dissident 184
American Haiku Archives 465
American Letters and Commentary 185
American Literary Review 185

American Poetry Journal Book Prize, The 413
American Poetry Journal, The 185
American Poetry Review, The 186
American Tanka 186
Amy Award for Poetry, The 413
Anabiosis Press Chapbook Contest 413
Anaphora Literary Press 378
Ancient Paths 186
Anderbo.com 186
Anderbo Poetry Prize 413
Anhinga Press 378
Annual World Haiku Competition & Annual World Tanka Contest 413
Antigonish Review, The 187
Antioch Review 187
Anvil Press 378
Aoife's Kiss 187
Apalachee Review 187
Appalachian Heritage 188
Apple Valley Review 188
Arc 189
Arc Poetry Magazine 189
Arc Publications 379
Ardent! 189
Aries 189
Arizona Authors Association 466
Arizona Literary Contest & Book Awards 414
Arizona State Poetry Society Annual Contest 414
Arkansas Review 190
Arsenic Lobster 190
Art Affair Annual Writing Contest 414
Artful Dodge 190
Art of Music Biennial Writing Contest, The 414
Arts & Letters Journal of Contemporary Culture 191
Art Times 191

Art Workshops in Guatemala 452
Ascent Aspirations 191
Asheville Poetry Review 192
Ashland Poetry Press 379
asinine poetry 192
Aspen Summer Words Literary Festival & Writing
    Retreat 452
Assent 192
Atlanta Review 193
Atlantic Center for the Arts 453
Atlantic Monthly, The 193
Atlantic Writing Competition for Unpublished Manu-
    scripts 414
Austin International Poetry Festival 453
Authors Guild, Inc., The 466
Autumn House Poetry, Fiction, and Nonfiction Prizes
    415
Autumn House Press 379
Avalon Literary Review, The 193
Avocet, A Journal of Nature Poems 194
Awakenings Review, The 194
Babel 194
babysue® 195
Backwaters Press, The 379
Baltimore Review, The 195
Barbaric Yawp 196
Barn Owl Review 196
Barrow Street 196
Barrow Street Press Book Contest 415
Bateau 196
Bayou 196
bear creek haiku 197
Bear Deluxe Magazine, The 197
Bear Star Press 379
Bellevue Literary Review 197
Bellingham Review 198
Bell's Letters Poet 198
Beloit Poetry Journal 199
Beltway Poetry Quarterly 199
Benedict Poetry Prize, Elinor 415
Beyond Centauri 199
Bibby First Book Award, The Patricia 415
Bible Advocate 200
Big Muddy 200
Big Pulp 200
Binghamton University Milt Kessler Poetry Book
    Award 415
Birch Book Press 380
Bitter Oleander, The 201
BkMk Press 380
Blackbird 201
Black Lawrence Press 380
Black Mountain Press 380
Black Ocean 381
Black Warrior Review 201
BlazeVOX [books] 381
Blood Lotus 201
Blood Orange Review 201
Bloomsbury Review, The 202

Blue Collar Review 202
Blue Light Press 381
Blueline 202
Blue Mesa Review 203
Blue Mountain Arts/SPS Studios Poetry Card Contest
    415
Blue Mountain Press 381
Bluestem 203
BOA Editions, Ltd. 381
Bock Prize, The Frederick 416
Bomb Magazine 203
Borderlands 204
Boston Review 204
Bottom Dog Press, Inc. 382
Boulevard 204
Boulevard Emerging Poets Contest 416
Bread Loaf Writers' Conference 453
Breakthrough Intercessor, The 205
Briar Cliff Review, The 205
Brick Road Poetry Book Contest 416
Brick Road Poetry Press, Inc. 382
Bright Hill Press Poetry Chapbook Competition 416
Brilliant Corners 206
Brittingham Prize in Poetry 417
Broken Jaw Press 383
Brooks Books 383
Bryant Literary Review 206
Burnside Review 206
Burnside Review Chapbook Competition 417
Button 207
Cable Book Award, Gerald 417
Caketrain 207
Calamari Press 383
California State Poetry Society 466
Calyx 207
Canadian Writer's Journal 208
Cape Cod Writers Center Annual Conference 453
Capilano Review, The 208
Caribbean Writer, The 208
Carolina Quarterly, The 209
Carolina Wren Press 383
Carolina Wren Press Poetry Contest for a First or
    Second Book 417
Carus Publishing Company 209
Cat Callan Humor Prize, Jamie 418
Caveat Lector 209
Cave Wall 209
CC&D 210
Celebration of Southern Literature 453
Cellar Door Poetry Journal 210
Center for Book Arts Poetry Chapbook Competition,
    The 418
Ceremony, a journal of poetry and other arts 210
Cerise Press 210
Chaffin Journal 211
Challenger international 211
Chantarelle's Notebook 211
Chapman 212
character i 212

Chariton Review, The 212
Chautauqua Literary Journal 212
CHEST 213
Chicken Soup for the Soul Publishing, LLC 213
Chizine 213
Christian Books Today Ltd 384
Christian Communicator 213
Christian Science Monitor, The 213
Cicada Magazine 214
Cider Press Review 214, 418
Cimarron Review 215
Claremont Review, The 215
Clark Street Review 215
Cleveland State University Poetry Center 384
Cleveland State University Poetry Center First Book 418
Cleveland State University Poetry Center Open Competition 419
Clockwise Chapbook Competition 419
Cloudbank 215
Cloudbank Contest 419
Coach House Books 384
Coal City Review 216
C/Oasis 216
Cobblestone 216
Coffe House Press 384
Cold Mountain Review 217
Colorado Prize for Poetry, The 419
Colorado Review 217
Columbia 217
Common Ground Review 217
Common Threads 218
Commonweal 218
Comstock Review, The 218
Concrete Wolf Poetry Chapbook Contest 419
Confrontation 219
Congruent Spaces 219
Connecticut Review 219
Connecticut River Review Poetry Contest, The 419
Connecticut River Review, The 220
contemporary haibun 220
Contrary 220
Convergence 221
Coteau Books 385
Cottonwood 222
Country Dog Review, The 222
CPR Editor's Prize Book Award 420
Crab Creek Review 222
Crab Orchard Review 222
Crab Orchard Series in Poetry First Book Award 420
Cranston Memorial Poetry Prize, Lois 420
Crazyhorse 223
Cream City Review 223
Creative With Words Publications 223
Crescent Moon Publishing 385
Cross-Cultural Communications 385
C&R Press 383
Crucible 224
Crystal Spirit Publishing, Inc. 386

CURA 224
Current Accounts 224
Curriculum Vitae 225
Cutbank 226
CWW Annual Wisconsin Writers Awards Competition 420
Dalhousie Review 226
Dana Anhinga Prize For Poetry, The Robert 420
Dana Awards in the Novel, Short Fiction, Essay and Poetry 420
Dancing Poetry Contest 421
Darkling Magazine 226
Dead Mule School of Southern Literature, The 226
Denver Quarterly 227
Der-Hovanessian Prize 421
Deronda Review, The 227
descant 227
devozine 228
Diagram 228
DIAGRAM/New Michigan Press Chapbook Contest 421
Dial Books for Young Readers 386
Dig Magazine 228
Diode Poetry Journal 229
Dirty Napkin, The 229
DISLOCATE 229
Diversion Press 386
DMQ Review 229
Dobie Paisano Project 421
Down in the Dirt 230
Dreamland Books Inc. 386
Drown In My Own Fears 230
Drunken Boat 230
Ducts 231
Dufour Editions 386
Earthshine 231
Eclectica 231
Eclectic Muse, The 232
Ecotone 232
Écrits des Forges 387
Ekphrasis 232
Eliot Prize for Poetry, T.S. 421
Eliot Prize, T.S. (UK, Ireland) 421
Ellery Queen's Mystery Magazine 233
Ellipsis Magazine 233
Emerging Voices 421
Epicenter 233
Epiphany-Where Creativity and Inspiration Evolve! 234
Epoch 234
Erskine J. Poetry Prize 422
Eureka Literary Magazine 234
European Judaism 234
Evangel 235
Evansville Review 235
Exit 13 Magazine 235
Eye on Life Online Magazine 235
Faber & Faber Inc. 387
Faber & Faber Ltd 387

FACES Magazine 236
Fantastic Books Publishing 387
Far Horizons Award for Poetry 422
Farrar, Straus & Giroux 387
Farrell Poetry Prize, Janice 422
Faultline 236
Fence Books 388
Fickle Muses 236
Fiddlehead, The 236
FIELD 237
FIELD Poetry Prize 422
Fifth Di..., The 237
filling Station 237
Finch Prize for Poetry, The 423
Fine Arts Work Center 454
First Class 238
First Edition Design Publishing 388
Five AM - 5 AM 238
Flarestack Poets 388
Flint Hills Review 238
Floating Bridge Press 388
Florida First Coast Writers' Festival Novel, Short Fic-
    tion, Playwriting & Poetry Awards 423
Florida Review, The 238
Floyd County Moonshine 238
Flyway 239
Fogged Clarity 239
Folded Word 389
Foliate Oak Literary Magazine 240
Folio, A Literary Journal at American University 240
Foothill 240
ForPoetry.Com 241
Fourteen Hills 241
Fourth River, The 241
Four Way Books 389
Four Way Books Poetry Prizes 423
FreeFall Magazine 242
FreeFall Short Prose and Poetry Contest 423
FreeXpresSion 242
Friend, The 242
Frogmore Papers, The 243
Frogpond 243
Front Street 389
Fugue Literary Magazine 243
Furious Flower Poetry Center 466
FutureCycle Press 389
Gargoyle 244
Gathering of the Tribes, A 181
Georgetown Review 244, 423
Georgia Poetry Society 467
Georgia Review, The 244
Gettysburg Review, The 245
Ghost Pony Press 389
Ginninderra Press 390
Ginosko 245
Ginsberg Poetry Awards, Allen 423
Gival Press 390
Gival Press Poetry Award 423
Glass 245

Godine, Publisher, David R. 386
Goose Lane Editions 390
Governor General's Literary Award for Poetry 424
Grain 245
Graywolf Press 390
Great American Poetry Show, The 246
Green Hills Literary Lantern 246
Green Mountains Review 246
Greensboro Review, The 246
Grove/Atlantic, Inc. 391
Guernica Editions 391
Guernica Magazine 247
Guggenheim Fellowships 424
Gulf Coast 247
Gulf Stream Magazine 247
G.W. Review, The 248
Hackney Literary Awards 424
Haight Ashbury Literary Journal 248
Haiku North America Conference 454
Haiku Society of America 467
Handley Prose Poem Prize, Kathryn 424
Hanging Loose 248
Harpur Palate 248
hArtworks 249
Hawaii Review 249
Hayden's Ferry Review 249
Highland Summer Conference 454
Highlights for Children 250
High Plains Press 391
Hippopotamus Press 391
Hiram Poetry Review 250
His Work Christian Publishing 392
Hodder Fellowship, The 424
Hoffer Award, Eric 425
Hofstra University Summer Writing Workshops 454
Hokin Prize, The Bess 425
Holiday House, Inc. 392
Holiness Today 250
Hollins Critic, The 251
Home Planet News 251
Homestead Review 251
HOOT 252
Horizons 252
Hospital Drive 252
Hotel Amerika 252
Houghton Prize, Firman 425
House of Anansi Press 392
Howard/John H. Reid Poetry Contest, Tom 425
Howe/Boston Authors Award, The Julia Ward 425
Hubbub 253
Hudson Review, The 253
Hull Memorial Poetry Prize, The Lynda 425
Hunger Mountain 253
Hungur Magazine 254
Ibbetson St. Press 254
IdeaGems 254
Idiom 23 255
Ilium Press 392
Illumen 255

Illuminations 255
Image 256
Indefinite Space 256
Indiana Review 256
Indiana Review ½ K (Short-Short/Prose-Poem)
    Contest 426
Indiana Review Poetry Prize 426
Indiana University Writers' Conference 455
Inkwell Annual Poetry Contest 426
Innisfree Poetry Journal 256
Insomniac Press 392
International Creative Writing Camp 455
International Women's Writing Guild 467
Interpreter's House 257
Intro Prize in Poetry, The 426
Iodine Poetry Journal 257
iota 257
Iowa Poetry Association 468
Iowa Poetry Prizes 426
Iowa Review Award in Poetry, Fiction, and Nonfiction,
    The 426
Iowa Review, The 258
Iowa Summer Writing Festival 455
Island 258
Italian Americana 258
Italica Press 393
Jabberwock Review 258
Jack and Jill 259
Jackson Award, Joseph Henry 427
Jackson Hole Writers Conference 456
James Books, Alice 393
Jerry Jazz Musician 259
Jewish Currents 259
Jewish Women's Literary Annual 259
J Journal 259
Johns Hopkins University Press, The 393
Journal of Asian Martial Arts 260
Journal of New Jersey Poets 260
Journal of the American Medical Association (JAMA)
    260
Journal, The 260, 261
Kaimana 261
Kaleidoscope 261
Kelsey Review 262
Kenyon Review, The 262
Kenyon Review Writers Workshop 456
Kerf, The 263
Knopf, Alfred A. 394
KotaPress Loss Journal 263
Kundiman Poetry Retreat 456
Ladybug 263
La Fovea 263
Lake Effect 264
Lamb Books, Wendy 394
Landfall/Otago University Press 264
Landon Translation Award, Harold Morton 427
Languageandculture.net 264
La Petite Zine 264
Lapwing Publications 394

Leading Edge 265
League of Utah Writers Contest 427
Ledge Annual Poetry Chapbook Contest, The 427
Ledge Hill Publishing 395
Ledge Magazine, The 265
Lee & Low Books 395
Left Curve 265
Les Figues Press 395
Les Figues Press NOS Book Contest 427
Lethe Press 395
Let's Write Literary Contest 427
Levis Reading Prize 427
Lilith Magazine 266
Lilly Poetry Prize, The Ruth 428
Linebreak 266
Lips 266
Lissette's Tales of the Imagination 267
Literal Latté 267
Literal Latté Food Verse Awards 428
Literary Juice 267
Literary Mama 267
Literary Review 267
LIT, The 468
Little Patuxent Review 268
Living Poets Magazine 268
Llenyddiaeth Cymru / Literature Wales 468
Loft Literary Center, The 468
London Magazine, The 269
Lone Stars Magazine 269
Long Life 269
Long Story Short, An E-zine for Writers 269
Los 270
Louisiana Literature 270
Louisiana Review, The 270
Louisiana State University Press 395
Louisville Review, The 271
Lullwater Review 271
Luna Bisonte Prods 395
LUNGFULL!magazine 271
Lutheran Digest, The 271
Lyrical Passion Poetry E-Zine 272
Lyric, The 272
MacGuffin National Poet Hunt Contest, The 428
MacGuffin, The 273
Madgett Poetry Award, Naomi Long 428
Madison Review, The 273
Magazine of Fantasy & Science Fiction, The 273
Magma Poetry 274
Magnolia Quarterly, The 274
Main Street Rag's Annual Poetry Book Award 428
Main Street Rag, The 274
Malahat Review Long Poem Prize, The 428
Malahat Review, The 275
Manhattan Review, The 275
Manoa 275
Marr Poetry Prize, The Morton 428
Massachusetts Review, The 276
Mature Years 276
Maverick Duck Press 396

McElderry Books, Margaret K. 396
Measure 276
Melbourne Poets Union National Poetry Competition 429
Mendocino Coast Writers Conference 456
Mennonite, The 276
MensBook Journal 276
Meridian 277
Merriam Press 396
Miami University Press 396
Michigan Quarterly Review 277
Mid-American Review 278
Midland Authors Award 429
Midwest Quarterly, The 278
Midwifery Today 279
Milford Fine Arts Council National Poetry Contest 429
Milkweed Editions 396
miller's pond 279
Minnesota Review, The 279
M.I.P. Company 279
Mississippi Review 279
Mississippi Review Prize 429
Missouri Review, The 280
Mobius 280
Moccasin, The 280
Mochila Review, The 281
Modern Haiku 281
Montevallo Literary Festival 456
Moonshot Magazine 281
Moon Tide Press 397
Moore Community Workshops, Jenny McKean 457
Moore Visiting Writer, Jenny McKean 430
Morton Prize in Poetry, The Kathryn A. 430
Motton Prize, Sheila Margaret 430
Mount Hermon Christian Writers Conference 457
Moving Parts Press 397
Mudfish 282
Mudlark 282
Mumford Prize, Erika 430
My Green Publisher LLC 397
Mythic Delirium 282
Napa Valley Writers' Conference 457
Nassau Review 283
National Book Awards 430
National Poetry Review 430
National Poetry Review, The 283
National Writers Association 469
National Writers Association Poetry Contest 431
National Writers Union 469
Nation, The 283
Natural Bridge 283
Naturally 284
Naugatuck River Review 284
Necrology Shorts 285
Nemerov Sonnet Award, Howard 431
Neruda Prize for Poetry, The Pablo 431
Nerve Cowboy 285
New Criterion Poetry Prize, The 431

New England Review 285
New Hampshire Writers' Project 469
New Issues Poetry & Prose 397
New Laurel Review, The 286
New Letters 286
New Letters Prize for Poetry 431
New Letters Weekend Writers Conference, The 458
New Millennium Awards for Fiction, Poetry, and Nonfiction 431
New Millennium Writings 286
New Ohio Review 287
New Orleans Review 287
New Rivers Press 398
New South 287
New South Writing Contest 431
New Verse News, The 288
New Welsh Review 288
New Women's Voices Chapbook Competition 432
New Writer, The 288
New Yorker, The 288
Niles Memorial Chapbook Award, Jessie Bryce 432
Nimrod 289
Nims Memorial Prize, The John Frederick 432
Ninety-Six Press 398
Ninth Letter 289
Nite-Writer's International Literary Arts Journal 289
Normal School, The 289
North American Review 290
North Atlantic Books 398
North Carolina Literary Review 290
North Carolina Poetry Society, The 469
North Carolina Writers' Fellowships 432
North Carolina Writers' Network 470
North Central Review 290
North Dakota Quarterly 291
Northwind 291
Norton & Company, Inc., W.W. 398
Notes on the State of New Jersey 291
Notre Dame Review 292
Now & Then 292
NSW Premier's Literary Award The Kenneth Slessor Prize 432
Nth Degree 292
nthposition 292
Nuthouse 293
Oberlin College Press 398
Obsidian 293
Ocean Magazine 293
Off the Coast 293
Ohioana Poetry Award 433
Ohio Poetry Association 470
Old Red Kimono 294
On Spec 294
Ooligan Press 399
Open Minds Quarterly 294
Open Season Awards 433
Orchard Books 399
Orchises Press 295
Oxford Magazine 295

Oyez Review 296
Oyster Boy Review 296
Packingtown Review 296
Painted Bride Quarterly 297
Palabra 297
Palettes & Quills 399
Paperplates 297
Paris Review, The 297
Parnassus 297
Passages North 297
Passion 298
Paterson Literary Review 298
Paterson Poetry Prize, The 433
Paterson Prize for Young Adult and Children's Writing,
    The Katherine 434
Paumanok Review, The 298
Pavement Saw 299
Pavement Saw Press Chapbook Award 434
Peace & Freedom 299
Pearl 299
Pearl Poetry Prize 434
Pearson Award, Judith Siegel 434
Pebble Lake Review 300
Pedestal Magazine, The 300
Pedrick Prize, Jean 434
Pegasus Review, The 300
Pelican Publishing Company 400
Pemmican Publications, Inc. 400
PEN American Center 470
PEN Center USA Literary Awards 434
PEN/Joyce Osterweil Award for Poetry 434
Pennine Ink Magazine 300
Pennsylvania English 301
Penny Dreadful 301
PEN/Voelcker Award for Poetry 435
Penwood Review, The 301
Peregrine 302
Perennial 400
Permafrost 302
Persea Books 400
Perugia Press 401
Perugia Press Prize 435
Peterson Poetry Prize, The Richard 435
Philadelphia Stories 302
Philadelphia Writers' Conference 458
Phoebe 303
Pima Writers' Workshop 458
Pinch Literary Award in Fiction and Poetry, The 435
Pinch, The 303
Pink Chameleon, The 304
Pinyon 304
Pirene's Fountain 304
Plainsongs 305
Plain Spoke 305
Plan B Press 401
Plan B Press Poetry Chapbook Contest 435
PLANET-The Welsh Internationalist 306
Pleiades 306
Ploughshares 306

PMS poemmemoirstory 307
PNWA Literary Contest 435
Pockets 307
Poem 308
Poemeleon 308
Poems & Plays 308
POESY Magazine 309
POETALK 309
Poetica Magazine, Reflections of Jewish Thought 310
Poetic Matrix, a periodic letteR 310
Poet Lore 310
Poetry 310
Poetry 2013 International Poetry Competition 435
Poetrybay 311
Poetry Church Magazine, The 311
Poetry International 312
Poetry Kanto 312
Poetry Northwest 312
Poetry Salzburg Review 313
Poetry Society of New Hampshire 471
Poetry Society of South Carolina, The 471
Poetry Society of Virginia Adult and Student Contests,
    The 436
Poetry Weekend Intensives 458
Poets and Artists (O&S) 313
Poet's Art, The 313
Poetse & Patrons Annual Chicagoland Poetry Contest
    436
Poets' Espresso Review 314
Poet's Haven, The 314
Poet's Pen, The 314
Poets' Podium 315
Pointed Circle 315
Pollak Prize in Poetry, Felix 436
Polyphony H.S. 315
Portland Review, The 315
Potomac Review 316
Potomac, The 316
Poulin, Jr. Poetry Prize, A. 436
Prairie Journal, The 316
Prairie Schooner 317
Prairie Schooner Book Prize 437
Presa 401
Press 53 401
Press 53 Open Awards 437
Princeton University Press 402
Prism International 317
Prism Quarterly 318
Provincetown Arts 318
PSA New York Chapbook Fellowships, The 437
Public Space, A 319
Puckerbrush Review, The 319
Pudding Magazine 319
Puerto del Sol 320
Pulsar Poetry Magazine 320
Pulse Online Literary Journal 320
Purpose 321
Pushcart Prize 437
Quantum Leap 321

Quarter After Eight 321
Quarterly West 322
Queen's Quarterly 322
Quiddity International Literary Journal and Public-
    Radio Program 322
Radix Magazine 323
Ragged Sky Press 402
Rag, The 323
Railroad Evangelist 323
Raintown Review, The 323
Rattapallax 323
RATTLE 324
RATTLE Poetry Prize 437
Rattling Wall 324
Raven Chronicles, The 324
RBC Bronwen Wallace Memorial Award, The 437
READER, The 324
Realpoetik 325
Redactions 325
Red Clay Review, The 325
Redheaded Stepchild 325
Red Hen Press 402
Redivider 326
red lights 326
Red Moon Anthology of English Language Haiku,
    The 326
Red Moon Press 402
Red River Review 327
Red Rock Review 327
Reed Magazine 327
Regina Book Award 437
Renditions 327
Rhino 328
Rialto, The 328
Ribbons 328
Rio Grande Review 329
Road Not Taken 329
Roadrunner Haiku Journal 329
Roanoke Review 329
Rockford Review, The 330
Rocky Mountain Rider Magazine 330
Ronsdale Press 402
Room 330
Rose Alley Press 403
Rosebud 331
Rose Poetry Prize, Beullah 438
Rudnitsky First Book Prize, Lori 438
Sacramento Poetry Center Book Prize, The 438
Sacred Journey 331
Sakura Publishing & Technologies 403
Salmon Poetry 403
Salt Hill Journal 331
Same, The 332
Samsara 332
Sandeen Prize in Poetry, Ernest 438
San Diego State University Writers' Conference 459
Sandy River Review 332
Sanskrit Literary Arts Magazine 332
Santa Barbara Writers Conference 459

Santa Clara Review 333
Saranac Review, The 333
Sarton Award, May 438
Saskatchewan Festival of Words 459
Saskatchewan First Book Award 438
Saskatchewan Poetry Award 438
Saturnalia Books 403
Scars Editor's Choice Awards, The 438
School for Writers Summer Workshop, The 461
School of The Arts at Rhinelander UW-Madison
    Continuing Studies 459
Schreiber Prize for Humorous Fiction & Nonfiction,
    The Mona 439
Science Editor 333
Scifaikuest 334
Seam 334
Seattle Review, The 334
Second Aeon Publications 403
Secret Place, The 335
SEEMS 335
Seneca Review 335
Sewanee Review, The 335
Sewanee Writers' Conference 459
Shearsman 336
Shearsman Books, LTD 403
Shemom 336
Shenandoah 336
Ship of Fools 336
Sierra Nevada Review 337
Skidrow Penthouse 337
Skipping Stones 337
Skipping Stones Honor (Book) Awards 439
Slant 338
Slapering Hol Press Chapbook Competition 439
Slate & Style 338
SleepingFish 339
Slipstream 339
Slipstream Annual Poetry Chapbook Contest 439
Slope Editions Book Prize 439
Slote Award, The Bernice 440
Slow Trains Literary Journal 339
Smith Memorial Award for Best Book of Poetry, Helen
    C. 440
Snow Monkey 340
Snow Writing Contest, Kay 440
Snowy Egret 340
Snyder Memorial Publication Prize, The Richard 440
Song of the San Joaquin 340
So to Speak 340
Soul Fountain 341
Soul Making Keats Literary Competition 440
South Carolina Review 341
South Coast Writers Conference 460
South Dakota Review 341
Southeast Review, The 343
Southern California Review 342
Southern Humanities Review 342
Southern Poetry Review 342
Southern Review, The 342

SOUTH Poetry Magazine 343
Southwestern American Literature 344
Southwest Review 344
Sou'wester 344
Sow's Ear 440
Sow's Ear Poetry Competition, The 440
Sow's Ear Poetry Review, The 345
Space and Time 345
Spaceports & Spidersilk 345
Spark Quarterly Writing Contest 441
SpeedPoets Zine 346
Spider 346
Spillway 346
Spinning Jenny 346
Spitball 347
Splizz 347
Spout Magazine 347
Spring 348
SRPR (Spoon River Poetry Review) 348
Stand Magazine 348
St. Anthony Messenger 348
Star*Line 349
Steamboat Springs Writers Conference 460
Steel Toe Books 404
Stepping Stones Magazine 349
Stevens Journal, The Wallace 367
Stevens Poetry Manuscript Contest 441
Still Crazy 349
Stirring 349
Stone Soup 350
storySouth 350
Storyteller, The 350
Stover Memorial Award, The Elizabeth Matchett 441
Stray Branch, The 350
Straylight 351
Stride Magazine 351
Strokestown International Poetry Competition 441
Struggle 351
Studio, A Journal of Christians Writing 352
Studio One 352
Subito Press 404
Subliminal Interiors, A Literary Arts Magazine 352
Subtropics 352
Summer Writing Program 460
Sunspinner 353
Sunstone 353
Sun, The 353
Swan Isle Press 404
Swan Scythe Press 404
Swenson Poetry Award, May 441
Sycamore Review 354
SynergEbooks 405
Takahe 354
Talent Drips Erotic Literary EZine 354
Tales of the Talisman 354
Talking River 355
Taos Summer Writers' Conference 460
Tarpaulin Sky 355
Tarpaulin Sky Press 405

Tar River Poetry 355
Tattoo Highway 356
Teacher's Voice, The 356
Tears in the Fence 356
Tebot Bach 405
Texas Institute of Letters Bob Bush Memorial Award for First Book of Poetry 441
Texas Institute of Letters Literary Awards, The 441
Texas Poetry Calendar 357
Texas Review 357
Texas Tech University Press 405
THEMA 357
Thick With Conviction 358
Think Journal 358
Third Wednesday 358
Thirty-Fourth Parallel - 34th Parallel 359
Tia Chucha Press 405
Tiger's Eye 359
Tiger's Eye Poetry Chapbook Contest 441
Tightrope Books 406
Timber Journal 359
Timberline Press 406
Time of Singing 360
Tin House 360
Toad Suck Review 360
Toasted Cheese 361
Todd Poetry Series Book Competition, Lena-Miles Wever 442
Tokyo Rose Records/Chapultepec Press 406
Torch 361
Travel Naturally 361
Tribeca Poetry Review 362
Tufts Poetry Awards 442
Tulane Review 362
Tule Review, The 363
Tundra 363
Tupelo Press 406
Turnstone Press 406
Turtle Magazine for Preschool Kids 363
University of Akron Press 407
University of Arizona Poetry Center 472
University of Arkansas Press, The 407
University of Chicago Press, The 407
University of Iowa Press 407
University of Nebraska Press 407
University of New Mexico Press 408
University of North Dakota Writers Conference 461
University of Wisconsin Press 408
Untreed Reads Publishing 408
Up and Under 364
Urthona Magazine 364
U.S. 1 Worksheets 364
U.S. Catholic 364
Utmost Christian Poetry Contest 442
Vallum 365
Valparaiso Poetry Review 365
VAN GOGH'S EAR 365
Varujan Award, Daniel 442
Vassar Miller Prize in Poetry 429

Vegetarian Journal 366
Vehicule Press 408
Ventura County Writers Club Poetry Contest With
    Two Divisions For Young Poets, Annual 413
Verandah Literary & Art Journal 366
Vermont Studio Center 461
Verse 366
View From Here Magazine, The 367
Vilcek Prize for Poetry, Marica and Jan 442
Virginia Quarterly Review, The 367
Wake Forest University Press 408
Washington Writers' Publishing House 409
Waterways 367
Wave Books 409
Weber 368
Wergle Flomp Humor Poetry Contest 443
Wesleyan University Press 409
Wesleyan Writers Conference 461
West Branch 368
Westerly 368
Western Australian Premier's Book Awards 443
Western Humanities Review 369
Western Reserve Writers & Freelance Conference 462
Westview 369
WestWard Quarterly 369
Whiskey Island Magazine 370
White Eagle Coffee Store Press 409
Wicked Alice 370
Wild Goose Poetry Review 370
Wild Violet 370
WILLA Literary Award 443
Willard & Maple 371
Willow Review 371

Windfall 372
Windhover 372
Windsor Review 373
Winter Poetry & Prose Getaway 462
Wisconsin Review 373
Wisdom Publications 410
Wolf, The 373
Wood Prize, The J. Howard and Barbara M.J. 443
Worcester Review, The 373
Wordsong 410
Words Without Borders 472
Working People's Poetry Competition 443
Write On!! Poetry Magazette 374
Write Place At the Write Time, The 374
Writer's Bloc 374
Writer's Chronicle, The 375
Writer's Digest 375
Writer's Digest Conference 462
Writer's Digest International Self-Published Book
    Awards 444
Writers' Federation of Nova Scotia 472
Writers Guild of Alberta 473
Writers Omi at Ledig House 463
Writers Room, The 473
Writing Disorder, The 375
Writing Workshop at Castle Hill 463
Wurlitzer, Helene, Foundation, The 463
Xavier Review 376
Yale University Press 410
Yemassee 376
Zylophone Poetry Journal 376
ZYZZYVA 376